THE ILLUSION OF LIFE 2

MORE ESSAYS ON ANIMATION

THE ILLUSION OF LIFE 2

MORE ESSAYS ON ANIMATION

EDITED BY
ALAN CHOLODENKO

POWER PUBLICATIONS

Published by
Power Publications
Power Institute Foundation for Art and Visual Culture
University of Sydney
NSW 2006 Australia
www.arts.usyd.edu.au/departs/arthistory/power

Managing Editor Victoria Dawson
Assistant Editor Kirsten Krauth
Consulting Editor Julian Pefanis
Executive Editor Roger Benjamin
Cover design Matthew Martin
Printed by Southwood Press

National Library of Australia Cataloguing-in-Publication data:

The illusion of life 2 : more essays on animation.

Includes index.
ISBN 9780909952341.

ISBN 0 909952 34 5.

1. Animated films. 2. Animation (Cinematography). I. Cholodenko, Alan.

791.4334

Acknowledgements

In terms of the conference that generated this book, I want first to express my gratitude to the major sponsors of the event: the Mari Kuttna Bequest, the Power Institute, the Faculty of Arts of the University of Sydney; the Japan Foundation; the Museum of Contemporary Art; Film Graphics; and Network 10.

Second, I want to thank the two Sydney host institutions and staff who so graciously helped to make this event come to pass: first, the Japan Cultural Centre, Mr Toshihisa Tanaka, Ms Rei Hamabe, Ms Kara Yamaguchi and Mr Masafumi Konomi; and second, the Museum of Contemporary Art, Leon Paroissien, Bernice Murphy, Julie Ewington, Therese Burnett and Barbara Maré.

Third, for giving us permission to screen the conference films, I want to express my gratitude to Tezuka Production Company and Mr Takayuki Matsutani, its President, for Osamu Tezuka's *Legend of the Forest*; Studio Ghibli Company and Mr Shinsuke Nonaka, its Deputy General Manager, for Hayao Miyazaki's *My Neighbour Totoro*; and Streamline Pictures and Carl Macek, its President, and Fred Patten, its Director of Marketing and Publications, for *Robot Carnival*; *Eight Man After*, vol. 1: *City in Fear*; and *Great Conquest: Romance of the Three Kingdoms*. As well, I want to thank Mr Kazafumi Nomura, President of A.P.P.P. Co., for *Robot Carnival* and Mr Yoshi Enoki, President of Enoki Films, for *Eight Man After* and *Great Conquest*.

Also, I wish to acknowledge profoundly Madame Barbara Gré, who gave the Power Institute the Mari Kuttna Bequest in Film, which helped me to realize the three events I have organized—*FUTUR◊FALL: Excursions into Post-Modernity* in 1984, *THE ILLUSION OF LIFE* in 1988 and *THE LIFE OF ILLUSION* in 1995. Madame Gré died in 2004.

Too, I want to thank Susan Shehadie, then Power Institute Public Education Officer, and Myra Katz, Christine Costello and Claudia Nemeth de Bickal, the administrative staff supporting me in my role as Head of the Department of Fine Arts during the period of the event.

As well, thanks to the Faculty of Arts, its then Dean Paul Crittenden, and its IT Unit, especially John Couani.

Also, I would like to thank Matthew Martin for his wonderful logo for the event, which appears on the cover of this book. Martin created the logo for *THE ILLUSION OF LIFE*, too.

And I would like to express my appreciation to Katherine Moline, for her fine design work on the conference program, taking over from Gregory Harvey when he left for America.

Thanks also to Boz Kappie for the t-shirts, Stephen Jones and Alan Butterfield for the technical assistance, and Andrew Dodds for the introduction to *anime* on video.

In terms of the book itself, for their assistance with the Japanese side of it, I express my gratitude first to Fred Patten, for generously sharing his encyclopaedic knowledge with me; second, to Buichi Terasawa and Junco Ito, for their gift to me of a most informative video on *anime*; third, to Professor John Clark and then postgraduate teaching assistant Michael Fitzhenry of the Department, for translation of certain texts and guidance on certain things Japanese; fourth, to Deborah Szapiro, for her advice on the local and global animation industry, including the *anime* scene; and finally, to Jeanette Amano, for her assistance as a facilitator of communication with Kosei Ono in Japan.

Also much thanks to David Denneen, Brian Sherman, Rae de Teliga and Michael Heins for their support.

As for the images which illustrate this book, I want to express my gratitude to the U.S. Air Force, for providing the images for Patrick Crogan's essay; to Tezuka Productions, for those for Pauline Moore's essay; and to Shawne P. Kleckner and the Right Stuf International, Inc., for those for Fred Patten's essay.

Thanks also go to Freida Riggs, who substituted for me, keeping the work on the book moving forward, when I was overseas in 1996 on study leave.

Thanks to Lisa Trahair, for her fine and helpful refereeing of the essays; and to Rex Butler, for reading my Introduction and offering astute advice on its finalizing.

Thanks to Greg Shapley, former Managing Editor of Power Publications, and to Victoria Dawson, its present Managing Editor, and Kirsten Krauth, Assistant Editor, for their help in bringing the book to press.

Thanks to all the authors in the book, for their incredible patience, perseverance, understanding and encouragement.

Finally, thanks to Elizabeth Day, who has lived this book with me, even as she has animated my life, for many years.

Alan Cholodenko
August 2006

Contents

This book is dedicated to and in memory of Chuck Jones,
guest speaker at *THE ILLUSION OF LIFE* conference in 1988.

As well, it is dedicated to and in memory of Madame Barbara Gré,
whose generous donation made it and its precursor,
and the events that generated both, possible.

INTRODUCTION

ALAN CHOLODENKO

I

THE ILLUSION OF LIFE 2: More Essays on Animation follows on from *THE ILLUSION OF LIFE: Essays on Animation* (1991), the world's first book of scholarly essays theorizing animation, published by Power Publications in association with the Australian Film Commission. Even as the first book was generated by an event—*THE ILLUSION OF LIFE*—the world's first international conference on animation and Australia's first large-scale international festival of animation (1988),[1] *THE ILLUSION OF LIFE 2* was generated by one—*THE LIFE OF ILLUSION*—Australia's second international conference on animation (1995). (For details of its program, see the Appendix.)

THE LIFE OF ILLUSION was mounted by the Power Institute of Fine Arts of the University of Sydney in association with The Japan Foundation and the Museum of Contemporary Art (MCA for short) and had the dual venues of the Japan Cultural Centre and the MCA's American Express Foundation Hall for its three day event. It was affiliated with *KABOOM!: Explosive Animation from America and Japan*, Australia's first animation exhibition, curated by Philip Brophy at the MCA November 12, 1994-March 5, 1995. Like *KABOOM!*, the subject of *THE LIFE OF ILLUSION* conference was post-World War II animation in the United States and Japan. It too had as its foci: in terms of the United States, the work of Robert (Bob) Clampett and Ralph Bakshi and more recent TV animation, especially John Kricfalusi's Ren & Stimpy; in terms of Japan, the work of Osamu Tezuka and Hayao Miyazaki and more recent techno-animation.

The overseas guests were Kosei Ono, Japan's leading expert on comics and animation, and Fred Patten, one of America's foremost commentators on *manga* (Japanese comics), *anime* (Japanese animation) and science fiction. These historians were joined by 17 Australian theorists of animation to produce an event with sophisticated and fascinating historical and theoretical perspectives, an event offering provocative, complex and challenging takes on animation, many mobilizing 'poststructuralist' and 'postmodernist' approaches to the subject such as informed *THE ILLUSION OF LIFE* conference and book. Some of the participating Australian scholars were already acknowledged for their essays in that book.

THE LIFE OF ILLUSION conference proved to be a worthy sequel to *THE ILLUSION OF LIFE*—event and book. With its publication, this new volume continues and extends the work in the theory of animation of *THE ILLUSION OF LIFE* and *THE LIFE OF ILLUSION* conference.[2] It provides an abundance of understandings, approaches, qualifications, correctives and challenges to scholars not only in animation studies but in Film (i.e. live action cinema) Studies. It proceeds on the supposition that animation studies and Film Studies are not separate, nor are they identical, and that the relations of one to the other call for intense, rigourous, scholarly theoretical inquiry. This is especially so as film, under the increasing impact of computer generated animation or imagery (CGI)—which we can simply call computer animation—reveals itself to be what it arguably was never not—animation! (a point which I shall elaborate in subsequent Parts of this Introduction). Indeed, *THE ILLUSION OF LIFE 2*, like its predecessor, offers rewards to disciplines across the spectrum—from the humanities to the physical sciences and technology (a point to which I shall return in Part IV of this Introduction.)

The remit of this Introduction is to characterize what has happened since the publication of *THE ILLUSION OF LIFE* to animation (Part I) and writing on animation (Part II), to contextualize further and describe the essays in this volume (Part III) and to present a final few key ideas and issues for the theorizing of animation (Part IV). The enormity of what has occurred means that there is much to cover. The length of this Introduction is testament to that enormity and byproduct of an effort to do justice to it and to how *THE ILLUSION OF LIFE* and *THE ILLUSION OF LIFE 2* relate to it for the reader (and the various constituencies composing it).

In this regard, in my Introduction to *THE ILLUSION OF LIFE* book, I suggested a number of reasons for that book and the event that generated it. *They are still apt* and apply to this book, animating it as they did *THE LIFE OF ILLUSION* conference; and I shall tease them out as I go.

The first reason was to begin to remedy the state of neglect in which animation had existed both as a film practice and as an object of theoretical inquiry—the neglect of animation by the popular and mass media forms of publication and legitimation and by the institution of Film Studies. But before I address what has happened in terms of that neglect since the publication of *THE ILLUSION OF LIFE* in 1991 (Part II), I will sketch in this first Part what has happened to animation as a film practice since.

What has happened is a quantum increase, expansion and diversification in animation production, distribution, exhibition and consumption around the world. It would not be amiss to call it a renaissance even, especially as, meaning rebirth, it is a term of animation. First, there has been an explosion of animation films in the classic drawn mode (or in the computer simulation of it) from the commercial studios in the United States and Japan—the two powerhouses in the field. (Japan is number one and the United States number two at present.)[3]

In the U.S., taking off from *The Little Mermaid* (1989)—the subject of an essay in this volume—Disney has produced over a dozen animation features for theatrical release, including *Beauty and the Beast* (1991), *Aladdin* (1992), *The Lion King* (1994)—the subject of two essays herein—and most recently *Home on the Range* (2004). In combination with Disney, John Lasseter's Pixar Animation Studio has brought to the big screen *Toy Story* (1995), *A Bug's Life* (1998), *Toy Story 2* (1999), *Monsters, Inc.* (2001), the Academy Award winning *Finding Nemo* (2003)—which surpassed *The Lion King* as the highest grossing animated film of all time—and *The Incredibles* (2004). DreamWorks SKG has made *Antz* (1998), *The Prince of Egypt* (1998), *The Road to El Dorado* (2000), the Academy Award winning *Shrek*

(2001), *Spirit: Stallion of the Cimarron* (2002), *Shrek 2* (2004)—poised to surpass *Finding Nemo* as the highest grossing animation film ever—and *Shark Tale* (2004). MTV Productions and Paramount Pictures have given us *Beavis and Butt-head Do America* (1996); Nickelodeon *The Rugrats Movie* (1998), *Rugrats in Paris: The Movie* (2000), *Jimmy Neutron: Boy Genius* (2001) and *The Wild Thornberrys Movie* (2002); Turner *Tom and Jerry: The Movie* (1992), *Cats Don't Dance* (1997) and with Warner Bros. *Quest for Camelot* (1998); Warner Bros. *The Iron Giant* (1999), *Osmosis Jones* (2001) and *The Polar Express* (2004)[4]; and Blue Sky Studios and Fox Animation Studios *Titan A.E.* (2000) and *Ice Age* (2002).[5]

As for the lush array of feature animation films made in Japan—the subject of six essays in this book—I need to first observe that while Hayao Miyazaki was producing more and more features for domestic release in Japan in the 1980s, Katsuhiro Otomo's *Akira* (1988) led the charge of *anime* into theatrical release in the West. It was a watershed moment for not only the animation relations of Japan and the U.S. but world animation. 1991 and beyond has seen Miyazaki's *Porco Rosso* (1992), *Princess Mononoke* (1997) and the Academy Award winning *Spirited Away* (2001)—which also won the Golden Bear for Best Film at the 2002 Berlin Film Festival and is the top-grossing film to date in Japan—arrive in the West and, like *Akira*, gain theatrical release. (In fact, since 1996, Walt Disney Enterprises has distributed Miyazaki's Studio Ghibli films in the U.S. and Canada, while more recently, Columbia Tristar has distributed Shinichiro Watanabe's *Cowboy Bebop* (2001) and DreamWorks Satoshi Kon's *Millennium Actress* (2001). (Kon is increasingly emerging as one of contemporary Japan's most significant animators.)

At the same time, feature films from other key Japanese directors and what are now over 20 studios have been released on video (including animation films made specifically for video release, called *OVAs*—Original Video Animations, sometimes written OAV*s*—Original Animation Videos) and DVD overseas, including in Australia. These include Hiroyuki Kitakubo's *Roujin-Z* (1991), Kenichi Sonada's OVA *Rhea Gall Force* (1989) and OVA series *Bubblegum Crash* (1991), Hideki Takayama's *Overfiend* film trilogy (constructed from his 1987 OVA series *Urotsukidoji*, released in English in the early '90s), Hiroshi Fukutomi's *Battle Angel Alita* (1993), Buichi Terasawa's *Takeru* (1993), Isao Takahata's *Pom Poko* (1994), Mamoru Oshii's *Ghost in the Shell* (1995) and *Patlabor 2* (1995), Satoshi Kon's *Perfect Blue* (1998), Otomo's *Spriggan* (1998), Hiroyuki Okiura's *Jin-Roh (Man-Wolf)* (1999), Kitakubo's *Blood: The Last Vampire* (2000), Yoshiaki Kawajiri's *Vampire Hunter D* (2000), Fumihiko Takayama's *Patlabor 3* (2002), Kon's *Tokyo Godfathers* (2003), Otomo's *Steam Boy* (2004) and Oshii's *Ghost in the Shell 2: Innocence* (2004).

Second, there has been an increasing popularity of model animation, for example, *James and the Giant Peach* (1995), a hybrid combining model animation (plus some computer animation) with live action (at head and tail), a U.S./UK production joining Walt Disney Pictures, Allied Filmmakers and Skellington Productions. Especially popular has been claymation, singularly that of England's Nick Park and Peter Lord and their Aardman Animation feature *Chicken Run* (2000) and their wonderful Wallace and Gromit shorts—films like *A Grand Day Out* (1990) and the three Oscar winners: *Creature Comforts* (1990), *The Wrong Trousers* (1993) and *A Close Shave* (1995). As well, and following in the Oscar-winning footsteps of Aardman, Australian Adam Elliot's Academy Award winning claymation short *Harvey Krumpet* (2003) calls for mention. Acknowledgement must also be given the puppet animation of *Team America: World Police* (2004), by *South Park's* Trey Parker and Matt Stone, among other things a homage to the '60s TV series *The Thunderbirds*.

Third, there has been the increasing proliferation of 'hyperhybrid' 'live action' films using special effects animation, likewise increasingly computer animated—usually science fiction and/or horror films, but some transposing favoured comic book superheroes to the screen.[6] Taking off from James Cameron's *The Abyss* (1989), these have included such American films as his *Terminator 2: Judgment Day* (1991), Robert Zemeckis' *Death Becomes Her* (1992), Tim Burton's *Batman Returns* (1992), Francis Ford Coppola's *Bram Stoker's Dracula* (1992), Steven Spielberg's *Jurassic Park* (1993), Chuck Russell's *The Mask* (1994), Zemeckis' *Forrest Gump* (1994), Ronald Donaldson's *Species* (1995), Roland Emmerich's *Independence Day* (1996), Tom Shadyac's *The Nutty Professor* (1996), Zemeckis' *Contact* (1997), Emmerich's *Godzilla* (1998), George Lucas' *Star Wars*: Episode

1—*The Phantom Menace* (1999), Larry and Andy Wachowski's *The Matrix* (1999), Bryan Singer's *X-Men* (2000), Simon West's *Lara Croft: Tomb Raider* (2001), Chris Columbus' *Harry Potter and the Philosopher's Stone* (2001), Sam Raimi's *Spider-Man* (2002), Ang Lee's *The Hulk* (2003), Jonathan Mostow's *Terminator 3: Rise of the Machines* (2003), and Quentin Tarantino's *Kill Bill*, Vol. 1 (2003) and *Kill Bill*, Vol. 2 (2004). The list is enormous and growing daily.[7]

And fourth, there has been the advent of totally computer animated feature animation films, starting in 1995 with John Lasseter's *Toy Story*, followed by Pixar's other features, as well as those of DreamWorks SKG, plus Fox's *Ice Age* (2002) and Disney's *Dinosaur* (2000). And to these must be added Hironobu Sakaguchi and Moto Sakakibara's *Final Fantasy: The Spirits Within* (2001), an American/Japanese co-production. In this regard, one must also cite the pioneering totally computer animated shorts from John Lasseter and Pixar: *Luxo Jr.* (1986), *Red's Dream* (1987), *Knickknack* (1989), *Mike's New Car* (2003), and Lasseter/Pixar's three Academy Award winning shorts—*Tin Toy* (1988), *Geri's Game* (1997) and *For the Birds* (2000).

This proliferation and saturation of film animation for theatre and home (on videos and DVDs, as OVAs from Japan) is also complemented by the increase in the number of animation film festivals. The well-established annual international ones—at Annecy, Bristol (The Animation Festival, Bristol has morphed into Animated Encounters there), Los Angeles (the Los Angeles International Animation Celebration has been revived in World Animation Celebration Los Angeles), Ottawa, Zagreb, Hiroshima, Krok (in Russia)—and the new one—Cartoons on the Bay (in Italy)—have been supplemented by local ones, including in Australia. While *THE LIFE OF ILLUSION* gave the Australian premiere to five *anime* as part of the event (see the program in the Appendix), Australia's first *anime* festival—the *JAPANIME* festival—was held in Sydney in 2000, followed two years later by Sydney's second—the *JAPANIME 02* festival (also presented in Melbourne, Brisbane and Canberra)—both curated and directed by Deborah Szapiro. In their wake, a number of *anime* features have been screened in Sydney, the latest being the *Miyazaki Showcase* of five films. Australia also has the Brisbane International Animation Festival, created by Festival Director Peter Moyes, and the Melbourne International Animation Festival.[8]

There are as well signs of the gradual acceptance of the animated film on the larger festival circuit. Miyazaki's win at Berlin two years ago is testimony, as is the acceptance into competition at the Cannes International Film Festival of *Shrek*, and more recently, of both Oshii's new *Ghost in the Shell 2: Innocence* (2004) and *Shrek 2*. So, too, is the new Oscar for Animated Feature Film.[9] Locally, the Melbourne International Film Festival has included animation programs curated by Philip Brophy, featuring the work of Osamu Tezuka and Studio Ghibli.

Beyond such modes of distribution, exhibition and consumption of animated film lies television, where the use of animation is a staple. It even has dedicated channels—Cartoon Network, Nickelodeon, Fox Kids and the Disney Channel—offering an incredible range of animation, from—to select among too many—*The Bugs Bunny Show, The Tom and Jerry Show* and *Tiny Toon Adventures* to *The Simpsons, Ren & Stimpy, Dr. Katz, Professional Therapist, Beavis and Butt-head, King of the Hill, South Park* and *Futurama*, from *Pokémon* and *Sailor Moon* to *Bubblegum Crisis: Tokyo 2040* and *Neon Genesis Evangelion*, from *Crapston Villas* and *Pond Life* to Eastern European and Australian art animation, and—in terms of made-for-television computer animation—from France's *Les fables géométriques* (1989-1992) and *Insektors* (1993) and the Canadian studio Mainframe Entertainment's 1994 'ReBoot' series to The Simpsons' episode *Homer*^{3} (1995) (with its partial use of computer animation) and Japan's *Robot Wars*—Japan's several decades of cel animated robot series and the English-speaking world's *Robotech* morphed into computer generated 3D form.[10]

Furthermore, animation—be it film, video or computer animation—on TV is used for commercials, for station and program idents, and for MTV rock video clips, most notably Michael Jackson's computer animated *Black or White* (1991), directed by John Landis and produced by Pacific Data Images (which also did the computer animation in *Homer*^{3}). Jackson's clip has received much popular comment, as well as scholarly attention, for its use of morphing.

Then there is the computer, where more and more animation

is coming on-line. The computer offers animated games (as does video), advertisements, even sites explicitly dedicated to animation, including cataloguing, exhibiting and promoting it.[11]

In other words, we have experienced an exponential leap of animation in our media, in the systems which deliver it and in its popularity, too. Indeed, for Ben Crawford, the animation in our media is but a part of a larger process, one that he maps in his essay in this volume: the expansion, following the Disney model, of commercial animation into an animation entertainment-industrial complex, one composed of networks proliferating ever increasing forms and experiences of animation, including through merchandising, licensing of character properties, marketing cross-promotions and tie-ins, studio stores, theme parks, websites (including The Animation World Store on awn.com), etc.

To pass from description to overt theorizing here: for me this immersion in animation in and by the media (even including the entertainment-industrial complex as media) has increasingly, uncannily, brought something uncanny 'home': animation 'itself'. Put simply, we are increasingly discovering that we and the world swim in a sea of media, and vice versa. And we are increasingly finding that the nature of not only what swims in that sea but of that sea itself is animation 'as such', which for us it has always been. In other words, for us, not only do all the media (film, television, the computer, etc.) show animation, they are *themselves as media* of the order of animation. The media are animate—animators, animated and animating. In my Introduction to *THE ILLUSION OF LIFE*, I claimed that not only is animation a form of film, film—all film—is a form of animation. (I will return to this claim in Part II.) To extend that point: not only is animation a form of the media, the media—all media, including film—are forms of animation, or rather forms of reanimation: reanimators.[12]

And that animation/reanimation in and *of* media has reached tidal wave, or better tsunami, proportions, what I call *hyperanimation*—an increasingly extreme, increasingly engulfing phenomenon, in terms of not only all aspects and modalities of context and performance but all aspects and modalities of form and content. This tsunami is for me signified by the Matthew Martin logo that graces the cover of this new volume, one aptly after the Japanese artist Hokusai. And I should add: after the Greek sea god Proteus, too, singular sign for me of the reanimations, the 'transformations'—the 'extreme makeovers', the 'ultimate transformations'—occurring 'within' and 'without' the media, including not only within but between the 'West' and the 'East'. As well, Proteus is inescapably for us singular figure of Sergei Eisenstein's notion of 'protean plasmaticness'—that formless form that, giving all form, is itself ungivable as such[13]—which is for him the essence of animation, sign for me of the *animatic*, which various of the essays in this book in different ways instantiate.[14]

And this animation tsunami applies to the fans, too. The new generation is not composed only of kids (not that Chuck Jones and the folks at Warner Bros. animation ever thought its audience was). Animation has now on offer a range of products for consumers of all ages, genders, etc., from kids to adolescents to adults (though for me, and in ways that are profound for the thinking of animation, they all qualify at the same time as 'kids of all ages'!). Here Japan has been for us the leader, its *anime* offering a significantly wider range of genre, subject matter and theme than classic Western animation. Indeed, as Deborah Szapiro declares, in Japan, animation films are 'part of the mainstream'[15]; and they are becoming increasingly so in the West (although we could as well say that they have already become so if we include computer animated feature films, especially the hyperhybrid 'live action'/animation films, in our consideration[16]). Australian correspondent Alexa Moses states:

> The animated feature film is experiencing a popularity not seen since the glory days of Disney. That's backed up by the $37 million box office returns for *Finding Nemo*, which made it Australia's highest earning film last year. *Shrek II*…is already the top-grossing animated film of all time in the US.[17]

As for the fans, there is a Japanese term for one who is fanatically devoted to *anime*—'*otaku*'—a term well known across the English speaking world, this itself a sign that animation is increasingly taking 'centre stage' globally for 'kids of all ages'.[18] A new generation of consumers is ready to immerse itself and disappear in this sea of animation in and of the media. And crucially, the increasingly extreme, *hyperanimate* life and motion in and of this sea increasingly reanimates the world and its fans (ourselves) in its animation, for fans become hyperfans. Or shall we not say simply *fanatics*, as defined by Chuck Jones in terms of his rules for one Wile E. Coyote:

> RULE 3. 'THE COYOTE COULD STOP ANYTIME—*IF* HE WERE NOT A FANATIC. (REPEAT: 'A FANATIC IS ONE WHO REDOUBLES HIS EFFORT WHEN HE HAS FORGOTTEN HIS AIM'.—GEORGE SANTAYANA).[19]

Such redoubling cannot but recall Jean Baudrillard's definition of the ecstatic, of *hypertelia*—that extreme, exponential process of pushing things to the limits where they at once fulfill and annihilate themselves—precisely characterizing contemporary hyperreality, increasingly the only 'reality'. It is a process of escalation, of intensification, of maximalization,[20] where things function all the better for having been liberated from their idea, content, referent, aim, etc., a process privileged by the cartoon and by the contemporary form of animation—hyperanimation—even as experiencing and partaking in such animation becomes the sole passion of the hyperfan.[21] It is a passion encapsulated for me in these words of Baudrillard: 'Since the world drives to a delirious state of things, we must drive to a delirious point of view'.[22]

For us, the media, the world and the fans have been caught up in the same hyperreal, hyperbolic, hyped-up, 'ground-breaking', 'envelope-pushing', 'mind-blowing', 'adrenalin-rushing', 'jaw-dropping', 'eye-popping', 'ear-shattering', 'hair-raising', 'heart-pounding', 'heart-stopping', 'breath-taking', 'nerve-wrenching', 'gut-wrenching', 'bone-crunching', 'in your face', paroxystic, ecstatic, hypertelic game of pushing things to their limits, 'over the top', 'to the max', 'to infinity and beyond!'—an 'action-packed', 'high-impact', 'high performance', 'performance-enhanced', 'dynamite', 'totally awesome', 'stop you in your tracks', 'drop dead', 'scare you to death', 'life-threatening', 'death-defying', 'block-busting', 'roller coaster', 'collision course', 'thrill ride', at 'warp speed', at 'terminal velocity'—adventure on 'the brink of disaster', catastrophe, apocalypse—singularly exemplified and performed for us by post-World War II hyperreal, hypertelic film animation in Japan and the U.S. The extreme states and extreme sensations of explosive entertainment! (Implosive, too, at the same time.) 'Fast films', like fast food, offering a 'quick fix', a 'quick change', all 'super-sized' and 'at the speed of live'.[23]

Or, on the other hand, it can be slow, or rather, hyperslow. The only requirement is that, whatever the process, it be hyper, that is, the *'more x than x'*, and that it apply to *all* qualities, categories, operations, etc., and in *all* spheres, *the subject included*—for example, the hyperfast (the faster than fast), the hyperslow (the slower than slow), the hypertrophic or hyperlarge (the larger than large), the atrophic, or hypersmall (the smaller than small), the hyperobese, the hyperobscene, the hypersexual, the hyperviolent, the hyperterrorist, the hyperhostage, the hypergraphic, the hypershocking, the hyperloud, the hypersoft, the hyperdefined (hi-fi), the hyperindefined, etc. All things tend in the direction of the hyper. Here, media become hyperanimate *hypermedia*, hyperreal, pure and empty, third and fourth order simulations, viral vital virtualities, virtual realities, living and moving in the world and us, as at the same time the world and we live and move in them, *hypercryptically*, *hyperanimatically*, making it increasingly impossible to say which is which—which media, which world, which ourselves[24]—the immersing effect of media in the immediate by media, hence world and ourselves, become *immedia*.[25] All things tend in this direction: the *hypermediatic*.

II

Since 1991, the neglect of animation as a film practice by the popular and mass media forms of publication and legitimation has been on the wane, especially it seems in light of two key developments.[26] One was the explosion in production and consumption of both American and Japanese feature length animation, including the increasing dissemination of the latter to the West (something whose nature and implications I consider in Part III of this Introduction). In this regard, as I indicated in Part I, Australia had its first animation exhibition in 1994-1995—*KABOOM!*—and appositely it was on the post-World War II animation of the United States and Japan. It itself played a part in this dissemination and popularization of animation in general and post-World War II American and Japanese animation (and popular culture) in particular. (*THE LIFE OF ILLUSION* conference played a part, too.) *KABOOM!* attracted large crowds keen to experience an audio-visual sensorium of intense, dizzying, extreme sound/image bombardment that for Brophy (and myself) is characteristic of the manic, hysterical, psychotic post-World War II cartoon world. Also, it generated significant media coverage, served to educate people in the history of the commercial animation dominating the post-World War II period and landscape, and was encapsulated in a book (detailed later in this section).

The other key development for me in animation's leap in popularity, its taking 'centre stage' in the 1990s, was digitalization. Live action film increasingly became computer animated, animation films became totally computer animated, and video and computer games (to say nothing of the computer, period!) came to dominate the lives of a new generation of kids and kids at heart. (Several essays in this volume bear upon this development.) Such digital reanimation—in and of film, the computer, the mass media 'in toto'—seemed to receive increasing attention, considerable reportage and almost universal approbation from the popular and mass media and from an expanding legion of fans. (The increasing consideration given this development in academic texts has been far more mixed, ambivalent, in response, even in some quarters opposed, as it has been linked to, even seen as the engine of, the increasing virtualization of reality, and vice versa—the reanimation of reality itself as virtual, hyperreal.)

As for the neglect by the institution of Film Studies of animation as a film practice and as an object of theoretical inquiry—Film Studies having regarded animation as the most inferior and inconsequential form of film or not a form of film at all, rather a form of graphic art—little progress is visible to this reporter. Here, I would add: the neglect of animation by disciplines other than Film Studies, too. Whether attending Film Studies conferences or those of other disciplines in the United States or here in Australia, I have perennially found—and continue to find—the terms 'animate' and 'animation' used with monotonous regularity in papers; yet they always remains taken-for-granted, unexamined terms in their own right (as does the perennial expression that something has 'a life of its own'). Perhaps that will change, even as the Society for Cinema Studies—the world-wide organization of Film Studies academics—(which has continued to have a panel or two on animation at its annual conferences) has changed its name recently to the Society for Cinema and Media Studies, as the animation so pervasive and integral to the media ever increasingly draws attention to itself and insists it be acknowledged and addressed.[27] Not that that is assured, of course. Film historians and theorists writing of the changing, reanimating, face of cinema over the last 30 or so years under the impact of animation may well continue to ignore the pertinence, even as they use the terms, of animation.

As for animation studies, since 1991 it has continued to grow. In terms of institutional events, the Society for Animation Studies held its fifteenth annual conference in September-October 2004 at the University of Illinois at Urbana-Champaign. In addition, the Animation Research Centre of the Surrey Institute of Art & Design, University College, staged a two day conference, *Animated 'Worlds'*, July 10-11, 2003, at Farnham Castle. (Of course, even the creation of such a Centre, which happened in 2000, is itself indicative). Closer to home, there was a one day symposium organized by Patrick Crogan and held at Artspace, in Sydney, May 16, 2003, entitled *Ludic Moments: Computer Games for the Time Being*. Crucially, insofar as the computer game—like all that is computer *animated*—is a form of animation, conferences on computer games are conferences per se on animation.[28] Simply put, the computer not only expands considerably but profoundly reanimates what can be understood to be the purview of animation studies.[29]

Even as animation in and of film, television, the computer—the mass media—has boomed since *THE ILLUSION OF LIFE*, so has English language publication on animation.[30] This veritable explosion (or again tsunami) has by my count generated at least 140 new books to date (and there have been nine reprinted, revised, second or third editions as well, including the reprinting of the first manual and book on animation film—E.G. Lutz's *Animated Cartoons: How They Are Made, Their Origin and Development* (Bedford, Mass.: Applewood Books, 1998), published in 1920 by Charles Scribner's Sons.

These new books include both the popular (at least 86) and the academic (approximately 54), and they have been supplemented by issues of popular magazines and by two dedicated academic journals.[31] While *Animation Magazine, Animatrix,* and *Animato!* continue to publish, there has been a proliferation in particular of popular magazines for *anime* fans, so much so that one might speak here also of a tsunami of popular publications on the subject.[32] The two academic journals are: *Animation Journal,* edited by Maureen Furniss, founded in 1991; and *Animatrix,* a graduate student publication of the UCLA Animation Workshop, first published in 1984.[33]

As well, there have been special issues devoted to animation in non-dedicated academic (and non-academic) journals[34] and articles on animation in non-dedicated issues of non-dedicated academic (and non-academic) journals.[35] Moreover, on the World Wide Web, one can access considerable material on animation.[36]

The vast majority of these popular books on animation are on American animation (70 out of 85), especially Disney and his studio (35), maintaining Disney as the number one subject of such books, from Robert Feild's *The Art of Walt Disney* (New York: Macmillan, 1942) to today.[37] As for other Hollywood studios, Warner Bros. is represented by Chuck Jones' *Chuck Reducks: Drawing from the Fun Side of Life* (New York: Warner Books, 1996)—his lovely, rich supplement to *Chuck Amuck: The Life and Times of an Animated Cartoonist* (New York: Avon Books, 1989)—as well as by Hugh Kenner's *Chuck Jones: A Flurry of Drawings* (Berkeley, CA: University of California Press, 1994).[38] MGM is represented,[39] including in texts related to the work on Tom and Jerry there of William Hanna and Joseph Barbera.[40] More recent American film animation—both cel and CGI—is also covered[41]; and made-for-TV animation gets a look-in, too.[42] And there are encyclopedias on American animation.[43]

After the United States, the nation with the second largest number of popular publications in English since *THE ILLUSION OF LIFE* is aptly Japan. The fact that the animation of these two nations has dominated English language publication over this time frame is itself indicative of why not only *KABOOM!* but *THE LIFE OF ILLUSION* conference and this book were called for. There are a substantial and burgeoning number of guides to *anime*, many by Helen McCarthy,[44] as well as a popular introduction to Japanese animation—Antonia Levi's *Samurai from Outer Space: Understanding Japanese Animation* (Chicago: Open Court, 1996). And Fred Patten, our conference guest, has just published his *Watching Anime, Reading Manga* (Berkeley: Stone Bridge Press, 2004), a collection of essays and reviews of the last 25 years.

Finally, there are several 'encyclopedic' texts not delimited to U.S. animation to assist both the fan and the scholar.[45] There are still practical and technical guides to animation being published.[46] And there are even books now on collecting animation art,[47] acknowledging the massive growth globally in the marketing of cels, quite a few of which command prices of thousands of dollars.

As I declared, the academic books on animation that have appeared since the publication of *THE ILLUSION OF LIFE* number around 54. (To these might be added the sections on animation of *The Oxford History of World Cinema*, edited by Geoffrey Nowell-Smith, and *An Introduction to Film Studies*, edited by Jill Nelmes.)[48] Also, I would mention that Giannalberto Bendazzi's *Cartoons: Il cinema d'animazione 1888-1988* now exists in revised, updated, English language translation as *Cartoons: One Hundred Years of Cinema Animation* (London: John Libbey, 1994). Due recognition must also be given essays on animation in non-dedicated academic books as part of the boom in animation scholarship.[49]

Most of the academic books are in the areas of animation history (be it national, studio, individual, artistic, authorial, generic, industrial, audience reception, economic, social, cultural, ideological, institutional, commercial, 'mainstream', 'avant-garde/experimental', etc.) and animation aesthetics. Again, as in the popular area, the majority is American/Hollywood animation (28); and Disney again figures strongly (17), and in both categories—history and aesthetics.[50] (As with the popular, a number of the academic texts focus on Disney theme parks.) In addition, and at long last, there is a collection of scholarly essays focusing exclusively on Warner Bros. animation: *Reading the Rabbit: Explorations in Warner Bros. Animation*, edited by Kevin S. Sandler (New Brunswick, NJ: Rutgers University Press, 1998). And there are four texts that follow on from Leonard Maltin's groundbreaking *Of Mice and Magic: A History of American Animated Cartoons* (New York: McGraw-Hill, 1980), surveying the history of the American animated cartoon and industry.[51]

As for Japan, there are but a few scholarly books in English: the anthology of Brophy's exhibition—*KABOOM!: Explosive Animation from America and Japan* (Sydney: Museum of Contemporary Art, 1994); Susan J. Napier's *Anime from* Akira *to* Princess Mononoke: *Experiencing Contemporary Japanese Animation* (New York: Palgrave, 2000); and the *anime* section of the anthology *Animation in Asia and the Pacific*, edited by John A. Lent (London: John Libbey, 2001), which includes an essay by Fred Patten on the subject. To this book list must be added the special issue on *anime* of the journal *Japan Forum*, vol. 14, no. 2, 2002, edited by Thomas Lamarre, which I will, along with the first two items, address below.

Beyond these publications, there are the first general introductions to animation history and aesthetics in English—by Maureen Furniss and Paul Wells, which I shall also comment on below[52]—and other first texts on their respective topics in English.[53]

For me, all the academic books published since *THE ILLUSION OF LIFE* are required reading. There are many important publications among them. Some are standouts for me. In the area of history and aesthetics, I must first single out a text that was published before *THE ILLUSION OF LIFE* but which I did not see before we went to press: Donald Crafton's *Emile Cohl, Caricature and Film* (Princeton: Princeton University Press, 1990), the follow on book from his groundbreaking *Before Mickey: The Animated Film 1898-1928* (Cambridge, MA: The MIT Press, 1982)—a meticulously researched, richly conceptualized, lushly illustrated volume on this pioneering animator that, like its predecessor, has much to offer the animation theorist.[54] Also dazzling is Norman M. Klein's *Seven Minutes: The Life and Death of the American Animated Cartoon* (1993), a text of great intellection and erudition, incredibly nuanced description, and profound speculation about not only the Hollywood cartoon but animation 'as such'.[55]

Here, turning to the matter of the theory of animation, I must first advise that for us no text is devoid of theory and theorizing. In fact, for us, all texts theorize and are 'in-formed' by theory, including a theory or theories of animation, including of what animates them as texts and what they animate (just as every film is so 'in-formed' for us), *regardless of whether theory is explicitly addressed as a subject*. Indeed, a text like Klein's is incredibly learned, steeped in theory and rich in theorizing, though the book does not explicitly foreground them, focusing on animation aesthetics and history (industrial and social).

This being said, since the publication of *THE ILLUSION OF LIFE*, a small number of books have explicitly brought the theory and theorizing of animation—the explicit focus and project of *THE ILLUSION OF LIFE* and this new volume—to the fore. They *all* pioneer in and contribute to the study of animation, including, to varying degrees, in the areas of the theory and theorizing of animation. They warrant thorough analysis and evaluation of that theoretical work, including as it relates to ours, necessarily impossible in this limited space. I hope that even this cursory identification and characterization may serve a salutary function for the interested reader, who I in any case encourage to engage with and evaluate for him- or herself these texts, including their work in the theory and theorizing of animation. They are (in terms of chronological order):

• *KABOOM!: Explosive Animation from America and Japan* (Sydney: Museum of Contemporary Art, 1994)—with essays scholarly (including Brophy's lovely 'Ocular Excess: A Semiotic Morphology of Cartoon Eyes') and popular, and interviews conducted by Brophy and others with key animators, including Ralph Bakshi, John Kricfalusi, Mike Judge, Hayao Miyazaki, Rumiko Takahashi and Katsuhiro Otomo. *THE ILLUSION OF LIFE 2* is for me its companion, even as the conference on which *THE ILLUSION OF LIFE 2* is based companioned the *KABOOM!* exhibition, not only sharing its foci and its organizer but its organizer's radical belief in the radicality of the 'mainstream' cartoon, where for Brophy 'animation achieves its most brutish yet most dynamic form'.[56]

Its extreme manifestations are found for him as for me precisely in post-World War II American and Japanese animation. Such 'mainstream' cartoons are for us more radical than the 'radical', counter-'mainstream', alternative animation text, be it political (of a Marxist or other putatively subversive or transgressive political persuasion) or in the fine arts tradition of avant-gardist animation.[57] I put it thus: insofar as animation is of the order of the limit, the cartoon is the limit of animation, the limit therefore of the limit, the extreme form, performance and measure of all animation.

• *A Reader in Animation Studies*, ed. Jayne Pilling (London: John Libbey, 1997)—the first and still only collection of selected essays from the Society for Animation Studies annual conferences. It has 21 essays in all, including five by William Moritz, with a 'Theoretical Approaches' section containing four. The essays are divided between commercial (Disney, John Kricfalusi) and 'independent' animation (both traditional and more recent 'European' fine art—the Czech Jan Svankmajer; the England-based Americans the Brothers Quay—and contemporary feminist). While focusing mostly on cel animation, the anthology includes an essay by Michael Frierson on clay animation, essays by Lev Manovich and Andy Darley on computer animation, and one other essay obviously relevant to *THE ILLUSION OF LIFE* and this new volume: Luca Raffaelli's 'Disney, Warner Bros. and Japanese animation'.

• Maureen Furniss' *Art in Motion: Animation Aesthetics* (London: John Libbey, 1998) and Paul Wells' *Understanding Animation* (London: Routledge, 1998)—the first general introductions to animation aesthetics in English. These are clearly required readings for anyone interested in animation, wide-ranging celebrations and mappings of the animated film and what the authors propose as its aesthetic specificities. Furniss' book is explicitly meant as a course textbook or for general reading, Wells' is for the more advanced reader. While they both take up animation theory in a self-declaredly necessarily limited way, still I must say that I find certain aspects of that work problematic, especially to the degree that their theoretical models are aligned with and framed by what is for me a limited in scope, reductive, undertheorized and undeconstructed Cultural Studies model focused on identity that seems today to pervade the academy and that bears strong linkages with late '60s French and English Marxist film theory, its cultural politics, its simple either/or taxonomies (eg. either reactionary or radical), its commitment to reveal the mode of production, expose the illusion and liberate the viewer from their ideological interpellation in and mystification by the commodified and commodifying, fetishized and fetishizing capitalist bourgeois film text and apparatus, etc.[58] Just for openers, such paradigms for me mistakenly exclude the experimental from the traditional/orthodox and at the same time the traditional/orthodox from the experimental—the near century long history of experimental, independent and abstract film animation and their by now long established (some would say petrified) canonical codes and conventions for 'subverting and transgressing'.

• *Reading the Rabbit: Explorations in Warner Bros. Animation*, ed. Kevin S. Sandler (New Brunswick, NJ: Rutgers University Press, 1998)—the first collection of essays dedicated to Warner Bros. animation, all attempting, writes Sandler, 'to map the theoretical and historical implications of Warner Bros. animation in terms of its place not only in animation history but also in American cinema and popular culture'.[59] The essays, many of which are fine, provocative, stimulating, range widely in subject and cover the entire history of Warner Bros. animation. Several seem powerfully invested in Cultural Studies' considerations of class, race, and gender and 'discourse theory'. Sandler's Introduction offers an important analysis and even partial critique of Warner Bros.' '90s return to animation.

• Eleanor Byrne and Martin McQuillan's *Deconstructing Disney* (London: Pluto Press, 1999)—to my knowledge the only text endeavouring to do what my '*Who Framed Roger Rabbit,* or the Framing of Animation' essay in *THE ILLUSION OF LIFE* did, that is, bring Derridean deconstruction to the theorizing of animation.[60] The subject here is Disney animation, more particularly, the New Disney, even the NDO (New Disney Order), from *The Little Mermaid* on. I find this a difficult, quirky, highly uneven text in many regards, not without considerable theoretical problems, including in its treatment of Disney pre-*The Little Mermaid*, Baudrillardian simulation (including its place in their analysis) and even, most crucially, deconstruction itself. Occasionally, acute theoretical insights concerning animation erupt but then as quickly disappear, presented as they are in all-too-brief, byte-size, schematic assertions, as if self-evident, rather than as argued, developed articulations. This is a problem compounded by their text being for me impossibly riven between the promotion of an undeconstructed, Marxist politics-based Cultural Studies *and* at the same time its deconstruction, at once an undeconstructed Marx *and* a Marx deconstructed by Derrida.

• *Meta-Morphing: Visual Transformation and the Culture of Quick-Change*, ed. Vivian Sobchack (Minneapolis: University of Minnesota Press, 2000)—the first and only English language book to my knowledge on the history and theory of digital animation, or more precisely, of the shape-shifter that is the digital morph. The book takes its place for me in animation studies, not only because the morph is avatar of the key figure and process of animation—metamorphosis—but because digital animation is subsumed by definition within animation. Though Sobchack and others in the book use the term 'computergraphic' when referring to the digital morph and the digital technologies enabling as well as exceeding it and treat animation as a genre of film, the term 'computergraphic' easily translates as digitally or computer *animated*. It is a book replete with informative, stimulating and challenging essays, including that of the editor. (Her Introduction is excellent, too).

• Susan J. Napier's *Anime from* Akira *to* Princess Mononoke: *Experiencing Contemporary Japanese Animation* (New York: Palgrave, 2000)—the first and to my knowledge only scholarly introduction to *anime*, focusing on that key Cultural Studies and postmodern issue of identity (here Japanese)—personal, sexual, national, etc. For Napier, animation's 'emphasis on metamorphosis can be seen as the ideal artistic vehicle' to express postmodernism's 'obsession with fluctuating identity', even as '*anime* may be the perfect medium to capture what is perhaps the overriding issue of our day, the shifting nature of identity in a constantly changing society'.[61] While differing from us in foregrounding the artistic, Napier, like ourselves, places animation 'centre stage' for contemporary culture in terms of issue, medium and vehicle. Hers is an insightful, innovative, accessible, well written text.

• Esther Leslie's iconoclastic, thought-provoking *Hollywood Flatlands: Animation, Critical Theory and the Avant-Garde* (London: Verso, 2002)—the only book to my knowledge to host 'a number of encounters between animated films, figures of the avant-garde and modernist critics'.[62] These include the encounter of avant-garde artist Sergei Eisenstein with Disney and those of European modernist critics Walter Benjamin, Theodor Adorno, Max Horkheimer and Siegfried Kracauer with Disney and Fleischer Brothers cartoons (and varyingly with the work of each other, too). In light of such animating encounters, the critics for Leslie 'developed their thoughts on representation, utopia and revolution...'[63] For them, Leslie notes, '...cartoons...are set inside a universe of transformation, overturning and provisionality'.[64] It should be noted that the Critical Theory in the book's subtitle refers to that of the Frankfurt School (though I can find it nowhere stated in the book), with which Benjamin et al were associated to different degrees, not the contemporary variety associated with Derrida, Samuel Weber and others. While erudite and ground-breaking in many regards, Leslie's text for me could profit in multiple regards from (an understanding of) the work of that contemporary variety, as could just about every academic text published to date on animation.

To this list of books must be added the special issue of *Japan Forum*, vol. 14, no. 2, 2002, mentioned earlier, devoted to the theory of *anime*.[65] Edited by Thomas Lamarre, its six essays form the first and to my knowledge only scholarly collection published on the topic. The issue contains some highly provocative, ambitious, in many regards rewarding essays, including Mark Driscoll's 'From Kino-Eye to *Anime*-Eye/*ai:* The Filmed and the Animated in Imamura Taihei's Media Theory'; Livia Monnet's 'Towards the Feminine Sublime, or the Story of "A Twinkling Monad, Shape-Shifting Across Dimension": Intermediality, Fantasy and Special Effects in Cyberpunk Film and Animation', focusing on *Ghost in the Shell* and *The Matrix*; and the editor's 'From Animation to *Anime*: Drawing Movements and Moving Drawings', on modalities of Miyazaki's ethico-aesthetic philosophy.

There are affinities, to varying degrees, between these ten publications and *THE ILLUSION OF LIFE*, in terms of, on the one hand, the ideas, issues, topics and themes it raised and foregrounded as crucial for the theorizing of animation, and, on the other, the theoretical approaches and theorists it privileged for that enterprise—ideas, issues, topics, themes, theoretical approaches and theorists which this new volume continues to foreground and privilege. In fact, a number of the ideas, issues, topics and themes *THE ILLUSION OF LIFE* privileged are later foregrounded by other writers. For example, the key relation of animation to Freud's uncanny—which Robyn Ferrell implicitly in her essay 'Life-Threatening Life: Angela Carter and the Uncanny' and I explicitly in my Introduction privileged—is raised by Furniss; Wells; Byrne and McQuillan; Sobchack in her Introduction to *Meta-Morphing* (but in terms of digital media); Napier; and Monnet in *Japan Forum*.[66] The crucial importance to the theorizing of animation of Eisenstein's notion of protean plasmaticness—posed and engaged with by Keith Clancy in his 'ΠΡΗΣΤΗΡ: The T(r)opology of Pyromania' and Keith Broadfoot and Rex Butler in their 'The Illusion of Illusion' in *THE ILLUSION OF LIFE*—is raised by Michael O'Pray in his essay in *A Reader in Animation Studies*; Furniss; Wells; Leslie; Sobchack in her Introduction (again in terms of digital media) to and Matthew Solomon in his article in *Meta-Morphing*; and Monnet in *Japan Forum*.[67]

In terms of the theoretical approaches and theorists *THE ILLUSION OF LIFE* privileged for the theory and theorizing of animation, I must say that it is not for us only a question of remedying the theoretical neglect of animation. It is a question of *how* that neglect is remedied. For example, it is a key point of my Introduction to *THE ILLUSION OF LIFE*—indeed the first premise of the book and this sequel—that not only is animation a form of film, film—all film—is a form of animation. There is an historical component and a theoretical one (not that they do not commingle) to this premise/point. The animation apparatus of Emile Reynaud's Théâtre Optique, which entertained over 500,000 spectators at the Musée Grévin in Paris from 1892 to 1900, possessed all the elements of the cinematic apparatus minus photography, suggesting (and inverting the conventional wisdom in the process) that cinema (that is, live action film) is animation's step-child. Indeed, from the outset of film, the cinematic apparatus was described in various ways as an animator of images, turning still inanimate photographic images into mobile animated cinematographic ones, thereby providing 'the illusion of life'.[68]

This means that cinema cannot be thought without thinking (its relation to) animation. It means that, insofar as animation's logics, processes, performances, etc., operate in all film, *including live action*, the theorizing of animation must by definition be a theorizing of all film. Therefore, animation's logics, processes, performances, etc., must be brought to bear upon such theorizing, including of live action (in its various modes and genres). Such a rethinking of all aspects of film through animation and animation theory must have the most profound consequences for (all) film theory—its reanimation as film animation theory—and for Film Studies—its reanimation as Film Animation Studies. Its key consequence for me in terms of live action would be to make live action a special case, a conditional, reduced form, of animation.

Here it is important to state that I am not the first to claim that film per se is a form of animation. Writing in 1973 of Reynaud, the acclaimed animator Alexandre Alexeïeff stated:

> It is certain that the invention of 'cinema' had been patented by Reynaud who did not have enough money to sue the Lumière brothers and win.
>
> Anyhow, it is legitimate to consider cinema as a particular kind of animation, a sort of cheap, industrial substitute...which was destined to replace the creative work of an artist, such as Emile Reynaud, with photography of human models 'in movement'.[69]

Also that year, Ralph Stephenson declared of Reynaud: 'He not only invented a technique, he originated a new art and was the first to develop the animated film (indeed the cinema if by *cinema* we mean movement, not photography) into a spectacle'.[70] Even earlier than Alexeieff and Stephenson, Taihei Imamura, as Driscoll tells us, had the same idea, positing animation as prior to and the basis of film.[71] And Eisenstein made the point even earlier, in *Eisenstein on*

Disney, when he posited animation as the essence of film.[72]

Will Straw characterized the startling, provocative nature of the thesis of *THE ILLUSION OF LIFE* as follows: 'The claim that film studies might require a theory of animation as its core cannot help but seem audacious when it is first encountered'.[73] As audacious as it seemed in 1991, when I challenged with it Donald Crafton's limited and limiting assertion in *Before Mickey*—'the animated film is a subspecies of film in general'[74]—it remains so still. And not just to film scholars but, and in a sense astonishingly, to most animation scholars.[75] For the overriding tendency—perhaps better to call it the orthodoxy—on the part of animation scholars continues to be to treat animation as a genre, a form, of film, perhaps as a way of seeking to legitimate animation by giving it a place within cinema and its history, without going the extra and radical step we take, which is to see all film as a form of animation.[76] (I have more to say about this restricted approach in the next pages.)

That all film is a form of animation has a profound implication for computer animation: it is not the case that only recently, with the advent of digital animation, film became animation. It has *never not* been animation. An often cited recent expression of this point is Lev Manovich's assertion: '*Born from animation, cinema pushed animation to its periphery, only in the end* [digital cinema] *to become one particular case of animation*'.[77] But I would qualify: for me, the 'in the end' to which Manovich refers is always already in the beginning. As I proposed in 1991 in *THE ILLUSION OF LIFE*, cinema was never not a 'particular case of animation', and Film Studies never not a particular case therefore of animation studies—the consequence of our inverting the convention wisdom by thinking of cinema as animation's 'step-child'. Such a turn, such a spiraling return by Film Studies and film theory to animation, from which they came and from which they never departed, marked and marks for me a certain turbulence, a certain violence, a certain 'uncanny' fatality, to animation itself.

But Manovich's perception of such an historical 'development' itself registers something profound, profoundly ironical. Animation—too long taken for granted, too long considered either too 'familiar' *or* too 'strange' by Film Studies, the cinephiles of live action cinema, the popular and mass media, etc.—suddenly *uncannily* metamorphoses/morphs into something of paramount, even singular, importance, into something at once strangely familiar and familiarly strange, that is, into something *uncanny*, which it was never not.

The computer-generated metamorphosis of live action cinema into what it was never not—animation—and the hypersaturation by such computer animation of American cinema are two of the most compelling reasons why animation and animation theory must be taken into account by Film Studies and film theory (and by all other relevant constituencies), in order to understand such cinema and the uncanny process of its advent, even as the uncanny metamorphosis of animation into 'live action', including in computer animation and *anime,* is a potent reason for animation theorists to take into account film theory.[78]

Related to this thinking of all film through animation is the other, groundbreaking, radical aspect of *THE ILLUSION OF LIFE*, and this new volume: our privileging of 'poststructuralist' and 'postmodernist' approaches for the theory and theorizing of animation. Here for the sake of concision and brevity I repeat these two contextualizing paragraphs from the Introduction to the first book:

> ...as a way of acknowledging the nature and significance of the work already done [in the study of animation], perhaps it would be more apt to see this book as endeavouring to reanimate animation studies by endowing it with subjects, themes and approaches not heretofore brought to thinking and writing about animation film nor for that matter, at least explicitly, about animation: subjects the criteria for addressal of which are not their aesthetic merit nor inherent propriety and good taste; themes and approaches not of the banal humanist ilk, not pietistic and platitudinous, not naively empiricist or 'exclusively' historical, not focused only on the subject as animated and animating authorial (and artistic) agency, not taking animation as only productive and 'life asserting', not reductivist and simplistic. Rather, these essays seek to account for the complications, implications, duplications, perplexities, indeterminacies and dilemmas which for them animation marks, including animation's special association with the 'abject', the double, the 'uncanny', the sublime, seduction, *différance*, disappearance and death—all those improper, unseemly things which

> would likewise count as reasons for the 'exclusion' of animation by Film Studies. And in articulating animation with these complications and associations, these essays are reanimating not only animation studies but the very idea of animation.
>
> In this regard the approaches to animation in almost all the essays by film theorists in the book are informed by 'post-structuralist' and 'postmodernist' critiques of that mix of literary semiology, Althusserian Marxism and 'Lacanian psychoanalysis' that coalesced in a theory of film in the late '60s in France and was disseminated worldwide primarily by the English film journal *Screen*. Thus it might be suggested that the film theory brought here to the thinking of animation film and animation as idea represents the very latest approaches to their subjects, bringing the latest theorization of film together with the latest theorization of animation, which is also to say that this animation theory is also and inevitably film theory, animation/film theory [and film animation theory] endeavouring to reanimate not only animation theory and animation studies but film theory, Film Studies and the very idea of film.[79]

Here I need to make a qualification. As we learn from Imamura, Eisenstein and from writers in France—in the '20s and '30s, those associating animation with Surrealism, especially such writers as Gus Bofa and Marcel Brion, and in the '40s with the work of Giuseppe Lo Duca—animation theory has already existed. So we are in that sense reanimating animation theory in accord with the theoretical givens and trajectories that we privilege.

THE ILLUSION OF LIFE animated its animation theory on the basis of its *critique of and challenge to* 'existing film theory'—that of the prevailing model of late '60s Marxist film theory—as well as its *critique of and challenge to* existing approaches to animation. However, while the theory being developed in *THE ILLUSION OF LIFE* was, and that here in this second volume is, a critique of 'existing film theory' and a critique of modeling not only film but animation on such film theory, it would be a mistake to presume that that film theory should simply be ignored by animation (film) theorists. For me, as a matter of scholarship and intellection, that theory must be worked through in its own terms to see what it can and does offer both in its specificities and as a model, as well as to see how a model has been and can be animated. Moreover, insofar as live action film is a form, a special case, of animation, (that) film theory can be of assistance in theorizing animation, even as the theorizing of animation can be of assistance in querying and challenging (that) film theory, its terms, axioms, claims, etc., especially given that that late '60s Marxist film theoretical model still (in my opinion) largely pervades Anglo-American Film Studies. The powerful criticism that it, and Cultural Studies, have received for their simple oppositional thought (and for their other shortcomings, too) from the 'poststructuralist' and 'postmodernist' approaches privileged in and by *THE ILLUSION OF LIFE* seems to have as yet little purchase in Film Studies and far less in animation studies.

In my Introduction to *THE ILLUSION OF LIFE,* among other things, I indicated that simple oppositional thinking calling for simple inversion of dominant and subordinate relations is not enough, especially not for the thinking of animation (and the animation of thinking!). Beyond the simple either/orism of late '60s Marxist film theory and of Cultural Studies (either reactionary *or* radical, passive *or* active, oppressed *or* liberated, object *or* subject, false *or* true, male *or* female, etc.) lies the commonalty of their exclusive emphases on: *pure production,* foremost *the production of identity* (in all possible forms, including self-identity—including the fetish cliché and alleged panacea of 'self-reflexivity'—as well as in terms of author, genre, gender, sex, race, religion, nation, etc.), complemented by *the production of power* (and the power of production), *the production of desire* (and the desire of production), and *the production of the social* (and the social of production); *the ontological,* on the *meta-,* including of metaphysics, on fusion, union, presence, essence, truth, meaning, reality, identity, self-identity, etc.; *the subject and his desires; representation* and *theories of representation* (and misrepresentation) of reality (including therefore ideology); *sameness and difference;* and *a banal criticality.*

What is for me missing from all this is the considering at the same time, to say nothing of privileging, of, respectively, the *limits of production* (and of reproduction) in *all* its forms, its *dissemination, seduction,* reversion, undoing, etc.; the *hauntological*—

the deconstruction/dissemination of the ontological, of the meta-, of fusion/union, etc.; *the object and its games;* the so-called *'crisis of representation', the catastrophe of the reality-principle,* even *simulation* and *theories of simulation;* Derridean *différance,* to say nothing of Baudrillardian *Seduction, Illusion, Evil, radical Exoticism,* irreducible, irreconcilable *Otherness;* the *critical theory* of Derrida, to say nothing of the *fatal theory* of Baudrillard.

To which critiques we would add: the sense at times of the patchwork, the pastiche, of radical eclecticism (surprisingly, that anything goes...and goes with anything else—the antithesis of scholarly rigour, resembling ironically nothing so much as a set of postmodernist tastings, a smorgasbord, thin on, if not devoid of, theoretical substance, where elements war with and among each other, a war that itself goes unobserved, much less commented upon, as does its effect upon the 'whole' smorgasbord; and what I call the 'scholar in the bubble' syndrome, that is, the writing of destruction, ruin, catastrophe, including to identity and self-identity, without reflecting (on) that in the writing itself, on the author's own ability to write, to claim what they claim, as if they, including their very identity, could be the exception to, could stand outside of, protected, safe and exempt from, what they write about, what they claim. (This includes writing critically of postmodernism in a postmodernist style of pastiche, radical eclecticism, etc., that embodies precisely what the writer is criticizing!)

The lack of purchase by animation studies of these critiques is not surprising, for a number of reasons in fact. One would have to be that most writers in animation studies seem unacquainted not only with such critiques but with the model (and texts forming that model) of which they are critiques. It is intriguing that, while late '60s Marxist film theory writing forms in varying aspects a clear precedent for certain theoretical writings in animation studies, it rarely is cited in them, pointing to a significant lack of knowledge of not only that work but of the way in which their writing on animation is arguably retreading the same path and opening itself to the same criticisms. So here is another persuasive reason why animation studies needs to address and engage with Film Studies rather than ignore it the way Film Studies has ignored animation and animation studies.

The message seems clear: Film Studies needs to take account of animation and animation theory. And animation studies needs to take account of film and film theory, of the issues, debates, logics, terms, axioms and suppositions that have marked its theorizing, the critiques and challenges they have called forth, the transformations (or lack thereof) they have undergone, etc. It needs to take account of Film Studies, of *its animation* and *reanimation* since its advent as a 'discipline' in the late '60s.

It is thus promising that, in contrast to Pilling's criticizing *THE ILLUSION OF LIFE* as the attempt 'to graft existing film theory onto animation'[80] (which I would insist it crucially was not and did not do, at least not in her sense), in his report on the 2003 *Animated 'Worlds'* conference, Edwin Carels acknowledged 'three prominent names in the field of film theory' and celebrated the following:

> The fact that Laura Mulvey, Kristin Thompson and Vivian Sobchack are now willing to focus their attention and apply their ideas on certain aspects of animation is a strong signal that the field of animation studies is gaining maturity, and that its 'ghetto' is opening up to a wider range of discourse.[81]

Of course, the effort to 'take account of' Film Studies and film theory, to help the field to mature and to open it up to theoretical approaches not up to then informing it were key goals and projects that *THE ILLUSION OF LIFE* put into play for animation studies—not only in its single-minded commitment to the theory and theorizing of animation but in its mobilizing of 'poststructuralist' and 'postmodernist' approaches to achieve those objectives.

Though it is disappointing, in many ways it is not surprising that Film Studies still in largest measure ignores animation and that animation studies likewise does Film Studies, and that most animation studies academics seem to want to keep animation as not only merely one form of film—a point made earlier—but also at the same time a form that is completely autonomous and different from all other film forms, preeminently live action. For me, even to take animation as a form, genre, of film would mean that any theorization of it would be valuable for theorizing film as such, therefore of obvious importance to not only animation studies but Film Studies. But if one accepts the orthodoxy that animation is an autonomous form of film—a form, genre, of film completely different from all other kinds of film—animation would have nothing to do with nor to tell us about other modes of film and would leave the animation theorist in no position to theorize film as such. Of course, our second step, taking all film as a form of animation, puts the animation theorist in a singular position to theorize film as such. Indeed, for me, animation comes to irretrievably, always already perturb, disseminate, denegate, seduce, as do the 'poststructuralist' and 'postmodernist' approaches privileged by us, any marginalizing, excluding, isolating, 'ghettoizing' and/or 'safekeeping' of animation on the part of any entity whatsoever, including Film Studies and animation studies.

For me, intimately implicated in this 'isolating' and 'safekeeping', this 'ghettoizing' effort,[82] is what still overridingly animates animation scholarship (as it does Cultural Studies, to which we shall return)—the issue of identity—in this case, the drive to define animation's identity, to seek a specificity to it, to establish its uniqueness, its essence, to distil (it into) its pure form, one significantly, even completely, different to live action. (That effort takes on a modernist cast when animation is claimed or assumed to be purely modernist in nature.) That in turn is one part of the overweening focus of Anglo-American academics on the subject of identity—and the identity of the subject—in all its forms, including personal, sexual, national, etc. For me, any thinking of animation cannot delimit itself to the thinking of the subject and its desires—including for identity, in all its forms—and of production and appearance—including, again, of identity, in all its forms—cannot delimit itself to the thinking of the subject as (putative) master and commander of all it surveys—but must at the same time consider what Anglo-American theorists (including animation film theorists) have typically ignored, that is, the object and its games, games superior to the subject—*the life of illusion* of objects, the life of *the animatic apparatus* and its modes of seduction, play, dissemination and disappearance, a life and modes bearing privileged relation to the cartoon, the child, the looney, the primitive, savage and primal, the nonhuman, the object, the world and the universe, and vice versa.

To sum up: in order to begin to accomplish the goal of remedying the neglect, preeminently theoretical, of animation, our modus operandi in 1988 was, and remains so now, to operate on two fronts simultaneously. To proceed in a way that would seek: 1. to reanimate Film Studies and film theory, and 2. animate, or rather reanimate, animation studies and animation theory, retheorizing film and film theory through animation and animation theory as film animation and film animation theory, respectively.

To remedy that theoretical neglect—of not only animation film but film animation—necessitated approaches that would 'do justice' to the complexities of what animation most profoundly and compellingly is. For me, the 'discipline' of Film Studies, especially as one finds it in America over the last three plus decades, is dominated by theoretical models, logics and assumptions that do not do justice to film because they are reductive, banal, and ironically, 'static'. In a word, they are not *animated*—itself testament to the lack of acknowledgement by Film Studies that film is a form of animation.

It makes no sense to bring 'inanimate' theoretical models, logics, structures, etc., to the thinking of animation, be it film or any other kind of animation. Rather, such thinking calls for the models, logics, processes, performances of animation 'itself', the complex, fatal and dynamic logics of animation, of animation as the animatic. Which in turn means for us bringing to the thinking of animation and film a bevy of approaches—'poststructuralist' and 'postmodernist'[83]—that are themselves animate, animated, animating—themselves animatic.

Let me pause to say: I theorize the *animatic* as not only the very logics, processes, performance and performativity of animation but the very 'essence' of animation—*the animation* and *animating* of *animation*. The animatic subsumes animation, is its very condition of at once possibility and impossibility, at once the inanimation in and of animation and animation in and of inanimation. The animatic is that nonessence enabling and at the same time disenabling animation as essence, including Eisenstein's protean plasmaticness as essence (which is why I put essence in quotation marks). Not only is the animatic uncanny, the uncanny is animatic. The animatic is not simply different but *radically*, irreducibly Other.

The animatic is precisely for me best described, exemplified and performed by the 'poststructuralist' and 'postmodernist' approaches privileged in our two volumes for the theorizing of animation—by their logics, processes, performances and performativity, likewise impossible of solution or resolution. These approaches not only offer the richest ways to theorize the animatic, they are the most isomorphic with it, the most, as it were, informed by and performing it.[84]

One other point demands mention. The much touted 'turn away from Grand Theory' in Film Studies and the call for such a turn in animation studies are not only misguided, they are, indeed, ironical. To wit, Pilling's explicit 'casting out' of *THE ILLUSION OF LIFE* from animation studies by subsuming the book within and making it subject to David Bordwell's notion of and attack on Grand Theory is *itself* based on Grand Theory, the Grand Theory she, like Bordwell (and Noël Carroll), embrace and propound: the Grand (ie. totalizing) Theory that Grand Theory is per se unacceptable, devoid, of no value.[85] Indeed, it would be hard not to argue that an Objectively Ironical process turns the much heralded so-called 'turn away from Grand Theory' at the same time into a turn toward it—the special effect for us of animation as the animatic. Indeed, given the errors, misunderstandings and reductions 'informing' the Anglo-American version of late '60s French film theory, one might even venture the proposition that 'Grand Theory' in that version has yet to begin, making the call for a 'turn away' from it decidedly premature.

The Grand Theory of animation that there is and can be no Grand Theory of animation has come with a corollary, as well ironical, Grand Theory, that only 'piecemeal theorizing'[86] and '"piecemeal" approaches that concentrate on individual films'[87] are worthwhile and legitimate. For me, working on both fronts simultaneously—global theory and 'piecemeal theorizing', including 'small analyses' of individual texts—is not only necessary but unavoidable, for they, like the global and the local, are inextricably coimplicated. Which means that it is only through one that one can 'arrive at' the other, and any effort to suppress one thereby only causes it to assert itself all the more.

The 'poststructuralist' and 'postmodernist' approaches we privilege are explicitly at work within almost all the essays in each volume and establish theoretical consistencies within each volume as well as across the two of them, generating (and now doubly reinforcing) the 'theoretical coherence' that Will Straw in his review highlighted as a strength of the first book.[88] Their thinking of the animatic and its apparatus necessarily rethinks the cinematic and its apparatus, as they necessarily rethink film as film animation, even as they perform the animatic—all of which contributes profoundly to the binding of the essays in a theoretically 'coherent' project.

The relentless, 'single-minded', global pursuit of that common theoretical project has allowed at once the remedying of not just a single neglect but a dual neglect on the part of both Film Studies and film theory and animation studies and animation theory (and by other 'disciplines' that use the discourses of animation without engaging with it): 1. the theorizing of film 'as such' as a form of animation; and 2. the theorizing of animation as a form of 'philosophy'. The theorizing of the first at once calls for the rethinking of all aspects of film through animation and opens the door to thinking animation beyond film (including theorizing all other art and media forms as forms of animation—drawing, painting, sculpture, photography, TV, video, computer, new media, etc.). The theorizing of the second, of animation as a form of 'philosophy', of philosophizing (and I would add, the theorizing of philosophy as a form of animation—the animating of concepts), calls for the thinking of animation far beyond conventional notions of it, far beyond its pervasive modeling in terms of just aesthetics and/or Cultural Studies. It also calls for rethinking the terms of that pervasive modeling. It certainly calls for thinking animation beyond those texts that frame animation (and believe it can only be so framed) in terms of either internal states of consciousness (where one is never far from the clichéd descriptions 'surrealist', 'surrealist dream imagery' or 'hallucinatory') or external depictions of cultural formations, the either/or of a banalized Freudian or socio-political (even Marxist) model (often accompanied by another either/or, that of either 'self-conscious' or 'un-self-conscious' artists/authors/texts).

The remedying of that dual neglect calls for theorizing animation in the widest, grandest and deepest ways possible, as a concept and process 'whose purchase', as I wrote in my Introduction to *THE ILLUSION OF LIFE*, 'would be transdisciplinary, transinstitutional, implicating the most profound, complex and challenging questions of our culture, questions in the areas of being and becoming, time, space, motion, change—indeed, life itself'.[89] For me, these approaches to animation, to film animation, to animation 'as such', open the door to the theorizing of all animation as a form of the animatic. Put simply, they animate animatic understandings of animation, while at the same time performing the logics and processes of the animatic (about which I will have more to say in the pages ahead).

In terms of such approaches, in his review of *THE ILLUSION OF LIFE*, John Conomos asserted:

> Indeed the book's *raison d'etre* focuses on its various postmodernist perspectives that are not only specifically concerned with the thinking of animation, but which challenge us to rethink our most basic concepts of the cinematic apparatus and film in general.[90]

This thinking of all film through animation and all animation through the animatic (and its apparatus) opened up by the theoretical approaches we privilege remains a bulwark to our enterprise.[91] In pursuit of such rethinking of the cinematic apparatus and film in general as animatic apparatus and film animation, *THE ILLUSION OF LIFE* and this new volume are—to use a term of animation—'inbetweeners' operating between film and animation, Film Studies and animation studies.

Here let me recall those contemporary French 'philosophers' I named as privileged for the theorizing of animation in my 1991 Introduction, thinkers whose differing work I have nonetheless characterized for convenience (but in any case too swiftly, globally and unproblematically) with the abbreviation '"poststructuralist" and "postmodernist" approaches': Jean Baudrillard, Hélène Cixous, Gilles Deleuze, Jacques Derrida, Luce Irigaray, Julia Kristeva, Jacques Lacan[92] and Michel Serres, and the noted American theorist Samuel Weber. To this list I added such other key relevant figures, cited in the essays, as Gaston Bachelard, Roland Barthes, Georges Bataille, Maurice Blanchot, Jorge Luis Borges and Paul Virilio.[93] In addition to 'contemporary French thought', *THE ILLUSION OF LIFE* privileged classical Greek philosophy—the 'Presocratics' (Keith Clancy foregrounded Heraclitus), Socrates, Plato, Aristotle—the work of Kant and Hegel, Nietzsche, Freud, etc., as well as of Walter Benjamin, Sergei Eisenstein, etc. This new volume continues to valorize all of them, while extending the list to include, most notably, Thomas Hobbes, Henri Bergson, Edmund Husserl, Martin Heidegger, Pierre Klossowski, Philippe Lacoue-Labarthe, Slavoj Žižek and Gayatri Chakravorty Spivak.[94] This list is not, nor could it be, comprehensive.[95]

The contemporary French thinkers that we have privileged still turn up but rarely in academic publications on animation to date. Three of the texts explicitly dedicated to the theory and theorizing of animation make no mention of them. And where they do appear, in most cases, including in the majority of the remaining publications explicitly dedicated to the theory and theorizing of animation, it is in a very spotty, occasional, minimal, slight, superficial and eclectic manner. Their work has rarely garnered attention, to say nothing of knowledgeable, sophisticated, rigourous, scholarly attention, to say nothing moreover of affirmation, in animation studies. In the few places where it has been referenced (including under the rubric of 'poststructuralist' and/or 'postmodernist thought'), it is almost always misunderstood and/or reduced to only one of its multiplicitous and even clashing terms and dimensions. Its richness and complexity receive little, if any, play, to say nothing of acknowledgement. Postmodernism gets flattened into a matter only of aesthetics—pastiche, parody, irony, quotationality, eclecticism, play, etc. (typical of swathes of American academic publications where postmodernism receives passing reference and Fredric Jameson is the only authority mobilized on the subject). And 'deconstruction' as a term, which seems everywhere used, seems almost everywhere misused, as deconstruction as a practice and process (including as process of animation as the animatic) seems almost everywhere misunderstood. In all these cases, it is never informed by Derrida's work (except for Byrne and McQuillan in part). Such ignorance of deconstruction is often combined with hostility toward it.

Such thinkers are most in evidence, and explicitly so, and most mobilized to theorize animation—which includes theorizing those topics, issues, objects, figures, etc., key to and privileged in and by *THE ILLUSION OF LIFE*, and this new volume—in but a few publications to date: the books by Byrne and McQuillan (1999) and Napier (2000), the *Meta-Morphing* (2000) and *Japan Forum* (2002) anthologies. Such use obviously varies in terms of the thinkers addressed, their number, and the intensity and extensivity of their deployment. (And its accuracy, too.) It is lovely to see thinkers we privileged, for example Derrida and Kristeva, likewise privileged in these texts, Derrida by Byrne and McQuillan, Kristeva by Napier.[96]

Which is why for me it is these four explicitly theoretical texts (to which I would add Klein's *Seven Minutes*) that have the most in common with *THE ILLUSION OF LIFE* and this new volume. And, given the fact that *Meta-Morphing* and the *Japan Forum* issue are anthologies and these thinkers seem to be most massed and deployed (and deployed by a number of authors in certain ways consistent with *THE ILLUSION OF LIFE*) there, they, of all the publications to date on the theory of animation, have for me the greatest affinity to *THE ILLUSION OF LIFE* and this new volume. They most share with us the aspiration to a grand vision of what animation is, in their case the grand vision of what the digital morph is (*Meta-Morphing*) and of what *anime* is (*Japan Forum*), and the commitment to the sophisticated, complex theorizing required of and by animation. They accept the challenge it poses to theory, to thought, including mobilizing the demanding, wide-ranging intellection of the thinkers privileged in and by *THE ILLUSION OF LIFE*.

So at long last, there are two publications that in these key regards have a significant affiliation with our 1991 book, and with this new volume, too, with its essays on digital animation and *anime*.[97] Indeed, insofar as morphing is crucial to digital live action cinema—as evidenced by *Meta-Morphing's* essays—and *anime* bears crucial relations to 'live action' cinema per se (Lamarre so situates the essays even in the title of his Introduction, 'Between Cinema and *Anime*'), *Meta-Morphing* and the special issue of *Japan Forum*, like *THE ILLUSION OF LIFE* before them, not only serve animation studies but Film Studies. Thus, by definition they exemplify one key project of *THE ILLUSION OF LIFE* and this new volume: to retheorize, that is, to reanimate, the theory and history of cinema in and through animation.

I would add: for me *Meta-Morphing* and *Japan Forum* have a significant affinity with each other in the key parallelism linking their theoretical objects, for digital animation and post-World War II *anime* are for me the hyperreal forms/avatars of their respective antecedents.[98] To be more precise, the digital morph, like such *anime*, takes up a place for me in the theorizing of animation in terms of Baudrillard's third and fourth orders of simulacra. For me, the morph is the cold, disenchanted, viral, fractal, clonal, pure and empty, hyperreal, *metastatic* form of that enchanted form *metamorphosis*. Put otherwise, the morph is metamorphosis in its metastatic expression. It is the disillusion of life, not *the illusion of life*—except for the possibility, unprovable like its opposite, that it is merely the avatar of metamorphosis, of the illusion of life, of that first order of the enchanted, seductive form of illusion, a detour always already, strangely, uncannily, returning to that from which it departed.[99] In either case—metamorphosis or metastasis—it is never not a case for us of what we call *lifedeath*. Put simply, digital animation is the reanimation of animation in its/the hyperreal form of lifedeath.

In sum, few of the 54 scholarly/academic texts published on animation since *THE ILLUSION OF LIFE* engage directly, explicitly, intensively, extensively, rigourously and sophisticatedly: 1. with the topic of the theory of animation 2. in the explicit theorizing of animation 3. in the explicit animating of animation theory 4. with and in all three—respectively the topic and projects of *THE ILLUSION OF LIFE* and now *THE ILLUSION OF LIFE 2*. The vast majority of such publications to date do not acknowledge—much less embrace, valorize, or mobilize—the theorists and theoretical approaches, the 'poststructuralist' and 'postmodernist' perspectives, privileged and advanced in and by *THE ILLUSION OF LIFE* (nor, it should be said, the topics, ideas, issues, figures, themes, etc., we have privileged, the claims we have advanced, the understandings we have generated). While the majority of the publications dedicated to the theory and theorizing of animation acknowledge the 'French theorists' (the term including those non-French thinkers theorizing within the 'orbit' of that French work) we have privileged, of that majority four do so but slightly, four do so more committedly and significantly. In fact, it is the non-French theorists we have privileged, Freud and Eisenstein most notably, who, at least numerically, dominate the theoretical publications, turning up together in six of them (seven if one wants to read the mention of the protean in Napier as referencing Eisenstein though he is never explicitly named), with Freud appearing alone in an additional three, making Freud the number one thinker utilized in these publications.

At this point in our assessment of how the scholarly publications on animation since *THE ILLUSION OF LIFE* compare with it, and with our new volume (and our new volume with them), I need to add Cultural Studies, to which I have given passing reference. Like the late '60s Marxist film theory model, with which, as I indicated earlier, it has significant affinities, the Cultural Studies model is one which *THE ILLUSION OF LIFE* and this new volume challenge, radically, unqualifiedly so, as do the theorists and theories the essays in the two volumes draw upon and privilege.[100] This cannot be said of most of the publications explicitly focused on the theory and theorizing of animation. Such publications align animation and animation studies to varying degrees with Cultural Studies, framing animation with the topics, terms, assumptions and modelings that form Cultural Studies' matrix of concerns and approaches (something Leslie at least in one key regard explicitly wants to contest). While in at least half of them that affiliation is slight, partial, occasional and restricted in application (especially in the case of the anthologies, where variability also is introduced in terms of the individual essays collected), to the degree that they possess such an affiliation, they are at loggerheads with their privileging of theorists and theories we likewise privilege, as well at loggerheads with certain of their readings of their textual objects. As a result, such texts are for me the site of internecine warfare.[101]

All of which makes *THE ILLUSION OF LIFE* and *THE ILLUSION OF LIFE 2* radically different, in terms of almost all academic publications to date both on animation and on film, and which not only animates but maintains the animate(d) and animating nature of the two volumes. They are for me in largest measure singular, pioneering and fresh, at once 'timely', 'early' and 'to come', for *both* animation studies and Film Studies.

Which means that the work we began in 1988 with *THE ILLUSION OF LIFE* conference, published in 1991 in *THE ILLUSION OF LIFE* book, extended in 1995 with *THE LIFE OF ILLUSION* conference, and now publish here, has still just begun.

III

Here I must pause to clarify. The title of the conference from which this book is drawn—*THE LIFE OF ILLUSION*—was and is not just a simple playful inversion of *THE ILLUSION OF LIFE*. It evokes for me a powerful, seductive, playful thought: with animation one is always dealing not only with the illusion of life but with the life of that illusion, an implication already in and at play in *THE ILLUSION OF LIFE* (the book included). We would put it thus: insofar as film animation simulates the world and the subject, offering an illusion of life, animation as the animatic would be the very seduction of that simulation and doubling, the very life of (that) illusion itself.[102]

Here a second key point: by the term 'the illusion of life', I did not in my Introduction to *THE ILLUSION OF LIFE* nor elsewhere intend to, nor did I, nor do I now, circumscribe the theorizing of animation with Disney's definition of the term, that is, animation aspiring to a realism of depiction such as one associates with classic Hollywood live action cinema, that is, to a theorizing of animation that would be delimited to such simulation.[103] Not only did I trace the term back to the Lumière Bros.' definition of cinema at cinema's 'advent',[104] I was inspired by and inscribing in this term Baudrillard's treatment of illusion in the largest sense—the illusion of the world, of reality:

> The principle fundamentally and from the very beginning is that there is *no* objectivity to the world.
>
> But nevertheless one has to recognise the reality of the illusion; and one must play upon this illusion itself and the power that it exerts.[105]

This is what I sought (and seek) to evoke by these terms—*the illusion of life* and *the life of illusion*—the radical illusion of the world, its great game of putting into play, its artifice, its irony, its humour, and to propose, as I did in that Introduction, that 'animation film, film animation and the animatic apparatus offer us this animating gift of *the illusion of life*',[106] doing so through their gift of *the life of illusion*—the seductive life of their images and of the apparatus that delivers and performs them.

Such gifts remain alive, animated, for me in the first volume and are so in this second one, whose projects are several: to examine key aspects of post-World War II film animation, as well to consider, though in far fewer essays, video and computer animation, the animation entertainment industry and 'meta'-theoretical issues of animation. Through such theorizing, the book hopes to convey to the reader a powerful sense of the 'centrality' of animation to contemporary culture and the contemporary world, indeed to culture and the world 'as such'.

The 16 essays in this book are divided into five sections. The first three sections focus on post-World War II studio animation in Japan and the United States. The final two address, respectively, the 'expanded'[107] field of animation post World War II—including, among other things, the shifts from cel to digital animation and (arguably) from animation as an object to animation as an intertextual (corporate) field—and issues of a more general theoretical nature.

But before characterizing these sections and essays, I want to offer a brief contextualizing of the book's specific 'historical' and theoretical project: to investigate the animations of post-World War II Japan and the U.S. to see what they say not only about themselves but about animation 'as such'. And in the case of a number of the essays, to examine the processes at play not only within but between those animations, as well as within and between post-World War II Japan and the U.S., and across them—the crossover of film animation and nation animation.

That animation is 'central' to the contemporary world—indeed, the world as such—is singularly exemplified for us in terms of these two nations—each state and its culture not only extreme but singular in its own right—and the 'world-shaking', not only extreme but singular relations between them—animated relations that have been 'centre stage' since the beginning of World War II. Such relations have been for me singularly played out in and performed by their film animations, film animations that have themselves been 'central' to contemporary culture and the contemporary world.

This 'centrality' served as instigation, as animating agency, for our conference and this book. While American animation continues to dominate the post-World War II global landscape as it did the pre-war, by the mid-1990s *anime*, characterized by Annalee Newitz as Japan's 'chief cultural export',[108] had spread across the globe, its popularity only increasing since, including in the U.S. Today, it stands as sole worldwide competitor to American animation, even as what it singularly exemplifies—Japanese popular culture (including video and computer games)—stands as sole worldwide competitor of American pop culture.[109]

It is in the domain of popular culture—preeminently in the realm of animation and comics—that for Frederik L. Schodt a profound interchange, a cross-pollination, has occurred and is occurring between these two nations, nations not only foes but friends, not only mirrors but models, to paraphrase the title of his key book *America and the Four Japans: Friend, Foe, Model, Mirror.* Already in 1994, he declared: '...in the last ten years Japanese animation and comics have stormed into young America's consciousness'.[110]

For me, a game of seduction and simulation has been at play within and between post-war Japan and the United States, a game of challenge and outbidding, of seduction through simulation of and hyperconformity to the other, imitating the other better than the other imitates itself. Such a game is for me marked in the post-apocalyptic, post-nuclear hyperanimations of both post-war Japan and the United States and in the relations between them—relations played out within these films, in their production histories and in the economic, technological and cultural relations between the nations.

In such a context, the pushing by *anime* of Disney cute into hypercute—the more cute than cute—becomes an event of profound import, as does the nonacknowledgement by the Disney Company of *Kimba the White Lion* as a source of *The Lion King*. The pushing as well by *anime* of the speed, violence and war of Warner Bros.

cartoons into hyperspeed, hyperviolence and hyperwar is another highly loaded event. We would say that the hyperform of *anime* redoubles not only *anime* but live action, making it—hyper*anime*—more live action than live action, as exemplified for me by *Akira* and *Ghost in the Shell,* even as the hyperform of live action redoubles not only live action but *anime*, making it more *anime* than *anime*, as exemplified by *The Matrix* and *Kill Bill*. Put otherwise: as hyper*anime* challenges and outbids not only *anime* but American live action and hyperlive action (*Akira* and *Ghost in the Shell* re *Blade Runner, Alien, The Terminator*, for example), American hyperlive action challenges and outbids not only live action but *anime* and hyper*anime* (*The Matrix* and the *Kill Bill* films, for example, although the *anime* in *Kill Bill* seems for me to outbid its hyperlive action).[111]

All these hypertelic processes are thinkable as modes and games of competition between Japanese and American animation and between Japan and the U.S.[112] One might even postulate a war between and among them to outbid each other as animation, exemplifying and performing the *animus* (animosity) for us never not in animation.[113]

Here it is crucial to state: for me, the events played out within these animations are doubled by these animations being *themselves* events in and of the cultures that have produced them and been produced by them, as well as events in and of the transcultural relations between these nations, relations across the board: in the political, economic, social and sexual realms, in the areas of science and technology, in the realm of 'culture', the media, etc. In other words, for me, in the wake of 'the apocalyptic closure',[114] as Brophy characterizes it, of World War II—the dropping of the Atomic Bomb by the U.S. on Japan[115]—post-World War II animation in the U.S. and Japan underwent a mind-blowing metamorphosis, a generic/genetic transformation into a hypercharged, superconductive, nuclear-powered, chain reactive, delirious, excitingly excessive, extreme mode singularly exemplary and performative of the hyperreal processes in play in film, television, the computer, etc.—the mass media—the cultures and nations of Japan and the U.S., and the world in general.[116]

In consequence, the world (and the subject, too) is increasingly revealing itself to be animated, to be animatic, to be hyperanimatic, in the very terms of what is singularly in play in these post-World War II animations of Japan and the U.S. and in the relations between them. (And to say 'post-World War II' does not mean that one is post war, that war ceases. To the contrary, it can take other forms, including economic, technological, personal, cultural, including therefore what is at play in and of these hyperanimations of Japan and the U.S. and in the relations between them. War morphed into hyperwar.)

Jean Baudrillard writes of seduction in his essay *The Evil Demon of Images*: 'To begin to resemble the other, to take on their appearance, is to seduce them, since it is to make them enter the realm of metamorphosis despite themselves'[117]—the animatic effect. But the upshot of such seduction is the impossibility of saying who/what is imitating whom/what. Not only do the events within the films and of the films make it impossible to determine where the films end and, as they say, 'the real world' begins, they even, I would suggest, make it impossible to determine where the culture of Japan ends and that of America begins—not that perfect fusion of yin and yang that Schodt envisions of the relation of Japan and the U.S. but that (con)fusion marking the animatic process of the life of illusion.

This is to say that for me the animations of each country and their relations to each other declare that the cultures and nations of post-war Japan and the U.S. are 'in themselves' not only animated but animatic and in a not only animated but animatic relation to each other—the animatic not only indistinguishing film and reality, film and world, but film animation and nation animation, animating an increasingly definitive lack of differentiation between and among them.

If the term so often used to characterize *anime* has any purchase—'Japanimation'—what would be for me the animation of Japan, there would be a spectre that haunts the animatic relation between the two nations, one that I have called 'Jap*anime*rica'. This term stands for me as *the state of play* of animation not only between Japan and the U.S. but within them, singularly exemplified and performed by their film, video and computer animations, the state of play 'centre stage' in and of the world today.

Hence, we would say, even as *THE ILLUSION OF LIFE* had as its primary objective to begin to remedy the scholarly neglect of animation, *THE ILLUSION OF LIFE 2* has as one of its major purposes assisting in the remedying of the dearth of scholarly publication on 'Japanimation' and 'Jap*anime*rica', as well as contributing to scholarship in the other areas of its remit, and continuing to do so with theoretical approaches whose general lack of utilization it is at the same time remedying.

Now, to the essays.

The first section of the book consists of five essays on Japanese animation. It collectively canvasses and excavates key aspects of *anime*—its history, its two dominant post-World War II transgeneric figures/modes of cute and the apocalyptic, its aesthetics—its textual codes of image and sound—certain pertinent psychoanalytical, philosophical, social and cultural contexts, etc., its leading animators—especially Tezuka, Miyazaki and those given to a more techno, violent ilk, like Otomo, Takayama, Oshii and Anno—and major, indeed increasingly canonical, animations, especially Tezuka's *Astro Boy* and *Kimba the White Lion*; Miyazaki's beloved corpus, including *Nausicaa, Laputa, My Neighbour Totoro* and *Princess Mononoke*; Otomo's *Akira*; Takayama's *Urotsukidoji* (the Overfiend series); Oshii's *Patlabor* and *Ghost in the Shell;* Hideaki Anno's *Neon Genesis Evangelion*, etc.

The section takes off with 'The Long Flight of *Manga* and *Anime*: The History of Comics and Animation in Japan', a highly readable, delightful personal sketch by our overseas conference guest Kosei Ono of the history of these two interrelated forms, offering us tasty insights from the perspective of someone who grew up in Japan with them. Though not an academic theoretical piece, it offers, like Chuck Jones' in *THE ILLUSION OF LIFE*, a wealth of observations, insights and anecdotes to theorists of animation.[118] Ono's capsule historical overview—from 1917 to the final decade of the 20th century, with emphases on wartime propaganda animation, the work of Tezuka (especially *Astro Boy*) and Miyazaki—has many virtues, not least that of introducing us to the fact that *anime* did not commence post-World War II in the 1960s with *Astro Boy* but goes back to the second decade of the century and had a significant conversation with U.S. animation before and during World War II.

Ono's essay is followed by Pauline Moore's 'When Velvet Gloves Meet Iron Fists: Cuteness in Japanese Animation'. It addresses precisely one of the key features of *anime* as well as of popular culture in general in Japan—cuteness (*kawaii*)—which is also one of the features of most interest to Westerners. Moore argues that cuteness is a phenomenon that plays a profound role in and across *all* forms of *anime*, from the gentlest to the most violent and sexual, and proposes a tripartite historical and generational model of its elaboration in *anime*.[119] She continues, extends and deepens Ono's personal and social contextualizing of *anime*, foregrounding a Japan traumatized by and living on in the wake of The Bomb, and expands the purview to include consideration of the 'philosophical', enlisting especially Freud's uncanny and Derrida's deconstruction, including of tele-techno-communications, in the thinking of cuteness and of the cross-cultural relations between Japan and the U.S., relations for her played out in exemplary fashion between *anime* and Hollywood animation.

In her essay 'Hybridity and the End of Innocence', Jane Goodall takes the thematic of innocence and experience in animation as her subject (a topic also broached by Moore)—the innocence and experience of the animated worlds created, of the animators' approaches to the medium itself, and of genre and taxonomy—and selects three sites for its examination: the Golden Age of Warner Bros. cartoons, the experiments of Ralph Bakshi in America (*Cool World*) (she also makes passing comment on Zemeckis' *Who Framed Roger Rabbit*) and the animations of post-World War II Japan (represented by Takayama's *Urotsukidoji*). For Goodall, hybridity in animation has itself undergone a metamorphosis, losing its innocence and beginning 'to admit its resonances as one of the most insistent thematics of an era obsessed with difference, cloning, grafting and taxonomic slippage', an era whose definitive experience is that of anxiety.[120]

The next essay, William D. Routt's '*De Anime*', situates animation—the illusion of life—in what animates it—the life of that illusion—which he locates, after Aristotle's treatise *De Anima*, in the internal life—in motivation: 'soul, mind, psychology'—be it of character, text, medium. And he instantiates this, as well as comes to complicate it, by offering a heuristic reading of the very popular *manga Gunnm*, known in English as *Battle Angel Alita.* His reading includes comics within the orbit of animation and treats both the *manga* in which the tale is drawn and the two OAVs into which it was made—*Rusty Angel* and *Tears Sign*—as different ways of not only thinking about but experiencing, being animated by—even being possessed by—soul. Indeed, if Goodall focuses on the author (and the character authored, too) as animator, Routt proposes a theory of the reader and spectator as *animator*, whose reading and spectating animates soul in character and text, in *manga* and *anime*, even as these animate the reader and spectator.

The final essay of the first section—Philip Brophy's 'Sonic—Atomic—Neumonic: Apocalyptic Echoes in *Anime*'—jumps off from and extends his 'The Animation of Sound' in *THE ILLUSION OF LIFE.* What that essay was to image-sound relationships in Disney and Warner Bros. cartoons this companion piece is to image-sound relationships in *anime*, offering specific instantiation with a number of key films—*Patlabor, Laputa, My Neighbour Totoro, Akira* and, like Goodall, *Urotsukidoji.*[121] Brophy argues that post-'60s *anime* pushes beyond Disney classicism, organicism and *symphony* and Warner Bros. modernism, mechanism and *cacophany* to the *polyphony* of image-sound recordings of the life of apocalyptic, post-nuclear energies—animating energies that create, destroy and rebirth worlds, energies in maximal, dynamic interaction. For Brophy, it is the *anime* boom of the early '80s that achieves what he understands as this radicalizing by *anime* of the animatic apparatus, the terms of which he analyzes in detail, including considering how *anime* narratively foregrounds and graphically depicts the materialization of energy.

The three essays composing the second section of the book focus on American post-World War II animation, specifically the work of Bob Clampett and Ralph Bakshi (two of the three American animators featured in *KABOOM!*) and that of Disney, offering fresh, innovative, fascinating takes on their respective subjects. The section starts with Richard Thompson's 'Pronoun Trouble II: The Missing Dick'—an essay that, like Ono's and, as we will see, Fred Patten's, takes the reader back before the post-War period, here to the years of World War II, to commence and contextualize its analysis. At the same time, the references in the essays of the first section to pre-World War II and wartime Disney, Warner Bros. and Fleischer cartoons, as well as to Bakshi's post-war work, form a felicitous cross-connection with and lead in to this section.

Thompson's essay revisits Clampett's wonderful cartoon *The Great Piggy Bank Robbery* (1946), focusing on issues of stylistic differences among the Warner Bros. animation directors; the inscription of the war in the cartoon[122]; what the cartoon says about the nature of cartoon character and narrative in that war/post-war period; and the relation of the cartoon to Hollywood live action feature films of the era, notably to Orson Welles' *Citizen Kane* (1941), as well as to those of an earlier time, especially for me Buster Keaton's *Sherlock, Jr.* (1924). Departing from the 'received wisdom' on Clampett as the creator of arguably the daffiest, nuttiest, whackiest work of all the Warner Bros. animators, Thompson animates a Clampett *heretofore unknown*, one he inducts into a post-*Citizen Kane* cinema of ambiguity, indeterminacy and interminably thwarted detection—including of character (the 'pronoun trouble' of self-identity), narrative, etc.[123]—and that links Clampett's Daffy with Chuck Jones' Daffy as Thompson treated of the latter in terms of 'the postwar mentality—our world view, our angst'[124] in his 1980 essay 'Pronoun Trouble'.

The following essay—Edward Colless' 'Between the Legs of the Mermaid'—proceeds from the supposition that 'Every story is the excuse for an image', an image animated by lust. Colless teases out the aesthetic complexities of not only Hans Christian Andersen's tale 'The Little Mermaid' and Disney's 1989 animated feature version of it but an image from the ever popular television program *Baywatch*—one of another 'Anderson', the likewise ever popular Pamela. And he does more: through his reading of bodies in various metamorphoses, mediums and media, he articulates the complex figurations and performances of soul and (its) animation that these stories and images animate. For Colless, like Routt, what these stories and images speculate on, what is at stake in them, is the very nature of soul. Soul and its metamorphoses—from myth to melodrama to orgy, from *pneuma* to pseudo to pneumatic, from seduction to production to fascination.[125]

The final essay of this section is Freida Riggs' 'The Infinite Quest: Husserl, Bakshi, the Rotoscope and the Ring', an especially timely essay given Peter Jackson's *Lord of the Rings* trilogy (2001-2003), as well as the keen interest in rotoscoping among animation scholars these last few years. Riggs brings the work of Deleuze (and Félix Guattari) into an animated, indeed *animatic*, relation with that of Edmund Husserl, even as she brings them into such a relation with that of Ralph Bakshi and his animated feature *The Lord of the Rings* (1978). Not only does Riggs offer a reply to Bakshi's claimed 'treachery' to animation in his use of the rotoscoping technique in this feature, she advances a notion of animation as *becoming* that of necessity makes any definition of animation itself subject to animation—to animation as becoming—to animation as rotoscoping, at once trope and device exemplifying and performing the turn of animation. For Riggs, Bakshi not only turns live action into animation but (re)turns it to it, revealing its roots in, its nature as, animation.

The third section of the book features one essay only, 'Simba Versus Kimba: The Pride of Lions',[126] by the conference's other overseas guest speaker, Fred Patten. It provides a careful, detailed, measured account that takes the reader from a brief summary of Tezuka's career and of his *Kimba the White Lion*, focusing on public awareness of them in America, to an overview of the production of Disney's *The Lion King* (1994) and of astonishing similarities between it and *Kimba*. He then prizes open the heated controversy that erupted over Disney's denial that *The Lion King* was derived from *Kimba*, analyzing and assessing its key features in what is an assiduously researched, scrupulously documented and compellingly argued examination, one sufficient in my opinion to rock the pride of the Disney Studio. Like a number of the essays, it acknowledges and operates in the space between Japan and the U.S. and their animations, showing how the national is never not international.

The fourth section—The 'Expanded' Field of Animation—concentrates on three areas of major import for animation studies: 1. the relation of live action and animation 2. video and computer games, the electronic, digitally animated mediascape, the city, flight simulation, the military and war, and 3. animation in the entertainment industry, with focus on the commercial exploitation of intellectual property and character licensing. These areas are most relevant for thinking the contemporary global 'transformations'/ 'reanimations' of animation, including of film and other media (video, the computer, etc.), including the reanimation by those other media of film animation.[127]

The section commences with a consideration of the relation of live action and animation in Rex Butler's 'Allegories of Animation: *Schindler's List, E.T.* and *The Lion King*'. In this complex, iconoclastic take on the films of Steven Spielberg, not only does Butler (after film critic Adrian Martin) situate Spielberg's work, and the post-Spielbergian Hollywood cinema, in terms of that of Frank Capra, he brings the thinking of Freud, Lacan and Žižek to the analysis, privileging Freud's uncanny and Lacan's Real in terms of animation in general and what for Butler is Spielberg's impossible aspiration to return (his) live action cinema to animation, more precisely, to animation as animism, and vice versa.[128] But Butler goes further than this, animating an even more radical Spielberg. Extending the piece he co-wrote with Keith Broadfoot in *THE ILLUSION OF LIFE*, 'The Illusion of Illusion', he turns Spielberg and Disney (read in terms of *The Lion King,* linking this essay to Patten's) into two of the great critics, rather than great exemplars, of the nostalgic postmodern of Fredric Jameson—critics whose films for Butler are far more radically deconstructive of capitalist ideology than the so-called 'radical materialist' cinemas of the 1960s and '70s.

Next come two essays on video and computer games, the electronic, digitally animated mediascape, the city, flight simulation, the military and war. The first, by David Ellison, 'Animating Architectures: Panic Styles for Troubled Cities', offers a futurist blueprint of Los Angeles post the 1992 riots—a blueprint for me increasingly of the present and uncannily increasingly resembling the L.A. of *Blade Runner* and *The Terminator* movies, as well as the Neo-Tokyo of *Akira*, and vice versa. Ellison's blueprint operates across the widest terrain, mapping images of the stealth architectures, advertisements and electronic, illuminated screens that animate the simulated life of the contemporary, virtual (non)city, the city of the militarized New Electronic Order,[129] the city of and at war. Ellison foregrounds the uncanny nature of the urban architectural tele-technological scanscape in terms of the Gulf War and that other 'Gulf War'—the one between 'whites and blacks, suburbans and urbans, the info rich and info poor'—as well as in terms of Nintendo and *Street Fighter*—the transforming of war into television, video and computer war game, a war of and over images.[130] Intriguingly, in its concerns and theoretical framings, for me Ellison's essay does for the U.S. what Moore's does for Japan, as well as marks, like Moore's and Patten's, certain 'special' effects of Japanese animation—be it film, video (including games), computer (including games), etc.—on the U.S. Moreover, it anticipates and has important things to say about recent global events, including aspects of '9/11' and Gulf War II.

In his essay 'Logistical Space: Flight Simulation and Virtual Reality', Patrick Crogan takes up, like Ellison, the topic of the military, war and animation. Crogan focuses on the key subject of flight simulation, to which he brings the profoundly germane thinking of Paul Virilio. Addressing what he nominates, after Virilio's writings on speed, war, technology and the world today, 'the logistical space of flight simulation', Crogan argues that the 1960s' substitution by computer-based flight simulation of videographic and 'infographic' space for the model terrain boards of analog-based simulations, heralded since as a definitive technological rupture and a major moment in the development of Virtual Reality, was rather an 'accidental' acceleration of a tendency already well marked in the post-war period, a tendency toward what Virilio calls 'pure war'—the collapse of the distinction between 'wartime-space' (as an exceptional state) and 'peacetime-space', between, more generally, the military and non-military relation. For Crogan, flight simulation, in the logistical space it, as progenitor and model, has animated—the space of Virtual Reality—not only founds a new generation of technology for the animation of 'artificial realities', it becomes a virtually perfect figure of this tendency toward 'pure war' and of the dilemma it poses to critical inquiry into (and I would add: to critical theory of) contemporary technological developments.[131]

Here I must make several more general points. First, Crogan's essay activates a powerful relation between the reanimating of every aspect of the 'non-military' sphere by Virilio's tendency to pure war and games like *F/A-18 Hornet Strike Fighter*, which exemplify and perform that reanimating in the 'domestic' space. At the same time, it generates a powerful relation between that tendency and such games and the theorists, ideas and games animating Ellison's 'domestic' blueprint. Second, in the light of what these two essays and Moore's mark—the logistical, *diagrammatological* reanimation of the world by its animate(d) and animating image technologies, its image generators, analog and digital, past and present—animation becomes crucial to understanding the most profound features, processes and changes marking the post-war period in all its spheres and dimensions, from the largest to the smallest—features, processes and changes which, while undergoing maximal acceleration for Crogan since '9/11', still mark the contemporary world, a world of logistics (a term Ellison uses too), a world (not only a city) of and at war.

In this regard, these two essays interconnect with *all* the essays in the book that engage with the post-World War II period, especially those that address it in terms of adversarial, agonistic, war and warlike activities, technologies and relations, including Ben Crawford's essay to come. Their foregrounding of war suggests, as I did earlier, that the post-World War II period was anything but post war.[132] War is a dominant figure, form, event, process animating the 'post-war' period right down to today, with Gulf War II and the 'War Against Terror'; and film and other media animations are enlisted in and serve, increasingly so, as weapons of war, of Pure War (Virilio), of information war (Virilio), of hyperwar (what would be pure and empty war) (Baudrillard), etc. The *animus* never not there in animation, the war that has never not been happening therein, makes J. Robert Oppenheimer's words spoken after the detonation of the first nuclear device at Trinity Site July 16, 1945—'Now I am become Death, the destroyer of worlds' (words from the *Bhagavad Gita*)—never not 'uttered' by animation itself, including film animation.

Third, even as essays in the book treat in varying ways of post-World War II *anime* as marking the passage from classic Hollywood and Japanese drawn animation to a hyperreal form of graphic animation film and film animation—where, I would propose, the term *graphic* itself takes on a charge of hyperspeed, hyperviolence, hyperwar, hyper*animus*—the essays of Ellison and Crogan mark a parallel metamorphosis (morphing) in the passage (including of 'live action' cinema) from analog to digital animation modes, from old to new media animation technologies and what they digitally animate—hyperreal animation (including hyperreal 'live action' 'cinema', a 'cinema' of Virtual Reality), 'animated' 'film' and 'film' 'animation' (where cinema morphs into 'cinema' and film into 'film').

Lastly, Crogan's remarks on the impact of technologies of digital animation—of Virtual Reality and digital special effects cinema—on the increasing blurring of the distinction between 'live' and 'animated' (and 'real' and 'artificial', including of 'Virtual Reality's undoing of any clear distinction between "live interaction" in the real world and in the animated milieu that comprises "artificial reality"') bear upon other essays taking up such subjects and effects.[133]

The last essay of this section is Ben Crawford's 'Intertextual Personae: Character Licensing in Practice and Theory'.[134] It outlines a groundbreaking understanding of animation in the context of the commercial exploitation of intellectual properties, and as well disputes, as did his irreverent, 'politically incorrect' essay in *THE ILLUSION OF LIFE*, 'Saturday Morning Fever', some of the major criticisms by sociologists of animated children's entertainment. Crawford not only argues that licensed product merchandising is an integral element of animated films, more radically he proposes that the flourishing of character licensing 'explodes or mutates the object of Animation Studies'. In consequence, the animated film calls for situating in the context of the animation intertext, which forms for Crawford a part of the entertainment industry. Crawford thereby reanimates the object of animation studies and Film Studies as the intertextual in general and the intellectual property in particular, an industrious, animated 'object' whose purchase is global and whose understanding requires that animation studies, Film Studies and Cultural Studies look beyond the text and embrace the disciplines of marketing and business strategy.[135]

The final section of this collection contains three essays of a more general theoretical nature on animation. Each includes consideration of the animatic, the uncanny and the mechanical. The first is a rare and lovely addressal of the subject of sound in animation—Annemarie Jonson's 'Porky's Stutter: The Vocal Trope and Lifedeath in Animation'. For Jonson, that stutter serves as a clue to the thinking of animation itself, a thinking which draws a relationship between the conventional theorizations and definitions of voice and of animation and which, building upon the work of Derrida, Freud, Thierry Kuntzel, Barthes, Virilio, Spivak and Norman McLaren, posits the complicity of voice and animation not in their co-plenitude but in the intervallic cut—the stutter or stammer—which renders both voice and animation at once possible and impossible. Furthermore, as part of her exegesis of 'the thanatic economies' of cinema, consciousness and voice—which is to say for her (as for me) the lifedeath economy of animation as the animatic—Jonson treats not only the cartoon but 'experimental animation'—in particular the flicker film work of Paul Sharits—making the flicker film exemplary of film animation itself.[136]

In his essay, 'Animation 1: The Control-Image', William Schaffer takes up Deleuze's characterizing of the classic drawn cartoon film as a kind of minimal cinema. Through consideration of Deleuze's four technical preconditions of cinema, Schaffer turns Deleuze's characterization back against itself, illustrating where Deleuze's own thinking of these preconditions, therefore of the cartoon itself, falls short. Schaffer posits a radical difference between the live action image and the cartoon image, one residing in what he calls the interval of control, that is, the 'direct interaction [by the maker-controller] with every interval of the any-instant-whatever generated by film'. Using Chuck Jones' *Duck Amuck* and The Road Runner cartoons as his premiere exemplars, and drawing upon the work of Norman M. Klein on the cartoon allegory of control, Schaffer advances a reading of the controller-animator and what it animates—the cartoon—as figuring and performing the animatic abyss of the impossibility of control, which is none other than the interval of control itself.[137]

The last essay in this volume is my 'Speculations on the Animatic

Automaton'.[138] It takes off from that part of my Introduction to *THE ILLUSION OF LIFE* where I posited the crucial relevance to the thinking of animation of the debates of the animists and mechanists over the nature of life and motion, the human and the machine. As well, it follows on from my initial formulation in that Introduction, and in my '*Who Framed Roger Rabbit*' essay in that book, of a theory of the filmic/cinematic apparatus as animatic apparatus. The essay not only focuses on and explores these debates and that formulation, it seeks to extend them by situating that apparatus within the debates, and vice versa. In so doing, it continues the project I began in *THE ILLUSION OF LIFE*—and the work I have done subsequently on animation—to develop not only a theory of animation but an *animatic* theory of it. To that end, I bring to these debates and that formulation the ideas of many thinkers, especially J. David Bolter, Mary Shelley, Donald Crafton, David F. Channell, Eisenstein, Derrida, Freud, Philippe Lacoue-Labarthe, Deleuze, Baudrillard and Plato. The essay includes consideration of singular ways in which *Blade Runner* exemplifies and performs these debates, that apparatus and their commingling.

The book contains two appendices: 'Fred Patten's Annotated Chronology of Pertinent Works and Publications Relevant to *The Lion King* and to the Controversy' (where his extensive endnotes are to be found); and the complete program of *THE LIFE OF ILLUSION* conference, which generated the essays in this book.

As is evident from my descriptions, in their theorizing of animation, these essays have multiple interconnections, sharing not only theoretical approaches but a number of ideas, issues, topics and themes only a few of which I have been able to highlight here. These form a network, a matrix, of subjects, of concerns, for us privileged by not only post-World War II animation but animation 'as such'—linking these essays not only among themselves but with those in *THE ILLUSION OF LIFE*. These include, notably: war, the military, violence, speed, trauma, horror, death, disappearance; innocence and experience, including sexual; metamorphosis, transformation, mutation, becoming; the uncanny, including issues of home, the domestic, comfort, refuge, safety (and, in Thompson's essay, we would suggest, the piggy bank as (a) safe and anything but), and what always already enables and at the same time threatens home et al., producing anxiety, uncertainty, etc.; the animatic; energy; the soul; the wave, liquid, the fluid (see Part I re Matthew Martin's logo); the corporation and incorporation; the in-between, including in the form of what happens between nations, between their animations and across them; the author; identity and self-identity; genre; the animation apparatus of image, sound, and image-sound relations and technologies, including of film, video, the computer and media in general—and what they animate, including Virtual Reality; modes of transportation, including flight (in multiple forms and modes).

IV

In this final Part, I want to present a number of key ideas and raise a number of significant issues for the theorizing of animation.

It has been suggested by Thomas Looser that 'film is, arguably, *the* art of the twentieth century, and even perhaps the central medium of modernity'.[139] This would translate for us as: film as a form of animation is *the* art of the twentieth century and even the 'central' medium of modernity. Indeed, in *Understanding Animation* Wells insists upon the modernism and modernity of animation, while in *Animation and America* he goes so far as to claim that animation is intrinsically modernist—which seems to mean for him, as in *Understanding Animation*, that it is per se politically radical, spiritual, humanist and socio-politically progressive as a form.[140] Moreover, he asserts that 'the current place of animation' is as '*the* intrinsic language not merely of film, but all contemporary visual, communications, and design cultures'.[141]

But I would propose more, less and other. First, unlike the majority of those who write on animation, for me animation is not only an art. And it is not only the life and motion of a genre of film, of cinema, of film 'as such'. It is far more. It is idea, concept, process, performance, medium and milieu; and it invests all arts, media and communications. (In other words, all arts, media and communications are forms of animation). It invests all sciences and technologies. It invests all disciplines, faculties, knowledges (including the history of philosophy, the history of ideas), fields, practices, discourses and institutions. It invests all relationships (of whatever kind: personal, social, national, sexual, etc.). It invests all life and movement, as it invests all thought. It invests not only the subject, it invests the object, the world, the universe itself. That's why it is more than only a human practice. It is a process, performance, medium and milieu of world, of universe. What might be called the at once 'squash and stretch', elastic, plastic, animated—indeed animatic—nature of 'all'. It is not only the human that is at stake in animation, it is the world, the universe—everything which is the case.

Second, for me, film animation (and video and computer animation, etc.)—indeed animation 'as such'—has been the 'central' medium of not only modernity but postmodernity, thought after Lyotard as that which precedes, accompanies and follows a period of modernity. For Lyotard, the postmodern is that which at once enables and disenables the modern (with all the consequences, philosophical and otherwise, attendant upon that).

Third, insofar as for me there is no essence to animation, animation is not intrinsically anything. Insofar as there is no proper, propriety nor property to it, it is always already, never not, expropriated. Therefore, it could not be wedded nor appropriatable to anything, including, by definition, any socio-political, ideological, cultural position or persuasion. (Insofar as any attempt to appropriate it automatically expropriates it, and vice versa, in this sense it is never not expropriated from the will, desire and control of the human.)

Fourth, the 'poststructuralist' critiques of structural linguistics and semiology, including Deleuze's critique of Christian Metz's linguistic semiology of cinema and Derrida's grammatological critique of Saussurean semiology, are fatal to any simple assertion that animation is a language, to say nothing of when the term is taken in the loose, impressionistic sense marking its popular usage. Animation is more and other than a language.[142]

Fifth, to develop what I said in Part I, since *THE ILLUSION OF LIFE* was published, animation—indeed, the animatic—has increasingly come forward, presented itself, as the most compelling, indeed singular process of not only contemporary film but the contemporary world. We live in a world increasingly animated, increasingly animatic (at the same time acknowledging that, like film, the world was never not animated, animatic). This means that the logics and processes of animation, of the animatic, of which film animation provides singular exemplification and performance, offer the best description of not only film animation but the contemporary world (and the subject therein). The implication is clear: we need animation film theory, film animation theory, animation theory 'as such', to understand film, the world and the subject. And we need television animation theory, video animation theory and especially computer animation theory as these media increasingly pervade and reanimate the mediascape, or rather immediascape, of the world and the subject, an immediascape, world and subject increasingly hyperanimated, hyperanimatic—the pure and empty, virtual forms of animation and the animatic.

Here a related point. In his review in *Film Quarterly*, Summer 1993, Richard Leskosky, then President of the Society for Animation Studies, declared that *THE ILLUSION OF LIFE: Essays on Animation* 'heralds (and argues) the arrival of animation studies as a valid discipline equal to and separate from cinema studies but with a wealth of critical practice relevant to cinema scholars as well as animation scholars'.[143]

For me this lovely comment must be qualified in two regards. First, animation (therefore animation studies) is relevant to *all* disciplines and *all* scholars, operating in, integral to and performed by all of them. Second, if by 'discipline' one means something coherent and entire unto itself, something at peace and in a state of 'oneness' with itself, an irresolvable, indeed aporetic, problem is harboured here. It is a problem denegating any and all efforts to animate and institute a discipline—any discipline—so conceived, including the discipline of animation studies. For animation itself, animation as the protean plasmatic as we reread it, as the animatic—that very singularity of animation, the very animation of animation—renders that discipline at once possible and impossible.

Therefore, a discipline must be thought otherwise, through animation as the animatic, thought, after Derrida, for example, not as a form of presence, essence, the ontological, but as what is at once enabled and disenabled by dissemination, the hauntological—as by definition indisciplined, or rather, at once disciplined and indisciplined. A discipline so thought would be at once the discipline of indiscipline and indiscipline of discipline. In any case, for us such a form of 'discipline' would always already inhabit and spectre a discipline figured purely as ontological.

If *THE ILLUSION OF LIFE* and this new volume offer singular exemplification of and compelling theoretical insights into such a lively 'discipline' as 'animation studies'—one not only animated but animatic—then it will have made a contribution, not to the creation of the discipline of Animation Studies—whose departure arrives with, if not before, its 'arrival'—but to animation studies, a term Leskosky insightfully puts, like cinema studies, in lower case, a term for me always to be thought as in quotation marks, always, after Derrida, *sous rature* (under erasure). Animation studies so conceived not only studies animation, which for us all 'disciplines' do—making animation studies the 'discipline' of all 'disciplines'—but is obedient to the very processes of animation as the animatic, as all 'disciplines' are.

Sixth, the animatic is prior and superior to animation, the condition of at once the possibility and impossibility of animation. Here it counters all tendencies to think of animation as fullness of being, presence, essence, as pure positivity, including, crucially, as metamorphosis *so thought*. While animation privileges becoming over being, the dynamic over the static, the mobile over the fixed—indeed, it shows and performs the impossibility of being, the static, the fixed—the animatic deconstructs and seduces such an opposition, likewise showing and performing the impossibility of becoming, the dynamic, the mobile.[144]

The animatic is an in-betweener. It would be what lies and operates between, forms the milieu, and at once enables and disenables all binary oppositions as simple oppositions. It is the in-between of inanimate and animate, death and life, non-motion and motion, non-metamorphosis and metamorphosis, the child and the adult, female and male, etc. In terms of the 'both/and, neither/nor, at the same time' of Derridean *différance*, it would be, for example, that which is both inanimate and animate, neither inanimate nor animate, at the same time. Moreover, it lies and operates *within*, always already incorporating the between inside, thereby disseminating all possibilities of fullness, totality, wholeness, including of identity and self-identity, disseminating the very possibility of definition, denotation, the literal, fact, etc., 'as such'. The animatic thus makes every discipline always already between disciplines, interdisciplinary, an in-betweener.

The animatic: the groundless 'ground' of all arts, media, disciplines, institutions, etc., and of the subject, of culture, of world 'as such'.

In his review of *THE ILLUSION OF LIFE*, Guy Johnson wrote these powerful words—words acknowledging that animation is a provocation, a challenge—words which for me characterize this present volume, too, and with which I will conclude this Introduction:

> What...essays in *The Illusion of Life* make clear is that animation is out to unsettle. This collection of essays is most concerned to write out some sophisticated reasons for alarm, and succeeds for as long as the reader is determined to seek the experience of feeling this world, of solid forms and fixed points, move.[145]

Note: The 'original' catalyst for the book was *THE LIFE OF ILLUSION* conference, March 3-5, 1995, at which all of the essays in the book were presented but for two—Annemarie Jonson's and my own. See note 97, as well as the Appendix for the full program of papers. Since then there has been ongoing development and editorial dialogue which has led to the present collection. A few of the essays have been deliberately left as studies of animation in the '90s because of their value at the least as considerations of recent cultural history, notably those of Kosei Ono, Pauline Moore, David Ellison and Ben Crawford.

NOTES

1 For details of the first conference, consult *THE ILLUSION OF LIFE: Essays on Animation*, ed. Alan Cholodenko (Sydney: Power Publications in association with the Australian Film Commission, 1991), especially its Appendix.

2 I would have called the book *THE LIFE OF ILLUSION* but for the fear expressed by a number of colleagues that people would mistake it for *THE ILLUSION OF LIFE* book. I have more to say about this phrase 'the life of illusion' in Part III of the Introduction.

3 For coverage of 'alternative', 'independent' modes of animation practice both within and outside the U.S., consult the classic Robert Russett and Cecile Starr, *Experimental Animation: Origins of a New Art*, rev. ed. (New York: Da Capo Press, 1976), for the period up to its publication. Note: since 'experimental animation' also goes by the names 'avant-garde cinema' or 'experimental cinema', and in its abstract mode is included in the subcategory 'abstract cinema', this *one* form of animation *is* covertly recognized as cinema by those who theorize film. Therefore, the many film books devoted to it are also relevant.

4 As well, we should note that Warner Bros. released new cartoon shorts in the '90s—*Invasion of the Bunny Snatchers* (1992), *Carrotblanca* (1995) and *Blooper Bunny* (made in 1991 but released in 1997), along with Chuck Jones Film Production's *Chariots of Fur* (1994); *Another Froggy Evening* (1995); *Superior Duck* (1995); *From Hare to Eternity* (1996); *Pullet Surprise* (1996), directed by Darrell Van Citters; *Father of the Bird* (1997), directed by Stephen Fossati; and *A Tail to Tell* (2001).

5 Also *The Swan Princess* films from Nest Entertainment. Mention should also be made of the Ireland-based feature animation work of American Don Bluth, including *Rock-A-Doodle* (1991), *A Troll in Central Park* (1994), *Thumbelina* (1994), *The Pebble and the Penguin* (1995) and *Anastasia* (1997). And we must also mention, in Australia, Yoram Gross Film Studio's *Blinky Bill the Mischievous Koala* (1992), *Dot in Space* (1994) and *Joseph the Dreamer* (2002), in stop motion animation. Acknowledgement too must be given Raoul Servais' *Taxandria* (1996), a Belgian production; Michel Ocelet's *Kirikou and the Sorceress* (1998), a France/Belgium/Luxembourg production; Ocelet's *Princes and Princesses* (2000), a French production; and Sylvain Chomet's *The Triplets of Belleville* (2003), a France/Belgium/Canada/United Kingdom production.

6 Not only are Hollywood 'live action' feature films increasingly marked in some way by the computer (marked to the point where it can be

claimed that most if not all Hollywood live action films are animated), so too is the cel animation still being produced there. As for Japan, some of the feature animation films made with cel animation use computer animation for aspects of the work, for example, *Ghost in the Shell* and even *Princess Mononoke*. The fact is, of course, that the pencil and pen can be, and are increasingly being, traded in for the computerized version, including in Japan; and the computer can simulate cel (and all other modes of) animation, as it can simulate live action.

7 To this list we would add Luc Besson's *The Fifth Element* (1997), a French production, with digital effects by American companies. Also, we need to add several hybrid cartoon animation/live action films (and incorporating digital effects): 20th Century Fox and Turner Pictures' *The Pagemaster* (1994) and two produced by Warner Bros.—*Space Jam* (1996) and *Looney Tunes: Back in Action* (2003). Moreover, especially given that we are based in Australia, we must acknowledge the computer animation work in Chris Noonan's *Babe* (1995) and George Miller's *Babe: Pig in the City* (1998), both from Kennedy Miller Productions in Sydney. Also, the Australian Alex Proyas' stunning *Dark City* (1998), with U.S. producers, as well as his *I, Robot* (2004), call for citation, as does Michael Rymer's U.S./Australian co-production *Queen of the Damned* (2002). Across the Tasman, there is Peter Jackson's *Heavenly Creatures* (1994), a U.S./New Zealand/German production, and his *Lord of the Rings: The Fellowship of the Ring* (2001), *Lord of the Rings: The Two Towers* (2002), and *Lord of the Rings: The Return of the King* (2003), a U.S./New Zealand production.

8 Furthermore, the occasional compilation animation film programs of the annual Tournées of Animation, as well as Spike and Mike's 'Sick and Twisted' Animation Festival, have come to Australia and been screened at art house-type cinemas.

9 Intriguingly, to the degree that Hollywood 'live action' feature films are increasingly computer animated, the category Oscar for Animated Feature Film, instituted in 2000-2001, should ironically apply to them, too, even as, in another register, as we posited in the Introduction to *THE ILLUSION OF LIFE*, all films are animations, meaning all feature films qualify.

10 Two key texts on computer animation that I have drawn upon for some data are Robin Baker, 'Computer Technology and Special Effects in Contemporary Cinema', in *Future Visions: New Technologies of the Screen*, eds. Philip Hayward and Tana Wollen (London: BFI, 1993); and Maureen Furniss' chapter 'Animation and New Technologies',

in her *Art in Motion: Animation Aesthetics* (London: John Libbey, 1998).

11 Especially that of Animation World Network, which has links to a number of other animation-related sites. (Its address: awn.com)

12 Here I need to qualify, for animation for us is always already reanimation.

13 In fact, Eisenstein finds in Hokusai an example of this very quality. See Sergei Eisenstein, *Eisenstein on Disney*, ed. Jay Leyda and trans. Alan Upchurch (London: Methuen, 1988), p. 19. In animation film, Eisenstein singles out the transforming animals in Disney's *Merbabies* (1938) as protean plasmatic. Other filmic examples of it include Felix The Cat; the eponymous 'live action' figures of John Carpenter's *The Thing* (1982), Woody Allen's *Zelig* (1983), the T-1000 in *Terminator 2: Judgment Day* (1991) and the T-X of *Terminator 3: Rise of the Machines* (2003), as well as Dracula in Francis Ford Coppola's *Bram Stoker's Dracula* (1992); Tetsuo at the end of Katsuhiro Otomo's *Akira* (1988); the Genie in Disney's *Aladdin* (1992), etc. To these we would add Jim Carrey as actor/body, the most astonishing 1990s 'live action' incarnation of the principle, in *The Mask* (1994)—the title itself tellingly attesting to the never revealed/unveiled as such character of the protean plasmatic, for which every revealing is at the same time a re-veiling. On the protean plasmatic, see Keith Clancy's 'ΠΡΗΣΤΗΡ: The T(r)opology of Pyromania' and Keith Broadfoot and Rex Butler's 'The Illusion of Illusion' in *THE ILLUSION OF LIFE*. It should be noted that Matthew Martin's figure shows not just a duck emerging from the wave but an appropriately cartoonish and therefore appropriately hybrid duck/human with five fingers and swimmer's goggles, marking the logic of the Bororo—at once human and bird (for me thinkable, after Jacques Derrida, as both human and bird and neither simply human nor simply bird at the same time)—that Eisenstein himself mobilizes in his text (p. 50).

14 I develop what I mean by the animatic in the other Parts of the Introduction.

15 Deborah Szapiro, '*Manga* Daiquiri', smh.com.au, October 11, 2002.

16 To say nothing of that further complicating point that all films are animations.

17 Alexa Moses, 'Child's Play Creates Monster Box Office', *Metropolitan, The Sydney Morning Herald*, June 17, 2004, p. 15.

18 *Anime* fandom typically operates at universities. For example, an *anime* convention was held here at the University of Sydney in 2002 by the university *anime* club, with an attendance of 500 people, both from

the city and the New South Wales countryside. The next year the club joined with that of the University of New South Wales to stage the *Animania* convention, attracting around 1400 people, the biggest *anime* convention in Australia. (Until then, Melbourne's *MANIFEST* held the record with 1300 in attendance.) A yet more ample event occurred in 2004, with several thousand attending; and *Animania* 2005 is in planning.

19 Chuck Jones, *Chuck Amuck: The Life and Times of an Animated Cartoonist* (New York: Avon Books, 1989), p. 225.

20 See Baudrillard, 'Ecstacy and Inertia', *Fatal Strategies*, ed. Jim Fleming and trans. Philip Beitchman and W.G.J. Niesluchowski (New York/ London: Semiotext(e)/Pluto, 1990). See also Rex Butler, 'Towards a Principle of Maximalism: Jean Baudrillard's *Cool Memories*', *Hermes*, 1991.

21 Hyperanimation would be at once the fulfillment and annihilation of animation, its pure and empty, virtual form, so any reference to it as animation would call for that word's putting in quotation marks: 'animation'.

22 One of the two opening epigraphs to Jean Baudrillard's *The Transparency of Evil: Essays on Extreme Phenomena*, trans. James Benedict (London: Verso, 1993), published originally as *La Transparence du Mal: Essai sur les phénomènes extrêmes* (Paris: Galilée, 1990). The epigraph in French reads '*Puisque le monde prend un cours délirant, nous devons prendre sur lui un point de vue délirant*'. I much prefer 'delirious' to Benedict's translation of *délirant* as 'delusional'. In terms of the hypertelic process, see Baudrillard, 'After the Orgy', *The Transparency of Evil*, p. 6.

23 The last expression said by Shepard Smith of his *The FOX Report* on the FOX News Channel.

24 Indeed, hyperfans find it increasingly impossible to distinguish themselves from whom and what they are fans of, are increasingly more whom and what they are fans of than whom and what they are fans of, etc.

25 On the mediatic, on what Baudrillard describes as the 'conversion of the mediatized into the immediatized', see Baudrillard, 'Aesthetic Illusion and Virtual Reality', in *Jean Baudrillard, Art and Artefact*, ed. Nicholas Zurbrugg (London: Sage, 1997), pp. 20-21. What the media perform they likewise make their content, that of animation/ reanimation. One key example is the plethora of makeover shows and home renovation shows on TV these last few years (makeover and renovation being synonyms for reanimation). Such shows, like all the

extreme phenomena imaged in the media (extreme sport and extreme fighting being two other notable examples, to say nothing of extreme news and current affairs), increasingly declare, animate and double that radically uncertain hyperreality that the media apparatuses themselves likewise increasingly animate, even as they at the same time increasingly present themselves as the cure for that to which they in no small part contribute, as Samuel Weber so characterizes TV in 'Television: Set and Screen', *Mass Mediauras: Form, Technics, Media*, ed. Alan Cholodenko (Sydney/Stanford: Power Publications/Stanford University Press, 1996), pp. 126-128, as well as '*Deus ex Media*: Interview by Cassi Plate of the ABC' therein, pp. 161-163, including his remarks on the uncanny, spectral reality of TV.

26 Supplemented by the other developments described in Part I.

27 The 2004 Society for Cinema and Media Studies conference had two animation panels: *Special Effects and CGI: Histories and Trajectories*, chaired by Bob Rehak; and *Japanese Anime: History, Theory, and Practice*, chaired by Kumiko Sato.

28 See Patrick Crogan's essay on computer animation in this volume. Dan McLaughlin heralded the need for the discipline of animation to move into the digital era in his 1996 UCLA paper 'Into the Digital: Revolution or Evolution? or the Retooling, Retraining, Rethinking of Film/TV & Animation'. Maureen Furniss includes computer animation in her *Art in Motion: Animation Aesthetics* (1998), as does Paul Wells in his *Understanding Animation* (1998), as well as in his more recent *Animation and America* (2002) and *Animation: Genre and Authorship* (2002).

29 Yet even at *Ludic Moments*, when the word 'animation' was used by presenters (Crogan excepted) and participants, it was without any acknowledgement that it is a term calling for engagement in its own right and that computer animation is subsumable within animation studies. Here a related point: games (including those played by apparatuses such as film, television and the computer, doubling the play of terms like 'video games' and 'computer games') are of the order of animation, likewise falling therefore within the purview of animation studies. See my Introduction to *THE ILLUSION OF LIFE*, pp. 32-33, note 23. Therefore, for me all publications on the computer, including on computer games, on television and video, including video games, and on games in general are by definition publications on animation. Addressing them (with one exception) lies outside the scope of this Introduction.

30 For a list of non-English language publications, consult the Bibliography in Giannalberto Bendazzi, *Cartoons: One Hundred Years of Cinema Animation* (London: John Libbey, 1994); and Jayne Pilling's Introduction to *A Reader in Animation Studies*, ed. Jayne Pilling (London: John Libbey, 1997), pp. xv-xvi and p. xviii, notes 30-31 and 33-34.

31 Two points: 1. a number of these publications straddle the popular and the academic; and 2. popular, fan-oriented texts can be rich resources for animation scholarship, even as academic texts can hold treasures for the animatophiliac.

32 Magazines 'totally' or partly dedicated to *anime* include *Animerica, Anime FX, Anime Fantastique, fps, Mangazine, Protoculture Addicts, TOON Magazine, V.Max, Newtype USA, Gaigin!* and *AnimePlay*. In addition, *Animation Magazine* and *Animato*! carry articles on *anime*.

33 For an extended review of English language animation publications, see Maureen Furniss, 'Animation Literature Review', *Animation Journal*, Spring 1999.

34 Notably, 'The World According to Disney', *South Atlantic Quarterly*, vol. 92, no. 1, Winter 1993, edited by Susan Willis; the Animation issue, *Film History*, vol. 5, no. 2, June 1993, edited by Mark Langer and published by John Libbey; the Special Issue 'Cartoon: Caricature: Animation', *Art History*, vol. 18, no. 1, March 1995; the 'Art & Animation' issue, *Art & Design*, vol. 12, no. 3/4, March-April 1997, edited by Paul Wells; and the issue of *Japan Forum*, vol. 14, no. 2, 2002, on *anime*, edited by Thomas Lamarre. For a list that includes non-English language dedicated journals and special issues of non-dedicated journals, see the Bibliography in Bendazzi's *Cartoons* (though that is now 10 years old).

35 Including Patrick Crogan, 'Bugs, Daffy and Deleuze: The Out-of-Field in Chuck Jones' *Duck Amuck*', in *Hermes Papers 1990* (published by the University of Sydney Union); Sean Griffin, 'Pronoun Trouble: The "Queerness" of Animation', in the 1994 'Do You Read Me?: Queer Theory and Social Praxis' issue of the University of Southern California's *Spectator*, edited by Eric Freedman; a number in *Screen*, including vol. 33, no. 4, Winter 1992 (plus occasional articles in other of its issues); Cynthia Chris' 'Beyond the Mouse-Ear Gates: The Wonderful World of Disney Studies', in *Afterimage*, vol. 23, no. 3, November/December 1995; and my essay, 'The Illusion of the Beginning: A Theory of Drawing and Animation', in *Afterimage*, vol. 28, no. 1, July/August 2000. There are many more. See, for instance, on Disney alone, the dozens of articles listed in Janet Wasko's notes to her *Understanding*

Disney: The Manufacture of Fantasy (Cambridge, England: Polity Press, 2001).

36 Animation World Network, which I mentioned in Part I, is home to *Animation World Magazine*, to which Fred Patten is a regular contributor on *anime*. It is also home to *VFXWorld*. See also *fps: The Magazine of Animation*; and *toonhound*, the British online magazine. See too Richard Llewellyn's site, *Richard's Animated Divots (Diversions on Various Topics)*.

37 These 35 publications on Disney from 1991 on include several more biographies of Walt Disney, a number of books on Disneyland and/or Disney World, two books on *Snow White*, an encyclopedia of Disney, a book on the use of Mickey Mouse in the works of other artists worldwide, books on Disney trivia, a book on Disney insignia, a book on Disneyana, a book on the Mickey Mouse Club, as well as Michael Eisner's autobiography, *Work in Progress* (New York: Penguin, 1998), and two books on him.

38 Other books on Warner Bros.: Jerry Beck, *I Tawt I Taw a Puddy Tat: Fifty Years of Sylvester and Tweety* (New York: Henry Holt & Co., 1991); and Jerry Beck and Will Friedwald, *Warner Bros. Animation Art: The Characters, the Creators, the Limited Editions* (New York: Hugh Lauter Levin, 1997).

39 In John Canemaker, *Tex Avery: The MGM Years, 1942-1955* (New York: Turner, 1996).

40 In T.R. Adams, *Tom and Jerry: 50 Years of Cat and Mouse* (New York: Crescent Books, 1991), as well as in the autobiographies—Joe Barbera, *My Life in 'Toons: From Flatbush to Bedrock in Under a Century* (Atlanta: Turner Publishing, 1994); and Bill Hanna (co-authored with Tom Ito), *A Cast of Friends* (Dallas: Taylor Publishing Co., 1996). For Hanna and Barbera post-MGM, there is T.R. Adams, *The Flintstones: A Modern Stone Age Phenomenon* (Kansas City: Turner, 1994).

41 In this category, publications from the Disney company Hyperion include: Frank Thompson, *Tim Burton's* Nightmare Before Christmas: *The Film, the Art, the Vision* (New York: Hyperion, 1993); John Lasseter and Steve Daly, Toy Story: *The Art and Making of the Animated Film* (New York: Hyperion, 1995); and Jeff Kurtti, A Bug's Life: *The Art and Making of an Epic of Miniature Proportion* (New York: Hyperion, 1998). There is also Don Shay and Jody Duncan, *The Making of* Jurassic Park (London: Boxtree, 1993); and Mark Cotta Vaz and Patricia Rose Duignan, *Industrial Light & Magic: Into the Digital Realm* (New York:

Ballantine, 1996)—supplementing Thomas G. Smith, *Industrial Light & Magic: The Art of Special Effects* (New York: Ballantine, 1986).

42 With The Simpsons books, like *The Simpsons: A Complete Guide to Our Favorite Family*. Also calling for mention are the books by Aardman animators Peter Lord and Brian Sibley: *Creating 3D Animation: The Aardman Book of Filmmaking* (New York: Harry Abrams, 1998); and *Cracking Animation* (London: Thames and Hudson, 1998).

43 For example, Jeff Rovin, *The Illustrated Encylopaedia of Cartoon Animals* (New York: Prentice Hall, 1991); Jeff Lenburg, *The Encyclopedia of Animated Cartoons* (New York: Facts On File, 1991); and Hal Erickson, *Television Cartoon Shows: An Illustrated Encyclopedia, 1949 through 1993* (Jefferson City, NC: McFarland, 1995).

44 Including Helen McCarthy, *Anime!: A Beginners' Guide to Japanese Animation* (London: Titan Books, 1993)—the first English language book on *anime*; Helen McCarthy, *The Anime! Movie Guide* (Woodstock, NY: The Overlook Press, 1996, 1997); Helen McCarthy and Jonathan Clements, *The Erotic Anime Movie Guide* (Woodstock, NY: The Overlook Press, 1998); Jonathan Clements and Helen McCarthy, *The Anime Encyclopedia: A Guide to Japanese Animation Since 1917* (Berkeley, CA: Stone Bridge Press, 2001)—the most comprehensive guide to *anime* to date—and her monograph *Hayao Miyazaki, Master of Japanese Animation: Films, Themes, Artistry* (Berkeley, CA: Stone Bridge Press, 1999)—the first English language monograph on a Japanese animator. As well, there is Trish Ledoux and Doug Ranney, *The Complete Anime Guide: Japanese Animation Video Directory & Resource Guide*, ed. Fred Patten (Issaquah, WA: Tiger Mountain Press, 1995); Gilles Poitras, *The Anime Companion: What's Japanese in Japanese Animation?* (Berkeley, CA: Stone Bridge Press, 1999); Gilles Poitras, *Anime Essentials* (Berkeley, CA: Stone Bridge Press, 2000); and Patrick Drazen, *Anime Explosion!: The What? Why? & Wow! of Japanese Animation* (Berkeley, CA: Stone Bridge Press, 2002).

45 The lovely synoptic *The 50 Greatest Cartoons as Selected by 1,000 Animation Professionals*, ed. Jerry Beck (Atlanta: Turner Publishing, 1994), largely American animation; David Kilmer, *The Animated Film Collectors Guide: Worldwide Sources for Cartoons on Video and Laserdisc* (London: John Libbey, 1997); and Andy Mangels, *Animation on DVD: The Ultimate Guide* (Berkeley, CA: Stone Bridge Press, 2003), including *anime*.

46 Preston Blair, *Cartoon Animation* (Laguna Hills, California: Walter Foster Publishing, Inc., 1994); Richard Taylor, *The Encyclopedia of Animation*

Techniques (London: Running Press, 1996); and Michael O'Rourke, *Principles of Three-Dimensional Computer Animation: Modeling, Rendering & Animating with 3D Computer Graphics*, rev. ed. (New York: Norton, 1998).

47 Jeff Lotman, *Animation Art: The Early Years, 1911-1953* (Atglen, PA: Schiffer, 1995); and *Animation Art: The Later Years, 1954-1993* (Atglen, PA: Schiffer, 1996).

48 *The Oxford History of World Cinema*, ed. Geoffrey Nowell-Smith (Oxford: Oxford University Press, 1996), with sections on animation authored by Donald Crafton and William Moritz; and *An Introduction to Film Studies*, ed. Jill Nelmes (London: Routledge, 1996), with an animation section by Paul Wells.

49 For example, Freda Freiberg, '*Akira* and the Postnuclear Sublime' and Ben Crawford, '*Emperor Tomato-Ketchup*: Cartoon Properties from Japan', in *Hibakusha Cinema: Hiroshima, Nagasaki and the Nuclear Image in Japanese Film,* ed. Mick Broderick (London: Kegan Paul International, 1996). Also my essays '"OBJECTS IN MIRROR ARE CLOSER THAN THEY APPEAR": The Virtual Reality of *Jurassic Park* and Jean Baudrillard', in *Jean Baudrillard, Art and Artefact*, ed. Nicholas Zurbrugg (London: Sage, 1996); and 'Apocalyptic Animation: In the Wake of Hiroshima, Nagasaki, *Godzilla* and Baudrillard', in *Baudrillard West of the Dateline*, eds. Victoria Grace, Heather Worth and Laurence Simmons (Palmerston North, New Zealand: Dunmore Press, 2003).

50 Including such texts as Stephen M. Fjellman, *Vinyl Leaves: Walt Disney World and America* (Boulder, CO: Westview Press, 1992); Russell Merritt and J.B. Kaufmann, *Walt in Wonderland: The Silent Films of Walt Disney* (Baltimore: The Johns Hopkins University Press, 1993); Kathy Merlock Jackson, *Walt Disney: A Bio-Bibliography* (Westport: Greenwood Press, 1993); *Disney Discourse: Producing the Magic Kingdom*, ed. Eric Smoodin (New York: Routledge, 1994); *From Mouse to Mermaid: The Politics of Film, Gender, and Culture*, eds. Elizabeth Bell, Lynda Haas and Laura Sells (Bloomington: Indiana University Press, 1995); *Inside the Mouse: Work and Play at Disney World*, The Project on Disney (Karen Klugman, Jane Kuenz, Shelton Weldrep and Susan Willis) (Durham, NC: Duke University Press, 1995); Alan Bryman, *Disney and His Worlds* (London; Routledge, 1995); Steven Watts, *The Magic Kingdom: Walt Disney and the American Way of Life* (New York: Houghton Mifflin, 1997); *Designing Disney's Theme Parks: The Architecture of Reassurance*, ed. Karal Ann Marling (Montreal: Canadian Center for Architecture, 1997); Carl Hiassen, *Team Rodent: How Disney Devours the World* (Toronto: Ballantine,

1998); Robin Allan, *Walt Disney and Europe: European Influences on the Animated Feature Films of Walt Disney* (London: John Libbey, 1999); Eleanor Byrne and Martin McQuillan, *Deconstructing Disney* (London: Pluto Press, 1999); Henry A. Giroux, *The Mouse That Roared: Disney and the End of Innocence* (Lanham, MD: Rowman & Littlefield, 1999); Sean Griffin, *Tinker Belles and Evil Queens: The Walt Disney Company from the Inside Out* (New York: New York University Press, 2000); Janet Wasko, Mark Phillips and Eileen Meehan, *Dazzled by Disney?: The Global Disney Audience Project* (London: University of Leicester Press, 2001); Janet Wasko, *Understanding Disney: The Manufacture of Fantasy* (Cambridge, England: Polity Press, 2001); and John Canemaker, *Walt Disney's Nine Old Men and the Art of Animation* (New York: Disney Editions, 2001).

51 Norman M. Klein, *Seven Minutes: The Life and Death of the American Animated Cartoon* (London: Verso, 1993); Stefan Kanfer, *Serious Business: The Art and Commerce of Animation in America from Betty Boop to* Toy Story (New York: Scribner, 1997); Michael Barrier, *Hollywood Cartoons: American Animation in Its Golden Age* (Oxford: Oxford University Press, 1999) (devoted to close analysis of them); and Paul Wells, *Animation and America* (Edinburgh: Edinburgh University Press, 2002).

52 Maureen Furniss, *Art in Motion: Animation Aesthetics* (London: John Libbey, 1998); and Paul Wells, *Understanding Animation* (London: Routledge, 1998). As well, in terms of an overview of animation globally, in addition to Bendazzi's *Cartoons*, Paul Wells' *Around the World in Animation* (London: BFI/MOMI, 1997), a small survey of the subject in terms of animation aesthetics, must be mentioned.

53 And to my knowledge still the only ones focused on their respective topics: *Women and Animation: A Compendium*, ed. Jayne Pilling (London: BFI, 1992); Michael Frierson, *Clay Animation: American Highlights 1908 to the Present* (New York: Twayne Publishers, 1994); *Dark Alchemy: The Films of Jan Svankmajer*, ed. Peter Hames (Trowbridge, England: Flicks Books, 1995)—not only the first English-language publication on this leading European animator but at the same time, and at long last, the first large scholarly English language publication on European animation; Karl Cohen, *Forbidden Animation: Censored Cartoons and Blacklisted Animators in America* (Jefferson N.C.: McFarland & Co., 1997); and Paul Wells, *Animation: Genre and Authorship* (London: Wallflower, 2002). Also, three books I will address below: *A Reader in Animation Studies*, ed. Jayne Pilling (London: John Libbey, 1997); *Meta-Morphing: Visual Transformation and the Culture of Quick-Change*, ed. Vivian Sobchack (Minneapolis: University of Minnesota Press, 2000); and Esther Leslie,

Hollywood Flatlands: Animation, Critical Theory and the Avant-Garde (London: Verso, 2002).

54 And one which I forgot to mention in my Introduction (thanks to Adrian Martin for reminding me)—Thierry Kuntzel, '*Le Défilement*: A View in Close Up', *Camera Obscura* 2, 1977, an uneven but nonetheless suggestive text for the theorizing of animation.

55 Also impressive, at the least, for their historical scholarship and research zeal, are: Eric Smoodin, *Animating Culture: Hollywood Cartoons from the Sound Era* (New Brunswick, NJ: Rutgers University Press, 1993); Bendazzi, *Cartoons: One Hundred Years of Cinema Animation*—the first 'encyclopedic' history and critique of film animation around the world, the standard reference text; Robin Allan, *Walt Disney and Europe: European Influences on the Animated Feature Films of Walt Disney* (London: John Libbey, 1999)—a treasure trove of primary material based on archival research and interviews, lavishly illustrated, studying the impact of European culture on Disney and his artists; and Michael Frierson, *Clay Animation: American Highlights 1908 to the Present*—the first and only book to chart its subject's history, distinctive qualities, leading artists and future.

56 Brophy, 'Explosive Animation', Introduction to *KABOOM!: Explosive Animation from America and Japan*, p. 9.

57 In this regard, Brophy in 1994 stands against what will come to be advanced in 1998 by Furniss and Wells.

58 In terms of English Marxist film theory, see, for example, Peter Wollen's model taxonomy (articulated in 7 categories, like Wells') of radical versus reactionary cinema, itself modeled after Brecht, in Wollen's famous essay on Jean-Luc Godard, 'Counter Cinema: *Vent D'Est*', *Afterimage* 4, Autumn 1972.

59 Sandler, *Reading the Rabbit*, p. 4.

60 Here I must note: in my own publications, I say much about some of the key ideas, issues, topics, themes, theoretical approaches and theorists I take up in necessarily brief manner in this Introduction (especially the uncanny). So, rather than repeatedly referencing those publications here, but for the odd citing, I simply ask the interested reader to consult them, in particular: '*Who Framed Roger Rabbit*, or the Framing of Animation', in *THE ILLUSION OF LIFE*, on the hybrid live action/cartoon animation film, its history and its logics after Derrida; '"OBJECTS IN MIRROR ARE CLOSER THAN THEY APPEAR": The Virtual Reality of *Jurassic Park* and Jean Baudrillard', on live action

film, classic and digital animation, the live action/computer animation 'hybrid' of Spielberg's film and its hyperreal features, processes and logics thought after Baudrillard; 'The Illusion of the Beginning: A Theory of Drawing and Animation', on the drawing side of the graphic, supplementing my '*Who Framed Roger Rabbit*' essay, on the writing side of the graphic. 'The Illusion of the Beginning' was meant to help to remedy the paucity of writing theorizing drawing and the relation of drawing and animation; 'Apocalyptic Animation: In the Wake of Hiroshima, Nagasaki, *Godzilla* and Baudrillard', on *anime* in general, *Akira* in particular, and the relation of Japan and the U.S., including as figured in their respective animations, thought through the work of Baudrillard on Seduction, simulation and hyperreality; 'The Crypt, the Haunted House, of Cinema', in *Cultural Studies Review*, vol. 10, no. 2, September 2004, on the spectre, the Cryptic Complex, of film, of animation, thought after Derrida; and 'Still Photography?', in *Afterimage*, vol. 32, no. 5, March/April 2005, on photography, film, animation and the Cryptic Complex, thought after Baudrillard, including his photographs.

61 Napier, *Anime from* Akira *to* Princess Mononoke, p. 12.

62 Leslie, *Hollywood Flatlands*, p. v.

63 ibid.

64 ibid., p. vi.

65 Also to be added, though there is no room for their consideration either, are Paul Wells' latest books, *Animation and America* and *Animation: Genre and Authorship*, which can be seen as extensions of his earlier work in the theory and theorizing of animation. His seeming reassertion of the orthodox notion of the sovereignty and total control of the animation auteur is problematic for me, as was Terrance R. Lindvall and J. Matthew Melton's reassertion of it in their essay in Pilling's anthology. Here two general points must be made: first, the terms 'author' and 'genre' (and 'gender', for that matter) are themselves terms of animation, indicating that animation subsumes them in its logics. Second, despite simplistic readings (by animation theorists, among others) of his 'The Death of the Author', Roland Barthes does not simply do away with the author. He reanimates it, making the reader the author, even as the author remains a spectre of the text—never captured as such, always lost as found and found as lost.

66 See my Introduction to *THE ILLUSION OF LIFE*, pp. 28-29. The privileged relation between animation and the uncanny has been

an abiding thematic and object of inquiry of my writings since that Introduction. (Its second instantiation is my essay in this volume, presented in 1991 at the Society for Animation Studies conference. Four more essays have followed to date.) Five essays, including mine, in this new volume explicitly take up the uncanny, a number more use the term without addressal, more open themselves up profoundly to consideration in terms of its logics, especially where the home (and such cognates as the family, the familiar, etc.) is object of consideration and it is caught up in a dynamic where something strange and threatening has invaded it and made it metamorphose into something increasingly unfamiliar while at the same time the strange and threatening has metamorphosed into something increasingly familiar, 'home-like'. For me, the advent of film had such an effect. For Samuel Weber, it was the TV, with its uncanny reality, displacing the hearth as/at the centre of the 'home'. See Weber, *'Deus ex Media'*, *Mass Mediauras*, p. 162.

67 Additionally, Klein not only raises it but engages with Keith Clancy regarding his take on it. Napier writes of the protean but without mention of Eisenstein.

68 I cannot rehearse all the elements and aspects of this claim, including the theoretical, here, so I ask the reader to consult my Introduction to *THE ILLUSION OF LIFE*. As well, see my '"OBJECTS IN MIRROR ARE CLOSER THAN THEY APPEAR"', note 19; my 'The Illusion of the Beginning'; and my 'The Crypt, the Haunted House, of Cinema'.

69 Alexandre Alexeïeff, Preface to Bendazzi, *Cartoons*, pp. xix and xx.

70 Ralph Stephenson, *The Animated Film* (London/New York: The Tantivy Press/A. S. Barnes & Co., 1973), p. 26.

71 Driscoll, 'From Kino-Eye to *Anime*-Eye/*ai:* The Filmed and the Animated in Imamura Taihei's Media Theory', p. 280.

72 See my 'The Illusion of the Beginning' on Eisenstein.

73 Will Straw, *'The Illusion of Life: Essays on Animation'*, *Film History*, vol. 5, no. 2, June 1993, p. 252. I must qualify Straw: as I develop later in this Introduction, for me, unlike Eisenstein and most animation theorists, animation has no essence, has no core, nor therefore does what it enables.

74 Crafton, *Before Mickey*, p. 6, quoted in my Introduction to *THE ILLUSION OF LIFE*, p. 22.

75 Not only is the standard position espoused, just for openers, by Furniss in *Art in Motion* and Wells in *Understanding Animation*, Michael O'Pray asserts: 'Cholodenko...understands animation, perhaps unhelpfully, as that which pervades all film...'; and he states this without explicating

why I propose it and/or why he considers it perhaps unhelpful. Michael O'Pray, 'The Animated Film', *The Oxford Guide to Film Studies*, eds. John Hill and Pamela Church Gibson (Oxford: Oxford University Press, 1998), p. 434. Even O'Pray's use of the word 'pervades' is but a pale and partial reflection of what I advance in my Introduction to *THE ILLUSION OF LIFE* regarding the relation of animation to film.

76 Sean Griffin and Livia Monnet concur that all film is a form of animation. See his 'Pronoun Trouble: The "Queerness" of Animation', p. 107, and her 'Towards the Feminine Sublime,...', p. 226.

77 Lev Manovich, *The Language of New Media* (Cambridge, MA: The MIT Press, 2001, 2002), p. 302. Manovich is quoted by Lamarre, 'Introduction: Between Cinema and *Anime*', p. 184, and Monnet, 'Towards the Feminine Sublime,...', p. 226.

78 This privileged relation of animation to the uncanny is re-evidenced for me not only in the '80s-'90s return of digital animation to animation but in the '70s/'80s return of Tom Gunning's cinema of attractions in the form of what he calls the 'Spielberg-Lucas-Coppola cinema of effects' (Gunning, 'The Cinema of Attraction: Early Film, Its Spectator and the Avant-Garde', *Wide Angle*, vol. 8, no. 3/4, 1986, p. 70)—what would be the uncanny reanimation of not only cinema but animation, for Gunning's cinema of attractions is always already animation of attractions. See my 'The Crypt, the Haunted House, of Cinema'.

79 Introduction to *THE ILLUSION OF LIFE*, pp. 14-15.

80 Pilling, Introduction to A *Reader in Animation Studies*, p. xiv.

81 Edwin Carels, 'Theories on Real Phantasies', *Society for Animation Studies Newsletter*, vol. 17, issue 1, Spring 2004, p. 4.

82 Carels has his own sense of it.

83 I put these terms in quotation marks because, while they carry high recognition value and are therefore serviceable, they have been deemed unsatisfactory, by Derrida and Baudrillard for example, as labels of their work.

84 The animatic is something Philip Brophy, in his own way, and I have been writing about for well over a decade.

85 Pilling, Introduction to *A Reader in Animation Studies*, pp. xiii-xiv plus p. xviii, note 19.

86 Noël Carroll, 'Prospects for Film Theory: A Personal Assessment', *Post-Theory: Reconstructing Film Studies*, eds. David Bordwell and Noël Carroll (Madison: The University of Wisconsin Press, 1996), p. 41.

87 Animation Research Centre Conference Web Announcement for *Animated 'Worlds'*.

88 Straw, *'The Illusion of Life: Essays on Animation'*, pp. 251-253.

89 Introduction to *THE ILLUSION OF LIFE*, p. 15.

90 John Conomos, *'The Illusion of Life'*, *Agenda* 21, 1992, p. 46.

91 Not only are all films animations, all films for us thematize and perform animation in all its modes, as does the apparatus that likewise performs it. On the theme and performance of the reanimation of the hero as an aspect of 'the fascination of animation as the fascination with metamorphosis', see my Introduction to *THE ILLUSION OF LIFE*, p. 34, note 26. That fascination includes the one great subject, theme and performance of all narrative, as of all life: the uncanny reanimation of life and death, eros and thanatos—and their subforms: sex and violence. For us, each film not only animates the world and does so animatically, each *is* (to paraphrase the title of the Animation Research Centre's conference) an animated world—indeed, an *animatic* world—including animating theories of it, and vice versa. In such a light, all of film's modes and apparatuses, like all those of narrative and life, including spectatorship, call for retheorizing through the logics, processes and performances of animation, of animation as the animatic.

92 One of the thinkers I privileged in my Introduction to *THE ILLUSION OF LIFE* is Jacques Lacan (p. 24). Here I must correct Maureen Furniss' characterization in 'Animation Literature Review', *Animation Journal*, Spring 1999, that the essays in *THE ILLUSION OF LIFE* 'rely heavily on poststructuralist and postmodernist critiques of French film theory employing semiology, Althusserian Marxism and Lacanian psychoanalysis' (p. 67). Unfortunately, Furniss has removed the quotation marks that I placed around 'Lacanian psychoanalysis' at one point in my Introduction (p. 14), quotation marks meant to indicate (not very effectively, it appears) that Lacanian psychoanalysis was misunderstood and misused by English film theorists drawing on late '60s French film theory, including Laura Mulvey, in her famous 'Visual Pleasure and Narrative Cinema'. (Mulvey's 'Lacanian' model for live action cinema in that essay has in turn been invoked by Paul Wells for animation without critique of her misuse of Lacan. Wells, *Understanding Animation*, pp. 53-57.)

93 In note 33 of my Introduction. Michel Foucault, Maurice Merleau-Ponty and Jean-François Lyotard were also privileged in the book. I neglected to mention them.

94 Husserl *is* mentioned in *THE ILLUSION OF LIFE* but just in passing (in Lisa Trahair's essay), whereas he is foregrounded in this new volume

(in Freida Riggs' essay). Such continuity can even be found in Matthew Martin's logo, which inscribes and is inscribed in not only Proteus but the first of the Presocratic philosophers, Thales. Thales' first principle of animation was water, the animistic *arche* of everything. The logo takes us from Thales to Heraclitus and his famous comment on the river—'we do and do not step into the same rivers; we are and are not' (quoted in Keith Clancy, 'ΠΡΗΣΤΗΡ: The T(r)opology of Pyromania', in *THE ILLUSION OF LIFE*, p. 246)—and his notion that 'everything flows', everything is in a state of perpetual flux, in other words, in a state of perpetual metamorphosis.

95 For example, Bakhtin is privileged for the thinking of animation in terms of his writing on carnival (preeminently exemplified for him by Rabelais' *Gargantua and Pantagruel*) by Lindvall and Melton in their essay in *A Reader in Animation Studies*, Wells in *Understanding Animation* and Napier in *Anime from* Akira *to* Princess Mononoke; and in terms of his analysis of novelistic chronotopes of metamorphosis and their literary metamorphosis by Sobchack in her essay in *Meta-Morphing*. In addition, Kafka, Paul de Man and Avital Ronell are valorized by Byrne and McQuillan. (See the role of Kafka and Paul de Man in Samuel Weber's *Mass Mediauras*. Weber is acknowledged by Byrne and McQuillan too.) Antonin Artaud and Jean-Luc Nancy should be added, too.

96 While my '*Who Framed Roger Rabbit*, or the Framing of Animation' privileged Derrida for the thinking of animation, Peter Hutchings' 'The Work-shop of Filthy Animation' privileged Kristeva, in terms of her notion of abjection, as does Napier. Napier also privileges for such thinking, as I did in my Introduction to the book: the uncanny; the protean (as I indicated earlier, she does not mention Eisenstein though); metamorphosis; simulation; and animation as a medium, for me '...the very medium within which all, including film, "comes to be"' (my Introduction, p. 29), which position I repeat in my '*Who Framed Roger Rabbit*' essay (p. 213).

97 It should be noted that these essays on digital animation and *anime* were presented in 1995 at *THE LIFE OF ILLUSION* conference. (Indeed, 14 of the 16 essays in the book were presented there). Mine was presented in 1991 at the third Society for Animation Studies conference, in Rochester, NY, while Jonson's was a 1995 University of Sydney M.A. by Coursework essay for the first year of my theory of animation—film, television and computer—Honours course, a temporal testament to the pioneering nature of these essays. *Meta-Morphing* comes out of

a panel at the 1996 Society for Cinema Studies conference, a panel of the same name organized and chaired by Sobchack with three of the four panelists contributing essays to the book 'based on their earlier presentation'. Sobchack, Introduction to *Meta-Morphing*, p. xxiii, note 6. The special issue of *Japan Forum* was generated by a conference organized by Livia Monnet at the University of Montreal in 1999 entitled 'Japanese Pop Culture'.

98 See my '"OBJECTS IN MIRROR ARE CLOSER THAN THEY APPEAR"' and 'Apocalyptic Animation'. That affinity between *Meta-Morphing* and the *Japan Forum* issue is also marked in the fact that Monnet draws on four essays from *Meta-Morphing*, those of Kevin Fisher, Norman M. Klein, Angela Ndalianis and Sobchack herself, and Lamarre draws on one, that of Klein.

99 As Baudrillard speculates on his two irreconcilable hypotheses—undecidable between them—of The Perfect Crime of virtualization and the Radical Illusion of Seduction in *The Perfect Crime* (London: Verso, 1996), pp. 5, 74, as well as in the tellingly titled *The Vital Illusion*, ed. Julia Witwer (New York: Columbia University Press, 2000), pp. 53, 55.

100 Indeed, *THE ILLUSION OF LIFE 2* does have a number of essays (those of Ono, Moore, Goodall, Ellison, Crawford) that include consideration of issues that are key staples in the stock-in-trade of Cultural Studies—for example, sex, gender, race, nation—that is, issues of identity—as did the essays of Ferrell and Diprose and Vasseleu in *THE ILLUSION OF LIFE*. But, as with the Ferrell and Diprose and Vasseleu essays, such issues are treated here in ways radically different from, even 'opposed to', the banal, either/or, 'static', 'inanimate' modelings of Cultural Studies.

101 Of the four theoretical publications I have singled out, in this regard Byrne and McQuillan's text seems far from our volumes, *Meta-Morphing* less so (four out of its 12 essays appear to me marked by Cultural Studies modelings), Napier and *Japan Forum* even less so.

102 Here I also need to clarify and qualify something I said in my Introduction to *THE ILLUSION OF LIFE*, where I maintained that the Webster's Dictionary definition of animation I quoted poses animation as at once both endowing with life and endowing with motion. That definition can be so read by simply adding meanings 1—'to give life to; bring to life'—and 4—'to give motion to; put into action…'— but it need not be so read. The four different meanings it offers can be, but need not be, read as compatible, individually and collectively. So for

us, that 1 and 4 are never not combined (but at the same time without one being subsumed in the other) is a reading, argument and conclusion I make based on a Derridean theorizing, one that does not simply combine 1 and 4 either but deconstructs their relation in an animatic 'definition' of animation.

Even as my theorizing made animation as film and animation as idea (concept, process, etc.) inextricably coimplicated (see my Introduction to *THE ILLUSION OF LIFE* pp. 15-16), so it made life and motion inextricably coimplicated. Moreover, for us one must not only think both cycles, or rather spirals, of life and motion at the same time, the thinking of each must be of the 'whole' spiral, not just of the 'up' phase of each. This is a key point for us: the passage from the animate to the inanimate is as much a part of animation as is the passage from the inanimate to the animate.

103 Here a second caution: simulation is itself not a simple thing nor does it take a single, simple form. See Baudrillard, 'The Precession of Simulacra' and 'The Orders of Simulacra', in *Simulations*, trans. Paul Foss, Paul Patton and Philip Beitchman (New York: Semiotext(e), 1983). Of relevance too is his four phases of the image in the former, pp. 11-12. As well, consult Deleuze's 'Plato and the Simulacrum', *October* 27, Winter 1983.

104 Introduction to *THE ILLUSION OF LIFE*, p. 20.

105 Baudrillard in 'An Interview with Jean Baudrillard' conducted by Edward Colless, David Kelly and Alan Cholodenko, in Baudrillard, *The Evil Demon of Images*, ed. Alan Cholodenko (unnamed) (Sydney: Power Institute Publications, 1987), p. 45.

106 Introduction to *THE ILLUSION OF LIFE*, p. 21.

107 I put 'expanded' in quotation marks because animation as a 'field' is never not expanded for me. For example, animation film and film animation form the expanded field of live action film, animation 'as such' is the expanded field of animation film and film animation, etc.

108 Annalee Newitz, '*Anime Otaku*: Japanese Animation Fans Outside Japan', *Bad Subjects* 13, April 1994, p. 11, quoted in Napier, *Anime from* Akira *to* Princess Mononoke, p. 5. See more generally Napier's first and second chapters 'Why *Anime*?' and '*Anime* and Local/Global Identity' for historical and cultural details. See also the essays by Kosei Ono, Pauline Moore and Fred Patten in this volume.

109 Napier declares, 'At this point, it [*anime*] is the only real alternative to American popular culture...' Quoted in Robin Gerrow, 'An *Anime*

Explosion: Challenging Themes, Complex Characters Make Japanese Animation a Global Phenomenon', The University of Texas at Austin website, June 13, 2004. utexas.edu.features

110 Frederik L. Schodt, *America and the Four Japans: Friend, Foe, Model, Mirror* (Berkeley: Stone Bridge Press, 1994), p. 40. In terms of recent film animation, such cross-pollinating was at work in *The Matrix*, as explicitly evidenced in the DVD *The Animatrix* (2003), a collaboration between the Wachowskis and Japanese animators, producing what the jacket idealistically describes as 'a visionary fusion of CG-animation and Japanese *animé*...' Another key filmic indicator: Quentin Tarantino's *Kill Bill, Vol. 1* (2003), with animation by Japan's Production I.G, and *Vol. 2* (2004).

111 See my 'Apocalyptic Animation', p. 243, note 9, on such morphings of cartoon animation into live action, and vice versa, including these words: 'The hypervitality of *Akira, Jurassic Park* and *The Matrix* is in the wake of their and the world's radical loss of meaning, truth and identity, in the wake of their and the world's radical loss of reality and film—loss of animation in *anime* and live action in digitally animated "film"'.

112 If Disney animation seeks to simulate live action (that particular understanding of 'the illusion of life'), even to outbid it, to be more live action than live action, to make live action metamorphose into itself, and it into it, then not only does *anime* seeking to be more live action than live action, etc., become hyperreal avatar and outbidder of that Disney project and aspiration, so too does digital animation that seeks to simulate live action, to be more live action than live action, etc. Here, insofar as its very project seems to be to simulate digitally Disney animation, John Lasseter's'/Pixar's animation becomes singular exemplar of not only hyperanimation but of hyperDisney animation, the pure and empty form of Disney animation.

Another fascinating example of the dual metamorphosis, the crossover, of animation into live action and of live action into animation: *The Simpsons*—now the longest running sit-com in TV history—as cartoon animation more live action than live action 'against' *Married...with Children* as live action more cartoon animation than cartoon animation.

113 See my 'Apocalyptic Animation' essay, which is an extended elaboration of this issue of war and *animus*, considering *anime* in general, *Akira* in particular and the post-World War II relations between Japan and the

U.S., including as inscribed in and performed by the *anime*, through the games of seduction, simulation and hyperconformity of Baudrillard.

114 Brophy, 'Explosive Animation', *KABOOM!*, p. 9.

115 Along with the apocalypse of the A-Bomb, the Holocaust serves as the other key event of World War II that for Baudrillard inaugurates and characterizes hyperreality.

116 The impact—another highly loaded word—of the mass media has been profound, arguably pushing the world into the more (and less) real than real—the hyperreal—in the process exploding, but more so imploding, the givens of that zone of referentiality that went under the name of reality, givens such as truth, meaning, value, presence, essence, ground, centre, the constitutive human subject, identity, self-identity, subjectivity, fact, definition, the reality principle, representation, etc., even as they at the same time implode the distinction between themselves and the world, making it impossible to say which is media and which is world. See Baudrillard, *The Evil Demon of Images.*

117 Baudrillard, *The Evil Demon of Images*, p. 15. The realm of metamorphosis is that of animation. To think animation is to think the metamorphosing of one kind of life and motion into another, as Erwin Panofsky told us in his definition of animation. (Quoted in my Introduction to *THE ILLUSION OF LIFE*, p. 20.) In my Introduction, I posited metamorphosis as a key figure, process and performance of and for animation and of and for its thinking.

118 In his new book, *Wrong About Japan* (Sydney: Vintage, 2004), Peter Carey writes of the 'tantalising information' (p. 37) Ono communicated to him about aspects of the culture of Japan.

119 While Moore argues that cute in post-World War II Japanese animation is itself already apocalyptic—already a form of the apocalyptic, we would say—insofar as she reads cute in a deconstructive manner, it could be argued that not only is cute in Japanese post-World War II animation (a form of the) apocalyptic, the apocalyptic therein is at the same time (a form of) cute, a point William Schaffer made to me in conversation.

120 In the course of her reflections, Goodall offers a salutary corrective to those who automatically read binary oppositions in terms of difference (and I would add: in terms of the dialectic), forgetting or ignorant of dualism (and its historical and theoretical tradition). Unlike the dialectic, dualism in no way allows of synthesis, solution and resolution, rather is caught in the interminable, irresolvable agonistics/war of the

dual/duel. See in this regard Goodall's marvelous book *Artaud and the Gnostic Drama* (Oxford: Oxford University Press, 1994).

121 Not only does Brophy's essay in this volume crucially take off from and extend his 'The Animation of Sound' in *THE ILLUSION OF LIFE*, it also relates to his 'Ocular Excess' article in *KABOOM!*, as well as to his 'The Architecsonic Object: Stereo Sound, Cinema & *Colors*', in *Culture, Technology & Creativity in the Late Twentieth Century*, ed. Philip Hayward (London: John Libbey, 1990). Like 'The Animation of Sound' and his essay in this volume, 'The Architecsonic Object' is excerpted from his in-progress work *Sonic Cinema: Technology, Textuality and Aural Narratology in the Cinema*.

122 As Brophy emphatically put the war in Warner Bros. cartoons in his essay in *THE ILLUSION OF LIFE*, even condensing in his final endnote Bugs' famous 'Of course, you realize, this means war', quoted by Chuck Jones in his talk in the book 'What's Up, Down Under?'

123 For me, Thompson's analysis opens the Clampett text to not only a Lacanian reading—say after Christian Metz's 'The Imaginary Signifier' or Slavoj Žižek's *Looking Awry* (including Žižek's treatment of Lacan's little object a, what Rosebud in *Citizen Kane* is for me)—but a Deleuzian one, based on Deleuze's nominating *Citizen Kane* as the first film of the time-image, that which for him cinema is never not. (That includes Edwin S. Porter's *The Great Train Robbery*!, whose title anticipates Clampett's.) See Deleuze, *Cinema 2: The Time-Image*, trans. Hugh Tomlinson and Robert Galeta (Minneapolis: University of Minnesota Press, 1989). For me, it is uncanny that the reporter in *Citizen Kane* who plays the detective, who goes in search of the meaning of Rosebud, is named, like the author of this essay, Thompson; and insofar as his face is never seen, he too is missing in a way from the film, as is what he seeks: Rosebud. All of which points toward another 'dick' missing from writing about animation for far too long: Richard Thompson.

124 Thompson, 'Pronoun Trouble', in *The American Animated Cartoon*, eds. Danny and Gerald Peary (New York: Dutton, 1980), p. 227. 'Pronoun Trouble' was a later, different version of Thompson's '*Duck Amuck*', published in the landmark special issue on The Hollywood Cartoon of *Film Comment*, January-February 1975.

125 That Colless' essay is still timely is marked for me by 'Life after *Baywatch*', which aired on Australian TV November 19, 2003.

126 Patten's essay is included in his just published book *Watching Anime, Reading Manga* (Berkeley: Stone Bridge Press, 2004). I had hoped and

expected to have it out in our present volume before it appeared in his own collection, but that was not to be.

127 Perhaps, taking a page from Samuel Weber's book *Mass Mediauras*, we should speak of mass medianimations, even mass immedianimations.

128 I would add: insofar as it works across live action and animation, Butler's essay links up with the many other essays in this book that do so—Moore's, Goodall's, Brophy's, Thompson's, Colless', and as we will see Crogan's, Crawford's and Schaffer's, even mine—most without acknowledging, much less foregrounding and engaging with, that addressal, taking for granted that all film is a form of animation. But however broached, the including of live action in animation is for me a form of the 'expanded' field of animation. In this and other regards, insofar as Spielberg is inscribed in what Tom Gunning calls the 'Spielberg-Lucas-Coppola cinema of effects', Butler's treatment impacts upon and inflects Gunning's. Gunning, 'The Cinema of Attraction: Early Film, Its Spectator and the Avant-Garde', p. 70.

129 The acronym of New Electronic Order—NEO—is the name of the hero of *The Matrix*.

130 Including drawing from Baudrillard's *The Gulf War Did Not Take Place*, trans. Paul Patton (Sydney: Power Publications, 1995). In terms of the uncanny nature of what Ellison describes, see our note 66.

131 The image of the hybrid bug-eyed pilot in his VCASS (Visually-Coupled Airborne Systems Simulator) Helmet perfectly illustrating Crogan's essay and its key thesis of pure war as reanimator cannot but recall *The Fly* in both its earlier and more recent incarnations, which institutes a relation with Lisa Trahair's essay 'For the Noise of a Fly' in *THE ILLUSION OF LIFE*. Also, his consideration of flight and animation also links up with Ono's treatment of *anime* in general and Miyazaki's work in particular (and wherever else this topic comes up in these essays).

132 Gay Alcorn, 'The Return of Evil', *Spectrum, The Sydney Morning Herald*, August 28, 1999, p. 7s, contains this statistic: between 1945 and 1985 there were 150 wars and only 26 days when no war was underway in the world.

133 Parenthetically, Ellison's and Crogan's essays take it as a given that, as I proposed earlier, computer games are a form of computer *animation*, therefore are 'by definition' subsumed within 'animation studies'.

134 I would note: Ben Crawford's '*Emperor Tomato-Ketchup*: Cartoon Properties from Japan', in *Hibakusha Cinema: Hiroshima, Nagasaki and*

the Nuclear Image in Japanese Film, supplements this essay, as well as those on *anime* in this volume.

135 For me, the characterizing by Crawford of the global marketing activities of the 50 to 100 media and entertainment corporations involved in this enterprise as strategic, tactical engagements with their adversaries intriguingly relates to Ellison's and Crogan's essays on war (Crawford even cites *Street Fighter* in passing), as well as to Ono's, Moore's and Patten's on the relations between U.S. and Japanese animation. Indeed, his mention of Disney, DreamWorks and Nintendo networks his essay with a number of those in the book. Too, his consideration of issues of innocence and experience links at the least with Moore's and Goodall's essays, as his treatment of intellectual properties connects at the least with Moore's consideration of cute merchandise.

136 In its concern for thinking voice in terms of Aristotle's *anima* (or *psyché*) as principle of life, Jonson's essay links with Routt's and Colless', as in its concern for thinking sound in animation—the animation of sound and the sound of animation—it links with Brophy's in this volume as well as in its predecessor.

137 It should be noted that Schaffer's essay offers a criticism of all those who simply embrace a notion of the absolute control of the animator/author.

138 This paper, which I first presented at the 1991 Society for Animation Studies conference, is mistitled in the 'List of SAS Conference Papers' in *A Reader in Animation Studies*, p. 276, as 'Speculations on the Animatic Automation'. Pilling indicates her information is derived from the SAS newsletters. Indeed, it has been mistitled in the 'List of SAS Conference Papers' on the SAS website. In any case, for me automation is always haunted by the automaton.

139 Thomas Looser, 'From Edogawa to Miyazaki: Cinematic and *Anime*-ic Architectures of Early and Late Twentieth-Century Japan', *Japan Forum*, vol. 14, no. 2, 2002, p. 297.

140 See Wells, *Understanding Animation*, pp. 21, 183, 227; and *Animation and America*, Introduction and Chapter 1.

141 Wells, *Animation and America*, p. 160.

142 On Derrida's replacement of Saussure's semiology with grammatology, see Derrida, *Of Grammatology*, trans. Gayatri Chakravorty Spivak (Baltimore: The Johns Hopkins University Press, 1976), p. 51; and Derrida, *Positions*, trans. Alan Bass (London: The Athlone Press, 1981), the chapter entitled 'Semiology and Grammatology: *Interview with Julia Kristeva*'. Wells' standard claim that animation is a language

recalls an earlier Film Studies analogue, precisely Metz's linguistic semiology of cinema and Deleuze's critique of it.

143 Leskosky, *Film Quarterly*, Summer 1993, p. 43.

144 It is an easy step to claim that all those writing on/theorizing becoming by definition are writing on/theorizing animation.

145 Guy Johnson, review of *THE ILLUSION OF LIFE*, *Animation Journal*, Fall 1993, p. 86.

1 Japan

THE LONG FLIGHT OF *MANGA* AND *ANIME*: THE HISTORY OF COMICS AND ANIMATION IN JAPAN*

KOSEI ONO

FROM 1917 TO THE END OF WORLD WAR II

The history of Japanese animation can be traced back as far as 1917. One year earlier, the French animation series *Fantoche* by Emile Cohl was released in Japan; and its influence was immense. Indeed, there is a record of a simple animated film made in Japan that very year.[1] It was nine years before the first animation was made in China, and Japan and China used different methods. In 1926, influenced by American animators the Fleischer Brothers, Wan Lai Ming made his first animation short in China using cels (celluloid). On the other hand, the first animated film in Japan was made by shooting pictures drawn on paper. Use of cels in Japan did not become widespread until the 1930s. And, until then, most of the animated films in Japan consisted of *kirie*, cut-out pictures. Sometimes, the paper used was not plain colour paper but *chiyogami*, beautiful multi-coloured woodblock prints with intricate patterns.

These methods were popular at the beginning. But at the end of the 1920s, animation using silhouette pictures emerged; and the contents consisted mainly of fairy tales and folklore. In the 1930s, with the development of the talkie, the animated film became a popular medium for both educational and entertainment purposes. And with the expansion of militarism in the final years of the decade, animated films in this country began to reflect the national policy.

A 1938 animation short has a fighter plane with the *hinomaru*, the sun design of the Japanese flag, for example. There is a scene where an animal character pilots this plane and flies it to rescue a friendly plane; but a cloud in the shape of Popeye blocks its way. This incorporation of Popeye is probably due to the fact that American animated films, especially those of the Fleischers and Disney, were popular in Japan; and so Japanese children were familiar with Popeye and Mickey Mouse.

The most popular children's *manga* at this time was *Norakuro*. It was about the adventures of a stray dog who joins an army comprised of all canine troops. It was serialized for 11 years in a boys' magazine and later printed in ten hardcover volumes. Although the content is similar to *Sad Sack* in America, the difference is that the dog is promoted in rank every year and finally becomes a lieutenant. In 1934, *Norakuro* became a short animated film. And after the war, it was serialized for television without the military background. *Norakuro* is a rare case insofar as it was made in both *manga* and *anime* before and after the war.[2] Shortly before his death in 1988, the creator of Norakuro, Suiho Tagawa, confessed that the character was inspired by the American comic character Felix the Cat.

Norakuro was one of many long story comics produced for children, a genre that, under the influence of American comic strips, became popular in the 1920s. Production of such comics increased, such that, by the latter half of the 1930s, originally written long story comic books were 120 to 160 pages in length per volume and were published as hardcover books inside cases. It was a unique form developed in Japanese comics.

In 1938, the Internal Affairs Ministry of Japan ordered the publishing houses to decrease the publications of comics and comic series in magazines. In 1941, this ministry was especially hard on long story comics. Pages of comics in children's magazines decreased and eventually disappeared. Japan was in a state of war, and the government decided that precious paper was not to be wasted on such ludicrous things as comics.

When the war in the Pacific broke out in December of 1942, production of propaganda animation was launched; and some of the cartoonists who were out of work joined in. From 1943 until Japan's defeat in 1945, six animated propaganda films were sponsored by the Navy and one by the Army. These were shown along with live feature films at the theatres.

Among these propaganda animations is *Momotaro no Umi Washi* (*Momotaro's Sea Eagles*), directed by Mitsuse Seo in 1943. This is a 37 minute piece about Japan's attack on Pearl Harbor, with Momotaro, the most popular fairy tale character, as the hero. Never before was there an animation film of this length, and it was publicized as the first full-length animation film in Japan.[3] According to the legend, Momotaro, along with his retainers—a dog, a monkey and a pheasant—destroys a band of demons on Onigashima Island, which means Demon Island. In the film, though, Momotaro, dressed like Admiral Yamamoto, is the commander of an aircraft carrier and commands the attack on Demon Island, which looks exactly like Hawaii. Despite the film's propaganda, the animals, such as bunnies and monkeys, are adorably drawn. In the scene of the attack on the island, all the enemy soldiers are presented as demons, with horns on their foreheads. A fat demon falling into the sea and struggling is an obvious reminiscence of Popeye's nemesis, Bluto, whose voice from the Fleischer Brothers' Popeye animation series is used for this scene. *Momotaro no Umi Washi* became a record hit, drawing a mass audience consisting mainly of school children.

Among the dozens of propaganda animation shorts that were produced during the war, *Kumo to Tulip* (*The Spider and the Tulip*) stands out. This 16 minute short by Kenzo Masaoka was released about the same time as *Momotaro no Umi Washi*. It was a piece totally free of any wartime elements, even though the whole nation was coloured by war. The story is about a girl ladybug who is blown away one stormy night. She is pursued by a spider and rescued by a tulip. With its flexible movements and beautiful music, this poetic piece could be well compared in quality with Walt Disney's *Silly Symphonies*.

With the tremendous success of *Momotaro no Umi Washi*, the Ministry of the Navy accepted the challenge of an even bigger project: the production of a sequel. *Momotaro Umi no Shinpei* (*Momotaro's Divine Sea Warriors*) was produced with Mitsuse Seo again as director. The plot takes up the adventures of the Navy paratroops, with Japan's successful campaign in Singapore as the backdrop. Compared to *Momotaro no Umi Washi*, *Momotaro Umi no Shinpei* is marked with heavier propaganda; and the pleasant atmosphere of the earlier work is more or less eliminated. There is a scene where Momotaro's squadron attacks the enemy base, whose soldiers, indulging in a game of cards, are taken by surprise. As the enemy, with their hands raised, surrender, we see among them Popeye, a can of spinach falling from his hand! On the other hand, there are several quite soothing scenes, such as the one where Momotaro teaches Japanese to the animals.

With a year and nine months spent on the production, the 74 minute *Momotaro Umi no Shinpei* reached the technical peak of Japanese animated films made to that date. It was released in April of 1945, four months before the war ended. Air raids by the Americans were becoming intense in Tokyo and Osaka; and in consequence, this finest achievement of wartime Japanese animation was ironically seen by few people. But there was one secondary school boy who visited an almost vacant theatre in Osaka to see the film over and over. This boy was Osamu Tezuka.[4]

Even though the importation of American films was banned during the war, there were prints of American animated films in Shanghai and Singapore, cities that were occupied by the Japanese. The Japanese military confiscated those prints and sent them back to Japan. In fact, the Ministry of Education held screenings of them while *Momotaro Umi no Shinpei* was being made. That audience was very limited, consisting of animators and cartoonists involved in propaganda animation, the purpose of the screenings being to provide them with American references. Among the films screened at the time were the Fleischer Brothers' *Gulliver's Travels* and Disney's *Snow White and the Seven Dwarfs* and *Fantasia*. The animator of *Momotaro Umi no Shinpei* viewed *Fantasia* and was greatly shocked by its vastly superior technical quality. Indeed, on that basis, he came to the firm conclusion that Japan could not win the war.

THE POST-WAR YEARS

With Japan's surrender in the summer of 1945, the animators who had worked on propaganda films lost their jobs. But the publication of new magazines and the revival of those interrupted during wartime created a demand for cartoonists. As the production of new animated films had not yet begun, some animators became comic book artists to make a living. Mitsuse Seo, the animator who directed the two Momotaro films, was one of them, turning to writing comic paperbacks for children. Between 1945 and 1950, such paperbacks, printed on coarse paper and all original publications, were abundant. All kinds of comics for children sold well, especially the ones by Tezuka, satisfying the thirst from the wartime years, when the populace was deprived of entertainment.

Magazines for children were also affected by the war. When they reverted after the war to their original, non-propaganda style and content, the cartoons returned. While the pages were still few in number, considerable space was given to comics and illustrated stories, those in the adventure genre being especially popular.

What returned in multitudes to the theatres were American films. Disney's earlier animated features, such as *Snow White and the Seven Dwarfs*, *Pinocchio* and *Bambi*, were highly successful, most of the theatres so crowded that people could not get in. Many elementary schools sent pupils in groups under the teachers' supervision to see Disney animated films as part of the students' extra-curricular activities.

Such school trips to see American animated films were common and frequent. As for feature films, Tarzan movies were popular among children; and this was reflected in Japanese comics. As well, American comic strips, like Chic Young's *Blondie,* were translated and published. All of these triggered the admiration of the Japanese people for the American life style.

From 1945 to 1955, nearly 50 animation shorts were made in Japan. Most of them were for educational purposes and shown in schools. That means that these shorts were not geared for general release to be seen by a mass audience.

In 1956, Toei, one of Japan's five major film studios, established Toei Doga (Toei Animated Film Co. Ltd.) to produce its own animated films. By doing so, it opened the market for the theatrical release of animated films and thereby broke away from the restriction that such films be made for educational purposes and not for pure entertainment. In this way, Japanese animation was born as an industry. In 1958, Toei Doga made the first Japanese animation feature film in colour,[5] the 78 minute *Hakuja-den* (*Legend of the White Serpent*), directed by Taiji Yabushita and based on a Chinese legend.[6] It was extremely successful, screened on a double bill with a live action feature. The animators laboured hard to compete with Disney's works, and their enthusiasm is well reflected in the film's fine finish.

From 1958 to 1963, Toei Doga produced six animation features. Since there was no other Japanese company making animation for theatrical release, Toei Animation monopolized the market. All its animated films drew their subject from Japanese and Chinese fairy tales and folklore, as well as from such western tales as *A Thousand and One Nights*.

But Toei Doga's uncontested position was to take a blow when Japan's first animation series for television was aired: *Tetsuwan Atom* (*Astro Boy*), by Osamu Tezuka. In the immediate post-war years, Tezuka charmed children with dozens of his original comic books. In the 1950s, he was the most popular cartoonist among children; and many monthly magazines for children ran long-term series by him. *Testsuwan Atom* first appeared in one such monthly in 1951. The story featured a super power robot boy who led a life much like a human child and even went to school. The robot was amicable and loved by children across the nation.

By the end of the 1950s, almost all the pages of children's (both boys' and girls') magazines were occupied by comics. One of Tezuka's achievements was to present a new style in comics after the war, breaking away from plain humour to cultivate works of greater narrative character; and the comic series began to take this new form initiated by him. In addition to humour, the comics now had intricate story lines, a mass of characters, even characters of ambiguous nature, not clearly defined as either good or evil.

It is not generally known that the Japanese word for comics—*manga*—was used in a broader sense more than a century earlier by the *ukiyoe* artist Hokusai Katsushika to refer to humorous drawings. In the 1950s, the term *story-manga* emerged to describe the new type of comics popular among children. Sources of narrative, such as movies, theatre, radio dramas and printed matter (including comic books, magazines and literature), had long been enjoyed by Japanese children. But as it became established as a new type of narrative, *story-manga*, which included elements of both literature and picture books, witnessed a rapid increase in its share of the market. At that time, Japan was heading for economic growth; and the appearance of more publications accompanied it. Children's magazines, although they did not have the word *manga* in their names, were in reality comic magazines.

THE BIRTH OF *TETSUWAN ATOM* (*ASTRO BOY*) AND JAPANESE TV CARTOONS

Television broadcasting began in Japan in 1953. American sit-coms and animated cartoons were aired in abundance and were greatly cherished by children. The Japanese could now stay home and watch such live action drama series as *Superman*, *Highway Patrol* and *Rin Tin Tin*, as well as such animations as Disney's shorts, the Popeye series and Terrytoon's *Mighty Mouse*. From 1960 on, Hanna-Barbera cartoons, such as *The Flintstones* and *The Jetsons*, were also broadcast; and the Japanese children loved them.

In other words, the Japanese children were exposed to, and became accustomed to, television's weekly narrative cycle. Major publishing houses quickly followed suit. In 1959, two boys' comic weeklies were published, to be followed by an equivalent for the girls in 1962.

With this as the background, Osamu Tezuka realized his long held dream of establishing an animation studio in 1962. The first animated film produced by Tezuka's Mushi Production that year was a 39 minute experimental piece titled *Aru Machikado no Monogatari* (*Stories from a Street Corner*). It was a love story, but the man and woman did not move. They were represented by posters instead. The subject was determined by the low production cost and short production period. There was no dialogue, just music. Though I do not recall the exact number of cuts (and while some portions were done in full animation), I feel confident in saying that it was a work with the largest number of cuts for its running time. The result was indeed refreshing.

After this film, Tezuka launched the production of *Tetsuwan Atom* in the 30 minute television slot. On January 1, 1963, ten years after the birth of television in Japan, *Tetsuwan Atom* commenced broadcasting. The ratings were tremendous. Over the following four years, until the end of 1966, 193 *Tetsuwan Atom* episodes were aired.

To encourage the network and the sponsors to accept the first televising of a work of animation, Tezuka used low cost production to strongly appeal to them. He later confessed that the production cost of one episode was 450,000 yen. At the rate back then, it was approximately $1,250 U.S. dollars. Now, 30 years later, the production cost of a 30 minute television animation in colour is 8 million yen, or $80,000 U.S. dollars. To keep production costs to a minimum, Tezuka cut down the number of pictures. For a 30 minute cartoon, he used 1,000 to 1,300 cel drawings, and even as few as 900 at times, which sometimes meant watching one picture for three seconds.

Gisaburo Sugii, a veteran animator who entered Mushi Production after four years experience at Toei Doga and worked as chief animator for the first episode of *Tetsuwan Atom* TV cartoons, remembers the time Tezuka talked to him about the movement of the boy robot.[7] Sugii discovered that the script said 'Tetsuwan Atom is surprised. Three second shot'. So Sugii tried to draw three second movements of the surprised robot. 'What are you doing?', Tezuka said. 'Going to move Tetsuwan Atom', replied the chief animator. 'No, don't move him', Tezuka stated, and added 'This is not necessary'. 'No movement for three seconds?' Sugii could not believe it. 'No', his boss said. 'Forget the movement. This is not animation. This is just a TV program. If we have a really strong story, viewers will not care about movements'. 'B...but, absolutely no movement, sir?' 'No'. Finally, Tezuka compromised and permitted Sugii to make Tetsuwan Atom blink his eyes once.

Sugii was terribly uneasy until he saw the finished film, and he was truly amazed to discover the cartoon was not marred by such minimal movement of the main character. This anecdote illustrates how confident the master of *story-manga* was about his new method of making cartoons. And his 'this-is-not-animation' became a sort of standard of Japanese TV cartoons (and even of theatrical features after this cartoon).

Tetsuwan Atom paved the way for the emergence of the TV *anime* industry. But since the industry determined production costs on the basis of *Tetsuwan Atom*, it had to struggle within a low budget. When reprimanded for this, Tezuka responded that if he had sought a much higher budget, the television company and sponsors might not have agreed to air *Tetsuwan Atom*.[8]

The success of *Tetsuwan Atom* spawned new television cartoons by the dozens. Even Toei Doga, which until then had monopolized theatrical releases, began to make cartoons for television, too. The result was that television *anime* conquered the world of children with its new form.

Since *Tetsuwan Atom* first appeared as a comic book, many television cartoons that followed after were taken from the print medium as well. Or rather, a popular comic book was made into TV cartoons; and they served as feedback to the original printed matter, causing sales of the original comic books to increase and occasionally leading to the publication of comic books taking up episodes which were especially created for the animated version.

It may be symbolic that the first television cartoon hero in Japan was a robot. At the end of 1963, the year *Tetsuwan Atom* was broadcast, *Tetsujin Niju-hachi-go* (*Gigantor*) was also serialized. So, in fact, *Tetsuwan Atom* became a pioneer for the countless robot cartoons to follow. But Tetsujin was nothing like Tetsuwan Atom, who was not merely a chunk of metal but was created to replace a child killed in a traffic accident. Though Tetsuwan Atom was a robot and possessed of super powers, he behaved like a human child. He went to school, and even at times was more human than his human counterparts. Indeed, he had the heart of an angel and often wavered between his robot and human qualities. He was a mechanical doll that wanted to become human but could not and was characterized by the Pinocchio syndrome. In fact, in a way, he was Tezuka's futuristic version of Pinocchio. Although the puppet becomes a human boy at the end of the classic Italian tale, Tezuka's robot boy never gets a human body nor does he grow up. He can be understood to symbolize the moratorium situation of Japanese children who fear becoming adults.

Such a human robot was unique, as were the characters and the world surrounding him. Nothing equivalent to Tetsuwan Atom has been created since. By contrast, Tetsujin (Gigantor), as the name implies, was an enormous machine for destruction, with no thinking power, designed to be remote-controlled by humans. The countless TV robots to emerge in Japan are all descended from him, their prototype, not from Tetsuwan Atom. Even with its limbs severed, Tetsujin moved with what remained of itself. In this respect, the Transformers, with various parts functioning independently and becoming a different machine when those parts were assembled differently, could have been inspired by Tetsujin. Mazinger, created ten years after Tetsujin, was a brainchild of cartoonist Go Nagai, who had dreamed of operating a robot as one would drive a car. Mazinger was the dream realized, a device to amplify the operator's own power. Yoshiyuki Tomino's *Mobile Suit Gundam* was born in this lineage; and between the late 1970s and the beginning of the 1980s, this robot and *super mecha* (machine) genre brought on an extraordinary animation boom.

But this boom did not arrive just by itself. 1963, the year of the birth of both Astro Boy and Gigantor, was a turning point for post-war Japan, as it entered the phase of high economic growth with which for decades thereafter Japan was synonymous. In 1964, the Olympic Games were held in Tokyo, prior to which the Bullet trains began to operate, running on the Tokaido Line connecting Tokyo with Kyoto and the Osaka-Kobe district. One effect of the Tokyo Olympics was the drastic increase in the number of households with television sets. Years later, Japan would become famous for its industrial robots.

The 1960s was also the time when the post-war baby-boomers were entering college. The intense education boom had already begun, and the children had to spend more time studying. Children disappeared from alleys and parks and were forced to study with private tutors and in drill classes. Parents sought to have children enroll in prestigious schools, even preparing them from kindergarten so they might later be able to attend a famous university and then join a major corporation. Parents without doubt believed that this was the only way their children could have a happy and stable life. The children also began to share their parents' values and went voluntarily to drill classes.

But even these children needed an escape into fantasy as a form of entertainment. Television became their major source of entertainment, in response to which the Japanese animation industry mass-produced animated films for television and later for the theatre. Many of these films were of robot battles. Since these robots were machines created for combat, the cartoons in which they appeared had many scenes of explosions and destruction. At times these cartoons were criticized as being too violent. Regardless, new model robots were produced as often as automobiles. There is no doubt that Japanese animation achieved an unprecedented development in, and of, this genre.

Since the mid-1960s, the cultural environment of children in Japan has been comprised mainly of a flood of weekly comic magazines, TV cartoons (likewise on a weekly cycle) and theatrically released cartoons as extensions of the other two media. And it was through them all that children were most commonly provided with narrative entertainment. The consumption of an extraordinary amount of stories in printed matter, on the television tube and on the silver screen became a form of child culture.

MIYAZAKI'S NEW ATTEMPTS IN ANIMATION

Amidst the flood of animated images being produced and consumed in the 1980s, a new attempt in animation was born when, in 1984, Hayao Miyazaki released his independently produced, full-length theatrical animation *Kaze no Tani no Nausicaa* (*Nausicaa of the Valley of Wind*). Miyazaki had formerly worked at Toei Doga, where he had made a number of animated features, including *Lupin Sansei: Cagliostro no Shiro* (*Lupin III: Castle of Cagliostro*), and TV series, such as *Mirai Shonen Conan* (*Future Boy Conan*), before he went independent in 1982.

Contrary to the trend, *Nausicaa* was not based on a world classic, folklore, a popular comic book or an extension of a TV cartoon. It was derived from his own comic book story and was a totally original creation. The story features the adventures of a young heroine, whose name, Nausicaa, Miyazaki borrowed from Greek mythology. Compared to other Japanese animations, *Nausicaa* had something rare: a well constructed plot. The film also presented the creator's message without being preachy, and the characterization of the heroine was certainly attractive.

But its major strength was offering the satisfaction of watching a *worthwhile* animation, a pleasure for which animation fans had longed. In truth, there were other works portraying the world after a nuclear holocaust; but by introducing this heroine who may be able to save the earth from destruction, *Nausicaa* cleverly combined the topical problem of nuclear apocalypse with that of pollution and ecology.

What especially impressed the audiences of *Nausicaa* were the scenes where, in its full animation form, the heroine flies in the sky as freely as a bird. It was with Tetsuwan Atom's flight that post-war Japanese animation had prepared for a take-off, but Nausicaa perfected that flight. And the period in between *Tetsuwan Atom* and *Kaze no Tani no Nausicaa* can be taken as a taxiing onto the runway or as a test flight. While Tetsuwan Atom took off into the sky by jet drive, Nausicaa, the princess of the people, living in the Valley of the Winds, took off on a kite. The kite is propelled by a jet engine; but it is basically a super kite, and the heroine cleverly rides the wind, thus earning her the name 'the wind worker'. Nausicaa and the kite flew through the atmosphere in harmony with nature.

Though still an adolescent, Princess Nausicaa demonstrates qualities of an independent woman. At the beginning of the film, she kills a number of enemy soldiers with her sword. This is a very important and necessary scene which makes the film powerful and meaningful in quite a different way from Disney-style animation features. It is derived from the Russian animated film *The Snow Queen*, made in the '50s, whose strong-willed gipsy girl aiding the heroine is Nausicaa's model. And Nausicaa's friendliness to the giant worms parallels that of the heroine in *Mushi Meguru Himegimi* (The Princess Who Loved Worms), a story written by a woman writer 1,200 years ago. Yet Miyazaki ingeniously utilizes this motif in a world set 1,000 years from now by adding the satisfaction of the freedom of flying.

Kaze no Tani no Nausicaa was both a critical and box office success, the first animated film to achieve this distinction in the history of Japanese cinema. It attracted the grown-up audience, especially young women. Groups who had never shown interest in animated films were charmed by this piece and drawn to the theatres. Even though the popularity of animation in Japan had been strong and sustained, the fans up until then were limited to enthusiasts. But *Nausicaa* broke this barrier and expanded the audience to the general level, raking in almost all the domestic film awards of the year.

While the story in the film was complete and provided a satisfactory ending, Miyazaki continued writing the comic story. The seventh volume was finally published, and the story came to its end after 12 years. (The comic book version, translated into English, is published in the United States.) The ending of the comics is therefore different from that of the film version. At the end of the film, an old woman praises Nausicaa as if she were a deity. At the end of the comics, we see that Miyazaki did not want her to be a god. She is not simply the saviour of Earth from the destruction of nature and other ecological problems. Miyazaki portrays her with more complexity, a heroine who can be the symbol of the good as well as equipped with the potential for evil, that of a destroyer.

In style, the comic book *Nausicaa* is drastically different from most of the comics in boys' comic weeklies. It is not designed to match the rapid weekly cycle of the Japanese comic book readers. Rather, it takes the style of the French *bande dessinée* and is written and drawn with utmost detail. Unlike Tezuka, who was basically a cartoonist even though he made animated films, Miyazaki put, and still puts, animation first.

Following *Nausicaa*, Miyazaki made the original theatrical animation *Tenku no Shiro Laputa* (*Laputa: The Castle in the Sky*) in 1986. In this film, too, the main protagonist is a girl; and she makes her first appearance by descending from the sky to come to stand in front of a boy. She wears a pendant, and the stone mounted on it has the magic power of anti-gravity. The girl's name is Sheeta, borrowed from the name of a princess in the *Ramayana*, the Indian mythological text. In the film, the heroine is captured by sky pirates but is rescued by the boy by his operating an aircraft which floats in the sky like a kite.

Like *Nausicaa*, *Laputa* introduces many types of aircraft, including an enormous aeroboat and a dragonfly-like flying machine. Characters operating these craft race them to their destination, an island in the sky called Laputa. Needless to say, this name is taken from Jonathan Swift's *Gulliver's Travels*; but instead of being a gigantic magnetic stone, Laputa here is an island which floats by the power of anti-gravity.

In 1988, with his original theatrical release *Tonari no Totoro* (*My Neighbour Totoro*), Miyazaki for the first time does not set his story in an imaginary place or time but in Japan. The location is perhaps the suburbs of Tokyo in the late 1950s, when high rise modern buildings did not yet exist. The overall atmosphere is rural, or rather, pastoral, with farms and forests to stir our nostalgia. The plot features two young sisters coming from the city. They meet Totoro, a giant, spirit-like guardian of the woods. Totoro can only be seen by those who believe in its existence. The younger sister, the first to believe, rides Totoro; and it flies through the sky. There is also a catbus,[9] which has that strange Cheshire Cat smile from *Alice in Wonderland*. With the girls on board, the catbus speeds through the air, not high up in the sky, but on the level of the telephone poles.

Kiki, the heroine in *Majo no Takkyubin* (*Kiki's Delivery Service*), made in 1990, is the daughter of a witch who becomes an apprentice witch. She leaves her parents' home and sets out for the city to support herself. To be a witch, she must learn to fly skillfully on a broom. Like the path of a car driven by a teenager learning how to drive, her flight is erratic; but Miyazaki presents her as enjoying her upside-down or off-course flights.

As the story unfolds, a young man makes his appearance and takes an interest in Kiki. While she is busy practicing how to ride the broom, he is also preparing to fly. In his case, the aircraft is not a broom but a human-powered airplane. The young man tries to fly but repeatedly fails. In the world of Miyazaki, it is the women who have the power of magic, not the men.

In his 1992 *Kurenai no Buta* (*The Crimson Pig*), set in the Adriatic Sea in the 1920s, the main protagonist is a male pilot of an aeroboat;

but a young girl becomes his mechanic. She seems to be waiting for her turn to fly, and we can easily assume that she will some day be another Nausicaa.

Flight in Miyazaki's films takes various forms: horizontal, vertical and hovering. All these forms are presented in a way that only animation can express. His scenes of flight induce in us a feeling of physiological ecstacy and spiritual liberation, and are at times very sensuous. Miyazaki himself admits he has been strongly attracted to flight since he was a child and that when he became an animator, he was greatly moved by Peter Pan's flight in Disney's eponymous film.

Miyazaki's films are targeted at an audience ranging from children to adults, including both sexes, and significantly at those who are not animation enthusiasts.

The recent Japanese animation scene is also characterized by another type of animated film, one with a highly restricted audience. One major example of this species is Mamoru Oshii's 1995 feature *Kokaku Kidotai* (*Ghost in the Shell*), based on Masamune Shirow's cyberpunk comics of the same title. While the original comics are often cartoony and filled with humour, Oshii's version is more serious and set in a complicated near-future society somewhat resembling that of Ridley Scott's *Blade Runner*. This film attracts the so-called *otaku*, a new generation of *manga* and *anime* enthusiast who supports this kind of Japanese animation. Though Katsuhiro Otomo's *Memories* (1995) must have been targeted to a general audience, it was this new generation of *anime otaku* that in reality mainly supported it.

THE PRESENT SITUATION

1997 initiated a new epoch in Japanese animation with the release of two animated films of completely different character. Both were controversial, both were phenomenal cultural events. One was *Mononoke Hime* (*Princess Mononoke*), by Miyazaki, which opened as a summer season blockbuster. Three months later, adults and children of all ages and both sexes were still setting out to the theatres in multitudes. The film, the most expensive *anime* to date, had the largest audience attendance of any film (not just *anime*) ever in Japan, putting *E.T.* and *Jurassic Park* to shame.

The story is set in feudal times, somewhere between the fourteenth and sixteenth centuries. Miyazaki presents the confrontation of technology and nature by means of two warring entities: a group of humans with the industrial skills of refining, smelting and the manufacture of firearms; and the deities of the beasts and plants of the woods. The confrontation occurs when the industrial group attempts to preserve its iron plant by destroying the woods, the home of the deities.

The hero is a teenager who is involved in the confrontation but gradually begins to take an interest in nature when he meets a girl who was brought up by the deities of the woods.

Although the drama in the film unfolds as an adventure story with an array of characters, Miyazaki grounds the film in the question he poses: can humans live in harmony with nature? It is this question that forms the basis of most of his films; and in *Mononoke* he takes its consideration to a higher, more complex and uneasy level. In it, he breaks from the simple message of living in harmony with nature that had up til then given him the image in Japan of 'ecologist' or 'keeper of Totoro'. In this film, Miyazaki looks annoyed with such a message and label, suggesting that it is not so easy to live happily with nature.

In this regard, this film is less satisfying but far more realistic in attitude than his earlier work. The shift Miyazaki created in the different ending in the comic book version of *Nausicaa* is reflected in *Mononoke*.

Miyazaki's motif of human characters flying is not present in *Mononoke*; but his technical and artistic genius is at its peak, creating near perfect movements and metamorphoses. The film's integration of hand drawn and computerized images is beautifully executed, an amazing technical achievement. The exquisite images lure the children in the audience; and the theme is an intelligent and—despite the fantasy coating of an adventure set in the middle ages—contemporary one for grown-ups. In not offering a clear-cut ending, the film leaves the audience to think deeply about the future of the world we live in.

In sum, in terms of story, technique, complex approach to subject matter, controversial ending and box office success, *Mononoke* breaks new ground for *anime*. In this regard, it is interesting that Tezuka, who admired Disney greatly, invented the Japanese style, *manga*-based, story-telling *anime* with very limited (but effective) animation; that Miyazaki, who grew up with Disney animated feature films and read Tezuka's *manga* when he was young, developed non-*manga* based, original animated features with strong story content and superb expression; and that Disney has distributed *Mononoke* and videos of earlier works by Miyazaki in the United States and Europe. It has been announced that Miyazaki's next film will have a budget of a bigger scale and is set in the future (the twenty-first century), when earth suffers from overpopulation, intense pollution, plagues and terrorism.

The other hit *anime* is *Shin-seiki Evangelion: Shito Shinsei* (*Evangelion: Death and Rebirth*), directed by Hideaki Anno and released in the spring of 1997. Originally aired as a TV cartoon series (1995-1996), the story, set in the future, is about a giant mechanical organism that protects a city-sized citadel from unknown outside forces. It is interesting that this TV cartoon series began to become popular after the broadcasting had finished and finally has proved to be the most talked about *anime* series among young audiences since *Gundam*. Besides the battle and destruction sequences, the series stresses the anxieties of fourteen year old boys and girls who are selected to mount the Evangelion mechanical organisms to control them. Curiously, almost nothing is explained: what are the Evangelion? What is the purpose of the organization controlling the citadel? Whom are they fighting? Why must only fourteen year olds be chosen for the task... With so many questions unanswered, the audience must try to find their own answers.

These mystery elements seem to appeal especially to young people. As if to respond to this, many books with unique hypothetical answers have been published, a phenomenon which has never before existed in Japan. Yet *Evangelion's* popularity does not rely solely on this riddle-solving. While the sequences of people are shot in very limited animation, the battles are in full animation, dynamic, beautiful and stylish.

The sequel, *Air: Magokoro-o-kimi-ni* (*End of Evangelion*), was released in July 1997. Instead of answering all the questions raised by the first *Evangelion*, the sequel maintains most of them. Nevertheless, younger audiences are lured to the theatres, particularly youths around the same age as the Evangelion operators, because they feel they can identify with the mentality of these characters. It is interesting that the director is not very enthusiastic about answering questions or solving riddles. Instead, he focuses on the psychological aspects of the main character, a fourteen year old boy. The boy lacks confidence, having anxieties about his identity and trouble in communicating with others. Director Anno carefully describes the boy's dilemma: the fear of contact with other people and the fear of not having a friend. All the adolescent Evangelion operators in this *anime* have a trauma of some kind, and the fact that they have not conquered the trauma seems to make them better controllers/ synchronizers of the bio-machines. The characters of *Gundam* have the same type of anxieties, but they are much older and experienced in life.

Another interesting attempt in *anime* is *Perfect Blue* (same title in English), directed by Satoshi Kon, produced in 1997 and released in 1998. It is a psycho thriller about a pop idol who becomes a victim of a mysterious stalker. This graphically sophisticated *anime* has drawn much attention since it takes up a subject which reflects the problems plaguing our society now.

Evangelion and *Perfect Blue* seem to criticize unexpectedly Miyazaki's tour de force *Mononoke*. How to get along with nature? It's surely a serious problem. And it's too obvious that it's not easy to live happily together with nature. But the real, immediate problem is how to survive in the city of today. Both *anime* seem to say this. In both films, the living spaces of the main characters are fetishistically described: artificial, clean, well-lit.

Animated films with such intricate or complicated plots are reflections of the situation of Japanese *manga*. In this essay, I traced the history of Japanese animation in its relationship with that of *manga*. Many of the animated works in Japan reflect the diversity of *manga*. Some *manga* artists are even at the same time animators, like Katsuhiro Otomo, who is now preparing a new *anime* feature,

Steam Boy. The Japanese audience who are accustomed to, and enjoy, the variety of styles, subjects and complex story lines of *manga* can easily access animated films with highly elaborate content, such as Miyazaki's *Mononoke*.

As many scholars of modern Japan point out, *manga* has become a part of our culture. As literature, films, music and other arts are reflections of the society, so too are *manga* and *anime*. *Manga* depict almost every aspect of life in Japan, from pure entertainment to educational, instructive and even metaphysical fields. Yet it is of interest that the wide variety of *manga* and *anime* seldom covers politics and social issues as in the American animation *The Simpsons*, which seems to be a paragon of black humour emerging from the relationships and behaviour of the family members. With the majority of Japanese wishing to 'belong' to a group, the Japanese society is said to be built on homogeneity; and its people may not have had enough training to express their opinions or be ready for confrontations.[10]

Still, in the current *anime* scene, animators of the generation after Miyazaki are pursuing their individual styles and themes. Unlike his films, theirs are not necessarily family entertainments.

NOTES

*Editor's note: where possible, to assist readers, English language titles of the *anime* Kosei Ono references are taken from *The Anime Encyclopedia: A Guide to Japanese Animation Since 1917*, eds. Jonathan Clements and Helen McCarthy (Berkeley, CA: Stone Bridge Press, 2001) or other reputable sources, and are italicized. Otherwise, Ono's literal translations are used and are not italicized.

1 The person who made the first animation in Japan was Hekoten Shimokawa, a current events cartoonist for newspapers. Making animated films strained his eyes; and after five films, he withdrew from animation. Prints of many of the earlier works of Japanese animation are lost, including all of Shimokawa's.

2 The word *animation* came to be used in Japan around the second half of the 1960s. Until then, works of animation were referred to as *manga* movies or *do ga*, meaning moving pictures. In the 1960s, along with cartoons on television, non-commercial artistic and experimental

animated films were made by individuals such as Yoji Kuri and Renzo Kinoshita. Their creators referred to their works by using the English word *animation*. This term was added to the Japanese language vocabulary in the 1970s; and by shortening it in the Japanese way, the expression *anime* was born. It has become a household word.

3 It may be noted that the first full-length animation in Asia was made by the pioneer of Chinese animation, Wan Lai Ming, and his brothers. Made in 1941, it was titled *Princess Iron Fan* and was 72 minutes long.

4 In his diary written during the war, Tezuka mentions how he was impressed by the film. He even drew some of the film's scenes in the diary.

5 For the record, the first colour animation in Japan was made in 1948 as Fuji Film's test film.

6 Before this feature, they produced a beautiful black and white short *Koneko no Rakugaki* (*Doodling Kitty*), directed by Yasuji Mori in 1957. In this animation, a variety of animals play on the roof of the locomotive drawn on the wall. The widespread presence of cute and cuddly characters in Japanese *anime* possibly came from this work.

7 Kosei Ono's interview with Gisaburo Sugii on January 23, 1996.

8 In reality, Tezuka was not solely an animation producer. Since Tetsuwan Atom was his own brain child, he held the copyrights to all uses of this character. So even though the actual production cost was more than the budget he received from the television companies, he was able to break even through the sale of merchandising goods. Other animation producers were not so fortunate because they were not the authors of the stories nor creators of the characters. Almost three and a half decades after the birth of *Tetsuwan Atom* TV cartoons, the general working conditions of animators have improved very little. For example, a young man graduating from an animation school and beginning work for an animation studio may only receive a salary which is less than half of a college graduate's starting salary as an office worker.

9 Japanese film director Akira Kurosawa had seen all of Miyazaki's films; and when he was on a television talk show with Miyazaki soon after the release of *Totoro*, he told the animator that he especially enjoyed this catbus sequence in the film.

10 While the Japanese pride themselves on understanding each other without any or little verbal exchange, this in return has nurtured ambiguity, especially in decision making. This ambiguity can be seen in the boy in *Evangelion*, whose indecision and awkwardness in voicing his opinion are often found in recent Japanese youth.

When Velvet Gloves Meet Iron Fists: Cuteness in Japanese Animation

PAULINE MOORE

> SHE: . . . on the fifteenth day too.
>
> Hiroshima was blanketed with flowers. There were cornflowers and gladiolas everywhere, and morning glories and day lilies that rose again from the ashes with an extraordinary vigor, quite unheard of for flowers till then.[1]

In the midst of the devastation and suffering caused by the dropping of the Atomic Bomb on Hiroshima, such an unnatural blooming of flowers, caused by the heat of the atomic blast itself, must have seemed miraculous. It can be seen retrospectively as a moment of reanimation, a rebirth, albeit in a mutated form, offering the Japanese people qualified hope for the future.

These themes of reanimation, rebirth and mutation predominate in Japanese *manga* and *anime* and are regularly linked to both the threat and promise of science and technology in the wake of The Bomb. For me, it is the cute figures of *manga* and *anime* that, in their uncanny and ambivalent nature, singularly articulate and incarnate this event and process, an event and process spanning U.S. A-Bombing, occupation and imposition of its culture upon Japan and Japan's adopting, adapting and replying to it, rising out of it 'with an extraordinary vigor'.

In this essay I will explore some of the contradictions at work in this event and process via the notion of cute, as it has been adopted from America, and then adapted and transformed by Japanese popular culture since World War II.

Today the word *cute* is used primarily to denote persons, animals or things that are attractive, pretty and/or charming to us in some way. This designation has come to replace the word's earlier, eighteenth century definition as clever, sharp, cunning and/or shrewd (from *acute*), a signification that is used rarely, if at all, today. Nevertheless, even when not explicitly declared to be operative, this earlier and markedly opposed definition is, I would argue, still active, exerting a covert, unacknowledged and troubling influence on our relation to such objects.

For me, this is something that the Japanese adoption of cute from America is always telling us, including in its *manga* and *anime*: there can never be a solely benign figure of cute as pretty, attractive, charming. The cute characters and things found in the most recent generation of *anime* not only play out this ambivalence, this undecidability, in the word itself but make it overt. Such *anime* has developed the cute figure to explicitly evidence the word's range of opposing qualities, that is, the figure is *at once both* attractive and clever, pretty and cunning, charming and shrewd, comforting and discomforting. As well, such *anime* shows that the process at work in cute is not simply additive but rather disseminative, a process that indetermines and suspends distinctive opposition in an inextricable, uncannily coimplicated and coimplicating figure—what would be an attractive cleverness and clever attractiveness, a pretty cunningness and cunning prettyness, etc. In fact, what we see evidenced is the way in which key terms semantically associated with cute—*cunning* and *canny*—in themselves, as well as together with cute, uncannily evidence and play out the disseminative process in the word and figure of cute.

The word *cute* would be an undecidable or a homonym for Jacques Derrida, the undecidable or homonym marking the disseminative process that is 'always already' at work within *any* word, thing, situation or text.[2] Such terms not only reveal such processes, they perform them. And crucially, their operation accords for me with the processes of animation and acculturation themselves. It is impossible to explore these processes in clear-cut oppositional terms or by referring to some fixed or pure point of origin. There is an animating principle—the *animatic*—a principle of dissemination, of transformation, at work in them.[3]

CROSS-CULTURAL RELATIONS AND *ANIME*

Not only does the cute figure as cute—at once charming and cunning, therefore neither (simply) charming nor (simply) cunning—embody and perform this undecidable process, so too does the appearance of the cute figure in a Japanese context, insofar as, imported from America, and from Disney cartoons in particular, it is an example of cross-cultural exchange between America and Japan from that time to the present. As cross-cultural, it operates in an undecidable realm, one that lies between cultures, in that chiasmatic crossing space of cultural exchange—the in between. It is a figure that looks in two directions at once—both East and West—mirroring the fraught history of cultural exchange between Japan and the United States in the last two centuries.

Of course, to say 'in the last two centuries' is to raise up another mirror essential to this history and exchange, the mirror of our technological media. In this regard, for Derrida, our tele-techno-communications have intensified a process never not happening. Not only are place, identity, origin, presence, and any effort to fix their specificity, 'always already' displaced and disseminated, our reproducing, or rather, animatic tele-technologies like film, television, video, fax and modem—which transport and transpose information, images and events from somewhere to somewhere else—all the more displace, disseminate, our idea or sense of place, all the more reveal that 'a place' is 'always already' 'the possibility, chance, or threat of [its] replacement'.[4]

So place is never simply a given, rather place is always already displaced, including Japan and America. And tele-communication technologies all the more set in motion—that is, displace—place, and our idea of it. Place becomes both here and there, neither here nor there, at the same time. What this means is that such technologies do not just repeat the place and/or the event, they displace, replace, transform and even create such places and events. Better, they *reanimate* such places and events, endowing them with *their* life and motion at the same time, a life and motion not only inscribed in but performed by these technologies and what they transmit, including, for our purposes, *manga* and *anime*.

This process of dissemination, of the animatic, that is never not happening and that is intensified in the twentieth century thanks to our media technologies has reached the point where the world is now 'globalized', that is, networked in and by a web of tele-techno-communications that spans many places and cultures and that exists without any specific point of origin. This net, this web, has brought about the sense of a global culture that, while it might seem to incorporate, transmit, present and produce cultural specificity, is never not engaged in its dissemination.

Insofar as the cross-cultural relations between Japan and the United States have been sited in this net, this web, these cultural relations of the crossing, as disseminative, have been intensified further, a process of forgetting and remembering that is never not happening in terms of place, identity, origin, presence, including the identity of a place and nation called Japan or America. Any effort to fix their specificity only reminds us that that process has never not been happening in the undecidable operations of cute itself, as demonstrated in Disney animation (with *its* origins in European and specifically German kitsch) and *manga* and *anime*, indeed, even in the very word *cute*.

The cute face that Japan re-turns towards America in its *manga* and *anime* is at once both familiar and strange. It is uncanny (*unheimlich)*—a face at once familiarly strange and strangely familiar, a face that simultaneously comforts and disturbs, that at once comforts in its disturbing and disturbs in its comforting. It is a cross-cultural image—neither Japanese nor American, and yet both at the same time. Insofar as cuteness in Japanese animation reanimates and comments on processes of cultural exchange that have occurred between Japan and America, it enacts a haunting at once of both the West and the East, both America and Japan, by operating at the same time as a forgetting *and* a reminder of what both cultures had seemed to be prior to World War II. In the wake of Hiroshima and

Nagasaki, the comforting qualities of the cute figure are inextricably linked to the discomforting qualities of horror and grief associated with The Bomb and its aftermath, life after this event marked essentially by the capacity for absolute destruction/death. After the dropping of the Atomic Bomb, a split for us occurred in the history of the world, one that continues to drag its monumental past along with it. This past is traumatic, a lived experience that, despite having to be continuously repressed from consciousness, retains an active, although unacknowledged, role on a day to day level.

As J. Laplanche and J.-B. Pontalis define it, trauma is related to 'the idea of a violent shock, the idea of a wound and the idea of consequences affecting the whole organisation'.[5] Another useful way of thinking about this is that a shocking event in an individual's life exists in the psyche as a '*foreign* body' insofar as it is unassimilated by consciousness but still exerts influence. We could say that the events of Hiroshima and Nagasaki, as they were visited on Japan by America, exist as a foreign body in the collective psyche of the Japanese people, a psychic trauma that would be doubled by America's actual occupation of Japan after the war. The necessary repression of this trauma demanded by that occupation in no way alleviated the wounding that Japan suffered at Hiroshima and Nagasaki and after, a wounding that is still an active and defining moment in contemporary Japanese life,[6] one that has separated Japan, and indeed the world, from the illusory idea of the past as solely comforting.

The destruction of Hiroshima on August 6 and Nagasaki on August 9, 1945, has changed Japan and the rest of the world forever. At the level of popular and mass culture, the experience of destruction reveals itself by cloaking itself in the language of the imagination, where it then appears in forms of expression like *manga* and *anime*, forms that are writing an unofficial history of this cataclysmic event. They live out, that is, reanimate, the trauma of The Bomb, as do the cute figures found therein. These figures offer comfort, and yet they continually deny such a possibility. Their eyes, moist and welcoming, are pools that mirror the nuclear explosion just as clearly as the camera flash.[7]

According to Philip Brophy, the Japanese cartoon character with large, exaggerated, rounded eyes is 'a new terrain: neither east nor west; neither human nor inhuman'.[8] For Brophy, too, this cute figure is an undecidable. It bridges the gap that opens between two cultures while at the same time mutating to create a new form—'neither east nor west, neither human nor inhuman'. But for me, even while being neither, such figures are still both at the same time—an idea that Brophy gestures towards but does not fully elaborate. He states that '...Japan was the largest producer of celluloid dolls world-wide between the early 1910s and the late 1930s, bearing the ubiquitous stamp "Made In Japan"',[9] an observation that this paper will extend and give further insight into by exploring elements within Japanese culture that give rise to the adoption of cute. The strangely new figure in *anime* is new only insofar as it incorporates both East and West, human and inhuman characteristics. Because of its uncanny, undecidable appearance, Western viewers are unsure of what they are seeing. They seem to be Occidental eyes, but they may not be. This is the indeterminate space that these figures inhabit—between cultures—but with very real attributes of both. These cute figures occupy a place which, although particular, is also anywhere, everywhere and nowhere, simultaneously.

The cute figure appears here as an attempt to reconcile such incommensurables as past and present, self and other, East and West, Japan and America, an attempt that it—as *itself* irreconcilable—at the same time not only shows to be but renders impossible. In this way, this figure provides us with a fascinating alternative view of Japanese culture and customs in the period following World War II. Insofar as post-World War II *anime* is an acknowledgement and performance of The Bomb and of the effects it has had on traditional Japanese culture, it provides an oblique commentary on issues relating to the environment, sexuality, violence, science, consumerism and cultural exchange. It lives out—animates—questions and problems that are difficult, if not impossible, to explore directly.

The post-war period in Japan is in many ways one of contradiction: hope for the future accompanied by a sense of mourning and even melancholia for the past. Peace had arrived, but at what cost? By repressing the past and embracing a vision of the future that relied on the development of technology in support of democratic values, Japan leapt forward to meet its future. With the rise of capitalism and the aid of a rapidly burgeoning economy in the late 1950s and early 1960s, Japan was able to 'forget' its most recent past and sense of failure. Production blossomed; and technology developed at such a rapid rate that Japan soon surpassed its former conquerors and occupiers, who also became its teachers and sponsors.

At the same time, there was a proliferation of the graphic art medium on a mass scale.[10] After World War II, an aesthetic of cuteness (*kawaii*) is increasingly applied in *manga* and *anime* to the depiction of animals and children, to the point where it becomes one of their two dominant figures, the other being the apocalyptic. Of course, what I am suggesting is that cute is already *itself* apocalyptic in post-World War II *manga* and *anime*. This aesthetic was applied as well across a wide range of objects, from cuddly toys and dolls to miniaturized electronic items, clothing, musical styles and cars. As in the West, cuteness sells! As such, it is critical that we understand what is at stake in such big sales and such a pervasive and yet maligned aesthetic.[11]

It is possible to make anything seem cute by reducing its size, making it appear babyish (in which case size is less important), colouring it in a certain way (either pastels or 'pop-py' brightness) or by accentuating a sense of roundness (its cuddliness or 'huggability') (Fig. 1). Above all else, it must appear to pose no threat to the viewer/owner. On the contrary, it must arouse feelings of protectiveness towards itself, thereby soothing, placating and comforting its viewer/owner. While these objects hold sway, animating this illusory and charmed realm, the world of aggression and violence seems banished from its frontiers, indeed seems to cease to exist. However, this is not to say that these objects are able to magically charm anyone at any time. In fact, their soothing qualities are only activated by the willing viewer.[12]

Fig. 1. *Pinoko Says, 'I Love Doctor'* (*Osamu Tezuka* exhibition catalogue) © 2007 Tezuka Productions

As Kosei Ono's paper in this book attests, the Japanese were keen fans of American animation prior to World War II. That this interest should continue after the war with the American occupation is in a sense not surprising. In contrast to a landscape of devastation and defeat, the world of American animation, particularly that of Disney, offered Japan a comforting (but not solely comforting, as I would remind the reader) way to bridge past, present and future. America had visited destruction, but it was now there to help heal and rebuild.

In this scenario, one itself of reanimation, it is Disney's Mickey Mouse that functions for Japan, as it did before the war, as a symbol of boundless optimism, a figure operating without a memory per se, a figure that is, and always was, cheerful and happy, despite any adversity that crosses his path. Mickey Mouse does not age; and although the style of his figuration may alter over time (in which case it can be viewed historically), in a more general sense, he is kept suspended in an ageless a-historical time and place. Mickey Mouse, as he exists in both American and Japanese popular culture, can be seen as an elision of historical memory; and in this way, he is uncannily comforting and disturbing at the same time. In this manner, he crosses the boundaries of cultural and historical specificity and appeals on a universal level, a movement that the cute image in *anime* is now making in re-turn.

OSAMU TEZUKA AND THE GENERATIONS OF CUTE IN *ANIME*

The cultural exchange between Japan and America in the twentieth century produced three generations of cute in *anime*. The first generation is the style developed by Disney and then adopted and adapted by Japan before, during and just after World War II. It is a style that remains close to Disney and therefore to earlier modes found in Euro-kitsch. Its ostensible aim was to lead the viewer into experiencing an uncomplicated, naive and innocent state of being. Examples can be found in Kosei Ono's paper in this book.

The second generation, which I suggest exceeds and mutates the qualities of the first, is what I call the *hypercute* (or what the Japanese call *kawaii* as a more general and widespread cultural phenomenon); and it is found in *manga* and *anime* from the mid-1950s onwards. It is this style of characterization that Osamu Tezuka, the creator of *Astro Boy*, developed most fully during the course of his career. It seeks to ecstasize—that is, push to the limit, to its pure and empty form—cuteness as hyperpretty, hyperattractive, hypercharming—in a word, hyperbenign, as happens in Tezuka's *Unico* (1981), Hiroshi Fujimoto's *Doraemon* films (starting in 1984—the *manga* started in 1964), Hayao Miyazaki's *My Neighbour Totoro* (1988), Junichi Sato's *Sailor Moon* (1993), and other films and OAVs (Original Animation Videos) too numerous to mention here.

For me, the search for a purely benign form of cute never achieves fulfillment. If the persistence of cute after the trauma of The Bomb and during the period of U.S. Occupation and thereafter marks something traumatic, troubling, *repressed*, therein, the hypercute marks the intensification of that trauma, that repression, to the point where it might explode or turn into its opposite, thereby revealing its opposite was always already there and operative, even though unseen.

In its turn, the third generation, which I call the *acute*, marks the explicit return of the repressed, making this trauma overt by visibly displaying malign characteristics at the same time as the benign ones which ruled generations one and two. It not only displays cuteness as both pretty and cunning, charming and shrewd, benign and malign, at the same time, it disseminates it in accordance with the very logic of cute. The acute is found in such *anime* as Mamoru Oshii's *Urusei Yatsura—Beautiful Dreamer* (1984), Katsuhiro Otomo's *Akira* (1988), Masahisa Yamada's *Galactic Pirates* (1990), Satoshi Saga, Kengo Inagaki and Junichi Watanabe's *Green Legend Ran* (1992), Hiroki Hayashi's *Tenchi Muyo!* (1992), Hirohide Fujiwara's *Moldiver* (1993), Kinji Yoshimoto's *Plastic Little* (1994), Mamoru Oshii's *Ghost in the Shell* (1995) and Anno Hideaki's series *Neon Genesis Evangelion* (1996-1997).

So each generation of cute in its own way reanimates, embodies and performs the trauma of nuclear devastation and the reconstruction of post-war Japan. But while the cute figure of the first two generations is on its surface tied to a utopian innocence unmarked by obvious trauma, the acute figure of contemporary *anime* shows itself as at once utopian and dystopian; and it fights back 'in the name of' an always already lost utopianism and innocence, against the misappropriation of cute by corporate Japan—an anti-establishment theme that recurs consistently in contemporary *manga* and *anime*. Unlike the first two generations, this figure presents itself as having passed beyond childhood; but instead of reaching adulthood proper, it is suspended in the teenage realm between childhood and maturity.

It is important to recognize that these three categories are neither exclusive of, nor sharply delimited from, each other. In fact, a figure like Mighty Atom/Astro Boy becomes at once the inheritor of Disney cute, the figuration of hypercute and the precursor of the acute, insofar as he *shows* himself to be both charming and cunning, peaceful and aggressive, human and machine, at the same time.

Mighty Atom, the half-human, half-robot character created by Osamu Tezuka in 1951, subsequently appeared in animated form for the American market as Astro Boy in the 1960s.[13] He underwent a significant change from '50s Japan to '60s America, from being tall, mechanical and robotic (Fig. 2) to shorter, smaller, rounder and more childlike—in a word, more cute. Despite Tezuka's original intention of creating Mighty Atom as a parodic figure, he retailored him in this way, as Astro Boy, to suit the American market. This latter style is typical of Tezuka's subsequent use of Disney-esque cute, as can be

Fig. 2. Astro Boy—Astro Boy Plays the Role of Ambassador (*Osamu Tezuka* exhibition catalogue) © 2007 Tezuka Productions

seen in such animated series as *Kimba the White Lion* (1965-66), *The Amazing Three* (1965-66) and the feature *Unico*.

Nevertheless, the shift from the parodic, taller and even more adult (ostensibly acute) figure of Mighty Atom, produced for the local market, to Astro Boy, who is more childlike and innocent, that is, cuter, for the American market, is an interesting confluence of the three generations of cute to which I have been referring. Although Astro Boy assumes the covert and disguised/repressed mode of cute, created in accordance with the American taste for Disney, I would argue that it adds to the complexity of the overall phenomenon. In fact, we can regard this alteration as further evidence of the extensive repression that Japan was forced to undergo by a 'peaceful' American occupation. This entry into the global market is, although problematic on many levels, a clever strategy by Tezuka himself; and for me, it is an example of Japan's general adaptability to the demands of foreign influence. In fact, the history of Mighty Atom/Astro Boy is a crucial one in Japanese cultural production, one where cute, once again, embodies this highly mobile, dynamic and shifting terrain between cultures, a process that, as I have already highlighted in relation to the word cute itself, is fundamental to the qualities found in this undecidable figure.

Tezuka's cute figures are naive and childlike; and they evoke a return to a sensuous and pre-logical, comforting mode of existence. Yet Tezuka places them in complex and over-coded narrative structures, subjecting them to hostile forces and events, against which, instead of taking flight (as Bambi did), they stand and fight. In this way, cuteness changes its guise and starts to toughen up, starts to develop ingenuity, initiative and independence, and prepares the way for the acute figure of contemporary *manga* and *anime*. It could be said that cuteness starts to reveal its other face—that of cunning, cannyness, shrewdness, acuteness.

Astro Boy is both charming and canny, innocent and experienced. He knows whom to serve and what to protect. As a robot who replaces a dead human boy, he re-presents science and technology in the guise of his cute, friendly, benign face and illustrates that they can work 'for' humankind and not against it. This strategy shows how, in post-war Japan, an understandable suspicion of science and technology was overcome by popularizing them as the means for future national success and prosperity. Rather than being treated as opposed to nature, technology was elevated to the status of the supernatural, in line with Shinto religious belief that all objects (natural or 'man'-made) are endowed with a soul. This creed provided the ideal ground for the implementation and realization of a national project promoting science and technology.

But Tezuka's own project, including for Mighty Atom/Astro Boy, was far from being a simple cosmetic. For him, the popularization and elevation of science and technology called for acknowledgement of their accompanying dangers. His view was that an excess of belief in their beneficial powers ignored their destructive potential, even as an excess of belief in their destructive powers ignored their beneficial potential. A tendency towards either extreme needed to be acknowledged and then tempered. Throughout his work, Tezuka placed emphasis upon recognizing and guarding against the dangers of technology while at the same time stressing the urgency of a more positive and constructive approach to the application of this form of knowledge. For him, technology and science must be made to work for the world. He felt that, just as technology ceaselessly questions and challenges us on a material and philosophical level, we in turn must actively engage in a questioning of it. The appearance of Mighty Atom in the early 1950s was the first attempt at such a questioning and challenge in *manga* and *anime*.

Following after Tezuka, there is a new generation of animator who continues to adopt and adapt, although in ways undreamt of before.[14] Stylistically like Tezuka, their work is fast paced, colourful and often humorous. It continues his commentary on science and technology while bringing his style of animation to such topics as sexuality, the environment, capito-consumerism and the ambiguities of cross-cultural fertilization. It extends, and indeed exceeds, Tezuka's project by creating new forms of cute and new genres of *anime* for them. These are the animators who have taken the velvet glove of Tezuka and re-made it to fit an iron fist. To endure the increasingly hard-edged nature of movement, narrative and character, etc., these cute figures have been made acute. These half grown-up figures rage through technological landscapes of death, destruction and danger with an attitude that will not be controlled or ameliorated.

AMAE AND ITS INCORPORATION IN *KAWAII*

As I have proposed, the cute figures of *anime* can be viewed from an historical perspective, firstly, in terms of The Bomb and the post-war cross-cultural exchanges between America and Japan, and secondly, in terms of an internal history of *anime*, that is, generationally—as cute, hypercute and acute. In this way, these figures serve to illustrate the fluid and mutative—animatic—processes of exchange that have occurred between Japan and the Western world in the twentieth century and which intensify after World War II. It is the acute figure, as the inheritor and current incarnation of the previous two generations, that explicitly embodies and gives visual demonstration of these processes.

But the cute figure can also be viewed as a social and psychological phenomenon relating to elements internal to Japan's culture. So before addressing further the second and third generations of cute, I will pause to explore an aspect of Japanese culture that may account for the adoption of cute and the appearance of the *kawaii* phenomenon in Japan. Rather than erroneously seeing the adoption of cuteness by Japan as a case of straightforward cultural imperialism, that is, treating Japan Inc. as the (s)pawn of America Corp., we should ask what else is at stake in the proliferation of *kawaii* in Japanese animation and of cuteness in twentieth century popular culture.

Despite appearances to the contrary, Japan's social fabric is not as hierarchically, paternalistically structured as is assumed. The mother-child relationship is highly valued; and in Japanese social life, it exists alongside that of patriarchal authority. It is within this relationship that, I would propose, we witness a phenomenon of importance to our understanding of *kawaii*. That phenomenon is *amae*. *Amae* refers to the relationship between mother and child. According to Takeo Doi, a Japanese psychologist, the Japanese word *amae*, while denoting a phenomenon that is universal, at the same time denotes one of particular and peculiar importance in Japanese culture. In it, the mother-child relationship involves the concepts of indulgence (of the child by the mother) and dependence (of the child on the mother), a dependence allowing the child to indulge itself. In Japan, this state is regarded positively, as beneficial to both parent and child. Insofar as the distinctions between self and other, subject and object, seek their dissolution in it, it tends to unification and identification. At the same time, given that the relation between mother and child also entails the first instance of separation for the child, in a broader sense, that is, when applied to relations between self and other in an adult environment, *amae* is the psychological attempt to circumvent the sense of alienation that human subjects experience by existing in the world.[15] As Doi states:

> A relationship between two people becomes deeper the closer it approaches to the warmth of the parent-child relationship, and is considered shallow unless it becomes so. In other words, no relationship between people is a real relationship so long as they remain *tanin* [persons unconnected with oneself].[16]

Even though the *amae* relation is at odds with contemporary industrialized urban life, it functions as a social ideal with profound implications for a whole range of customs and values in Japanese culture. In the wake of the trauma occasioned by World War II and The Bomb, the comforting qualities of cute have served as a reminder and regenerator of the private maternal space associated with *amae*. For me, cute re-presents that maternal space displaced to the public and mass arenas. And it is the tele-communications technologies of which Derrida writes, as mentioned earlier, that seek to reanimate that space in those places, even as they at the same time inescapably displace it, a space that, in any event, as *plenum* is, for us, after Heidegger and Derrida (to say nothing of The Bomb), never not *always already* itself displaced, (dis)enabled by the disseminative process itself.

At the same time, as both a figure of healing and a foreign import 'MADE IN THE USA', the cute figure is also a perpetual reminder of this cataclysmic period in Japanese history. One could thus say that the tele-communications technologies double what is already at work within the cute figure (as well as within the word cute). Although the cute figure operates as a place of intimacy and comfort for the Japanese viewer, at the same time it operates to disrupt, disturb and displace that intimacy and comfort and in part figures elements that are alien (*tanin*) and hostile to Japanese culture and therefore to the *amae* psychology itself. So *kawaii*, the reanimation of *amae* as well as of cute, is therefore irreparably, irretrievably ambivalent in its means, aims and results.

Via a doubled movement of identification with the object itself as cute and with what it objectifies—innocence and vulnerability—*kawaii,* as the incorporation of *amae,* transfers the private qualities of this relation onto a range of public objects which simultaneously reanimate feelings of dependence, protection and indulgence in the viewer. When the *amae* psychology has been displaced to the public, corporate arena by the demands of industrialization and by the anxiety or alienation that that industrialization produces, *kawaii* seeks to reanimate a sense of generalized comfort in that public space. The *kawaii* phenomenon, seen in both the lack of cynicism and the indulgence both masculine and feminine subjects bear towards cute objects and things, is the cultural marker of this deeper social need, a need, for us, increasingly impossible to fulfil.

Insofar as the loss of intimacy and comfort brought by industrialization, mass urbanization and the tele-communications technologies doubles the trauma of the war, The Bomb and foreign occupation, the need for *kawaii* is intensified and complicated, even as it grows more incapable of satisfaction. In response to the need for *amae* within the Japanese psyche, *kawaii* is produced by the mass culture machine—including in *manga* and *anime*—for a populace that cannot get enough of it. When viewed in this light, the proliferation of *kawaii* alongside of the acute figures of contemporary *manga* and *anime* begins to tell another story.

For art critics Noi Sawaragi and Fumio Nanjo, the *kawaii* phenomenon is the symptom of a problem deeply submerged in the Japanese psyche.[17] For them, institutional and interpersonal power structures are disguised and made to appear neutral by being presented as cute. Figures of power are thus presented as harmless, innocent and childlike; and the public is seduced into believing that it will be well looked after by, and because of, this appearance. The public adopts a childlike acceptance of a seemingly vulnerable authority, a relation which is continually reinforced privately and publicly, and which compounds the systemic oppression of individualism.

Takeo Doi is of like mind.[18] He proposes that all who occupy a high position in Japan are supported in their role by those around them and that those who embody dependence to its greatest degree are the ones most qualified and likely to occupy positions of power. For him, figures like the Japanese Emperor ruled, and rule, by dependence and identification rather than by confrontation or opposition.

Akira Asada, a Japanese philosopher, is also critical of the machinations of a psychology of dependence.[19] Rather than analyzing Japanese culture via the cute figure of the Emperor—the centralized figure who once acted as the focus of *amae* but is now 'missing'—he dissects the role of the Japanese Corporation. For Asada, Japan is caught in the throes of what he calls Infantile Capitalism, a situation which, although it might appear at first glance to be totally anarchic, is for him an anarchism that can only exist within the protected maternal sphere produced by the *amae* structure of Japanese culture. Thus, instead of being childlike, the Corporation is maternal; and as such, it incorporates the hierarchical employee structure within itself. For Asada, the Japanese family, structured at its deepest levels by the maternal space of *amae* indulgence, is in turn embedded in a social body whose allegiance is to the Japanese Corporation, which forms a kind of extended family within which *amae* operates as an integral and organizing component. A displacement has occurred, one where *amae* persists and enlarges its scope of operation to benefit The Corporate State. As a result, we would say the individual subject has been *incorporated*; and it is the *kawaii* phenomenon that registers the disturbed nature of this process. For me, the acute figures in contemporary *anime* fight back not only against the destruction of innocence by The Bomb but against the misuse of intimacy by corporations, including those of tele-techno-communications, a battle that can only be waged by adopting, as we shall see, an approach that is paradoxically disobedient to the demands of *amae* itself.

Like the two earlier figures of cute in *manga* and *anime*, the acute figure in contemporary *manga* and *anime* comments on elements internal to the Japanese psyche while at the same time, in its own way, drawing attention to, and revivifying, the troubled history of cultural exchange between Japan and America that coincides with it. The acute figure is representative of a new generation of Japanese, a generation that has been brought up on and internalized American cultural values such as individualism and freedom of expression and is therefore less inclined to accept the restrictions placed upon it by traditional Japanese modes of conduct like *amae*, with its group dynamic, in today's world.[20]

THE GENERATIVITY OF HYPERCUTE AND ACUTE

To reiterate: in Japanese animation, Disney cuteness undergoes a transformation, mutation and reanimation (Fig. 3). Although still referring to the protected space of the child, a utopian space that is comforting, nurturing and benign, the cute Japanese figure at the same time propels us toward a dystopian world ruled by the terror of absolute annihilation, a world of devastation and degeneration, one which is repressed in the first and second generations of cute but explicitly expressed in the third. Incorporating elements that have arrived from elsewhere, the cute figures of *manga* and *anime* and of the Japanese Corporation itself—which has marketed cute to Japan and the world—are witnesses to, and transformers of, the character of Japan and its relation to the rest of the world.

As I indicated earlier, second generation cute, while still operating within the formulae of the Disney style of cute, exceeds and accentuates its parameters in the form of the hypercute. In films like *Unico* and *Doraemon*, all of the characters are babylike, appealing and comforting. They utilize a mode of excessive roundness, a mode that suggests comfort, nurturance and hope, qualities associated not only with *amae* but with the power of healing itself. If open to this form of expression, the viewer experiences the delight and comfort of a utopian space that is childlike, playful and innocent. Nevertheless, such experience is always qualified. In a film like Miyazaki's *My Neighbour Totoro* and in Tezuka's series *Astro Boy* and *Kimba the White Lion*, for example, there are unsettling elements of loss, sadness and threat. This is especially true of *My Neighbour Totoro*, where Totoro itself appears menacing at first sight but is not, and where the mother's absence from home, in hospital with an unspecified illness, casts a strange sense of impending doom over the entire film.

Fig. 3. Astro Boy Attacking Giant Robot, *The Treasure of Zolomon* (*Osamu Tezuka* exhibition catalogue) © 2007 Tezuka Productions

Of course, for me, these moments are a sign of the larger processes at work disrupting any purely benign, utopian presence in these films and in cute. The hypercute image may take us to the place of *amae* indulgence, but it never stays there for long. Indeed, it is always already on its way back. What this image evinces is the *uncanny* character of such a return to the maternal space, as well as the uncanny nature of the cute figure itself. Cute images open up the possibility of a *heimlich* (homelike, familiar, comforting, secret) space, a place for 'being-in-the-world', a place to experience the enchantments of the imagination. But, just as the viewer is starting to feel comfortable, this place/space begins to look decidedly *unheimlich* (at once both comforting and anxious, secret and estranged, familiar and unfamiliar, homelike and not-at-homelike). Like the large rounded eyes of these characters, which seem to be 'Occidental eyes but may not be', the undecidable, uncanny phenomenon of cute in Japanese culture accords with Freud's explanation of the uncanny return, which is always a 'stand-in' for death. It is thus death that returns in *kawaii* in post-World War II *manga* and *anime* and death that haunts all of its phases, a process which Freud called the return of the repressed.[21] Like the uncanny word cute itself, the cute beings of Japanese animation reflect the undecidable, ambivalent conditions of comfort *and* anxiety, home *and* homelessness, remembering *and* forgetting, trauma *and* repression in the wake of The Bomb and that are found at the same time in Japanese culture today.

As I have proposed, all three generations of cute are associated with experience—the experience of The Bomb and its aftermath; but while generations one and two repress that experience, generation three explicitly evidences it. Beyond that, acute (generation three) figures, having grown up with technology and corporatization, experience a different landscape, and experience it differently insofar as, unlike the cute kids of generations one and two, they have passed into their teens. The acute beings of the post-Tezuka generation have slimmed down considerably, are taller and less rounded, and no longer exhibit a babyish figure. They have grown up a little, having arrived at that troubled and troubling time we call early adolescence—a time of acne and existential angst, of budding sexuality and simmering rivalries and hatred—a moment in a child's life when a definite sexuality begins to form. The child, born of mother technology, now talks back. Instead of embodying the dependence of *amae*, it seeks independence; and instead of soliciting indulgence from others, it indulges itself, without seeking authorization for it. As I have already suggested, this shift is one that moves from an Eastern to a Western perspective, from the *amae* desire for unification to Western individualism and independence.

Nevertheless, as I proposed earlier, Mighty Atom, as the precursor of the acute figure, complicates this reading somewhat. The assertion of independence by Mighty Atom is uncannily closer to the acute in form, and yet further away from it in intention, than is Astro Boy. I would suggest that this situation must be read historically or generationally and that Mighty Atom, rather than embodying some notion of Western independence, is the figuration of an understandably ambivalent relation within Japanese culture to technology itself.

With the acute figure in contemporary *manga* and *anime*, on the other hand, the narrative emphasis has shifted considerably; and the themes and issues being explored are of interest to a burgeoning Americanized youth culture.[22] However, although the newly found 'independence' of Japanese youth appears to be a Western form, there are just as many elements and inconsistencies that confound such a reading. As I have already insisted, it is impossible to retain simple oppositions of East and West, dependence and independence, for long insofar as, in accordance with the principles of mutation, undecidability and dissemination played out by *kawaii* and the acute figures of *manga* and *anime*, such oppositions are always already coimplicated in and by each other.

Cuteness has come a long way. Instead of explicitly appealing to us to return to a space where we imagine and dream, cute figures now explicitly warn us of the dangers involved in submitting to the charm that such a repressed space offers, one that is now perceived as never not possessed of malign as well as benign qualities. These 'knowing' figures take us half way and then laugh at our gullibility. They are not only hypercute, they are, like the undecidable word *cute* itself, and like its undecidable synonyms *cunning* and *canny*, uncannily at once charming and crafty, pretty and shrewd. And in their battle against an often awesome enemy, they are gifted with special powers, those of levitation, mutation and transformation, that is, gifted with the powers of animation itself. For example, in a series like *Galactic Pirates*, in which a fatal, nihilistic game of images and concepts is being played out in a world dominated by 'mind control', advertising and consumerism, the cute character has become self-referential and ironic and in this way serves to show the errors of a naive or innocent (impossible in any case, it suggests) way of looking at the world.

One of the most prominent features of acute *anime* is the way in which cute figures have become sexualized while at the same time remaining strangely asexual. This (a)sexuality is achieved by the age group of the characters, the mobility of role-playing between masculine and feminine characteristics by both sexes, and by trans-sexuality—the animatic form of sexuality, the last of which we shall address shortly.

As teens, these characters are between the child and the adult. As hybrid cross-cultural figures, they are between East and West, Japan and America. And as figures of the between, they play with a range of Eastern and Western feminine and masculine roles. These characters have the ability to mutate and animate one aspect of either the masculine or the feminine and to as quickly mutate into the other, a back and forth that conflates the sexes until there is no sexuality left at all. Theirs is a world ruled by fluidity, where gender difference is sent into orbit and where both sexes bleed into each other. They are hybrid beings. Like the cute boys, the cute girls in serials like *Moldiver*, *Plastic Little* and *Galactic Pirates* are smart, tough and streetwise. The girls are often given active leading roles; or else they come to assume these roles during the episode, whereupon they enact a transformation from the passive feminine to the active masculine position. The boys themselves may dissolve into fits of giggling, an inner transformation that leaves them confused and breathless. The girls at this point appear to be tougher than the boys, while still retaining the power to seduce. They are able to turn the boys to jelly just by looking at them. But this is not just a case of role reversal. Instead, the roles become entangled. Boy meets girl and girl turns aggressive; girl meets boy and boy turns shy. The traditional gender roles in Japanese culture with which *anime* seem to be playing—the *geisha* as shy, retiring and subservient; the *samurai* as aggressive, confronting, deadly—meet Western feminism head on and settle somewhere between East and West, Japan and America, masculine and feminine.

The sexualization that is created is an awkward one. Just as the girls are not yet women, the boys are not yet men. Their sexuality exists between innocence (ignorance) and experience (knowledge). They almost know. And their sexuality is explosive, one that is about to reach full bloom. Muscles tighten and bulge, budding (often nippleless) breasts quiver, and white panties flash momentarily in a tantalizing glimpse that teases. A flicker of fantasy is inserted into the narrative; and for a micro-second, the action stops. It is at this moment, of the suspension of activity at the height of its movement, that an adult sexuality intrudes momentarily into this teen realm. We are witnesses here to a strangely asexual mode of pornography, a teen-porn that covers as much as it shows, where explicit genitalia is, if not hidden altogether, only hinted at, and where the girls and boys tease us as much as they do themselves. This suspension enacts the transfer of one state of being to another, attaining a moment of inertia where neither innocence nor experience gains transcendence. The viewer is presented with the highly ambivalent and undecidable nature of these figures. They seduce, but only momentarily. By occupying a zone between child and adult, male and female, the intervallic uncanny nature of acuteness as an undecidable is accentuated.

In addition to girls and boys who are neither fully sexualized nor completely innocent, literal anatomical transsexuality is another trick up the sleeve (or in the glove?) of the Japanese animators.[23] While the cute figure of *anime* is always intervallic, between categories, for example, between East and West, Japan and America, the acute figure of *anime* is as well between child and adult, male and female, innocence and experience, and overtly so; and now as transsexual, it is able to transport itself across the physical boundaries of the sexes—from masculine to feminine and then back again—which series like *Moldiver* and Rumiko Takahashi's *Ranma 1/2* (commencing 1987) explore. For me, this is the extension of an asexuality present in cute leading beyond sexual difference and where sexualization is pushed to its limit. Giggling and teasing one moment, tough and cynical the next, girls are literally transformed into boys (*Moldiver*), while gauche, shy and yet tough boys are turned into girls (*Ranma 1/2*). They seem to have turned into one protean simulacrum of sex—a vertiginous descent into the duplicity, trickery, cunning, cannyness and shadiness of sexual indifference that allows for any and every form of simulation of sexual difference.

The 'boys' and 'girls' of the acute phase bear the mark of what Jean

Baudrillard likewise calls 'transsexuality'. They are beings that play with sex but derive no pleasure from it. They are creatures of artifice (another synonym for cunning), prosthesis, mutation, anxiety and confusion. Baudrillard calls it 'A postmodern pornography,...where sexuality is lost in the theatrical excess of its ambiguity'.[24]

As an example of this condition, Baudrillard analyzes a contemporary American celebrity who spectacularly embodies the interval between child and adult, male and female, and who in a bizarre twist, I would suggest, sheds further light on the Japanese situation. That person is Michael Jackson. Despite reaching adulthood, he remains the model of the 'innocent and pure child'.[25] As a result of his reconstruction by plastic surgery, he has erased the markings of both his sex and his race. For Baudrillard, he is 'the artificial hermaphrodite of the fable...child-prosthesis, an embryo of all those dreamt-of mutations that will deliver us from race and from sex'.[26]

In Michael Jackson's music video *Scream* (1995), set in a space capsule, with Janet Jackson singing back-up vocals, images of acute figures from *anime* are projected behind the siblings. The effect is uncanny. Michael and Janet look remarkably like these animated characters. Both Jacksons resemble asexual mutants (aliens?), with small tightly drawn noses and mouths and large kohl-rimmed eyes. Are Michael and Janet simulating the animated characters that appear behind them or are the animated characters simulations of Michael and Janet? Who is simulating/animating whom? Another turn of the cycle is thus visible here: from animation exported from America to Japan to *anime* exported from Japan to America, here we see *anime* now being re-turned from America to Japan![27]

For me, this video offers us a graphic demonstration of, and insight into, the nature of the process of cross-cultural exchange that has operated between America and Japan in terms of *anime* since World War II. As Ben Crawford said at *THE LIFE OF ILLUSION* conference, Tokyo Disneyland is a place with its own character, a topsy-turvy version of American kitsch, a form of adaptation that could only happen in Japan. He observed that cultural imperialism may exist, but it is always intercepted half-way by, in this case, the Japanese. As I would argue, rather than simply being invasions by a cultural form that arrives from elsewhere, such re-makings, such re-animations, are re-placements that attest to a process of 'active importation', a means of reply, response, and even resistance, to what is commonly, mistakenly, seen as a one-way traffic. This is often, although not always, achieved by the selection of elements that appeal in some way; and if they do not quite fit, then they are 'made' to fit. That is, they are re-made to suit the occasion. What is re-made is a hybrid form, the strangeness and dynamism of which defeat any simple analysis couched in oppositional terms. It is a form that embodies, and at the same time disembodies, two cultures simultaneously.[28]

For Derrida, the act of quotation—of the masculine by the feminine, of the adult by the child, and of America by Japan, and vice versa—would be a transference that 'drives mad the very inside of place'.[29] The bi-cultural, asexual and sometimes transsexual acute figure embodies a zone that is 'anywhere' and 'nowhere'—the trans-cultural—a zone in which Japan has re-played, re-made and re-invented America such that one can no longer distinguish original from copy, where the copy is no longer just a copy. Here we have to deal with a cultural hybrid that flourishes to the point of parody or even monstrosity. The mirror laughs, grimaces, flashes, taunts and derides. Much to the dismay of some, it even winks back. The exportation of *anime* to America is just such a wink; but, as the Michael Jackson video clip shows, it is now, as could be expected, being re-turned in turn. The game is one where Japan, in re-making itself, re-makes America, and where America, in order to compete, must return the serve.

In his opening remarks to the conference, Alan Cholodenko stated that the relation between Japan and America is a 'game of challenge and outbidding, of seduction through simulation of and hyperconformity to the other, imitating the other better than the other imitates itself'. The Jackson video clip confirms this. Like the cute figure found in *manga* and *anime* and the Japanese Ameri-cult teenager, this clip, and the Jacksons imaged within it, are simulacra. Such forms are not copies, as some would like to think. Instead, simulacra supersede the opposition of original versus copy, in our case taking the place of, that is, re-placing, America and Japan. The process we are confronted with in their cross-cultural exchange is a series of reanimations as the dissemination of the (increasingly) simulacral: of Japan by America (after World War II), of America by Japan (in *manga, anime* and Tokyo Disneyland), and in the latest twist, of a back and forth exchange between America and Japan that, like the stock market, is happening daily.

TRADING PLACES

Technologization has had a manifold effect on Japan. Adopted as Japan's hope for the future after The Bomb, it has permeated Japanese society and culture. Nevertheless, the specificities of everyday life in Japan resist and transform the influences that flow in from what has become a global technological and cultural matrix (a new figure of the maternal being and space). *Kawaii*, as a reanimation of both Disney cute and *amae*, has been, and is, one of Japan's ways of dealing with this adoption of technology and its contemporary globalization, as well as with the demands exerted on it by an enforced foreign cultural invasion.

The relation between *kawaii* and *amae* is now, and has always been, one that aids the Japanese, as individuals and as a nation, to assimilate foreign influences, deal with a rapidly changing world and soothe traumatic psychic wounds. But the 'foreign object' of psychic trauma is irrepressible, unexpellable and unassimilable; and it is the cute figure that registers the agonistic nature of this attempt and failure at exclusion and/or introjection in relation to both traditional and industrial Japanese culture. By quoting Disney-esque innocence and vulnerability, this figure attempts to heal; but in the process of doing so, it, at the same time, wounds anew, recriminating by acting as a felt reminder of the corruption and destruction that such qualities have undergone at the hands of America, then by corporatization itself. Historical memory intrudes like an architectonic plate that shudders, closes in on itself, before tearing itself apart anew. In this way, Japanese cuteness is animatic, a simultaneous and ambivalent configuration—a hybrid, a mutant—of two opposing modes of animation, that of regeneration and degeneration. When rounded eyes turn square, when miniature mouths open wide in vehemence and rage, when velvet gloves meet iron fists, the repressed returns in a show of hyperanimated aggression. The assault is shocking, intense, uncanny and unexpected; and when it is over, the viewer cannot remain unchanged or unaffected.

Cuteness, in the history of Japanese animation, has thus assumed a very complex role. Like the flowers reanimated in, and by, *Hiroshima Mon Amour*, Japan's cute figure has lived through, and risen from, the ashes of The Bomb. Through this figure, there has been an attempt to speak the unspeakable, bridge the abyssal and defuse the fatal. It fixes us with its orb-like eyes, in which fantasy and reality, past, present and future, are reflected, eyes that have seen too much—the flash and the aftermath of an atomic explosion. With it, we arrive at the haunted house of twentieth century world history, where the event of nuclear fission reconfirms the always already doubled possibility of life and death, reconstruction and annihilation. Beyond the nuclear explosion lies the threat of the viral. If Mighty Atom/Astro Boy configure the nuclear, then the acute figures of contemporary *manga* and *anime* speak in the name

Fig. 4. *The Amazing Three* (*Osamu Tezuka* exhibition catalogue) © 2007 Tezuka Productions

of viral mutation and contamination, of globally networked systems that are always already threatened by viral invasion, even as they themselves perform it.

In today's strangely animated, simulacral, global world of cross-cultural pollination, hybridization and mutant transfiguration, the cute figure of Japanese animation can no longer be explained or interpreted as an example of mere borrowing or adaptation. Not only has it undergone a remaking, a mutation, it has in turn remade, mutated, this world in its image, in its wake. It is a sign of a world economy and history that are alive, animated, only by dint of the process of exchange. It is this figure that is 'trading places' and is now being exported to America with the label 'MADE IN JAPAN'—even as it is on the way back again (Fig. 4).

NOTES

1 Marguerite Duras, *Hiroshima Mon Amour*, trans. Richard Seaver (New York: Grove Press, 1961), p. 19. A footnote on this page tells us 'This sentence is taken almost verbatim from John Hersey's admirable report on Hiroshima'.

2 For Derrida, such terms as *pharmakon*, *supplement* and *trace* are undecidables, that is, 'unities of simulacrum, "false" verbal properties...that can no longer be included within philosophical (binary) opposition, ... resisting and disorganizing it, *without ever* constituting a third term...' Jacques Derrida, *Positions*, trans. Alan Bass (Chicago: The University of Chicago Press, 1981), p. 43. Homonyms, he writes, '"inscribe" *différance* within themselves: they are always different from themselves, they always defer any singular grasp of their meaning' (p. 100).

3 Alan Cholodenko declares in the Introduction to *THE ILLUSION OF LIFE* that animation is 'always already' the re-animation of both movement and life, both of which need to be 'thought through each other'. The animation process gives life and movement to things, events and states of being 'frame by frame'. It is marked essentially by this interval (from frame to frame). See his Introduction, *THE ILLUSION OF LIFE: Essays on Animation*, ed. Alan Cholodenko (Sydney: Power Publications in association with the Australian Film Commission, 1991), pp. 15-16. Animation is therefore the intervallic moment itself, one that occurs between stasis and movement. As such, it flickers constantly between

life and death in a shimmering dance that produces an 'illusion of life'. It occasions the emergence of the troubled and troubling realm (for thought) of the double, of simulacra, of the uncanny, of magic and perversity.

4 Derrida, 'Faxitexture', in *Anywhere*, ed. Cynthia C. Davidson (New York: Rizzoli, 1992), p. 24.

5 J. Laplanche and J.-B. Pontalis, *The Language of Psycho-analysis*, trans. Donald Nicholson-Smith (London: Karnac Books and the Institute of Psycho-analysis, 1973, 1988), p. 466.

6 To extend and enlarge on this point, one could say that Japan's own history of aggression prior to World War II (against China) is repressed alongside of Japan's defeat by atomic warfare, a process that complicates Japan's relation to itself and to America even further. These repressed elements, as repressed, would always be on the verge of returning in other forms. Although this essay will approach *anime* via its relation to America and Western culture in a post-World War II context, one could do a range of other readings that explore the return of traditional elements, like samurai and geisha culture, and the way these interact with the introduction of foreign concepts and issues.

7 See Philip Brophy, 'Ocular Excess: A Semiotic Morphology of Cartoon Eyes', in *KABOOM!: Explosive Animation from America and Japan* (Sydney: Museum of Contemporary Art, 1994), pp. 53-56.

8 ibid., p. 56. In this essay, Brophy explores the use of what 'seem' to be Western eyes in Japanese animation. He traces a history of ocularity, firstly, in relation to the baby and the cadaver, then, in relation to '[d]olls, comics and animations' (p. 44). For him, these eyes, more dead than alive, reflect a morbidly mortal history that extends from the early nineteenth century to the present. It is the history of industrialization, of mass production, mass extermination and the utopic striving for an idealized happiness for all. He argues that the Japanese, by embracing an

> Americanised therapeutically-designed version of Euro-cute...have been attracted to the hyper-iconic status of these grotesque figures which 'cry out' in sad-eyed silence; and that the Japanese have been able to imbue these postwar signs with a mystical resonance which remembers the past precisely by appropriating images designed to aid in forgetting it. (p. 49)

While agreeing with this view, I suggest that rather than being reminders of apocalyptic destruction alone, they are also signposts to an element in Japanese society that is fundamental and pervasive on a private and public level.

9 ibid., p. 48.

10 Japan's long history of graphic art (in woodcuts, especially) was well suited to the adoption of European and American graphic and animated styles of art practice. Cute figures, which appear with increasing frequency in Japanese graphic art from the later nineteenth century onwards, are variously derived from European caricature, Disney and Fleischer cartoons, American comic strips like *Blondie* and Disney comic book and animated features. For a comprehensive history of Japanese *manga*, see Frederik L. Schodt, *Manga! Manga!: The World of Japanese Comics* (New York: Kodansha International, 1983).

11 With its enormous range of both benign and malign cute characters, *Pokémon*, originally a game for 'Game Boy' by Nintendo, is another example of this aesthetic. It became the latest phenomenon to reach America, and then Australia, from Japan; and it was a bigger hit than anything that had preceded it.

12 My views on the qualities particular to the cute image and its effect on the viewer are informed by Gaston Bachelard's work on the poetic image. These images work on a momentary level; and they transport the viewer into the space of the imagination, an event that can only happen to a viewer who is open to the particular qualities of this form. Although not seen as round, these images evoke the experience of roundness in the viewer. For Bachelard, this experience of roundness accords with the state of being prior to socialization. For me, cute images, themselves composed of circles, curves and spirals rather than sharp angles and straight lines, evoke the comfort, wholeness, self-containment and generative promise that Bachelard associates with the roundness of the poetic image. See Gaston Bachelard, *The Poetics of Space*, trans. Maria Jolas (Boston: Beacon Press, 1964, 1969). I would like to thank Paul Adams for this reference.

It must be stressed that Bachelard's book is a prolonged meditation on one moment or side of how the poetic image affects the viewer's response. His exclusion of the ambivalent and uncanny aspect of these images and the viewing process itself is a conscious strategy on his part; and in his introduction to this book, Bachelard states that

> On the other hand, hostile space is hardly mentioned... The space of hatred and combat can only be studied in the context

> of impassioned subject matter and apocalyptic images... [I]t soon becomes clear that to attract and to repulse do not give contrary experiences. The terms are contrary. (Introduction, p. xxxii)

This paper is therefore an act of recontextualization, situating his account of the poetic image in relation to an apocalyptic context, an approach that foregrounds the uncanny and ambivalent nature that is always already happening in the world of things and human subjects.

13 The following information and all the images in this essay were taken from the exhibition catalogue *Osamu Tezuka* (Tokyo: The National Museum of Modern Art, Tokyo, and the Asahi Shimbunsha, 1990). I would like to thank Rick Tanaka for allowing me to borrow this catalogue on several occasions.

14 To name a few of their works that came onto the market in Australia in 1995: *Galactic Pirates*, *Moldiver*, *Green Legend Ran* and *Tenchi Muyo!* These were serialized for television and were subsequently released for the export video market.

15 The views of Martin Heidegger, who has had a marked influence on Japanese philosophy since World War II, are pertinent to this issue. For Heidegger, the realm of general public opinion brings about a tranquilized sense of 'Being-at-home', while anxiety about 'where' that is ('in the face of which') causes the existential mode of the 'not-at-home'. It is only by being anxious, 'in the face of which', that the subject is individualized and is able to open itself to its own potentiality for existence *as* Being-in-the-world. That is, it can only experience 'being-at-home' by way of anxiety about 'where' that is. The realm of comfort and 'being-at-home' is thus always already accompanied by the threat of loss, injury and homelessness; and it is the latter that provides the conditions or ground for the former to 'take place'. See Martin Heidegger, *Being and Time*, trans. John Macquarrie and Edward Robinson (Oxford: Basil Blackwell, 1962, 1985), pp. 149-165, H114-H127; pp. 232-233, H188. For me, the *amae* relation and psychology is an attempt to circumvent this state of anxiety; and I would suggest that for a nation that was, and is, the object of cultural invasion, industrialization and trauma, it is a pragmatic and everyday method of attempting to do so.

16 Takeo Doi, *The Anatomy of Dependence*, trans. John Bester (Tokyo: Kodansha International, 1973), p. 36. I would like to thank Professor John Clark for this reference.

17 See Noi Sawaragi and Fumio Nanjo, 'Dangerously Cute', *Flash Art*, no. 163, March/April 1992, p. 75.

18 See Doi, *The Anatomy of Dependence*, p. 58.

19 See Akira Asada, 'Infantile Capitalism and Japan's Postmodernism: A Fairy Tale', in *Postmodernism and Japan*, eds. Miyoshi Masao and H.D. Harootunian (Durham: Duke University Press, 1989), p. 276.

20 The issues that arise in relation to the question of freedom and individualism, as they are set up philosophically in opposition to determinism, are too complex to enter into here. Instead, I would suggest such aporetic and contradictory American cultural values as individualism and freedom of expression accord with Jean Baudrillard's idea of a hypercapitalist mode of production. For him, this mode operates beyond the grasp of the industrial, the social and the individual. It is where everything, including culture, cultural values, individual subjects, individuality itself, circulates as a sign with no reference to any materiality whatsoever, including that of production or class. It is a hyperreal situation that extends, indeed pushes to the limits and beyond, the founding conditions of the Enlightenment and capitalism, where reason and unreason, free will and determinism, are inextricably intertwined. For me, Japanese youth culture operates in accordance with the conditions of hypercapitalism, in a mode of simulation that exceeds any simple oppositional logic propagated by the conditions of the industrial age.

21 See Sigmund Freud, 'The "Uncanny"' (1919), The Pelican Freud Library, vol. 14, *Art and Literature*, ed. Albert Dickson and trans. James Strachey (Harmondsworth: Penguin Books, 1985), pp. 363-364. On the privileged relation between animation 'as such' and Freud's uncanny, see Alan Cholodenko, Introduction to *THE ILLUSION OF LIFE*, pp. 28-29.

22 Japanese teenagers constitute a significant youth culture that is a huge target market for *manga* and *anime*. It therefore comes as no surprise that Japanese youth doubles and is doubled by a fantasized range of cute and acute figures which they influence and with which they identify. These teenagers, like the characters of *manga* and *anime*, inhabit a world of pop-rock, comics and dressing up; and they define and use *kawaii* in different ways. The phenomenon includes not only *kawaii* itself but also *kireii* (pretty, clean) and *omoshiroi* (interesting and fun). But while the Japanese teenager participates in a form of rebellion that is largely pseudo, it is the cute figures of *manga* and *anime* who fulfil their fantasy in a dramatized recreation that marks a significant

change in the nature of the relation of *anime* to *amae*. These figures no longer seek indulgence by adopting a charmingly childlike manner. They now demand it aggressively.

23 Instances of transsexuality can be found in Japanese traditional culture in the figure of the *onnagata*, a female impersonator who is related to the theatre, homosexuality and prostitution. Nevertheless, because of the ambivalent, undecidable, cross-cultural nature of the cute figure found in *anime* and its acute anatomical limit case—the transsexual—this relation is complicated.

24 Jean Baudrillard, *The Transparency of Evil: Essays on Extreme Phenomena*, trans. James Benedict (London: Verso, 1993), p. 22.

25 In the light of Jackson's subsequent child molestation charges, this observation is not without a sense of irony. It seems that, instead of delivering us from race and sex, he is now at once the aggressor and victim of both. His childish voice and girlish giggle have become the sinister external signs of some hidden internal bent, an association that is too close for comfort. For many, despite his professed and 'proven' innocence, he is guilty.

26 Baudrillard, *The Transparency of Evil*, pp. 21-22.

27 *The Powerpuff Girls* series, screened on the Foxtel Cartoon Network, seems to be a good example of this tendency. Nevertheless, in an article in *The Sydney Morning Herald*, its American animator, Craig McCracken, has strongly denied the influence of Japanese animation on his own work—a curious parallel with what the Disney organization did with the work of Tezuka in regard to *The Lion King*.

28 For an account of the remake, see Lisa Trahair's essay, 'For the Noise of a Fly', in *THE ILLUSION OF LIFE*. For Trahair, after Derrida, the remake is of the order of the 'in-between'.

29 Derrida, 'Faxitexture', p. 23.

Hybridity and the End of Innocence

JANE GOODALL

INNOCENCE AND EXPERIENCE

Animation is a medium strongly identified with the popular culture of early childhood. It has also proved its capacity for catering to the sado-erotic fantasies of an adults-only audience. A marked preoccupation with the thematic of innocence and experience in animation narratives may be partially explained by this polarity in its audience appeal. This in turn has something to do with the contradictory potentialities in the role of the animator, whose relationship with the creature being sketched into an adventure can slide between sentimental playfulness and the most extravagant abuse.

In manipulating the cartoon character, the animator also plays manipulative games with genre and taxonomy. The opportunity to play at taxonomic slippage is apparently irresistible when the difference between a cat, a duck and a rabbit is, literally, a slip of the pen. The slip may be 'innocent'—a happy accident—or it may be a calculated sleight of hand through which the not-so-innocent sophistry of a designing intelligence slips into the naive world of cartoon adventure. At the other end of the spectrum, the animator becomes libertine and allows prurient fantasy to dictate what happens when every possibility is taken to extremes. While the animated creatures violate each other in every imaginable way, the animator violates them by putting them through hyperbolic becomings, weird transformations, abject dissolutions.

There are 'innocent' and 'experienced' approaches to the medium of animation itself, and these in turn are bound up with the accumulation of experience within it. Animators draw on established tropes, genres and narrative patterns, then manipulate them to create a feedback loop through which increasingly knowing references and techniques are added to the repertoire. This knowingness is essential to the *anime* tradition in Japan, which can be seen to epitomize the 'experienced' end of the spectrum. It is a tradition that seeks extremes, and the *Urotsukidoji* series has made its mark for its thoroughgoing commitment to extremism.

If there is a polar opposite to the ethos of *Urotsukidoji*, it is the world of Warner Bros., as evoked by Chuck Jones in his wilfully ingenuous address to *THE ILLUSION OF LIFE* conference in 1988.[1] What, then, of the space between these polarities? If it is not a continuum, perhaps it is a collapsed space of mysterious and dramatic conversions. Ralph Bakshi's *Cool World* explores such a space, while spinning a dualistic narrative in which innocence and experience continually threaten to collapse into each other.

In selecting these three sites for discussion, I am concerned to avoid the implication of a simple continuum, even though they follow in chronological sequence. The image of accumulation is more appropriate, especially when linked with the idea of the feedback loop through which generic sophistication inevitably escalates. In this discussion, I have located the polarity of innocence in American animation, that of experience in Japanese animation and the zone of convergence/conversion in an American work. Clearly, there are implications to be explored here and essentialist conclusions to avoid. I am interested in the ways in which these three distinct sites speak to each other on a common theme.

DIES IRAE

> Mankind, you are an ignorant race. How foolish it is to believe that your kind rules the earth. Know now that you are not alone. There are unseen worlds that exist parallel to yours. These are the worlds of the Makkai, the race of demons. And the Jujinkai—those that are half human and half beast. There is an ancient legend,

> a prophecy, foretelling the appearance of a super being every 3,000 years. He is called the Chojin—a god above all Gods—the Overfiend. The Chojin will appear through the body of a human, and he will unite the three worlds. And with his power, he will create a new world—a world of peace and harmony. His time has now come. Ignorant humans, the truth shall now be revealed.
>
> Opening speech in *Urotsukidoji: Legend of the Overfiend* (1989)

Who or what might speak this? Whatever it is is speaking from a position that is other to that of all the species from all the orders of being: demons, man-beasts, humans, gods. Whatever it is is taking an exultant overview of a drama involving the implosion of all structures that enable difference and taxonomy. It is a narrator's voice and sounds suspiciously authorial. It speaks with the license to know all and to conjure the play of images that is to follow. As the voice speaks, a sea of fire plays across a dark void, suggesting an inferno of destroyed or yet-to-be-conjured beings: a catastrophic interval, perhaps, between creations, where the only existence is an imageless potency.

It is tempting to read these opening frames of *Urotsukidoji* as an allegorical representation of the animator as Chojin, exulting in a world-making power which can steer between utopian innocence and infernal experience. The circus of perversions, violations and havoc that is to follow attempts to take the generic extremism of *anime* as far as it can conceivably go. (The cover notes for the video cassette proclaim 'a sickening tale of horrendous violence and supernatural forces beyond the imagination.') The Blakean ideas of experience as active, dynamic, violent, fiery, sexual, adult, knowing and of innocence with its tinsel tears as a necessary counter-creation have a certain kind of fit with the world of *Urotsukidoji*. Blake associates experience with excess and energy, often manifested in scenes of hyperactive becoming such as this one, which might be a description of the becoming of the sea monster Nagumo in *Legend of the Overfiend*:

> ...the nether deep grew black as a sea, & rolled with a terrible noise; beneath us was nothing now to be seen but a black tempest, till looking east between the clouds & the waves, we saw a cataract of blood mixed with fire, and not many stones' throw

> from us appear'd and sunk again the scaly fold of a monstrous serpent...[2]

As an alternative to the Deleuzian view of metamorphoses and becomings (considered by Keith Clancy in his essay in *THE ILLUSION OF LIFE*[3]), I'd like to suggest the continuing relevance of some older paradigms to the phenomenon of species confusion in animation. Late twentieth century cosmologies take an 'innocent' view of creation, in that they assume a cosmos that is innocent of design. The worlds created by the animator, though, are totally designed and thus recall archaic cosmologies (such as those of the Gnostics, the alchemists or Hinduism) infused with volition, in which the dynamics are dualistic. Blake is an especially relevant point of reference, in that he nominates innocence and experience as dualistic principles, lined up with the dualities of good and evil, pastoral and wild, water and fire. In his visions of innocence, you can tell a lamb from a bird, a worm from a snake, a flower from a clod of clay, a good from an evil angel. In the visions of experience, the category divisions are always threatening to dissolve, so that all beasts merge with each other to form 'reptiles of the mind'; the elemental structures of the created world erupt in cataclysmic imbroglios of sea, sky, earth, blood and fire.

These are visions, though, which belong to the revolutionary ethos of the late eighteenth century. In the late twentieth century, the thematic of 'experience' has absorbed a combination of exoticism, decadence and belatedness from the last *fin de siècle* in Europe. It is a thematic with Orientalist tendencies: the weary sensualist traverses the regions of the East in the bid to make a complete collection of human experience. The *anime* industry knowingly exploits this kind of cultural appetite as it seeks to expand its markets in the West while at the same time drawing on an apparently insatiable and traditional demand for sensual odyssey in the home market.

Whether Eastern or Western, the spectator whose delusions of centricity are addressed by the voice from the void in the overture to the *Urotsukidoji* saga shares in a political history about to be luridly evoked through a drama whose central theme is the end of empire. The *Return of the Overfiend* trilogy charts the downfall of Caesar, imaged as an overblown cyborg body confined to an armchair in the depths of his palace, where he is serviced by sex slaves as he sends out tentacular waves of power to control events in the world at large. Here is a considered and drawn out portrait of terminal identity, the phenomenon Scott Bukatman investigates in a study which emphasizes the species-warping effects of the organic-technological interface.[4] Through his incestuous fixation on his daughter Alector, also a cyborg creation, Caesar is progressively undermined by emotional dependence as his body begins to dislocate itself into dysfunctional parts. As this happens, his presence becomes ever more bulbous, solid and pain-ridden until his final scene, which more resembles a primitive *sparagmos*[5] than the 'ecstatic dissolution of the body'[6] as some kind of electronic apotheosis.

Reflecting on its own denaturing capabilities, the human species has become the anxious species. In heralding a terminal identity crisis for the human, the voice that opens *Legend of the Overfiend* speaks for our times, which are characterized, according to Bukatman, by 'a massive upheaval in the understanding of human *being*...'[7] No longer just an innocent form of imaginative license for the animator, hybridity in animation has begun to admit its resonances as one of the most insistent thematics of an era obsessed with difference, cloning, grafting and taxonomic slippage.[8] The end of the millennium brought with it a consciousness of over-accumulated experience and of about-to-be punished hubris. Where better to see its realization than in the cartoon world, which has always afforded an escape from experience through its constant reconversion to innocence?

HAPPY DAYS

> I've never overcome the wonder of that, that for over 57 or 58 years people have paid me for what I enjoy doing. You can't ask for better than that.[9]

So said Chuck Jones, the eternal beaming child, who gave the audience at *THE ILLUSION OF LIFE* conference an insider's view of the Golden Age at Warner Bros. as a working world in which the boss talked like Daffy Duck—'Well, boyth, put in a lot of jokthes'—and blissfully failed to recognize himself as a source of inspiration. ('Jethuth Chritht, that's a funny voith. Where'd you get that voith?')[10] Here, the first law of collegial relations was never-say-no. To refuse anything was to be complicit in the primary offence against innocence:

> I've often wondered how human beings survive when you think that for the first six months of our lives or so we're carried around in this wonderful cocoon, with warm milk and love and beautiful boobs, you know, to lean on—and then all of a sudden we decide it would be fun to explore a waste paper basket or take a drink out of the toilet and somebody says, 'NO!' Jesus, at that point, it's a wonder anybody survives.[11]

If innocence is incompatible with knowingness, how can it be so knowing about itself without turning into disingenuousness? This is a paradox that Chuck Jones negotiates for the time being by wilfully embracing the infantile, this being a form of innocence that is free of idealization. To be infantile is to live in a world that is happy or tragic according to whether or not it complies with demands for instant gratification; the infantile is the domain of license, in which perverse impulses reign unchecked. It is perverse, rather than disingenuous, for an adult to be wilfully infantile. Jones makes infantilism into the raw material of a sophisticated comic art. It is at once a game of sabotage and a gleeful refusal of limits.

The lure of the looney toons world is license. Almost any law that holds good in the natural world can be broken. The laws of nature are flouted not just in the kinds of images that are created but in the kinds of action and active relationship that can be generated between the images. To an extent, all kinds of cinema can do that, but only to an extent. The limiting factor is the live body of the actor. No stunt-man could fill in for Ren or Stimpy, the current inheritors of the looney tradition.

These points may seem too obvious to be worth making. So, like the toon body, they need a bit of a stretch. Specifically, the cartoon world offers license to experiment with bodies that are not bound by natural limits. The animate image is always potentially anarchic, as the looney looney looney Bugs Bunny very quickly taught his creators. The body image of the cartoon character can run amuck. It's an elastic, plastic, pliable body always returnable to the form in which it was originally conceived, with no signs of wear and tear, no matter what it has been through. Bodies are squashed flat and instantly return to 3-D. Bumps disappear as quickly as they arise, eyes boing out of the head and straight back in again, limbs distend and snap back into shape. It all sounds a bit like an innocent kind of surrogate sex for the boys at the drawing board, which maybe it is, although for the moment that's by the by.

License is balanced by certain kinds of restriction. The sensations of a cartoon character do not last beyond the frames in which they're drawn and are limited to what can be portrayed through a range of easily readable visual signifiers; there's not much scope for overlay or ambiguity. This is a restriction which also in a way contributes to license. The extreme things that happen to the cartoon body are as momentary in their personal impact on the character as they are on the body itself. Anything can happen, and nothing leaves any enduring effects. While the Keystone Cops and the Three Stooges could pretend to enjoy a childish freedom from the enduring consequences of irresponsible action, the animator did not have to pretend. No creator could be more free of responsibility towards his creature. If Victor Frankenstein had worked for Warner Bros., think of the tedious cultural angst we'd all have been spared.

In-experience, in the most literal sense, is a defining quality of the cartoons of the Golden Age. While anything could happen to any of the characters in the worlds conjured up by the animators, none of these characters was ever portrayed as having what could be properly called an experience. A classic toon was in the most literal sense never marked by experience and so could never become experienced. It repeated its adventures, with all their habitual errors and pleasures, *ad infinitum*. It knew whim and compulsion, but not the tyrannical continuity of desire. Its a-sexual body could have every imaginable adventure without injury or perversion.

The cartoon body was characterized by the sharpness of its delimitation: it was outlined and differentiated so as to ensure instant recognition even in shots where it was caught at the flash point of the 'kaboom!' Warner Bros.' first toon was Hugh Harman's Bosko. According to Rudolph Ising, 'It was supposed to be an inkspot sort of thing. We never thought of him as human, or as an animal. But we had him behave like a little boy'.[12] Bosko looked like a composite of the animation codes for mouse and monkey, and his generic indeterminacy may account for his failure to achieve a place in the pantheon of cartoon superstars. Audiences, however young, rapidly became toon-literate and adept at telling a duck from a rabbit from a pig by a couple of key signifiers. Anthropomorphism was standard, but otherwise, species definition was an art practised in good faith. Chuck Jones, so his audience learned, was a taxonomist from way back, when, as a boy, he lived in a house owned by the world's leading authority on guano:

> So there was this entire library of books on guano. So you may be sure that I know a great deal more about guano than any of you do. Pelican guano is different than bluebird guano and so on. Doesn't vary so much in colour as it does in quality.[13]

Species coding was such an exact art that a category distinction could be made with a single stroke, as when a cat walking under a trail of spilling white paint acquired a neat white stripe down its back and became the skunk Pepe Le Pew. The recognition of difference is incited as an act of infantile triumph rather than called for as a disciplined and constraining knowledge practice.

The compulsive role-playing of Daffy Duck works precisely because, beneath his promiscuous evocation of human types, he is, unequivocally, a duck. Albeit he is a vehicle for all the most perverse characteristics of his several animators, a container of 'multitoons',[14] a breacher of limits and a breaker of frames, Daffy is only once in his career subject to anything approximating an identity crisis, when he marches into the midst of a frame and crows like a rooster. Jones' *Duck Amuck* (1953) is late Daffy, and some tensions between creature and creator are allowed to surface. The Duck is quite unjustly accused of running amuck; in fact he's nearly run off his feet trying to keep himself properly coded to the set, which his capricious animator keeps changing from frame to frame until he is driven to a moment of direct confrontation: 'All right, enough is enough. This is the final, the very very last straw. Who is responsible for this? I *demand* that you show yourself! Who are you? Huh?' (Daffy's emphasis). When he finds that it is not just his costume but his *imago* that is thrown out of order by the games being played on the drawing board, Daffy encounters the mirror stage not as subjective experience but as the unruly autonomy of the signifiers. Changing his costume is Daffy's speciality—but the prospect of changing his body formation, and so losing his species definition, threatens to collapse his whole repertoire. Here, then, species confusion is a way of disempowering the animate character.

MUTINY AND MUTATION

Duck Amuck is an innocent little game of control between animator and creature, where the animator assumes all the initiatives and does all the rule-breaking, while the creature just does his damnedest to keep the codes in order. The switch from innocence to experience in the realms of animation is marked by the increasingly determining role of the toon character, who inevitably discovers sexual desire, as the animator discovers a desiring relationship with it. Bakshi's *Fritz the Cat* (1972) had all the signifiers of desire and sexuality, but it is in *Who Framed Roger Rabbit* (1988) that we first meet a toon who has made sexual desire her element. Jessica's definitely got it and cruelly exposes the truth that Betty Boop never did have it, any more than did any of Jessica's precursor chanteuses from the Tex Avery repertoire. Innocent games in which panties are removed—albeit too fast for the average video player to catch[15]—lead to progressively confusing imbroglios with the eroticised toon body, so that Bakshi in *Cool World* (1992) finds himself fronting up to the whole issue of species regulation, and in the process, finds himself dramatizing the interface between innocence and experience.

The character charged with policing the segregation of human and animate species is Frank, a young guy who has got sucked into the cartoon world, or 'Cool World', as a consequence of a tragic accident. Frank is responsible for killing his mother in a vehicle crash that no toon would have failed to survive. The experience is too much for him, and the Cool World provides an almost instant escape from it. Almost, because for the first few moments after the translation, he's manifesting the effects of an emotional trauma that is entirely outside the capacity of any of the toons—or 'doodles', as Bakshi calls them—to register. Later in the story, he meets a toon girl who's hankering after the real thing and tries to explain: 'Let me tell you something about over there. It hurts over there. It gets lonely over there. They got a war over there. They got eight million ways for you to die over there and all of them are permanent'.

In other ways, though, Frank is an innocent. He never 'did it' in the real world, having come straight from fighting in the war to killing his mother in a motor bike crash. And now his job is to prevent any of 'it' happening with the doodles in the Cool World. I don't know quite how a Freudian would gloss this, but clearly the fall from innocence in the realms of animation involves the acknowledgement of an Oedipal dynamic between character and animator. The biggest threat to the sterility of the Cool World is Jack, a character who is marked by guilty experience. Sent to jail for murdering his wife's lover, he created the doodles with his pen from the confinement of his cell; and now, having served his sentence, he's out in the world, or out wavering between two worlds, being lured towards a dangerous consummation by the most seductive of his own creations, Holly Wood. Holly not only would, she's determined to do it at all costs and on her own initiative.

We all know now to take the seductions of the image seriously. Why is it that the Warner boys never seem to have done so, never took the license to show the toon body as far more extravagantly endowable with codes of desirability than any human body, if only it is licensed to *be* desiring?[16] Holly is pure, unadulterated seduction. In every scene she enacts a pantomime of escalating desire, which summons up demons in the form of a pack of low grade mutant doodles, a carnival of desires run rampant, but able to gratify themselves only through surrogacy. They remain in-experienced, but they're not exactly innocent. Having attached themselves to Holly as the vehicle of a desire that could get realized, they 'wanna watch'. Voyeurism, in the classic literature of libertinage, is one of the first steps by which the innocent enters the world of experience. The lunatic toon mutants are powerless and get left behind when Holly *makes it* to the real world by luring Jack into the act of intercourse. Mutation itself is innocent and inconsequential within the confines of the Cool World. The only kind of species crossing that matters is the human/toon (or in this case noid/doodle) crossing, because it threatens the animator's control systems.

Holly's first real experience is not sex but the mirror stage where, unlike Daffy, what she encounters is not a pack of signifiers but a delimited body. Nevertheless, her determination is to use this new body to get anything she wants; and as what she wants ultimately is power, the first thing she does is steal her animator's pen. (Her masculine animator naturally assumes she needs the phallus to complete her translation from sex object into a desiring subject.) Holly's ultimate objective is to steal the spike lodged in the fluorescent sign on the top of a Las Vegas skyscraper, because she's learned that this is the origin of the life force in the animate world. The spike will unleash a flood of cartoon life into the real world and turn her once and for all from a created object into a determining subject. But the plan backfires—literally and spectacularly—when the spike switches her back into a toon and in the same moment converts Jack into a supertoon. Jack gets to make the authorial closure. Swaggering across a landscape that pans out into a framed square in a comic book, he crows: 'What a beautiful landscape... We could put a house over here; we'll raise kids over here; we'll put a studio over here (I'll still draw of course)... We'll be deliriously happy, Honey poo'.

Holly may have to suffer the narrative foreclosing on her, but at least she gets the last word: 'Pencil dick!' And so the toon world is sealed off again from the real phallus. A Lacanian would no doubt gloss this at length, but for the moment I'm after a simpler point: the innocent cartoon worlds of Warner Bros. acknowledged power relations only in the form of contests between their characters. *Duck Amuck* is a rare instance of the Warner Bros. animator directly alluding to his creative dominance and flaunting his power to exploit his creature. What is common, though, is for the creatures themselves to acknowledge this power relation inversely, by making themselves difficult to control. Warner Bros. characters fall into the distinct categories of the bossy, the cute or the looney, each of which offers generic ways of giving authorial determination the run-around. The addition of the genus 'seductive' (with Jessica Rabbit and Holly Wood) introduces a different level of negotiation between creature and creator. The qualities of bossiness, cuteness or looniness will trigger particular kinds of action and reaction in the story, but the animate character who is seductive acquires direct manipulative influence over the animator. He animates her. She turns him on. He produces her. She seduces him. He gets sucked in by the power of his own fantasy, to which the process of animation has granted autonomy. The relations of control between desire and representation have always been volatile and reversible.

CROSSINGS AND CONFUSIONS

The treatment of the toon world/real world interface in American animation as equivalent to the innocence/experience interface is itself founded in a kind of innocent binarism. Clearly both the binarism and the innocence are under threat, but they're hanging in there, with the help of traditional closures that leave the toon world intact. 'That's all, Folks!' No repercussions. No compulsive repetitions. Of course we all know Daffy and Bugs and Porky will be back; but their new adventures will bear no trace of the old, which are erased from the record every time the 'end' board goes up.

A Derridean view of the framing of animation would alert us, though, to the disingenuousness of these definitive reassertions of the frame and its containing function, these graphic closures. Animation even in its most innocent forms is a fallen discourse. 'As forms of the *graph*', says Alan Cholodenko, 'animation, film and cinema are contaminated and contaminating concepts, concepts drawn from, to and of the nature of drawing'.[17] What the graph 'contaminates' is, paradoxically, speech. The replacement of graphic closure by vocal closure in *Legend of the Overfiend* may then be construed as an attempt to reinstate 'the fullness of presence, the living presence of *logos*, speech as a living, animate discourse'.[18] The territories of innocence and experience are, of course, always already crossed; but *Urotsukidoji*, at the experienced end of the spectrum, is ready to acknowledge this, while the world of the Looney Tunes is firmly in denial. The voice-over statement which opens *Legend* is repeated to close it. Here, where the world has been shown to end recurrently for the last twenty minutes of the film, repetition is the only available form of closure. Return and repetition compulsion are generically integral to *manga* and *anime,* whose stories build by accumulation from one episode to the next. The Overfiend not only returns four times—to date—it spawns different series, each with its own repetitions.

The *anime* tradition is intrinsically pornographic, and the violation of innocence is generic to pornography. Violation means more than sexual assault, which in pornographic narratives commonly belongs to a programmatic education in perversion. It is not just virginity that has to be destroyed but innocence itself. Audiences of *anime* are drawn by the lure of a license opposite to that which operates in the worlds of Bugs and Daffy. It is still the license to flout the laws of nature by presenting the animate body in processes which would be physically impossible to the biological body, but this time there is a determined attempt to show the animate character getting experience. The innocent cartoon body is still the dynamic centre of the action, but this time it is interactive with forces whose violence and sexuality are drawn in earnest. To draw sex and violence in earnest and in the pornographic spirit which offers spectatorship as surrogate participation involves the invocation of live action. The properties of cartoon bodies must be modelled on those of biological bodies in certain respects if their activities are designed to be erotic. What is at issue here is a different order of cross-over between 'live action' and 'animation' than that which is celebrated in *Who Framed Roger Rabbit* or *Cool World.*

Typically, the violations to which *anime* submit the innocent body are phallic and technological. The analogy between the real world/animate world interface and the monitor screen as interface between actual and virtual being is made an explicit feature in *Adventure Kid* (1993), a film also made by the *Urotsukidoji* team. Norikazu, the Kid in question, is a naive teenage hacker, who spends his time absorbed in screen war games while his girlfriend Midori hangs around looking bored and occasionally innocently kicking her legs in the air (showing her white knickers, of course). These two are paralleled by an experienced couple, Norikazu's overweight father and his young mistress, who play childish sex games in explicit detail and call each other 'naughty boy' and 'naughty girl'. The only games Norikazu and Midori play are video games—until they suddenly get sucked through the screen. Precipitated bodily into the war zone in Norikazu's computer, the innocents are menaced with various forms of violation supposedly more real than those they play with from the other side of the screen.

The status of the body in these scenes is full of ambiguities. What *is* the status of the animate body in a virtual environment? This is what Norikazu seems about to find out when he is plucked from a scene of virtual tragedy and brought naked to face his 'maker', a scientist with glowing eyes, the mad animator who proclaims: 'You are powerless here. You are helpless in my world'. What Chuck Jones does to Daffy is child's play in comparison with what Norikazu and Midori are subjected to, but that there is a comparison at all puts the innocence (or should I say infantilism) of Chuck Jones into question. When might a discourse of perversity suddenly recast itself as one of perversion?

Species confusion is not itself a significant feature in *Adventure Kid*. Yet, in its concern with transition, violation and violent displacement, this work peripherally reflects the obsession with hybridity that is central to *Urotsukidoji*; and it highlights the traumas peripheral to hybridity, which here is more than just an innocent matter of mixing codes on the drawing board. The opening frames of the *Legend*, with the prophetic voice-over, are followed by images of an orgiastic mass of bodies whose activities produce monstrosity not through generational mutation but apparently as a spontaneous consequence of intercourse itself. The beasts of the Makkai disguise themselves as humans; and when they become sexually aroused, they begin to explode into multiple erections: they sprout vast jaws from which evil serpent tongues rush out, eyes burst from their sockets on great ropes of sinew, hands blow up into writhing tentacles. The human girls who are the victims of this are impaled from every angle. Hybridity and monstrosity, instead of being the outcome of intercourse between different species, are instead expressions of the immediate transformational impact of connection between heterogeneous bodies. All evil bodies in the *Urotsukidoji* series are tentacular and build to orgasmic explosions of power in which their emanations shoot across vast fields of space to encompass and penetrate their targets. Tentacles are not gender specific: evil females are also prone to turn psychotic impaler, especially at the moment of orgasm. Bodies that contain the forces of good irradiate. There is no version of the body, whether human, divine or monstrous, that is allowed to be self-contained. Bodies that appear to be so, like those of virginal girls, are always subject to sudden attacks of multiple penetration. Nor is there any clear demarcation line between the penetrated and the penetrators. Even the Overfiend Nagumo, whose cosmic tentacles are the most powerful and devastating of all, can be counter-penetrated by enemy forces.

The spectacular corporeal *mélange* continually erupting on the screen is associated with forms of fusion and confusion in orders of meaning and value. Ultimately, no one is sure whether the Overfiend is good or evil. This question becomes progressively more urgent as the saga develops. In spite of its name, the Overfiend is heralded in the early episodes as the other of the powers of evil. It is the bringer of a cosmic destiny which must move through cataclysmic implosion into a final harmonic blending of its three orders. The diverse hybridities portrayed by the animators may be the pathognomies arising from a condition of failed harmony in the orders of creation.

They are also an opportunity for the animators, an invitation to technical virtuosity and conceptual license. They are expressive, perhaps, of certain tendencies in the animation process itself. If animation in its innocence was always hiding from an inevitable disingenuousness, animation that has deliberately sacrificed innocence to licentiousness knows more about itself. Innocent animation evoked a world of creatures whose difference from each other depended on the mutual trust of a code shared between the animator and the spectator and founded securely in the observable differences of the natural world. The act of recognition invited was one of infantile triumph associated with the process of learning to read through symbol recognition. To put it simply, different animals were the mainstay of animation, with the human included as just one of the several species making up the *dramatis personae*. In *manga* and *anime*, coding and the reading of codes belong to a very different kind of contract, or complicity, between animator and spectator, as Sandra Buckley explains:

> What facilitates the production of meaning is the reader's ability to synthesize the censored, incomplete frame within...the context of the entire repertoire of pornographic codes operating within the comic genre. For example:

nurse	therapeutic treatment (sadomasochism)
schoolgirl in uniform	object of pedophilic desire
stiletto heels	bar hostess
candle	torture device
conch shell	cunnilingus[19]

And so on. In the *Urotsukidoji* saga, there is very little constraint from censorship; but its female figures are coded according to established erotic genres or 'species' (schoolgirl, kooky nympho, evil temptress, magical virgin). These figures are constantly subject to violation; male figures are more prone to mutation and metamorphosis. While species definition, variation and confusion seem to be the main interest of the animators here, not a single animal appears in the entire cycle—not a pet dog or cat, not a bird in the sky, not a snake or a wild beast. All these creatures are evoked from time to time through the bizarre transformational behaviours of the humanoid figures, but none ever appears as an animal proper. It is as though the animators have left the innocence of the natural order to explore perversions and permutations in the orders of representation.

In *Urotsukidoji II: Legend of the Demon Womb*, two male characters are shown moving along a continuum from innocence to experience; and the stages of their progress are marked on their bodies. Myuni Hausen, the villainous Faustian overseer of the late stages of the saga, is shown as a schoolboy being whipped and abused, then as his father's adolescent apprentice, then gaining power as he embarks on his own megalomaniacal enterprise. Through these phases he grows in stature; his face elongates and becomes marked with 'character lines', first subtly, then through definitive mutations, until half his features are a machinic assemblage. His victim is Takeaki, a clean cut would-be Karate Kid, sexually inexperienced and resistant to initiation. Takeaki acquires monster blood by means of transfusion from his cousin (who is the beast Nagumo in disguise) and begins to experience mutation. The imaging of this mutation shows striking analogies with the portrayal of Tetsuo's mutations in *Iron Man* (1988) and *Body Hammer* (1992). Aside from the visual parallels—the body form losing its boundaries as something much larger, more powerful and dangerously chaotic bursts from within—there is similarity in the constant determination to portray the experience of mutation as both agonizing and agonistic. It is an experience which is tormenting and which is resisted.

The dynamics of experienced animation are built on violation as the prototypical mode of action, whereas those of innocent animation are based on the chase. The chase works with spatial distance and emphasizes autonomy and, of course, species difference: cat chases bird, man chases duck, wolf chases rabbit. Violation collapses distance and concentrates on interminglings. It defies species difference and works to erode it through genetic mutation, as well as through actual acts of perverted intercourse. But the *Urotsukidoji* project becomes more complex as it progressively involves the physical with the metaphysical and as its preoccupation with the perversion of forms slides towards a preoccupation with forces and force fields. In *Urotsukidoji III: Return of the Overfiend*, the characters or agents belong to an archetypal taxonomy. There is the gigantic destroyer-beast Nagumo; the numinous baby Imi, who will grow into the most powerful principle of good or of evil (this always remains in doubt); the sorcerer Faust (alias Myuni Hausen); the degenerate tyrant Caesar; Alector the idealized maiden; and the man/boy/beast Amano Jaku, who witnesses all. It is he who is the titular 'wandering kid'. The action is a combination of narrative events and abstract, intersecting fields of power. Innocence and experience, the most starkly demarcated values in the narrative, also become confused through the course of the action. In its last phase, the disintegrating and revolting Caesar is redeemed when Alector, his exquisitely innocent daughter creation, returns his incestuous love.

What is going on here is something other than the kinds of becomings, multiplicities and differences that Deleuze and Guattari celebrate in *A Thousand Plateaus*.[20] The dynamic of *Urotsukidoji* is dualistic, and dualism and difference belong to incommensurable modes of thought. Post-structuralist thinking too readily assumes that binarism and dualism are the same thing. Binarism, as Lacan taught his students, is the beginning of difference, a structural principle which supports multiple and proliferating differentiations. Difference founds order and taxonomy, stabilizes signs in sign systems and so enables cognitive control. It is, of course, asking to be sabotaged, but Lacan, Derrida and Deleuze are not its first (nor, arguably, its most effective) saboteurs. Dualism is the enemy of difference from of old. It is not structural but dynamic. It is not about signifiers but about forces. Whether its chosen principles are good and evil, innocence and experience, feminine and masculine, reason and energy, or any other of the great metaphysical oppositions, dualism remains volatile and is always dramatic because it is always agonistic. Each of the two sides devours subdivisions in an all-consuming drive to confront its other head-on; and, as the different forms of the created world line up on either edge of the one great divide, the ultimatum looms, inevitably, as implosion. There is something inherently catastrophic about dualism. To read *Urotsukidoji* in Deleuzian terms would be to miss out on its dynamics. It would also be to miss the particular qualities of its humour, for this saga is very humorously knowing about dualism. Here, it is helpful to bring in the matter of cultural context and, with it, some intercultural politics. Karel van Wolferen provides a useful summary account:

> [The] alleged absence of any fundamental duality in traditional Japanese thought is extolled even today. Contemporary theorists on the national character proudly proclaim that Japanese prefer to live with intellectual ambiguity. The well-known populariser of Zen in the West, Suzuki Daisetz...never tired of pointing out the shortcomings of Western 'dualistic logic'.[21]

The voice-over recital which is repeated as the opening to each episode of *Urotsukidoji* warns that the last laugh will be on 'ignorant humans' who still believe in metaphysical divisions. Here again, there is commonality with the poetic epics of Blake, which lampoon the dualistic consciousness even while they engage in the most spectacular and compelling exercises in dualistic imagining.

NOTES

Thanks to Alan Cholodenko for helpful suggestions during the redrafting of this essay, and thanks to him and to Peter Blacklock for their help with research materials.

1 Chuck Jones, 'What's Up, Down Under?', in *THE ILLUSION OF LIFE: Essays on Animation*, ed. Alan Cholodenko (Sydney: Power Publications in association with the Australian Film Commission, 1991).

2 William Blake, *The Marriage of Heaven and Hell*, in *Blake: Complete Writings*, ed. Geoffrey Keynes (London: Oxford University Press, 1966), p. 156. The punctuation is Blake's own and its eccentricities are deliberate. He took the view that the structures of language should not be allowed to constrain its energies.

3 Keith Clancy, 'ΠΡΗΣΤΗΡ: The T(r)opology of Pyromania', in *THE ILLUSION OF LIFE*.

4 Scott Bukatman, *Terminal Identity: The Virtual Subject in Postmodern Science Fiction* (Durham: Duke University Press, 1993).

5 *Sparagmos* was the term for the ritual dismemberment of the victim in the Bacchic orgies.

6 Bukatman, *Terminal Identity*, p. 244.

7 ibid., p. 10.

8 For an essay that addresses the complexity of hybridity in animation through a Derridean analysis, see Alan Cholodenko's '*Who Framed Roger Rabbit*, or the Framing of Animation', in *THE ILLUSION OF LIFE*.

9 Jones, 'What's Up, Down Under?', p. 37.

10 ibid., pp. 39 and 40.

11 ibid., p. 46.

12 Ising quoted in Steve Schneider, *That's all Folks!: The Art of Warner Bros. Animation* (New York: Henry Holt and Company, 1988), p. 34.

13 Jones, 'What's Up, Down Under?', p. 38.
14 Schneider, *That's all Folks!*, p. 150.
15 The sleight of hand (and eye) was only discovered with the advent of digital video technology enabling frame by frame inspection.
16 It was at MGM that Tex Avery created his showgirl 'Red', the precursor of Jessica Rabbit and Holly Wood as a toon siren so licensed.
17 Cholodenko, '*Who Framed Roger Rabbit*, or the Framing of Animation', p. 214.
18 ibid., p. 216.
19 Sandra Buckley, '"Penguin in Bondage": A Graphic Tale of Japanese Comic Books', in *Technoculture*, eds. Constance Penley and Andrew Ross (Minneapolis: University of Minnesota Press, 1991), p. 187.
20 Gilles Deleuze and Félix Guattari, *A Thousand Plateaus: Capitalism and Schizophrenia*, trans. Brian Massumi (Minneapolis: University of Minnesota Press, 1987).
21 Karel van Wolferen, *The Enigma of Japanese Power* (London: Macmillan, 1989), p. 241. There is a nice irony here, in that Suzuki Daisetz appears not to recognize his own East-West thinking as a form of dualism.

or soul and mind, if

De Anime

WILLIAM D. ROUTT

ON THE SOUL

Do these women have souls?
Can these drawings live?[1]

As you see already, this essay turns on the substitution of things for other things. But the pun of the title is not merely an accident. Animation is 'the action of imparting life, vitality, or (as the sign of life) motion'. It is 'the state of being animate or alive'.

In the late nineteenth century, before the cinema and when these definitions were propounded, the usage of the word to signify 'representation of things as alive' was obsolete and rare.[2] Under this heading *The Oxford English Dictionary* (*OED*) also quotes Thomas Hobbes' *Rhetoric* from 1688: 'Animation is that expression which makes us seem to see the thing before our eyes'. One of the minor global effects of the cinema has been to make Hobbes' rhetorical sense of 'animation' the one most commonly encountered these days. When most people use the word, they mean movie cartoons. Or perhaps not. 'Animation' is to 'cartoon' almost exactly what 'cinema' or 'film' is to 'movie'.

Hobbes' sense of 'animation' is, broadly speaking, metaphorical; and metaphors are interesting partly because of the way in which they preserve original sense at the same time that they make new meanings. Metaphorical usage makes almost any phrase of contemporary language a vehicle of history, representing the past inescapably in all speaking and writing. No matter how many times or in how many contexts we use 'animation' to mean 'cartoons', the senses of imparting life or being alive continue to be evoked. And, of course, the reverse is true as well. The word confuses literal and figural meanings, presentation and representation.

These things being so, in the interests of clarity and common sense (and for the time being) I reject Hobbes' metaphor. Animation is not the representation of life. It is the action of imparting life. It is being alive. Or, put in another way and one that is perhaps more reasonable, I should like to be more precise about what the illusion is we are talking about, the type of representation evoked by the word 'animation'. In the effort to avoid charges of essentialism, discussions of representation and illusion almost always ignore what is being represented. In them all illusions are illusions—as if that was ever what was important about illusions. Against that spirit, this discussion will treat the illusion of life as seeming to see the thing before our eyes, and will speculate about the life of that illusion.

'Animation' comes to us via the Latin *anima*, which the *OED* glosses as 'air, breath, life, soul, mind'. But that is not all—for *anima* is symbiotically related to a gendered partner, *animus* (a relation metaphorically exploited by Jungian psychology). The feminine form, *anima*, moves from air to mind as the *OED* indicates; while the masculine, *animus*, traces a line from soul to mind to reason to feeling to willing.[3] Eric Partridge interprets the relation slightly differently:

> *animus* (s *anim-*), mind, spirit, is a parallel to *anima* (s *anim-*), spirit, soul. Strictly, *animus* is the thinking principle opp both *corpus*, body, and *anima*, soul: and *anima* (hence, ult, *animus*) is orig 'breath of air', hence breath of life, hence the soul, whether of the living or of the dead.[4]

He goes on to note the English transformation of *animus* into 'feeling of hostility' and the movement of *anima* towards 'animate' and 'animation'—all in an entry headed by the word 'animal'. *Anima* is the more generous and inclusive term, subsuming *animus* in many respects. But Lewis and Short's *A Latin Dictionary* argues that *animus* actually has historical priority—masculine narrowness and linearity preceding feminine inclusiveness—'...so that Cic[ero] was theoretically right, but historically wrong, when he said, ipse animus ab animâ dictus est...',[5] which can be roughly translated by a non-Latinist like myself as 'where Ego was, Id shall be'.

In the *OED*'s list of meanings for *anima*, 'life' occupies the midpoint, 'air' and 'breath' coming before it and 'soul' and 'mind' after. There is a sense of historical linearity there, or perhaps theory masquerading as history again. In any case, the list is a story of transformation that anyone might read. It is, I would guess, a story told many times, and one I am retelling here illogically, by beginning in the middle with animation—the state of being alive.

I suppose that one of the first things which might strike one about the ideas of 'life' clustered under *anima* is their invisibility. Who has seen the wind? Or breath or soul or mind, for that matter? Perceptions of these things are matters of feeling, not really of seeing or even of hearing. Indeed, it seems that life cannot be apprehended by the physical senses at all. Air, which can be felt on the skin, is not by itself a sign of life; and breath—which some people believe they see when they observe water condensing in cold weather—is surely nothing other than air that lives, sensorially indistinguishable from any other air. As for soul and mind, if they can be apprehended at all, their apprehension depends on senses other than physical ones.

Nonetheless, common sense says that there is a distinction that makes a difference between a dead body and a live one and that the life in the latter may be something we cannot see or hear or smell or taste or touch. It is no wonder, then, that imagination has filled this void with dreaming. Or, put in another way, life cannot be present in and of itself. It can only be represented, mediated—incorporated—in its effects, like breath. This may be another argument for rejecting the special, rhetorical sense of animation as the representation of life. The rough metaphor dissolves into all the other senses of the word if 'the state of being alive' can be known only as an effect of life, that is, through representation. Or, put in another way, if what seems is what is, then the perception of the effects of life is sufficient evidence of life itself. Whether this is the case or not, the alliance of life with things we cannot see or hear or smell or taste or touch redirects the crazy question of how drawings live along lines that may result in a reasonable answer.

If physically life is an emptiness, mentally we fill the emptiness with imagining—and broadly speaking, with motivation. By this I only mean that the various senses of *anima* which I have listed all have to do with motivation in one sense or another. The most fundamental test of life (a notoriously inaccurate one) is whether things seem to move of themselves or not. This is motivation in its crudest form. It is also life represented, life observed—animation in the sense of movie cartoons.

I want to stress that point because of the way in which the thinking about *anima* rapidly abandons the view from outside in favour of various routes to the interior. In the treatise by Aristotle which used to be known commonly as *De Anima*, the philosopher is not much interested in how we might or might not be able to discern whether something else is alive or not. Instead, he concentrates on inferences about motivation that seem to use internal experience as their common reference point, that are, in other words, broadly speaking, phenomenological. He makes a hierarchy of motivation in which actual locomotion, when it occurs at all, is an effect of nutritive, perceptive and/or thinking impulses that originate inside the organism, setting the stage for what David Bordwell would one day call 'classical narration'.

De Anima used to be translated as 'On the Soul'. For Aristotle, life was not the movement of a thing but the internal or psychic cause of that movement: its soul. In these terms, then, animation would seem to be the representation of the effects of soul, allusions of a soul. Do these women have souls? One answer might be, 'if they are animated, they do'.

We can go further than this. *De Anima* is Latin. The treatises of Aristotle were composed in Greek. In Greek, Aristotle wrote about *psyché*. *Psyché* suggests '*breath of life, ghost, vital principle, soul,* anima',[6] a cluster of sense unsurprisingly quite like the *OED*'s for *anima*. But *psyché* also has a familiar, perhaps ominous, ring in English—and indeed, the treatise that was once known as 'On the Soul', from the Latin, is nowadays called 'Psychology', presumably from the Greek. In a circular, yet linear, way, I have come to the idea of 'mind', the last link in the *OED*'s chain of meaning, by repeating the Ciceronian error of substituting theory for history.

Metaphors, I have said, are verbal constructions in which history plays a part. 'Animation', which we use metaphorically to refer to movie cartoons when the word is nothing other than a metaphor in its most literal sense, has connotations of motivation, soul and psychology that go directly to the question of how drawings live. Animated drawings live by definition (or so I think), and their life is based in their motivation: soul, mind, psychology.

MANGA

The *manga Gunnm* translates as 'Gun Dreams', but it is known in English as *Battle Angel Alita*.[7] The character of Alita, or Gally as she is known in Japan, has been extraordinarily popular in Japan and the United States. Undoubtedly there are many reasons for her popularity, among which I should like to give first preference to the high quality of Kishiro Yukito's artwork and writing. Covers of the U.S. version of the comic show an almost parodic, constantly transforming, sexual object, while the narrative deals with the common, and popular, *manga/anime* theme of female empowerment through technology (*Bubblegum Crisis, Venus Wars, Genocyber, Ghost in the Shell*) and quite consciously sets up several transformative and oppositional series, radiating from the transformed human-machine Alita (or Gally) as the centre. Not unexpectedly for this type of work, *Battle Angel Alita* is grounded in a complex interplay of innocence and decadence, technology and spiritualism, eroticism and gore, in which ideas originally posited as opposites come to be represented as the same.

The underlying 'problem' (narrative enigma) of the nine issues of Part 1 of the *manga* is precisely Alita's soul and its relation to her body or bodies. Moreover, the question of the soul seems to act as a strong structuring thematic throughout the entire series, inflecting and interfering with a more easily read thematic of feminine longing and masculine lust.

Alita is introduced as a head and part of a torso, which the cyber doctor, Daisuke Ido, identifies as 'a genuine human being',[8] although it is clearly at least partly mechanical. The torso displays the outline of one breast and is obviously intended to be sexually attractive. However, Ido's interest at this point does not appear to be sexual. He has found something rare, and the only words he uses to characterize that rareness identify it as what it does not appear to be, that is, human. The cyber doctor apprehends what we, who look at the drawing, cannot see: Alita's soul, the invisible principle of animation. And that soul is human.

This last is no minor point. In the *manga* world, machines move and perceive and think, which is pretty much the entire repertoire of bodies motivated by what Aristotle would call a human soul. It is notable that Ido can recognize this machine's humanity even without evidence of motion, perception or thought, that is, without the classical evidence of the presence of a soul, thus suggesting that humanity consists in none of these and is even more mysterious, and significant, than soul alone. At the same time, Ido's ability to sense the presence or potential of humanity in the emptiness *behind* or *beneath* the machine's sculpted materiality is surely an ability to read blank spaces, to hear silence, to apprehend the void.

In the beginning, then, Ido instructs the reader by correctly interpreting the signs of the text. He is Alita's model reader—from the outset, her animator. In this role, of course, he merely represents and repeats the reader's animating activity, reminding me, perhaps, that I animate the comic with my reading.

The unmoving, unperceiving, unthinking part of the human machine Ido has found can be brought back to consciousness; but it has lost its memory. If Ido's assertion of humanity places a human soul in this machine virtually by decree, its lack of memory announces that certain elements of that soul usually considered crucial are still to be discovered. This soul is merely a site, a named emptiness. It is 'soul', rather than this specific being's particular soul. Ido expects Alita to remember what she has forgotten in time.

As the first move in assigning specificity to the human machine Ido names it.[9]

Then he attaches Alita to a 'beautiful' body.[10]

All of Ido's motivations may not be directly articulated. As the *manga* develops, Alita seems to treat him as a father; but it is possible that their feelings about one another are more complicated. Some of the complexity of those feelings is conveyed in the *manga* indirectly, via the reader. The reader and Alita suspect that Ido is destroying women to get the best parts for his girl machine.[11] We say that the reader *identifies* with Alita at this point; but the process is actually one of *projection*, a textbook case of *supplying motivation*. At the same time, of course, the mad desire that would drive Ido to kill is also a projection of ours (and Alita's). In both instances, blanks are being filled in as the narrative calls upon the reader's commonplace ability to supply motivation—that is, to attribute souls to characters.

In fact Ido is hunting the destroyer. We have read him wrong. But we have also read Alita right (which our guide, Ido, does not do in this instance); and her ability to imagine such evil of him, masked in our projection, belies the empty innocence of a soul without memory. Indeed, this subplot about the murderer of women leads to Alita's first memory: '*panzer kunst*', a particularly remarkable fighting technique, which she uses to destroy the real serial killer.[12]

Alita's first memory is, then, how to move (including how to kill). She finds she knows the *panzer kunst* instinctively, without having to consider how or what to do. The *manga* defines this technique as the 'armored arts', which inscribes her memory on her surface, connecting unconscious and body, animating, motivating.

In the second issue, Alita determines to become a 'hunter-warrior' like Ido. Ido does not want this, but eventually he relents and throws Alita's pretty girl clothing into the canal in recognition of her right to be herself.[13] Structurally, of course, she is becoming Ido, not herself. But her desire is expressly shown as originating within, in her soul, in memories she cannot quite grasp. Ido is a trigger, not a model, for her choice of profession.

In the same issue, a new plot line introduces Makaku[14] (whose name is not given until page 24 of the issue following). At this point, Makaku seems to be an inarticulate male-mechanical body with an overwhelming passion for eating brains, an addiction in fact. Although Makaku's addiction is as physical as one could want in cartoon black-and-white ('Schlurrrp!'), the mirrored parallel with Alita seems deliberate. Alita is a soul (brain, mind) needing a (female) machine body; Makaku is a (male) machine body in search of brains (minds, souls). They are destined for each other.

Alita sets out to confront Makaku and eventually succeeds in boring into his eye, after her body has been destroyed. Makaku picks her up immediately after he has been wounded. He identifies her as 'GIRL!' and tries to suck her brains with his tongue.[15] Throughout the series, Alita is identified by others as a 'girl'; and Makaku is associated with inarticulate sound. There is a kinship here, between Alita's girlness, her ideal embodiment, and Makaku's beastliness, his carnal spirit.

Soon after, the essential Makaku is revealed as a head on a flexible mechanical trunk: a snake. ('It's like Nietzsche said, the mind is nothing but a plaything of the body. GWAHAHAHAHAAA', it remarks.)[16] However, lest crude Freudian—or even Nietzschean—soul reading run away with our *manga* reading, it is mete that we remember that Makaku's major feature is an immense mouth of grinning teeth.

Ido, grievously wounded himself, painfully takes Alita's torso back to the city ('The Scrap Yard'), vowing to give her a proper body. He replaces Alita's (battered) beautiful body with the mechanical body of a 'berserker', an alien warrior of unknown, but definitely lethal, capabilities.[17]

The berserker body as it is found is male, but can be 'set' to female, and is, by Ido. Unremarkably in this genre, gender pervades all life, including the life of machines. But, also unremarkably, gender is something which is 'set' (albeit by someone else), not something unalterable. Apparently what are unalterable are the tendencies, instincts, of the body (to kill, addiction to brains, and so on) and the soul (*panzer kunst*, to be a hunter-warrior).

During the operation to place her self into the new body, Alita dreams of Ido, flashing back over her time with him. As she repeats her defeat of the serial killer, she finds herself rocketing upward.

> Wh-what AM I? This—this POWER! Where does it COME from!? Inside me is ANOTHER me struggling to break free! If I can just fly a little farther... I can almost see her, touch her!... (FWSH)... My body! [Alita's body is vapourized, and Makaku's face appears gigantically behind her as she falls.] GWAHAHAHA.[18]

The reference to near death experience is clear and significant, but the parallel the dream draws between Ido and Makaku seems just as significant. Both of them have done things to Alita's body, and their interference both aids and impedes the desire of her soul. In the dream, it does seem that Alita can only find herself and fulfil her soul's desire in death. Thus far in the story, her body—that is, the one Ido first gave her—has been the material means to finding that identity: life and the body have been the foundations for her self. But that body has been destroyed by Makaku and is now being replaced by Ido. Makaku's destruction of her body paradoxically frees her in the dream to fly up to find her self (apparently using that body in a denial of it). And it is Ido's replacement of that body which calls her back from finding out who she really is. She is stopped from realizing her soul's desire when Ido replaces her soul in a new body, thus the implied dissolve from Makaku's face to Ido that ends the dream.

Not long after, Ido wonders if the berserker body will affect Alita's mind, making her more grown up and less like a girl. Alita reassures him: 'I know what you're worried about, Ido, but believe me, no matter *how* I may seem to change from this point on, I'll still be the Alita you know always'.[19] The perdurance of soul is being asserted here, and perhaps something else: this is the end of Alita's search, her soul's desire is satiated, she is herself—a girl, as Pinocchio is finally a boy.

But if Alita's search is ended, Makaku's is not. He too needs a new body; and, disguised as an old woman, he gains access to an awesomely large and superior male body.[20] Searching for Alita, he invades an underground bar; and there is a confrontation involving his new weapon, 'the grind cutter', which operates like a sewer rooter and is snakily phallic. When she first sees it in action, Alita says, 'You think this is a *threat*?!'[21] However, Makaku has five of them; and, using them all, he is indeed able to knock the cyborg girl *hors de combat.*

Instead of finishing her off, Makaku snatches up a baby and, like Rumpelstiltskin, stamps a hole through the floor, plunging down to the sewers beneath the city. Alita hesitates for a moment before the bat hole he has made, which is one hellaciously big *vagina detenta.*[22]

No wonder Alita pauses before jumping in. But another reason for pausing is that the story is about to take her to what lies unseen beneath the surface, that is, to another dimension of the soul.

What lies beneath the Scrap Yard (the city) is, to be sure, not Alita's soul (or, at least, it is not to be attributed directly to her soul), but Makaku's—at the same time the soul of the city, and by extension, of humanity itself. Where the desire of Alita's soul had taken her up and toward the light, Makaku's desire draws her downward, into the pit—equally a place of death.

Ido says that if Alita survives this combat, it will be because of her berserker body, not her *panzer kunst*—her body, not her soul. But it is the 'survival mode' of the body (its software, its mind) 'connected to the cerebral cortex deep inside her brain' which is her hope.[23] Not her body, but her body's soul, will save her.

By way of parallel and contrast, Makaku asks the computer built into *his* body to figure out what Alita can do. The computer is a 'boarhead' codpiece, that is, the mind of this machine is figured as a male sexual organ.[24] It is hard to imagine a more forceful image of the brain as beast. Eventually, after the computer turns out to be wrong about when she has defeated him, Makaku rips it off and hurls it into the walls of the sewer where it explodes. The action again confounds a simple gendered interpretation of his exaggerated masculinity while emphasizing the genre's privileged distinction between humans and machines, souls and intellects.

Makaku knows better than the computer because he knows this deep place intimately. In particular, he knows when and where the filth of the surface will be dumped—just in time to forestall Alita's attack and to restore his faltering fortunes.[25] For a moment, it seems as though the tide of battle will turn again in the beast machine's favour; but Alita has already severed the dangerous arm that is equipped with those five grind cutters, although this is not apparent until he attempts to use it. His stroke completes her action; and he falls into the cesspit, emasculated, disembodied.[26]

Makaku is not finished yet, of course. For his last trick, he wraps his metallic snake-like body around Alita and tells her that if she uses the plasma power she has been relying on up to this point, she will explode everything (obviously including herself). She counters with electromagnetic force and discovers that the monster is already near death. He then ignites the gas. ('Let's blow ourselves to hell—together!')[27]

In the heart of the explosion, Makaku explains himself by recounting his past as a sewer dweller, living on the refuse of the surface world, wounded by surface dwellers, saved by an unidentified scientist, like Ido, and given the body that best suited 'the desire that lies hidden at the bottom of your heart'—his soul's desire.[28] Makaku, the beast, has been made by his memories, by his soul.

A panel of yelling Alitas is launched at us while Makaku's words burst in tiny explosions: 'Despise me!... Smash me to pieces!... Burn my soul to a cinder!'[29] The unexpected juxtaposition emphasizes the significance of these words for Alita; but indirectly it also assigns the words to Alita or to us to apply to Alita, underscoring their symbiotic kinship. The words call for the annihilation of the soul as well as the body—a kind of death different from the one Alita had previously nearly experienced and one fitting the place in which she finds herself now. But still, death is what Makaku wants, just as it is what Alita wanted earlier. And annihilation, of course, is what he gets.

Once again, and at the very end, motivation is evoked by Alita's words, motivation by something ungraspable or inexplicable. 'I don't know if it's a sin or something to be proud of...if it is hatred or sadness...but I am moved to tears—by something I can't exactly explain...'[30] As it has been throughout these first nine issues, *reading* is invited here at the end—reading in the sense of creating fiction, motivating, making psychology, imagining souls. That is animation.

ANIME

Rusty Angel and *Tears Sign* are OAVs (Original Animated Videos) based on Parts 1 and 2 of the *manga Battle Angel Alita*. Two versions of the OAVs on one video cassette were issued for the English-speaking market, one subtitled and one dubbed. The subtitled version wisely opted to preserve direct English translations of Japanese names, rather than squaring with Fred Burke's translation for Viz Comics. Thus, in the subtitled version, the protagonist's name is Gally, among other differences. I have elected to use these names here, partly for the sake of accuracy (my work is based on the subtitled version) and partly as a means of keeping the comics and the videos distinct.

Many of the more complex, grotesque and extreme elements of the *manga* have been excluded or toned down in the OAVs. For example, a great deal involving the end-of-level monster of the first OAV, called Grewcica, is different from what pertains to Makaku, his double in the first series of the comic. Indeed, this is hardly the same monster. His brain addiction is not so graphically shown. He is the serial killer. He is not essentially a head on a spinal column. There are no sewers; there is no baby and no boarhead computer. The prolonged combat is much abbreviated and ends with Gally slitting him from guggle to zatch, which has the effect of blowing up his cyber body. There is no revelation of a traumatic childhood, no sympathy evoked and no strong reason for drawing a parallel between him and Gally.

Perhaps more to the point, the OAVs are not overtly about Gally's soul, as the first series of the *manga* is about Alita's soul. When Ido finds the head and torso that is Gally, he uses an electronic device to determine that she is alive—that is, a machine detects her life and instructs us in our viewing.

In the *manga*, Alita's life and her humanity are more or less coterminous. In the *anime*, Ido says 'she's human alright' only when Gally's consciousness is restored. *First* she is alive, *then* she is human. In the next line of dialogue, Gally's humanity is directly attributed to her *brain* ('It's uncanny how well the brain's been preserved under those conditions'), thus invoking a purely biological notion of humanity. But it is at this point also that the *anime* first adopts her point of view, confounding the biological with the spectatorial-cinematic. In some sense, Gally's soul is ours.

Not a great deal is made of Gally's missing memory; and what little reference there is occurs in dialogue. (Gally: 'I have no memories, no past'. Her friend, Yugo: '...no memories to haunt you'.) Gally is given only one body in the OAVs, and nothing about its special nature is suggested. In the terms I am using here, this suggests that whatever extraordinary fighting power she has comes from what she is to begin with, from her soul—not, as in the *manga*, partly from the soul of the berserker body. Her powers are not known until they are deployed. (They are not given names like '*panzer kunst*', and she experiences no intimations of her past.) She operates entirely through intuition. ('A flash of rage called inside me and then I sprang'.) Gally's soul seems to supply her with instinctive skill and no memory; but memory is integral to Aristotle's concept of the human soul, so Gally's soul may be something less or more than Aristotle's: inhuman.

When Gally determines to become a hunter-warrior, Ido speculates that the desire may stem from a repressed memory. ('But why a Hunter? Is it some demon hidden in your untapped memory?') Still, he allows her to fulfil her wish; and *Rusty Angel* ends with the exchange about her always being herself from this point on, which occurs about halfway through Part 1 of the *manga*. *Something* from within (instinct, inarticulate memory) has made Gally into what she is; and this, at least, recalls Aristotle, who suggests that the soul fashions us, or ought to do so.

But the animation of an *anime* is not the same as the animation of a comic. Whether this woman has a soul is not really in question. I must begin again if I am to animate animated images aright, that is, to write of how they live.

There are three characters in the OAVs who do not appear in Part 1 of the *manga*: Chiren, Yugo and an unnamed *ronin* figure.

Chiren is a scientist about Ido's age and his former partner. She is originally from Zalem, the city of the upper classes that floats above Scrap Iron City, where all the action of the *manga* and OAVs so far has taken place. Her overweening desire to get back there sets up a conflict with Ido, who is also a native of Zalem but has no wish to return. It also sets up a parallel between her and Yugo to which I shall return in a moment.

Chiren moves the thematics of the OAVs decisively into several related areas. She functions as Gally's Bad or Inadequate (M)other/Sister, just as Ido takes the part of her Good Father. Chiren remakes Grewcica especially to destroy Gally—in order to prove herself Ido's superior in scientific skill. But eventually she also saves Gally and Yugo at the cost of her own life, presumably because she empathizes with and respects Gally's love for Yugo (that is, perhaps she sees herself in Gally's mirror).

In addition, Chiren represents the upper classes of Zalem. She thinks that being in Scrap Iron City is beneath her, and she despises the inhabitants of the place except for Ido. As one of the principal villains in the OAVs and an older, upper class woman, Chiren first cathects the spectatorial hostility inspired by her actions opposing Gally on to the convenient otherness of her age, class and gender, then transforms those feelings into atonement.

Yugo has been imported into the first OAV from Part 2 of the *manga*, where he is known in the English version as Hugo.[31] The seven issues of Part 2 are all about Alita's relation with Hugo, which is also the primary focus of *Tears Sign*. That relation is depicted in *Rusty Angel* with scenes, very like some of those in the *manga*, in which Gally is attracted to Yugo and listens to his dreams of going to Zalem. Near the end of *Rusty Angel*, there is a brief shot of Yugo removing a spinal cord from something in a back alley. He is doing everything he can, even things that are wrong, to get the money to go to Zalem.

Much of the evil desire suggested in the *manga* is deflected in the *anime* by Gally's intense interest in Yugo. For example, Ido's indulgent reaction to Gally's attraction to Yugo underlines the paternal role he takes in the OAV and helps to assuage any suspicion of his having any other kind of interest in Gally. There is not much, if any, conflict within Gally. In the *manga*, Alita goes through a lot of 'what is happening to me?!' *angst*, which seems appropriate to an early adolescent; but in the *anime*, Gally seems to accept almost everything about herself, if not about the way the world treats her, with fervent single-mindedness.

The result in *Tears Sign* is a subtle rewriting of what emerges as *amour fou* in Part 2 of the *manga*. The difference is perhaps best exemplified in the denouements of the two. In both cases, Yugo/Hugo, wounded and delirious, tries to climb the tubes connecting the lower city to the upper. In the *manga*, Hugo's madness is horrific, but predominantly tragic, just as Makaku's horrible madness becomes tragic in the first series of the *manga*. This is because *we feel for them*. We identify with them, as well as with Alita in her love or hate for them.[32] In the OAV, however, costuming and movement combine to overwhelm the tragedy. Yugo crawls up the tubes like some desperate insect. Although there is pathos in what he is doing, it is also repellent. Whatever motivates him has passed beyond our ken. Perhaps he is a demon.

Chiren and Yugo, who share the desire for Zalem, demonically *motivate the narratives* of the OAVs. They are the only characters with articulate, strong and focused desires. They both compromise their integrity in order to get to Zalem, and they both die because of that desire. These are the 'most human' characters in the OAVs, the most internally driven, most psychologized. They are the ones who fail, also the ones most certainly with souls.

The unnamed *ronin* character is, like Chiren, an addition to the OAVs that does not occur anywhere in the *manga*. But, where Chiren and Yugo are characters whose motivations are more important than their actions (at least until Yugo's attempt to climb to Zalem), the unnamed *ronin* has no discernible 'inner life' until he tells Gally that he is fighting her because she has beaten him to various important hunter-warrior prizes. He is, in other words, the most demonic character of all.

This empty figure gathers mystery about itself. It watches impassively as Gally defeats Grewcica, then reappears in time to kill Yugo for the bounty placed upon him. It seems to exist primarily for formal purposes: to provide a climactic spectacular combat for Gally that would otherwise not take place in the second OAV—that is, to fill a hole. But, for just that reason, the unnamed *ronin* takes on the resonance of a dream image. Unnamed fears and desires are cathected on to it, and its implacable logic becomes the soul's unreason. This combat is Gally's destiny, a test that in some sense she has made for herself, against a figure that evokes both Ido and Yugo: the hunter-warrior father and the lover who must die because he is not as good as she is.

There is a particular moment of significance near the climax of *Tears Sign*. Yugo is held by Gally's gradually failing grip, about to drop into the void from one of the tubes leading to Zalem. Loving her now, when it is too late, he bids her farewell. As he speaks, around his face the short black hair is agitated, perhaps by the wind we know is perpetually sighing through and around the tubes, but perhaps also or instead by the action of their souls. Slowly, he slips away.

The agitation of Yugo's hair recalls privileged moments throughout the two OAVs of Gally's hair moving, shifting, waving. Her hair speaks her self. A gesture is amplified, given volume, by the corresponding movement of hair. The hair reacts to events, signs her perception. And it shows emotion, internal feeling. In certain ways, Gally's moving hair resembles the grounding bass in music, the deep breath of the soul that gives life to melody and harmony.

AS ONE POSSESSED

Now this manifestation of soul in the OAVs is quite unlike the more discussable, more intellectual dynamics of soul in the *manga*. It brings us back to the sense of soul as mere life, rather than the more familiar place of communitarian psychology. In so doing, it restores a certain measure of the blankness of the concept, its 'mechanistic' faculty. But the blankness in its turn restores certain aspects of the mystery the comic seeks to dispel. As life, soul becomes a surface we cannot see and cannot be certain about. We know these women have souls, but we cannot ever fully grasp what makes their figures live. This is a sensation of quite a different order from Alita's sense of being moved by something inside that she cannot explain.

I do not mean to suggest that the cinema entails abandoning the kind of psychologizing that fuels still fictions—only that it warns against being too certain about that kind of understanding. In the cinema, soul is movement, that is, it is animation. But in the cinema, movement is transformation, change. It is *sensational*. Meaning is derived from sensing, and such a meaning is altogether fluid.

The *manga* are 'deeper', a property of words. When readers are moved by *manga*, they are moved 'profoundly', moved by a transference of animation from psyche to psyche. The OAVs are, correspondingly, 'higher', a property of sensation. When they provoke feelings, the emotions are changeable, too agitated for analysis, as quickly gone as they appear. Cinema moves us 'superficially'—that is to say, kinetically, in a communication of life as waves, the way sound hits the eardrum. *Manga* and cinema *are animated*, but the cinema *animates* too. It makes us cartoons.

Because I cannot stop the movie it goes on and it takes me with it I am we are like a net in its ocean the film surrounds us with its animation flows through and around our porous selves. It possesses us! The film is the soul here (the soul according to Plotinus); and we and Alita and Yugo and Chiren and Ido are what the soul makes alive. The film is a demon who makes us dance by dancing for us with us through us like cartoon characters like people in photographs in the cinema we are animated by something outside!

Now I write Jean-François Lyotard's words again, write them over differently and the same, combining them with my own and the words of others—as I have done since the beginning of this piece. It cannot be me writing here, but neither is it Lyotard.

We are heteromata because our soul is outside us. The concatenation of postures constituting the mime of the attack follows a scenario. This scenario is what is dictated to us, we play it. So we hear instructions, and carry them out on our bodies. This carrying out is an interpretation and presupposes not only that the orders are heard, but a subtle listening to what the scenario demands.[33]

The animated image ceases to support the argumentation of the cine-scientists, it greases the dialectic. Grasp me if you can. But it will be or has been too early or too late. Is a movement graspable? The animated image is possessed, but I cannot possess it. The possessed image is damned by virtue of its being an ontological essay on time.[34] *Animation reveals this because it is also a possessed state,*

slipping

out of control

along the spider's track.

Angel and demon

gun dreaming.

NOTES

This piece would not exist if it were not for Alan Cholodenko, to whom I am most grateful for the opportunity to write about *manga* and *anime*. Dena Gleeson and Judy Routt did most of what was necessary to prepare the images that accompanied its presentation at the conference. Judy made the T-shirt. Rick Thompson contributed more than he knew to its writing. This version is dedicated to Philip, who didn't hear it and, as always, to Diane.

1 The origin of most of these words is Jean-François Lyotard's 'Speech Snapshot' (1980), in his collection *The Inhuman: Reflections on Time*, trans. Geoffrey Bennington and Rachel Bowlby (Cambridge: Polity Press, 1991), p. 129. The second line is a modification of the Lyotard.

2 See Alan Cholodenko's recourse to Webster's Dictionary in his Introduction to *THE ILLUSION OF LIFE: Essays on Animation* (Sydney: Power Publications in association with the Australian Film Commission, 1991), p. 15 and the discussion following.

3 Charlton T. Lewis and Charles Short, *A Latin Dictionary* (Oxford: The Clarendon Press, 1879), pp. 120-121 and pp. 123-124.

4 Eric Partridge, *Origins: A Short Etymological Dictionary of Modern English* (London: Routledge & Kegan Paul, 1958), p. 18.

5 Lewis and Short, *A Latin Dictionary*, p. 123.

6 F.E. Peters, *Greek Philosophical Terms: A Historical Lexicon* (New York: New York University Press, 1967), p. 166.

7 *Battle Angel Alita* continued to be published in the U.S. up to Part 8, no. 9 (1998), the end of Alita's story. The issues referred to in this essay have been reprinted as *Battle Angel Alita Graphic Novel* and *Battle Angel Alita Graphic Novel: Tears of an Angel* (both San Francisco: Viz Communications Inc., 1994).

The title change may be of interest to some. According to his own account, Fred Burke, who is credited with the English 'adaptation' of the first series, renamed *'Gunnm' 'Battle Angel Alita'* in order to attract readers ('Battling with Angelic Alita!', *Animerica*, vol. 1, no. 8, October 1993, p. 9). The English adaptation makes a point about the unsuitability of Alita's name that now makes no sense: 'Wait a minute—wasn't that your cat, the one that died last month? Wasn't it a boy?' (Yukito Kishiro, *Battle Angel Alita*, trans. Fred Burke, Sterling Bell and Matt Thorn (San Francisco: Viz Communications Inc., 1992), Part 1, issue 1, p. 9). Burke's marketing-driven decision—which, not accidentally, has given him a certain prominence—quite clearly is at variance with Kishiro's more complex naming strategy.

In quotations of *manga* dialogue throughout this text, I have eliminated most distinctions between balloons and panels, repunctuating where it seemed necessary.

8 Kishiro, *Battle Angel Alita,* Part 1, issue 1, 1992, p. 8.
9 ibid., p. 9.
10 ibid., pp. 14-17; and see Part 1, issue 2, p. 6.
11 ibid., pp. 17-22. For Ido's darker side, see also Part 1, issue 2, pp. 18-21. ('I kill for my own sake, nothing more, nothing less'.)
12 ibid., pp. 24-28.
13 ibid., issue 2, pp. 4-17.
14 ibid., pp. 11-15, 19-27.
15 ibid., issue 3, pp. 4-13.
16 ibid., pp. 22-23.
17 ibid., pp. 24-31; issue 4, pp. 4-19.
18 ibid., pp. 14-17.
19 ibid., issue 5, pp. 6-7.
20 ibid., issue 4, pp. 28-29.
21 ibid., issue 6, p. 11.
22 ibid., p. 24.
23 ibid., issue 7, 1993, p. 10.
24 ibid., issue 8, p. 6ff.
25 ibid., p. 19.
26 ibid., p. 26.
27 ibid., issue 9, pp. 4-15.
28 ibid., pp. 18-23.
29 ibid., p. 25.
30 ibid., p. 27.
31 ibid., Part 2, issues 1-7, 1993.
32 The *manga* sequence of Hugo's climb occupies the last half of *Battle Angel Alita,* Part 2, issue 7 (p. 14ff). He begins the climb in a trenchcoat; and his face evidences a blank, benign madness, until he returns to himself at the very end.
33 The origin of most of these words is Lyotard's 'Speech Snapshot', p. 131. Even as the opening words of that essay were reproduced in the opening words of this essay, so also is its closing here. I have drastically altered the *sens* of Lyotard's piece in order to include those words here. His essay is about photography, for one thing; and the original of this passage is not about us, for another.
34 ibid., p. 134, and see previous note.

Sonic—Atomic—Neumonic: Apocalyptic Echoes in *Anime*

PHILIP BROPHY

INTRODUCTION

Perhaps more than any other medium, filmic animation—the hysterical unleashing of dynamic movement resulting from the wilful animation of the inanimate—is precisely suited to visualizing the invisible lines and fields of energy which exist in our physical reality and beyond. And more so than the Western animation with which we are familiar, Japanese animation (*anime*) is founded on a discursive metaphysical visuality, combining animist beliefs with the medium's fantastic flexibility. While these ideas are symbolically contained in animation from Japan's immediate post-war period,[1] the visual tempo, orchestration and polyphony of post-'60s *anime* expresses a high-keyed formal interplay between energy and its depiction. Specifically, energy is manifested as the monitoring, graphing and recording of the invisible. Scenes abound where lightning bolts crackle across the screen, breaking up space, objects and people. Very often, this energy comes from a character or from an object recently acquired by the character. Characters' psychological states are similarly outlined by superimposed swirling lines and imported optical backgrounds—visual devices transposed from a long calligraphic legacy in *manga*.[2] But while *manga* often used these devices to describe interiority, *anime* exploits the dynamism of movement to affect directly the physical world—to graphically thrust upon us this collision between energy and its depiction. These manifestations of invisible energy are demonstrated by the tangible transformation of the atmospheric conditions of a spatial environment—where, quite simply, a force leaves the body, mind, psyche, soul, etc., and *energizes space.*

With greater rigour than Western animation, *anime* employs a concept of *linear* energy where a causal 'line' of energy is contracted from one point to the next in either dispersive wave form or concentrated beam form. While Occidental thought will readily exemplify this by analogous systems like electricity (where man tames nature through 'inventive containment', then allows energy to pass territorially along a controlled line), Oriental thought provides a more immediate and corporeal model: *chi. Chi* is the energy that exists in anyone and anything. It can be hidden, exposed, tapped, exercised, abused. From the many martial arts through to disciplines like *Tai Chi,* one channels this energy as a linear flow coursing through the body. This type of transference of invisible *chi* occurs in a range of energy manifestations in physical reality—from the stature of one's standing body to the slice of the samurai sword to the brush stroke of calligraphy. All are marked embodiments of channelled energy. Each example—the shape of the body, the slice of the sword, the calligraphic character—is a visual mark which is held in place by the *latent dynamics* of an invisible energy controlled by the body.

Animation is the privileged mode of what I call *the apparently-visual* world. It shows and reminds us that the world we see around us can be viewed as the markings and recordings of energy fields, transmissions and events—from the concentric rings tabulated to estimate a tree's age to the volcanic formations evaluated to gauge major geological transformations. Once one accepts that all matter is but momentarily held in place by unseen energies and forces whose change alters its condition, then the visuality of things is no more than a slight optical algae: slippery, alive and essentially non-objective. What we 'see' is a disconnected moment from a more expansive and enveloping continuum of events.

In this regard, the *animatic apparatus*—as a catalogue of machinic, technological and textual effects born of filmic animation—is the prime means by which we can perceive and comprehend the apparently-visual of the medium's verisimilitude as the result of frequency relationships in time and space. As I have postulated in 'The Animation of Sound',[3] the production of cel animation requires all sounds and images to be calculated and engineered according to temporal and spatial ratios of variance. Before any sense, meaning or effect can arise from an animated sequence, time (speed, rate, duration) and space (foreground, background, periphery) have to be arranged, orchestrated and conducted. While this is deftly conveyed through the acute timing and musical command of the wartime and post-war work by the Disney and Warner Bros. studios, the medium's potential for further mobilizing and radicalizing the animatic apparatus is not critically evident until the boom of *anime* in the early '80s.

It is in Japanese cel animation that the dynamic interaction between gesture, event, sound and image reaches an apogee, combining extreme mannerism with post-atomic contemplative states. Consequently, organic energies (air, water, steam, fire, and so on) collide with and/or fuse *immaterial* energies—psychic, cosmic, extra-terrestrial, spiritual, ectoplasmic. While we can easily see, for example, bodies, sword cuts and brush strokes around us, characters in the post-nuclear realm portrayed in '80s sci-fi *anime* just as easily sense *espers*[4] and feel psychic beams whose visual markings (their existence, their presence) exist in an immaterial domain.

Not surprisingly, the sonic—that most invisible yet most palpable energy—surfaces to govern the textuality of *anime*. Far from having the soundtrack submerged by *anime*'s imagery, image is immersed in *anime*'s soundtracks. This inversion of audio-visual logic (where convention dictates that sound subscribe to image) creates a *neumonic* effect, whereby sound is both material and referent. 'Neumonic' effects are the law court's hammer bang, radio's electronic whoops that command our attention, theatre's off-stage rooster crow and cinema's off-screen crickets that locate us within the story's time frame. These are not simply 'sound effects' which are interpreted at a base semantic level but sonic effects which buzz our aural consciousness and signal that a sign is being signified. Our brief analysis of the following scenes from '80s/'90s *anime* establishes some introductory concepts of (a) how the materialization of energy is narratively foregrounded in Japanese animation, and (b) how such audio-visualizations evidence textually and signify neumonically the nature of sound in our physical reality.

AKIRA

SCENE: Tetsuo attempts to escape the hospital

The character Tetsuo in *Akira* (1987, directed by Katsuhiro Otomo) is a quintessential *post-nuclear being*—one born of conditions which both redefine our physical reality and allow for the re-invention of the human form. He symbolizes the newness of such a being and in his naivete and innocence confuses his unique energy with adrenalin power, sending him to a state of abusive excess. His power is conveyed by his ability to exist beyond the putative constrictions of physical existence: he transforms physically; he projects psychically; he transports himself between spatial and temporal dimensions. Tetsuo's anger often erupts in a series of *shock waves,* hurling balls of energy which emanate from his being and rupture his surrounding physical surfaces. When he is trapped in the hospital corridor and is severely threatened, a psychic ball of energy erupts and pushes out the architecture of the corridor. Tetsuo's destructive bent is rendered by the recordings of power he leaves upon his immediate environment.

That image of Tetsuo left standing in the hospital corridor, centred by the negative spherical ball which breaks up the walls, floor and roof of the corridor, is one in which he has encoded or *recorded* his anger energy onto and into the physical surface of the corridor. This is exactly what happens in the aforementioned examples of the sword and the brush. We could break all these examples down thus:

agent	instrument	energy source	surface	mark
samurai	sword	arm/torso	victim's body	slice in the victim's flesh
artist	brush	arm/hand	paper	ink on the paper
Tetsuo	mind	psychic power	hospital corridor	curved indentations on walls, floor and ceiling

This model is nearly identical to the often-used characterization of how sound works, where sound waves are visually described as if air is water and the sound waves are like the concentric rings which form when one throws a stone into a pond. It is also analogous to the functioning of vinyl recording and speaker design (based on these same principles of expanding and contracting waves of energy) and can be broken down schematically as follows:

agent	instrument	energy source	surface	mark
thrower	stone	arm/hand	water	concentric ripples
sound	2 objects	collision between 2 objects	air	expansion/ contraction of air pressure
record lathe	diamond cutter	vibrations from recording	vinyl	spiral groove
record/ CD	speaker	vibrations from recording	speaker cone	inward and outward movement of speaker cone

AKIRA

SCENE: SOL satellite sends laser beam to the stadium to destroy Tetsuo

In the process of defining his post-nuclear being, Tetsuo undergoes the transition from dumb punk to psycho-techno Gargantuan.

Most of his scenes chart the upscale shift in degree from the human former to the post-human latter. In the first stadium confrontation between Tetsuo and Kaneda (and then between Tetsuo and the SOL satellite beam), the transition is symbolized by a fight between the *material* and the *immaterial*. This is represented respectively by visual displays of *spherical* and *linear* recordings of energy. Tetsuo is a material being battling the purity of a laser beam from Kaneda's gun, an immaterial line of energy which slices through all molecular density. Typical of post-'80s sci-fi *anime*, characters are defined by the nature, type and level of their energy. All post-nuclear beings have strange powers; the specificity and identity of their powers are the crux of their scenarios.

Remembering that in *anime* these powers and forces energize the space within which they occur, we find that *Akira* positions all spaces and environments to *capture the recordings of energy waves and lines*. Atomic bomb blasts leave huge craters downtown; an *esper*'s piercing scream shatters glass buildings; psychic energy causes subterranean chambers to rise and rupture the overground, etc. At its most extreme, the architecture of *Akira* is rendered not as solid form but as a network of recordable surfaces. Logically, the soundtrack of *Akira* highlights how energy waves and lines perform in this manner by exploring the various ways that sound can be temporally split from image, for we most notice the effect of sound when it does not obey the constricture of image. In Western photo-cinematic action films, the big boom of a dynamite explosion is always in sync with the visual ball of flame. In *Akira*, the sound of destruction is *asynchronous*. As a single percussive incident, it is mistimed to the visual moment of destruction; as an aural passage, it is delayed from the visual sequence of destruction.

The SOL satellite showdown exemplifies both forms of asynchronism. When Kaneda tries to shoot Tetsuo with a laser gun, Tetsuo hurls an energy ball toward him. As the veins build on his forehead in a spread of humoral tributaries, so does the concrete break up due to vein-like fault lines fanning out as if feeling the shock waves of an earthquake. The synchronous relation between the dynamic events (caused by agent, instrument, energy source and the mark on a surface—charted above) is thus extended and established as a running counterpoint to the visual action. Contrast this, for example, to the archetypically Western climax in *Carrie* (1976, directed by Brian De Palma): she twists her neck, eyes the door, the door instantaneously slams shut on cue to a violin stab. In *Akira*, instead of seeing and hearing one simultaneous explosion, we see and hear a gradual build-up of energy, from its projection to its eventual detonation. Following the breaking apart of the concrete on which he stands, Kaneda registers the loud explosions around him; but he is then caught off guard by the silence that follows, as falling pieces of concrete rain down on him. His reactions to the situation are as out-of-sync as the elaborately orchestrated soundtrack.

When the SOL satellite beam is first sent down to the stadium, the audio-visual delays in the Kaneda-Tetsuo fight are transformed into a complete dislocation between sound and image. The atmosphere becomes enveloped by a bright blue haze; a deadly silence befalls the scene; a thin ray of light appears; the gravity is altered as small pebbles slowly rise—and then the soundtrack erupts in a series of explosions as the ground is carved up by the beam, as if it is a gigantic samurai sword slicing across it.[5] Then, in response to this audio-visual rupture, Tetsuo beams himself up and past the threshold of the earth's atmosphere. There in space—where no sound exists due to the absence of atmosphere which could audibly register sound waves—Tetsuo rips apart the SOL satellite. Visual explosions appear, but the soundtrack is dead silent. The paradoxical quietness of this audio-visual dislocation is generated by a *dimensional split*, exporting us into a truly metaphysical realm wherein we can ponder the operation of sound-image relationships within such dimensional warps and shifts. On numerous occasions in *Akira*, the most devastating destruction is depicted in either total silence or with naught but a soft vocal tone or subtle deep rumble. In these scenes, the energy is so intense it appropriately appears to be beyond the recording range of the soundtrack. In *anime*, when the sound is so severely dislocated from its image, the apocalyptic 'big bang' is nigh but will never be heard.

LAPUTA

SCENE: Sheeta and Pazu clasp the levi stone and chant the 'charm of ruin' to destroy the sky castle

The balance of energies—how they lock into and against each another—is a fragile system. While we may intellectually appreciate the relations between microcosms and macrocosms, *anime* is notable for its reverence and respect of the same. Every energy source has its own threshold, its own location, its own environment of manifestation. One slight touch and everything is put out of balance. The apocalyptic finale in *Laputa* (1986, directed by Hayao Miyazaki) pictures this well. The monstrous, archaic construct of the floating sky castle suggests an unworldly presence of power, due to the gravity-defying spectacle of a solid rock castle floating in the air—an environment which also contains its own gravitational force governed by the central levi stone. When Sheeta and Pazu speak the charm of ruin ('Balse!'), they dislodge the sky castle's mystical power core, causing the whole energy system of the massive hovering rock to collapse and uncover the marvellous organic root system which drew life and sustenance from the ground surrounding the stone.

Sheeta's levi stone pendant is a miniature version of the sky castle's huge levi stone. This stone not only allows bodies to levitate. It also gravitationally binds bodies to it. As the sky castle falls apart, the inner core of energy—a bright blue spherical apparition—is revealed as the energy ball which attracts all surface material of the island (stone, ground, tress, roots, etc.). Just as the slight alteration of an underground tectonic plate can effect a major earthquake, so does the utterance of 'Balse!' cause the whole sky castle to collapse. Each creates a sonic vibration that unsettles a previously still surface—as the stone thrown in a pond creates concentric ripples. The sky castle's destruction is a visual rendering of the apocalyptic finality under which many pan-Pacific islands exist: any island enjoys stasis and equilibrium until sonic, tectonic and oceanic waves disturb it.

Characteristic of Hayao Miyazaki's eco-sci-fi,[6] the levi stones of *Laputa* are succinct visual symbols of macrocosmic eco-geological energies which hold the earth in place: planetary gravity, physical density, oceanic currents, and so on. The core levi stone of *Laputa* is remarkably similar to the deathly white orb which opens *Akira*. Each is a ball of energy that disturbs and destroys. In *Akira*, the energy ball sends a series of *outward shock waves* which raze the metropolis. In *Laputa*, the energy ball *inverts energy waves* to create a self-contained gravitational force for the floating island. Both are invisible energies which determine the visual landscapes of their environments; both exploit the animation medium's capacity to render such energies visible and determine the direction of their flow.

PATLABOR

SCENE: Fight between Ohta in a Shinohara and a renegade labor in a city canal

Patlabor (1991, directed by Mamoru Oshii) features many scenes where re-programed renegade industrial robots ('labors') wreak havoc by recklessly careering through Tokyo. In many respects, this figure of the gigantic monster or robot trampling the city underfoot fuses the gigantic spectral presences found in *yokai* folklore (beings the size of mountains suddenly materializing to destroy villages) with the mid-'50s to mid-'70s Toho cycle of monster movies (*Godzilla, Mothra, Ghidrah, Rodan, Gamera,* etc.). The stylized Toho movies particularly delight in destroying dioramas of Tokyo again and again and again. The semiotic baggage of *Godzilla* is too dense to detail here (nuclear radiation/mutation, urban decimation, American imperialism, post-war traumatization, etc.). Suffice to say that Japanese post-war entertainment embodies destructive principles and aesthetics, the legacy of its own nuclear devastation. *Patlabor* exhibits this base impulse to re-imagine the destructive, wherein the city—its landscape and architecture—is treated as the *surface* across which an agent of destruction leaves its visible mark. From helicopter view (uncannily recalling the telescopic perspectives of World War II air-borne bombing raids), the renegade labor has carved a line across the architectural order of the city's town planning. Like the calligrapher's ink on paper, the groove cut into the vinyl disc or the film of aerial bombing, the labor's path of destruction is clearly *recorded*.

In *Akira*, when Tetsuo turns the SOL satellite's laser beam against the earth below, shafts of light pierce the clouds, causing a rain of laser destruction to fall on Neo-Tokyo. Typical of much post-nuclear apocalyptic *anime*, lines, rays and beams of intense energy fall randomly across a metropolis, causing chaos and destruction, not unlike the infamous black rain of Hiroshima and Nagasaki. Despite the Western ignorance of the subtextual scarring which lines the underbelly of popular Japanese imagery, *anime* remains remarkably attuned to the effect Japan's past has on its current psyche. Irony is deeply folded into *Patlabor's* contemporary image of the city: the urban/domestic elements of police, citizens, robots and criminals are the agents of energy control and abuse. Rather than rays, beams or waves of light and sound carving up the landscape, here it is people and machines that tear the social fabric and architectural blueprint. As Ohta in his Shinohara droid battles the malfunctioning labor, he causes an equal amount of damage. Police and the criminal element wage their war, but the power and energy of each adversely affects the surrounding environment.

GIANT ROBO

SCENE: Dr Franken von Vogler short-circuits all Shizuma drives, causing the Notre Dame black-out

In a sublime fusion of the Gothic with the apocalyptic, an early scene from *Giant Robo* (1992, OVA series directed by Yasuhiro Imagawa) opens with the huge church bells of Paris' Notre Dame Cathedral clanging with the bodies of dead scientists—the death knell of old science for the city of the future. While these bells are not integral to the story of *Giant Robo*, the image of the bell is highly relevant to notions of sound.

The spherical design of bells allows them to resonate harmonically-tuned frequencies, so that sound waves created within the bell generate a complex sonic event which rings the whole bell, causing it to vibrate and send out a clear and rich tone capable of carrying across great distances. In essence, a bell is half-ball and half-megaphone: the dome of the upper-half rings and resonates while the aperture of the lower-half amplifies the ringing. When a bell resonates, it becomes energized by the force brought to bear on it and sends out a series of shock waves. The image of the bell's spherical upper-half is thus remarkably similar in both image and function to the sky castle's spherical lower-half in *Laputa* and the erupting spherical upper-half of the nuclear white orb in *Akira*.

Once the bells of Notre Dame have sounded, an expanding set of shock waves emanates from the central cathedral to eventually surround Paris. As a negative energy field drains the city of power, all lights are extinguished from the centre out to create a black hole. The knelling bells ring across the city and ominously signify the event of the energy drain; the blackout silently and visually follows the pattern of concentric circles which *neumonically replicates* a bell's own spherical wave formation. Once again, the visual is the recording of energy waves which rupture a material surface. Actually, the blackout is a macro-circle of energy drain that follows a micro-circle or internal circumference of Dr Shizuma's underground laboratory, which has risen to the surface to create a circular island of black energy, which then drains the surrounding area and later the globe.

As in many horror and Gothic-inspired scenarios, the earth covers the past, the dead and the forgotten. While Occidental Gothic sets its scenes near a graveyard of buried dead bodies who return to life to haunt the living, the 'Oriental Gothic' of *Giant Robo* functions according to a pan-Pacific logic: tectonic plates on the ocean floor are themselves markings of the earth's life in a previous epoch, waiting to rise up and destroy the present through a cataclysmic earthquake. The earth *is* the past. Dr Franken von Vogler—presumed dead and buried in the past—returns to haunt the prosperous city running on the Shizuma drives he invented by literally raising his underground laboratory to the surface to create a black hole of oppression.

MY NEIGHBOUR TOTORO

SCENE: King Totoro, Satsuki and Mei summon the tree to grow from the seedling patch

Just as destruction can result from an epic drain of energy (prominently figured in *Giant Robo* and in much post-apocalyptic scenarios from the East and the West), creation can embody what would normally be a destructive force. The energy utilized in the advent of either force grows from its opposite. Most examples discussed so far evidence ways in which a surface is ruptured, scratched, engraved, distorted, encoded, etc., by an *energized instrument* whose vibrations change facets and features of the surface, and thereby the surrounding space. In *My Neighbour Totoro* (1988, directed by Hayao Miyazaki), a key scene reverses this.

When King Totoro wills the tree to grow from the seedling patch, the tree sprouts forth from the earth: the ground is an energized surface which reacts to King Totoro's will and hyper-accelerates the tree's growth. In keeping with Miyazaki's perspective on the role eco-systems play in shaping our environment, the living earth gives birth to a living tree. This bi-polar model of energy flow—that which energizes and that which is energized—can be discerned in the mirroring of the underground root network by the overground branch structure. Here instruments and surfaces are energized *by each other*. The animated simulation of time-lapse photography portrays the invisible time line of the tree's life force, thereby acknowledging that the moment of our perception (the 'image' of the tree) is but a momentary intersection with another continuum (the 'life' of the tree).

As we have uncovered thus far, the apparently-visual world around us can be surmised as the recordings of past and dormant energy fields. The expansive terrain of post-'60s *anime* also freely inverts this metaphysical precept to project forward and view the apparently-visual as ground for that which might come to exist. Thus, the flat earth is a potential forest; the still pond has subsumed the stone thrown into its depths; a post-nuclear civilization is built upon the craters of death caused by bombs of the past. In fact, these are the key subtexts, commentaries and themes which drive the bulk of contemporary *anime*.

But perhaps the most forceful demonstration of this relationship between the latent/invisible/hidden energy of the ground and the manifest/visible/exposed energy of the tree lies in the haunting resemblance the sprouting form bears to the infamous 'mushroom cloud' of atomic bomb blasts. Consequently, such an image can cast the tree as violently rupturing the earth or cast a bomb blast as being part of a life-death cycle for a city. Each are exemplars of the bi-polar energy flow that is—philosophically, at least—accepted as the nature of life more by the East than by us in the West. This scene in *My Neighbour Totoro* is poignant and elegiac, yet it does not shy away from the power of metaphor it employs.

UROTSUKIDOJI

SCENE: The advent of Lord Chaos' reign and the Chojin in Akemi's womb in Osaka Temple

The sprawling *Urotsukidoji* (1992, directed by Hideki Takayama, the saga so far numbers nine episodes in two series, totalling just under ten hours) features most of the metaphysical and meta-textual aspects of Japanese animation discussed above: a fusion of dimensions; a collapse of space; an implosion of time; a collision of energies; an explosion of audio-visual conventions, and so on. Also, the numerous apocalyptic closures of *Urotsukidoji* clearly site an ongoing textual dialogue between linear energy lines which carve and slash cities and spherical explosions which engulf and digest complete atmospheres. Working within the operative generic codes of Japanese erotic horror animation, *Urotsukidoji* is distinguished by two co-joined sonic features which are pertinent to our discussion of neumonic functions in *anime*.

The first is the interpolation of on-screen dialogue with voice-over thoughts. Logically, a confounding complex of narration arises when a range of characters from different yet simultaneous dimensions psychically communicate with each other in which-ever dimension they momentarily reside, as well as engage in their own flashbacks, which occur in various dimensions where further psychic communication is carried on between dimensions. What is particularly noticeable in *Urotsukidoji* is how much plot and character development exists at this level, giving rise to intriguing narrative implications rarely explored in Western cinema. While the image track maintains a fixed location for a set scene, the soundtrack is fluid and multiple. Voice—inhabiting multiple locations—is the vehicle by which the soundtrack registers dimensional warps and demonstrates the neumonic role of the dialogue.

The second sonic feature of *Urotsukidoji* is the metaphorical use of sonar and aural figures to shape both narrative and soundtrack. In the film's climactic conclusion, the central character—Amano Jaku—engages in a dialogue with the as-yet unborn Chojin (Overfiend), who has been transported to the womb of Akemi and left to hibernate in the Osaka Temple. Akemi is suspended in a non-space, hair floating upward, as concentric rings of luminous sound waves emanate from her womb, while maidens chant to keep her alive in the Temple. The womb is a crucial symbol here, the sonar-tactile environment which shapes human experience to a remarkably sophisticated level prior to 'birth'. Enveloped in such a hyper-sonic domain, Chojin transmits his voice like a telepathic heartbeat across the converging dimensions resulting from Lord Chaos' destruction. At every level, this scene resounds with the sonic. Energy—that essence of the universe which is at the core of *Urotsukidoji's* labyrinthine plot—is materially centred in the womb of the unborn and psychically projected via waves of sound. At this point let us recall the still water disturbed by the catapulted rock, the earth by tectonic fractures, the metropolis by nuclear detonations. Now, the womb—symbolically and neumonically a universal drum of life in *Urotsukidoji*—is disturbed by the emergence of the Chojin, whose birth causes parallel dimensions to cataclysmically fold into each other.

Let us compare this to an Occidental vision of the nuclear demise of the metropolis in the live action film *Fail Safe* (1960, directed by Sidney Lumet). The final scene is a montage of still photos of New York married to a continuous high-pitched drone signifying the melted telecommunications between New York and Moscow. Such a finality rarely occurs in Japanese animation, as the soundtrack usually voices, announces or predicts that which shall ensue. Put simply, worlds (including Earth) often end; but music, sound effects and voice inevitably continue past the image, indicating literally or symbolically that life forces still exist and energy still radiates. The irony that *Fail Safe* surrenders in light of this comparison is that it attempts to end the world by de-animating both image (as photograph) and soundtrack (as silence)—the exact opposite of the audio-visual combines which drive much *anime*. Symbolically, we could liken the cyclical, open-ended nature of Eastern narrativity and its metaphysical dismissal of foreclosure to the acoustic phenomenon of *reverberation*, wherein the acoustic event always carries past its occurrences in both time and space and—most importantly—within a frame we can audibly perceive. In terms of *anime* narratives, this means that their story lines feverishly flow well past our Western barriers of death, matter and force.

AKIRA

SCENE: Opening title sequence

Somewhere between the audio-visual ruptures explored in the endings of both *Urotsukidoji* and *Fail Safe* is the opening title sequence to *Akira*. A flash appears on the horizon's edge, a huge ball of black energy grows and expands its circumference in sheets of white fallout, gravitating silently toward our location and engulfing the screen in silent white. *Fail Safe* is mute and immobile, incapable of witnessing and evidencing the very destruction which defines the purpose of its story. *Urotsukidoji* perversely images—excessively, repeatedly, continually—all that *Fail Safe* cannot bring itself to show. Rather than staging apocalyptic scenarios for spectacle, *Akira* positions us to experience a nuclear blast—and to live through it. Its white silence is a deathly visitation in the act of narration: we witness, we die, we live on.

Sound—the life of the sonic, the energy of its waves—orients this narration in profoundly mystical and life-affirming ways. The white screen gives way to the standard aerial cartographical perspective;

but this time the city is reborn, and the frail remnants of central Tokyo are held by thin bridges to the surrounding mainlands. The shimmering red and orange, the sinuous bridges, the pulpy morph of Tokyo's remains all evoke the image of a heart. And at its dead centre: the monstrous gaping crater left after the bomb drop which created Neo-Tokyo.

Accompanying this black void is the truly earth-shattering sound of taiko drums uniformly pulsing in huge, single, metronomic explosions. Herein lies perhaps the major *neumonic signifier* that shapes the fantastic, post-nuclear textuality of *anime*. The crater we see is the still and dead recording of an energy event (the bomb drop) which has left a physical impression of its energy field (as in the example of Tetsuo's rage in the hospital corridor). Remembering the concave aspects of previously discussed examples of speaker design, water displacement and bell tone, let us now note the structural relationship between a drum skin and its resonating chamber. Once struck, the drum skin is momentarily rendered concave, then convex, then a series of fluctuating shapes between the two, modulated by the proportionate shape-shifting of the drum chamber. In line with the symbolic purpose of *Akira's* political project, the neumonic signification of the figure of the crater can be summarized thus: just as the surface of the drum skin is traumatized by the force brought to bear on it, so do a nation's landscape and its inhabitants suffer an analogous psycho-geological scarring. And just as explosions in Japanese animation are rendered asynchronous, so does the present in *Akira reverberate* its past.

The figures of white screen + silence and black screen + sound stand at diametrically opposed peripheries of animation's audio-visual range, coupling visibility with deafness and audibility with blindness. They are the edges of the medium, signposted to declare that all spatio-temporal events in between can exist. It should be noted that all audio-visual texts have the potential to articulate radical sound-image configurations (as indeed does momentarily occur in Western live action cinema), yet it is in *anime* that their conventional fixity is liquefied as a vast reservoir of metaphysical possibilities. *Anime's* audio-visualization of energized spaces, surfaces, instruments and beings and their resultant neumonic and symbolic effects posit ways in which the latent can be manifested, the potential realized, and—most importantly—the sonic visualized and the visual 'auralized'.

NOTES

This paper has been excerpted from the in-progress work *Sonic Cinema: Technology, Textuality and Aural Narratology in the Cinema*. Some points on *Akira* and *My Neighbour Totoro* were previously raised in (a) the lecture *Apocalyptic Scenarios in Japanese Pop Culture*, delivered at the 1992 Melbourne International Film Festival, and (b) profiles on Katsuhiro Otomo, Hayao Miyazaki and *Urotsukidoji*, written for the exhibition catalogue *KABOOM!: Explosive Animation from America and Japan*, published by the Museum of Contemporary Art, Sydney, in conjunction with its eponymous exhibition of 1994. Thanks to Alan Cholodenko for his comments.

1 Japan's assimilation of Western culture is arguably heightened during the post-war American Occupation. Following America's departure from Japan in 1952, the '60s is marked by refractions and mutations of all Japan had assimilated, giving us their peculiar re-invention of a technological future under an Eastern logic. This period is as vital to the formation of contemporary Japanese culture as America's post-war baby-boom is to its own. It is generally regarded that the animation industry in Japan blossoms with the formation of the independent Mushi Studio under the leadership of Osamu Tezuka in the early '60s (culminating in the successful sale of *Tetsuwan Atom—Astro Boy*—to NBC in America).

2 The acknowledged *sensei* of virtually all modern *manga* conventions is Osamu Tezuka. Many stylistic traits of visualizing the inner psychological states of a character were defined in numerous of Tezuka's works between the mid-'60s and mid-'70s like *Eulogy to Kirohito*, *MW* and *Black Jack*. See 'Glimpse of a Fantastic World'—my program notes to the Osamu Tezuka Retrospective in the 1995 Melbourne International Film Festival catalogue.

3 An investigation of relationships between sound and image as engineered in the process of animation is detailed in my 'The Animation of Sound', in *THE ILLUSION OF LIFE: Essays on Animation*, ed. Alan Cholodenko (Sydney: Power Publications in association with the Australian Film Commission, 1991).

4 *Espers* is a Japlish term for beings who have extrasensory perception. Such characters—human, cyborg and robotic—have been staples of *anime* since the early '80s.

5 It has taken a decade for Western photo-cinematic action movies to even attempt this 'demetered' dramatic timing. The explosions of *Independence Day* (1996, directed by Roland Emmerich), for example, may have 'plausible' perspectival shifts (the corridor of death down Main Street USA has some slight delays which have been labouriously storyboarded for redundant comprehension), but the orchestral cues persist with moronic on-beat timing. Once again, nineteenth century Occidental musical conventions nullify the aural power of the soundtrack. Western cinema is neurotic when it comes to music cues, pathologically fearful that an audience will not 'feel' the 'mood' on cue. *Anime* is consequently as difficult for Spielberg fans to experience as free jazz is for Country & Western fans.

6 See 'Magic, Mayhem, Maelstroms'—my program notes to the Studio Ghibli Retrospective in the 1997 Melbourne International Film Festival catalogue.

2 The United States

Pronoun Trouble II: The Missing Dick

RICHARD THOMPSON

Over the past two and a half decades, Chuck Jones' *Duck Amuck* (1953) has become the Warner Bros. cartoon of choice to exemplify modernist sensibilities of various sorts, largely because the film makes itself so available as an example of self-reflexivity and as a catalogue of the material conditions of cinema. (In 1980 I wrote an article, 'Pronoun Trouble',[1] which called attention to some aspects of the film and so may be partly responsible for this privileging.) *Duck Amuck* finds Daffy Duck at the mercy of narrating forces determined to destroy (some of) the illusions expected in animated films. He is frustrated by an inappropriate soundtrack, childishly drawn backgrounds, distortion and violation of frame lines, etc. *Duck Amuck* is, of course, not the only animated film to work this area; but its extremity as an example, in conjunction with the new importance given to self-reflexivity (a staple of film comedy from early in the silent period) and related issues in the film theory of the 1970s, conjoined to privilege it.

If we want an example with which to examine the nature and changes of the post-World War II Warner Bros. cartoon, *Duck Amuck* is not a bad choice, particularly given its explicit questioning of character stability. Daffy Duck, the star of the film, is improperly drawn, coloured, voiced, backgrounded and sometimes erased, all in service of the questions: 'who am I?' and 'what does it mean to be who I am?' Certainly, since 1975, *Duck Amuck* has received far more attention than other post-war Warners cartoons, measured by articles, citations and book space devoted to it.

But Robert Clampett's *The Great Piggy Bank Robbery* (1946), among post-World War II Warner Bros. cartoons, provides a very different set of strategies and features, which have to do with World War II proper (as a source of images, iconography, reference) and with developments in Hollywood feature films across the war years. In this way, it is a model as valuable as, and complementary to, *Duck Amuck*.

Four topics flow from looking again at Robert Clampett's *The Great Piggy Bank Robbery*[2]: 1. the World War II years as a period of significant change for Warner Bros. animation; 2. a revised view of Clampett; 3. implications of the selection of cartoons put forward as models to represent the nature of post-war Warners animation; and 4. the relation of those cartoons to developments in Hollywood feature films of the period.

THE WAR AND CARTOON DEVELOPMENTS

Recent attention has been given to the WWII/post-war period of studio animation. For Philip Brophy, the World War II period marks the development of the cacophonous Warner Bros. cartoon. In contrast to classic Disney animation, which he terms symphonic, the elements of the cacophonic are: effects of speed; exigencies; excitations; explosions; syncopative deformation; and modernist deflation.[3] This notion implies a rearrangement of cartoon structures and operations, a movement toward extremes, including forms of self-consciousness ('modernist deflation'). One notable area of this ecstatic process is the increasing amount of attention given to character. By the end of the war, Warner cartoons have foregrounded character as the prime mover of the narrative, the focus of attention. Animated cartoons had always marketed themselves around series characters or 'stars' who continued through many individual cartoons, and this of course continued after the war. The significant shift in post-war Warners characters is their movement beyond the functional, instrumental needs of plot and gag into reflection on their feelings about situations, often taking the form of soliloquy (talking to themselves, and so to us) or else direct address to the audience, using these sorts of speech to present a more complex character than the pre-war Bosko, for instance.

Wartime cartoons expanded their imagery of violence to keep abreast of military topicality. *Blitz Wolf* (Tex Avery, 1942) and *Draft Horse* (Chuck Jones, 1942) are among many examples of war-time cartoons which show excessive and inescapable firepower and present this as legitimately anxiety-producing. In our example, *The Great Piggy Bank Robbery,* one sequence involves machine guns, hand grenades and a John Woo body count. The film also includes references to aircraft carriers, fighter planes, strafing and hand-to-hand combat techniques. Films such as these use a great many explosions (as an immediate index of unleashed, kinetic and indiscriminate energy), changing the aural rhythm and punctuation of the cartoons and adding to an effect of faster pace, narrative velocity.[4] The 'world' in which cartoon characters operated had usually been a dangerous place, and certainly this intensified in cartoons made during the war. Some uncertainty and disillusionment may have accompanied the post-war loss of a single clear focus for hostility (the Axis); and so, not surprisingly, animators found other targets. Notably, many post-war cartoons used metaphors for the interiorization of such violence, often with characters at the mercy of their own bodies and their own minds.

While Brophy is concerned with the cacophonic and the explosive, in *Seven Minutes* Norman M. Klein sees post-war cartoons as having two overall themes: consumerism and the domestic family unit.[5] The cartoons repeatedly use the family and consumerism as examples that such things cannot be counted on and cannot count for much, certainly not for stability nor for permanence. An implication of Klein's analysis is that what prevails, outlasts, returns, connects and *can* be counted upon to maintain its promise are character itself and the cartoon as form. In the face of cacophonic and explosive threat, the failure of consumerism and family, and rapid post-war change, character can be depended on to remain. Just to stay, to continue. No more than that.[6]

Threats to this particular security blanket, then, are extreme indeed when they arise—as they do in *Duck Amuck* and *The Great*

Piggy Bank Robbery. While the same threat powers each film, their responses are very different: Clampett's film is manic, over-the-top, and invites categorization as an anything-can-happen-in-a-cartoon film; *Duck Amuck* carefully pursues a single idea with Jones' usual syllogistic logic.

CLAMPETT AT WARNER BROS.

Brophy compares Walt Disney's production method, which he terms studio factory, with the Warner Bros. production unit organization in which four or five directors would each head their own separate production unit with their own writer, animators, background artist, etc. Some of these directors' units have come to be associated with particular methods or concerns. Tex Avery's films tested or emptied things of meaning by repetition, escalation or the sabotaging of logic. Conversely, Chuck Jones' films developed single syllogisms to an obsessive scale. On the other hand, Friz Freleng's films used very traditional comic technique in a functional, transparent style. It is hard to place Clampett's unit as the others have been because the sample is smaller. His unit produced fewer cartoons than the other major Warners units, his tenure at Warners running from 1935 to 1946 (therefore, not extending into the post-1947 period most familiar to general viewers today via television and video cassette circulation).[7]

A widespread view across a range of animation comment has held that rather than having a central concern, concept or vision, Clampett films have an operating principle marked simply by excess, an apoplectic race to follow gag with gag as rapidly as possible—a frenzy tending toward the out-of-control—as opposed to the cool, calculating construction work of the other animators. Seen by himself and others as a Harold Lloyd figure, Clampett was the personification of tireless ambition, a dynamo of self-promotion, a man without the need of a modest bone in his body. His work has often been situated as mainstream, with the slight negative implication that it is conservative in relation to his more formally experimental, subversive and intellectually sophisticated Warner Bros. colleagues and downright prim compared to the libidinous

Avery.[8] In Greg Ford's view, he was a craftsman of the frantic

> in whose madness there was even less method than in Avery's, and whose most undisciplined sproinging rubbery character-motion gave him some of the most eminently stretchable-bendable characters in Cartoon History, and whose anything-for-a-laugh temperament prophesized today's Sick or Black Humor...[9]

He has not been seen as notable for his work with structure or development, but rather as having a surrealist streak (*Porky in Wackyland* (1938) is the usual citation for this).

The *KABOOM!: Explosive Animation from America and Japan* exhibition, curated by Philip Brophy, and *THE LIFE OF ILLUSION* conference, convened by Alan Cholodenko, called specific attention to Clampett's work and prompted my retrospective interest. I had remembered *The Great Piggy Bank Robbery* as a simple parable about male role-playing which would confirm the received opinion regarding Clampett's work. But the film was not as simple as I had remembered.

THE FILM

The story has three sections: the first is set on a farm where Daffy Duck, the hero, apparently lives; the second is a fantasy dream sequence in which Daffy Duck plays Duck Twacy, private detective, and moves from Twacy's office to a haunted mansion; the third returns to the farm as Daffy Duck recovers from his dream.

The film begins with a long (in duration and proximity) left-to-right pan across an airbrushed farmyard scene backed by pastoral panpipes.[10] As the image cuts to the first shot of Daffy Duck, the soundtrack changes to agitato urban music—Raymond Scott's 'Powerhouse'—the sounds of excitement and impatience. Having established an ideal farm, the film wastes no time easing into its narrative concerns. Daffy's first line is 'Sufferin' succotash! Why don't he get here?' This opens a continuing device through the film: pursuing that 'he', that question, as possible answers are paraded past. 'He' who? Which 'he'?

Apparently not the postman, who is the next figure presented. All we get of him is a skirting-board cartoon metonym—a hand, letters, a postbox. He has brought Daffy a comic book featuring his hero, Dick Tracy. So for the moment, the 'he' in question is either the comic book hero, Tracy, or some other manifestation of Tracy for which the comic book stands. The arrival of the comic is a major event and is marked as such by a barrage of signing: a musical crescendo accompanying an elaborate long shot of Daffy tearing away from us across hills and dales against a cliché sunset or sunrise (even though the preceding and following shots take place at mid-day). Daffy arrives at his secret, private spot especially reserved for just this activity. Before opening the book, he savours the coming experience: 'You're here at last, and you're mine, all mine. I can hardly wait to see what happens... *I love that man!*'[11] Daffy then reads the story, acting or re-enacting it for us with such abandon that he knocks himself unconscious, but not before exclaiming, 'Oh boy! If only I could be Dick Tracy—I'd show those goony criminals!'

Clampett's *Piggy Bank* Daffy is more acutely expressive than versions of the character from other production units. The deployment of line, volume and elasticity in drawing the character's mouth, tongue and saliva creates a precise and simultaneous visual equivalent of his juicy, lubricious diction. Aurally and visually, the character presentation starts at a high pitch. (In the context of wartime iconography, perhaps this is the character as explosion. It is certainly highly cacophonous.) Awaiting the postman, Daffy coyly hides behind the postbox pillar, pretending not to be impatiently waiting, a pretense he can't maintain as his eyes, now independent of each other and his head, slide around the pillar to peek, looking like distended breasts. Similarly, encountering a gruesome threat to Tracy as he reads his comic book, Daffy slaps his hands over his eyes and shouts, 'Ooh, I hate to look!', at which point his eyeballs force their way from between his laced fingers back toward the threatening page. This first sequence also initiates the film's extreme use of noise rather than words, along with its modelling of words as noise toys ('Oh, a-go-ny, AG-OH-KNEE!'). Unlike versions produced by Jones or Freleng, for whom characters are vehicles for or conveyors of expression, Daffy Duck in this film simply *is* expression, often an expression of contradiction—the simultaneous and equal realization of opposites. (I can't look; I must look.)[12]

THE DREAM SEQUENCE

Unconscious now, in his fantasy, Daffy becomes a present version of something unshown by (absent from) the film: Dick Tracy, an extremely popular character created by Chester Gould as a newspaper comic strip hero in 1931.[13] This initiates a general induction of World War II-centred material—film noir, hardboiled writing, military iconography—and a more specific induction, from the World War II period, of villains—figured as grotesques—from Gould's daily strip.[14] *Dick Tracy* was at the height of its popularity in the late 1940s, appearing not only as a daily and Sunday comic strip but as a radio show, movies, comic book and book-length reprints series, not to mention marketing tie-ins. As the strip developed, Gould began to create a gallery of grotesque villains whose names reflected their physical abnormalities, beginning with The Blank in 1937 (no features, an unmarked facial surface), followed by Pruneface, Little Face, B.B. Eyes, 88 Keyes, The Brow and Flat-Top. The drawing of Tracy's jaw-line and nose became more and more exaggerated, exceeding the limits of anatomical probability by the time of *Piggy Bank Robbery*. The strip's drawing style developed from an undifferentiated, utilitarian presentation of busy frames into a bold, expressionist use of line, edge and shadow, still in harsh black and white (eschewing the various grey tone processes taken up by most other comic strip artists in the 1940s), but by the mid-1940s using much more black than in the 1930s. By this time, Gould's strip had become markedly more cinematic than in the 1930s, showing a new concern with unusual shot angles, more effective organization of emphasis in the frame and much greater attention to varying the nature of frames as they succeed each other—an understanding of close-up, medium shot, etc., and their interrelation as editing if not montage.[15] Jules Feiffer remembers comic book and comic strip artists of the period paying attention to this:

> We were a *generation*. We thought of ourselves the way the men who began movies must have. We were out to be splendid—somehow. In the meantime we talked at our drawing tables about Caniff, Raymond, Foster. We argued over the importance of detail. Must every button on a suit be shown? Some argued yes. The magic realists of the business. Others argued no; what we wanted, after all, was *effect*. The expressionists of the business. Experiments in the use of angle shots were carried on. Arguments raged: Should angle shots be used for their own sake or for the sake of furthering the story? Everyone went back to study *Citizen Kane*. Rumors spread that Welles, himself, had read and learned from comic books![16]

Daffy's impersonation differs from the Tracy original in two ways: he becomes a private eye rather than a policeman like Tracy; and he does not become Dick Tracy, he becomes Duck Twacy. At the point when urban nighttime replaces the farm's pastoral sunshine, the film becomes a case of the missing (or substituted) Dick, which re-complicates the search for the 'he', which is not fully satisfied by the partial or split identity offered by Duck Twacy. There is now an unrecovered excess, a Dick—which we've never seen but have been referred to—traded for a Duck serving as Dick. 'Not fully satisfied' certainly for narrative reasons. Just as the initial mechanism of walking is falling forward (the second mechanism is interrupting the fall by putting a foot down), narrative moves forward by 'falling' into openings, absences, spaces; and, as this is the middle of the film—that is, the narrative is not ready to stop yet—satisfaction must continue its deferral. But in a larger sense, the possibility now arises that the logic of the film may not include satisfaction.

Daffy, as detective 'Duck Twacy', turns down offers to investigate missing piggy banks as too minor to bother with (beneath the dignity of a Private Eye), judging others harshly: 'Why don't people take care of their piggy banks?' Two points here: Daffy takes the high moral ground vis-à-vis others; and he defines the terms of the problem as piggy banks per se rather than whatever they might contain or represent. The possible contents are ignored, a non-issue, an emptiness.

With a self-congratulatory flourish, Daffy opens his office safe to demonstrate his own prudential care—and horrors! His own piggy bank is missing. The safe is entirely empty, too. (It only ever held his piggy bank.) This is an instance of Sylvain du Pasquier's doubled inversion logic of gag structures: in the first half, the container—the piggy bank—is important and the contents are not; in the second half, the container—the safe—is unimportant and the contents (missing) *are* important.[17] The over-the-top reaction to the comic book's arrival is here echoed in the inflating of the significance of this calamity through a trope of losing and then belatedly remembering one's identity. Twacy frantically telephones for help: 'Calling Duck Twacy! Calling Duck Twacy! Come in, Twacy!' Then a double take: 'Hey! What's the matter with me! *I'M* Duck Twacy!'

Daffy/Twacy begins his mission, which is not to solve a crime (wave)—this will happen subordinately—but to retrieve his own piggy bank. Not its contents. The possibility that it might contain anything is never mentioned. In fact, the bank is now personalized by being named. It is not a he but a she: Velda.

It is at this point in the narrative that, in an earlier draft of this essay, I made an error. I assumed the usual sequential relation between a cartoon parody and its (apparently) prior model. I presented Velda as a very topical reference to Mickey Spillane's first Mike Hammer novel, the pop culture icon *I, the Jury* (1947), a huge best-seller[18] in which Velda is Hammer's secretary and, when kidnapped, quest object. As does Duck Twacy, Mike Hammer uses extreme violence rather than ratiocination: shooting first often saves the trouble of having to frame a question. In that earlier draft, I said: 'This is notable not in service of some case for Clampett's awareness of film noir (which as a concept and term would not begin to have much circulation until the 1955 publication of Raymond Borde and Etienne Chaumeton's *Panorama du film noir américain*) but rather as an example of the Clampett unit's quick response time and smart selection of references across a range of popular U.S. media'. Certainly, like *Dick Tracy* and *Dragnet*, Mike Hammer was a frequent parody subject in the 1950s. (See particularly Walt Kelly's 'Mucky Spleen: The Bloody Drip' and his sequel, 'The Bloody Drip Writhes Again (from Gore Blimey)'[19]; and the 'Girl Hunt Ballet' in Vincente Minnelli's *The Band Wagon*.)

But this blithe assumption of cartoon's automatic subservience to other media conveniently ignores chronology. The cartoon was released in the middle of 1946. *I, the Jury* was published in 1947, a year later. The unusualness of the name Velda raises the possibility that Spillane swiped her from a Daffy Duck cartoon, a possibility perhaps slightly increased by the fact that Spillane's first writing jobs were doing story continuity for comic books. He was part of the world of commercial comic art. On the other hand, both *The Great Piggy Bank Robbery* and *I, the Jury* may well be drawing upon currents flowing through popular fiction at the time. Or both.

Hitting the streets, Twacy takes part in two brief blackout scenes which again fall into du Pasquier's 1-2 inversion patttern. Taken together, the two scenes show Twacy actually undertaking a search, a journey toward locating his piggy bank, in this sense, a necessary bridge between Twacy's realization of his lack and the spectacular concluding set piece of Twacy's story. In the first scene, Twacy stalks the sidewalks with magnifying glass, looking for clues; bumps into Sherlock Holmes doing the same, coming from the other screen direction; and asserts dominance by dismissing the great detective: 'Scram, Sherlock, I'm working this side of the street!' No progress toward solving the mystery problem, but a pointed contribution to the paradigmatic development of Twacy's character, as well as a reminder that *Piggy Bank Robbery* follows in the footsteps of the watershed dream/detective film, Buster Keaton's *Sherlock, Jr.* (1924), as does *Duck Amuck*, in its own way. In the second scene, Twacy encounters a tram driven by Porky Pig (a cameo role). The tram's destination window reads 'GANGSTER'S HIDEOUT', a location also pointed to by proliferating arrow signs. Twacy boards and duly arrives at the old dark house in which his story will finish. In this scene, progress is made toward solving the mystery, but that progress is supplied to Twacy rather than by Twacy.

Twacy explores the house, alternately exhibiting bravado and cowering terror. Finally, he is confronted by a coven of Chester Gould's *Dick Tracy* bizarre villains: Bat Boy, Neon Noodle, The Wolf Man, Rubber Head, and so on. Twacy takes them on. (This is the scene referred to above in which a great deal of military technology is represented.) Finally, Daffy tricks most of the grotesques into a closet, locks the door and laces it with machine gun fire. Then he opens the door in a climactic low-angle shot borrowed from William Wellman's *Public Enemy* (1931), the one in which James Cagney's mummy-wrapped body pitches into the camera. Typically, in Clampett's excessive recreation, dozens of bizarre, bullet-riddled bodies tumble forward domino-fashion.

The most serious menace comes from Rubber Head, the corrective end of a lead pencil. Rubber Head corners Twacy, taunting 'I'm gonna r-r-r-rub ya out!', which he proceeds to do, erasing Twacy from the screen, metaphorically threatening to remove Twacy/Daffy from the film entirely.[20] Twacy perseveres. Over the bodies of his enemies he enters a vault filled with all the missing piggy banks he had no time for, now given an increased value not only indexed by Twacy's own bank having been stolen but also by the combat, the deaths, the threat of erasure, that have passed since the scene in Twacy's office. (It is worth noting here that the film never explains how Twacy's bank was stolen, a Sphinx-like cryptic approach to plot points associated with Howard Hawks' *The Big Sleep* (1946) or Jacques Tourneur's *Out of the Past* (1947).)

In any case, as one would expect in a post-war Warners cartoon, niceties of plot are less important than character. Locating his Velda, Twacy clasps it to his body (which he had so recently lost, if only briefly, providing another—quickly closed—avenue for the question: 'He who?'). He showers it with kisses—and not the derisive, mocking kisses earlier versions of Bugs and Daffy have reserved for Elmer Fudd either. Kisses of passion and desire. Twacy speaks to it, to Velda: 'My own, my very own little piggy bank!'

RESOLUTION (?)

The Great Piggy Bank Robbery is articulated by such delirious, hysterical moments: the arrival of the comic book; the identification through reading it which results in un-(or other-)consciousness, the transport into the dream state; the threat of erasure; the saving release of ecstatic machine gun firepower. This moment of reunion with Velda is one of them. Transformed by its own excess of energy, the dream ends and is replaced by a return to the pre-dream diegetic situation: back on the farm, but this time in a medium shot of the pigpen we first saw fleetingly at the end of the film's first shot. Twacy is now gone—or he is Daffy again? Yet the power of his passion for Velda bridges the transition between the two diegetic worlds. Daffy is now embracing not a miniature model of a pig (Velda the piggy bank) but a full-size, live sow, who flirtatiously asks him if he'd like to dance.

With knowledge (the delayed realization of the substitution of real for replica—the realization of the pig), Daffy's desire turns to disgust. Beyond language for once,[21] he makes a 'Ptui!' gesture and sound and exits the frame. This is unusual for a post-war Warners cartoon, the final images of which are nearly always of the cartoon's star(s). But here, the ultimate image is that of the sow, a new player, who closes the dialogue by recovering the film's opening claim—*'I love that man!'*—and redirecting it: *'I love that duck!'* Once again, the film has arranged for the object of the speech of desire to be missing, absent or deferred. Whatever the piggy bank represented in the dream sequence cannot be sustained or matched in the daily world.

Not quite as austere as *Duck Amuck* (doggedly committed to its one-joke structure), The *Great Piggy Bank Robbery* is a rare case of a cartoon carried by just one character and consistently interested in that character's inner state. In place of character interaction (that is, in the absence of a co-star as opponent or foil), the narrative pursues a process of deferral or slippage, a shuffle which continually puts off (or aside) stabilizing the key referent, persistently rejigs questions and potential answers regarding the object of closure. Starting with the vexed and sometimes gender-misleading pronoun 'he', it slips from the comic book to 'Dick Tracy' to Duck Twacy to a (missing) piggy bank (Pig 1, the fetish version) to the real pig, the sow (Pig 2, the real and rejected pig) to, finally, the unspecified (and unspecifiable, because off-frame). At its conclusion, the film leaves unanswered questions, among them, who or what is desired? And who desires?

ROSEBUD

Seeing the film in this way allows relations to be drawn with other post-war film developments. As today television is frequently the raw material of television comedy, so live action features were for studio cartoons. At Warner Bros. in the 1930s, a popular format was the Hollywood revue cartoon, featuring gags strung together around a situation—a night at the Brown Derby, for instance—rather than a narrative, in which one-liners, black-outs and short skits featured caricatures of popular stars of the day. (Robert Clampett did more than his fair share of these, with gusto. Of all the Warner animators, he seems most frequently to refer to film material in his work.) This earlier recycling of Hollywood material was restricted to citation and exaggeration of physical appearance, voice, tag lines, mannerisms, and the recreation of key moments and iconic and generic images from popular features. *Great Piggy Bank Robbery*'s induction of Chester Gould's graphics, military imagery and hardboiled, noir iconography is a post-war continuation of this surface parody/caricature procedure, imitating characteristics through exaggeration.

Standing between such 1930s revues and *Piggy Bank* are major changes. The single event with which film history usually represents these changes is *Citizen Kane* (1941). Three months before its release, Orson Welles said of the hero, Kane: 'He is never judged with the objectivity of an author, and the point of the picture is not so much the solution of the problem as its presentation'.[22] It is at this moment that a new sort of popular cinema becomes possible, one in which films can be deliberately ambiguous, contradictory, non-judgmental, enigmatic. It is in this context that Velda the piggy bank joins Rosebud, Dashiell Hammett/John Huston's Maltese Falcon and the summary wisdom of Preston Sturges' *Sullivan's Travels*[23] (all from 1941). These things—objects, names, words—are used throughout their respective films as lightning rods to attract and condense an expectation of meaning or significance far greater than that which is finally delivered; and while this disparity may occur in films and fictions of other periods, what is of interest here is that films of this period and type raise it to an explicit level. It is an issue in these films' address to the audience, making an ironic (in the precise sense of irony: a difference in levels of knowledge) point or joke about that misplaced expectation of meaning as closure or closure as satisfaction. These (narrative) rhetorical questions shrink upon inspection and in so doing strategically open up correspondingly larger narrative areas for which they become the negative space (or obverse/reverse), and so, in a clever way, also the signpost. The search for Rosebud fails but at the same time sets out all the issues *Citizen Kane* wishes to parade.[24]

The Great Piggy Bank Robbery fits interestingly into the films flowing from *Citizen Kane*—quest films, melodramas of desire, enigma films, film noir. Clearly, in this film Clampett raised his recycling of material from feature films to a new level, one including but no longer limited to play with characteristics, appearances, imitation. The film inducts larger, more complex narrative devices. One is that key figure of post-war American film and fiction, the detective, used: 1. to structure and direct the narrative, to double it over upon itself so that it becomes also the story of its own past; 2. to express a world view and set of values commonly called hardboiled; 3. to examine notions of truth—what can and cannot be known, discovered, analyzed; and 4. to index the individual and social cost of seeking such knowledge. Duck Twacy is more Mike Hammer than Philip Marlowe. He retrieves his Velda not by using his brain but by out-shooting the mob. Daffy Duck's participation in the detective fantasy has produced change—a trajectory from the anticipation of the fulfilment of desire to rejection and disgust reminiscent of Welles' *The Lady from Shanghai* (1947)—but no progress. *Great Piggy Bank Robbery* is one of many 'empty quest' films which call attention to the hollowness of answers, the final results of achieving a mission, completing a search.

Like many contemporary features—Otto Preminger's *Laura* (1944), for instance, or Fritz Lang's *The Secret beyond the Door* (1948)—*The Great Piggy Bank Robbery* enfolds its detective activities within desire and desire's vehicle, obsession. Daffy desires his comic book. He is obsessed with Tracy and with becoming Tracy, which he does, at the same time establishing a new desire object, Velda. But the theme of such films is the futility of desire. Desire is unfulfillable, is always one step beyond what can be had. Clampett builds his film around a dream sequence, a frequent narrative feature of the period. (See Dmytryk's *Murder, My Sweet* (1944); Leisen's *Lady in the Dark* (1944); Hitchcock's *Spellbound* (1945); *Secret Beyond the Door*.) By proposing a second state of consciousness or reality within the film's world, dream sequences automatically set in motion a comparison between these two states, making explicit the status of both as subjective, arbitrary or unstable constructs. (Each of the interview flashbacks in *Citizen Kane* does this work as well). *Piggy Bank Robbery* also uses the dream to centre the theme of *l'amour fou*, first raised with relation to the *Dick Tracy* comic book and in the dream transferred to Velda—a passion beyond reason, its own first and last principle, and consequently doomed, if not outright destructive (Lang's *Scarlet Street* (1945); Garnett's *The Postman Always Rings Twice* (1946); Vidor's *Duel in the Sun* (1947); Lewis' *Gun Crazy* (1949)).

The film does its most impressive work of induction at a third level of structure, the deepest one. It is not structured as a series of progressive-sequential-dependent actions moving toward a final accomplishment or contest which will result in apparent closure (as most of the studio cartoons of the period were). On this level, *The Great Piggy Bank Robbery* is built on a series of deferrals. The answers supplied to the film's questions are never sufficient as answers, as finishes of their respective sub-narratives. Instead, they serve to change the question or to substitute a new one (the mechanism and the rhythm of the stage magician's one-ahead principle), denying the narrative—and the audience—specifics and certainties, keeping the narrative moving, certainly, but not in the usual simple linearity, rather in a step-slide, step-slide pattern. This post-*Kane* pattern is that of the cinema of ambiguity and of the ongoing futility of desire; and for *The Great Piggy Bank Robbery*, it can only be concluded by Daffy's removal.[25]

NOTES

1 Richard Thompson, 'Pronoun Trouble', in *The American Animated Cartoon: A Critical Anthology*, eds. Danny and Gerald Peary (New York:

E.P. Dutton, 1980). A different, earlier version appears as '*Duck Amuck*', *Film Comment*, vol. 11, no. 1, January-February 1975.

2 A Looney Tune, released July 20, 1946. Director: Robert Clampett. Story: Warren Foster. Animation: Rod Scribner, Manny Gould, C. Menendez and I. Ellis. Layouts and Backgrounds by Thomas McKimson and Philip De Guard. Voice characterization: Mel Blanc. Musical Direction: Carl W. Stalling. Source: Jerry Beck and Will Friedwald, *Looney Tunes and Merrie Melodies: A Complete Illustrated Guide to the Warner Bros. Cartoons* (New York: Henry Holt and Company, 1989), p. 169. The version consulted for this paper is included in the laserdisk collection *The Golden Age of Looney Tunes*, vols. 1-5 (Culver City: MGM/UA Home Video, 1992). This collection, along with *The Compleat Tex Avery* (Culver City: MGM/UA Home Video, 1993), provides a deep sampling of the pertinent work of Clampett and his colleagues.

3 Philip Brophy, 'The Animation of Sound', in *THE ILLUSION OF LIFE: Essays on Animation*, ed. Alan Cholodenko (Sydney: Power Publications in Association with the Australian Film Commission, 1991).

4 In this way, cartoon explosions are very like the bass drum accents developed in the World War II and immediate post-war years by bebop jazz drummers Kenny Clarke and Max Roach in that they were surprising, catching the audience unexpectedly, and so rearranged the rhythmic pattern. Suggestively, jazz musicians of the period referred to these big bass coups as 'dropping a bomb'.

5 Norman M. Klein, *Seven Minutes: The Life and Death of the American Animated Cartoon* (London: Verso, 1993), Chapter 20, 'Chase Cartoons after 1947: Consumer Graphics', pp. 206-217.

6 *The Great Piggy Bank Robbery* is one of a few examples of threats to this 'staying'. The erasure of Daffy by the giant pencil Rubber Head is the threat at its most concrete as the continuity guarantees of the Daffy character are lost from the visual track and carried only by the soundtrack. *Duck Amuck* is the frequently cited and extreme example.

7 Reversing the general movement of animation production from independence to a place in the large studio structure, Clampett left Warners in 1947 to establish his own production company. In 1949, he made an extremely successful move into television with a children's puppet show, *Time for Beanie* (later an animated TV series as well). Clampett was an excellent marketer of his characters and of himself. Years before Jones or Avery gained any wider public recognition, Clampett became one of the two animated cartoon producers known by name across

the land. (The other was Walt Disney.) He consolidated this in the 1970s in a series of campus lectures and public appearances. See Jeff Lenburg, *The Great Cartoon Directors* (New York: Da Capo Press, 1993), pp. 119-121. This success and public profile, along with his penchant for claiming to have 'invented' major characters such as Bugs Bunny and for not sharing credit with his collaborators, probably fuelled his colleagues' criticism of him. In the late 1970s, Chuck Jones privately circulated a six page letter of December 11, 1975 from Jones to Avery (with Avery's handwritten marginal responses) attacking Clampett's claims in considerable detail.

8 'Sex? It either embarrassed—as when the silkworm knits a brassiere for Porky Pig in *Porky's Party* (1938), triggering a mortified blush—or disinterested him [Clampett]'. Patrick McGilligan, 'Robert Clampett', in *The American Animated Cartoon: A Critical Anthology*, eds. Danny and Gerald Peary, p. 153.

9 Greg Ford, 'Warner Brothers', *Film Comment*, vol. 11, no. 1, January-February 1975, p. 13. See also Tim Onosko, 'Bob Clampett: Cartoonist', *The Velvet Light Trap*, no. 15, Fall 1975; and Mike Barrier and Milton Gray, 'Bob Clampett', *Funnyworld*, no. 12, Summer 1970.

10 The airbrushed look always seems to idealize its subject. This is helped by its stylistic echo of the paintings of Thomas Hart Benton.

11 It is misleading to say, 'Emphasis added—RT', because nearly all of Daffy's dialogue is emphasized by delivery, diction, gesture. It is all bold face verging on headline type. The Daffy Duck in the Chuck Jones unit's post-war cartoons mutters, sneers, complains, agonizes, and for moments of particular emphasis raises his voice. By contrast, screaming and shouting are the default setting for Clampett's Daffy. But I do want to call particular attention to these four words.

12 Sigmund Freud comments on such phenomena in 'Fetishism' (1927), The Pelican Freud Library, vol. 7, *On Sexuality: Three Essays on the Theory of Sexuality and Other Works*, ed. Angela Richards and trans. James Strachey (Harmondsworth: Penguin, 1977); and 'Splitting of the Ego in the Process of Defence' (1940), The Pelican Freud Library, vol. 11, *On Metapsychology: The Theory of Psychoanalysis*, ed. Angela Richards and trans. James Strachey (Harmondsworth: Penguin, 1984). The extension of this line of thought into film theory is usefully summarized in 'The Spectator' section of Chapter IV, 'Psychoanalysis', in Robert Stam, Robert Burgoyne and Sandy Flitterman-Lewis, *New Vocabularies in Film Semiotics* (London: Routledge, 1992), pp. 146-158.

13 *Dick Tracy*'s first appearance was on Sunday, October 4, 1931 in the

Detroit Mirror. Daffy's ecstatic relation to the arrival of his comic book displaces everything else. He apparently has no life other than a vicarious one as reader/audience, exactly the situation of Al Capp's comic strip hero L'il Abner, who avidly awaited the arrival of another parody of Dick Tracy—Fearless Fosdick—with a key difference: in Capp's version, reading Fosdick distracted L'il Abner from the domestic and sexual obligations expected by his wife, Daisy Mae. I have not yet been able to establish whether or not Fosdick preceded *The Great Piggy Bank Robbery*; in any case, the two parodies interestingly intersect at an obsession with a comic book hero which displaces (other) sexual activity.

14 At least two are specifically cited from Gould's strip: 88 Keyes, named in Twacy's on-screen dialogue, and Flat-Top, not named but drawn à la Gould.

15 See Chester Gould, *The Dick Tracy Casebook: Favorite Adventures, 1931-1990* (New York: St. Martin's Press, 1990); and Chester Gould, *The Celebrated Cases of Dick Tracy, 1931-1951*, ed. Herb Galewitz (New York: Chelsea House, 1970). For the expressionist claim, see particularly the reproductions on pp. 204 and 218 in Pierre Couperie et al., *Bande dessinée et figuration narrative* (Paris: Musée des arts décoratifs, 1967).

16 Jules Feiffer, *The Great Comic Book Heroes* (New York: Dial Press, 1965), p. 51. See also pp. 29-30.

17 Sylvain du Pasquier, 'Buster Keaton's Gags', ed. and trans. Norman Silverstein, *Journal of Modern Literature*, vol. 3, no. 2, April 1973.

18 Spillane and/or his publishers claimed that his Mike Hammer novels had sold more copies than the Bible.

19 In Walt Kelly, *Uncle Pogo So-So Stories* (New York: Simon & Schuster, 1953), and Walt Kelly, *The Pogo Peek-A-Book* (New York: Simon & Schuster, 1955), respectively.

20 Clampett uses this opportunity to break the production code censorship guidelines—in a dream sequence, of course—joining a long line of Hollywood studio feature filmmakers who delighted in the in-joke game of getting around these restrictions. As Rubber Head erases Twacy's image from the screen, Twacy comments on his own disappearance: 'Fantastic! And furthermore, it's unbelieva...', at which syllable he vanishes from the shot, erased. One beat, then an adjacent door opens screen left, Twacy sticks his head out and utters the completing, and production code proscribed, syllable: 'Bull!' As Gloria Grahame would have said had she been in this film instead of Minnelli's *The Bad and the Beautiful* (1952), 'You're a very naughty boy, Bobby Clampett...

I'm happy to say'. As I indicated in note 6, the erasure device figures prominently, later, in *Duck Amuck.*

21 A comico-logical conclusion to the film's various efforts to turn words into physical things.

22 Orson Welles, '*Citizen Kane* Is Not About Louella Parsons' Boss', *Friday 2*, February 14, 1941, p. 9. Reprinted in *Focus on Citizen Kane*, ed. Ronald Gottesman (Englewood Cliffs: Prentice-Hall, 1971), p. 68. A useful recent summary of critical positions around *Kane* and a revaluation of the film upon its fiftieth anniversary is Laura Mulvey's *Citizen Kane* (London: British Film Institute, 1992).

23 At the conclusion of this complex, sophisticated comic epic, the hero sums up the results of his quest for truth and the meaning of life in the final words of the film: 'And I'll tell you something else: there's a lot to be said for making people laugh...did you know that's all some people have? It isn't much...but it's better than nothing in this cockeyed caravan... [He shakes his head reminiscently] Boy!' Preston Sturges, *Five Screenplays by Preston Sturges*, ed. Brian Henderson (Berkeley: University of California Press, 1985), p. 683. This may be at the shaggy dog end of Rosebud, but it is the same mechanism.

24 One of the blackest versions of this is Samuel Fuller's *Shock Corridor* (1963), another quasi-newspaper film, in which an investigative reporter goes underground in a state mental hospital to answer the question, 'Who killed Sloan with a knife in the kitchen?' The question repeats during a *Kane*-like, Kurosawa *Rashomon*-like set of overlapping and differing eyewitness acounts which, again *Kane*-like, serve to provide a rich critique of the U.S. at the time. The reporter hero, Barrett, finally solves the murder mystery; but the cost of that knowledge is that he himself becomes terminally insane.

25 So while Feiffer's comic artists went back to study *Citizen Kane* for its innovative expressionist style, Clampett may have gone back to study it too, but for its treatment of character and narrative, of the enigma of identity and the futile pursuit of desire, as well as for its irresolvable ambiguities of meaning, truth and reality in and of the world.

Between the Legs of the Mermaid

EDWARD COLLESS

Every story is the excuse for an image. This is no exception. My image is both familiar (to the degree of being overexposed) and also obscure (if not cryptic, then murky). It is a frame grabbed from a scene in the perennially popular TV series *Baywatch* of the character CJ Parker, played by Pamela Anderson. In the scene from which this image is lifted, CJ has been accidentally knocked unconscious while out on a rescue mission in the surf and is slowly sinking underwater. The still image is ambiguous because, as a low angle shot taken most likely in a studio tank, there is no incidental scenery to provide clues about this story: no weed, no fish, no white water, no other characters. The only scenery to speak of is a naturalistic light from above filtering down through the water, breaking up, dancing about, silhouetting CJ's body. And of course, this is complemented by a necessary but unnaturalistic light from the sides and below to 'fill' the silhouette of Pamela Anderson's well known and voluptuous figure. Her body is, justifiably, the essence of this image; and this body becomes unreal because its setting is devoid of any signs of scale, proportion or dimension. The water in which CJ is drowning is consequently a strangely empty or at least abstract substance which envelopes and suspends her in order to expose, for a momentary delight, the actor's luxuriant body. The odd, artificial flicker of light in the water around her abstracts time as well as space. There is no functional 'up' and 'down' in the image, nor is there any practical meaning to 'before' or 'after' what her body is doing. This moment of delight disengages from the story much like a spent rocket stage falling away in orbit.

Water is the focus for the dramatic action of *Baywatch*. The climaxes usually require 'ironman' or 'ironwoman' athletic prowess in water or on its edges. The show's slow passages illustrate casual beach sports by extras. If anyone lounges about, sunbathing for instance, it is still healthy recreation and so a type of activity because it is organized around the warm California sun and the *mythos* of bathing—its baptismal, regenerative powers which depend upon its cultivated pleasure. The show's lifeguards are more like the retinue of Dionysius than officiating Baptist priests: they guide the rest of us toward the orgy. All activity in *Baywatch* is conducted under the supervision of *erōs*, which is to say all the action in the show is ultimately erotic.

But this is no cheap paradise; people still get into trouble on the beach. The characters deal with persistent social and personal problems—divorce, bereavement, career rivalry, lovers' tiffs, drug abuse, debt—and there are also natural calamities, like storms, landslides and earthquakes frequently afflicting the beach community. All the scores, however, get settled in the water. The water is the medium both for the show's conflicts and for their usually agreeable resolution. This water is, after all, the *Pacific* ocean—an ocean you could (if you respected its currents and winds) cross on a dinghy, an ocean that doesn't race in the way the Atlantic does.

When this water consumes a lead character like CJ Parker—an iconic figure of the contemporary Californian beach girl—it becomes an abstraction of the TV show's 'real' Pacific ocean. Something like an essence of that ocean (and thus of the TV show's iconography) is claiming her—absorbing her and yet keeping her intact. In this image, she is like a specimen preserved in formaldehyde, except that there is no container visible and so no limit to the medium in which she hovers. It is as if there is no violence to the image because one cannot imagine it any other way. Pamela Anderson is floating in the depths of this water on the condition that CJ exists as a phantasm on the TV screen.

This is quite unlike the way an ocean can consume characters in movies such as *Jaws*, *The Deep* or *The Abyss*. In those movies, there is a dramatic and often violent traffic between submarine and out-of-water experiences—a contest between limited conditions of existence; and the distinction between the two states is like a fault line, gash or split in the characters which is exploited if not as a metaphoric flourish then as a structural motif. This is beautifully illustrated by the low angle shots, from a shark's point of view, of the naked thrashing legs and straining thighs of the female swimmer at the start of *Jaws*. The thematic division between water and land (represented by the opposed allegiances of the lead characters) is embodied in our view up at swimmers' legs opening and closing as they 'tread water'—particularly so (as in the film's opening sequence) when the physical vulnerability of the legs to a carnivorous appetite is eroticized as a sexual exposure.[1]

In *Baywatch*, the sexual exposure of the body does not require this sort of physical vulnerability. Sex here is a portrayal of power, and that power is manifest in the body's physique or exercised in a field of action which demonstrates the physique. This is an exposure which is exhibitionist without being explicit, no matter how much it shows. Its sex is externalized and aestheticized as the form of the body (forming an impenetrable exterior, or rather an exterior which yields nothing to analysis or interpretation). It is in part like the nudity of any model, whether in a life drawing class, on a catwalk or in a body building contest. It is, in other words, a civilised nudity: the sovereign beauty of a body that is designed for exhibition and yet can act as if its display is natural to it. Artificial, cosmetic, refined and yet also unselfconscious, unaffected, graceful. It is not surprising that the popular estimate of *Baywatch*'s erotic appeal usually settles on the aerobic vigour and surgical enhancement of its female actors' bodies, notably Pamela Anderson's. These are bodies in peak natural condition, ripe, ready, alive; but they are bodies which are also suspiciously unnatural in their voluptuousness. Their beauty is compromised precisely because it is supreme; and so it is not an idealizing beauty but a 'camp' aesthetic that popular taste responds to in *Baywatch*, detecting an enjoyable travesty of natural beauty.[2]

Popular taste barely does justice to the aesthetic complexity of *Baywatch*. On that Californian beach, nature and artifice parody one another in the way that CJ's slick, red lycra maillot seamlessly doubles the extravagances of her flesh. Nothing is concealed or revealed by this costume that is not already evident; and so, generally speaking, natural beauty is enveloped in a second, slick skin which masks it in order to rival it. CJ's costume is indistinguishable from Pamela Anderson's body, precisely so in order to compete with its voluptuousness. It copies the contours of her body, but her body is destined to outdo the costume's distinctive shape. Each stretches and swells according to the enticements of the other, yet in competition.

This is how the abstract water envelopes her body in my image of her. The water in which CJ's limp body drifts is a parody of water, unnatural in appearance—that is, it does not look quite like the sort of water it pretends to be—and irrational in narrative function. It is more a fantasia than a fiction. It is not a 'made up' water, integral to the story. It is instead a 'costume' water, part of Pamela Anderson's make-up for the shot. It has no measure or shape other than as the enhancement of the absolute body it envelopes. Nature, in *Baywatch*, is a cosmetic treatment of its own form, a masquerade that eclipses nature in order to enhance its truth.

It is appropriate, thus, to say that in *Baywatch*, Pamela Anderson is both more real and less real than any woman, but particularly more and less real than the woman she plays. This unreality is the very core of her erotic identity.[3] No matter what role she plays, she is destined to be at once more and less than that role. In this image, she floats like an anaesthetized angel in an air that has thickened around her, as if the legendary, pneumatic quality of her own body has magically affected her surroundings. This gives the image a certain occult quality, like a 'spirit photograph' from the late nineteenth century. Indeed, her limp yet voluptuous suspension in a domain that is fluid but without turbulence, that is light but unilluminating, that is thick but without resistance, could be seen as an original speculation on the very nature of the soul. In this image, there is little of the cultural lineage of women dissolving in the whorls or eddies of water (from Leonardo's studies in natural philosophy of wind, water, blood, libido to the late nineteenth century academic and Symbolist fantasies of erotic engulfment, of women whose bones fuse with their flesh in beautiful and pliant volumes). Look at her hair: it is motionless—or at least slowed down to an illusion of possible motion. It is as if the excesses of her form have been revealed as the condition for her weightlessness. Look at her expression: she is both possibly alive and possibly dead in the ambiguous medium that suspends her motion.

It is an image worthy of theological as well as mythological attention. Or at least the attention of a spiritualist medium, for in another image a little later from the scene, we see how the bubble of her soul breaks, as surely as her breath billows out from her lungs through throat and mouth, like ectoplasm in a séance. If she sings a seductive song, it is obscenely materialized as the skin of air that erupts from her mouth and bulges in the languid convulsion of a jellyfish.

Every story is the excuse for an image. All right. Now for my excuse. It comes from a remark made by a sixth century theologian, Fulgentius, which could almost be a motto: 'lust scatters all that it possesses'. But this excuse comes with a story, a story of lust that requires permission for a slight digression. This is a cheat: from Pamela Anderson to Hans Christian Andersen. And it is the route to another image, no less murky or occulted than that of CJ; and one that also speculates on the nature of the soul. What is the story behind this image? Hans Christian Andersen's story is as enchanting as it is cruel and morbid. A little mermaid falls in love with a prince whom she has saved from drowning in a shipwreck. Unable to pursue her courtship of him on land, she seeks help from the sea witch, who agrees to make her human, or at least human in appearance. But this is for a considerable price. The little mermaid will receive legs so as to be able to walk upon the earth, but she can gain these only in exchange for her voice. (She has the most beautiful voice among all mermaids.) With a richly macabre metaphoric turn, Andersen adds a cruel property to this mermaid's costly legs: with every step she takes on earth, her feet will feel as if knives are cutting deep into them. Indeed, her feet will even bleed with each step.

Her legs, both a prize and a wound, will take her among humans and will bring her to the man whom she loves. Yet even with her legs, the mermaid cannot truly be human. What she lacks as a mermaid—with or without legs—is a soul, and she can only gain a soul through a stroke of white magic that comes with the commitment of total love. The prince must give up his other loves for her (that is to say, he must give up his parents and marry the girl). Alas, in Andersen's story, the mermaid's love is not returned. The prince mistakenly believes that the one who saved him from the sea is another girl, and he marries her in a mistake he never knows he has committed. The morning after the prince's wedding night, the little mermaid dies, drowning in the sea, a soul-less being (that is to say, a being whose desire remains unconsummated). At least her self-sacrifice and endurance do not go totally unrewarded. The fate of most mermaids, we are informed, is to dissolve and become sea foam. As she dies, the little mermaid finds herself floating, disembodied among the daughters of the air. She becomes, in other words, a breeze (the *pneuma*); and as a breeze she may one day be redeemed and granted a soul by God.

Evidently Hans Andersen's story is a wonderfully evocative mix of Greek and Oriental mythology, of medieval folk tale and modern psychological insight. The mermaid herself is a contradictory and even complex character: greedy, impatient, rebellious, impulsive and reckless, but also dutiful, courageous and kind-hearted. She is both plaintive, submissive and also heroic, faithful and adventurous. Her suffering is exquisite in its cruel irony—enough, one imagines, to please temperaments like that of Edgar Allan Poe or Oscar Wilde. This complex personality of the protagonist adds an especially modern sentiment to the familiar legends of mute, stoic female heroes and fairy creatures seeking embodiment in order to marry mortals. 'The Little Mermaid' has justifiably become a classic parable on teenage love and desire, on the balance of enthusiasms and allegiances that shape the passage through puberty and adolescence.

The Disney adaptation of 1989 has some notable and obvious differences to the original Andersen; but the most obvious one is perhaps the least interesting: in Disney's version, the little mermaid (now given the name of Ariel) gets her man.[4] The happy ending, however, is not easily won (either for the scriptwriters or the mermaid). It requires an apocalyptic confrontation between the mermaid's father, King Triton, and the sea witch, an octopus called Ursula—a battle comparable in scale to the havoc wreaked by a Japanese over-fiend in an *anime*. The sexual symbolism tips into black comedy as the titanic Triton's phallic power (represented in his trident) is taken from him in a series of clever legal manoeuvres by Ursula, and Triton is physically reduced to a withered and pathetically limp polyp on the ocean floor. He remains an impotent, shrunken weed until the young prince comes to his and Ariel's rescue. Steering solo through Ursula's terrifying storm, the prince rams the firmly erect bowsprit (which is jutting out above the voluptuous figurehead on the bow) straight into Ursula's belly. This proves fatal to the sea witch, who loses her grip on the magical trident. The sea turns calm again; and the trident drifts down to the sea bed to Triton, restoring his authority along with his former stature.

In order for the Disney version to sustain a happy ending, it reconfigures in the *dénouement* much of the mythic content as family disputation and bonding. Myth is translated into the idiom of melodrama. For Andersen, the story proposes a difficult correspondence between sexual desire and spiritual fulfilment, between the attainment of sexual experience and the possession of a soul. For Disney, sexual desire and sexual experience are located entirely within the exchanges between father, daughter and malevolent mother figure, played through travesty and caricature. The spiritual prize in Andersen's story has been dispatched as unconvincing sentimentality and moralizing. Disney's objective is pragmatic: happiness within the terms of a divided family setting. In this manner, the story becomes a burlesque of *The Magic Flute*, with Ursula performing as Queen of Night to Triton's Sarastro, as if the opera were directed by John Waters. Ursula is a confronting and monstrous demon, but also elusive. She can be interpreted as the absent mother of Ariel, a surrogate and corrupting influence, a diabolical version of Auntie Mame instructing Ariel in feminine wiles or as the divorced wife of Triton, stewing with solitary alcoholic envy and dreams of revenge. When she seduces Ariel into the deal, inside her vulval cave she sings like Lotte Lenya and struts like an obese diva in a Kurt Weil cabaret. The Disney sea witch is a marvellous piece of misogyny, a huge and comically grotesque transvestite, a showgirl with the dress sense of Divine. She is also a predatory vagina, which is exposed in the forms of her writhing body. Her torso, her black dress and her waving tentacles are all fashioned from the one globular substance. What is beneath her skirt is obscenely explicated in the form of the skirt itself, as it divides into eight groping, undulating and slithering phallic tentacles.

Innocence cannot possibly survive in such a bestiary, and the happy ending in the Disney version is by no means a triumph of ingenuousness or purity. Hans Andersen's mermaid can gain a soul only if her prince commits himself to her in an act of love by which he relinquishes his attachments to his parents. This is a test for the prince. He must graduate from filial love to erotic love. That is to say, he must become a man; and he does this even by marrying the wrong girl. It is a test for the mermaid, too; but if she is being asked to become a woman, it is with a different commitment to *erōs*. Her spiritual salvation, as it is offered paradoxically by the sea witch, depends on being able to seduce the prince with her speechless body—her image—rather than through the ethereal beauty of her voice. She fails to do this. But Andersen's unhappy ending implies that she has kept her spiritual innocence and purity. Her reward is offered in a lyrical coda which depicts an incorporeal bliss opposed to the erotic satisfactions she pursued. The Disney version's happy ending, on the other hand, is possible only by rendering the Andersen story secular and parodic. Ariel does not wish for a soul, she wants happiness with her man. Her desire is profoundly erotic. It is also practical and carnal. In Andersen's story, the mermaid's new legs incorporate stigmata of her desire: they hurt and bleed as she steps on the earth. This is the moral and physical price she must repeatedly pay for erotic experience. Painful as it is, she will dance for the prince and convert her suffering into a beauty that she hopes will be equivalent to the beauty of her lost voice. Ariel's legs, however, do not have this metaphoric function. Instead, they open and close. She is amused by them and enjoys them. They are the means for attaining her happiness; and as we will see, it is their acquisition rather than their use which is painful. It is a pain not transcended but forgotten.

In Disney, the existence of Ariel's soul is never raised as a problem. When the deal is proposed, Ursula addresses Ariel as 'you poor unfortunate soul', ironically putting her already into the category of her previous victims and slaves. What counts is who possesses that soul, and it is the mistake of Ursula's victims to have signed theirs away to the witch. Ariel gives up her soul, manifested in her voice, in order to have a body that can occupy the world of humans and that can embrace a man. It is the soul's relation to the body that provides the moral caption to this film. The Disney story is based on a pattern of unalterable ontological divisions: water from land, animal from human, adolescent from adult, child from parent. Ariel straddles all of these when she trades her voice for legs, that is to say, trades her soul for a body that can accomplish desire. The metaphoric sequence of feminine sexual organs is literalized when, in silhouette against electric fumes bursting forth from Ursula's great vulvic cauldron, Ariel's fish tail splits into two naked human legs. The cloud that engulfs Ariel's body as it is transfigured is the malign, vaporous essence of Ursula's corrupt sexual desire. (It first takes form as grotesquely long feminine fingers poking inside Ariel's mouth to touch and take her voice.) Ariel's 'getting of wisdom' happens in a sequence that pushes the animation to its most delirious abstraction, signalling both the transition through puberty for her (the menarche) and dramatizing her hazardous identity with the pseudo-mother, Ursula.

What is particularly striking about this sequence in the movie is that the sudden appearance of bare legs on Ariel immediately renders her, like Eve after the first bite, naked. The narrative indicates so much when, after she is brought to the surface and to shore by her friends (Flounder the fish and Sebastian the lobster), their first task is to find her some clothing. This is actually one of those anomalies of sexuality which anthropomorphic animation in general, and Disney animation in particular, thrive upon. Donald Duck, for instance, was clothed quite decently by wearing only a cap and a sailor shirt. But in an episode when he lost his shirt, he covered his 'groin' from the viewer in embarrassment, imitating the gesture of a human male. Through this caricature of human modesty, the absence of the shirt exposed a part of the body that was already and necessarily exposed. In Ariel's case, she is also already naked as a mermaid, since her tail is her bare flesh. This is a disingenuous nakedness. We see her petite breasts are covered, by shells of course, in the form of little hands cupped over her in modesty. This is obvious yet soft eroticism. It is sweetly tantalizing. Her tail is something else. It is the focus of the film's true eroticism, which is hard and more compelling. The junction of any mermaid's tail with her human torso is always a difficult pictorial problem. Ariel's fish tail joins to her waist with a soft furl outward of a veil-like surfeit of skin, as if it could peel delicately away from her. Her tail is a costume which fits her like an aerobic leotard and is also her naked skin.[5] It has the same relation to the human body as Pamela Anderson's maillot. And, like Ursula's obscene skirt, Ariel's tail manifests what it conceals: her legs will part when the desire is strong enough.

In a brief note on the film in her book on fairy tales, *From the Beast to the Blonde*, Marina Warner pays particular attention to the price Ariel pays Ursula for receiving a mature and ready human sexuality (in the form of her legs).[6] Ariel's voice is the siren's song, the mermaid's call for love. (The three ascending notes are identifiably Ariel's leitmotif throughout the film's score.) Contrary to Ursula's account of what makes men find women attractive ('baaaahdy language', she offers, waggling her huge rump), it is her voice that is Ariel's most important attribute, more important than her bodily beauty. Indeed, as her essential quality (her soul, although not named as such), Ariel's song is her true identity. The lack of voice renders Ariel, in the prince's eyes at any rate, merely an image which he must try to match against his fragmentary memory of the girl who saved him from the sea. Ariel's appearance to him is a secondary property—and an inessential aspect—of her voice. Since she no longer possesses her song, the Ariel who possesses legs (and the essential means for consummating her love of the prince) is a false copy of the Ariel who is 'the little mermaid'. This copy is capable of uttering only the language of the body. The moral implications of this separation between image and essence are Platonist, as they are in Hans Andersen's story; but the Disney version's audacious—and sexually riotous—conclusion, in which Ariel regains her voice and gets her man, compromises Andersen's morality.

Andersen can only offer his mermaid a reprieve which does not alter the terms of her fatal deal with the sea witch. Because the prospect of her transformation into a breeze is an aftermath to the narrative action (she is, after all, dead), this appears as a mawkish addendum to the story, a sentimental gift of the narrator to the dead spirit. This is not a complaint against Andersen's ability as a story teller. His sentimentality is an expressive medium for his theology. And while Andersen's story may be sentimental, it is far from coy. The scene in which his mermaid's voice is taken from her has a startlingly direct and simple violence: 'stick out your tongue', the sea witch orders, and then the witch cuts the little mermaid's tongue out. It is a shocking metaphor for the sacrifice required of this young girl in order for her to assume a carnal as well as emotional relation with a man. Nothing so grotesquely practical happens in the Disney version, in which the dealings between all characters are based on intrigue and sly misinterpretation. Ursula captures the ethereal glow in Ariel's throat by sorcery and seduction, storing it in a little vulval shell (a parody of the image of Ursula as a gargantuan, talking vulva). Ariel must break her silence to prevail against the witch, to win the heart of the prince and keep her human form. She can only do this once that little shell—the sign of her virginity, possessed in a travesty of its meaning by Ursula—is broken open and her voice, sparkling like Tinker Bell, finds its way back to her, rising up her legs and into her, up into her heart and throat.

For Marina Warner, the imagery of the mermaid's voice stolen and regained is the emblem of the power of the female storyteller. It is the secret power of the spinner, the crone, the old wife, all captured in a fabulous figure of Mother Goose. The fairy tale is the voice of the mother heard in the nursery: that 'acoustic mirror'. Fairy tales attempt to restore the bliss of maternal engulfment by pretending to a world of nursery certainties. They also record that maternal voice's obliteration, Warner claims, never more so than in the tales of silenced mermaids. Sirens' songs are bewitching; but their enchantments threaten entanglement and erasure, and so will be done away with. The heroines who deftly weave their spells of love will be punished for their enchantment. When a boat sinks, as Andersen tells it, the mermaids welcome the sailors to the ocean, singing to them of how beautiful it is. But the sailors do not understand, and by the time they reach the mermaids' palaces and gardens at the bottom of the ocean they are dead. The rapture of the deep that drowns a man in the mermaid's voice is a pure beauty. But the story of the little mermaid is an impure thing that excuses the image of a carnal embrace. The little mermaid relinquishes her weightless, balletic self-absorption in order to win and give herself to a living man. That timeless rapture becomes possession, possession by a lust that confuses the domains of the mortal and the fabulous and so disturbs the boundary between the figurative and the real. A story is the excuse for an image, an image animated and scattered by lust.

NOTES

1 The sexual imagery in *Jaws* (1975, directed by Steven Spielberg, script by John Milius) is wonderfully clear while still being rich with macabre humour. In the opening scene, a young woman at a beach party late at night lures a young man toward the water to go skinny dipping. Her invitation has a casual, sexual offer implied in it. But he passes out in a drunken stupor at the water's edge as he ineffectually tries to remove his jeans to go in after her: 'I'm coming', he pants...but fails to. She calls to him in exasperation as she paddles about naked in the deep moonlit water. When the White Pointer shark finally grabs her legs, we only see her from above the water line: at first with a look of surprise, then being thrown about as if in a vigorous sexual bout. Blood clouds the water around her, but there are no visible signs of physical violence to her body during the attack. To interpret this scenario as a phallic vengeance on the female character for her expression of desire would not only be humourless but would also fail to recognize the sexual ambiguity of the shark throughout the film. The most explicit violence is enacted on the Ahab styled shark hunter Quinn, who is bitten in half as the enormous shark mounts his boat from behind in an hysterical version of a monstrous mating routine (the sexual act alluded to in the film's opening sequence). The artistic confusion of phallus and *vagina dentata* is, of course, not a discovery of *Jaws*. As with the equally celebrated *Aliens* series, this is an exaggeration and sophistication of figurative and iconographic ambivalence discernible in creatures from science fiction cinema of the 1950s, as well as in some of the predatory demons of 1940s horror. It is also worth noting that the menace directed toward children in *Jaws* is associated with conflicts between parental figures. This may have been a directorial touch. Similar scenarios occur, for instance, throughout Spielberg's *Jurassic Park*, in which the two children are often hanging in space with their legs thrashing about,

much like the swimmers in *Jaws*, while the carnivorous dinosaurs hunt them. These orphaned children are exposed to the predatory aggression of creatures who, as products of the laboratory (and hence also parent-less), embody pure appetite. The protection of the children is associated with the recovery of parental roles which have been displaced in a conflict between artifice (mechanical and commercial processes of production) and nature (sexually reproductive and alimentary functions). Family and food are equivalent in *Jurassic Park*.

2 The more obvious 'camp' qualities of *Baywatch* are inherited from the beach party movie cycle of the 1960s. But the TV show also appropriates photogenic iconography from the overlapping traditions of bathing beauties and sports pin-ups. To some extent, the masquerade of professional work which supports the show's hedonism resembles the Rococo usage of the 'bather' as subject matter: usually a thinly disguised mythological setting of Diana at her bath, for instance. This would be similar also to the thematic content of Renoir's neo-Rococo bathers: a luxurious pleasure in summertime eroticism theatricalized by a pagan or mythicizing pretext which is not intended to be convincing. Most of the 'mythicizing' elements of *Baywatch* concern perfection of body-image, through athletic prowess or therapeutic issues in American ego psychology. I recall an episode, for instance, in which an immense, carnivorous octopus which lived in a grotto attacked, unsuccessfully, one of the young female lifeguards in the team. The sequence of the attack allowed some striking, and only vaguely sadistic, imagery of rubber tentacles wrapping around and squeezing the woman's sumptuous figure. The counselling she received in order to cope with the trauma helped the woman overcome her—admittedly implausible—condition of *anorexia nervosa*.

3 This is not to say that her erotic appeal lies in her artifice. The artificiality of Pamela Anderson's body is quite different to that of, say, Madonna's. For the latter, the morphological variations of physique are cued to various roles, or pseudo-dramatic *personae*. In that sense, the varieties of Madonna's femininity are like the *personae* of a drag queen. They are not just image-conscious, they are parodies of images. On the other hand, Pamela Anderson's appearance relies on an invariant form which doubles a role indistinguishable from her. Her phantasmic appearance is much like that of Kim Novak's character of Madeleine in *Vertigo* (1958, directed by Alfred Hitchcock), who is played by Novak's other character in the film, Judy.

4 Written and directed by John Musker and Ron Clements; songs by

Howard Ashman and Alan Menken; original score by Alan Menken; produced by Howard Ashman and John Musker. Walt Disney Pictures in association with Silver Screen Partners IV, 1989, The Walt Disney Company.

5 This is a common feature among fantasy mutants, notably those creatures montaged from several species (centaurs or minotaurs, for instance) whose conjoining is at a genetic level, unlike products of vivisection, such as Frankenstein's monster, where surgical scars clearly delimit the bodily fragments. The visualization of the join becomes more critical in modern fantasies of mating between machines and organisms. David Cronenberg's remake of *The Fly* (1986) especially confronted this problem in the final mutation of the man-fly with the machine that created it. The final hybrid creature was shocking in its pathos, precisely because it was an unsustainable life form. (Less successful was the merging of flesh and electric technology in the same director's 1983 *Videodrome*.) Cyborgs do not escape this difficulty either. Schwarzenegger's 'terminator' (in James Cameron's movie of 1984) concealed the join between mechanism and living tissue by having its machinic parts completely enveloped in naked skin. Bodily nakedness is the paradoxical result of the effort to conceal the naked scar of the joinery. This is amusingly parodied in Tim Burton's beautiful fairy tale *Edward Scissorhands* (1990), whose eponymous protagonist (created by a childless elderly man in the manner of Pinocchio, but made of mechanical instruments rather than enchanted wood) wears a gothic-punk black leather outfit. At first, when the visiting Avon Lady encounters and befriends him after the death of his 'father', Edward appears like a caricature of Michael Jackson. She takes him home and gives him her husband's clothes to wear, which he dutifully puts on over his leather outfit. His surrogate mother takes this for granted, and so we realize that his leather outfit is actually his naked skin. He is a naked wild child, whose body has been exposed all along; but we only see his nakedness as it disappears when he is putting on the garb of his surrogate father.

6 Marina Warner, *From the Beast to the Blonde: On Fairy Tales and Their Tellers* (London: Chatto & Windus, 1994), pp. 396–408.

The Infinite Quest: Husserl, Bakshi, the Rotoscope and the Ring

FREIDA RIGGS

BECOMING-ANIMATION

Between the idea
And the reality
Between the motion
And the act
Falls the Shadow...[1]

T.S. Eliot

...Robert De Niro walks 'like' a crab...[2]

Gilles Deleuze and Félix Guattari

Gilles Deleuze and Félix Guattari are thinkers of animation. Although Deleuze takes but slight note of animation at the beginning of *Cinema 1: The Movement-Image*, his and Guattari's work is about processes which are traditionally associated with, and still definable as, those of animation. At the same time, their writing *performs* such processes, aligning the authors with animation through both the content and form of their work. In texts devoted to philosophical and literary themes and in his two books about cinema, for instance, Deleuze sets out to create new concepts, concepts which animate both cinema and philosophy: 'Cinema and philosophy are brought together in a continuing process of intercutting. This is philosophy as assemblage, a kind of provoked becoming of thought'.[3]

Yet the notion of becoming precedes these theorists. Without wishing to trace its beginnings, I will in this essay consider becoming as it informs the work of phenomenologist Edmund Husserl. Husserl's search for the telos or idea of knowledge is forever thwarted by the processes and revisions of his facts on the way to this telos. It is thwarted, in other words, by *becoming*. The thinker must admit, therefore, that the only being is becoming. The continuous and mobile nature of becoming is an example of the way animation pervades the work of Husserl. Husserl's quest is one for identity, whereas Deleuze and Guattari emphasize the radical difference at the heart of becoming; but the debt to Husserl cannot be ignored.

In addition, becoming is Deleuze and Guattari's reply to the relatively static concept of structuralism, to that structuralist position which proposes correspondences and relationships between the terms which it attempts to arrest and classify. Becoming puts into question the very idea of classifiable terms, as it '...lacks a subject distinct from itself;...it has no term, since its term in turn exists only as taken up in another becoming...'[4] The example of De Niro walking '"like" a crab' in a certain film sequence implies that something crablike enters into the very essence of the image and serves as an instance of the human becoming-animal. This instance appears among many other examples of becoming which Deleuze and Guattari take not only from film but from literature, science and myth. Becoming, in the authors' specific sense, does not only apply to the human-animal configuration but encompasses a multitude of comminglings: becoming-woman, -child, -animal, -vegetable, -mineral, -molecular or -particle. However, lest we conclude that there is some design to this list of becomings, the authors stress that becomings are not evolutionary but symbiotic (or 'involutionary', so long as this does not imply regression), resulting in alliances between very disparate entities which, in themselves, are unimportant to the principle of becoming: 'What is real is the becoming itself, the block of becoming, not the supposedly fixed terms through which that which becomes passes'.[5]

In the light of these becomings, De Niro's sideways gait is not merely the result of the human actor imitating the crustacean. Rather, it is a fusion of the crab with the image of the actor, a fusion with the speed of the image, resulting in a haecceity—a thisness, a hereness and nowness—in other words, a crabness. In this sense, becoming is not what Deleuze and Guattari call a 'molar' species, that is, what is able to be understood through form.[6] Becoming belongs instead to a 'molecular' process, which is a dynamic interchange of molecules and particles at rest and in motion in and through which the human enters the zone of the animal, and vice versa.[7]

A becoming bears no resemblance to either of the two entities involved in its process (e.g. human/animal, man/woman, adult/child, etc.). Crabness is as radically *different* from De Niro as it is from a crab. For Deleuze and Guattari, such difference serves as a questioning of traditional methods of thinking which presuppose the unshakeable existence of truth and error. Difference reaches beyond these propositions to *animate* truth and error in what Deleuze and Guattari call the 'vegetal' model of thought. Like a rhizome, difference is mobile, constantly in the process of becoming. In other words, just as truth and error could be imagined as multiplicities rather than as fixed states, so difference can be thought as multiplicity, as process, as becoming. As difference, becoming is a figure that rearticulates some of Deleuze's ongoing concerns: issues of difference and repetition, as well as of the original, the copy and simulation.[8]

In terms of the latter, let us recall that for Plato, a hierarchy of representation installs supreme value in the original, places at one remove from the original the 'good copy', which is good insofar as it resembles the nature of the original, and places at second remove from the original the 'bad copy', so denigrated by Plato as simulacrum or mimicry. For Deleuze, however, simulation is not simply a false copy but is of a different order altogether, one which '...calls into question the very notions of the copy...and of the model'.[9] I would say that Deleuzian simulation is an animatic process that animates (or reanimates) the original and the good copy as it becomes radically different from them.

Considered from the point of view of Deleuzian becoming,

difference and simulation, animation is a form/figure/process that exceeds more traditional characterizations and definitions of it. More than being the imitation, the illusion, of life, it has a life of its own—the life of illusion. More than possessing only the narrow specificity of drawn, photographed, scratched or computer-animated images imbued with movement on the screen, animation encompasses any and every project concerned with giving life and movement. In such a light, Deleuze can *himself* be seen as an animator, giving a new and different life and movement to the terms and concepts with which he philosophizes. As an animator-philosopher, Deleuze forms concepts as 'assemblages' across disciplines, 'assemblages' which Hugh Tomlinson and Barbara Habberjam call a 'cutting [*découpage*]' that 'groups under a single concept things that one would have thought were different, and…separates from it others which one would have thought very close'.[10]

THE INTERBECOMINGS OF BAKSHI AND HUSSERL

This essay attempts to invent a relation between the work of the philosopher Edmund Husserl and the filmmaker Ralph Bakshi. After Deleuze, we can describe this relation as the becoming of two animators: the becoming-Bakshi of Edmund Husserl and the becoming-Husserl of Ralph Bakshi. Just as human becoming-animal is neither actual nor metaphorical but rather an area of indeterminacy, a rejection of the border between human and animal, so the becomings of philosopher and filmmaker blur borders—between disciplines, between different periods of history, etc. The result is a 'molecular' process which is unique and autonomous, that is difference in its purest form.

Through the evocation of Husserl and Bakshi, I am reanimating history—the history of the 'father of phenomenology' of the late nineteenth and twentieth century and that of the creator of 'adult animation', whose mass appeal reached its apotheosis in the 1960s and '70s. But this reanimation is of a history which considers resurrection not as a good or faithful copy of an original but as something other, a new and altered form of the old, as difficult to fix and classify as that which it attempts to repeat and double. No more than its resurrected form can the historical referent, itself neither pure nor atextual in the first place, be delivered in an unmediated way. If the resurrected form is an altered form of the old, the old is an altered form of the new. Both change and become different with every telling, with every reincarnation, simulation and becoming. Historical commentary, as Deleuze proposes, leads a double existence, where the repetition of the former text changes both that text and its newest manifestation. They continue to repeat themselves *in one another*, each time with a significant difference, for at the very core of repetition lies an irreconcilable order of difference.[11]

It is this very difference, this very impurity of the referent, that summons forth its reinvention, while a pure and immutable referent (if that were possible) would remain deaf to the call of its own repetition. Of this process of reinvention it might be said: history is reanimated with every telling. But even here, the prefix 're' could evoke the concept of similarity rather than the irreconcilable alterity of repetition. It would therefore be more precise to remove the 're' and view history as animation, for in the context of this essay, to animate is always already to reanimate. So when I propose to animate history, it is both the process of becoming and the unfixable, already animate nature of the referent, with its equally unfixable signifying resurrections, upon which I shall concentrate in my attempt to (re)invent the figures of Edmund Husserl and Ralph Bakshi.

Today, the work of both these men no longer enjoys the attention that it received at the peak of their popularity. However, textual evidence shows that neither has been forgotten. Each year, we see new books, articles and discussions about Husserl; and Bakshi is still working and influencing younger directors, notably John Kricfalusi. But it is neither the popularity nor the more recent lack thereof that draws me to conjecture on the mutual becomings of these two men. It is the passion with which each of them confronts his goals, goals which, as I shall argue, are impossible to achieve. It is the passion with which Husserl poses the explicit question which he articulates and develops throughout his work: what is the essence of consciousness and its objects? It is the passion with which Bakshi asks the question never explicitly stated but evident in his willingness to experiment and to take risks, to risk censure and failure: what is the essence of animation?

If the referent is always animated, always in the process of becoming, a stable referent or essence is unattainable. In consequence, the *quest* of the thinkers-animators becomes more significant than the fact that their ever-mutating goal can never be realized. In the same way, this essay will not and cannot retrieve and redeliver an essential Husserlian phenomenology or an essential Bakshian animation but can only remain obedient to the principles of animation/becoming sketched above. Thus, through the coupling of seemingly disparate figures—phenomenology-film animation and Husserl-Bakshi—this text can only repeat both phenomenology and animation in their mutual becoming while seeking out the difference that this repetition and juxtaposition imply.

To facilitate this investigation, I will introduce the notion of the Idea as it pertains to the philosophy of Husserl and to Bakshi's *The Lord of the Rings* (1978). I have chosen to analyze this film, rather than some of his more successful or better known films, because it is an example of what Bakshi considered a new form of filmic animation and demonstrates his willingness to risk his reputation in order to realize his vision.

Published in the United States between 1954 and 1956, Tolkien's epic trilogy, *The Lord of the Rings*, drew a small but devoted following. It was not until the 1960s that its use of fantasy to represent the conflict between good and evil coalesced with a particular consciousness, one which was becoming aware of social inequality and injustice. The consciousness that was being shaped by mind-expanding drugs was receptive to the novel's allegorical approach as it was to its ethical concerns, thus ensuring its success.

In the books, a hobbit named Frodo, living in the third age of Middle Earth, inherits a magical ring which is coveted by dark and dangerous forces. He must destroy the ring to ensure universal peace and undertakes a perilous journey to Mordor where he will throw it into the fire. It is no surprise that Bakshi, the maker of adult, politically committed animation associated with the '60s counterculture like *Fritz the Cat* (1972) and *Heavy Traffic* (1973), should choose to film a text which had the quest for peace as its central concern.

Bakshi's first job was with CBS Terrytoons, where he eventually became supervising director. He moved to Paramount and became interested in the radical politics of the '60s. This led to his first feature, one which made his name as one of the first producers of adult animation, an adaptation of Robert Crumb's underground comic, *Fritz the Cat*. Through the figure of Fritz, a character 'who paid lip service to the counterculture but whose only real interest was getting laid',[12] Bakshi exposed much of the hypocrisy of his time. His film shocked many of his viewers, in particular Robert Crumb himself, who killed Fritz off in his final comic after depicting him as exploited by two Hollywood characters (caricatures of Bakshi and Steve Krantz, the film's producer). Nevertheless, Bakshi's angry characterization of Fritz established the filmmaker's reputation. The film was also the first of many personal artistic statements that he would make through the medium of animation. His response to Crumb's disapproval is telling:

> His criticism was very severe at the time, but I'm not ashamed about it. I was out to make personal films, and I wasn't doing Robert Crumb's 'Fritz the Cat' at that point. I was doing Ralph Bakshi's 'Fritz the Cat'.[13]

Bakshi continued to make films which were both personal and controversial. *The Lord of the Rings* was no exception. The task here was to translate a cult epic which depended on a dense and multifaceted narrative into the visual medium of film. It needed to be faithful to the book so as not to disappoint the vast number of Tolkien devotees, but at the same time it needed to appeal to lovers of animation and Bakshi fans who had come to expect a radically auteurist adaptation of the novel.

Bakshi's and Frodo's tasks are parallel and intertwined. Both happen to be in a place and time that require actions which call for courage and integrity. Frodo has been entrusted with the disposal of the master ring made by the dark lord, a ring which possesses power over men and elves and cannot be used for good. A timid hobbit, he needs to overcome all the obstacles that the dark forces put in his way and narrowly escapes dark riders, orcs, snowstorms and other disasters on his perilous journey. Around him is a world in chaos where few can be trusted. Allegiances shift as the power of the ring entices allies to become enemies. Great battles are fought between the champions for good and the evil warriors.

Around Bakshi, too, was a world in chaos; and the battles which had begun with the making of *Fritz the Cat* would continue after the screening of *The Lord of the Rings* when, as we shall see, the film incensed many critics. Working in an environment where power had too long resided in the wrong hands both in the larger world of politics and in the smaller world of filmmaking, Bakshi needed to play a small part in ridding the world of the metaphorical ring. The choice of subject for his film was a criticism of the status quo, an attempt to play a part in altering the reactionary nature of the pre-1960s society. In his own field, he needed to wrest the ring from the Disney-dominated world of animation and throw it into the fire; and he did this by reinventing an old technique—rotoscoping—and using it in a new and personal way.

Bakshi had already adopted rotoscoping in his earlier film *Wizards* (1977). Although the publicity released by *Centerpiece* (a *Special Features* branch of *The New York Times* Syndication Sales Corporation) stated that this was a 'never-before-tried process', its use by Bakshi represented a return to early animation insofar as rotoscoping had been developed and patented in 1917 by Max and Dave Fleischer.[14]

Rotoscoping enables the animator to trace live action film frames onto animation paper placed on glass, the film illuminated from below by means of a modified projector which advances it frame by frame. The Fleischers used rotoscoping to animate Koko the Clown, who appeared in a series of cartoons which all began with his emergence from an inkwell. Koko was well received, as an article in *The New York Times*, February 22, 1920 shows:

> This little inkwell clown has attracted favorable attention because of a number of distinguishing characteristics. His motions, for one thing, are smooth and graceful. He walks, dances and leaps as a human being, as a particularly easy-limbed human being might.[15]

One could conjecture that it was because of these qualities that Bakshi chose this technique to animate *The Lord of the Rings*, a film which required abundant movement and action. After shooting in the Mojave Desert and in Spain, Bakshi edited the film into a two and a half hour live action movie. Practically every one of the 900,000 frames of the film was then enlarged and traced. In a promotional text of the time, he makes a number of points about his approach, which I have here rendered in summary form. He did the first drawings himself, declaring: 'If you just trace live action directly, it looks tacky. So I interpreted what those (traced) shapes looked like so they'd be interesting'. He calls this process a 'moving illustration', one which suits his goal of making animation for adults. Although this technique is unsuitable for 'Disney's dancing mice', Bakshi adds, realism is what he strives for in adult animation: 'With real live timing you get more of the personality and attitude of the characters. You can now animate subtle nuances—people's sighs and touching each other'. The rotoscope permitted the use of difficult shots as well as that of 1,000 extras, all of them traced, all of them moving. Bakshi's enthusiasm is obvious when he says: 'The thrill of getting those numbers moving through the screen flawlessly is—my God—that's a lifelong dream for an animator. I think I've blown animation wide open'.[16]

One could read this last declaration, 'I've blown animation wide open', in many different ways. It could mean that animation has been expanded, enlarged, perfected. Or it could have the opposite meaning, that of ripping it apart and annihilating it. Or perhaps the meanings are not mutually exclusive. Perhaps it is only the expansion, enlargement and perfection of animation that can permit its ripping apart and annihilation, and vice versa. One thing seems certain: to blow animation wide open is anything but a transparent assertion. Its varying meanings will be traversed over the remainder of the essay.

In any case, for us it is clear that through the sheer scale and innovative use of an early technique, Bakshi did indeed break new ground. The colossal masses of Black Riders, the horses, the battles were a far cry from the lone figure of Koko; and the technique of rotoscoping was certainly expanded and enlarged, even if some critics questioned that it was perfected. And he did rip apart more conventional forms of animation. But in doing so, he performed a double act of annihilation, for in the act of annihilating the conservative and prescriptive characterizations of what animation should be, he unwittingly came close to annihilating his own reputation as animator. Whereas the maverick experimental filmmaker who dared question received ideas about the *content* of animation was mostly praised for his success, the innovative filmmaker who dared question received ideas about the *form* and *technique* of animation was, more often than not, pilloried for his transgression.

Although *The Lord of the Rings* (the first half of a two-part film, the other half of which has never been completed) was hailed by some reviewers as a sophisticated breakthrough in animation, most reviewers were very critical—about its incompleteness and its incomprehensibility to the uninitiated, on the one hand, and its failure to satisfy Tolkien devotees, on the other. One of the main criticisms of the film was its treachery to animation in its use of rotoscoping.[17]

It is outside the scope of this essay to comment in detail about these reviews, to write yet another review or to pass judgment upon the film. Given Bakshi's stated aim—to blow animation wide open through his use of rotoscoping—my analysis of this film will consider the implications for animation of his use of this technique. I therefore intend to focus on the film mainly as a catalyst that enables us to think animation differently.[18]

In this regard, of special interest are some of John Canemaker's withering criticisms of Bakshi in a review available in the Celeste Bartos Film Study Center of The Museum of Modern Art, New York.[19] I should stress at the outset that my intention here is not simply to criticize Canemaker, whose contribution to the practice and scholarship of animation has been undeniable, but to draw attention to a particular set of criteria used by him and others to theorize animation. Through this set, we can locate and understand the philosophical attitude which underpins Canemaker's evaluation and suggest alternative approaches based on philosophical suppositions I consider more in keeping with Bakshi's project, approaches that not only bear a privileged relation to animation but are themselves animated.

Here are three of Canemaker's harshest claims against Bakshi and *The Lord of the Rings*:

(1) 'It's so easy to fool the moviegoing public these days: you can make a live action film embellished with special effects, call it animation, and people will believe you…';

(2) '…in its heavy reliance on traced-over live action footage, the film displays an unbelievable distrust of the medium of animation. Bakshi shot the entire film in live action first and then a staff of "tracers" (they do not deserve the designation of animators) worked over the footage';

(3) 'The contempt for animation Bakshi had as a minion and later the boss of the infamously cheap Terrytoon cartoon factory in the 1950s has come out in *Rings*, his anti-animation feature'.

In sum, Canemaker assumes the role of defender of animation and charges Bakshi with being deceitful, hypocritical, duplicitous—fobbing off to the public what Bakshi calls animation but is in fact live action.

In drawing a proprietary line around what he considers to be animation, Canemaker does not explicitly declare what animation *is*, only says that what Bakshi makes is not animation, indeed is anti-animation. The closest he comes in fact to defining animation is in his statement that '(t)he principles of animation developed at Disney's to create an "illusion of life" can be adapted to any graphic style', and that adherence to these principles would have made for a more 'visually exciting' interpretation of Tolkien. These foundational principles, which need only be 'adapted to any graphic style', are given as the essence from which subsequent animation, if it is to be successful, should be derived. A deviation from these principles is a transgression that more than impoverishes the medium, it turns its back on animation itself.

Canemaker's moves are classically essentialist: he takes one form/practice/style of animation, that which stems from the foundations laid by Disney, idealizes it and declares it to be the essence of animation, automatically excluding everything else from the magic kingdom. His highly charged and derisive language—'fool', 'unbelievable distrust', 'not deserve', 'contempt', 'minion', 'infamously cheap'—strongly images a scenario of the elect and the damned, the true believers and the false prophets. Within the kingdom are the Good, the true; outside lie the Evil, the deceivers and manipulators.

I would suggest that, in making such moves, Canemaker falls prey in part to his critique of Bakshi. It could be claimed that *he* has unbelievable distrust of the medium, fixing it in the rigid inanimate vice of one and one only form and definition, which he postulates as the eternal, unchanging ideal of animation. In so doing, he turns his back on the history of animation, on all those who actually believe in and think they have been contributors to a history of animation beyond Disney. Perhaps Canemaker intuits Bakshi as pushing Disney animation to its limits, going Disney one further and not liking where that takes animation and what it says about Disney.

Canemaker for me comes very close to subscribing to Plato's vision of earthly forms striving to emulate as good copies an unchanging and unchangeable—in a word, *inanimate*—Ideal. He likewise comes very close to situating Bakshi's work in terms of Plato's critique of the bad copy that I articulated above after Deleuze. To tie animation to an inanimate, unchanging ideal is to deanimate it, to tie it to being instead of to becoming, to tie it to Disney's illusion of life rather than to the life of illusion. It is, by means of prescription and proscription, to deprive animation of its life and to arrest it of its movement. It is to substitute for the dynamic, fluid and changing life and movement of animation an inertness, stasis and rigidity, both on a formal and conceptual level. It would be a life devoid of life, a movement devoid of movement.

From such a perspective, it would be Canemaker who would be anti-animation. It would be he who would fall prey to the logic and operations of the simulacrum, the mime Bakshi, as the latter calls into question the very notion of the copy. It would be he who would fall prey to animation as a Deleuzian becoming that, as I indicated above, exceeds more traditional characterizations and definitions of it. Moreover, in seeking to exclude Bakshi from animation, Canemaker tellingly repeats the move by film studies to exclude animation from itself. The animatic nature of *live action*, indeed the debt *it* owes to animation, *is* animation, is not acknowledged by Canemaker.

Against the Platonic 'calm, ordered life of the soul governed by reason', Bakshi pits 'the disorderly and passionate life of the soul moved by poetry'.[20] I would propose that he too posited an Ideal, but crucially one which would animate the static Ideal of Plato. In seeking to find a form of animation which would most compellingly transmit the nuances of Tolkein's adult fantasy and transform the way we think of *The Lord of the Rings*, he based his Ideal on an excessive view of what animation is—a view that does not confine animation to one form of film but arguably sees film *as such* as a form of animation. For me, his Ideal would blow wide open both animation as a form of film and film as a form of animation. It would transform live action into cartoon animation, and vice versa.

He thus would be a hybrid animator, an animator of the hybrid, who wears the caps of live action animator as well as cartoon animation director. If the live action auteur is an animator, Bakshi could be considered the exemplary auteur, one reason for, or effect of, his first shooting live action, then transforming it by rotoscope into cartoon animation. We could say that, by this turning device (the roto in rotoscope is from the Latin *rota*. wheel), Bakshi is not only turning live action into animation but (re)turning it to it, revealing its roots in, its nature as, animation, challenging thereby the restricted understanding of live action with animation. Thereby too he pushes the form, even as he does his own role, beyond the limits prescribed by Canemaker, into the realm of becoming.

For me, Bakshi's project is no different from that of any auteur, be they makers of live action film or cartoon animation. Nor, in his search for an Ideal form for his film, is he so different from Canemaker. One might feel impelled to say that both simply have a different Ideal, but it would be wrong, for it would miss a crucial difference. Because Canemaker's Ideal is static and limiting, animation for him, even when manifested in a large and varied corpus of work, cannot change nor influence the Idea itself. It is always the Idea which dictates the form which any animation must take, its value residing in being a 'good copy', a copy which remains faithful to the Idea.

Bakshi's Idea also dictates the form of animation and live action film; but in return, the form of animation and live action film changes and trans-forms the Idea. There is a reciprocity in flux which ensures that neither animation, live action film nor their Idea remain the same. It could therefore be said that while live action film and animation (re)animate each other, they simultaneously (re)animate and are (re)animated by the Idea of animation and live action film. *The Lord of the Rings* is (re)animated by the Idea of animation at the same time that the Idea of animation is (re)animated by *The Lord of the Rings.* The Idea of animation and its factual example, *The Lord of the Rings*, are in a perpetual and mutual becoming which constantly forces us to rethink both the Idea of animation and its example, the film itself.

And the process of animation conceptualized by Bakshi extends further. He is himself caught up in the process of becoming. If in Platonic terms he refuses to make a 'good copy' of the Ideal form, a 'failure' which would be a form of success for him, he also fails to fix his own animated Ideal, fails to attain a form of animation which would serve as the conceptual essence of all animation. In other words, one could suppose that in Canemaker's world, the Ideal may be unattainable, but only one type of true and good copy is fit to represent it. He therefore fixes his style of animation to conform as closely as possible to that Ideal. In the world of Bakshi, where the Ideal is constantly changing, animation itself must be animated and change, something which, in its turn, acts upon and changes the Ideal, and so on. Bakshi attempts, through the example of *The Lord of the Rings*, to establish a new Idea of animation, a meeting of film and concept which could become the foundation for subsequent animation. However, if Bakshi does establish a new Idea of animation, this Idea is only a step in the process of further developments of the form. *The Lord of the Rings* can become a foundation for animation only if we admit that this foundation is transient, temporary and will itself be displaced. Like Frodo's attempt to save the world from evil, it can exist only as quest, as deferral to infinity, and therefore cannot be conceived in traditional terms as stable and permanent. Just as Bakshi himself freed the Idea of animation from its imprisonment in the drawn image, so will his own Idea continue in its path to freedom, a freedom which he himself has made possible. He cannot fix the essence of animation in and by rotoscoping, any more than it can be fixed, by Canemaker or anyone else, in and by drawn animation.

Although it may seem that this search for essences indicates a certain Platonic leaning in Bakshi's approach which would take him closer to Canemaker, there is in fact a subtle difference, one which in fact brings him closer to Husserl and takes him further from Canemaker. Bakshi's Ideal of Ideals would be the redefinition of his chosen discipline through the eventual fusion of the concept of animation with its worldly example on film. That fusion has certainly not occurred with *The Lord of the Rings* or rotoscoping. The very animation of the Ideal precludes the attainment of the Ideal of Ideals. Here, Bakshi's quest resembles not only that of Frodo but that of Husserl. Like Husserl, who vainly searches for a foundation for philosophy, a 'true' philosophy which would be the product of the eventual coincidence of the Idea and its examples in the world, Bakshi will never find a foundation for animation, a 'true' animation; but in the process, both men force us to reconsider their particular disciplines and open up the potential of those disciplines. The Ideal of Ideals does exist for both men, albeit at a point in infinity; but whereas Plato's Ideal will always remain beyond the reach of its earthly simulations, Husserl and Bakshi are striving for that albeit impossible time in the future when fact and Idea will coincide.

In their mutual striving for the Ideal of Ideals, we glimpse the becoming-Husserl of Bakshi and the becoming-Bakshi of Husserl. Husserl's impossible Ideal was the attainment of the a priori principles of all human experience and understanding, whereas Bakshi's Ideal, perhaps not as lofty as that of Husserl but equally impossible, was to develop the type of animation which would most eloquently, and even definitively, bring Tolkien's *The Lord of the Rings* to life and thereby reanimate animation itself. This text was the culmination of many of Bakshi's personal and political concerns. Further, its position as an icon for its time made it the perfect vehicle for the pursuit of his Ideal. It represented a merging of his personal and artistic quests and called for a radical form to express a radical political content.

So this essay is about failure. It is about the failure to attain the Ideal of Ideals and the failure of this Ideal of Ideals to arrest its mobility and deliver itself to the thinker and the animator as a fusion of material fact and evanescent concept, as a fusion of thing and Idea. If the Ideal of Ideals cannot live up to its promise of coincidence of the Idea with the thing in the world, it is because it is only ever a promise, one which can never be fulfilled.

The notion of failure, however, only applies if we accept the terms advanced by the thinker Husserl and the artist Bakshi and the impossibility of attaining the Ideal of Ideals. But if we examine the separate and conjoined becomings of thinker/artist, we see a process, a quest, calling for addressal in its own right. The project of this essay—or better, its own quest—will be the elaboration of this quest. It will be about Husserl's painstaking method of paring down all the inessentials of experience to find an essence, about his seeking the ideal balance between an intersubjective self and the world. It will be about Bakshi's painstaking redrawing of thousands of live action stills, seeking the ideal balance between live action and animation, an attempt to illustrate through the essence of *The Lord of the Rings* the essence of animation. It will also be about Frodo's quest to rid the world of the tool of danger and destruction, the One ring, at the same time ridding it of evil and discovering the essence of good. We shall see how all these quests cannot attain their Ideal; and we shall also see that it is the quest itself which is 'essential' rather than its impossible realization.

Before continuing, I shall attempt a brief overview of Husserlian phenomenology and the role of the Idea in Husserl's thinking. As I shall approach his philosophy in general terms, there will be important omissions because only the facets of Husserl's thinking which are relevant to this essay will be addressed. For the purpose of this text, I will begin by proposing that Husserlian phenomenology is the quest for meaning, or more exactly, for the meaning of meaning, the meaning that meaning has for us. As Paul Ricœur so elegantly puts it, 'Phenomenology begins when, not content to "live" or "relive", we interrupt lived experience in order to signify it'.[21] Meaning for phenomenology has priority over self-consciousness, and the object of consciousness is not an object in the world but meaning. Robert C. Solomon, in his characterization of phenomenology, explains: 'If an *act* has any meaning, that meaning is its object, and if an act has any object, that object is its meaning'.[22]

Thus, phenomenology is primarily about the formation of

meaning and signification, which means that Bakshi, in his quest for a meaning for animation, or more precisely, for the meaning of the meaning of animation, could be regarded as a phenomenologist.

What must be stressed is that when we speak about the 'phenomenon' in phenomenology, we are not speaking about an object. Neither are we referring to a consciousness. Rather, we are drawing out the *relationship* between an object and consciousness. It is this denial of some kind of quasi-realist 'in-itself' of the object which Ricœur considers Husserl's greatest strength:

> Husserl can...maintain the transcendence of the perceived with respect to consciousness...all the while denying the existence in-themselves of the things perceived. This difficult and original setting up of the problem of reality is phenomenology's essential philosophical contribution.[23]

The very discipline of phenomenology is an object without an in-itself, an object which cannot be stabilized. Phenomenology is not a rigid doctrine but a method forever under self-scrutiny, forever in process, forever animated, forever becoming. Phenomenology is a quest, an ongoing adventure; and its goal of a foundation for pure meaning through an intersubjective lived world or *Lebenswelt* is an impossible one. The fact or quest will only coincide with its Idea or goal at infinity, which is to say that they will never coincide. We see an illustration of the unending quest, the ongoing adventure, in *The Lord of the Rings*. Our last encounter with Frodo is from the back. We, together with Frodo and Sam, undertake a journey into a hostile and seemingly infinite landscape where Mordor continually recedes and where Frodo's chances of ridding himself of the ring become increasingly remote.

Bakshi, too, is on a quest; and his search for the essential meaning of animation through the world of rotoscoping is, as I have posited, equally impossible. Just as there cannot be an in-itself of phenomenology, there cannot be an in-itself of animation. Animation can only ever exist in the gap between its realization and consciousness of it. In other words, the phenomenon 'animation' is not a particular object but a relationship, or the Shadow that for T.S. Eliot falls between the idea and the reality, between the motion and the act. Nevertheless, like Frodo, both phenomenologist and animator strongly believe in that final coalescence of thing and concept and attempt to open the possibility for its attainment.

The emphasis of phenomenology is on potency rather than act, process rather than product. The *de jure* teleology of Husserl's thinking is endlessly deferred by the *de facto* process of its realization. Similarly, the process of animation continues, forever experimenting, forever deferring its impossible goal of finding the one telling way to employ the medium. Here we can see radical difference in the Deleuzian sense, in that knowledge, experience, history or the object (in this case animation) can be grasped only reflectively, and thus are subject to the phenomenological process of *Nachverstehen*, that process which repeats but always 'inadequately'—which repeats as difference. That the end is never realized, cannot be realized and—as we shall see—*must* not be realized is the basis of Husserl's philosophy and Bakshian animation.[24]

The Lord of the Rings illustrates quite literally both the process and the unattainable promise. The film does not come to a conclusion; and the elusive, mobile Ideal is never reached. The ring will not be disposed of until the promised sequel, which never comes. Rotoscoping will not 'blow animation wide open'. We are left with the *de facto* or 'real' object, which is nothing more nor less than its process of realization[25]—all the stylistic and thematic elements which make up *The Lord of the Rings*: colour, music, drawn animation and rotoscoping and the process of the narrative. However, if we consider that this process, while not attaining its telos of essential animation, nevertheless demonstrates the primacy of process and the value of striving, we could argue that Bakshi has indeed 'blown animation wide open'. He has countered the premise of theorists like Canemaker that there is only a limited body of work that can call itself animation, a stance based on their belief in an essence of animation which would be an inanimate Ideal.

Therefore, when Bakshi asks, in an interview with Michael Musto, why the realism of Rockwell's paintings and N.C. Wyeth's illustrations for *Treasure Island* works better than that of photographs, it is not because he or anyone else considers photography intrinsically inferior to illustration but because their paintings and illustrations better realize his own aesthetic at this stage of his development. In other words, their work best solicits the Ideal towards which his animation strives.

When Michael Musto asks why he adopts realistic visual effects when *The Lord of the Rings* is hardly a realistic story, Bakshi replies:

> The structure was real… The reason you love *The Lord of the Rings* [and here he means the book] is because you believe it, and to break that belief would hurt the fantasy.[26]

The 'real' structure of which Bakshi speaks emphasizes the *de facto* film on the screen; and the effect reminds us of what Norman M. Klein says about the developers of rotoscoping—Max and Dave Fleischer: 'It is an irony peculiar to the Fleischers [and now to Bakshi] that they used illusion and live action to emphasize the autonomy of the screen, rather than to evoke a nineteenth-century Academic pastoralism as Disney did'.[27]

And it is also that belief—that Husserlian relationship of an inter-subjective consciousness with the object, Tolkien's trilogy—that Bakshi attempts to preserve; and the 'success' or 'failure' of the project is not as relevant as the process he uses to realize his Ideal. Indeed, the project itself could best be seen as the process of animation, the becoming of animation, the animation of animation.[28] Thus, when Canemaker leaps on Bakshi's words and says,

> [i]t is *my* great belief that cartoon and animation are not real. No amount of hype and rotoscoping can make them real. Animation transcends reality and functions best in the realm of the fantastic, the abstract, the caricatured norm,

he does not see that the animation of which he speaks is no less 'real' than Bakshi's, that animation as such is the factical exemplar of an Ideal of animation towards which Canemaker aims, an Ideal which, in his words, 'transcends reality', an Ideal which still remains exactly that—an Ideal—albeit a very different one from Bakshi's. The *process* of animation, whatever factical form it may take, is the only 'truth' of animation for Bakshi, a stance finding a parallel in the words of Jean-François Lyotard. In a statement which embodies the process of becoming, Lyotard says: 'There is no absolute truth, as postulated by dogmatism and scepticism alike; rather, truth defines itself in process, as revision, correction, and self-surpassing ...'[29]

Almost twenty years later, in his interview with Philip Brophy in *KABOOM!: Explosive Animation from America and Japan*, Bakshi twice hints that his interest lies in the *de facto* object, in the form which a film takes. This form, in its process of experimentation, constantly changes the Idea of animation, which in its turn will change the form of not only this film but the next. Although he is not specifically referring to *The Lord of the Rings*, he speaks about the joy of creating motion, which he says is an art form, and adds: 'I was only interested in underground animation, in the art form'.[30] What Bakshi calls the 'art form' can be read as the animation of animation, that is, as the progressive realization of a form of animation which solicits the Idea he calls 'underground'. The art form is not static but in constant dialogue with his Idea; and the Idea, in its turn, will continue to influence Bakshi's filmmaking.

This dialogue can be understood further through an elaboration of the Husserlian dialectic of the Real and the Idea, a dialectic which André de Muralt addresses in his book *The Idea of Phenomenology: Husserlian Exemplarism*.[31] De Muralt argues for the exemplarity of the Real and the Idea, and the following is indebted to his investigation.

Husserl uses science as his point of departure to discuss his notion of the Idea. Ideal science and real science are exemplars of one another: the Ideal will be the ideal example of real science, while real science will be the factical example of Ideal science. In other words, the Ideal exemplar is elicited from the fact at the same time as the factical becomes exemplary through its relationship with the Ideal. The relationship becomes animated as both the Ideal and the factical examples reciprocally act and are acted upon and are both constantly transformed. Here we see the difference from the commonly accepted static and immutable nature of the Platonic Idea.[32] Students of Husserl's phenomenology might argue that the Husserlian Idea does suggest a totality; but, as de Muralt asserts, it can only ever be an *assumed*, unattainable, imaginary, contingent totality, a totality 'as if' (*Quasi-totalitat, Als-ob*).

Thus, the Idea, an infinite pole which is always unattainable, can only be gleaned from the progressive realization of real data which exist in the world. Here again, we can turn to Bakshi's film and glimpse from the real data—the animation techniques, the development of the 'art form', as well as the character development—the Idea towards which it strives, the Idea as a new form which will speak to adult lovers of fantasy. For Husserl as for Bakshi, the movement from the real to the Ideal does not travel in one direction only, but rather in a reciprocal movement: just as the worldly facts strive to realize the Ideal, so the Ideal becomes constituted by progressive factical realization structured by time, something which binds the Idea to history.[33] We note here that the historicity of the Idea is Husserl's most radical departure from Plato. Husserl's Idea is an open-ended construct, characterized by the fundamental form 'and so forth', or *Grundform des Und-so-weiter.* One may therefore look at science as either an idealization of real science or a progressive realization of Ideal science. As de Muralt says:

> ...here we have a new way of expressing the reciprocal exemplarity of the idea and the real: it can equally well be said either that the idea is realized or that the real is idealized.[34]

Indeed, one could go further to propose that both can be said at the same time.

But if the Idea of animation is historical, temporal, always in a state of transformation, can there ever be such a thing as 'pure' uncontaminated animation? The answer is, of course, no, for as we enter the animated world—be it early animation, Bakshi's work or Beavis and Butt-head—and recognize that world with its own specificities and peculiarities, we also recognize and are guided by our own world and the whole range of historical, cultural and technological concerns which go into making it our world. So, for instance, the cartoon seen in the '60s is different from the same cartoon seen in the '90s. At both times the Idea of animation is solicited; but in the later case, the Idea has been changed by history. Who is to say which is pure? And what, in this case, could pure animation be? Each factical example of animation—be it drawing on cels, rotoscoping, computer animation or virtual reality—stretches, bends and transforms what we mean when we speak of animation. In other words, through Husserl's theorization of the Real and Ideal, the Idea is acted upon by every factical example of animation; but in its turn, every factical example is acted upon by the constantly changing Idea.

When we say that the factical example and the Idea 'act upon' one another, we are of course speaking of animation. To speak of animation, as we have seen, is not to discuss only the variety of forms by which movement on a surface can be delivered. In the sense of giving both new movement and a new life, Husserl has animated and been animated by Plato's Idea; Bakshi has animated and been animated by Husserl; Deleuze and Guattari have animated and been animated by Plato, by Husserl and by Bakshi. Further, it is hoped that this text has been animated and animates, breathes new movement and life into the figures and into the Idea which it solicits.

There have been and will be other texts, other Ideas, on the same subject. This demonstrates the historicity, the animated nature, of the Idea, for if the Idea is in flux, always moving, always acted on by the real, and vice versa, always open to change, it is obviously temporal or historical. The temporality of fact and Idea was a site of much self-questioning by Husserl. While his goal, as I read it, was to reach a utopia where fact and Idea would coincide, a fixing which would therefore render the product of that coincidence ahistorical, throughout this search for a foundationalist discipline he knew that until that coincidence—an impossible event—occurred, fact and Idea must remain animated, temporal, historical through and through. One could therefore say that the historicity of the Idea is both the triumph and the grand failure of Husserlian phenomenology. Phenomenology expects the Idea to be at the same time nothing and something. On the one hand, the Idea is nothing, as its existence is given only by the fact which strives towards it. On the other hand, it is always something, for it is that which gives existence to the fact which it regulates and determines. It is that which makes the fact possible, yet it is also that which the fact can never realize. This therefore makes both the Idea and the fact mutually contingent, unfathomable, unknowable and impossible, at the same time that both are reciprocally necessary.

We further encounter some of the difficulties and aporias of Husserl's thinking when we examine the role played by time in his philosophy. Individual transcendental consciousness is Ideal, as is the collective lifeworld or *Lebenswelt*. Although the Ideal has been shown to be different from Plato's, Husserl nevertheless strives (although impossibly) for an Ideal which will be atemporal, infinite, beyond time, and which therefore cannot have a history. Yet for Husserl, consciousness must have a sense of internal time and a relationship with the Other and with the world. This relationship cannot be static, cannot exist outside time, outside history. But if consciousness is Ideal, ahistorical, it cannot also be temporal or historical. Within this insoluble aporia of the simultaneous temporality and atemporality of Ideal consciousness lies what I have so far called Husserl's failure. In Ricœur's words:

> The *Lebenswelt* is never actually given but always presupposed. It is phenomenology's paradise lost. It is in this sense that phenomenology has undermined its own guiding idea in the very attempt to realize it. It is this that gives to Husserl's work its tragic grandeur.[35]

Although it would be absurd (or would it?) to apply the words 'tragic grandeur' to Bakshi, we could posit here that he too failed in his attempt to 'blow animation wide open' through his use of rotoscoping, and that, fatalistically, he expected to be misunderstood by the likes of Canemaker. 'I'll be creamed by your establishment and creamed by your Tolkien fans', he said to Michael Musto, 'and somewhere in the middle I'll sit there bleeding. I sit there dead'.[36]

Yet in a very important sense, neither Husserl nor Bakshi did fail. For what would have happened if they had reached their Ideal? If science were to reach its telos, the opposition between the Ideal and the real, immanence and transcendence, would no longer make sense. Science would no longer *have* meaning, it would *be* meaning; and this notion is as absurd for science as for other cases which concern phenomenology, such as perception, judgement, even phenomenology itself. For it is a question neither of the fact's independent existence nor of its inability to coincide with the Idea. Rather, it is the case that they *must* never coincide if we are to think phenomenologically, because, as we have seen, phenomenology is about process and relationships, about animation, rather than about fixity and dogma.

If phenomenology were realizable, finalizable, there could be no phenomenology. The Idea can no more be divorced from the crude empirical fact which strives to realize it than the fact can be severed from its quest for the Ideal. In the film, Frodo and Sam do not reach Mount Doom. 'There's that Mount Doom again, Mr Frodo', says Sam, 'the one place in all the world that we don't want to see and that's the one place we're trying to get to'.

Likewise, if Bakshi had 'blown animation wide open', if the film *The Lord of the Rings* had realized the Idea of animation, if rotoscoping had become a pure form of animation, there could no longer be any other examples of animation. There could no longer be a practice called animation.

And thematically, pure goodness could not be realized either, even if Frodo had succeeded in his quest. For the Idea of pure good is untenable, unrecognizable, unrealizable by any worldly fact that strives to realize it. The figure of the ring can never be closed, and neither can the analogous figure of the wheel, as the *rota* in rotoscope, and Bakshi's use of it, tell and perform for animation and for us.

We notice how many examples of obligatory non-closure and non-coincidence are literally represented in the film: the non-coincidence with themselves of Bakshi's lines, which always seem to be multiplying, shimmering and shifting; the non-coincidence of rotoscope with drawn animation; the non-coincidence of animation with live action; and the non-coincidence of Frodo's quest with his goal, which, like Bakshi's and Husserl's, could be taken as a metaphor for non-coincidence itself, non-coincidence as such.

So we can perhaps see Husserl's labour as an endless deferral of Ideality, an Ideality which he hopes will one day be attained by his successors. He writes:

> The author sees the infinite open country of the true philosophy, the 'promised land' on which he himself will never set foot...

> Gladly would he hope that those who come after will take up these first ventures...[37]

He thus bequeaths his quest to his legatees. But his legatees, for instance, Deleuze and Guattari, turn away from the absolutes which are impossible to attain. Instead, they focus on the notion of non-coincidence in Husserl's thinking, rather than on the impossible achievement of an unreachable Ideal.

And Bakshi's work may indeed be an aesthetic and critical failure. It may be long, boring, incomplete and incomprehensible. But in the non-coincidence with its own or anyone else's Ideal of animation, it displays an audacity and a willingness to question canons and prescriptions about his chosen form of expression. So, in a sense, he does 'blow animation wide open'—open to questions about what is proper to animation, about the possibility of ever achieving an uncontaminated Ideal animation. Like Husserl, he opens the possibility for his own legatees, in this case for animators who are willing to take risks, willing to experiment with their medium and to animate animation, instead of considering animation simply as drawn cels put into motion. In the process, and *by means of* the process, these animators transform both the medium and its Ideal.[38]

Perhaps Frodo speaks best for Bakshi, Husserl and the primacy of process in his reply to Sam at the end of the film. Sam is worried about the fact that they are running out of food, that their food will only last them until they reach Mount Doom, and wonders what might happen after that. Frodo says:

> *After that*, when the ring goes into the fire, *after that*...I wouldn't worry, dear Sam. Just to get there, just to get there—but the ring is so heavy now.

NOTES

1 T.S. Eliot, 'The Hollow Men' (1925), in T.S. Eliot, *The Complete Poems and Plays, 1909-1950* (New York: Harcourt, Brace and Company, 1934, 1952), p. 58.

2 Gilles Deleuze and Félix Guattari, '1730: Becoming-Intense, Becoming-

Animal, Becoming Imperceptible...', *A Thousand Plateaus: Capitalism and Schizophrenia*, trans. Brian Massumi (Minneapolis: University of Minnesota Press, 1987), p. 274.

3 Hugh Tomlinson and Robert Galeta, Translators' Introduction to Gilles Deleuze, *Cinema 2: The Time-Image* (Minneapolis: University of Minnesota Press, 1989), p. xv.

4 Deleuze and Guattari, *A Thousand Plateaus*, p. 238.

5 ibid.

6 See Samuel Weber, 'The Unravelling of Form', *Mass Mediauras: Form, Technics, Media*, ed. Alan Cholodenko (Sydney/Stanford: Power Publications/Stanford University Press, 1996), where Platonic and Kantian notions of form are shown to 'unravel', where form de-forms itself. Deleuze and Guattari, however, for the sake of their argument, propose a more conventional notion of form so as to pit the molar against the molecular.

7 Deleuze and Guattari write:

> You become animal only molecularly. You do not become a barking molar dog, but by barking, if it is done with enough feeling, with enough necessity and composition, you emit a molecular dog. Man does not become wolf, or vampire, as if he changed molar species: the vampire and werewolf are becomings of man, in other words, proximities between molecules in composition, relations of movement and rest, speed and slowness between emitted particles. *A Thousand Plateaus*, p. 275.

8 See, for instance, Deleuze, *Difference and Repetition*, trans. Paul Patton (New York: Columbia University Press, 1994); Deleuze, 'Plato and the Simulacrum', trans. Rosalind Krauss, *October* 27, Winter 1983; and Paul Patton, 'Anti-Platonism and Art', in *Gilles Deleuze and the Theater of Philosophy*, eds. Constantin V. Boundas and Dorothea Olkowski (New York: Routledge, 1994).

9 Deleuze, 'Plato and the Simulacrum', p. 47. See also Lisa Trahair's discussion of animation through Plato's 'good' and 'bad' copies in 'For the Noise of a Fly', in *THE ILLUSION OF LIFE: Essays on Animation*, ed. Alan Cholodenko (Sydney: Power Publications in association with the Australian Film Commission, 1991), pp. 190-192.

10 Hugh Tomlinson and Barbara Habberjam, Translators' Introduction to Deleuze, *Cinema 1: The Movement-Image*, trans. Hugh Tomlinson

and Barbara Habberjam (Minneapolis: University of Minnesota Press, 1986), p. xii.

11 See Deleuze, *Difference and Repetition*, especially the 'Introduction: Repetition and Difference'. It seems that some of the arguments in this chapter relate to Edmund Husserl's idea of the reciprocal exemplarity of the Real and the Idea, to be discussed below.

12 Charles Solomon, *Enchanted Drawings: The History of Animation* (New York: Wings Books, 1989, 1994), pp. 268-269. The information in this paragraph on *Fritz the Cat* comes from Solomon.

13 Bakshi quoted by Kirk Honeycutt in *Special Features* (New York: The New York Times Syndication Sales Corporation, 1978), n.p. This is promotional material available at the Celeste Bartos Film Study Center, Museum of Modern Art, New York.

14 See Solomon, *Enchanted Drawings*, p. 30.

15 ibid.

16 The Bakshi quotes and information provided in this paragraph are from Honeycutt, *Special Features*. n.p.

17 For positive commentary, see Aljean Harmetz, 'Bakshi Journeys to Middle Earth to Animate *Lord of the Rings*', *The New York Times*, November 8, 1978, p. C17; the similar approach adopted by Michael Musto in 'What's a Hobbit?', in *The Weekly News*, November 16, 1978, p. 67; glowing reviews by William Carlton, 'Frodo Lives & So Does *the Ring*', *The Daily News*, November 19, 1978, n.p.; C.J. Henderson, '*The Lord of the Rings*', *Questar 3*, March 1979, pp. 32-34 and 62; and James Delson, 'The Arts', *Omni*, December 1978, pp. 26 and 135. For negative commentary, consult John Canemaker's review, entitled 'John Canemaker reviews *The Lord of the Rings*', November 16, 1978 (see note 19 below); David Ansen and Stryker McGuire's equally negative review, 'Hobbits and Rabbits', in *Newsweek*, November 20, 1978, pp. 79-81; and Paul Gray's criticisms in 'Frodo Moves', *Time*, November 20, 1978, p. 78.

18 Bakshi's return to rotoscoping is, of course, not only a return to an earlier period in animation but an inscription in the form of its name of the whole tradition of philosophers' toys that were precursors to both animation and live action cinema, even as such toys were prior to the artificial distinction between these modes of film. Such toys included Joseph Plateau's Phenakisticope, Simon von Stampfer's Stroboscope, Eadweard Muybridge's Zoopraxiscope and Emile Reynaud's Praxinoscope.

19 The review is entitled 'John Canemaker reviews *The Lord of the Rings*',

with the byline 'John Canemaker, NYC 11/16/78'. Efforts to determine where it was published have proven fruitless. The following quotes are taken from it.

20 The quotation distinguishing the Platonic philosopher and the poet for Plato is that of Patton on Deleuze in 'Anti-Platonism and Art', p. 151. For me, both Deleuze and Bakshi enact that poet.

21 Paul Ricœur, *From Text to Action: Essays in Hermeneutics, II*, trans. Kathleen Blamey and John B. Thompson (Evanston: Northwestern University Press, 1991), p. 40.

22 Robert C. Solomon, *From Hegel to Existentialism* (New York: Oxford University Press, 1987), p. 174.

23 Ricœur, *Husserl: An Analysis of His Phenomenology*, trans. Edward G. Ballard and Lester E. Embree (Evanston: Northwestern University Press, 1967), p. 9.

24 Husserl, however, pursues adequation as his Ideal. Factual non-coincidence nevertheless anticipates Ideal coincidence.

25 Here we can note that the real is neither the material film nor the theories of animation which Bakshi brings to the film through rotoscoping, but the *process* of realizing the theory through the film, and vice versa—the process of becoming. We can refer back to the quote by Deleuze and Guattari: 'What is *real* [my emphasis] is the becoming itself' (note 5).

26 Bakshi quoted in Musto, *The Weekly News.*, n.p.

27 Norman M. Klein, *Seven Minutes: the Life and Death of the American Animated Cartoon* (London: Verso, 1993), p. 59.

28 Such becoming of animation encompasses the becoming-Deleuze of phenomenology; the becoming-Husserl of Deleuze; the becoming-phenomenology of animation, etc. All these becomings are reciprocal and mutable. They animate this text and are animated by it.

29 Jean-François Lyotard, *Phenomenology*, trans. Brian Beakley (Albany: State University of New York Press, 1991), p. 62. Which means we can speak too of the becoming-Bakshi of Lyotard, and vice versa.

30 'Bakshi Interview: Philip Brophy talks to Ralph Bakshi', in *KABOOM!: Explosive Animation from America and Japan* (Sydney: Museum of Contemporary Art, 1994), p. 92.

31 The following two paragraphs are drawn from André de Muralt, *The Idea of Phenomenology: Husserlian Exemplarism*, trans. Garry L. Breckon (Evanston: Northwestern University Press, 1974). These are points made throughout his text.

32 I am using this characterization of Plato's Idea, one which is commonly espoused in texts and dictionaries of philosophy, and one which I believe underlies Canemaker's approach, although earlier I have

proposed after Deleuze that the Platonic Idea is itself unstable, that the 'bad copy' or simulation is not a bad copy at all but is of a different order. See Deleuze, 'Plato and the Simulacrum'.

33 In this specific sense, history and historicity are used to emphasize the temporal dimension crucial to the understanding of Husserl's fact and Idea.

34 de Muralt, *The Idea of Phenomenology: Husserlian Exemplarism*, p. 25.

35 Ricœur, *From Text to Action: Essays in Hermeneutics, II*, p. 14.

36 Bakshi quoted in Musto, *The Weekly News*, n.p.

37 Edmund Husserl, 'Author's Preface to the English Edition', *Ideas: General Introduction to Pure Phenomenology*, trans. W.R. Boyce Gibson (London: George Allen & Unwin, 1958), p. 29.

38 We can now include, among Husserl's legatees, Peter Jackson, who divided Tolkein's epic into three parts for his *Lord of the Rings* trilogy. While the first part, shown in 2002, and the second, in 2003, compose a live action film with state of the art special effects, their debt to Bakshi's animated feature cannot be ignored. The overall aesthetic of both parts—dark and foreboding—is reminiscent of their precursor; and the Black Riders bear an uncanny resemblance to the much maligned rotoscoped figures that threatened Frodo in the earlier film. Other parallels exist, but merit more space than can be given in this essay.

3 Japan and the United States

Kimba races to the rescue. This dramatic run cycle appeared in many episodes, animated over different backgrounds. © 1966/2007 Tezuka Production Co., Ltd/Mushi Production Co., Ltd. Image courtesy of The Right Stuf International, Inc.

Simba Versus Kimba: The Pride of Lions*

FRED PATTEN

INTRODUCTION

The February 27, 1995 *Los Angeles Times* quoted the Disney Company's Roy E. Disney as saying that *The Lion King* 'would be the most profitable movie of all time, with about $800 million in profits from its box office, video sales, merchandising, and other sources...'[50] In addition to the technical excellence of its animation, its great popularity was generally attributed to the strength of its characters and story: the maturing of a lion prince, Simba, from an insecure cub to a strong ruler of all the animals of the jungle.

However, this was not the first time that this plot appeared in animation. One of the major works of Japanese animation is Osamu Tezuka's 1965-1966 *Jungle Emperor*, known in the West as *Kimba the White Lion*.[3] This is the story of the maturing of a lion prince, Kimba, from an idealistic but often naive cub with self-doubts to a confident leader of all the animals of the jungle.

Similarities between the two titles were immediately noticed and commented upon, at least partly because of Disney's publicity emphasis of its claim that *The Lion King* was its first animated feature

*Endnote numbers reference the entries in 'Fred Patten's Annotated Chronology of Pertinent Works and Publications Relevant to *The Lion King* and to the Controversy' in the Appendix. Hence, they do not follow standard numerical sequence, as is observed in the other essays.

which was an entirely original studio-developed story, not based upon any previous folk tale or literary work. During the three or four months after the release of *The Lion King*, the issue generated considerable controversy in America and in Japan. This was exacerbated by Disney's further claim in the July 14, 1994 *San Francisco Chronicle* that 'None of the principals involved in creating *The Lion King* were aware of Kimba or Tezuka', according to 'Howard Green, spokesman for Walt Disney Pictures'[25] (p. D1). This assertion seemed improbably ignorant to both American and Japanese critics, since Osamu Tezuka was internationally famous as 'the Walt Disney of Japan' and since the *Kimba* TV cartoons had been widely shown on American TV from 1966 until the early 1980s.

This essay presents a brief summary of the career of Osamu Tezuka and of his *Kimba the White Lion*, with an emphasis on public awareness of them in America. An overview of the production of Disney's *The Lion King* is next presented, and similarities between it and *Kimba* are addressed. Finally, Tezuka's international reputation as an award-winning animator and Disney's expertise in the animation industry are discussed in relation to Disney's claims of a lack of awareness of Tezuka or of *Kimba*. While the essay draws support for its position from the work of Fred Ladd, Trish Ledoux, Frederik L. Schodt and Toren Smith on the matter, its conclusions are those of the author alone. I have undertaken this essay to collate evidence from many diverse sources and to add my own personal knowledge acquired over two decades as an enthusiast and expert on both American and Japanese animation.

A BIOGRAPHICAL SKETCH OF OSAMU TEZUKA

Osamu Tezuka is widely revered in Japan as the founder of its comic book and animation industries. He was not the first to create either comic books or animation; but, like Disney, he came into a nascent industry and became its trend-setter.

Osamu Tezuka was born on November 3, 1928 in Osaka. He entered college as a medical student just after World War II. He was also a precocious cartoonist and an enthusiast of animation. In 1946, at the age of 18, he published his first professional comic book.

Shortly after obtaining his physician's license, he was forced to concentrate upon one career or the other; and he chose cartooning.

The Japanese comic book industry scarcely existed before Tezuka. His career and this artistic literary form evolved together. Tezuka gave 'comic book artist' a completely different interpretation to that which it had in America. He was essentially a visual novelist and short story writer. He produced his own stories of varying lengths for a wide variety of magazines.

Among Tezuka's early artistic influences were the American animated cartoons and newspaper comic strips from the Disney and Fleischer studios. Tezuka later acknowledged his debt to the *Mickey Mouse* newspaper strip drawn by Disney artist Floyd Gottfredson and to the Fleischer Brothers' 1939 *Gulliver's Travels*. One of Tezuka's few graphic adaptations of someone else's work was an authorized Japanese comic book version of Disney's *Bambi*, published in 1951.[2] Frederik L. Schodt, Tezuka's personal English translator for many years, has said that Tezuka considered Disney to be his idol.[57]

His works included children's picture books, fantasy-adventure comics for boys, fantasy-romance comics for girls, raunchy humour for men's magazines, psychological thrillers and historical novels for serious adult magazines, political cartoons, poster art and advertising art. He was instrumental in establishing the Japanese cultural attitude that cartooning was not limited to children's entertainment but was an acceptable medium for the presentation of fiction for all age groups.

In 1961, Tezuka created Japan's first TV animation studio. The existing studios were all concentrating on the famous Disney formula of high-quality theatrical animated features based on traditional folk tales. Japan's most elaborate feature up to that time was Toei Animation's 1960 *Sai Yuki* (brought to America in 1961 as *Alakazam the Great*), an adaptation by Director Taiji Yabushita of Tezuka's own 1950s comic art interpretation of the classic Chinese *Monkey King* legend. (The aforementioned artistic influences from Gottfredson's *Mickey Mouse* and the Fleischers' *Gulliver's Travels* are noticeable here.) Nonetheless, Tezuka recognized that the animation establishment was ignoring a public demand for modern and futuristic cartoon adventures on film, as demonstrated by the increasing sales of comic books featuring those plots during the previous decade.

Tezuka's studio, Mushi Productions, premiered its first TV series on New Year's Day 1963—*Mighty Atom* (*Tetsuwan Atom,* meaning actually Iron Arm Atom but conventionally translated as Mighty Atom)—brought to America later that year as *Astro Boy*. It was an instant, great success, so much so that within two years, a half-dozen other TV animation studios had sprung up in competition.

While turning his back on the Disney formula of remaking the classics in his pioneering of this new genre, Tezuka did not turn his back on another signature feature of Disney's animation, that is, he followed Disney's lead in concentrating on characters rather than on gags or action or flashy visuals. *Mighty Atom* was most easily symbolized by its futuristic setting and its little boy robot star. But what won it a devoted following was its strong characterizations, generated through the personal interactions of a regular cast of characters. Tezuka refined this Disney formula in his second TV series, *Jungle Emperor*, or *Kimba the White Lion*, which many feel was really his best work.

After that, Tezuka fell victim to his own determination to remain an artist rather than a businessman. He was not interested in repeating the same things *ad infinitum* just because they made money. Ironically, what befell Mushi Productions was basically what befell the Disney studio after Disney's personal attention shifted to his EPCOT project and he let his staff take complete directorial control over his features. In Tezuka's case, he began to concentrate on avant-garde animations, such as *Pictures at an Exhibition* (1966), a *Fantasia*-like production of Mussorgsky's musical classic, with the individual 'pictures' being satiric political cartoon commentaries on aspects of contemporary society; and *One Thousand and One Nights* (1969), a feature length version of the classic *Arabian Nights* tale which was faithful to the mature eroticism of the original work. These garnered critical acclaim, but they were not commercial successes.

Mushi Productions continued to produce TV series, but they lacked the strong characterizations that had gone into *Astro Boy* and *Kimba*. In 1971, Tezuka left Mushi Productions for a new studio, Tezuka Productions. Although Tezuka Productions has produced numerous commercial projects—and is still doing so today—Tezuka's own attention remained upon short, experimental films which he personally took to animation festivals around the world, where they invariably won major awards. The most famous examples are *Jumping* (1984), *Broken-Down Film* (1985), and *Legend of the Forest* (1987). Osamu Tezuka passed away from cancer on February 9, 1989, working to the end.

THE PUBLICATION AND POPULAR INFLUENCE OF *JUNGLE EMPEROR* IN JAPAN

Although Tezuka produced over 500 different comic art stories during his life, among his top ten and the first to win critical acclaim was *Junguru Taitei*, translated into English by Tezuka himself as *The Jungle Emperor*, but more idiomatically *King of the Jungle*.

This was his first major work. It began publication in a children's magazine, *Manga Shonen* (*Boys' Comics*), in November 1950.[1] It was the story of an intelligent African lion, named Leo in the Japanese version, who tried to improve the lot of all animals. It was an adventure fantasy with talking animals, not a realistic nature novel; and it explored concepts of civilization in comparison to natural instinct. It showed how issues that seem simplistically right or wrong to a child can look much more complex to an adult, and made the point that a full life is bound to encompass both happiness and tragedy.

Jungle Emperor was a serious children's novel in cartoon form, and it was almost immediately recognized as such. Its serialization took three and a half years to complete; the final installment was in April 1954. The first book reprints of its over 500 pages appeared while it was still being serialized. It has been almost constantly in print, in editions ranging from a *de luxe* boxed, hardbound single volume to inexpensive paperbound sets of three or four volumes. Tezuka slightly revised the story several times, and the final version was published in 1977.

To give some perspective, Tezuka's *Mighty Atom* (*Astro Boy*) began in another comic book, *Shonen* (*Boy*), in April 1951. This was more of a comic book series in the American sense. It consisted of numerous serialized short stories which Tezuka kept spinning out. There was originally no planned conclusion to the series, although Tezuka wrote one in the late 1960s. During the great popularity of the *Mighty Atom* TV series, the commercial pressures on Tezuka to produce more comic book adventures grew to the point where he admitted becoming heartily sick of having to hack out new stories. But despite the fact that the *Jungle Emperor* TV program was also extremely popular, Tezuka was never seriously tempted to expand that finished novel (as distinct from his fine-tuning of the existing pages).

Jungle Emperor became a national institution. This was due to the TV cartoons as much as to the novel. They were broadcast from 1965 to 1967, and their characters—slightly modified from those in the cartoon novel—became merchandising idols. A unique aspect of this was that, in Japan, unlike in America, Leo and his girl friend, Lya, matured, married and had cubs of their own. Therefore, the Japanese *Jungle Emperor* merchandising included additional characters unknown in America. This merchandising consisted of the usual range of Disney, Hanna-Barbera or Warner Bros. style cartoon character toys, items such as childrens' towels and band-aids, calendars, and so forth.

But awareness in Japan of *Jungle Emperor* did not stop with the completion of the TV cartoons. Mighty Atom and Leo became the standard character-emblems of Tezuka and his cartooning empire, just as Mickey Mouse and Donald Duck have remained permanently associated with Walt Disney in America, long after their animated cartoons ceased production. A symphonic suite arrangement of Isao Tomita's music for the *Jungle Emperor* pilot episode became a Japanese children's musical classic, comparable to Prokofieff's *Peter and the Wolf*; and it is still in circulation. The adult Leo became the cartoon mascot-logo of the Seibu Lions, one of Japan's top baseball teams. In the 1970s and 1980s, after serious animation fandom developed in Japan, numerous books on the *Jungle Emperor* TV cartoons were published, giving full details about their production history and staff and credits for each episode. Leo toys and other juvenile merchandise have continued to appear every year, keeping up with the times as concerns computer games, PVC figures and the latest in packaging design. One of Tezuka's last business decisions was to authorize a remake of the *Jungle Emperor* TV series by Tezuka Productions. This was considered by both his staff and the public as largely a memorial to him. It was serialized as 50 weekly episodes from October 1989, eight months after his death, through September 1990, in a 7:30 p.m. prime time spot.[13]

ANALYSIS OF THE PLOT AND THEME OF *JUNGLE EMPEROR*

Jungle Emperor is primarily the story of a lion, Leo, who is the heir to a kingdom of jungle animals near Kenya. He is born on a ship taking his captured mother to a European zoo, so all that he initially knows about his heritage is the little that she has time to tell him—that he is the son of a jungle king who was killed by human hunters and that he must escape and return to help the animals. Leo does escape from the ship, but he ends up in the port city of Aden. Since he is still a cute cub, a human boy is allowed to temporarily keep him as a pet.

Leo's experiences in this family situation, and his growing friendship with the boy Ken-ichi, lead him to realize that humans are not automatically bad—they can be good or bad. When, after various adventures, Leo returns to the jungle and assumes the leadership of the animal kingdom, he has two ideals that he enthusiastically wants to put into practice: first, animals and humans should live together as fellow inhabitants of the same world, not as distinct life forms separate from each other; and second, the animals themselves should imitate humans in building a cooperative civilization instead of fatalistically accepting the harsh law of the jungle as an immutable natural order.

Tezuka commented at a presentation to the Cartoon/Fantasy Organization in Los Angeles in March 1978, at which this author was present, that his inspiration for *Jungle Emperor* was in part his disagreement with the philosophy of nature and intelligence expressed in Disney's *Bambi*. Tezuka felt that if the forest animals in *Bambi* had been as self-aware and mutually social as they were depicted, they would not have remained so fearful and remote from man. They would have recognized man as just another animal like themselves and tried to communicate with him. This led to his own story in which the animals of Africa realize the advantages of civilization and try to take advantage of them and try to get man to recognize them as social equals. Tezuka always felt that both 'nature' and 'civilization' were aspects of the same real world, rather than separate worlds, and that both the advantages and disadvantages of each needed to be taken into account. (In some of his other works, notably *Phoenix*, begun in 1954 and revised and expanded during the rest of his life, Tezuka describes a futuristic, overly mechanized civilization that has totally lost touch with nature, leading to its self-destruction.)

As Leo matures, he gradually learns more about his ancestors and the special role of his white lion dynasty. He also discovers that some of his initial expectations were unrealistically simplistic. For example, he learns that carnivores do not eat other animals just because they are ignorant or uncaring of the virtues of friendship. Carnivores cannot voluntarily switch to grazing like the herbivores—they would starve to death. Leo does the best that he can, sometimes cutting back on his goals, sometimes proving to the other animals that cooperation does work better than 'every animal for itself'. Leo finds a girl friend; when they become adults, they marry and have two cubs. After other triumphs and tragedies, Leo joins a human scientific expedition searching for a rare mineral atop Mount Moon. One of the members of this expedition is the father of Leo's childhood human friend. At the climax, Leo sacrifices his own life to save Ken-ichi's father. *Jungle Emperor* ends with an affirmation that Leo's son, Luné (who has had his own adventures in a long subplot in New York City), has returned to the jungle and will carry on Leo's peaceful animal civilization and his ideals of a brotherhood of all nature that includes man.

THE ANIMATED VERSION OF *JUNGLE EMPEROR*

There are significant differences between Tezuka's cartoon art novel and the animated adaptation of *Jungle Emperor*, differences that issued from Tezuka's desire to distribute his work in the United States and the conditions that attached to this aspiration. Previously, *Mighty Atom* had been acquired for the American market by NBC, shortly after it debuted in Japan on January 1, 1963; and it premiered in America as a syndicated series, *Astro Boy*, in September 1963. NBC's money was a welcome windfall; it enabled Tezuka to increase the production values of the later episodes.

In 1965, Tezuka felt ready to animate *Jungle Emperor*. He had no trouble preselling it to Japan's Fuji TV network, but he also wanted to get NBC's money into its production and from the start. His proposal to NBC was for a serialization of his novel, from Leo's birth to his heroic death. This was completely foreign to American ideas for children's television, but NBC liked the concept of a friendly, altruistic lion who promoted brotherhood and cooperation. They offered Tezuka enough money to film *Jungle Emperor* in colour rather than in black-and-white, if he would agree to some changes. The story should concentrate on the animals in Leo's kingdom and downplay the humans. Leo should remain a cute cub and never grow up, and *certainly* never die! In fact, nobody should ever die. NBC wanted an upbeat series with violence at a minimum. Finally, the story should be restructured into self-contained episodes that could be shown in any order rather than as a serial.

Tezuka was very unhappy. But he did want to produce *Jungle Emperor* in higher-quality, colour animation; and he wanted to introduce his story to American audiences, so he agreed to NBC's terms. Nevertheless, he tried to keep as close to his original story as NBC would allow. There were references in flashback to Leo's experiences in the humans' civilization before he came to the jungle—a sequence that NBC had wanted removed. In addition to the deaths of Leo's parents (NBC had conceded that this was too integral to the plot to be removed), there were occasional fatalities, or clear references to mortality. In the episode *Dangerous Journey*, when the old mountain goat who has a fever soliloquizes about going off by himself to spare the other animals from catching his disease, it is obvious that he expects to die. As the episodes were sent to America, NBC kept telling Tezuka to 'lighten up', which he promised to do, but went on inserting as much drama as he could get away with.

The animated *Jungle Emperor*, then, was not really to either Tezuka's or NBC's credit. It was an uneasy, grudging mixture of American and Japanese cultural styles. In the novel, Leo might have a bloody fight with some large animal, such as an elephant, who refused to abide by his policies of cooperation. This may have been plausible where Leo was an adult lion, but it was not credible that a little cub could defeat such massive animals. The solution was to make Leo a super-cub, with unusual strength as well as his unique white colouring. That way he could easily overpower his adversaries and then deliver a moral lecture to them, without needing to maul them into submission. It also made Leo more like a super-hero, with which American juveniles were comfortable.

If the animated *Jungle Emperor* is to any single individual's credit, that person is its director, Eiichi Yamamoto. Tezuka kept an eye on the general story line, but he gave Yamamoto free rein in adapting the 533 page novel into 52 separate episodes. It was Yamamoto who gave *Jungle Emperor* its subtle but crucial changes. He had to replace story evolution with character development. Since the animated version's setting was fixed in the jungle animal kingdom during Leo's childhood, the focus had to shift to the animals themselves and their social relationships. Tezuka had drawn the juvenile Leo as the cub equivalent of an eight year old human. This was too young for a plausible kingdom-founder, so Yamamoto portrayed Leo as a husky 11 or 12 year old, approaching adolescence. Yamamoto combined most of Leo's various animal antagonists into a single villain, a brutish one-eyed lion who had seized the vacant jungle throne after Leo's father's death. He turned this villain's assistant, Tot (a comical black panther), into a much more sinister henchman, and gave Tot's old comedy relief role to two new stooges, a couple of laughing hyenas. (The idea was briefly considered of having them be lieutenants who would pass the villain's orders down to a whole pack of hyena goons, but the TV animation budget did not permit the addition of so many characters.)

Most importantly, Yamamoto created the large supporting cast of Leo's friends. A couple had been minor characters in Tezuka's novel. Others were invented by Yamamoto. The cast included Mandy, the old baboon father-figure and advisor; Coco, the comically pompous parrot who appoints himself as Leo's herald and news-gatherer; Tommy, the well-meaning but often inept gazelle; the several animal children; and the older, larger animals who are initially skeptical of Leo's lofty ideals and are gradually won over to become Leo's supporters. Some of the minor characters, such as the hedgehog, might appear only for a few seconds in every seventh or eighth episode; but when they did, they stood out from the others and were completely in character with their previous appearances. This large, regular cast of individualized, likeable characters has been cited by fans in both Japan and America as what they liked best about the program.

Other notable aspects of the high quality of *Jungle Emperor* were the rich use of colour, also to Yamamoto's credit, and the background music, which was scored for a full orchestra by Isao Tomita before he became a prestigious composer of electronic music. When Tezuka agreed to produce *Jungle Emperor* in colour, he wanted its quality to be as high as possible. *Astro Boy*'s American producer, Fred Ladd, arranged for Tezuka and Yamamoto to send a Mushi animation team to Ladd's New York office where they were instructed in colour production by veteran former Disney animator Preston Blair.

There was also an unusual sequel. It rankled Tezuka that he had not been allowed to film *Jungle Emperor* as the life story of Leo. As soon as the 52 episodes that he was obligated to produce to NBC's standards were completed, he began a 26 episode sequel—*Susume, Leo!* (*susume* is a Japanese colloquial shout of daring encouragement, as for a cavalry charge or a football team's advance)—set about five years later. Leo and Lya were now adults; and the story continued roughly as it had in Tezuka's graphic novel, although Leo did not quite die in the final episode. (He survived to abdicate in his son Luné's favour and to a well-earned retirement.) This was shown in Japan as a direct sequel to *Jungle Emperor*. Tezuka offered it to NBC, which declined it. So it was not seen in America at that time.

THE AMERICANIZED *JUNGLE EMPEROR: KIMBA THE WHITE LION*

Jungle Emperor was produced in Japan for network broadcast as a weekly 7:00 p.m. prime-time program—Japan's first TV colour animation, although it was broadcast in black-and-white—beginning on October 6, 1965. Episodes were sent to America as soon as they were completed. Their Americanization was subcontracted by NBC to Fred Ladd, an independent producer who specialized in converting foreign movies and TV programs into English. Ladd had also produced *Mighty Atom* as *Astro Boy* since 1963, so he and his staff had some familiarity with Tezuka's films.

NBC gave Ladd the same instructions that Tezuka had received, with one important addition. NBC felt that the name, Leo, was too stereotyped for a lion, especially since it was the name of MGM's trademarked lion mascot-logo. Leo's name had to be changed to something more original. The decision was made by Ladd's staff to take the Swahili word for lion, *simba,* and change the initial letter. The result was Kimba, a catchy, euphonious and completely original name, and the obvious source of the American title: *Kimba the White Lion*[3] (Fig. 1).

In America, *Kimba* (and *Astro Boy*) were syndicated by NBC rather than being shown on its own network. NBC decided to wait until all 52 episodes had been converted into English before releasing them, so purchasing channels could air them as either a weekly or a daily program. *Kimba* first appeared on Los Angeles' KHJ-TV, Channel 9, in September 1966 in a 5:30 p.m. late afternoon time slot. It spread to other American cities in late 1966 and early 1967. (As a chronological reference note, Walt Disney died in December 1966.)

Kimba was immediately popular. It was subtly different from other TV cartoons. The colours, the backgrounds and the orchestral music had a richness that ranked with theatrical cartoons, not the TV animation of the day. However, the story format—half-hour adventures rather than six or seven minutes of gag humour—identified *Kimba* as a TV cartoon rather than a TV broadcast of an old theatrical short. *Kimba* also presented a richness of characterization which stood out amidst the shallow stereotypes of other TV cartoons. When *Kimba* first appeared, public attitudes toward children's television were such that it was commended for its positive moral values. Kimba was an approved role model for his strong ethics and his willingness to fight for good causes.

This gradually changed over the following decade. Standards for children's programing became stricter and encouraging fighting for any reason became frowned upon. Complaints began to come in from African-American pressure groups, not so much because Kimba himself was white (as animation fan legend today attributes

Fig. 1. *Kimba* Main Characters. On Left: Japanese *Jungle Emperor* Character Names. On Right: American *Kimba* Character Names. © 1966/2007 Tezuka Production Co., Ltd/Mushi Production Co., Ltd. Image courtesy of The Right Stuf International, Inc.

the reason) as because, in the few times that humans did appear in an episode, *they* were invariably white: big-game hunters, tourists on safari, scientific explorers, criminals hiding from the law. Africa seemed to have no black Africans living there.

But these complaints were not the reason for *Kimba's* disappearance in the late 1970s. The contract for the American rights expired in September 1978. Mushi Productions had gone bankrupt in 1973, following Tezuka's departure; and the rights to its properties were in litigation. Nobody in Japan had authority to sign a new contract for *Kimba*.

Meanwhile, in America, the federal government had issued an anti-monopoly directive forbidding television companies from both broadcasting and syndicating programs to other broadcasters. NBC had to close its NBC Films subsidiary. In 1971, *Kimba* was transferred, along with all of NBC's other syndicated programing, to National Telefilm Associates in Los Angeles. NTA continued to syndicate *Kimba* for as long as NBC's rights lasted. NTA withdrew *Kimba* from release on September 30, 1978.

However, one of the Japanese claimants of the *Kimba* rights, Fumio Suzuki, obtained a set of the 16 mm films and, representing himself as their owner, sold them to another TV distributor, Air Time International. ATI was a much smaller distributor than NTA, but it did continue to get *Kimba* on the air in some American cities through barter sales until it went out of business during the 1980s.

The rights to *Jungle Emperor* were in litigation in Japan through early 1997. Several American video companies over the years tried to license the *Kimba* video rights, without success. So during the time of *The Lion King's* production and release, the only videos in America of NBC's *Kimba* were unauthorized copies, either film-chained from worn 16 mm prints discarded by TV studios twenty years ago or copies of the videos of the final TV broadcasts that were dubbed by fans in the late 1970s and early 1980s. (Many of the *Kimba* videos sold at fan conventions show the commercial break logo cards of Los Angeles' KBSC-TV, Channel 52, which broadcast *Kimba* from August 1976 through July 1977.)

The sequel, *Susume, Leo!*, did finally come to American TV in 1984 on the Christian Broadcasting Network, under the title of *Leo the Lion*.

The quality of the American adaptation was atrocious, but at least all the characters retained their original Japanese names. It attracted little attention, even from the *anime* fandom that had developed by that time; and it also soon disappeared.

PLOT AND PARALLELS BETWEEN *KIMBA* AND *THE LION KING*

Ten years later, on June 15, 1994, the Disney Company released its 87 minute *The Lion King*, which has set new records for animation popularity throughout the world.[50] As a result of this acclaim, attention has been recalled to *Kimba the White Lion* and to notable similarities between the two. (See endnotes 18, 22-35, 37-49, 51-61.)

The protagonist of *The Lion King* is a lion cub, Simba, who is the heir to an African kingdom of animals. He is told from birth that, one day, this will all be his. But his father is murdered, and he is tricked into fleeing. Years later, as a young adult, he returns to claim his rightful position from its usurper and to reestablish the kingdom, which has fallen into ruin.

There are striking parallels between the two stories, but there are also significant differences. In *Kimba the White Lion*, as noted earlier, Kimba is concerned with friendship and social equality between the animals and mankind. In *The Lion King*, man does not seem to exist (although man is alluded to in the film's humour, such as the parody of the hyenas as marching Nazi troopers in Scar's musical number, and Timon's dressing in Hawaiian drag to dance a hula). Moreover, in *The Lion King*, it is implied that the animal kingdom around Pride Rock, reigned over by the lion dynasty, is peaceful and happy because this is the natural order of life. It also seems that this kingdom encompasses all of Africa, although this is contradicted when Simba flees from the kingdom by merely running from Pride Rock across the plains for a few hours and is suddenly beyond its borders. He must later be persuaded to return to the kingdom from his self-imposed exile. On the other hand, in *Kimba*, the natural order of life is the law of the jungle. Kimba's 'peaceful kingdom' is an artificial creation which must be established through deliberate persuasion and which only spreads slowly from a small nucleus in imitation of the evolution of human civilization.

Furthermore, Simba in *The Lion King* is a cocky and rather spoiled child who instantly evolves into a carefree older adolescent who rejects all responsibility until he undergoes a divine revelation which transforms him into an adult, enlightened ruler. Kimba is a young child only in the pilot episode. In the regular episodes, Kimba is about to enter adolescence, highly idealistic and obsessed with his responsibility to an almost pathological degree—there are several instances when he breaks into tears because of doubts about his ability to live up to his image of his father. (Kimba never knew his father, Caesar, alive; but the hunter who killed him had skinned him, and the animals later retrieved this trophy. One of the series' more memorable images—doubtlessly because it is so bizarre—is young Kimba going into a hut which has been turned into a shrine to Caesar to receive inspiration from his father's glassy-eyed pelt.) Kimba is aware of his lack of experience, and he constantly seeks advice from wise old Dan'l Baboon, instead of needing it forced upon him. Kimba does gradually grow in self-confidence, but not significantly in physical maturity. (He appears to be approximately the lion cub equivalent of a 10 or 11 year old human boy at his return to the jungle and of a 13 or 14 year old young adolescent in the final episode.)

Certainly, given that the reputation of the lion as 'king of the jungle' is a staple of folklore, going back at least as far as Aesop's fables 2,500 years ago, it is reasonable that modern fantasy writers might independently parody the court intrigue of a European-style monarchy by setting it in an African nation of anthropomorphized animals with a lion king. This can make it difficult to determine whether two similar stories are the result of coincidental development of the same source materials, or whether the later of the two stories was actually derived from the former. Simba is an obvious name for a lion protagonist. An article in the July 13 *Los Angeles Times* declared: '"The project was initially called *King of the Jungle* and, like most animated features at Disney, its development was evolutionary, taking years to create and refine", stated a Disney press kit'.[24] As noted earlier, *King of the Jungle*[16] is an alternate translation of Tezuka's *Junguru Taitei*—but the phrase is such a common metaphor for lions that it could easily be anyone's first choice for the title of a fantasy of this nature.

So what, specifically, are the parallels between the two films? Here are eight points of similarity which seem to go beyond reasonable coincidence:

(1) The personalities and roles of the major characters are established throughout both *The Lion King* and various of the 52 episodes of *Kimba the White Lion*. The parallels include: Simba and Kimba; their wise, noble fathers Mufasa and Caesar; their childhood sweethearts Nala and Kitty; the villainous lions Scar and Claw, and the panther Cassius (Scar combines elements of both); the wise baboon advisors Rafiki and Dan'l Baboon; the comically pompous bird major-domos Zazu and Pauley Cracker; the humourous loyal companions Timon and Pumbaa and Pauley Cracker (again) and Bucky Deer; and the evil, cowardly, yet irrepressibly silly, laughing hyenas Shenzi, Banzai and Ed, and Tab and Tom.

(2) The same plot operates. The wise lion king is killed, and the young prince is driven from home. He returns to find that the throne has been occupied in his absence by a brutal, scar-faced (the scar located over one eye) older lion, whom he must defeat in battle to become king.

(3) A wise, elderly mandrill baboon who had been the old king's friend becomes the prince's sardonic but kindly mentor. Also, a comically excitable bird of about the same size—a parrot in *Kimba*, a hornbill in *The Lion King*—plays a pompous functionary, a herald or its equivalent. The scar-faced lion villain is supported by a team of comic-relief cowardly laughing hyenas. In *The Lion King*, the evil Scar gives orders directly to the hyenas whereas in *Kimba*, Boss Claw has a black panther henchman who is his intermediary to the lower-class hyenas. In *The Lion King*, Scar is played as suavely sinister with an upper-class accent. In *Kimba*, Claw is a hot-tempered, brutal thug; but the black panther, Cassius, is suavely sinister with an upper-class accent.

(4) The prince as a cub meets a young lioness who becomes his playmate (Fig. 2). In *The Lion King*, they marry when they become adults; and the lioness bears his child to carry on the dynasty. In *Kimba*, there is a clear implication that Kimba and Kitty will wed

when they grow up. And in the *Leo the Lion* sequel shown on cable TV during the mid-1980s, this explicitly happens.

(5) There is an anti-carnivore and pro-herbivore stance. In *Kimba*, Kimba's initial dream of planting a farm for all animals so the carnivores can be friends with the herbivores seems stymied when he is made aware that carnivores cannot survive on plants. Just then, the farm is attacked by locusts; and the carnivores save the plants—and find a socially acceptable food for themselves—by eating the locusts (the episodes *Insect Invasion* and *The Gigantic Grasshopper*). Later, when they are about to run out of locusts, a friendly human scientist visiting the jungle discovers a vegetarian 'meat substitute' so the carnivores never have to prey upon other animals again (*A Revolting Development*). In *The Lion King*, Simba is taught to eat bugs so he can become a non-threatening social equal of herbivores.

(6) The image of a parent in the sky plays an inspirational role. In *The Jungle Emperor* novel, there is a memorable scene at the beginning where the infant Leo sees his mother's image in the stars at night and another at the end where young Luné sees the martyred Leo's image in the clouds over the savannah. In the TV cartoons, Kimba has a vision every few episodes of his mother or father in the stars, in the clouds or over a full moon (Fig. 3). In *The Lion King*, King Mufasa tells young Simba, 'Look at the stars. The great kings of the past look down on us from those stars. So whenever you feel alone, just remember that those kings will always be there to guide you'. Later, the adult Simba is inspired by Mufasa's image in the clouds.

(7) A stampede is a key event in the hero's life. In *The Lion King*, King Mufasa is killed while rescuing Simba from a tree in the midst of a wildebeest stampede. As a result of this stampede and his father's death, Simba is tricked into fleeing into exile. In the episode *Running Wild*, Kimba and his friends are threatened by a stampede of antelopes. Kimba must save Bucky Deer, who is clinging to a tree in the midst of the stampede. Later, Kimba is so despondent that he could not stop the antelope that he declares he is not fit to rule; and he runs off to sulk. Dan'l Baboon has to spank him and, to give him the understanding to take up his responsibilities again, give him a pep talk about how a leader is not expected to succeed every time as long as he perseveres.

Fig. 2. Kimba romping with his playmate Kitty. In Tezuka's complete *Jungle Emperor*, the two grow up and mate. The same designs are used for their children in the animated *Leo the Lion* sequel (which uses their Japanese names, the boy Luné and his sister Lukyo). © 1966/2007 Tezuka Production Co., Ltd/Mushi Production Co., Ltd. Image courtesy of The Right Stuf International, Inc.

(8) There are notable visual parallels between many scenes in both works:

1-A. *The Lion King*. Opening scene, 'The Circle of Life': pan over birds flying over the savannah, showing a panorama of all the animals of Africa, sweeping up to King Mufasa posing majestically on Pride Rock. 0:40 to 1:51.

1-B. *Jungle Emperor.* Opening title credits & theme song: from the adult King Leo posing majestically on a cliff, panning down over birds flying over the savannah, showing a panorama of all the animals of Africa. 0:01 to 1:57.

1-C. *Kimba*, Prod. #66-5, *Journey Into Time.* Another lion (King Specklerex) poses majestically on a cliff, with the Japanese Rising Sun in the background.

2-A. *The Lion King*. The wildebeest stampede. 32:08 to 32:30.

Fig. 3. Kimba, swimming exhaustedly after a storm, is inspired by the image of his mother Snowene in the stars. © 1966/2007 Tezuka Production Co., Ltd/Mushi Production Co., Ltd. Image courtesy of The Right Stuf International, Inc.

2-B. *Kimba*, Prod. #66-24, *Running Wild*. The antelope stampede. 1:32 to 2:20.

3-A. *The Lion King*. Zazu flies to Simba clinging to a tree in the midst of the wildebeest stampede, and tells him to hold on, his father is coming. 33:08 to 33:14.

3-B. *Kimba*, Prod. #66-24, *Running Wild*. Pauley Cracker flies to Bucky Deer clinging to a tree in the midst of the antelope stampede, and tells him to hold on, Kimba is coming. 8:23 to 8:28.

4-A. *The Lion King*. Lightning starts a fire, 75:00 to 75:05, and rain puts it out. 79:58 to 80:05.

4-B. *Kimba*, Prod. #66-42, *The Red Menace*. Lightning starts a fire, 0:38 to 0:47, and rain puts it out. 13:37 to 13:52.

5-A. *The Lion King*. During a fight in the midst of the big fire, Scar scoops a pawful of hot coals into Simba's eyes. 78:30 to 78:35.

5-B. *Kimba*, Prod. #66-8, *The Wind in the Desert*. During a fight in the hot desert, Kimba kicks burning sand into Claw's eyes. 22:32 to 22:37.

6-A. *The Lion King*. After Simba protests that he cannot handle the responsibilities of becoming king, Rafiki gives him a pep talk, including a sharp rap on the head to get his attention. 67:11 to 67:32.

6-B. *Kimba*, Prod. #66-24, *Running Wild*. After Kimba protests that he cannot handle the responsibilities of becoming king, Dan'l Baboon gives him a pep talk, including a spanking to get his attention. 13:49 to 14:23.

7-A. *The Lion King*. King Mufasa tells young Simba to 'Look at the stars. The great kings of the past look down on us from those stars…' 25:02 to 25:25.

7-B. *The Lion King*. Simba sees Mufasa's image in the clouds. 69:06 to 69:11.

7-C. *Kimba*, Prod. #66-1, *Go, White Lion!* Young Kimba sees his mother's image in the stars. 20:10 to 20:45.

7-D. *Kimba*, Prod. #66-9, *The Insect Invasion*. Kimba sees an idealized image of himself with his father, King Caesar, in the clouds. 22:21 to 22:26.

7-E. *Kimba*, Prod. #66-3, *Dangerous Journey*. Kimba sees his father,

Caesar, superimposed over a full moon. 14:38 to 14:53, and 17:40 to 18:00.

8-A. *The Lion King*. The cubs Simba and Nala playing. 17:07 to 17:30.

8-B. *Kimba*, Prod. #66-5, *Journey into Time*. The cubs Kimba and Kitty playing. 21:35 to 22:15.

9-A. *The Lion King*. Timon (omnivore) and Pumbaa (herbivore) teach Simba (carnivore) to eat insects and bugs so he can live with them without starving. 46:07 to 47:07.

9-B. *Kimba*. The sub-plot of Kimba getting the carnivores to live in peace with the herbivores by, at first, trying (unsuccessfully) to teach them to eat grass, then getting them to temporarily eat insects, and finally discovering a vegetarian 'meat substitute', is spread through three episodes: Prod. #66-9. *The Insect Invasion*; #66-27, *The Gigantic Grasshopper*; and #66-36, *A Revolting Development*.

A digression on the comparison of the opening scene of *The Lion King* and the original Japanese opening title animation of *Jungle Emperor*: the latter showed Leo as an adult; and since NBC did not want Leo/Kimba presented as a grown-up, NBC created its own opening title animation from several brief scenes from various episodes. Therefore, this original Japanese opening title animation was never shown in America as a part of *Kimba*. But it is shown in Japanese animation books; and it is included in the Japanese commercial videos of *Jungle Emperor*, which are accessible to the large number of American *anime* fans. Professional animators would know how to get copies.

WHAT MIGHT DISNEY HAVE KNOWN?
WHAT SHOULD DISNEY HAVE KNOWN?

Do these similarities seem strained? If they are significant, could they be coincidental, rather than evidence of inspiration from *Kimba* to *The Lion King*? These are obvious questions, but there is a third which is equally important: if Disney was not aware of *Kimba*, should it have been?

To quote from Christopher Finch's cover article in the May-June 1994 issue of *Animation Magazine:* 'Astonishingly, *The Lion King*—

initially called *King of the Jungle*—is the first Disney animated feature to be based on an original story idea. The rest were rooted in traditional tales or existing copyrighted material'.[17] The article tells how the concept was conceived by studio chairman Jeffrey Katzenberg as an animal story like *Bambi* but set in Africa, 'with the central theme being woven around a young lion coming of age and learning to take responsibility'. Katzenberg passed the idea to Roy Disney, Jr., head of the animation department, who assigned Tom Schumacher, producer of *The Rescuers Down Under*, to assemble a creative team to develop it. An article by Charles Burress in the July 11, 1994 *San Francisco Chronicle,* which was the first public news of the controversy, states that *Lion King* co-director Rob Minkoff said that he had 'joined the 4-year-old project in April 1992',[22] establishing that it started in 1988.

Two key points emerge from these articles. First, Disney maintained that *The Lion King* is its own original story. Second, it maintained that nobody in the Disney organization ever heard of either the *Kimba* TV cartoons or Osamu Tezuka. The July 11 *Chronicle,* citing a telephone interview with *The Lion King* co-director Minkoff, declares that 'Rob Minkoff said he was unaware of Tezuka's story during production'.[22] The July 13 *Los Angeles Times* quoted Minkoff directly: 'I know for a fact that [*Kimba*] has never been discussed as long as I've been on the project'.[24] *USA Today* on July 14 cited a Disney statement: 'No one associated with (*The Lion King*) had even heard of (*Kimba*) or...seen it'.[26] On July 18, the *San Francisco Chronicle* ran a follow-up.[29] Disney spokesman Howard Green clarified that the company had queried the artists who worked on *The Lion King.* Some admitted they had heard of *Kimba* or even seen it when they were young children. But Green affirmed that this meant only that some artists had a vague childhood memory of *Kimba* along with all of the other TV cartoons that had blended together in their subconscious. He repeated that none of the creative team who developed *The Lion King* were aware of *Kimba* or Tezuka. Mark Henn, lead animator for the young Simba, was quoted that he had heard of *Kimba* but never seen it and 'that the name Tezuka did not ring a bell'. Another unidentified Disney employee felt that it was 'totally reasonable' that *Kimba* had never been seen by 'many of the younger employees like [co-director]

Minkoff, who at 31 was barely 3 years old when *Kimba* aired'.

Here are some facts to compare with the Disney statements:

(1) Disney, the biggest animation company in America, takes pride in its global expertise in the field of animation, including its knowledge of popular animation worldwide. For example, Disney bought the animation rights to a major European cartoon star, André Franquin's Marsupilami, because Disney felt that it would be popular in America. In terms of *The Lion King*, an article in the *Wall Street Journal* on May 16, 1994, a month before the film's release, alluded to Disney's research into commercial and legal aspects of the movie, stating that 'When Disney consumer-products officials suggested the Lion King's name, "Simba", might run afoul of copyrights of a German toy maker of the same name, Mr. [Studio chairman Jeffrey] Katzenberg wouldn't hear about changing the name'.[20] If such research was carried out by Disney to this extent, it seems improbable that no references to Tezuka or to *Kimba* were ever found.

(2) Japan is one of Disney's largest markets outside America. Tokyo Disneyland is the popular success that EuroDisney is not. Disney executives regularly visit Tokyo. Most Disney features are on laser disc there, and the Disney company is on record about its concern that American film collectors can purchase Japanese laser discs of movies that have not been released to the U.S. video market, such as *Song of the South*. Aside from the fact that *Jungle Emperor* merchandise is still in every Japanese toy store, Osamu Tezuka is a giant of modern Japanese popular culture, widely known as *manga no kamisama*—'The God of Comics'. He appeared in Japanese TV commercials during the 1980s as a major celebrity endorsing computer products. In 1980, he starred in a Japanese TV special on Disney World—filmed on location—as a humourously clumsy tourist, in his own reprise of Robert Benchley bumbling around the Disney studio in Disney's *The Reluctant Dragon*.[6] (Also—extremely significantly—Frederik L. Schodt, Osamu Tezuka's translator, says that 'I personally accompanied him in the 1980s to...the Disney animation studios in Burbank, California',[57] although Schodt does not report the purpose of Tezuka's visit nor who among the Disney staff may have met him.)

Possibly more significantly, Disney's own '*The Lion King* Press Information' publicity kit distributed for the film's premiere contains this biographical note on co-director Roger Allers:

> Roger Allers (Director) makes his feature film directing debut on *The Lion King* following a prolific two-decade career in the medium that has included everything from character design and animation to story supervision... In 1980, Allers and his family moved to Toronto, Canada, where he worked for Nelvana Studios as an animator... This two-year assignment was followed by a return to Los Angeles, where he provided character design, preliminary animation and story development for the Japanese-produced feature, *Little Nemo: Adventures in Slumberland*. He went on to live in Tokyo for the next two years in his role as one of the animation directors overseeing the Japanese artists.[21]

How probable is it that none of the Disney executives visiting Japan, nor American animators who worked in Japan and later worked for Disney on production of *The Lion King*, ever ran across any mentions of Tezuka—widely publicized as 'the Walt Disney of Japan'—or of *Jungle Emperor*? The Tezuka Productions remake of *Jungle Emperor* received a prime-time weekly TV broadcast from October 1989 through September 1990 in Japan,[13] with significant coverage in the Japanese animation magazines, and was immediately thereafter released to the Japanese home video market. American *anime* fans were fully aware of this and had no trouble obtaining video copies. How could the Disney researchers who discovered the Simba toys in Germany have overlooked this current Japanese TV animation series?

(3) *The World Encyclopedia of Comics*, edited by Maurice Horn,[4] has been a standard American reference book on cartoons since 1976. Its entry on Tezuka notes: 'Influenced in large part by Walt Disney... Tezuka has in turn influenced countless numbers of Japanese cartoonists...' The illustrated entry on *Jungle Emperor* states: '*Jungle Taitei* was adapted into animated form; it was the first colour cartoon series produced for Japanese TV. *Jungle Taitei* was awarded the Silver Lion at the International Children's Film Festival held in Venice in 1967'. Many other comics and animation reference books include

entries on Tezuka or on *Kimba*. (See endnotes 5, 8, 9, 12, 15.) Have Disney's animators, who are experts on cartooning, most of whom entered the profession because of a personal love for animation, never even accidentally encountered these entries, to say nothing of having any interest in following them up? The claim that Disney's artists could not have known of *Kimba* because they were little children when the series started to be aired on American television in 1966 ignores the fact that it was shown constantly around America until the early 1980s, including on Los Angeles television. So people who were only three years old in 1966 might still have seen *Kimba* until they were in their late teens.

While the general public may be unaware of Tezuka and *Kimba*, the Disney staff consists of professionals in the animation industry, many of whom are personally animation aficionados. The July 18, 1994 *San Francisco Chronicle* further quoted an unidentified Disney source: 'I can guarantee they didn't use any Tezuka ideas. No one had any Tezuka books. I didn't bring in a *Kimba, the White Lion* to show them. I doubt they have a Kimba film in their library. That period of Japanese animation is scoffed at'.[29] Of course, this quotation from the unidentified Disney source is itself evidence that *somebody* at Disney *was* aware of Tezuka and of *Kimba*. It is an admission that Disney personnel were familiar enough with that period of Japanese animation to have an opinion of it, even if an unfavorable one; and Tezuka was too dominant a figure in that period for them to be unaware of him if they considered themselves knowledgeable enough about it to form a judgment. Moreover, the *Chronicle* noted a couple of paragraphs later: 'And in a couple of other Disney films, artists have acknowledged taking inspiration from a more contemporary Japanese animator, Hayao Miyazaki'. This is further evidence that the Disney animators are professionals who are aware of their Japanese colleagues.

The effort to assign Tezuka to an earlier, more primitive period ignores the fact that some of his most famous films were not only made after *Kimba*, they were given well-publicized film festival screenings in Los Angeles, as well as elsewhere in the United States. His *Broken-Down Film* was one of the hits at the first Los Angeles International Animation Celebration in 1985; and Tezuka was expected to personally bring his *Legend of the Forest* to the 1989 Celebration, though his death prevented that. His *Jumping* played in the 19th annual International Tournée of Animation, which premiered in Los Angeles in 1986 and later toured America.

Disney animators who were professionally aware of Miyazaki's Japanese animation of the late 1980s could not have been ignorant of Japan's highly publicized 1989-1990 remake by Tezuka Productions of the *Jungle Emperor* TV cartoons, any more than they could have been ignorant of the inclusion of his work in the Los Angeles International Animation Celebration and the 19th Tournée.

The likelihood of Disney animators knowing of Tezuka and/or *Kimba* is compounded by the fact that, in December 1990, ASIFA-Hollywood, the Hollywood chapter of the international professional animation community, presented its Winsor McCay Award 'for lifetime contribution to animation' posthumously to Osamu Tezuka, at its gala annual awards. Tezuka received a three page tribute in the awards' program book, and the text included an illustration of Kimba.[14] None of that year's other award recipients received more than a one page tribute. The award was presented by June Foray, a noted animation voice actress whose roles included Granny Gummi in Disney's *Gummi Bears* TV cartoons. Among the other animation industry notables listed in the program book as being present was Marc Davis, one of Disney's often publicized 'nine old men' senior animators, famous for working on Disney's theatrical features from *Snow White and the Seven Dwarfs* in the 1930s to *Sleeping Beauty* in the 1950s.

So as recently as 1990, America's veteran animation professionals, as well as its animation buff community, were well aware of Tezuka and respected his work. Are we therefore to believe that the present Disney professional staff is either unaware of him or considers him a boringly primitive antique? There is ample evidence that Disney's 1928 *Steamboat Willie* is hopelessly quaint by today's standards, but does this mean that modern animators should not be expected to know of it or to recognize Disney's name? To know Miyazaki but to never have heard of Tezuka, the famous 'father' of Japanese animation, is like an animator who takes inspiration from Chuck Jones but professes to never have heard of Walt Disney, Tex Avery or Friz Freleng.

The July 11 *Chronicle*, further citing the telephone interview with *The Lion King* co-director Rob Minkoff, reported: 'He said he is trying to find copies of the comics, which are out of print, and the TV series, which is out of circulation'.[22] Tezuka's *Jungle Emperor* graphic novel has never been published in English, but it is easily obtainable in Japanese community bookshops around Southern California. I personally saw the paperback three volume Kodansha edition when I went shopping for *anime* books in late February 1995.

I have attended numerous fan conventions since the late 1980s at which key Disney animation personnel, including Rob Minkoff, have given presentations on whatever feature was about to be released.[19] At those same conventions, unauthorized American *Kimba* videos were displayed for sale in the dealers' rooms, along with Japanese *Jungle Emperor* merchandise and videos of the 1989-1990 *Jungle Emperor* remake. Disney artists commonly attend fan conventions in Southern California to shop for their personal collections. Fan conventions invariably run video rooms which are often casual about the legality of the videos that are shown. I have attended screenings of *Kimba* episodes at which Disney artists were present, or art students were present who I know later went to work for Disney.

Did they work on *The Lion King*? Yes, at least some did. Did their knowledge of *Kimba* influence the development of *The Lion King*? They say not. But Disney says that nobody at its studio—or at least nobody who worked on *The Lion King*—or at least nobody who was in a position to affect the key story and character concepts in *The Lion King*—had ever heard of Tezuka or were more than marginally aware of *Kimba*. There is already strong enough circumstantial evidence to disprove this and to raise natural suspicions that Disney is trying to hide a smoking gun.

While the Disney management has adamantly insisted that the creative staff of *The Lion King* were unaware of Tezuka or of *Kimba*, the July 18, 1994 *Chronicle* reported that 'in interviews done outside official Disney channels', some of the creative staff indicated otherwise. 'One source who worked on the early stages of the film's development' was quoted: 'I certainly knew about *Kimba the White Lion'*, he said. 'Other people did too...' But the source also indicated that some Disney personnel it spoke to did not know: 'I remember saying in a meeting, "This is mighty similar to *Kimba the White Lion*", and I got a bunch of blank stares'. Of course, this statement itself put those issuing such blank stares on notice.

CONCLUSION

There are two major issues, calling for two lines of addressal. The first is based on the question of knowledge: was Disney familiar with Tezuka and *Kimba*?; what did it know?; and importantly, what should it have known?; and, more murkily, what might it have known but forgotten or suppressed and that returned in some way? The right of Disney to claim its authority and take pride in knowing world animation, its global expertise, is fully engaged here. Disney cannot have it both ways. Its animators and legal and commercial departments cannot claim to be knowledgeable as professionals/ experts/defenders of Disney copyrights, and also claim to be ignorant of Tezuka and *Kimba*. For Disney to claim such ignorance is to demolish its claim to world authority, to admit that authority is sham, as it likewise flies in the face of the tangible evidence of the tenacity and vigilance it exercises worldwide in the protection of its copyrights. And once it makes that claim to authority and displays such tenacity and vigilance, a presumption attaches to its activities such that even where it may not have actually known, it is held to the rule that it *should* have known to be the expert it claims to be and protector it has shown itself to be, a double pride.

So, even if Disney did not know of Tezuka—the 'father' of *anime*, the greatest Japanese animator, the man called 'the Walt Disney of Japan'(!)—to sustain its claim to expertise, it must accept that it should have known, even if just to know how Tezuka acquired and maintained that sobriquet, how he was treating and reflecting upon Disney both in and outside of his works, including *Kimba*.

Beyond the question of what Disney knew or should have known before or during the making of *The Lion King* lies its conduct after the release of the film brought formal notification of *Kimba* in July

1994. The failure of Disney to acknowledge what it then came to know compromised itself further. While Tezuka and Mr Takayuki Matsutani, President of Tezuka Productions, always felt that *Jungle Emperor* derived from an inspiration based upon Disney's *Bambi* and they were always at pains to acknowledge their debt, the Disney organization's claim that it had never heard of Tezuka—that Tezuka was too unimportant to have heard of—was a failure to reciprocate, a failure to acknowledge the acknowledgement of and homage to Disney by Tezuka in *Kimba*. If one might think of *Kimba* as not only a gift from Disney to Tezuka but a gift from Tezuka to Disney, Disney refused not only the gift but its acknowledgement.

Antonia Levi, in her book *Samurai from Outer Space*,[59] addresses an August 1994 open letter to Disney[33-35] signed by over 200 Japanese artists and supporters protesting Disney's failure to recognize Tezuka's professional stature:

> Disney's lawyers, apparently unable to grasp the fact that this was a question of courtesy rather than copyright infringement or punitive damages, responded defensively and with a level of legalistic arrogance unusual even for them. (p. 7)

In actuality, Disney did not reply to this letter at all; its arrogance was in ignoring it. In other words, Disney has treated the issue as a legal one, not an ethical one nor one of etiquette, of politeness. Disney's tactics of disavowal at the level of knowing/not knowing, including silence in the face of the professional and critical animation communities in Japan, have clearly expressed its position in mime as 'Not only did we not know before, but we refuse to listen now'. This has made Disney look bad, including looking ignorant where it claims expertise.

And that has contaminated the other area calling for addressal: originality. If Disney is so ignorant where it claims to be so knowledgeable, how can we trust its claim to the originality of *The Lion King*?

In terms of this second issue, I have enumerated many similiarities between *The Lion King* and *Kimba*. These beg the question as to what legitimate grounds Disney could appeal to claim *The Lion King* as original. Disney's disclaimer of no knowledge of Tezuka and *Kimba* is, while in some ways relevant, not conclusive as regards originality. While the complexities of the thinking of the relation of knowledge to originality, to say nothing of the complexities of the thinking of what originality is, lie beyond this paper, one key point can serve: although knowledge of *Kimba* can be read as compromising the claim of Disney to the originality of *The Lion King*, not knowing of *Kimba* would not automatically make *The Lion King* original. The question of originality transcends subjectivity, transcends the knowledge and intentions of the makers and what must be presumed of such. Rather, it involves a comparison focusing largely upon the objects themselves.

By means of such a comparison, I have shown the ways in which *Kimba* and *The Lion King* coincide. Of course, coincidence is in itself a complex phenomenon. There are those who treat it as automatically implying a lack of both subjective will and objective patterning, the happenstance workings of chance. Others would regard it as testimony to just the opposite, as at least the workings of destiny to impose or disclose objective patterning. In the present case, it appears to operate in two different ways. First, in the register of knowledge, coincidence so defined—either as chance or destiny—defuses the guilt of Disney. It suggests that one does not have to, indeed cannot, presume Disney knew of Tezuka and *Kimba* for it to have made *The Lion King*. In other words, and despite the common error of equating coincidence with cause-effect, one cannot presume that because *The Lion King* is similar to *Kimba* and *Kimba* was made before *The Lion King*, *Kimba* was the cause of *The Lion King*. So the argument of coincidence puts pay to cause-effect thinking. But second, coincidence so thought can itself in turn cause an effect. It can cause *The Lion King* to not be original.

In the case of *The Lion King* and *Kimba*, this matter is further complicated by their common source in folk tale, though it might be argued that such a source uncomplicates the matter insofar as it automatically annuls any claim to originality on behalf of either. (See, for example, the medieval beast fable *Le Roman de Renart*, dating from the thirteenth century, in which the European animals live in a parody of a royal court presided over by a lion king of beasts, King Nobel.) The plots of both films exhibit the morphology of the folk tale. We are dealing with a set of conventions, archetypes, etc., that repeat themselves. It is impossible therefore to talk of texts based on fable/myth in terms of their originality except where they depart from the conventions. So even if one grants Disney that it not only did not know but also cannot be presumed to have known of Tezuka and *Kimba*, that does not automatically make *The Lion King* original.

There is a more speculative question regarding Disney's knowledge: the question of conscious versus subconscious knowledge. What might a *Lion King* creator who had consciously forgotten watching *Kimba* on TV as a child have subconsciously added to the development of a similar story about a young lion ruler of a kingdom of animals?

Further, animators have had a reputation for decades of having irrepressible senses of humour and a penchant for practical jokes on each other and on studio management and of drawing hidden jokes into their cartooning. (See, for example, Jack Kinney's *Walt Disney and Assorted Other Characters: An Unauthorized Account of the Early Years at Disney's* (1988).) If some Disney artists were aware of *Kimba*, might they have added *Kimba* visual references to *The Lion King* as an in-group joke without admitting the source to their co-workers or their superiors? If this did happen, then what Disney thought it knew was less than what it actually knew.

In the end, as in the beginning, we cannot know what Disney did or did not know, nor can we say *Kimba* caused *The Lion King*. But we can say that Disney's declaration that it was ignorant of Tezuka and *Kimba* before and during the making of the film and its continuing maintenance of that ignorance after release of the film destroy its claim to global expertise in animation. And the similarities between *Kimba* and *The Lion King* and their common source in fable argue persuasively that any easy claim by Disney to the originality of *The Lion King* is sham. In both cases—knowledge and originality—Disney's pride is on the line.

EPILOGUE (1998)

This essay was originally written at the beginning of 1995 for presentation at *THE LIFE OF ILLUSION* conference. Since then, the 'Simba versus Kimba' controversy has diminished but not been forgotten. Neither has it been formally resolved.

The box office and merchandising records set by *The Lion King* still stand, emphasized by the failures of Disney's subsequent major animated features (*Pocahontas, The Hunchback of Notre Dame* and *Hercules*) to measure up to them. And the Disney corporation has not yet replied to the August 1994 letter of protest organized by Machiko Satonaka with over 200 signatures.[35]

The controversy continues to be mentioned in books, magazines and even television satires, at times reaching the status of a new urban myth. In an episode of *The Simpsons* TV cartoon program, a lion's head in the clouds says, 'You must avenge my death, Kimba... I mean Simba!'[53] A media fan magazine states that 43 legal suits were filed against Disney by the Japanese and that the lack of *Kimba* merchandise in America is due to Disney getting a court order banning it—all untrue.[54] David Koenig presents a full page 'Simba-Kimba Conspiracy' chart of parallels in his *Mouse under Glass: Secrets of Disney Animation and Theme Parks*,[60] inviting readers to form their own conclusions as to whether so many can all be by chance. Another fan magazine states that the similarities between the two are so numerous 'that the direct influence of that TV series [*Kimba*] is almost indisputable'.[55]

In July 1996, Disney announced its acquisition of the world-wide distribution rights for the animated features produced by Hayao Miyazaki, 'Japan's best-loved animated-film director', for Japan's Tokuma Shoten company. ('Disney Dives into Japanese Film Business', *Los Angeles Times*, Wednesday, July 24, 1996, p. D4.)[58] The article mentions that 'Disney executives say they control 65% of the Japanese market for children's videotapes'. This does not relate directly to the Disney-Tezuka controversy, but it is indicative of Disney's knowledge of the Japanese animation market, which emphasizes the implausibility of Disney's statement that it had never heard of Tezuka nor of *Jungle Emperor* (unless Disney would care to claim that it developed that expertise only during the two years after *The Lion King* was produced).

Has the controversy prompted new productions of both *Kimba* in America and *Jungle Emperor* in Japan? In January 1996, four *Kimba* video tapes containing two episodes each were released by United American Video under the title of *Kimba the Lion Prince*. These feature the original *Jungle Emperor* animation made by Mushi Productions in 1965-1966, but with completely new scripts and dubbing.[61] The new dialogue changes Kimba's adult lion nemesis from a stranger to his 'evil uncle' (just as in *The Lion King*); and the video sleeves display the slogan, 'The lion adventure that started it all!' The credits, indicating a Canadian production, remove all Japanese names (including Tezuka's!), except for the addition of a new credit for Fumio Suzuki, one of the claimants to the Mushi property in that studio's decades old bankruptcy proceedings. These *Kimba the Lion Prince* videos were poorly distributed and soon disappeared.

(In March/April 1997, the Japanese litigation over the rights to Mushi Productions' properties, including the NBC-produced *Astro Boy* and *Kimba the White Lion*, was finally resolved. Suzuki was barred from continuing to represent himself in America as the owner of those rights. Negotiations were conducted between 1997 and 1999 between the reorganized Mushi Productions and Shawne P. Kleckner of The Right Stuf International of Des Moines, Iowa, for an authorized American video release of *Kimba the White Lion*. *Kimba* was finally released on video in America by The Right Stuf International between April and October 2000, in a set of thirteen videos containing four episodes per volume, produced from NBC's original masters in episode number order.)

On August 1, 1997, Tezuka Productions released a new *Jungle Emperor* 104 minute theatrical animated feature in Japan. Produced in theatrical quality animation, this was the most lavish filmed adaptation of Tezuka's cartoon art novel to date. Although the feature is faithful to the original story, Tezuka Productions' choice of images for its publicity stills bore a resemblance to scenes in *The Lion King*, which many fans took to be deliberately provocative. In one, Leo's cubs Luné and Lukyo romp through the savannah under the guardian eye of the pompous parrot Coco, just as the hornbill

Zazu follows the young Simba and Nala. In another, King Leo battles a pack of hyenas to protect his cubs, as King Mufasa does to save Simba and Nala in the elephants' graveyard. (Publicity images from this feature are available worldwide by downloading from the Tezuka website in Japan: www.tezuka.co.jp.) How this new *Jungle Emperor* might have fared in comparison to the Japanese reception of *The Lion King* must remain theoretical, since it had the misfortune to be released less than a month after the July 12 premiere of Hayao Miyazaki's *Mononoke Hime* (*Princess Mononoke*), which instantly monopolized all critical and popular attention for months. Ironically, *Mononoke Hime* became the Japanese animated feature to set box office records in Japan of equivalent stature to *The Lion King* in America—and to be picked up by Disney for American and international distribution.

After three years, the Disney organization has not changed its official stance on *The Lion King*'s total originality or on its lack of knowledge of or interest in Tezuka and *Kimba*. But not all of the production staff of *The Lion King* are still as reticent. Some have left Disney for other animation studios and no longer feel bound by Disney management's orders of silence or feel that Disney's claim of their ignorance is demeaning to their professional expertise.

Bridge U.S.A., October 15, 1997, quotes Sadao Miyamoto, an animator from Japan who came to work at Disney, and whose 'very first film…[there]…was *The Lion King*': 'When I first saw the storyboards…I was taken aback, because they did look like [*The Jungle Emperor*]'. *Bridge U.S.A.* goes on to report: '…he also says it's clear that [*The Lion King*] has been influenced to some degree'; and 'According to Miyamoto, for people involved in animation, it's unthinkable that [Disney people] never even saw *The Jungle Emperor*. Moreover, the [person(s)] responsible for *The Lion King* admit(s) this'.[62]

Tom Sito, who has a Story screen credit on *The Lion King*, was willing to speak for the record in this essay in a December 6, 1997 telephone interview:

> We always knew who *Kimba the White Lion* was—and I had met Osamu Tezuka socially—but I don't think anybody involved with the development thought about the connection. Later one of the

> animators, as a joke, pinned up some photocopies from the *Kimba* comic book on the studio bulletin board, but by that time we were so far into production that it didn't affect anything.

Mark Kausler, who also has a Story credit, said in a similar telephone interview December 13, 1997:

> Probably some of the hundreds of people who worked on *The Lion King* never heard of Tezuka or *Kimba*, but there were certainly many who did. I had seen *Kimba* episodes off and on, from watching it on TV as a kid to seeing video copies screened at meetings of animation fans into the '80s. But animation fans are always watching as many different cartoons as they can. When Disney started *The Lion King* project, we were told it should be like Disney's *Bambi* set in Africa with African animals, but keep it from looking too much like *Bambi* with its animals versus Man theme. It was to star only animals; no humans at all. So we were thinking just about variations of *Bambi*. Nobody ever mentioned *Kimba*; and if any of us who knew of it thought about it, I guess we figured that since *Kimba* was always about the animals trying to get the humans to accept them as equals, the absence of humans in *The Lion King* made it obviously a different plot. It was no secret that *The Lion King* was inspired by the studio's own *Bambi* and featured similar elements such as a young animal prince surrounded by colorful and comical animal companions. Tezuka also made no secret that it was *Bambi* that was his inspiration for *Kimba*, so obviously two new films both based on the same original film will have many similarities.

So the knowledge by *The Lion King*'s production staff of Tezuka and of *Kimba* is now proven. And that has always been the basic issue. (Indeed, such knowledge opens the possibility that, considering the long tradition of high-spirited production staffers secretly inserting personal jokes into their films, some aspects of *The Lion King* may have been consciously intended by some Disney animators as a return gift to Tezuka, as Tezuka's *Jungle Emperor* was his gift to Disney, a return gift that Disney management did not know about but which Tezuka would have doubtlessly understood and appreciated!). It was Disney management's insistence that, despite its worldwide animation expertise, it had never heard of Tezuka or of *Kimba*—that they were not worthy of knowing about—which caused the entire controversy. To quote Frederik L. Schodt in his *Dreamland Japan*: 'Ironically, the entire controversy could easily have been resolved by a simple tip of the hat to Tezuka, either in the form of a film credit or a public statement'.[57] Instead, the affair has demonstrated the knowledge of Disney's creative staff—and the stubbornly willful ignorance of Disney's management.

ACKNOWLEDGEMENT

I would like to acknowledge Robin Leyden for supplying me with much of this information. In 1966, as a young fan, Leyden obtained a copy of NBC's *Kimba* publicity kit, including the 52 episode *Kimba the White Lion Story Lines* program guide. This seems to be the only original copy known to exist today. It has been photocopied for fans many times; and it is the basic source for NBC's episode titles and numbers and the episode synopses which establish the spellings of the characters' names. I would also like to thank Frederik L. Schodt, an expert on Japanese popular culture who served as Osamu Tezuka's personal translator many times, who provided some of the information regarding original Japanese publication and broadcast dates and the Tezuka Productions press releases.

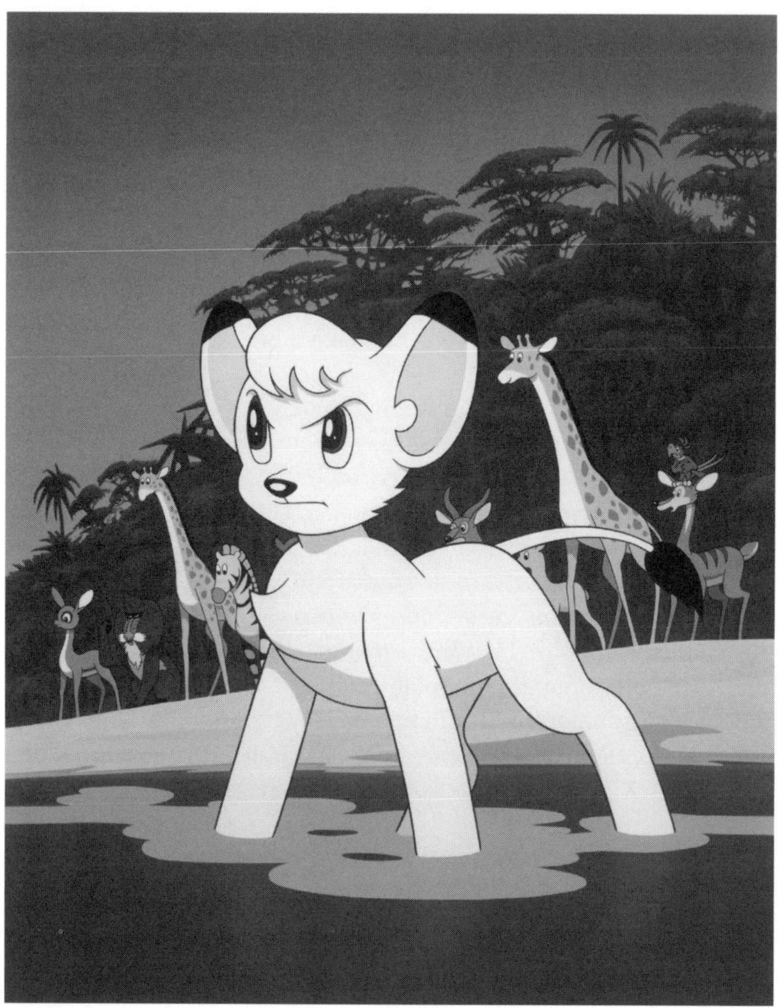

Kimba stands ready to defend the animals' cooperative kingdom from all threats. At far left (to his right): Dodie Deer and Dan'l Baboon. At far right: Pauley Cracker on the head of Bucky Deer. The others are nameless generic background characters. ©1966/2007 Tezuka Production Co., Ltd/Mushi Production Co., Ltd. Image courtesy of The Right Stuf International, Inc.

4 The 'Expanded' Field of Animation

A. Live Action and Animation

ALLEGORIES OF ANIMATION: *SCHINDLER'S LIST*, *E.T.* AND *THE LION KING*

REX BUTLER

> Spielberg's film portrays Oskar as a hero of this century. That is not true. Neither he nor I were heroes. We were just what we were able to be. In war we are all souls without destiny.[1]
>
> Emilie Schindler

The story of Steven Spielberg's *Schindler's List* is well known. It concerns the efforts of one Oskar Schindler, a prosperous German businessman, to save a number of Jews from the Nazi gas chambers by setting up a series of false factories at which they could work producing munitions for the war. The title of the film derives from the prodigious feats of memory of Schindler and his accountant Itzhak Stern in recalling the names of all those who had previously worked for Schindler in order that he might rescue them from the concentration camp to which they had inadvertently been sent. Thanks to him, those in his factory, unlike so many others of their faith, are able to walk free when the end of the war was finally declared.

Schindler's List, however, is not so much the story of these Jews as a moral study of Schindler himself. In it, we witness his transformation from hearty, beer-guzzling Nazi sympathizer to a covert resister of Nazism at great personal risk to himself. It is the aim of the film to explain this change, to show how the necessity for Schindler's choice arose.

There is a scene in *Schindler's List* where Schindler accidentally stumbles across the infamous massacre of the Jews at the Cracow ghetto in Poland while he is out riding with his wife. (Spielberg in the film shoots the scene from exactly the same position on top of a nearby hill from which the original Schindler would have seen it.) At the time, Schindler is still a fully-fledged member of the Nazi Party, enjoying the fruits of the Jewish slave labour in his factory. He watches as, far below him, the terrified inhabitants of the town are rounded up and shot by their tormentors.

But amidst this scene of carnage, an extraordinary moment occurs. In this otherwise black-and-white film, a small girl appears, individually hand-coloured in red, running across the courtyard of the ghetto and into hiding in an abandoned building. The sight seems to affect Schindler unaccountably, and he turns around on his horse and rides off. Later, he sees the same girl, again hand-coloured in red, being trundled away in a cartload of bodies from the concentration camp to be burnt. Schindler's conversion to the cause of the Jews—although there is no outward sign of it—is complete.

These two symbolic moments find their complement in the only other outburst of colour within the main body of the film, when Schindler, against all the rules of his Nazi bosses, allows the Jewish workers in his factory to light a candle to celebrate their Sabbath. (Colour is also used in the opening credits and epilogue of the film.) The flame of their candle is shown wavering back and forth in glowing yellow and gold, marking perhaps the only act of explicit defiance by Schindler throughout the narrative. (We will come back to this in a moment.)

As we suggest, the moral centre of the film is Schindler's decision to stand up to the Nazis. This is the dilemma it poses to its audience, each of whom must ask him- or herself: what would I do in similar circumstances? Would I rebel against the authorities or conform to them? But most reviewers had trouble with Schindler's change of heart here. (They often compared the enigma of his character to that of Charles Foster Kane in Orson Welles' *Citizen Kane*.)[2] Unlike most films of a similar kind, the moral turning points of *Schindler's List* are not clearly signposted; and that moment when Schindler first begins to oppose the Nazi regime is difficult to determine.

Of course, the obvious response to this is to say that, as in that scene with the little girl in red, Schindler is shocked by what he sees and vows to change it. But something is missing from this description. Some sense of Schindler's interiority prevents us from explaining his behaviour in such a cause-and-effect kind of way. (At the beginning of the film, for instance—and this is cleverly brought out by the use of deep-focus cinematography, which produces the impression of a great distance between Schindler and what he sees—he is quite capable of witnessing great brutality against Jews without being in the least affected.) Clearly, external circumstances alone are not enough to account for Schindler's actions. A transformation in the inner man is necessary as well.

But perhaps the key to grasping Schindler's character and our difficulties with it lies in something that both the critics of the film and the director himself tried to repress in discussions of *Schindler's List*: the fact that it was made by Steven Spielberg. It is by seeing it as similar to other Spielberg films, rather than—as critics have generally done—as different from them, that we might best understand *Schindler's List*.

* * *

The Australian film writer Adrian Martin, in a chapter entitled 'It's an Impossible Life' from his collection *Phantasms*, makes the point that Frank Capra's 1946 tearjerker *It's a Wonderful Life* forms a sort of generic prototype for the whole post-Spielbergian generation of Hollywood cinema. The reigning sensibility of this style of film-making, Martin argues, is not simply the substitution of fantasy for reality (this, after all, has been a staple of cinema everywhere from the very beginning) but their radical indistinguishability. Indeed, in a later chapter, 'Martin Scorsese's Indirect Aim', he notes director Martin Scorsese's refusal to mark the end of his film *The King of Comedy* as either fantasy or reality. As a result, it was impossible to determine, even for the actors within it, whether any of the film (and not just its ending) actually took place or was only the hallucination of one of its characters. It is this confusion, says Martin, that takes us to the heart of Scorsese's artistic vision: 'the impossible dream of personal identity that involves plunging into and becoming one's own fantasy image'.[3] And it is just this quality of *It's a Wonderful Life* that has made it so influential for the current generation of Hollywood filmmakers.

In the film, as we might remember, small-town George Bailey, at the moment of contemplating suicide by jumping off a bridge, is visited by his guardian angel Clarence, who shows him what life would have been like had he never been born. The idyllic hamlet of Bedford Falls where he lives would be an awful big city, run by the miserly scrooge Potter; his wife (in perhaps the one unrealistic touch in the whole film) would be a dried-up old maid; the friendly neighbourhood pharmacist would be in prison, unable to have been prevented by the young George from accidentally dispensing a poisonous remedy to a sick patient. The film, in other words, Martin argues, is an ingenious polemic for the maintenance of the *status quo* not by showing how good things are now but by showing how bad they would be otherwise, and, as such, is a subtle exercise in Hollywood-style ideological persuasion.

But Martin's real concern in this chapter is the spate of recent attempts to remake the film, from Robert Zemeckis' *Back to the Future* series to Bill Murray's *Scrooged* and *Groundhog Day* to Albert Brooks' *Defending Your Life* and Spielberg's own *Amazing Tales* television episodes. He wants to suggest that what these remakes are unable to do is perform the precarious balancing-act of the original, putting the *status quo* in doubt only finally to re-affirm it. They are unable to share Capra's belief in the populist ideals put forward at the end of the film, incapable of seeing them as still operative today. As Martin writes: '...they can only end up marking the yawning, aching abyss that opens up between that old dream and our new reality'.[4]

However, we would propose that, paradoxically, it is just this 'failure' that these remakes come to reveal about the original itself. For, in retrospect, an uncanny inversion can be seen to take place there, one that undoubtedly occurs beyond the film's 'direct aim'. Looking at that grasping, rapacious, money-driven world that Clarence conjures up as a result of George not existing, we cannot but be struck by the thought that this *is* in fact our contemporary reality and that the idyllic world of Bedford Falls is only a dream.

The true effect of the film, as Martin's comments on its remakes imply, is to show that the reality in which we live is only possible on the basis of the exclusion of a more profound 'reality'—but a 'reality' that is only accessible through dream (or the intercession of an angel).[5]

Now, what is the relationship between all this and *Schindler's List*? Critics have noted the film's sombre documentary style, its stark black-and-white photography, authentic period costumes and low-key acting. But we would argue, along the lines of Martin's reading of *It's a Wonderful Life*, that this is not an attempt actually to represent the Holocaust (an event that, perhaps by definition, remains unrepresentable). On the contrary, the panoply of documentary film devices is used there precisely to create a fiction. In other words, Spielberg acknowledges that the reality of the Holocaust is not to be represented as such but only in the form of fiction (the exclusion of which, however, reduces our lives to a kind of fiction). And, similarly, to go back to those episodes with the little girl in red we spoke of before, we would say that there too we have an intrusive, overdetermined allusion to childhood pleasures amidst the slaughter of the ghetto (the trembling, nostalgic feel of hand-coloured animation) but that it is only as a result of their failure adequately to represent the scene before him that Schindler is afforded some insight into its terrible reality.[6]

It is at this point that we might go back to the issue of Schindler's character and the critics' difficulty with Spielberg's account of his conversion to the cause of the Jews. As we say, the problem with explaining Schindler's change of heart—a limit Spielberg tries to take into account—is that it is not enough simply to say that external circumstances (the reality of Nazi brutality) force him to see the truth and mend his ways. Along with any change in the outer world, there must also be a transformation in the inner man; or this objective change must correspond to something that has already occurred within him. (It is this 'invisible' aspect of his conversion, this 'silent weaving of the Spirit', that leads to our sense of distance from Schindler and the critics' objection that we are never directly able to enter his character.)[7] To put it another way, to the extent that this change is not only external but also internal, it is possible that what we have in *Schindler's List* is a kind of fantasy, *that the entirety of the film after Schindler sees the girl in red did not really happen but is only a fantasy, a projection by him.*

It is just in this manner, however, that we might say that *Schindler's List* replicates the structure of *It's a Wonderful Life*, is in fact Spielberg's much-prized remake of Capra's masterpiece. For, in a way, Schindler saves nobody. That horrible fate which the incident with the little girl reveals to him does indeed come to pass. Schindler merely continues running his factory as he would if he were a devoted Nazi and the end of the war suddenly announced. Iconoclastically, we might even suggest that Schindler's list was a mere invention by Schindler (or, at least, we could never finally decide whether it was or not). It is possible, that is—as with George Bailey—that things would have turned out exactly the same without Schindler (the same factory would have been run by another and those same Jewish workers would have been set free at the end of the war). But—and this is the real effect of that post-Spielbergian confusion of fantasy and reality we spoke of before—it is just this fantasy which in fact produces and structures reality. Schindler's fantasy of saving the Jews might be just that, a fantasy; but it is nevertheless effective, not so much in actually saving those Jews as in saving Schindler himself. The film is a great parable about the benefits of doing good works not because they actually affect anything but because they are good for the person performing them. (However, of course, if everybody did as Schindler, the Holocaust might never have happened.) The key to the film, in other words, is an identification not so much with the Jews—they are its impossible Real with whom nobody can identify—as with Schindler himself. The film's anti-Nazi strategy, very ingeniously, is not to exhort us directly to identify with the persecuted but with Schindler's fantasy of rescuing them (as though we could ourselves).[8]

The effect of this mediation of the narrative through Schindler's fantasy, therefore, is that we suspend our disbelief with regard to its historical reality. More specifically, if we are sceptical about the events of the film (Schindler's attempt to avert the Holocaust), we remain transfixed, absorbed, by the gaze of their original, mythical, naive spectator—Schindler himself—who is still able to take them seriously. (It is perhaps for this reason that Spielberg shot that scene in the ghetto from exactly the same position from which Schindler saw it.) We know that the film is a fantasy, that from the beginning Schindler could have changed nothing about the objective fate of those Jews; and yet we live the film out, as with every Hollywood-style narrative, as though everything had not been determined, as though Schindler could have saved them.

And in this context, what finally is the significance of those moments of primitive, child-like animation involving the young girl we see in the film, which seemingly are that Real which appeals to Schindler and forces him to change his ways? They could be said to bear some analogy to what the psychoanalyst Jacques Lacan spoke of as the 'stain', that place in the image from which the image looks at you. (For, despite being removed and hidden away from the scene he observes, Schindler is struck by the impression that the little girl there is somehow able to see him, that the sight of her is meant for him alone.)[9] And this would be like the mute gaze of the Jews throughout the film—particularly that of Stern, his accountant—who never actually say anything or directly rise up against him but whose silent and insistent presence haunts him and leads to him feeling guilty.

This connection between animation and the notion of clear-seeingness is made apparent in that other moment in the film where colour is directly applied to the surface of the image, when Schindler allows the Jews in his factory to light a candle for their Sabbath. There is an extraordinary analogy made here between the candle, in its flickering and casting of shadows, and the cinematic apparatus itself. Its lighting, as we say, marks perhaps the only moment of actual rebellion by Schindler throughout the film; and it is the same liberatory possibility that Spielberg holds out for cinema itself in the making of something like *Schindler's List*. In both cases (the little girl in red, the lighting of the candle), animation represents a kind of response of the Real to the characters' fantasies (with regard to the little girl, that of Schindler; with regard to the candle, that of the Jews in the factory or Spielberg himself). In both, animation seems to offer a reverse look back to the audience that the rest of the film does not provide, an opening up of us to something out of the ordinary, something that is perhaps no longer or not yet able to be experienced. They are, as it were, moments of innocence or becoming, in which everything is not yet determined (or in which we are able to believe that everything is not yet determined). It is a childhood that is evoked in both cases, not only in what is seen (a young girl, a model of primitive cinema) but in the seer himself. And, in both cases, a key turning point of the plot is associated with animation (a change of heart in Schindler; the first act of overt resistance on his part), though this has not been noted by the critics, presumably because they do not want to consider the meaning of 'frivolous' animation in a supposedly 'serious' film like *Schindler's List*. (But it is perhaps in terms of this animation that we might look again at the often-made comparison between *Schindler's List* and Spielberg's *Jurassic Park*, which was released the same year. There too, animation—or let us say, re-animation—allows an upsetting of teleology within a system of narrative closure, the eruption of the past within the present or the present within the past.)[10]

We must, however, examine more closely this whole notion of the gaze or returned look implied in these images of animation, the way the Real there seems to respond to the characters' desires or fantasies. For, we would argue, another step is required properly to understand these sequences. We might begin by asking: whom are these episodes for, what kind of sight would be able to see them? A child's? Hardly. In *Schindler's List*, children are precisely robbed of their childhood and innocence. They are thoroughly immersed in the brutality and cruelty of the world. (We might think here of that terrible scene in the film where two children squabble over their hiding place in the bottom of a latrine during a search of their camp.) In this sense, we would say that, like every other Spielberg film—it seems strange to say this—*Schindler's List* is *nostalgic*. Or, to be more exact, it is made for a look that is now missing, for an impossible audience. And this audience might be—for who else could experience it as though it might have been otherwise?—the Jews who vanished in the Holocaust. The film is in part a testament—as the credits at the end show—to all those who actually experienced the Holocaust.[11] But, as is well known, no one has experienced the Holocaust and still remains alive; or no one who has experienced it has adequately been able to convey what it was like. (This is the problem of evidence the French anti-Revisionist philosopher Jean-François Lyotard speaks of in his book *The Differend*.)[12] So who could have seen the events Spielberg depicts in the death camps and ghettos? The film is made for this impossible gaze.[13]

And we would say this for all of Spielberg's films. Though they are, of course, hugely popular, they are made in fact for an audience that does not exist. Or, perhaps more accurately, they are made for an audience that is not of this world—an angel or an extra-terrestrial. Take, for instance, the sequence where the mother of the family in *E.T.* looks for the alien in one of her children's overstuffed cupboards after thinking she hears a disturbance upstairs. She cannot see him among all the other toys and dolls (other animatic replicas). But he can see her, just as her children can see him. Here in a nutshell is Spielberg's declaration of the audience for his films, those who can see *E.T.* and those who cannot. It is for an innocent gaze that the film is intended, just that ingenuous gaze which E.T. himself turns upon the world. (And, indeed, as has been often pointed out, the entire film is shot from the low-level point of view of a child, with adults frequently being seen only from below the waist.)

But who or what is E.T., anyway? He comes down to earth from another planet; and the question is, as with George Bailey in *It's a Wonderful Life*: is the way he sees things the most truthful or the most deluded? He trusts in the essential goodness of people. He believes what he reads in science fiction comics. (It is through one of them that he learns how to build the machine that allows his escape.) He takes for real the fate of the characters in cartoons. (When he watches *Tom and Jerry* on TV, he laughs when he sees Tom's tail being burnt and Tom going crazy. Indeed, he throws an empty beer can at Tom.) He is able, in other words, to suspend his disbelief in fiction. This is why he is able to follow the animation of the cartoons he looks at.

And Eliot, the young earth boy, and he share a telepathic relationship in the film, with each being able to intuit the other's thoughts and mental states. (Recall, for instance, the scene at school where Eliot becomes intoxicated while E.T. drinks alone at home.) The whole film, that is, is drenched in the atmosphere of what Freud calls the *uncanny*, in which spirits are real and the distinction between the living and the dead, the human and the alien, no longer holds. This is the world of *E.T.* in particular and of animation in general. And we would say that Spielberg's entire film is an attempt to go back to this uncanny world of animation—a world nostalgically conjured up for him by television. It is the childhood television experience that for Spielberg was that moment when he was able to believe in cartoons; and, as we say, he shoots *E.T.* from this impossible pre-conscious point of view. (As has been noted of Spielberg's films, it is their common absence of fathers, as with the unsupervised child-hood watching of TV, which is a license for the kind of fantasy we see in them. It is the absence of the Symbolic paternal law that allows that suspension of disbelief which is the Imaginary.)

But to unravel all this a little more slowly, let us ask a question: what is really being narrated in *E.T.*? In effect, the film is a type of *Bildungsroman* or apprenticeship narrative. The real story the film tells is the growing-up and maturing of the child Eliot through the loss of E.T. But what is involved in this loss of E.T.? In fact, what we realize—in just that confusion of fantasy and reality we looked at before—is that this animation, this animism, the whole existence of E.T., is possibly not true. He might only be a projection by Eliot (and this would be the true coincidence of the initials E.T. to stand in both for extra-terrestrial and for Eliot himself). The vision his innocence opens up for us can only remain a fantasy. Indeed, we might even say that our adult world is defined by the exclusion of the insight of someone like E.T. And, of course, this would be just like *It's a Wonderful Life*, where Clarence the angel appears only in a dream, or *Schindler's List*, where Schindler confronts the consequences of his actions as an hallucination or vision.

In each case, the horrible reality—the impossibility of the innocence and openness to new experience of E.T., the fact that George Bailey and Oskar Schindler save nobody—can only be revealed through a fantasy that appears to suggest the opposite. That is, to go back to *E.T.*, the story the film really wants to tell us is that E.T. does not exist, that his guilelessness and child-like credulity are impossible; but it can do this only through a plot that somehow makes us believe in these things. The Real can only be presented in the form of a fiction (as, again, the possibility that Schindler saved nobody can only be suggested through the Messianic fantasy that he did).[14] This would be the meaning too behind the critics' frequent comment that Spielberg, better than any other director, manages to put contemporary suburban everydayness and banality up on the screen. We would say he manages to do so, but only through fantastic, phantasmatic narratives that would be the very antithesis of this.

To make the point more clearly: each of Spielberg's films takes place under an absent paternal gaze. It is through this absence that his characters are able to believe in myths, archetypes, aliens, their own omnipotence in the world, all of which Freud spoke of in terms of the uncanny. (As an example of this omnipotence, let us recall the well-known scene from Spielberg's *Empire of the Sun*, in which young Jim answers a Japanese warship emitting Morse code signals with his own feeble pocket torch from a distant hotel window. When the ship moments later attacks Shanghai, he is convinced he has provoked it and rushes to apologize to his father: 'I didn't mean it! It was only a joke!') All these beliefs would constitute a kind of nostalgia in that sense in which someone like Fredric Jameson characterizes postmodernism, referring particularly to filmmakers like Spielberg.[15] Indeed, this nostalgia is something that Spielberg has spoken of as trying to recapture. But we would argue that, in fact, what we see played out in them—as in *It's a Wonderful Life*—is a profound engagement with the Real, the realization that this animation or animism does not exist. In this sense, we would say that Spielberg is a profound critic of that postmodern nostalgia he is portrayed in terms of, that his films subtly undermine the ideology they appear to put forward (through nostalgia, they aim to expose the impossibility of this nostalgia). In terms of that imagined returned gaze that appears to license their suspension of disbelief, that is, we come to understand that it is precisely nostalgic, does not in fact exist.

This issue of the nostalgic gaze is also at stake in a film like *Shane*—another important film for recent Hollywood—which the Lacanian social analyst Slavoj Žižek describes as a meta-Western (just as we would describe *E.T.* as a meta-science fiction film and Spielberg's films in general as meta-genre films). But this designation meta- does not mean that these films simply quote or parody elements of the various genres to which they belong (as someone like Jameson would have it[16]). Rather—and here we come back to this question of the missing, nostalgic gaze—just as *Shane* was a Western made when it was no longer possible to make Westerns, so *E.T.* is a science fiction film made when it is no longer possible to make science fiction films, impossible because no one believes any more in the possibility of other or alternative worlds.[17] The brilliance of *E.T.*, however, is that it manages to speak not of another world as alien but of *this* world. More specifically, it manages to alienate us from our world by making us realize that it is a fantasy construction brought about by the impossibility of that other world, the exclusion of something like E.T.'s point of view. In other words, paradoxically, it is the very failure of science fiction to visualize an alternative to this world which makes of this world its own science fiction. E.T., the extra-terrestrial, but also Eliot, the earth boy, are able to see—and are able to make us see—this world as another world, to turn us all into strangers in a strange land (again, the vertiginous banality of domestic interiors, of middle-class American life, the icons and paraphernalia of popular culture, etc.—and the final equivalence to be made here, of course, is between the initials E.T. and Earth itself).[18]

But we might think through the relationship between *Schindler's List* and this kind of nostalgia film in a little more detail here. (For *Schindler's List*, too, if we are to believe someone like Claude Lanzmann, the maker of *Shoah*, is a Holocaust film made when it is no longer possible to make Holocaust films.)[19] What ultimately is the aim of this nostalgia for Žižek? He writes in *Looking Awry: An Introduction to Jacques Lacan through Popular Culture*:

> ...the function of the nostalgic object is precisely to *conceal* the antinomy between eye and gaze—i.e., the traumatic impact of the gaze *qua* object—by means of its power of fascination. In nostalgia, the gaze of the other is in a way domesticated, 'gentrified'; instead of the gaze erupting like a traumatic, disharmonious blot, we have the illusion of 'seeing ourselves seeing', of seeing the gaze itself.[20]

That is, in the nostalgia film, as we have already remarked of *E.T.*

and *Empire of the Sun*, it is as though reality responds to you, comes about as a result of your actions or by being seen by you. Thus, in that sequence involving the little girl in *Schindler's List*, it is as though she looks back in response to Schindler looking at her; or more generally in the film, it is as though the Jews in the factory are saved because of him. But, as we argue, the dreadful insight Spielberg affords us through this suspension of disbelief is the possibility that there is simply no connection between this little girl and Schindler (for what real relationship could there be between a Jewish girl and a prosperous businessman in Nazi Germany?), that Schindler changes nothing concerning the objective fate of his workers, that his whole feeling of the girl looking back at him or even of his responding to her prior look could only take place *after* his initial identification with the Jews, which ultimately is only a fantasy to save himself, to protect him from that essential 'antinomy between eye and gaze', that is, from the Real.

This is to begin to think that the whole scene Schindler saw there with the little girl was 'staged' for him (as it was in reality, of course—and here we come back to the way that Liam Neeson, the actor, stands at the same point once occupied by the real Schindler), that his desire was already 'part of the game',[21] that his belief that he was helping the Jews and therefore outside of the system was in fact essential to its running, part of its operative ideology. But perhaps what this also opens up—and this is to lead us into the second half of this essay—is the possibility that Schindler already knows this, knows that his actions are futile, that he is only an actor for whom all things are appearances. But why then does he continue? And how is he able to make others follow him and thus save them (as well as himself) by making them believe that he can save them, that there is something to be done? In what sense is Schindler (like his Biblical prototype Moses, who also led his Chosen People to a Promised Land) a kind of king, a leader of men?

* * *

To begin to answer these questions, let us break off for a moment to consider a photograph. It shows Spielberg, the ex-Disney chief

Jeffrey Katzenberg and recording mogul David Geffen signing the papers setting up a new company, the aptly Freudian-named DreamWorks, a complete entertainment conglomerate, vertically integrated, covering all aspects of movie production, from the actual making of a film through to its distribution, the licensing of its sound recordings and its merchandising spin-offs. Why is Spielberg there with those other two and, more particularly, why this conjunction of Spielberg and Disney? A first, obvious answer (one that might be put by someone like Jameson): because both peddle a form of nostalgia. But perhaps another, more profound explanation might be given. Katzenberg, the ex-Disney chairman, had just made his name by overseeing the creation and launch of the animated feature *The Lion King*, the most profitable animated film ever made. And undoubtedly Spielberg could see the great affinity between his own work and *The Lion King*, an affinity whose real nature might escape us at first.

Of course, as everybody knows by now, *The Lion King* is the story of a young lion cub, Simba, who grows up to inherit the kingdom his father, Mufasa, left him and become ruler of Pride Rock. As such, it is a classic tale of patriarchy. And critics have not been slow to accuse the film of perpetuating racial and sexual stereotypes (especially in the casting of Whoopi Goldberg to voice the scheming hyena Shenzi and Jeremy Irons to voice the king's fey brother Scar). The film on a manifest level is conservative, preaches a continued allegiance to tradition, speaks of culturally specific values as though they were universal—accusations that have been levelled against myths and parables of kingship from time immemorial (Pascal, La Boétie, Hegel, Kantorowicz, etc.).

However, like Spielberg's own films, the message of *The Lion King* is perhaps more subtle and subversive than this. Let us examine just one sequence from it, a moment where—a bit like those scenes we have discussed from *Schindler's List* and *E.T.*—we have animation, as it were, allegorizing itself. (And here, furthermore, we see this animation arising diegetically within an animation film itself, that is, a moving image being watched by one of its characters.) It is a moment that occurs when Simba returns after a long period exiled from his fellow lions. He had mistakenly believed that he was responsible for his father's death, after causing him to come out looking for him when he had become lost. The kingdom of Pride Rock, under his evil uncle Scar, who had falsely encouraged him in this belief, has in the meantime fallen into disrepair and anarchy. But Simba does not quite possess the courage directly to challenge him, as some in the pride urge him to do. Then, suddenly, upon being led to a pool of water by the baboon magician Rafiki, he sees his own reflection changing into that of his father, Mufasa, who then appears to him as a vision out of the clouds, addressing him and urging him to 'Remember who you are'. It is at this point that Simba feels able to stand up to Scar. He wins a fight with him, forces him to admit that he lied (it was, in fact, Scar himself who caused the death of his own brother) and finally assumes his rightful place as the ruler of Pride Rock.

What we see in this sequence is that it is at that moment when Simba enters into a communion with his father that he first decides he is fit to become king. But how does his father appear to him? He appears nowhere in the real world, but only as a reflection in the water—precisely as an effect of animation itself. (Louis Marin says the same of royal portraiture in France in the seventeenth century: the king is first of all a portrait of a king.[22] And we might say the same of E.T., who in similar fashion first appears to Eliot's siblings from behind a TV set.) In other words, Simba, in order to become a king, must first identify with animation. Or, to put it another way, he must suspend his disbelief that what he is looking at is only a cartoon or portrait.

Now, it might be suggested that Simba at this point is never more under the ideological illusion of kingship, never more believes in the false notion of a natural-born king. But it is at just this moment too that he realizes that there is no king or that he himself must take on the mantle of the king for there to be a king at all. And it is after this that he also understands, having won his fight with Scar, that he did not in fact cause his father's death; that is, he breaks with his animistic belief that his actions have great consequences in the world (this was also his father's advice to him as a young cub).[23] At the same time, therefore, he both becomes king and realizes that there is no such thing as the king, that the king exists only as a result of others' belief in him (his own, first of all). And we might say it is exactly this insight into the king's non-existence that makes him a king; or, what is strangely enough the same thing, it is the one who can suspend his disbelief with regard to the king's existence who becomes king. Ordinary people might not themselves believe in the king, but they believe in him because others do. The king, however, needs no such intermediaries: as the analogy between the king and the sun in the film suggests, the king is immediately able to reflect upon himself, is equal to himself alone. He does not need anybody to believe in him before he believes in himself.

To conclude: ordinary people are in a relationship of what we have called the nostalgic gaze with regard to the king. They might not directly believe in him, but they believe that others believe; and this is good enough for them. This would be for us a working definition of ideology. But the royal subject might also see in a moment of insight that the secret of kingship is that there is really no such thing, that the gaze which precedes him is in fact his own.[24] This would be the end of that nostalgic overcoming of the 'antinomy between eye and gaze'. At this point, however, we sometimes see a very peculiar thing happen. In *Schindler's List*, for example, Schindler perhaps realizes that his ambitions are futile, that he will never prevent the Holocaust; but he carries on just the same. This would be the behaviour of a real king (and it would be another way of thinking the lesson Schindler gives to the crazed camp commandant Goeth, that the true exercise of power lies not in punishing but in sparing a man). Or think, for example, of Eliot in *E.T.*, who might realize that E.T. does not actually exist but who nevertheless carries on as though he does to end up being the leader of all the other children after they had at first bullied him and excluded him from their circle.

This is the 'genius', finally, of Spielberg and of every spectator of the film who also realizes in the end that E.T. does not exist but who could only have reached this conclusion by first of all believing in the film, by identifying with its child-like gaze. *The king is the place-holder of the void*. It is only through the king that we come to understand there is no actual locus of power.[25] Again, however, it is not through any immediate breaking down of this illusion that we come to grasp this but only through an identification with the king (or film).[26] It is only through the king that we can dream of another world, that we can desire and even desire the overthrow of the king. (And is this not ultimately the lesson of *It's a Wonderful Life* and of all the films that come after it: this alternative 'reality' is not to be directly presented but gestured at only through its very repression or impossibility, only as an absence which this world as the place-holder of the void allows us to think.)

In this sense, we might say that the 'idealism' of Spielberg and Disney offers a far more radical deconstruction of capitalist ideology than any of the so-called 'radical materialist' cinemas of the 1960s and '70s. It is better able to break with the current regime of the nostalgic gaze, that cynicism of not actually believing in anything oneself but only because others do, of believing that one maintains a distance from the ideologies and beliefs of one's own society. Against Jameson, we would say that it is appropriate to speak of Spielberg and Disney not as postmodern but as two of the great critics of the postmodern. For them, animation is neither more real than life nor merely an illusion. It is, rather, what we might call an 'illusion of illusion': that which, in its own impossibility, exposes this world as itself an illusion, the effect of a certain animation.

NOTES

I would like to thank Keith Broadfoot for discussions during the writing of this essay.

1 Emilie Schindler quoted in David Haskel, 'Schindler, "Selfish, Ruthless"', *The Sunday Mail*, Brisbane, March 31, 1996, p. 61. Of course, the point here is not to try to determine whether Schindler was actually like this or not but to think that the meaning of his actions is not determined once and for all, can be re-interpreted or 'requilted' in many different ways.

2 On the connection with *Citizen Kane*, see Miriam Bratu Hansen, '*Schindler's List* is not *Shoah*: The Second Commandment, Popular Modernism and Public Memory', *Critical Inquiry* 22, Winter 1996, pp. 307-310.

3 Adrian Martin, 'Martin Scorsese's Indirect Aim', *Phantasms* (Melbourne: McPhee Gribble, 1994), p. 152.

4 Martin, 'It's an Impossible Life', *Phantasms*, p. 163.

5 Slavoj Žižek proposes a similar reading of the film in *Tarrying with the Negative: Kant, Hegel and the Critique of Ideology* (Durham: Duke University Press, 1993), pp. 62-63.

6 This might be compared to the usual readings of the sequence, for example, that of Philip Strick:

> The authenticity of Spielberg's staging has three debatable flaws. The first, of course, is his use of a sudden detail of colour to pick out the red coat of a child who wanders among the carnage as the ghetto is destroyed, an event observed by Schindler from a hillside above the city. Since the quality of the whole celluloid image has to change in order to accommodate this touch of crimson, it seems ponderous, a purported insight into Schindler's normally enigmatic viewpoint that is both inconsistent (we, not Schindler, get a closeup of the little girl hiding under a bed) and unnecessary, since she could have been rendered just as noticeable by, say, a scarf or a hairstyle. When her body, still in red, is carried past under Schindler's gaze, her iconic fate becomes almost demeaning to the many other victims we have seen. Philip Strick, '*Schindler's List*', *Sight and Sound*, March 1994, p. 48.

It is, however, the meaning of this 'failure' that we prefer to examine here. The exhausted, by now conventional, choice of the colour red for the young girl would also have to be looked at in this light.

7 This is why it is interesting that perhaps Schindler's single direct attempt to save Jews, the bartering of his watch to save the Pearlmans, only occurs within a flashforward within a flashback authorized by the accountant Stern. In other words, we never see Schindler's change directly but only as a kind of future anterior or 'will have been'. It has both already taken place and is always deferred.

8 It is this that has perhaps led to that 'amazing and ambivalent' phenomenon Hansen notes occurring with the success of the film: the 'discovery of local Schindlers everywhere'. Hansen, '*Schindler's List* is not *Shoah*: The Second Commandment, Popular Modernism and Public Memory', p. 295.

9 This is emphasized by the fact that, amidst the chaos of the scene

below, no one but Schindler seems to notice the little girl crossing the street and entering the house.

10 On this eruption of the present within the past, the peculiar aspect of *Jurassic Park* is that it now seems as though the past was only possible in the first place as a result of its artificial resurrection by the present. However, what cannot thereby be explained is the presence of prehistoric fossils. In a sense, they are the Real which escapes this 'squaring of the circle' (Žižek, *Tarrying with the Negative*, p. 43). It is this problem of the dinosaur-and-the-egg around which the film revolves; or, to put it in Hegelese, what the film wants us to think is the 'infinite judgement' of 'The Spirit is a Bone'. It is this Real excluded by simulation, by the fantasy space to which everyday 'reality' must conform, that is also at stake in *Schindler's List*. On the aporias of *Jurassic Park* in relation to the work of Jean Baudrillard, see Alan Cholodenko, '"OBJECTS IN MIRROR ARE CLOSER THAN THEY APPEAR": The Virtual Reality of *Jurassic Park* and Jean Baudrillard', in *Jean Baudrillard, Art and Artefact*, ed. Nicholas Zurbrugg (London: Sage, 1997).

11 We think that one of the effects of the credit sequence at the end, also shot in colour—in which the actors are shown with the survivors on whom they are based—is the uncanny impression that these real life people have somehow *been brought back from the dead*.

12 Lyotard begins his book, which at once argues against the recent Revisionist attempts to deny the existence of the Holocaust and admits that in a sense we cannot simply refute them, with this premise:

> You are informed that human beings endowed with language were placed in a situation such that none of them is now able to tell about it. Most of them disappeared then, and the survivors rarely speak about it. When they do speak about it, their testimony bears only upon a minute part of this situation. How can you know that the situation itself existed? That it is not the fruit of your informant's imagination? Either the situation did not exist as such. Or else it did exist, in which case your informant's testimony is false, either because he or she should have disappeared, or else because he or she should remain silent, or else because, if he or she does speak, he or she can bear witness only to the particular experience he had, it remaining to be established whether this experience was a component of the situation in question. *The Differend* (Minneapolis: University of Minnesota Press, 1988), p. 3.

13 We might think here of that horrifying moment when the camera follows a group of newly processed women into a shower at one of the death camps and, as the taps momentarily fail to turn on, we are filled with the fear that they (and we) are about to be gassed. It is the paradox of this impossible gaze—at once witness to the 'moment' of the Holocaust but unable to live through it to narrate it—that we try to explicate here. (The same impossibility of actually knowing the Holocaust is raised by a group of Jewish women sitting around on bunks in one of the camps in the film.) It is perhaps worthy of note that Spielberg's film *Always* is also narrated from the impossible point of view of a dead pilot.

14 In this sense, the key to *Schindler's List* and its connection to *It's a Wonderful Life* might be brought out in a 'Jewish' joke one of the inhabitants of the ghetto tells: 'I woke up from a dream this morning. I was broke and sharing a room with 12 people I didn't know. Only to discover that I *was* broke and sharing a room with 12 people I didn't know'.

15 See Fredric Jameson, 'Postmodernism and Consumer Society', in *Postmodern Culture*, ed. Hal Foster (London: Pluto Press, 1985), p. 116. This argument is developed in Jameson's *Postmodernism, or, the Cultural Logic of Late Capitalism* (Durham: Duke University Press, 1992), especially the chapters 'The Cultural Logic of Late Capitalism' and 'Nostalgia for the Present'.

16 ibid., p. 113.

17 Indeed, we could even add to this sequence *Battleship Potemkin* as a film made when it was no longer possible to make revolutionary films—and it is fascinating to think that Spielberg's gesture of painting the little girl red comes from the red painted Communist flag hoisted above the battleship in that film. In *Battleship Potemkin* too, this red is perhaps not so much Symbolic as Real. It refers to something at once too soon (the mutiny celebrated in the film ultimately failed) and too late (by the time the film was made, revolutionary hopes were already beginning to fade). In other words, it might be possible to think *Battleship Potemkin* and its use of animation in the light of the issues opened up by *Schindler's List*, rather than the other way around. (My thanks to Lisa Trahair for drawing this comparison to my attention.)

18 We might compare *E.T.* in this regard to Nicholas Roeg's *The Man Who Fell to Earth*. The alien there has to appear on TV to appeal to his other world (as in a moment we shall see E.T. first appearing from behind a TV set). And, like E.T., he sees the world from a strange, distantiating

perspective—he develops a camera that takes photos from an impossible or non-existent point of view.

19 See Claude Lanzmann, 'Why Spielberg Has Distorted the Truth', *Guardian Weekly*, April 3, 1994, p. 14; and Yosefa Loshitzky, 'Holocaust Others: Spielberg's *Schindler's List* versus Lanzmann's *Shoah*', in *Spielberg's Holocaust: Critical Perspectives on 'Schindler's List'*, ed. Yosefa Loshitzky (Bloomington: Indiana University Press, 1996).

20 Žižek, *Looking Awry: An Introduction to Jacques Lacan through Popular Culture* (Cambridge: The MIT Press, 1991), p. 114. This could be interestingly read with a passage from *Tarrying with the Negative*, just after Žižek has discussed *It's a Wonderful Life*, where he remarks on the coincidence between this

> fantasy-gaze which immobilizes the subject, deprives him of his existence in reality, and reduces him to an object-gaze observing reality from which he is missing, and the Cartesian *cogito* which, at the height of its radical doubt, is also reduced to a nonexisting gaze acquiring distance from its own bodily presence, i.e., observing reality from 'behind its own retina'. Žižek, *Tarrying with the Negative*, p. 65.

21 ibid.

22 See Louis Marin, *Portrait of the King* (Minneapolis: University of Minnesota Press, 1988), especially the section 'A Portrait of Caesar, It is Caesar'. Readers might also refer to Marin's *Food for Thought* (Baltimore: The Johns Hopkins University Press, 1989), where the same arguments are continued. In terms of *The Lion King* itself, we might recall that Simba appears as a king even before this moment when he recognizes himself reflected in the pool of water, that is, when Rafiki predicts his re-appearance by drawing a picture of him on his cave wall (and the newly-born Simba was himself drawn and drawn upon by Rafiki).

23 Important to consider here would be the whole question of the elephants' graveyard as that point beyond which the lions cannot go and his uncle Scar's prohibiting him from going there, which precisely converts what is impossible into what is possible though forbidden. Along these lines, we might also think of Mufasa's paradoxical injunction for Simba to 'Remember who you are', to be himself. For, of course, exactly insofar as he does so, he is like his father, is not himself. We might say that it is just in coming to terms with this Symbolic deadlock that Simba grows up, becomes an adult, is fit to be king.

24 We might think here of Marin's analysis of the whole tradition of royal

ostentation or posing to attract the gaze. (See the chapter 'The King's Glorious Body', in *Food for Thought*.) This notion of the gaze one sees only being one's own is a way of understanding Lacan's statements where he, as does Žižek in his critique of the nostalgic gaze, distances himself from the possibility of a self-reflexive gaze, of seeing oneself seeing. Lacan states:

> There is no need for us to refer to some supposition of the existence of a universal seer. If the function of the stain is recognized in its autonomy and identified with that of the gaze, we can see its track, its thread, its trace, at every stage of the constitution of the world, in the scopic field. We will then realize that the function of the stain and of the gaze is both that which governs the gaze most secretly and that which always escapes from the grasp of that form of vision that is satisfied with itself in imagining itself as consciousness.
>
> That in which the consciousness may turn back upon itself—grasp itself, like Valéry's Young Parque, *as seeing oneself seeing oneself*—represents mere sleight of hand. An avoidance of the function of the gaze is at work there.

And ten pages later, Lacan declares, 'The gaze I encounter...is, not a seen gaze, but a gaze imagined by me in the field of the Other'. Jacques Lacan, *The Four Fundamental Concepts of Psycho-Analysis*, ed. Jacques-Alain Miller and trans. Alan Sheridan (Harmondsworth: Penguin, 1979), pp. 74, 84.

25 See on this the section '"The King is a Thing"', in Žižek, *For They Know Not What They Do: Enjoyment as a Political Factor* (London: Verso, 1991).

26 There is an analogy here with Lacan's mirror stage, where we might say that the child only becomes an adult by suspending the knowledge he has that the reflection he sees in front of him is only himself, that his recognition of it as another is mistaken. It is only in this way that he can learn the lessons—those of breaking with the Imaginary—that will finally make him an adult. And it is intriguing to consider that, looking at his own reflection in the water, Simba also goes through a mirror stage, an experience usually understood to be denied to animals. We might say that it is only by suspending, in a human-like way, the knowledge that he is merely an animal that Simba is able to learn the lessons that will ultimately make him a human adult. Of

course, we see this suspension of disbelief everywhere in cartoons, where animals carry on as though they were human. And this is something we might relate to that absence of the Symbolic Law of the father we spoke of above: cartoons, *par excellence*, are a world where the Law-of-the-Father is absent, both in the sense that they are only watched when one's father is absent and in the sense that we very rarely see functioning fathers within them. But, as we have tried to argue here, cartoons also constitute precisely the experience of the mirror stage in modern society. They are that place where children learn the lessons of adulthood, where they understand that if the paternal gaze is missing, it is only because they were that paternal gaze all along. We would like to relate this to what we take to be the quintessential experience in all animated cartoons: that moment when the cat or coyote pursues his prey along the road and across the thin air of an abyss. It is only, however, when he looks down and realizes what he has done that he actually begins to fall... It is to this mid-air point that we would say cartoons, Spielberg's *Schindler's List* and Disney's *The Lion King* all want to lead us.

4 The 'Expanded' Field of Animation

B. Video and Computer Games, the Electronic, Digitally Animated Mediascape, the City, Flight Simulation, the Military and War

Animating Architectures: Panic Styles for Troubled Cities

DAVID ELLISON

> SAN FRANCISCO (AFP)—The hottest-selling video game in the United States pits opponents of different ethnic backgrounds against one another in a brutal fight that ends with the loser lying bludgeoned and bloody on the ground. But against a backdrop of racial tension in US cities, *Street Fighter II* has stirred debate over whether it is a reflection of real life or could be construed as incitement to violence.
>
> 'It's a very destructive influence', said Charles Espalin, director of counselling programmes for the Los Angeles school district. Many of his students were involved in the riots that erupted in April. 'I could see where that could really generate some terrible events, if you have one group of kids attacking another simply because they are different'.
>
> 'Race Fights on Video', *The Independent* (London)[1]

In the weeks following the Rodney King riots, in the down time between panic and suburban armament, came the accusations. Who was responsible for this calamitous social upheaval? Here's the lineup: illegal immigrants, welfare queens, drug addicts, drug traffickers, the ever popular gangs and even Roosevelt's social reform policies, which had at last been revealed as the 'New Jack Deal'.

Among these was one other contender: the arcade game *Street Fighter*. Although it surfaced infrequently as a specific cause of the disruption, *Street Fighter* appeared as one of a series of demonized leisure pursuits that were claimed to have actually incited or contributed to the climate of violence.

This discussion in turn featured in a larger debate about the dispensations of public space, new urban forms and the role of technology in post-riot L.A. The riots created a crisis in public space where the fortifications of the built environment no longer seemed adequate to hold back the homeless, urban violence and racial tensions, where a new kind of safe space made possible by developments in telecommunications was fantasized about with an urgency normally associated with a sense of civil disaster.

But one of the problems with this anticipated move into the security of electronically altered space was the publicly accessible modes of electronic culture currently in circulation, such as TV, the counter-surveillance of George Holliday's video of the King beating and games like *Street Fighter*. This publicly accessible media presented a difficulty precisely because it operated as a prior consensual model of what constituted the electronic domain.

In the wake of the riots, a great deal of political energy was directed towards divvying up technology, an act of separation organized in crudely racial terms in an effort to sanitize what we have come to understand as the New Electronic World Order. This was an attempt to contract and purify the scope and shape of the electronic sphere.

In this paper, I will chart some of the preliminary efforts to effect this division in techno-culture, paying attention both to the means by which new technology was described and the efforts to construe certain less desirable modes. In particular, I will trace the vectors of the telecommunications and computing industries as they responded to the threat posed by the riots with new models of the urban.

The city that will emerge in this account is one with which we are becoming increasingly familiar through critical urban histories that trace the flight of capital away from the crisis-gripped city and towards corporate parks, gated communities and simulated public environments.[2] The brightly lit console screens of post-riot Los Angeles act out nervy little dramas that gesture towards a disseminated primal scene: the simultaneously generative and apocalyptic moment. The flaming mini-malls, besieged Korean grocery stores and the looting of Fredericks of Hollywood speak to the fiery undoing of the city, these emergent screens to its simulated restoration.

I am interested here in the anxious efforts to master the radiant light that played upon the roughcast stucco of riot-torn L.A. and the subsequent proliferation of illuminated screens (both electronic and architectural) that read as uncanny doubles of the burning wall. These rudimentary essays into the habitability of a newly animated wall are marked, as all such moves are, by traces of dispossession and violence, by the *unheimlich*. While Anthony Vidler situates the uncanny in terms of the insecurities of a *newly established bourgeoisie* not quite at home in its own home,[3] I suggest we should consider *post-riot gringo angelenos*, whose homes are not safe, but not breached, for whom 'location, location, location' refers to coordinates in the urban scanscape, for whom the domesticated terror of the uncanny irrupts in a vision of the living room as NORAD outpost, the deadliest of comfort zones.

The story told in this paper is of the dream images of this uncanny future (non)city, something like its hyperphysical blueprint etched in vanguardist architecture, in advertising, and most importantly, on the screen.

AT HOME...

Where will the inhabitants of this New Electronic Order dwell? In a Frank Gehry house, of course. Gehry, who, for critics like Mike Davis, best summarizes the increasingly militant retreat from public-minded design behind stealthy walls and fortified bunkers, has recently remodelled his Santa Monica home, replacing his signature raw plywood walls with gleaming stainless steel panels.[4] The decorative use of sheet metal is a constituent sign of the 'funk aesthetic' that distinguishes the work of a number of L.A. architects, including Frank Israel, Morphosis (Thom Mayne and Michael Rotondi), Elyse Grinstein, Jeffrey Daniels, Eric Owen Moss and Charles Moore.[5] As a material, stainless steel is featured widely in both domestic and corporate commissions, particularly in the most fetishized site in contemporary L.A. architecture: the warehouse conversion. Here the auratic, nostalgic spaces of an industrial culture fled south towards Mexico are re-fitted as micro-cities for the post-industrial labour force. Within these re-figured shells, design companies, advertising agencies and film and record businesses commingle in space cathected from the public sphere, weirdly coercive work sites complete with interiorized piazzas and 'streetscapes' lined with offices. Charles Jencks' description of Frank Israel's conversion of the old Eames studio captures both the imploded urbanism of the warehouse conversion and the obsessive use of sheet metal:

> One approaches this former warehouse, and modernist studio, by way of two tough billboards—one of grey sheet metal, the other a triangle of glass brought to a very aggressive point where you enter. After these and other acknowledgements of a hostile environment, one enters a tiny village turned inside-out. The arrival space is a yellow stucco tower open to the sky, with jutting balconies of—what else?—grey sheet metal. From this inverted Italian campanile one is shunted through a dark sheet metal tunnel, to arrive at the third building within a building—the conference room in the shape of an inverted cone. To the right one finds the main avenue of the village, with private streets and offices, placed under the grid of the exposed trusses. As in all these conversions metal gusset-plates, wooden beams and hanging duct-work are polished up to become essential icons of work and regular markers of space.[6]

The recursive use of metal in these buildings offers a phantom sign of 'industry' recuperated in its *luxe* form (polished, detailed, transcended), a technique in the service of the encyclopedic goals of these sites to encapsulate and restage the world in an anti-viral form. In a way, these spaces are like contorted versions of telecommuting, where, through some trick of feedback, the totality of public leisure space, domestic privacy and corporate identity have all ended up back at the place of work. Such an in-folding of work and play is characteristic of the re-animation of labour conceptualized by Ru Paul in the phrase 'work it girl', in which the machined (if not Taylorized) body of industry, leisure and sex is disseminated within an interchangeable house style.

What of the domestic sphere? The home site would not seem to lend itself to the use of metal cladding, except perhaps for practical security purposes. Gehry's Santa Monica refurbishment does suggest, at face value, a crude low-tech kind of armour; and as such, his renovations subscribe to the lexicon of defensive motifs that dominate much of his commissioned work. Put simply, this could be a mutation of the house as strong box, an aesthetic Gehry explored in his Spiller House of 1981, which made extensive use of corrugated iron and is oddly suggestive of Shankill Road battlements.

Gehry's work has always been attentive to the logistics of a siege life-style. But here and now, at home in Santa Monica, things are much calmer, as if the imperative to intimidate has receded in the face of new conditions. While stainless steel metal cladding *is* armour, it is also a reflective surface and, as such, draws on a very different notion of fortification, what Davis calls a 'militarized syntax' that is normally associated with downtown corporate architecture—specifically the use of mirrored glass as a kind of shorthand for high-tech, high-security smart buildings.[7] With references to the postmodern urbanity of the warehouse conversion and the sublimated hostility of the modernist glass tower, Gehry brings distinctly commercial design languages to bear upon the homestead. In this corporate merger with the *heimlich*, Gehry draws together two apparently incompatible spaces towards the production of a new space where, architecturally, the home lays claim to a share of the political and economic energy of the corporate urban core, and vice versa.

This transfer of energy from centre to periphery flickers across the light-bearing metal surface of the house in the red arc of brake lights, in the brilliance of the search beam that traces a seamless reflected line (of encrypted data?) from window to wall. These animated walls are screens that visualize a connecting loop from the glow of the work-station to the metal surface of the warehouse to the mirror skin of the tower to home.[8] Gehry's abundant use of polished stainless steel reveals the screen itself as a kind of armour and, inevitably, armour as a kind of screen.[9]

Gehry's modifications incorporate a derealizing stealth architecture that images the depthlessness of the screen, a new fortification made not of steel and brick but light and information. The *maison radieuse* will not enmesh itself in the old markers of home but rather source new uncanny metaphors of efficient domesticity: smartness, hardness, rapid response—techniques of war in the service of a California feeling.

INTEL INSIDE

The Intel Company graphically images this transfer of energy from the urban to the non-urban in an advertisement promoting software compatibility which ran in a number of magazines in 1993. A luminous purple sky frames modeled city towers rising out of a printed circuit board. The 'streets', really circuits, glow brightly as they converge on the Intel Processing Chip in the centre of the page and move towards their destination: a large suburban dwelling. The copy underneath reads: 'Software compatibility hits home'. Unlike the Gehry house—which acknowledges a looped connection to the urban core through metaphors sourced in corporate design—Intel in this ad insists on the unidirectional flow of movement away from the centre. The house literally drains energy from the city, animating white flight as the path of the data stream. The motivation for this flight is evasively narrativized through preexisting tropes of *film noir's* dark take on the city. We approach Intel's city from an extreme angle that offers a high angle view of the towers. They represent a clean, if somewhat anonymous, Pacific rim Modernism, but encountered from a *noir* vantage point. The viewer is dramatically suspended at that moment when the diurnal city reverts to its criminal underside. This is a city whose danger is not boldly announced but rather recollected, evoked from older and more pleasurable models of urban paranoia and menace. And in the space conventionally reserved for the voice-over promising stories of the city, we have copy that announces both the threat posed by the dangerous city—its ability to 'hit home'—and the compatible solution to that threat. The city drained of capital, information, resources and light is transformed, superseded by the safe on-line home that promises that the New Electronic Order is the cosy telecommunicational equivalent of suburbia.

The earnest realism that informs the modelling of Intel City suggests at least at some formal level a link with another very different small-scale environment: Norman Bel Geddes' 'Futurama'. The most popular exhibit at the 1939 World's Fair, Futurama depicted the American landscape of 1960 as an assemblage of arterial superhighways, colossal skyscrapers, radio-controlled cars and massive suspension bridges.[10] Sponsored by General Motors, Futurama was relentlessly optimistic in its vision of an automotive future where cars serviced a centripetal urban core. Intel City references Futurama, but implodes its polarities, exhausts its vision and re-phrases its future through the retro-ambience of *noir* stylistics. The nostalgia and faint malignancy of the Intel Cityscape, coupled with the centrifugal flow of data, offers a means of visualizing both the terminal point of the urban and the development of a new zone. In Scott Bukatman's words: 'Cyberspace arises at precisely the moment when the topos of the traditional city has been superseded'.[11]

Following the lines of data out of town, one arrives at 'Silicon Simi Valley', where the bright green plastic of the motherboard uncannily doubles as the well kept lawn surrounding the house. This doubling is important as it structures the intelligibility of the image. On the one hand, the location of the iconic house amidst the macro-circuitry of the board works to diminish the radical novelty of cyberspace, making it appear coherent and familiar. This is a place that we are invited to recognize as home, an invitation that in many ways summarizes the entire project under consideration. By recognizing home as the datasphere, we turn our old 'habs' into nodal points of energy and connection either through visual metaphors of our new allegiance to the telematic screen or through seductive new urban histories such as Intel's, or as we shall see, Nintendo's. These transformational narratives are the finishing moves of what Baudrillard identifies as the satellization of the domestic, the projection of the terrestrial habitat into the absolute space of simulation. For Baudrillard, we cease to be actors and become instead terminals of multiple networks:

> Television is the most direct prefiguration of this, and yet today one's private living space is conceived of as a receiving and operating area, as a monitoring screen endowed with telematic power, that is to say, with the capacity to regulate everything by remote control.[12]

On the other hand, the modelled Intel house figures the domestic in the sense that this advertisement offers the consumer technology geared towards the needs of a diasporic middle class. I want to consider how these needs are imaged.

Lodged between the on-line house and the twilight city is the black box that *houses* the Intel chip. The black box—that uncannily indestructible recorder of destruction—mediates, protects, filters and fortifies the suburban home. It also makes reference to recent catastrophe, its bulk ejected from the city in much the same way that flight recorders are found on the perimeter of tangled fuselage. Of course, the Intel City still stands, so disaster must either be imminent or read back into the (re-built) structures. Either way, the box is a place of refuge for data of what has not been otherwise saved and, as such, suggests a mode of salvationist architecture. The Intel chip signals its political allegiance to the suburbs over the city by occupying the same dimensions and latitude as the house, effectively mimicking its floor plan. From this location, Intel's trademark 'insideness' resonates in other contexts. Here Intel will always be inside as long as, say, Rodney King is outside.

As a protective barrier that substitutes advanced telecommunications technology for the residual technology of manpower, a chip for a boom gate, the black box located between the city and the house strategically rehearses the LAPD's shift from cops on the beat to cops on the keyboard.[13] The security putatively afforded by the chip-box lies in its mass (as toppled menhir, as barricade) and function as conduit, as a technology that acknowledges home as the definitive monitor. This idea of monitoring is enriched in the play of light snaking towards the house, the movement from kinetic stripe to diffuse glow assembling the constituent parts of a contemporary obsession. Movement outside the home is delineated in the greenish phosphor glare of the night scope, inside by steady white light softened by the orange fixture on the portico. Outside is motion detection, inside its emotional counterpart, the warm zone of the Oprah-sphere.[14] When the metaphysical difference between outside and inside is registered in colour-coded light, we are offered access to the monitor's optics.[15]

The sheer size of the Intel house becomes a means of imaging the on-line suburb's political power against what Mike Davis describes as the enervated city, the suburbanization of economic growth and the sense of independence from the crisis of the urban core.[16] Further, the house vividly captures the transit route of capital earmarked for urban infrastructure investment. Far from benefiting the city, this money, Davis tells us, is primarily targeted towards optical fibre and interstate highway projects[17]—centrifugal projects imaged in those luminous lines heading out of town, heading home...

'YOU WILL'

If race and the new technologies that respond to its pressures haunt the Gehry and Intel houses, a more intense statement may be found in a vision of the future brought to you by AT&T. In April 1993, AT&T launched its first corporate image campaign in three years, a $50 million network TV and print media blitz themed 'You Will'.[18] The campaign looks twenty minutes into the future of telecommunications to 'tell consumers...how high-tech their lives are going to become'.[19] Set in a rather incoherent, if not contradictory, future—a kind of channel-surfed hybrid of *Blade Runner*, *Thirtysomething*, Life-style Programing and *The Fugitive*—the ads are suffused with the quiet calm of the New Electronic Order, as well as being very attentive to current anxieties about the city. Structured as a series of questions tagged with the prescriptive 'You Will', each ad features three scenarios that phase between defense-minded technophilia and the under-specified utopian potential of telecommunications.

Above all, these ads sell security. In one sequence set in a darkened hallway (like Intel City, many of these scenarios rely on a pervasive sense of *noir*-ish gloom to carry the bulk of their negative urbanism), a woman evades an invisible but palpable threat through the use of a biometric voice recognition device to enter her secure apartment. ('Have you ever unlocked a door with the sound of your own voice?')[20] At home, kids avoid the dangers of the multiplex by dialling up (evoking) Eisenhower era sci-fi from the security of the living room. ('Have you ever watched any movie you can put your finger on?') In another scene, a white couple are safely directed through the city by a computerized street directory accessed through a dashboard-mounted display quite immune to the efforts of Damian

Williams to re-direct motorists through the violent intersection of Florence and Normandie streets, flashpoint of the riots. ('Have you ever crossed the country without stopping for directions?') This last scene, like the one featuring a car racing through sleek gates ('Have you ever paid a toll without slowing down?'), images the new logistics of transport thematized as 'getaway', an automotive future based on an internal logic of escape velocity enabled by Haussmann-ized tollways and digital maps. These new smart gates mockingly note the prior existence of physical barriers, now wholly inappropriate blockages in an age of speed and urban ambush.

AT&T's future also resolves lingering anxieties about women in the workforce by adapting any space to the intimacy demanded of maternal care. ('Have you ever tucked your baby in from a phone booth?') In this sequence, set in some kind of transport terminal, technology enables the seizure of semi-public space for private ends as a businesswoman lulls her child to sleep via the videophone. But there are possible dangers here. Unlike the analog phone, with its umbilical mobility, the vid-phone invites, even demands, a fixed gaze, thus presenting a potentially vulnerable back to the crowd. Yet here in the ad, propitiously, the transport terminal is virtually de-populated, serving as nothing more than an elaborately ambient frame for this moment of electronic bonding. The implicit play on (video)terminal/(transport)terminal is calculated to reassure. One has altered the conditions of the other, removing the homeless, the phone-card spotters, the scam artists, the pickpockets, the prostitutes, the cleaners, even the fellow commuters.

What remains are the police. In this ad, they are, I would suggest, presented as a phantasmatic projection, their anachronistic leathers recalling the uniform of early motorcycle patrolmen—something of an info superhighway visual pun. These 'clean' cops, retrieved from newsreel memory, affirm that telecommunications has now assumed the police function of space management. If anything, contra Intel, the cops represent the ubiquity of security-conscious technology through the rather outmoded trope of the beat.

It should come as no surprise that the scenarios discussed above foreground white actors. As a future, these ads promise an era where race relations will be volitional rather than a haphazard function of urban aggregation, if for no other reason than that, in the extraordinarily de-populated, electronically augmented and accelerated city, white Americans will no longer have to contend with the contingencies of a racially mixed crowd (or any crowd whatsoever). This is not, however, to suggest that African Americans are completely excluded from access to this technology. In a scene set in the electronic classroom of the future, a black student asks the professor on the screen: 'But where does Jazz come from?' ('Have you ever learned special things from far away places?') We do not hear the answer, which, if uttered, might provoke unease about the political and cultural claims of Pan-Africanism. Yet at least this is a partly articulated gesture of inclusion consistent with the self-proclaimed mission of telecommunications to create communities of mutual understanding, as in NYNEX's jingle: 'We're all connected, New York Telephone...'

But around the same time that some of the 'You Will' spots were promoting their vision of racial harmony, another version of the electronic future according to AT&T appeared in a now infamous edition of their in-house publication. The image depicts the globe criss-crossed by telegraph wires that carry conversations of cartoon characters representing their particular continent. Africa is represented by an ape.[21] This graphic crudely, cruelly and intuitively captures some sense of AT&T's mandate: a power has been conferred on telecommunications to supervise the global dispensation of livable space. The 'You Will' campaign evidences this mandate when it consigns minorities to specific locales—hospitals, schools and libraries—in other words, to the familiar, State-funded public spaces of the city. Admittedly, in AT&T's version, these institutions are technologically enhanced; but they remain, nevertheless, the residual institutions of a degraded public system. If current American funding trends indicate anything about the future, these sites as they appear in the ads are already ghosts, nothing more than a liberal memory of what might have been.

By contrast, whites are offered commuter and leisure space, space that is private, space coolly reclaimed from the contemporary violations of car-jacking and tourist murder. This kind of spatial division is clearest in the scene featuring a white businessman on the island of St. Thomas, who telecommutes to a meeting from his beach house—a meeting he daringly attends, as the narrator wryly observes, 'in his bare feet'.[22] Overlooking the beach, the businessman paces thoughtfully, stitching up a global deal that lies waiting to be assembled on and through the screen of his laptop. In the immediate background, black children frolic on the shore. Race relations are re-inscribed along the model of tourism as here business becomes leisure, a leisure made possible by the tele-screen, whose social force visibly diminishes the problems of race. In this fantasy, a group of black youth—certainly the basic unit of urban terror from the vantage point of the white suburbs—is reduced to playful children. This signals a return to a disturbingly older perception of African Americans as joyfully childlike and requiring benign supervision from the veranda (an attitude parodied in Herman Melville's *Benito Cereno*). In the spatial segregation made possible by the screen, business no longer needs the fortressing of downtown L.A. but may now relax, kick off its shoes and go native.

So far, I have traced the light that animates the uncanny walls of post-uprising architecture, from its flickering in houses that made ambit claims about the range and effectiveness of the domestic within information-based economies to its deployment on the tele-screens of the utopic outpost. I now turn to another kind of telematic screen, one whose instrumentality finds its nearest equivalent in the new arts of war. Of course, screen spaces capable of force need to be distinguished from video games 'responsible' for social unrest. Work to generate both the instrumental screen and the effort needed to separate it from other, illicit screens was performed by the Gulf War.

MARIO IN BAGHDAD

> [ABC Correspondent Cokie] Roberts: You see a building in a sight, it looks more like a video game than anything else. Is there any sort of danger that we don't have any sense of the horrors of war—that it's all a game?
>
> [General Norman] Schwarzkopf: You didn't see me treating it like a game. And you didn't see me laughing and joking while it was

> going on. There are human lives being lost, and *at this stage of the game...*, this is not a time for frivolity on the part of anybody.[23] [my emphasis!]

The question of video games as a source of social disruption in L.A. must be approached circuitously via Baghdad. The Gulf War re-shaped the political terrain of the new technologies. After all, it was the first war in history to be named after a home entertainment system: 'Nintendo War'. It emerged as something of a cliché during the war to refer to gun-camera and smart bomb footage as evidence of the transformation of war into a video game, specifically a Nintendo game. This phrase was spectacularly mobile, appearing haltingly on the lips of aged Congressmen, skirting through hundreds of editorials and even, in one of its most clever applications, providing a focus for the London fashion scene.[24] 'Nintendo War' drew attention to what was perceived to be a new mode of combat, where technology scrambled the supply of images that traditionally funded both war support and opposition.

Samuel Weber has called the Gulf Conflict a 'tele-war', a war fought quite literally at a distance but also employing a televisual aesthetic where fighting is 'much more like "zapping" than hand-to-hand combat'.[25] The tele-war invites us to re-examine our understanding of other tele-deployments: the telephone, television, the telecommuter of the on-line home, the tele- of the media. Criticism of the war as a video game contributes to this discussion of the tele- but in the quite specific terms of an ethical dissatisfaction constructed along aesthetic lines. 'Nintendo War' as trope authorized nostalgic comparisons that sought to undo some of the reviled hygiene of the tele-war, to read some gore back into it. Alison Gordon wrote:

> ...the Gulf War is the Nintendo War. When buildings are just targets, when human beings are no more than blips in a rifleman's night-vision sight, when 'enemies' are like super graphics on a fighter pilot's heads-up display screen, it's hard to understand that they bleed real blood and cry real-tears [*sic*] like our own.[26]

The practice of 'Nintendo War' required re-reading through

earlier modes of combat in order to register that this was in fact war, even if not a war of the golden age. John Voorhees stated:

> The 'instant war' is a week old now, and the networks have returned to sitcoms and commercials, occasionally interrupted by special bulletins. To one who remembers World War II newsreels seen only in movie theaters, the kind of instant coverage and international hookups provided by CNN and the networks this past week is like something from Buck Rogers.
>
> Those WWII newsreels showed death, all right, and the narration was heavy with patriotic sentiments. But thus far the Gulf war has been treated like some giant Nintendo game being played by the Pentagon; I almost expect to see the Super Mario Brothers at a Pentagon briefing.[27]

What is lost is not only some sense of the real (news-reel) but the ability to underwrite a coherent national act of will. Here an American war is being hijacked by the stylistics of a Japanese video game company whose most successful export features the antics of two frenetic Italians. We witness resistance to the theatre of war (a residual representational metaphor) becoming the home theatre of war, a setting where 'buy American' is one of many competing demands on the consumer-citizen.

When those older, putatively 'pre-technological' images of flesh, blood and twisted metal finally resumed centre stage (principally through footage of the so-called 'highway of death') within the visual-moral economy of battle, the war was swiftly brought to a 'humane' close. However, as much as the phrase 'Nintendo War' signalled the dissatisfaction of those who questioned the realism of surgical bombing, it also offered an alternative means of understanding the conflict, a new mode of journalism where events are reported by cameras housed in the nose cone of smart bombs, by computer simulations and by those technologies that make up the home entertainment system. This was a mode of warfare that seemed to capture America's sense of Robocop invulnerability—where the act of watching TV connected us as viewers in some vital way to the technology of destruction. Weber describes what we see on our screens:

> ...what we are shown is a building, and more exactly, a concrete wall. It is the most aseptic kind of target: the ugly wall is suggestive more of a barrier, to our sight, for example, than of a shelter that might house people more or less like ourselves. But it is a very symptomatic barrier: we want to see more, and yet were we to see more, we might react very differently. The wall of the target that we see on our TV screens is itself a screen: it prevents us from seeing human bodies, faces, limbs and what happens to them when they are subjected to the same sort of military-televisual 'scrutiny' of which we have so far been partial witnesses.[28]

If Baghdad's terminal architecture screens out the more vivid details of our scrutiny, it also enables new forms of narrative satisfaction. We return here to the wall as screen, but in an uncannily penetrable form. The very pre-condition of its vulnerability lies in its inability to deal 'smartly' with the laser light that plays across its surface, a micro-allegory of the on-line Intel house connected optically to a massive information infrastructure but failing to log on, instead blown to black. Here it is software incompatibility that hits home. It is worth recalling in this context the favourite motif among nineteenth century writers of uncanny literature, as characterized by Anthony Vidler:

> [It] was precisely the contrast between a secure and homely interior and the fearful invasion of an alien presence; on a psychological level, its play was one of doubling, where the other is, strangely enough, experienced as a replica of the self, all the more fearsome because apparently the same.[29]

Fearsome and yet pleasurable, a manageable terror kept aesthetically at bay, the screening of the doomed screen is also an empowering spectacle, where to witness is to participate. Judith Butler remarks:

> ...the television screen and its viewer [are] the extended apparatus of the bomb itself...transported from the North American continent to Iraq, and yet securely wedged in the couch in one's own living room... [W]e retain our visual distance and our bodily safety through the disembodied enactment of the kill that

> produces no blood and in which we retain our radical impermeability... The television screen thus redoubles the aerial view, securing a fantasy of transcendence, of a disembodied instrument of destruction which is infinitely protected from a reverse-strike through the guarantee of electronic distance.[30]

Butler's account easily networks with descriptions of the screen space of the 'information highway', of the Intel house, of AT&T's safely scary future of precisely what is promised in the new online era: instrumentality, security, invulnerability. Here the Powell Doctrine of 'overwhelming force' returns as lifestyle, effecting the militarization of domestic ease and leisure. In other words, far from being a criticism of the conflict, the 'Nintendo War' that empowered the armchair observer light years beyond their prior incarnation as moral spectators was actually read as one of its clearer justifications.

The Gulf War was in many respects a video game. But why Nintendo? Why not the Atari conflict or the Sega police action? Or, what would have been infinitely more honest, the Falcon 3.0 war. This high-res combat sim is produced by Spectrum Holobyte, the company responsible for flight simulator programs used by the U.S. military to train Gulf War pilots. An ad for Falcon appeared in a 1991 issue of *Video Games and Computer Entertainment* with the banner: 'The only simulation better than this one is still classified'.[31] Falcon 3.0 and games like it deliberately locate themselves on a continuum with hard-core defense technology, stamping a fun face on the military-aesthetic complex.[32] The public shared with the military at different intensities the ability to stage secure 'living-room' enactments of battle in the form of both computer-mediated entertainments and bomb footage that seemed to be governed by the same aesthetic of bit-mapped explosions and the simplified terrain of gamespace.[33]

Whether these enactments took place in the home, the Pentagon Briefing Room, at a Defense Advanced Research Projects Agency (DARPA) installation or on a pilot's heads-up display on a run into Baghdad, they relied on a common and increasingly familiar sequence of tasks: (1) locate the target within cross hairs; (2) use a remote pointer device to mark out a space on the screen; and (3) destroy the target in a flash of light. If Vietnam was visualized in terms of the spectacularly vulnerable embodiment of ground troops, the Gulf wasn't visualized at all.[34] We rarely witnessed imperiled American troops, having focused instead on the story told by smart bombs. The media emphasis on the screen shifted attention away from the body of the pilot/player, who re-emerged as an unseen (*stealthy*) controlling presence, an invisible consumer surrogate wielding technology as a putatively invulnerable prosthesis.

While these might be compelling reasons to view the Gulf War as a video game or at least as connected aesthetically, politically and socially to the video medium, there is still the question of the Nintendo tag. Did Nintendo's war-naming rights issue from their market dominance? The company's astonishing success in this regard is the product of a marketing strategy that targeted and successfully colonized the adult end of the vid game market. According to McKenzie Wark, Nintendo's appeal to the adult consumer is based on a strategic representation of video games as the logical extension of existing media (and I would add, military) forms. The appeal to familiar technologies effectively defuses resistance to potentially destabilizing novelty.[35] By contrast, Sega celebrates its break away status in the MTV-authorized terms of indie youth culture—precisely the culture, when localized in the arcades, that Nintendo evaded and subsequently reanimated (both literally and figuratively) in their first domestic terminals. With the release of *Donkey Kong* in 1980, Nintendo relocated video games to the home, a cross-over that translated the excitement of youth culture spaces into safer terms or at least safer terminals. This translation is mapped into the transit of white light flooding the Intel house. What Nintendo delivered to the homes of middle-America was an, albeit crude, working model of interactive media, one that effected—at the level of marketing rationale—a retreat from a notional public space.

It is this sense of Nintendo as a mode of private, domestic, interactive technology that is sutured to the global media event in the expression 'Nintendo War' to produce a glimpse of the fully functioning console of the future. In its most suspicious usage, the phrase 'Nintendo War' inaugurates the arrival of the domestic console with the force of armies, a screen that lets the player move out into the media event, interactively, interpretively and fearlessly. From this perspective, the nostalgia-oriented criticism of the representation of the war as a simulation of 'real' violence that I quoted above can be seen as rather convoluted advance press for a machine that promises stress management through the introduction of electronic instrumentality. It is important to distinguish those ambivalent critiques of war as simulation from the notion of incitement, which, as I will discuss in a moment, is reserved for a very different game-playing constituency.

The Nintendo console that emerges from the Gulf War is buttressed by a great deal of political force focused on the issue of interactivity. Obviously, I have the Clinton-Gore vision of a 'wired' America in mind, particularly as it fixates on citizens casting votes in the Electronic Town Hall, a machine that vigorously re-tools current conceptions of interactivity (i.e. the consumer choice of home shopping or leisurely pixel-pushing as democracy itself).

Similarly, we might consider the work of UCLA Professor of Psychology Patricia Marks Greenfield, who suggests that electronic gaming will produce a new breed of professionals. Her studies indicate that video game playing improves a player's spatial skills necessary for such professions as architecture and engineering.[36] In other words, Nintendo provides fast-track training for the builders and designers of future Intel houses, on-line gated communities, edge cities and corporate parks. Even as the Nintendo game effectively bridges the gulf between the Gulf War and the domestic American citizen/viewer, Nintendo operatives form the front line in the domestic 'Gulf War' between American whites and blacks, suburbans and urbans, the info rich and info poor. The retreat to the safe place in the suburbs is already part of this war, so too any activity that draws citizens towards the uncanny internal wall/ screen that opens the domestic out, even as it at the same time brings the global in.[37] The safe place is no longer simply, exclusively domestic because it is globally connected through the shared objectives of military simulation. In other words, interactive home leisure technology assumes strikingly global force.

Among those who have recognized this shift is former LAPD

Chief of Police Daryl Gates, who, although stripped of the right to secure the streets of Los Angeles, now does his work through the screen. Shortly after his resignation, Gates was hired by the Sierra On-Line Software Company to design games. His first, which goes by the absolutely chilling title of *Police Quest Open Season*, is, in his words, about giving 'computer users the opportunity to see what it's like to be a cop in L.A.'.[38] This computer-enabled merger of citizens and cops is consistent with the kind of fusions of TV viewers and bombs experienced during the Gulf War. In language that seems to trip over itself in a desire to incriminate, Sierra's press release announced that 'The game will draw heavily on Gates' 43 years in the LAPD with by-the-book procedures, real world pressures, photo-realistic backgrounds, and *video-captured actors*'[39] [my italics]. Fending off inevitable criticism, Sierra officials declared that in the game 'No one gets beaten up and there aren't any riots'.[40] Like the bomb screen that goes blank at the moment of detonation, Gates' game refuses to let us see certain aspects of police work.

The domestic Nintendo console is thus a social project, a means of thinking about the home as a zone of overwhelming force, a site that interactively polices, monitors and purchases but is magically exempt from the reverse strike. This also describes allied forces in the Gulf, who relied on 'over the horizon' technology to dominate the Iraqi forces. In this war, the opposing sides rarely occupied the same spatial (and to an extent, temporal) coordinates—a remote control war fought in the (and over) living room.

TV BREEDS INCITEMENT

I began this essay with the suggestion that the move into the electronic sphere was complicated by the presence of publicly accessible technology (like free to air TV, camcorder surveillance and arcade based gaming) and that many of the political initiatives following the L.A. riots could be described as attempts to demonize and racialize this (non-Nintendo) tech through the premise of inciting to riot. This can be seen clearly in the attack on television itself as a dangerously irresponsible medium. In the months following the broadcast of the King beating—arguably one of the most harrowing pieces of video ever seen in the United States—government (Senate Commerce Committee Hearings of 1993) and citizen-organized lobby groups joined forces to tell the networks that they had to stop violence on TV. *The New York Times* reported U.S. Attorney General Janet Reno's warning that 'unless [the television industry] moved immediately to stem the tide of shootings, stabbings and other mayhem beamed daily into the nation's homes, the White House and Congress would seek laws to do it for them'.[41]

In the absence of effective social programs, a kinder, gentler television was proposed. These acutely myopic critiques nervously identified a kind of twisted version of instrumental interactivity, where violence seen on the screen produced violence on the streets. If the collectively fantasized Nintendo console was to enable interactivity with minimal information feedback, television, according to its critics, created self-sustaining loops of information and action. For example, Richard Schickel commented:

> ...TV needed to offer perspective. Anchors everywhere plied field reporters with Big Picture questions. But that wasn't their job. Their job was to create a mythical city, a sort of Beirut West, views of which would keep many viewers frozen in fear to their Barcaloungers. *And, incidentally, send a few of them out to join in the vicious fun.*[42] [my italics]

In *Heteropolis*, Charles Jencks ventures a preliminary psychopathology of the interactive riot watcher as criminalized home shopper:

> [The riot was partly] motivated by greed and opportunism, and the psychic distance provided by a TV spectacle where others could be seen looting from burning shops as if they belonged to no one. 'Why not me too?' was the underlying assumption of the 'image looters'.[43]

For Jencks, the 'image looters' looted because of the image, because of coverage that derealized the mom and pop narratives of small business owners. For him, TV is culpable to the degree that it turns disaster into spectacle, human tragedy into a coldly observed simulation. Here, Jencks' language is rhetorically similar to that used by the critics of the 'Nintendo War', with an important demographic difference: in the case of the Persian Gulf, simulation presented a moral quandary for liberal Americans; in L.A., it gets Blacks and Latinos out on the street.

'FIGHT!'

In *The Practice of Everyday Life*, Michel de Certeau describes the street as the zone of lived space where ground level tactics resist the regulatory control implicit in aerial perspectives.[44] The Nintendo console dreamed by AT&T, Intel and the Gulf War attempts to reconfigure the car, the home, the beach, even the couch, from empowered aerial vantage points. Against this, *Street Fighter* was positioned as its name suggests, as a resistant, if not outlaw, street level tech. The street level has no official effectivity—this is one of the reasons why George Holliday's video of the King beating lacked juridical force. But it can unsettle. Most of the criticism (itself the means of effecting the division between good and bad technology) levelled at the game, and others like it (*Mortal Kombat*, for example), has been about its potential to incite violent behaviour rather than direct it strategically, as the Nintendo console is imagined to do.[45]

I am moving here from the animation of light on smart walls to specific gestures that enliven other screens: the *anime* of arcade-based vid games. When violent video games like *Street Fighter* are criticized, they appear as unsettling versions of the Nintendo console described above. Unlike its military-domestic other, *Street Fighter*'s violence is not subsumed in the trappings of decent dwelling.

To start the game, the player must select an identity from among an array of characters, including Guile, a Black American Marine; Ken, a White American martial arts student; Chun Li, a female Chinese Kung Fu specialist; E Honda, a sumo wrestler; Blanka, a 'mutant man beast from Brazil'; Dhalsim from India, whose fighting repertoire includes the 'Super Yoga Flame'; and Zangief, a Russian wrestler. These combatants meet on the streets of New York, Bangkok, Moscow and New Delhi, among other places, where they engage in hand-to-hand combat augmented by the occasional supernatural move—a feature that aligns *Street Fighter* with *wu xia pian,* the Chinese martial arts hero film of the 1920s. The game's fights are graphically arresting, with characters exhibiting distinct attack moves punctuated by digital sound effects on a screen that is unapologetically filled with violence, with bruised flesh and its victorious counterpart.

This violent screen of the publicly accessible arcade game is in critical dialogue with other more empowered screenspaces. The space management implied in AT&T's telescreen is brought to the surface in *Street Fighter,* explicitly thematizing the screen itself as a line of defense. AT&T's tasteful relocations of people of colour to an imaginary public sphere are subject to the return of the repressed in the *Street Fighter* scenario, where *all* turf is routinely contested. *Street Fighter* uncannily reads conflict back into the relative calm of electronic globalism.

This is all too close to the surface. Violence made to appear on the arcade screen is an intolerably honest reading of the Nintendo console. The arcade player is engaged in an unacceptable interface. In the face of this uncomfortable similarity, the notion of an incitable public stabilizes, shifting attention away from the emergent technology towards a pathologized reception: bad images incite, good images are implemented. 'Incitement' acts as an embargo, a refusal to allow public access to the pleasures of simulation at a moment when access to the kinetic screen assumes the status of an act of power itself.

Intriguingly, what disturbs about the game is not its violence *per se* but the epistemic violence it levels against the spatial and somatic logic of race, specifically in the visual field of race. Judith Butler has written that the visual is fully schematized by racism. How else, she asks, can we account for the line of inference drawn between the black, motionless, beaten body of Rodney King and the jury's conclusion that this body was in total control. King was 'hit in exchange for the blows he never delivered, but which he is, by virtue of his blackness, always about to deliver'.[46] Within the visual field of race, the black body is circumscribed as dangerous prior to any gesture.

Introducing a new twist, *Street Fighter* universalizes and

democratizes the racist phantasm of black bodies. It assumes that all races and species are capable of violence. In the game, all races, all genders, all bodies are presumed dangerous, oppositional and violent. Unlike the first person vantage point of the flight sim, the game not only obsesses over embodiment but openly fantasizes about the fluid inhabitation by the player at any one moment of a number of bodies, an incoherent disruption of the player/agent relationship.

It is the game's commitment to widely divergent body types as fighting identities that mounts a powerful challenge to the notion of the 'somatotype', a theory of criminality advanced by James Q. Wilson and Richard Herrnstein in their 1985 book *Crime and Human Nature*. Wilson and Herrnstein suggest that people of colour are more likely to be violent than the white majority and that there are anatomical correlates of crime.[47] They propose somatotyping as a means of measuring propensity to criminal behaviour. The types correspond to distinct body shapes, which they term mesomorphs, ectomorphs and andromorphs. In a sentence summarizing their explanation of crime, Wilson and Herrnstein write:

> An impulsive person can be taught greater self-control, a low-IQ individual can engage in satisfying learning experiences, and extroverted mesomorphs with slow autonomic nervous system response rates may earn honest money in the National Football League instead of dishonest money robbing banks.[48]

In this mendaciously scientific racism, the criminal is never required nor requested to speak on his or her own behalf, when their body speaks the truth of their character. It is this kind of racist typology that *Street Fighter* utterly subverts. While Wilson and Herrnstein characterize the dangerous criminal as hyperactive black men, *Street Fighter* confers hyperactivity on *everyone*, from, in one version of the game, a U.S. Air Force pilot (the ground zero subject of the Nintendo console) to a Sumo wrestler. Racist typologies are installed in bodies that completely repudiate the original designation, where men, women, ectomorphs, mesomorphs and Blanka, the mutant man beast, are simultaneously dangerous and vulnerable, where the screen records their violence before it goes blank. This violence incites urban terror, whereas the violence of the armchair strategist viewing smart bomb coverage of a video game as war, and vice versa, signals a new era in global and personal security.

The Gulf War and the Los Angeles riots mapped out the terrain of good and bad technology, an industry-based distinction made (again) in the cultural crisis of the post-uprising period—a distinction made to promote the role of good tech as a service provider of livable space. Of course, these technologies, imaged as rival screens, exist on a continuum, which makes the distinction particularly fragile. This can be seen in the lively cross-over between arcade and home-based games or in the cessation of the 'clean war' once the aesthetics of hard-core gaming took hold on the highway to Basra.

CONTINUE GAME?

I would like to close with one more corporate vision of the future, one that I think responds to *Street Fighter's* uncomfortable dialogue with the Nintendo screen and proposes an alternative model of interactivity.

In 1994, AT&T aired a television commercial for 'Truevoice', a fibre-optic phone connection service that promises exceptional clarity. In this ad, the human voice can overcome the attenuating effects of distance—geographical, anatomical or emotional. We see a white middle class woman receiving an ultrasound. She chats with the sonographer; but amidst her excitement, one detects anxiety: her husband has missed the ultrasound appointment. The phone rings, the technician smiles, the husband is on the phone. They talk, the wife's face registers relief. He asks, 'How's the little kicker?' The woman replies, 'Why don't you ask him?' She places the receiver against her swollen abdomen. He speaks: 'How's my big boy? Do you want to come out and play?' Cut to the woman's face, a look of surprise. Cut to the ultrasound screen: the foetus kicks.

Like many arcade and home-based games, the ad isolates the (kung fu) kick as the moment of intense pleasure but splits the perceptual apparatus between the screen and the body of the pregnant woman. We could read this as a rather feeble grab towards a phenomenology of immersive technology; but given the location of our foetal fighting-identity, other considerations must be brought into play. The womb is, after all, the agora of American politics, an inside/outside public sphere inhabited by (according to anti-abortion activists) 'virtual citizens'. This is a risky place to pitch a clear phone line, even one that promises intra-uterine telecommunications. Something else happens here. The moment of interactivity is radically re-defined. Where once the body of the player produced movement in the body of the screen-agent, either as street fighter or smart bomb, AT&T proposes instead the instrumental voice phrased not as command but as invitation. Specifically: 'How's my big boy? Do you want to come out and play?' It is this invitation that prompts the moment of kinetic pleasure. This softening, even liberalization, of interactivity (from command to invitation) attempts to stabilize the field, to establish a critical, irreducible difference from other modes of technology, to banish the continuum that links incitement technologies to instrumental ones. It is difference that is on sale here—cultural, racial and technological. In this ad, the enchanted white realm of the nuclear family—a ludicrous throwback even by the conservative standards of American advertising—draws the lineaments of the new product.

I have argued in this essay that one of the responses to the L.A. riots was to imagine a pathological technology (*Street Fighter*, free-to-air TV, etc.) in the hands of a pathological constituency. But I have proposed that the nominated technology replies with a rather emphatic no-vote on both counts. In response, enter AT&T 'Truevoice', which I would suggest offers to *geneticize* technological instrumentality, providing a way of finally dividing technology along sociobiological lines, not as pathology but as heredity. This is not so much the nuclear family as its nucleotide counterpart. We can see this when the mother-to-be twists the phone line that is both umbilicus and DNA double helix linked at one end to a virtual citizen and at the other to speculative investment in bio-tech start-up companies, industries that will soon be inviting us to 'come out and play' with new, very private modes of the human. The domestic Gulf War need no longer be fought with recourse to paranoid walls or interactive consoles. AT&T imagines instead a different solution, one that returns the company to a mastery over the pure telegraphic, this time not that of Morse but that of the manipulated code of life itself. Here the ability to implement instrumental technology is hard-wired into the white family: the 'Truevoice' of technology. The continuum that binds good to bad, anti-viral to viral technology is overcome by a return to an older notion of genetic difference imaged in the ultrasound of the foetus, an historically vulnerable satellite citizen who has learned, through technology, to kick ass. In a sense, 'Truevoice' provides us with a foundational myth in which we witness the subject who is always already on-line.

NOTES

I would like to thank Eva-Lynn Jagoe, Isabel Karpin, Tom Keenan, David Thomson and Andrew Ross for taking the time to discuss this as a work in progress. I am especially grateful to Alan Cholodenko for his patient and rigourous editorial assistance and his intellectual support.

1 'Race Fights on Video', *The Independent* (London), July 20, 1992, p. 12.

2 See, for example, Mike Davis, *City of Quartz: Excavating the Future in Los Angeles* (New York: Verso, 1990); Edward W. Soja, *Postmodern Geographies: The Reassertion of Space in Critical Social Theory* (New York: Verso, 1989); *Variations on a Theme Park: The New American City and the End of Public Space*, ed. Michael Sorkin (New York: Noonday Press, 1992).

3 Anthony Vidler, *The Architectural Uncanny: Essays in the Modern Unhomely* (Cambridge: The MIT Press, 1992), pp. 3-4.

4 For Davis' account of Gehry's architecture, see his essay 'Fortress Los Angeles: The Militarization of Urban Space', in *Variations on a Theme Park: The New American City and the End of Public Space*, ed. Michael Sorkin, pp. 167-169.

5 See Charles Jencks, *Heteropolis: Los Angeles, the Riots and the Strange Beauty of Hetero-Architecture* (London: Academy Editions, 1993), p. 66.

6 ibid., p. 67.

7 'Ramparts and battlements, reflective glass and elevated pedways, are tropes in an architectural language warning off the underclass Other. Although architectural critics are usually blind to this militarized syntax, urban pariah groups—whether young black men, poor Latino immigrants, or elderly homeless white females—read the signs

immediately'. Davis, 'Fortress Los Angeles', p. 159.

8 'The new monument is no longer the substantial spatiality of the building, but the depthless surface of the screen'. Scott Bukatman, *Terminal Identity: The Virtual Subject in Postmodern Science Fiction* (Durham: Duke University Press, 1993), p. 132.

9 Two of Gehry's recent public works make lavish use of reflective metal: the Weisman Museum in Michigan and the newly completed Guggenheim in Bilbao, Spain. The latter considerably ups the 'hardness' ante by replacing steel with polished titanium.

10 See Stephen Heller, 'Yesterday's World of Tomorrow', *Print*, vol. 48, no. 3, May/June 1989.

11 Bukatman, *Terminal Identity*, p. 122.

12 Jean Baudrillard, *The Ecstasy of Communication*, ed. Sylvère Lotringer and trans. Bernard and Caroline Schutze (New York: Semiotext(e), 1988), pp. 16-17.

13 The Los Angeles Police Department uses the Emergency Command Control Communications System (ECCCS), a digitalized communications system accessed via a keyboard mounted in the patrol car.

14 Intel's commitment to the political language of luminescence is seen in a recent ad that features a Pentium chip gliding through a mainframe, activating glowing functions in its wake. This looks back to a much earlier model of alleviating urban anxiety—street illumination.

15 Consider Sydney's Darling Harbour as an object lesson in the new optics, in particular, IMAX. This site of simulated vision perversely occupies coordinates that once commanded attention as scenic and strategic vantage points.

16 Davis, 'Who Killed LA? A Political Autopsy', *New Left Review*, 197, January/February 1993, p. 17.

17 ibid., p. 21.

18 Kate Fitzgerald, 'AT&T Dwells on the Future in New Ads', *Advertising Age*, April 26, 1993, p. 39.

19 ibid.

20 A related question—'Have you ever locked a door with the color of your skin?'—is discussed by Patricia J. Williams in her *The Alchemy of Race and Rights* (Cambridge: Harvard University Press, 1991), pp. 44-51.

21 The graphic was reprinted in *Time*, September 27, 1993, p. 15.

22 Los Angeles has more home offices than other cities, creating a subsequent loss in metropolitan office space. Where New York has twenty-eight square feet of office space per person, L.A.'s on-line home

workers have reduced the figure to fifteen. Jencks, *Heteropolis*, p. 66.

23 Quoted by James Van Derian in 'Lenin's War, Baudrillard's Games', in *Culture on the Brink: Ideologies of Technology*, eds. Gretchen Bender and Timothy Druckrey (Seattle: Bay Press, 1994), p. 272.

24 For Angel Biotek and Aki Sony, 'The Gulf War and Nintendo were the two most significant events of 1991'; and their 'Toyforce' range of '92 responded to both. Combining teddy bears, hand grenades and knitted camouflage-pattern jumpers, they explored their interest in '...corporate advertising, information technology, the Now world'. Quoted in Ekow Eshun, 'May Toyforce be with you', *The Guardian*, February 17, 1992, p. 35.

25 Samuel Weber, '*Deus ex Media*: Interview by Cassi Plate of the ABC', in Samuel Weber, *Mass Mediauras: Form, Technics, Media*, ed. Alan Cholodenko (Sydney/Stanford: Power Publications/Stanford University Press, 1996), p. 167.

26 Alison Gordon, 'Despite the Analogies Sports and War Are Not At All Alike', STAR*week* Magazine, *Toronto Star*, February 9, 1991, p. 66.

27 John Voorhees, 'Pentagon's Handling of News from the Gulf May Backfire', *The Seattle Times*, January 24, 1991, p. H1.

28 Weber, 'The Media and the War', *Alphabet City*, Summer 1991, p. 24.

29 Vidler, *The Architectural Uncanny*, p. 3.

30 Judith Butler, 'Contingent Foundations: Feminism and the Question of "Postmodernism"', in *Feminists Theorize the Political*, eds. Judith Butler and Joan W. Scott (New York: Routledge, 1992), p. 11.

31 Banner quoted by Deborah Heath in 'Computers and Their Bodies: Sex, War and Cyberspace', *The Electronic Salon: Feminism meets Info-Tech* (Electronically archived at Lewis & Clark College, Portland, Oregon), 1992, p. 21.

32 In the words of sim designer Sid Meier: 'Simulations present a filtered version of reality, and we only deal with the neat stuff'. Quoted in ibid., p. 19.

33 As Paul Patton has noted, within months of the end of the conflict, historians and simulators had constructed fly-through interactive, network capable sims of key tank battles. Armchair strategists can now fly through the battlefield in the so-called Simnet Flying Carpet, a stealthy virtual observer outpost. Paul Patton, Introduction to Jean Baudrillard's *The Gulf War Did Not Take Place*, trans. Paul Patton (Sydney: Power Publications, 1995), pp. 4-5. Unsurprisingly, Disney introduced a similar virtual flying carpet to allow aerial access to the pleasures of an Arabian market place in 'Aladdin's Magic Carpet Ride'. The now

defunct attraction was designed for Disney by Silicon Graphics, who also provided the supercomputer grunt used in military surveillance and simulation. Information provided via a telephone conversation with Fred Dupre, Library Assistant, Walt Disney World Library and Research Center, September 1, 1997.

34 Samuel Weber makes the point that this was a tactical decision on the part of the military, a lesson learned from media coverage of the Vietnam conflict. Weber, *'Deus ex Media'*, p. 163.

35 McKenzie Wark, 'The Video Game as an Emergent Media Form', *Media Information Australia*, no. 71, February 1994, p. 26.

36 See Laura Evenson, 'The Video Game Culture: How It's Changing Kids' Perception of the World', *San Francisco Chronicle*, May 25, 1993, p. B5.

37 See Alan Cholodenko's discussion of the film theatre as of the order of Derrida's double invagination, at once turning inside out and outside in, perturbing thereby the very distinction of inside and outside. Cholodenko, '*Who Framed Roger Rabbit*, or the Framing of Animation', in *THE ILLUSION OF LIFE: Essays on Animation*, ed. Alan Cholodenko (Sydney: Power Publications in association with the Australian Film Commission, 1991), pp. 228-235.

38 Gates quoted in 'Former LAPD Chief Gates to Design Video Game', *Newsbytes News Network*, February 2, 1993.

39 Sierra press release quoted in ibid.

40 Todd Copilevitz, 'Cop Culture: From TV to a New Video Game, the Intrigue of Police Work is Right at Your Fingertips', *The Dallas Morning News*, October 19, 1993, p. C2.

41 Reno quoted in Michael Wines, 'Reno Chastises TV Networks on Violence in Programming', *The New York Times*, October 21, 1993.

42 Richard Schickel, 'How TV Failed to Get the Real Picture', *Time*, May 11, 1992, p. 29.

43 Jencks, *Heteropolis*, p. 84. 'Image looters' is a South Central expression for reporters. Clearly, Jencks has another meaning in mind.

44 Michel de Certeau, *The Practice of Everyday Life*, trans. Steven Rendall (Berkeley: University of California Press, 1984), p. 93.

45 Parker V. Page, President of the Children's Television Resource and Education Center, and Professor Marsha Kinder are among the more outspoken critics of video game violence.

46 Butler, 'Endangered/Endangering: Schematic Racism and White Paranoia', in *Reading Rodney King, Reading Urban Uprising*, ed. Robert Gooding-Williams (New York: Routledge, 1993), p. 19.

47 I draw my account of Wilson and Herrnstein's work from Thomas L. Dumm's 'The New Enclosures: Racism in the Normalized Community', in *Reading Rodney King, Reading Urban Uprising*.

48 Wilson and Herrnstein quoted in ibid., p. 183.

Logistical Space: Flight Simulation and Virtual Reality

PATRICK CROGAN

> For once you are really flying it is the world that tilts, not the plane; it's the horizon that tips up when you turn, and settles back when you roll out, sinks when you climb, and rises when you dive. The plane remains a steady thing, a part of yourself, and you are not flying the plane—you are flying the world.[1]
>
> Samuel Hynes

> The world flown over is a world produced by speed.[2]
>
> Paul Virilio

I

The military development of flight simulation is routinely cited in histories and critical studies of digital imaging, Virtual Reality and cyberspace as a major influence in their emergence. For example, in his essay 'From Abstraction to Simulation: Notes on the History of Computer Imaging', Andy Darley states that the flight simulator is the 'progenitor and paradigm for work in the area of what is dubbed (oxymoronically) "artificial realities"'.[3] The production of these 'artificial realities' via the use of computer imaging technology and software is, argues Darley, pervasive today. This is not only because of the development of new computer-based forms of representation such as video games and Virtual Reality systems but also because computer imaging techniques have been incorporated into the standard recording and image-production equipment of the 'traditional technologies' of film, television and video (including, I would add, the 'traditional' forms of drawn and object animation). These traditional modes of generating 'artificial realities'—all of which I would propose could be described as modes of animating an 'artificial real'—have been taken over, says Darley, and their capacities have been enhanced or transformed in the process.[4]

If, for Darley, the flight simulator is the 'progenitor' of work in 'artificial realities', then I would say that it is the founder of a new generation of technology for their animation, a generation succeeding those of cinematographic and videographic animation. Used in this sense, the term 'animation' not only characterizes the entire process but also exceeds the bounds of the conventional opposition between live action and animation; and this is indeed appropriate because this opposition is becoming increasingly difficult to sustain under the impact of this new generation, whose various instantiations—including Virtual Reality and digital special effects cinema—blur easy distinctions between the 'live' and the 'animated' and the 'real' and the 'artificial'.[5]

Given the importance he assigns to it, it is curious that Darley mentions flight simulation but twice more in his text and only in passing. In a similar fashion, another historian of Virtual Reality, Myron W. Krueger, in his book *Artificial Reality II*, acknowledges the crucial relationship between 'the extensive history of flight simulation and heads-up displays' and Virtual Reality research and development and then goes on to say that he will not be dealing with that relationship in his history of Virtual Reality, offering no explanation for his decision other than that his discussion 'does not purport to be exhaustive or definitive'.[6]

Unlike such histories and critical studies, material has been published in techno-scientific journals that addresses quite explicitly the links between developments in flight simulation, computer graphics and related areas involving Virtual Reality. James L. Davis' contribution to a special section on flight simulation in the August 1993 issue of *Aerospace America*, 'Visual Systems: Generating a New

Reality', points out that the Image Generator component designed initially for flight simulation is the 'heart of any [computer-based] visual system' (such as Computer Aided Design software, spatial statistics simulation, scientific and medical image simulation, computer games, etc.).[7] Davis goes on to say that the generally accepted definition of Virtual Reality is basically a scaled-back version of '[t]oday's $12-million flight simulator [which] immerses the flight crew in an exact replica of a cockpit environment that looks, moves, and feels like the real thing'.[8] He concludes with an optimistic note about how the outlook is bright for bridging the gap between the expensive military/commercial airline simulator and the Virtual Reality entertainment industry, thanks to the possibilities offered by interactive multiple-user networks for spreading the costs of the technology.

Davis' optimism about the dissemination of leading-edge simulation technologies in the future is mirrored in the other articles making up this special section on flight simulation. For instance, Carl Lapiska, Larry Ross and Don Smart conclude their overview on flight simulation as follows: 'The products and pace of technology development will continue to amaze us. Only one thing is certain: [t]he potential is limited only by the boundaries of the imagination'.[9] And Brian F. Goldiez tells us that 'Education, medicine, and entertainment are other areas envisioned for DIS [Distributed Interactive Simulation] applications. Clearly, DIS will be a significant factor in the expanding use of simulation technology'.[10] DIS is a major initiative in the linking of flight simulators and will be examined later in this essay.

This optimism precludes any critical consideration on the part of Lapiska, Ross, Smart and Goldiez of the significance of the diffusion of this military-developed vision to so many aspects of human social-economic activity. The unsaid but pervasive implication is that such a diffusion has great possible benefits for humankind, including in 'spin-off' applications, and is in any event inevitable.

This preclusion of criticism by the explicitly instrumental approach is, in a curious way, symmetrical to the absence of focused critical attention on flight simulation's military origins and characteristics in the less instrumentalist, potentially more critical investigations of current technological developments, such as those of Darley and Krueger. The symmetry resides in the way both types of discourse fail to engage with what I would call the military/non-military relation, a relation that I argue lies at the heart of the phenomenon that these discourses take as their object. Even while addressing the crucial role of military and N.A.S.A. research in advancing computer image generation technology, the instrumentalist discourses of journals such as *Aerospace America* and *IEEE Computer Graphics and Applications* do not engage in explicit examination of the most crucial aspect of this relation, that is, its ethical and critical significance.[11] As Darley astutely recognizes, computer technology has flourished in a context which '...promotes—as perhaps its most fundamental tenet—a still dominant ethos of optimistic technophilia'.[12] However, I would suggest that, while he is concerned not to perpetuate such an ethos, his own text is critically impaired through its failure to examine flight simulation's paradigmatic relation to 'artificial realities' in particular, its influence on computer imaging in general, and crucially, their military origins.

My essay, then, will endeavour to remedy this critical neglect, examining flight simulation in terms of the military/non-military relation. As I have already indicated, the current technological developments in Virtual Reality and cyberspace are developments of what is a new generation of modes of animation which cannot but affect all the earlier forms of bringing 'artificial realities' to life. This new generation of 'artificial realities', based on computer-driven digital imaging, is itself animated by this military/non-military relation. Flight simulation is an exemplary instance of this new generation—I use the word advisedly as akin to animation—a global form of animation brought to life and put into motion by military research, objectives and modes of thought. And, like all modes of animation/generation, flight simulation has grown beyond the framework in which it was created and taken on 'a life of its own', not only in more recent commercial applications but in its influence on, and interaction with, the other forms of digital animation mentioned. As a result, flight simulation sits squarely across the military/non-military relation and the range of new 'visual systems'. My consideration of flight simulation, therefore, will enable me to understand the importance of the nexus between the military and the non-military spheres for the development of this new generation of animated 'artificial realities'.

My examination of flight simulation will be undertaken in the light of the work of Paul Virilio, French urbanist and foremost theorist of the military/non-military relation as it has influenced the development of technology, war, history, politics and culture. My consideration of Virilio's writings will enable me to formulate an answer to the question of the significance of the military source of flight simulation. This answer will be found in what I propose to call, after Virilio's notion of logistics, the *logistical space* of flight simulation, a notion I will discuss in detail below. We will see that this answer leads to a more profound problem concerning the task of understanding the nature of the relation. This problem has to do with the difficulty of distinguishing what is military from what is non-military in the phenomenon of flight simulation and, by implication, in the new generation of digital animation more generally.

Virilio's work postulates the existence in the post-World War II period of a powerful tendency toward the complete disappearance of the distinction between the military and the civilian spheres of economics, politics and culture. His term, for which he is perhaps best known—'pure war'—names this tendency. It is most evident, according to Virilio, in the 'fatal coupling' of the Soviet Union and the United States of America in the decades up to the end of the '80s and the resultant Cold War arms race. In this era of nuclear deterrence and the unprecedented escalation in weapons systems development and production, warfare overflowed its conventional spatio-temporal and epistemological framings and came to inhabit the political, economic and civilian spheres of the preparation for war. 'Pure war' is this overflowing of war into a 'pure' state of the permanent preparation for total war. The transformations set in train by this tendency toward pure war have been left largely unquestioned in most critical/theoretical accounts of culture in the post-war period.

That is why I described my characterization of the military/non-military relation as 'preliminary'. It is not so much that relation as its tendency to disappearance that I want to consider here in my examination of flight simulation.

Virilio's concern with finding the tendency latent in current phenomena is a crucial aspect of his attempt to delineate the new and the unforeseeable dimensions of these phenomena.[13] In searching for the tendency, Virilio tries to discern what he calls the 'change of level' in events. The change of level is like an accident hidden in developments which gives rise to the birth of an unforeseen potentiality. In this light, 'pure war' is, as we will discuss below, the accident of the Second World War's extreme political, technological and strategic undertakings. Virilio discovers this accident in the increased importance of logistics after the war.

This discovery is central to the challenge Virilio's approach poses to more conventional critical interpretations of phenomena such as flight simulation. What will become apparent, however, is that as the tendency towards the disappearance of the military/non-military distinction accelerates, a second accident occurs: the very possibility of the critical evaluation of this tendency is put into question. This impacts, necessarily, on Virilio's own efforts to interpret 'pure war' phenomena. This is to say that Virilio's work not only foregrounds the importance of addressing the military/non-military relation today but consequentially proposes the decreasing possibility of successfully doing so.

One might speculate that it is an intuition of the problematic nature of the task of addressing this situation that informs those writings commented upon above that fail to consider the military origins, developments and objectives of flight simulation. This would make those writings implicit, unconscious acknowledgements of the tendency Virilio marks toward the collapse of the distinction between the military and the non-military wrought by the military absorption and annihilation of the civilian sphere after World War II. If I am right in this speculation, however, it is Virilio's work that allows us to characterize these writings in this way.

This is why I believe that Virilio is the most pertinent theorist to consider in attempting to understand the impact and significance of flight simulation. In postulating the notion of the breakdown in 'pure war' of the military/non-military demarcation, Virilio has recast the critical perspective on the post-World War II era in which flight simulation has become influential and widely known. As well, he has broached the question of the very possibility of critical thought about the ongoing transformation of the 'real' world, of which transformation flight simulation—as a major influence on the development of computer imaging technologies—is a significant catalyst. This is a crucial question that must not be forgotten by any attempt to understand such a central element of contemporary 'reality'.

Bearing this in mind, let us look briefly at the history of flight simulation in order to introduce the themes that will most concern us in this essay: the logistical nature of the military interest in flight simulation beyond tactical and strategic concerns, and its consequences in light of the rapid expansion of the application of flight simulation technology in the '70s.

II

From the time in 1934 when the U.S. Army Air Corps purchased six of Edwin A. Link's 'Blue Box' flight trainers to train Army pilots for instrument flying in bad weather,[14] the history of the development of flight simulation has been the history of a military-driven development which has absorbed putative non-military technologies. Link's 1929 invention was based on air-driven organ technology and articulated flight controls with a motion simulator system without any visual display component. The use of the Link Corporation's 'Blue Box' as a training device multiplied during the Second World War when huge numbers of pilots needed to be trained in a short time due to the large-scale increases in the war's production of destruction. The war firmly established flight simulation as a component of military pilot training. Like the history of the aeroplane itself, it is impossible to characterize flight simulation's technological development independently of its military use.

With the advent of commercial video cameras in the early '50s, 'real-time visual feedback' for simulated flight became possible.[15] Cameras on motion platforms controlled by the simulator pilot through his flight controls moved over 'terrain boards' containing scale models of ground scenery. These terrain boards were, according to Davis, '...akin to those found in model railroading,...'[16] The video images produced by this coupling of the latest audio-visual technology with toy models were projected onto a screen substituting for the pilot's forward view out of the cockpit.

This amounted to what might be called a televisual miniaturization of reality for the purpose of more efficient and effective flight training. This process of reduction obeyed what Virilio would call a logistical imperative—a term which will be discussed in detail below. This televisual miniaturization gave way in the '60s and '70s to the animation/generation of the real by the computer, the next leading-edge technology advantageous to the development of simulation training for military pilots. The 'scene generator' software and hardware developed by Ivan Sutherland and David Evans in 1968 initiated the movement toward the sophisticated digital flight simulators developed in the '70s and '80s and, equally significant, the expansion of the flight simulation industry across military, commercial and entertainment sectors.

The idea for the scene generator came out of Sutherland's work on the first head-mounted display units.[17] Such pioneering work has made him a major figure in the history of Virtual Reality. In 1972, General Electric Company's Electronics Laboratory produced for the Navy the 'Advanced Development Model' (ADM) to test the effectiveness of Sutherland's 'Computer Image Generation' for flight training. The results were positive.[18] The ADM's set-up of three screens placed in front and either side of the cockpit meant that the simulator pilot's vision was now filled with close to 180 degrees of real-time visual feedback. Moreover, the possibility of simulating opponents within the virtual space of the 'mission' increased dramatically the combat-training potential of flight simulation—and its subsequent potential as a model for computer games such as Graphic Simulations Corporation's 1993 game, *F/A-18 Hornet Strike Fighter*.[19] The linking together of two or more simulators made virtual dogfighting and group mission simulation possible. As Lapiska et al. tell us: 'Aircraft and weapon systems developers could now evaluate the performance of the aircrew, aircraft, and weapons as a total system in a combat environment'.[20] Digital simulation expanded the use of the technology to include the development of new aircraft and weapons systems, as well as related applications, such as, more recently, air accident investigations.[21] The ADM is the starting point for the visual display component of today's 'top end' $12 million dome simulators.

The history of the development of flight simulation reveals how significant economic considerations have been in advancing simulation technology's role in pilot training and aircraft/weapons testing.[22] As mentioned above, Link's original 'Blue Box' units played a crucial part in matching 'pilot production', as it were, to the mass production of military aircraft during the Second World War. According to Goldiez, for aerospace organizations, the latest advances in simulator networking are 'critical to remaining economically competitive'.[23] And, as Lapiska et al. tell us, the U.S. Federal Aviation Authority (FAA) has had sufficient confidence in simulation fidelity since the mid-'70s to equate time in the simulator with time in the 'real' aircraft as concerns qualifying for pilot certification. This utilization of the simulator also has the advantage of 'freeing up' aircraft for revenue-generating activities:

> A simulator and training program approved to the highest level allowed by the FAA permits a pilot to obtain the type rating for that vehicle *without ever flying the actual aircraft*. A pilot receives classroom training, aircraft systems and procedure training, and flight training in the simulator, then takes the test with the FAA in the simulator and is approved to fly the real aircraft.[24] [my italics]

In *War and Cinema: The Logistics of Perception*, Virilio cites this decision to equate simulator time with time in the 'real' aircraft as an important moment in what he calls the 'process of derealization' affecting the post-World War II world.[25] The 'process of derealization' is Virilio's term for the impact of technologies such as cinema, television, video and the computer on conventional modes of perception and interpretation of reality. The effect of this proliferation of representations is being increasingly felt, he argues, in the era of computer simulation.[26]

The extension of flight simulation's '*mise-en-scène* of war'—in which instructors could teach students 'not just to pilot an aircraft with instruments but to pilot a series of startlingly realistic images'[27]—took place, Virilio argues, largely unnoticed. He links this expansion of the role and influence of simulation technology across the military and commercial sectors to the '70s oil crisis and the associated threat to military/industrial energy reserves. Indeed, the subtitle of Virilio's book, *The Logistics of Perception*, indicates that a central thesis of his text is the relation between the socio-economic phenomenon of the energy crisis and the 'process of derealization' affecting contemporary perceptions of reality. The very subtitle proposes this overflowing of military ways of seeing and organizing vision into all areas of visual culture.

Virilio's use of the term 'logistics' here represents a key instance of his interrogation of the military/non-military relation and how this has developed in recent decades. Logistics is generally associated with the economic, supply and transport considerations taken into account by military planning staff in their preparations for war or for maintaining standing armed forces. Manuel De Landa defines logistics as 'the art of assembling war and the agricultural, economic and industrial resources that make it possible'.[28] It has also gained a wider usage in describing labour and resource management and deployment more generally.[29] Virilio, for his part, has taken this term and pushed its implication—that war and the military cannot be considered as wholly separate from the socio-economic and cultural spheres—to the forefront in his texts. In this 'avant-garde' position, the term 'logistics' always announces a question for him about the overflowing of the military into every domain of life: the economic, the social, the political and the cultural.

In a more recent text in which he extends his analysis of this overflowing to the latest trends in military research, Virilio begins by claiming that 'our immediate perception is, in a sense, being corrupted—largely by the recent appearance of "*vision machines*" in the form of photocinematographic, video and infographic technology'. This 'corruption' amounts to a degradation of our ability to perceive reality because of the increasing influence of these 'vision machines' on human perception. The development of each of these technologies has been military-inspired to a significant degree, as Virilio had already demonstrated in *War and Cinema*. Restating *War and Cinema's* thesis about the 'process of derealization' that is in train today under the influence of these representational and simulation technologies, Virilio argues that 'these devices appropriate everyday images which as a consequence lose their ability to reflect reality'.[30]

We can immediately see the problem that I outlined in Section I: how can Virilio (or any other theorist/observer) recognize the contamination of the non-military by the military and account for it critically? If Virilio's analyses are valid, the theorist/observer can no longer accept with certainty that events or phenomena are purely non-military in nature. Indeed, the theorist/observer cannot even be sure that he/she stands outside the military in order to determine its diffusion into the realm of the non-military. In this light, the advent of video cameras, which I characterized earlier as a 'non-military' technology co-opted by military research, could no longer be characterized in so unproblematic a manner. Indeed, Virilio points out in a recent interview that video technology was developed after the Second World War in an effort to radio-control planes and aircraft carriers.[31] In the wake of the successful appropriation of 'everyday images' by 'vision machines', it would be impossible to establish whether one's immediate perception of the real has been corrupted and, if so, to what extent.

This problem, or rather aporia, not only confronts the substance of Virilio's critical project, it can be seen to operate at the formal and stylistic levels of his writing. Virilio's work is rapid. In short, it is a form of assault on traditional critical frameworks. It obeys Sun Tzu's famous military principle—speed is the essence of war—in its 'engagement' with conventional interpretations of events and technological developments. That Virilio follows this principle in order to keep pace with the tendencies unfolding in contemporary phenomena is indicative of the fact that the speed of technological and cultural change is to a significant degree a function of the influence of military principles in the supposedly non-military sphere.

To this extent, then, it might be argued that Virilio's work has itself been penetrated by a military logic and mode of thought at the level of the very form of his writing. But this would call into question the ability of Virilio's work to address the military/non-military relation with any certainty as it would problematize any easy assumption about the position from which he writes. In a way, however, this is precisely the point of my mobilization of Virilio in the consideration of flight simulation. After Virilio, the certainty of the meaning and stability of the terms in the military/non-military relation must be considered doubtful. It is his work above all that has made this apparent, even if the consequence is that his own project is itself rendered problematic. The rapid, provisional and questioning nature of his analyses represents an implicit acknowledgement and addressal of this problem confronting his own work. Indeed, it remains of necessity an ongoing problematic from which his investigations proceed.

So with an understanding of the limits imposed by and upon Virilio and ourselves with regard to this relation, let us turn now to the notion of logistics as Virilio employs it in order to describe how flight simulators have contributed to the 'process of derealization'. As I shall argue, flight simulators have performed a pivotal role in the spread of this visual regime that enacts the logistical indetermining of the distinction between the military and the non-military spheres, this visual regime I call the 'logistical space' of flight simulation.

III

What would this term 'logistical space' represent? We can get some clues from Virilio's response to a request to explain his use of the word 'logistics' in his extended interview with Sylvère Lotringer published in 1983 as the book *Pure War*. Virilio states that logistics first arises as an issue for military planning in the Napoleonic era, the beginning of the era of 'mass wars', and that the first person to use the term was the nineteenth century French military theorist Henri Jomini.[32] For this theorist, logistics was not limited to the subsistence of the new national army mobilized by Napoleon:

> [L]ogistics is not only food, it's also munitions and transportation... The trucks bringing ammunition and the flying shells

> bringing death are coupled in a system of vectors, of production, transportation, execution. There we have a whole flow chart which is logistics itself.[33]

Logistics as the management of a system of vectors requires a translation of economic activity, systems of transportation and armed conflict into a flow chart, a diagrammatic representation of an incredibly complex and dynamic reality. This process of translation produces an informational space where logistical problems are anticipated, mapped out and resolved. Virilio describes the advent of logistics as revolutionary because of its potential to refigure economics, politics and military strategy by subordinating them to the ever-increasing requirements of the logistical process. He sees in General Eisenhower's management of the D-Day invasion the culmination of an 'a-national logistical revolution', subsequently instantiated in an early post-World War II definition of logistics that issued from the Pentagon: 'Logistics is the procedure following which a nation's potential is transferred to its armed forces, in times of peace as in times of war'.[34]

This definition raises a crucial point. Were logistics taken to its 'logistical' conclusion, the transfer of a nation's potential to its armed forces would be, before anything else, the transformation of a nation *into* logistical potential. This is why Virilio will recognize in this definition a key to understanding what he calls 'the a-national logistical revolution'. The nation as origin of identity and as the locus of political and socio-cultural propriety disappears with the predominance of the logistical flow chart.

The decisive increase in importance and consequent proliferation of the logistical flow chart in the post-war period is the central element in the overflowing of the military sphere into the non-military sphere. The transformation of a nation *into* logistical potential leads to the transformation of the reality of the world of nations into a 'virtual reality'. That is to say, the traditional elements and relationships of socio-political and cultural reality become increasingly 'virtualized': all walks of life and all institutions, while maintaining their conventional appearance, tend to be determined more and more by the dictates of the logistics of perception, communication, politics, strategy, economics, and so on. Accepted modes of reasoning, interpretation and decision-making in these fields are subordinated to logistical considerations and survive only to legitimate processes they no longer govern.

To say that the 'logistical revolution' is the overflowing of the military sphere into the non-military sphere implies that military modes of analysis and organization—let us say 'military logic'—amount to logistics. Traditionally, however, logistics is not the only area exercising the minds of military thinkers. As De Landa has pointed out, there are three fundamental branches of military operations: tactics, strategy and logistics.[35] Historically, each branch required a different type of 'military logic' and was affected by different factors and considerations. De Landa suggests, however, that after World War II, logistics became the dominant mode in military thought, so that '...modern tactics and strategy would seem to have become special branches of logistics'.[36] Logistics overflowed into the other domains of 'military logic' at the same time as it overflowed into the non-military sphere.

The space animated by the flight simulator can be said to figure this transformation of a politico-strategic and economic real into a logistical diagram. Indeed, inasmuch as the flight simulator was the 'progenitor and paradigm' for computer imaging and visual simulation, this prototypical virtual space is an exemplary instantiation of the 'logistical revolution'.[37] Considered as a kind of logistical diagram, the virtual space of flight simulation is a descendent of two related representational traditions: the diagram and the map (itself a form of diagram). As I stated earlier, flight simulation is a new form of animation. It could be said, therefore, that its animated virtual space relates to the diagram in a fashion analogous to the way that the spatiality of a traditional animated cartoon relates to drawing. According to Michael Benedikt, both the diagram and the map exploit the power of René Descartes' insight into the translatability of algebra and geometry into each other. The Cartesian coordinate system for plotting mathematical equations in two-dimensional space has led, in Benedikt's terms, to the notion that '...*space itself* is something not necessarily physical: rather...it is a "field of play" for all information,...'[38] Diagrams and charts, then, are '...hybrids, mixing physical, energic or spatiotemporal coordinates with abstract, mathematical ones, mixing histories with geographies, simple intervallic scales with exponential ones, and so on'.[39]

For Benedikt, the proliferation of '*diagramming*' in the twentieth century—from 'simple bar charts and organizational "trees" through matrices, networks and "spreadsheets" to elaborate, multidimensional, computer-generated visualizations of invisible physical processes'—raises questions about the 'ontological status' of diagrammatic representation. The diagrammatic spatiality of these 'entities', he argues, exceeds the geography of the two-dimensional 'piece of paper or computer screen on which we see them. All have a reality that is no mere picture of the natural, phenomenal world, and all display a physics, as it were, from elsewhere'.[40] This 'reality' is, for Benedikt, the 'first evidence' of the 'materializing' of cyberspace and the precursor to cyberspace's 'parallel universe created and sustained by the world's computers and communication lines'.[41]

In light of our analysis of Virilio's work, this derealizing of physical space in favour of the materialization of a physics from 'elsewhere', so fundamental to the advent of cyberspace, can be seen as a logistical process.[42] The virtual space of flight simulation enacts this diagrammatical reanimation of the world as an informational 'field of play'. The simulator does not simply re-present a real space—even if its ever-increasing verisimilitude perturbs the clarity of the conventional understanding of the opposition between representation and simulation. This is a reanimation because it brings to life the world in a new way, one in which logistical considerations dominate over all others. But this new life of the world would be, in a sense, a living death because the possibility of traditional, non-logistical modes of interpreting and acting (political, ethical, strategic) wither in this world.

The dying away of these traditional modes of existence and critique in the new logistical world could even be considered to be an inevitable consequence of the process of (re)animation at work in this transformation of the real. As Alan Cholodenko has rightly pointed out in a discussion of the uncanny nature of animation's 'illusion of life', the generation of this illusion always has a relation to death. He suggests that:

> animation cannot be thought without thinking loss, disappearance and death, that one cannot think the endowing with life without thinking the other side of the life cycle—the transformation from the animate into the inanimate—at the same time, cannot think endowing with motion without thinking the other side of the cycle of movement—of metastasis, deceleration, inertia, suspended animation, etc.—at the same time, and cannot think the life cycle without thinking the movement cycle at the same time.[43]

Every form of the 'illusion of life', every generation of an animated real, has this linkage to disappearance and death, and must be so thought. I have argued that the generative movement toward the new forms of animation—with the development of flight simulation constituting an initiatory factor in this movement—must be thought in terms of the overflowing of the military into the non-military spheres and the consequent tendency toward the suspension of the real as traditionally conceived. That is to say, this movement is a process inescapably entailing degeneration, including of the capacity to maintain these spheres as exclusive and oppositional. Flight simulation's reanimation of the world as what Virilio calls the '*mise-en-scène* of war'[44]—of *pure war*—must be thought in relation to the multiple forms of degeneration that make up the loss of the conventional form of the real that is the 'other side' of this animatic process. The 'endowing with life' of the diagrammatic, informational world has this intrinsic link to the transformation of the hitherto animate real into a state of inanimation, or of suspended animation.

The *F/A-18 Hornet Strike Fighter* computer game is a good example of how this logistical reanimation of the world tends toward a living death of the real. The simulated three-dimensional space over the Middle East in and through which I pilot my F/A-18 in the Graphic Simulations Corporation game is a projection of that most unstable of geopolitical regions into a logistical dimension where strategic and tactical exercises can be played out in an experimental fashion that mirrors the laboratory-type conduct of the 'actual' Gulf War by the U.S.-led 'allies'.[45] The politico-strategic dimension is reduced to a residual 'pre-text' displayed in the 'Mission Briefing' window before I arm my plane for take-off.[46] Tactics and strategy have become here, as De Landa has indicated, 'special branches of logistics'.

In the 1980s, the U.S. Navy developed the Visually Coupled Airborne Systems Simulator (VCASS) or 'Super Cockpit' Project, a groundbreaking experiment in the 'activation' of the flight simulator's logistical space. The 'Super Cockpit' system responded to the trajectory of flight simulation technology toward head-mounted display systems (replacing the large and more costly domed simulators) by developing a 'virtual cockpit' that the pilot could wear

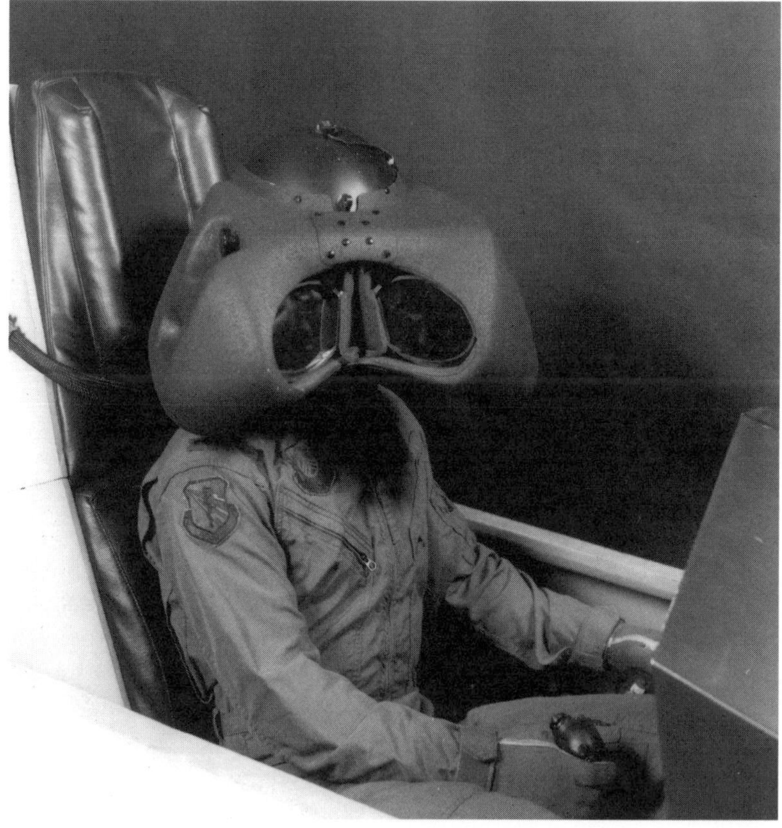

Fig. 1. Visually Coupled Airborne Systems Simulator (VCASS) Helmet. © 1985 Image Courtesy of Wright Patterson Air Force Base.

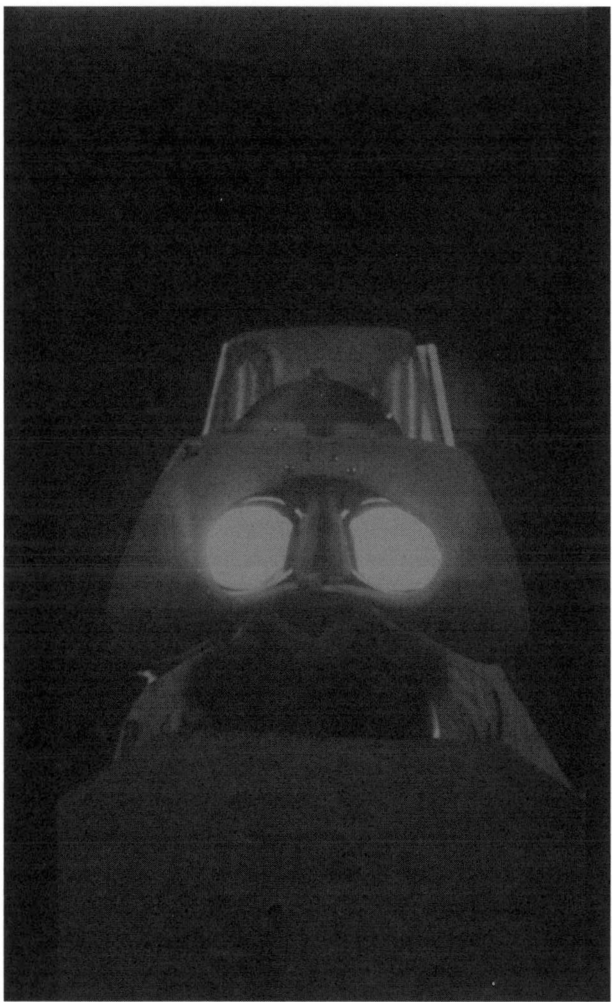

Fig. 2. Front view of VCASS Helmet. © 1985 Image Courtesy of Wright Patterson Air Force Base.

as a helmet (Figs. 1 and 2). One of the primary advantages of this system is the ability to 'supplement' the pilot's vision with a simplified, virtual view of the world (Fig. 3).[47]

Here is a description of the 'Super Cockpit' in operation:

> Once he was airborne, solid clouds obscured everything outside

> the canopy. But inside the helmet, the pilot 'saw' the horizon and terrain clearly, as if it were a clear day. His compass heading was displayed as a large band of numbers on the horizon line, his projected flight path a shimmering highway leading out toward infinity. A faint whine above and behind him to the left told the pilot...that his 'enemy'...was closing in...[48]

The pilot was now in combat in a virtual world which had been pre-planned and mapped out in advance to allow him to accomplish his mission objectives. The three major components of a flight simulator's visual system—the display, the image or scene generator and the database—were now essential not only to the success of the visual illusion in a 'real time' simulator but to the success of 'real' missions flown in the 'Super Cockpit'.[49]

The simplified, virtual environment generated by the 'Super Cockpit' as a substitute 'theatre of operations' for the military pilot

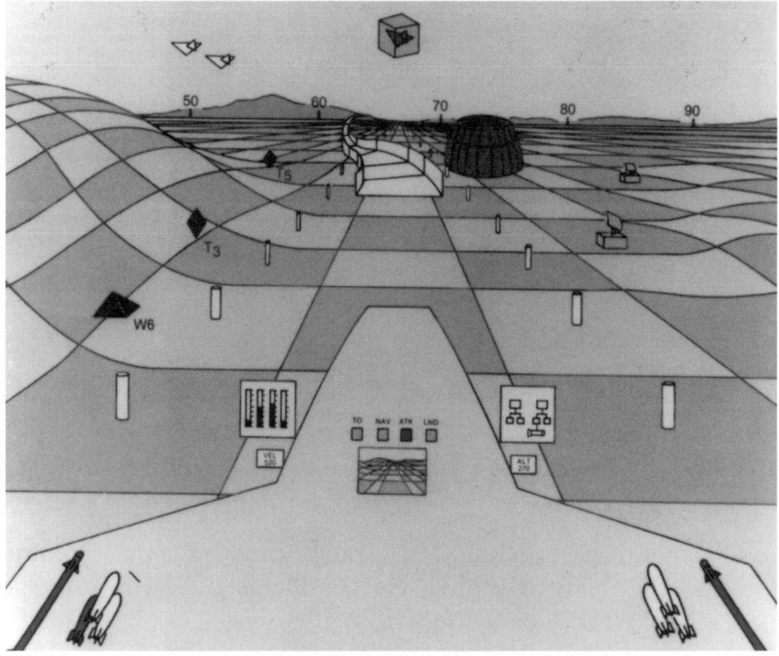

Fig. 3. Pilot's View through the VCASS 'Super Cockpit' Helmet. © 1985 Image Courtesy of Wright Patterson Air Force Base.

represents beautifully for us what Virilio would call the dromoscopic vision of the logistical tendency. Dromoscopy is a term coined by Virilio—among other related terms such as 'dromology' and 'dromocracy'—to describe a vision or perspective produced by speed. *Dromos* is ancient Greek for 'race', as in 'running race'. A dromoscopy is the view of one who is racing at speed.[50] This notion of the alteration of one's point of view 'at speed' is used by Virilio as a kind of hermeneutic to interpret the impacts of technological change which have affected the speeds of transport, communication, economic/military capacities, and the like.[51]

The simulator's virtual space is dromoscopic in its simplification of the real. One of the key trade-offs any visual simulation system faces is that between scenery complexity and screen update rates: the greater the complexity of the scene being rendered, that is, the greater the amount of information it contains about terrain, fixed structures and objects moving in the scene, the more the calculations required to generate the successive images needed to animate the virtual world. Flight simulation is a vision produced by a race: the algorithm against the clock. The stakes are 'realism' and effectivity. It was found that at screen update rates of less than 20 images per second, the simulation was ineffective because it was unrealistic. This need to maintain the flow of simulated images is balanced against the goal of achieving photo-realistic detail in the reproduction of the 'world flown over', a goal widely accepted, as Davis indicates:

> More recently the emphasis has been on 'photo-texture'. These are texture patterns created from a photograph of real-world objects. When used in the visual scene and *viewed from afar*, they increase realism dramatically.[52] [my italics]

The database must be selectively accessed by the image generator to enable a realistic but not over-complex virtual space to be generated. The sources of a flight simulator's database represent the major components of contemporary military topographical and territorial information-gathering: satellite pictures, topographical maps, aerial photographs, highway maps, photographs of important objects and on-site inspections.[53] In this regard, the image generator's treatment of the database can be seen to offer a logistical solution corresponding to the problem the military commander confronts in processing all the available information in the increasingly diminishing time allowed by the speed of modern weapons systems and at his increasing remove from the war zone necessitated by the scale and speed of modern warfare. Here is Virilio from *War and Cinema*:

> The level of foresight required by the geopolitical dimensions of modern battlefields demanded a veritable meteorology of war. Already we can see here the video-idea that the military voyeur is handicapped by the slowness with which he scans a field of action overstretched by the dynamic revolution of weaponry and mass transport. Only the further development of technology could offset this tendency to which it had given rise. For the disappearance of the proximity effect in the prosthesis of accelerated travel made it necessary to create a *wholly simulated appearance* that would restore three-dimensionality to the message in full.[54]

This restoration of the message from the battlefield in its 'wholly simulated appearance' was for Virilio a logistical necessity. And while it restored an illusion of depth to the complex and dynamic reality of modern war, animating the commander's illusion of the battlefield, it did not restore its strategic-political dimension. Rather, the 'video-idea' of supplementing the commander's vision with the 'real-time' technological simulation of the real led to the living death of the real discussed above.

This is what Virilio describes as the process of derealization that has spread with the infinite expansion of the 'military field of perception'.[55] In *War and Cinema*, he calls this process 'cinematic derealisation', referring to the cinematic dromoscopy of producing a moving, 'lifelike' vision by the successive superimposition of images at a certain speed. This 'cinematic derealisation' is a process of animation common to all visual systems using human retinal persistence in the generation of 'artificial realities'. To this extent, it would be better termed 'animatic derealization', a term which more precisely captures the paradoxical nature of this process which both brings to life a certain artificial reality—in this case a logistical one—

and at the same time degrades another reality, one that is taken to be authentic, true and preeminent, so that the clarity of the distinction between the former and latter realities dissolves.[56] Cinematic (animatic) derealization established itself in a realm where

> sequential perception, like optical phenomena resulting from retinal persistence, is both origin and end of the apprehension of reality, since the seeing of movement is but a statistical process connected with the nature of the segmentation of images and the speed of observation characteristic of humans. The macro-cinematography of aerial reconnaissance, the cable television of panoramic radar, the use of slow or accelerated motion in analysing the phases of an operation—all this converts the commander's plan into an animated cartoon or flow chart.[57]

Virilio's notion of the transformation of the commander's plan into an animated cartoon or flow chart immediately recalls flight simulation's animation of the logistical flow chart. It is evident that flight simulation is a model instance of this process of animatic derealization.

IV

One major initiative underway in simulation database development is Project 2851. This is a tri-service program organized by the U.S. Department of Defense, which, in the words of Davis, is '…striving to create a comprehensive database of the world, from which information can be extracted by the user to produce a working database for a particular location…'[58] This project is a vitally important component of recent efforts to network geographically distant simulators because it would provide a widely available and affordable basis for simulating the common virtual space required for networked simulators. A set of protocols called the Distributed Interactive Simulation (DIS) standards has been developed in recent years to achieve this networking goal. The DIS standards have been tested in hookups, such as in November 1992 when the Rockwell Corporation's 'AGF simulator' in Downey, California and the

Naval Training Systems Center F/A-18 simulator at a San Antonio Conference Center were networked so that the AGF and the Navy F/A-18 '...flew in formation in a simulated combat scenario over a fleet of three naval ships'.[59]

The DIS standards operate on the principles of time and space coherency. Project 2851's mapping of the world is set to satisfy the principle of spatial coherency, while 'Greenwich Mean Time obtained from a GPS [Global Positioning System] receiver is used to accomplish the time correlation'.[60] DIS is well placed to serve as a possible prototype for the much desired and imagined 'consensual illusion' of cyberspace, a situation which would make cyberspace *before anything else* a further extension of the logistical space I have been trying to theorize here.

In conclusion, let me recall the aporia confronting the attempt to consider the military/non-military relation by asserting that my theorization of flight simulation's logistical space must be considered as provisional. The logistical reanimation of the world must be understood as a tendency discernible in contemporary phenomena such as flight simulation and not as an accomplished fact. This imperative is dictated by the Virilian approach to flight simulation that I have adopted in this essay, for, as I argued earlier, Virilio's own work allows us to see both the necessity and the impossibility of accounting for the transformation in the military/non-military relation in the era of pure war. If, as Virilio's work suggests, this transformation is constitutive of the tendency toward pure war, then we who live in this era must call into question the certainty and finality of any account of what is military, what is non-military, and consequently of the becoming-military of the putative non-military, and vice versa.

Virilio's theorization of tendencies allows for this questioning and announces it as a crucial issue for critical work today. Insofar as his 'tendential' analyses amount to a rapid sketching out of potential (virtual) realities inherent in contemporary phenomena, this sketching out is, indeed, an animation of the virtual reality Virilio discerns in today's real, for critical interpretation is itself a form of (re)animating the world in, and as, an 'artificial reality'. As such, these tendencies pose questions both about the nature of these phenomena and the mode in which they can validly be brought to life by theoretical interpretation today. To recall our discussion of the imbrication of life and death in animation, Virilio's critical animations must be thought in terms of what is brought to life, to visibility, and what disappears and dies away in that appearing.

My analysis of flight simulation's logistical space, then, must be considered as a meditation not only on the tendency toward the reanimation of the world as an informational field of play for anticipating and solving logistical problems, it also raises questions about how the world is animated as such, the nature of its appearing as real and what is at stake in that 'real illusion'.

POSTSCRIPT

This paper was originally delivered in 1995, and has remained substantially the same through the processes of revision undertaken in the intervening years. While software and technical aspects of flight simulation computer games have moved on in significant ways—for instance, the innovation discussed in the final section of real time networked gameplay in a shared virtual space is now a standard option of flight simulation gaming—the principal elements of the simulation of virtual space and the design of gameplay remain the same. I was invited by the editor, however, to append a short postscript in order to bring the perspectives on computer simulation and gaming put forward in this paper into some dialogue with the post-September 11, 2001 context. I am grateful for the opportunity, even if it goes without saying that interpreting the logistical implications of '9/11' requires a far more extended consideration than is possible here. Nevertheless, two observations can be made that seem apt as a way of indicating the outline of such a consideration and the manner in which the tendency toward virtualization discussed here articulates with the politico-strategic dilemma of globalization that '9/11' confirmed as one of the key questions for the new century. Once again, insights from Virilio allow a swift crystallization of these key points.

In his examination of the Gulf War entitled *Desert Screen,*[61] Virilio discusses the logistical character of the way in which the 'war' was conducted. The Iraqi military threat was virtually eliminated in advance of the ground engagement by means of massive air superiority and total control over the radar and communications networks of Iraq by means of what Virilio calls the 'arms of communication'. The war, he says, resembled in many respects a televised arms marketing expo where the latest weapons could be demonstrated in a derealized space visible in the weapons' eye-views and in the charts and maps of the daily media briefings conducted by the U.S. military.[62] Virilio argues that even if the outcome of the Gulf War in a strictly military sense was clearly predictable, its consequences are 'incalculable' and 'uncontrollable...*politically speaking*'.[63] He speculates here about the necessary accident of the global real time mediatization of this logistical virtualization of real territory. He sees the potential for a myriad of unpredictable detonations of 'public opinion' across the globe with unforeseeable consequences.

This observation—that despite the massive effort at controlling both the enemy's capability and the mass media's dissemination of that effort, unpredictable, and therefore uncontrollable, consequences can and will follow—is given further elaboration in a subsequent text, *Strategy of Deception*,[64] a commentary on the U.S.-led NATO actions in the former Yugoslavia. Virilio characterizes herein the post-Cold War state as one in which the balance of power between the U.S. and the Soviet Union has been replaced by an 'unbalance of terror', one which proliferates in direct proportion to the increasing effort of the U.S. to deter threats to its absolute military superiority. This effort includes the new (in 1997) U.S. military doctrine of 'global information dominance', which includes retaining exclusive control over technologies of radar and satellite positioning and navigation so as to be able to withhold them from military opponents.[65] The virtualization of global space that allows 'the finding, tracking and targeting virtually in real time [of] any significant element moving on the surface of the earth'[66] is a crucial factor in the drive for total control over the potential enemy. The realization of this cyclopean, panoptical vision, as Virilio describes it, not only allows for the kind of interdictive military actions exemplified by the NATO campaigns in the Balkans, it also further escalates the unbalancing of political-strategic situations globally, so that the virtual map of logistical space will reanimate an increasingly unstable and unpredictable new world 'order', even as efforts to eliminate all contingent threats to 'domestic security' multiply. '9/11' would thus name the moment when this emergent dynamic of escalation and reanimation underwent maximum acceleration.

NOTES

1 Samuel Hynes, 'The Feeling of Flying', *The Sewanee Review*, vol. 95, no. 1, Winter 1987, p. 92.

2 Paul Virilio/Sylvère Lotringer, *Pure War*, trans. Mark Polizotti (New York: Semiotext(e), 1983), p. 84.

3 Andy Darley, 'From Abstraction to Simulation: Notes on the History of Computer Imaging', in *Culture, Technology & Creativity in the Late Twentieth Century*, ed. Philip Hayward (London: John Libbey, 1990), p. 53.

4 ibid., p. 39.

5 Alan Cholodenko, in his Introduction to *THE ILLUSION OF LIFE: Essays on Animation* (Sydney: Power Publications in association with the Australian Film Commission, 1991), argues that the live action/animation distinction has been challenged from the very beginning of film (and animation) history, starting with such hybrid live action/cartoon animation forms as the 'lightning sketch', which shows 'the animator...giving life in various ways to drawn characters' (p. 22). These hybrid forms have continued to trouble the framework through which animation is understood in relation to live action film as one of its 'subspecies', the most recent example of which, Cholodenko notes in 1991, was *Who Framed Roger Rabbit* (p. 23). (One might say *Space Jam* in 1997.) But in this new generation of animation, the 'dissemination' of the live action/animation distinction that Cholodenko theorizes (drawing on Derrida's notion of dissemination) can also be found in play in Virtual Reality's undoing of any clear distinction between 'live interaction' in the real world and in the animated milieu that comprises 'artificial reality'.

6 Myron W. Krueger, *Artificial Reality II* (Reading: Addison-Wesley, 1991), Chapter 4, 'Goggles and Gloves', p. 66. The heads-up display was developed as an aid to jet fighter pilots to enable them to keep their eyes on the action outside the cockpit. The display exhibits

crucial instrumentation readouts in real time in a transparent screen that underlays the pilot's visual field as he looks outside.

7 James L. Davis, 'Visual Systems: Generating a New Reality', *Aerospace America*, vol. 31, no. 8, August 1993, p. 26.

8 ibid., p. 29.

9 Carl Lapiska, Larry Ross and Don Smart, 'Flight Simulation: An Overview', *Aerospace America*, vol. 31, no. 8, August 1993, p. 33.

10 Brian F. Goldiez, 'Networks Extend Simulation's Reach', *Aerospace America*, vol. 31, no. 8, August 1993, p. 25.

11 Stephen R. Ellis' rather daring suggestion at the conclusion of his piece, 'What Are Virtual Environments?', that 'Life in virtual environments might also have social aftereffects…' stands out as an exceptional moment in the pages of *IEEE Computer Graphics and Applications*. *IEEE Computer Graphics and Applications*, vol. 14, no. 1, January 1994, p. 22.

12 Darley, 'From Abstraction to Simulation: Notes on the History of Computer Imaging', p. 51.

13 On his interest in the tendency, see Virilio in *Pure War*, pp. 39-42.

14 Lapiska, Ross and Smart, 'Flight Simulation: An Overview', p. 14. They tell us here that the Army pilots were employed at the time in transporting the U.S. mail. Thus, we see flight simulation linked to a key communications network, both military and non-military, at its very outset.

15 Ken Pimentel and Kevin Teixeira, *Virtual Reality: Through the New Looking Glass* (New York: Intel/Windcrest/McGraw-Hill, Inc., 1993), p. 34.

16 Davis, 'Visual Systems: Generating a New Reality', p. 26.

17 Pimentel and Teixeira, *Virtual Reality: Through the New Looking Glass*, p. 35. The corporation, Evans & Sutherland, has continued as a leading supplier of 'high-end' military simulators.

18 ibid., pp. 35-36.

19 *F/A-18 Hornet Strike Fighter* has a set of training missions, but the main action takes place in a Middle East theatre of operations based on the Gulf War. An additional set of missions, *F/A-18 Hornet 2.0: Korean Crisis*, was released in 1995. Generally speaking, it is typical of most flight simulation games for personal computers, although there are games such as *Microsoft Flight Simulator* which are based more on commercial pilot training models—themselves devolved from military simulations.

20 Lapiska, Ross and Smart, 'Flight Simulation: An Overview', p. 16.

21 See ibid.

22 Pilot safety and product security considerations are also frequently mentioned along with economic factors. See Lawrence J. Schilling and Dale A. Mackall, 'Flight Research Simulation Takes Off', *Aerospace America*, vol. 31, no. 8, August 1993.

23 Goldiez, 'Networks Extend Simulation's Reach', p. 22.

24 Lapiska, Ross and Smart, 'Flight Simulation: An Overview', p. 15.

25 Virilio, *War and Cinema: The Logistics of Perception*, trans. Patrick Camiller (London: Verso, 1989), p. 86.

26 ibid.

27 ibid.

28 Manuel De Landa, *War in the Age of Intelligent Machines* (New York: Zone Books, 1991), p. 105.

29 This more general usage of the term is already an indication of the diffusion of a military model to the 'domestic' sphere. And according to De Landa, the interrelation between military logistical considerations and the development of modern mass production has a long history. See his discussion of the interplay between the U.S. Department of Ordnance and private enterprise munitions producers from the 1830s onwards and the influence it had on the development of the 'American system' of manufacture and on the later formulation of the 'scientific principles of management'. De Landa, *War in the Age of Intelligent Machines*, pp. 30-31.

30 Virilio, 'Speed and Vision: The Incomporable [*sic*] Eye', *Daidalos: Berlin Architectural Journal*, vol. 47, March 15, 1993, p. 96.

31 See Virilio and Louise Wilson, 'Cyberwar, God and Television: Interview with Paul Virilio', *CTheory*, vol. 18, no. 1-2, April 1995, p. 4.

32 Virilio/Lotringer, *Pure War*, p. 15.

33 ibid., p. 16.

34 ibid.

35 See De Landa, *War in the Age of Intelligent Machines*, Chapter 1.

36 ibid., p. 106.

37 We might note here that the term *logistics* has another contemporary meaning, namely, as a term for mathematical or symbolic logic (my thanks to Paul Adams for pointing this out to me). Etymological research tells us that pre-nineteenth century, logistics generally meant reckoning or calculation. This would explain Jomini's adoption of the term *la logistique* in his account of the essential military skill for the modern era: that of coordinating the vectors of supply and combat. More specifically, logistics was a synonym for logarithmic calculation. While mathematical logic is generally thought to have begun with

Leibniz in the seventeenth century, it established itself in the nineteenth century with Boole and became a major branch of mathematical science in the twentieth century through the work of Bertrand Russell and others. Mathematical logic is at the foundation of Cybernetics, Systems Analysis and computer programing. The computer simulation industry—and flight simulation as the progenitor of visual simulation—is based on the computer and its abilities as an 'anticipation machine', or what Virilio calls an 'inference engine'. The predictive speed of computers depends on the application of the power of mathematical logic or logistics. It would seem, then, that the two senses of logistics—symbolic logic and military planning—have merged in the dominance of information technology over the contemporary experience of, and interaction with, the real.

38 Michael Benedikt, Introduction, *Cyberspace: First Steps,* ed. Michael Benedikt (Cambridge, Mass.: The MIT Press, 1991), p. 20.

39 ibid, p. 21.

40 ibid.

41 ibid., p. 1.

42 Benedikt's essay in the same book, on some principles for developing cyberspace, entitled 'Cyberspace: Some Proposals', betrays the powerful influence of flight simulation on his 'vision'. At one point, cyberspace is, for him, '...just a gigantic, active, and *spatially navigable* database...' (p. 149) [my emphasis]. Concepts of flight permeate his descriptions of this navigation, as in his discussion of a hypothetical cyberspatial experience in which one encounters an 'unidentified flying data object' (p. 157) and his suggestion that leaving cyberspace should be facilitated by an 'autopilot' (p. 172). Numerous allusions to the TV series *Star Trek: The Next Generation* (pp. 158, 169, 178) further indicate to what extent his conceptualization of cyberspace is linked to a model drawing heavily on that of flight simulation, for *Star Trek: The Next Generation* relies greatly for its appeal on its mainly computer-generated visual simulations of space flight and space combat.

43 Alan Cholodenko, Introduction, *THE ILLUSION OF LIFE,* p. 21.

44 Virilio, *War and Cinema*, p. 86.

45 This notion of the Gulf War as a kind of logistical experiment is a widely held one, if not always characterized in these Virilian terms. Perhaps the most vivid, if unwitting, example of this characterization of the Gulf War comes from Georgetown University's National Security Studies Professor, Anthony H. Cordesman, in his 'post-mortem' of the war entitled 'Why We Need to Police the World', in *The Gulf War Reader: History, Documents, Opinions*, eds. Micah L. Sifry and Christopher Cerf

(New York: Times Books, 1991). Cordesman describes how the U.S. military had learnt from the Korean and Vietnam experiences both strategically and politically, so that it was able to perform with 'full political support' and in such a way that 'Every tenet of the Allied air-land battle worked. The system functioned at a level of perfection virtually unknown in the fog of war' (p. 479). This characterization of the Gulf War as a system functioning in 'virtual' perfection confirms Virilio's thesis about the ongoing logistical transformation of war and politics into 'pure war'.

46 See, for instance the *F/A-18 Hornet Strike Fighter* briefing window for the mission entitled 'Hole in One':

Location: Saudi Arabia: Omar Kiam Base near Iraqi border
Time: 6.40 am
Conditions: Clear
Destination: Mt Shatrah

Notes: Enemy forces are finishing construction of a giant cannon (waypoint 1) which they intend to use on a neighboring country's civilian population. Intelligence reports that a nuclear shell has been developed for this gun making its immediate destruction imperative. You have been authorised by the President to use the B-57 [a tactical nuclear device] to destroy this target.

The Presidential authority to use nuclear weapons in this briefing represents the vestiges of the strategic-political realm in the era of the logistical necessity of weapons testing and preparation.

47 I use 'supplement' here in light of the Derridean use of this term to conceptualize a paradoxical situation wherein that which seems additional and extraneous to the positivity (the pilot's vision in our case) to which it is attached is also a replacement or a substitution that affects (and effects) that positivity integrally. See Jacques Derrida, *Of Grammatology*, trans. Gayatri Chakravorty Spivak (Baltimore: The Johns Hopkins University Press, 1974, 1976), pp. 144-145.

48 Steven Thompson, quoted in Pimentel and Teixeira, *Virtual Reality: Through the New Looking Glass*, p. 41.

49 This '80s project is only one experiment into a virtual cockpit system. More recent investigations have, according to Virilio, tried to create an 'intermittent electro-optical display' designed to come up on a transparent visor before the pilot's eyes as and when required for navigation and targeting decisions, leaving his/her vision 'absolutely

clear of unneccessary signals' the rest of the time. The pilot would fly the plane by using vocal and visual functions, that is, '...by staring at real or virtual buttons and saying ON or OFF at the same time. This is achieved by an infrared sensor which scans the back of the retina and detects the direction of the pilot's gaze' (Virilio, 'Speed and Vision: The Incomporable [*sic*] Eye', pp. 98-99). In this system, the pilot's intermittently 'virtualized' vision is thought to be a superior mode of facilitating his/her operations in the logistical space of pure war.

50 Virilio/Lotringer, *Pure War*, p. 42.

51 See Virilio, 'Dromoscopy, or Drunk with Magnitude', trans. Noel Sanders, *Frogger*, no. 10, October 1984.

52 Davis, 'Visual Systems: Generating a New Reality', p. 28.

53 ibid.

54 Virilio, *War and Cinema*, p. 59. In *The Vision Machine*, Virilio identifies the ability of simulation to satisfy the need for 'foresight' as the element which links the development of visual simulation technologies to the use of other computer simulation models in all kinds of commercial and economic forecasting in recent decades. This need has arisen as a necessary consequence of the constant acceleration of the speed of the occurrence of events in all fields of activity brought on by technical 'progress'. Having noted that recent studies of perception have asserted that seeing is a 'kind of pre-action partly explained by Searle's studies of "intentionality"', he goes on to argue that 'If seeing is in fact foreseeing, no wonder forecasting has recently become an industry in its own right, with the rapid rise of professional simulation and company projections, and ultimately, hypothetically, the advent of "vision machines" designed to see and foresee in our place'. *The Vision Machine*, trans. Julie Rose (Bloomington/London: Indiana University Press/British Film Institute, 1994), p. 61. This interrelation between flight simulation and other economic simulation models only emphasizes the profoundly logistical nature of flight simulation technology beyond its apparent kinship to a tradition of training in the tactics of warfare.

55 ibid., p. 69.

56 In relation to the 'animatic', I am indebted to Cholodenko's elaboration of the notion of an animatic apparatus that operates in a manner equivalent to Derridean dissemination and Baudrillardian seduction, an apparatus '...which indetermines and suspends the distinction between representation and simulation...[and] makes it impossible to say which is which, as it indetermines and suspends all things'. Introduction, *THE ILLUSION OF LIFE*, pp. 21-22.

57 Virilio, *War and Cinema*, p. 79.

58 Davis, 'Visual Systems: Generating a New Reality', p. 28.

59 Randall F. Baker, 'Combat Simulations from a Distance', *Aerospace America*, vol. 31, no. 8, August 1993, p. 39. You can already network missions in games like *F/A-18 Hornet Strike Fighter* and fly with or against other players using a modem. There is a newer game based on the United States Air Force's *A-10* ground support aircraft in which players can coordinate their air operations with people playing other games such as a tank simulation. These games must have databases designed from a common database.

60 ibid., p. 40. The Global Positioning System—a navigation and location system using 24 geo-stationary U.S. military-owned satellites—is making the world itself into a 'real time', animated map, the counterpart of Project 2851. Like the spread of simulation technology across military and non-military areas, the widespread commercial adoption of GPS represents an accelerating confusion of notions of military and civilian 'space'.

61 Virilio, *Desert Screen: War at the Speed of Light*, trans. Michael Degener (London: Continuum, 2002), published as *L'Ecran du désert* (Paris: Editions Galilée, 1991).

62 See ibid., p. 131ff.

63 ibid., p. 52.

64 Virilio, *Strategy of Deception*, trans. Chris Turner (London: Verso, 2000).

65 ibid., pp. 17-18.

66 U.S. Air Force Chief of Staff General Fogelman [*sic*], cited in F. Filloux, *'Le Pentagone la tête dans les étoiles'*, *Libération*, April 20, 1999, quoted in ibid., p. 18.

4 The 'Expanded' Field of Animation

C. Animation in the Entertainment Industry

INTERTEXTUAL PERSONAE: CHARACTER LICENSING IN PRACTICE AND THEORY*

BEN CRAWFORD

Animation has enjoyed a massive resurgence in the 1990s. The Walt Disney Company has experienced a phenomenal stream of successes with *The Little Mermaid, Beauty and the Beast, Aladdin, Pocahontas* and *The Lion King,* which at the time of its release achieved the third highest box office of all time. Other film studios have attempted to take some of the market and expanded the whole market in doing so—David Kirschner's *Pagemaster* from Turner and Fox, *Thumbelina* from Don Bluth Studios distributed by Warner Bros., *The Swan Princess* from Nest Entertainment, Turner's *Tom and Jerry* movie...

Animation has also flourished through the roles it plays in live action features, not only as the source material for live adaptations of cartoons like Universal's *The Flintstones* and *Casper* and Warner's *Batman* series but in the animation techniques used in the special effects of such 'live action' films as *Terminator 2* and the biggest box office generating movie to date, *Jurassic Park.*

The 1990s have also witnessed the continuation of the flourishing of children's television animation that started in the 1980s, which saw new shows from the majors, such as Disney and Warner Bros., new animation houses (Filmation, Harmony Gold, Saban, Marvel, etc.), as well as increased American and European adaptations of cartoons from Japan.

Recent years have also disproved the theory that, unlike the

Japanese, adults in Australia and some other Western nations are prevented from enjoying animated properties by a stigma which relegates them to the status of juvenile entertainment. *The Simpsons* was the first animated TV show since *The Flintstones* to sustain a prime-time (i.e. adult *and* child viewing) audience throughout the English speaking world, and its success has been followed by that of *Beavis and Butt-head, Ren and Stimpy,* and others. In Australia, *Looney Tunes* created a beachhead into the adult market by audacious programing by the Nine Network, which in 1990 scheduled it in the 5:30 p.m. time slot as the lead-in to the country's highest rating news program. Moreover, such cartoons as *Ren and Stimpy* and *Animaniacs* have succeeded in appealing to adults with their content despite being programed in children's viewing slots.

However, I would argue that to mark the flourishing and success of these programs and of the companies that have created them solely on the basis of the animation itself and the ratings, box office receipts and new audiences achieved is to do these programs and companies an injustice. The merchandising created by licensee companies on the basis of these programs is also a massively growing extension of these animation companies' businesses, one which I would propose is likewise a credit to them and calls for acknowledgement and accommodation on the part of the animation theorist.

Indeed, when all sales of licensed product are tallied up, the animated and animation-related films *Batman Forever*, *Jurassic Park*, *The Lion King* and the prior series of animated features created by Disney are the highest earning entertainment properties of all time. And as for the adult appeal of classic cartoons and recent TV animation, there could be no more conclusive evidence than the sales figures of adult-targeted licensed products. I would claim that this merchandising is an integral element of these films and calls for consideration in any evaluation of them. This is what this paper takes as its project.

ANIMATION THEORY, EVEN FILM THEORY, IS INADEQUATE

Paradoxically, such an acknowledgement means that character licensing is not merely a commercial cash-in on the art of animators.

Rather, it explodes or mutates the object of Animation Studies. In saying this, I am not suggesting that to date *animation* theory alone is inadequate in not coming to terms with animation properties. Such a claim would be too narrow in its ambit. Rather, I am saying that to date *film* theory also has been inadequate to the task of analyzing its properties in their contemporary context.

The entertainment industry has adopted a paradigm which conceives of cartoons as one of a multitude of vehicles for capitalizing on character properties. Film theory and animation theory must recognize this paradigm in order to understand the practices informed by it. To do so, they must open themselves to wider concerns beyond the film or animated text. A new theory acknowledging the topology of entertainment merchandising is required, one that is responsive to the revolution which has occurred in the entertainment industry's approach to the products that it creates. This theory must embrace the disciplines of marketing and business strategy rather than what Film Studies and Animation Studies have done largely to date—rejecting these disciplines on the basis of ideological biases—and come to terms with such strategies as globalization, licensing and integrated roll-outs of themed entertainment and consumer products. The object of this new theory is intellectual property, a concept whose definition is an array of 'brand values' and whose extension is as diverse as the fruits of capitalism itself.

THE MEDIA AND ENTERTAINMENT INDUSTRY

In the 1990s, the various distinct media and entertainment businesses—books, newspapers, magazines, movies, radio, music, TV, computer games, online services, etc.—have converged into a single, monolithic media and entertainment industry. Multinational conglomerates of media and entertainment businesses have emerged, interconnected by common ownership or strategic alliance, with a particular understanding of the potential of their union founded on the principle of synergy and on the legal concept of intellectual property as an asset which can be exploited via multiple creative, manufacturing and distribution processes.

Thus, we have the litany of massive diversified media and entertainment companies that form the landscape and horizon of any serious inquiry into popular media and entertainment: Time Warner, Disney, Sony, News, Viacom, Bertelsman, Thorn EMI, Microsoft, Pearson, Reed, TCI, Nintendo, Pony Canyon, Bandai, NEC, Marvel, Philips, Capcom, DreamWorks..., and, based in Australia, Village Roadshow, PBL and Fairfax. Although some of these companies are much bigger than others and some are closer to the global ideal than others, it is clear that there are problems with the stereotype of a half dozen companies dominating the entire media and entertainment business. The truth is closer to there being 50 to 100 players in the arena. And in addition to these companies, there are collections of allied independent businesses which either team up with the bigger players or with other independents. Each of these companies has certain resources (for example, many own animation production studios, television networks, amusement parks, book publishing arms, etc.) with which to exploit the properties it has created or which it otherwise owns; but it must rely on other companies to exploit these properties where it does not have the resources (for example, in the manufacture and distribution of toys, apparel, food, etc.). Thus, the licensing or consumer product divisions of these companies (which contract out merchandising activities to other companies) are an institutional line of flight, an opening to the totality of consumer capitalism through which their properties can flow.

From an economic viewpoint, then, rather than an oligopoly of media and entertainment companies, we have interconnected networks of companies operating in an abundance of oligopolistic marketplaces. This structure takes us far from a free market model to a type of macro-new-industrial-economics model in which global strategies are played out through virtually limitless related tactical engagements, property by property, product category by product category, territory by territory.

The secret route to and measure of success in this industry is considered to be achieving synergies between multiple coordinated licensing campaigns, with licensors, product distributors, retailers and promoters working together to maximize the potential of a property. The coordination meetings for these are a conspiracy theorist's dream come true, with representatives of the film and video companies, toy and apparel companies, soft drink and fast food companies planning for next year's fashions. Yet, while the coordination of the global roll-out of a property represents a nightmare-come-true for anti-consumerist conspiracy theorists, it equally represents the efforts of thousands of men and women in realizing the potential of each property in an adversarial context.

THE THREE COMPONENTS OF 'SYNERGY'

The concept of synergy which underpins the agglomeration of these businesses derives from a modeling of the media and entertainment business roughly in terms of three functions:

(1) The creation and acquisition of intellectual properties.

As an example of a portfolio of entertainment properties that can be put together by one of the big media/entertainment groups, we can consider that of Sony's new licensing company, Sony Signatures, which features an impressive range of properties, from the movies of Columbia Pictures to Tristar TV shows to Sony Music Artists like Mariah Carey and Janet Jackson. Sony's product portfolio extends to hardware, of course, but also to sport, where the properties under their control include one of Japan's biggest—J League, the national soccer organization.

As evidenced by this portfolio, character licensing properties do not necessarily start out as comics or cartoons. Each media and entertainment vehicle can provide a source for those intertextual personae which are then diffused across other merchandise categories, for example, the toys Barbie and GI Joe; the children's book character Babar; the movies *Friday the 13th* and *Alien* and the characters in them; the arcade game *Street Fighter II* and the characters in it; the console games *Super Mario Bros.* and *Sonic the Hedgehog* and the characters in them; the CD-ROM game *Myst;* promotional characters such as the Campbell's Kids and Ronald McDonald; and of course, human celebrities, most notably from the areas of sports, music and acting...

(2) The exploitation of intellectual properties via multiple networked creative, manufacturing and distribution processes.

There is, of course, nothing new about the practice of adaptation of an intellectual property from one medium to another. The character licensing industry is over a century old, developing from a cottage industry, where single toy, apparel or confectionary items were produced and sold under license from animators, comic strip artists and celebrities. Early exemplars include the Teddy Bear, licensed from Theodor Roosevelt by the Ideal Toy Company in the first decade of this century; the Disney-licensed Davy Crockett hat and Mickey Mouse watch; and the PEZ dispenser, issuing sugar candies from the throats of cartoon and comic characters.

Today, licensed characters are the 'software' developed specifically for a network of entertainment and consumer product industries. They appear in cartoons, in live action movies and TV shows, in musical sound recordings and music videos, in console, arcade and CD-ROM games, in theme parks, and in stage shows and shopping malls 'live'. They appear across the gamut of publications from educational materials to coffee table books to novelizations to colouring and activity books and magazines. They appear on trading cards and other collectibles, in household and stationery items, on a range of foodstuffs, in all manner of apparel, in concept retail outlets, and in virtually any other consumer product category.

The advantages of this networking include: 'instant branding'—it is more cost-efficient to transfer an image from one product category to another and leverage its brand equity than to develop an image from scratch; cross-promotion—the presence of a property across product categories and across the media used to promote those products increases awareness of the property and hence (if the property is deemed desirable by consumers) demand for licensed merchandise; and, of course, spreading of risk among specialist producers in each product category, minimizing the risk to the licensors and potentially ensuring them a predictable revenue stream.

(3) The adoption and adaptation of the management and marketing strategies developed by multinational consumer product companies.

Character licensing is only a small subset of the licensing universe. Technology, for example, is typically disseminated through licensing arrangements. And within the field of marketing, licensing of brands is frequently a component of franchising and agency agreements, allowing the international dissemination of those brands—be they Jim Beam, Playboy or Gucci. Licensing allows the owners of a property to maximize their market coverage without the cost of creating a multinational distribution infrastructure.

The current state of the haute couture industry represents a possible model for understanding the direction in which the animation industry is moving. Originally in the business of supplying exclusive tailored garments to the wealthy, such companies now earn the vast majority of their income from the broader market ready-to-wear, diffusion and bridge lines of apparel, from perfumes and from licensing arrangements. In the world of prestige products, licensing typically takes place by way of an exchange through which the licensee is able to use the signature, and in some circumstances the designs, of the licensor in exchange for obtaining design approval on its products and paying the licensor a percentage of its income. In 1987, Pierre Cardin made around U.S. $125 million by selling his name to more than 800 licensees in 93 countries, who sold merchandise worth more than $1 billion that year.[1] In that same year, Christian Dior had 300 licensees, who contributed 30% of their total turnover; and Yves Saint Laurent had 200, contributing 68% of total turnover.[2]

Like the fashion industry, the character licensing industry has established a growing international distribution network, fed by seasonal launches and re-launches that take place in a series of trade fairs (the New York Toy Fair, the Frankfurt Book Fair, the New York Licensing Show, etc.). And the international appeal of each property is ensured through a process which the people at Star TV in Hong Kong have named 'marketization'—a balancing between global brand values and regional, national and local preferences. For example, in many Asian countries, Disney characters are closely associated with educational values, while in Europe, the same characters are generally marketed as a fun diversion unrelated to learning. And while most characters from Warner Bros. and Disney animation may be appreciated in Islamic cultures, Porky Pig and *Winnie the Pooh* (which, of course, features Piglet) are not marketed in Moslem countries, as pigs are regarded by those nations as totally unacceptable as entertainment.

Marketization is taken so seriously by some licensors that it can even affect the actual costuming and graphic design of licensed characters. In Australia in 1994, international comic publisher Egmont introduced a Looney Tunes comic, *What's Up, Doc?*, which featured Bugs Bunny and Daffy Duck outfitted as American teen stereotypes—basketballers, rappers, surfers and skaters—to sell these characters to Australian children obsessed with Americana. During the same year, Warner Bros. Consumer Products entered into a cross-licensing arrangement with the Australian Rugby League, with artwork developed representing the Looney Tunes characters (even Tweetie Pie!) as a tough rugby squad, capitalizing on their popularity with adult males to add a fun, 'Hollywood' element to Australia's most popular sport. Meanwhile, in the board books using the Tiny Toons characters produced by Shogakukan in Japan, Hamton and his pals take on the distinctive exaggerated wide eyes and facial expressions typical of characters in local *manga* and *anime*.

CHARACTER MERCHANDISING, MARKETING AND BUSINESS STRATEGIES

Certain of the specific marketing and business strategies of character licensors are worthy of more detailed analysis. Such analysis is facilitated by making use of the Product Lifecycle theory, particularly as it has been applied to a phenomenon closely related to licensing properties—celebrities—in the book *High Visibility*, by distinguished marketing theorist Philip Kotler in collaboration with Communications Studies theorists Irving J. Rein and Martin R. Stoller.

The lifecycle pattern, comprising various permutations of emergence, growth, maturity and decline, applies to all marketed goods and services. In applying the concept to celebrity, the authors identified six career path patterns:[3]

(1) Steady-rise-to-the-top pattern. Cary Grant and David Ogilvy are examples.

(2) Overnight pattern. Neil Armstrong and Corazon Aquino are examples.

(3) Two-step pattern. Moving first to fame for a specialized audience, then later to fame for a mass audience. The careers of Willie Nelson and Bob Dole are examples.

(4) Meteor pattern. From obscurity to fame and back again. Rita Jenrette is the example. (If you cannot recollect Ms. Jenrette, that is precisely because of her 'meteor pattern' celebrity lifecycle.)

(5) Phoenix pattern. The example given is Tina Turner.

(6) Wave pattern. Deng Xiao Ping is an example.

Their argument that celebrity careers can be mapped in this way can clearly be extended to include entertainment properties, with a number of possible interpretations for the patterns they propose. The patterns can be viewed as mapping popularity or, more concretely, sales over time or market share (the proportion or percentage of total sales in a market attributable to a single property) over time. Alternatively, they could chart shifts between classes of consumers over time. For example, we might have collectors at the top and the mass market at the bottom of the x axis; or we might have different demographics, with adults at the top, teens in the centre and infants at the bottom of the axis.

Strategies employed to maximize popularity, sales or market share include licensors demanding increasingly large commitments from licensees, in terms of both non-refundable advances against royalties and promotional 'spends', to guarantee that merchandise sells through to the public. In many cases, some degree of training is now also provided by licensors to achieve these ends. These marketing efforts on the part of licensees not only operate as promotion for the TV cartoon or animated feature produced by the licensor. They also spread the potential earnings from a property across an abundance of product categories, reducing the licensor's reliance on the success of the filmed animation itself for funding its own development. This result is at best a win/win, at worst a win/lose, scenario for licensors and licensees, respectively.

Similarly, when it comes to reaching different markets over time, there is a dual motivation: firstly, to remain in the most profitable markets as long as possible; and secondly, to support the property as best as possible through its shifts from market to market. Certain such shifts, such as trickle down by age, appear virtually inevitable for some properties, with Teenage Mutant Ninja Turtles as an obvious example. The Turtles existed first in an underground comic book, appealing principally to teens and twenty-somethings. Throughout their career, their audience dropped in age, down to the pre-schoolers who now constitute their major market. Juvenile versions of other properties, such as *Disney Babies*, *Muppet Babies*, *Tiny Toons*, *Ultraman Kids*, etc., have been introduced to capitalize on the lucrative pre-school market and establish brand loyalty at a young age.

The techniques employed to maintain market positioning, to reach new markets and to sustain and increase hotness within character properties may involve developing the characters themselves—as the very successful personality change of Daffy Duck from Bob Clampett's and Tex Avery's manic/psychotic to Chuck Jones' frustrated/tempestuous shifted him from being a figure of awe for amateur surrealists to a global icon for those all too familiar with short tempers. Another example of this concept regeneration is the latest incarnation of the once shy and bland Casper the Friendly Ghost as an exuberant eight year old boy in the Universal Pictures movie. Since these regenerations are not always successful (think, for example, of the lacklustre big screen comebacks of Dick Tracy and The Jetsons), testing and refinement of properties has become a constant in their marketing.

PROTECTION OF INTELLECTUAL PROPERTY BY LAW

Protection of intellectual property by law is a crucial component of translating this creativity into profitable business strategies. No one who follows the news can have failed to witness the pressure placed on Western governments by their business constituents to force other countries to adopt and enforce laws to protect intellectual property. Nor can any realist fail to foresee that the single most crucial development that we will encounter in the harnessing of the commercial power of the internet over the next few years will be the rigid enforcement of copyright laws, clearing out the 'anarchic, amateur' *otaku* sites that have so captured the imaginations of utopian socialist media theorists. And, crucially for licensing purposes, it is necessary in countries operating under the Westminster system that this protection of intellectual property be extended in scope beyond the tort of passing off recognized by the common law. Thus, we not only have John Moore, ex-Warner Bros. Consumer Products Vice President Asia Pacific, praising the 1994 changes to Australia's Trade Marks Act, which made flavours, fragrances and other properties subject to legal protection. We also have the Character Licensing Act, which allows licensors to retain copyright in products which they license but do not produce themselves—a protection not offered in common law in this country. Yet, while the law supports the efforts of the media and entertainment industry to protect its intellectual property, it also regulates the industry, frequently under the influence of lobbyists and self-elected experts opposed to its flourishing.

EVALUATION OF THE VILIFICATION OF MERCHANDISING

Condemnation, indeed vilification, of merchandising and of children's marketing, entertainment and consumer culture is widespread in academic writing and journalism. These criticisms are discussed at length in the two most comprehensive scholarly studies of licensing in the toy industry to date: Ellen Seiter's *Sold Separately*[4] and Stephen Kline's *Out of the Garden*.[5] Both bring arguments to bear against such criticisms, but both remain hampered by the conceptual frameworks of the debate in which they engage. I will discuss their arguments and criticize these frameworks in a review of the seven main grounds for condemnation of merchandising and children's marketing:

(1) *Bad Taste.* Merchandising is viewed as kitsch, lowering the aesthetics of entertainment, apparel and household items to the cheapened level of advertising. The underlying assumption here is that there is a hierarchy of taste which extends from what is taken to be the lowest of cultural forms—advertising—to the highest ones, which embody loftier aims than selling, such as education and the imparting of spiritual values.

A classic exemplar of this condemnation is Tom Engelhardt's 'The Shortcake Strategy'.[6] This essay focuses on the creation of properties based on information gleaned from market research with the specific aim of exploiting the properties through toys with TV tie-ins. Engelhardt names this the 'Strawberry Shortcake Strategy' after one of the many girls' properties devised in the 1980s by a company called Those Characters from Cleveland, which also included the Care Bears, My Little Pony and Rainbow Brite.

Engelhardt's many criticisms of these girls' properties include their use of grating, sentimental, syrupy characters, storylines and dialogue and their debasement of the very nature of character, which he claims has been perversely

> ...born free of its specific structure in a myth, fairy tale, story, or even cartoon, and instead embedded...in a consortium of busy manufacturers whose goals are purely and simply to profit by multiplying the image itself in any way that conceivably will make money.[7]

As Ellen Seiter points out, Engelhardt's criticisms are in fact evaluations based on an inherited canon which privileges men while at the same time claiming a universalism of value and taste. Eschewing this canon, Those Characters from Cleveland (and companies like it) founded such properties as Strawberry Shortcake on detailed research into the attitudes and desires of young girls, which are incarnated and valorized in the properties. The cartoons using the properties, writes Seiter,

> [reached out] to the audience of little girls, and...this necessitated changing and adapting the conventions of the cartoon in significant ways.
>
> ...marketing for girls...created fictional worlds in which females were dominant. It...offered much more than the literary and media fare in which girls are nearly always required to identify with boys and men.[8]

In short, in their very failure to meet existing standards of 'good taste' and 'good entertainment', these properties for Seiter met the previously unrecognized demands of a subaltern social group.

Seiter draws on Pierre Bourdieu's work *Distinction*, which states that 'Taste classifies, and it classifies the classifier'.[9] She notes that criticism of the consumption patterns of subaltern social groups has a long tradition—both from the right, which views such 'hedonism' as a moral lapse, and from the Marxian left, whose literature of 'commodity fetishism' argues that capitalism blinds consumers to the authentic use-value and means of production of goods, depriving them of a true political understanding of their society. She argues, after Bourdieu, that such critiques flow from and re-enforce the ideology of dominant classes—of intellectuals, the middle class and adults—by attacking the consumption patterns of the less educated, poorer, and crucially, younger members of society. Such critiques seek not to comprehend the values of these groups but rather to subjugate them in an assertion of the superiority of the unquestioned values of the critics themselves.

(2) *False Consciousness.* Ideological criticism claims that merchandising falsely imbues mass-produced goods with an 'artificial' meaning, one that seeks to encourage conflict resolution through such undesirable and erroneous means as violence, gender stereotyping and other scenarios and attitudes portrayed and promoted in cartoons and entertainment properties. Such criticisms are sustained by Marxian theories of use-value and the determination of value in terms of production and by such doctrines as pacifism and feminism.

An argument against these claims can be mounted following the logic presented in Point One above. When successful, entertainment properties for young children meet needs of those young children which are not delimited by the strictures of feminist, pacifist or Marxian thought. Market research-based entertainment can enable children to experience their own world views through cultural artefacts which they do not have the power to create themselves. It also provides a common, peer culture, fostering a sense of community for young children that is otherwise restricted through family and other institutional power structures.

As for the claims that licensed characters represent 'false consciousness', occulting the true utilitarian value (or lack of value) or production cost of a T-shirt, pencil case or fashion doll, these proposals simply fail to come to terms with the fact that the human world is a world of symbolic values in which utilitarianism and cost accounting hold no position of natural privilege over any other system of meaning. The fatuousness of claims that a character design (or designer logo) printed on an item does not 'really' increase the value of that item can be made apparent with a comparison with the book publishing industry, which 'in the final instance' may be taken to be nothing more than paper converting—the production of interchangeable books, differentiated only by what (typographical) characters are printed on them.

(3) *Morally Corrupting.* Leisure and entertainment products are frequently viewed as 'corrupting', influencing children in particular in an undesirable manner, creating irrational consumerist desires which demand expensive clothes, new toys and junk food. These 'corrupting' effects are frequently contrasted both with the assumed innocence and natural imaginativeness of children and with the socially desirable effects assumed to result from traditional and educational products and activities.

Again, Seiter provides a compelling argument against this demonizing view as a 'smokescreen for elitism'.[10] Objecting to mass-marketed licensing properties for children, critics praise educational and traditional stories and toys, which, far from being exempted from consumerism, are ideas and products now produced for and marketed to parents, specifically, educated, upper-class parents, for whom these ideas and products are directly responsive to their values and assumptions. Seiter writes:

> What I wish to challenge here is the notion that total resistance to the commercialization of childhood by buying only 'quality' toys is possible. Instead, this route consists of participation in an *alternative* market that is in many ways equally manipulative and 'overcommercialized'. That alternative is more elite and its advertising and retailing more 'refined' in that it continually lays claim to higher aspirations. But it is a market nonetheless.[11]

To extend Seiter's argument beyond the category of toys, I would suggest that 'free imagination', the innocence of children and even anti-consumerism itself are values easily recuperated by business through intellectual properties, such as Montessori educational philosophies; 'quality' children's books and television shows informed by 'traditional family values' (as evidenced by George Bush Sr.'s famous preference for *The Waltons* over *The Simpsons*); and anti-consumerism music recordings, from Joni Mitchell's 'Big Yellow Taxi' to Crass' 'i ain't thick (it's just a trick)'.

(4) *Cultural Imperialism.* Mass-marketed entertainment properties are criticized for usurping the role played by traditional, national, regional, local and minority cultural forms, replacing them with the contrived output of Western, mostly American, minds that convey the values of their own particular capitalist culture. Globalization is perhaps the most feared and despised element of the current regime of entertainment and media companies, as it is thought to bring with it a homogenization of culture, particularly in an American style—although resentment of other mass-merchandised cultures, including those emanating from Japan and even Australia, also exists. Of course, such hatred of cultural globalization is very frequently little more than an expression of xenophobia and a conservative distrust of change.

By way of contrast, the Enlightenment ideal of cosmopolitanism remains in the enthusiasm for global 'marketization'. This would be not the parody of globalization—Coca-Colonization—that its opponents fall back on but rather a coexistence of local and global cultures, which is articulated, for example, in the kimonos emblazoned with *Fantasia* logos worn by children who perform at Tokyo Disneyland. (In fact, the management at EuroDisney might well have enjoyed smoother staff relations had they not insisted on American cotton-tail-style regulation underwear for their staff but instead allowed them to wear French lingerie on the condition that it bore Disney character emblems.)

As another example of the articulation of the local with the global, Japan's *Shonen Jump*—its 6 million weekly circulation making it the highest selling periodical in the world—was the launch vehicle for the property *Slam Dunk*, one of the publisher Shueisha's most successful properties. The property draws on the international basketball craze, which is largely the result of the superb marketing effort of the NBA, but is set in a *Hoosiers*-style competition among Japanese high schools. Far from being a foreign distraction from kendo classes, *Slam Dunk* is a uniquely Japanese property exported throughout Asia, where it competes successfully with properties from all over the world.

(5) *Exploitation.* Advertising and merchandising programs are condemned on the basis that they take advantage of the lack of critical faculties of children, of the parental urge to provide for their offspring and of widespread parental negligence. Such criticisms are underpinned by a presumption of superiority not only over children 'too young to know better' but also over their parents. For example, in Australia, lobby groups attempted to have the cartoon of Teenage Mutant Ninja Turtles banned from children's programing slots on the basis that it is an advertisement for toys, and thus somehow a lesser form of entertainment. This charge was rejected by the Australian Broadcasting Authority, which does nonetheless apply strict limits to the number and type of advertisements available during children's allocated viewing hours.

Such lobbying and regulation efforts have initiated clinical and field research into the issue of whether children are able to comprehend the difference between advertisements and entertainment programing. But I would propose that a similar effort has clearly been lacking in assessing whether such differences actually exist, whether the Platonic distinction implied between persuasion and education is sustainable, and, if such a distinction is sustainable, whether the researchers, lobbyists and regulators are on the side of Socrates or that of the Sophists.

(6) *Intellectually Moribund.* Critics of children's entertainment associated with licensing properties accuse the properties of being facile, repetitious and formulaic, stunting rather than developing the intellectual growth of their viewers. This commonly expressed accusation (put forward in books like Mary Winn's *The Plug-in Drug* and Neil Postman's *The Disappearance of Childhood*) is disproved at length by Robert Hodge and David Tripp in their *Children and Television: A Semiotic Approach,*[12] which reveals the enormous complexity of cartoons. In this book, Hodge and Tripp propose that children are fascinated by TV not because it turns them into 'zombies' but because they are engaged by the complex blend of aesthetic, narrative, visual, verbal and ideological codes presented in such programs as cartoons. And in her empirical studies reported in *The Lively Audience: A Study*

of Children Around the TV Set,[13] Patricia Palmer demonstrates that viewing TV is in fact an active experience for children, one that is instrumental in their attaining developmental goals.

Beyond the context of cartoons, character properties are packaged with the many diverse qualities implied by the term 'character', including a 'back-story'—a network of intrinsic narrative and relational associations which consumers bring to the comprehension of any representation of a character. Even the simplest of licensed characters, the smiley face familiar from Have A Nice Day badges and ecstasy tabs, is drawn from a symbolic order with which the typically fickle and discriminating user engages at a sophisticated level.

All this is not to say that I number myself among those who would situate *Scooby Doo Meets the Harlem Globetrotters* on the same intellectual or aesthetic plane as *Remembrance of Things Past*. However, I have found that many of the writings which claim that cartoons are lacking in meaning and complexity suffer from these same faults themselves.

(7) *Challenging to Adult, Particularly Parental, Authority.* This criticism is that children's entertainment and merchandising incite children to demand or become obsessed with properties and items of which parents, teachers and other adults disapprove, thus creating tension within the family and the classroom. Every time I hear this criticism of TV, merchandising and advertisements aimed at kids, I hear the protests of parents, teachers and others who have traditionally been able to control children through coercion and exclusion from society as they realize that theirs is a lost cause in the context of a consumer and media culture which seduces their children and invites them to join in with it. (For a detailed discussion of these issues in relation to animation, consult my 'Saturday Morning Fever' in the predecessor to this volume.)[14] As Stephen Kline phrases it:

> The merchants and marketers of children's goods...are not discouraged when they discover that peer perceptions, the love of stories, strong attachments to goods, vivid imaginations and a lively fantasy life lie at the heart of children's conversations and leisure preoccupations. Marketing's ethnography of childhood has validated children's emotional and fantasy experience, which the educational researchers have by and large avoided and

> derided. The marketers didn't have to assume that children's daydreams, hero worship, absurdist humour and keen sense of group identity were meaningless distractions or artefacts of immaturity. Rather, they recognized that these attributes were the deep roots of children's culture, which could be employed as effective tools for communicating with them.[15]

Although he advocates the serious study of marketing and media for children, Kline is no apologist for those institutions. Specifically, he argues that marketing activities to children should be limited, on the grounds that the values of 'autonomy', 'innocence' and 'quality' are not served by the commercially-orientated children's cultural industry. Kline fails to problematize such values or acknowledge that they themselves issue from an opposing ideology unwilling to admit children to the consumerist world of conformity, experience and trash in which adults indulge.

As for the argument that working-class parents cannot afford the licensed merchandise children are ostensibly incited to demand, Seiter astutely points out that business has also done parents the service of providing children with a very cheap form of entertainment via television and with low priced toys and promotional premiums.[16]

In sum, I would claim that all seven main criticisms of licensed merchandise should be regarded as strategies in the process of contestation over the hearts and minds of children. These strategies draw upon political and intellectual values which themselves are exempted from the criticism liberally applied to the children's entertainment industry. I would argue that this vilification of merchandising by cultural analysts, which merely seeks to combat or evade such consumerism, should give way to a study of licensing properties that acknowledges and analyzes their power in contemporary culture.

INTELLECTUAL PERSONAE

In his 1961 study of the effects of the media on social perception, *The Image*,[17] Daniel J. Boorstin introduces the phenomenon of the celebrity into what would now be termed 'cultural theory'. Boorstin contrasts this phenomenon with the traditional hero: 'The hero was distinguished by his achievement; the celebrity by his image or trademark. The hero created himself; the celebrity is created by the media'[18]; and he characterizes celebrities as 'the reflected images of our own emptiness'.[19] In so doing, Boorstin ushered in a now commonplace ideology which holds mediatization responsible for the undermining of humanist values.

However, while multinational media and entertainment companies are frequently seen in this light as degrading culture, dissipating values, quashing originality and destroying authenticity, I maintain that their actual strategy is quite the opposite. Their aim is to employ the tools of marketing to create brands that stand out among the generics, to fabricate recognizable icons in the morass of images, to create value in their properties which can be leveraged to make profits. By means of their entertainment properties, these companies are a new avant garde, revitalizing clichés, creating the extraordinary from the commonplace and setting a leading example that others follow. (Indeed, the terms 'creative' and 'genius' are these days far more commonly applied to cartoonists and special effects technicians than they are to artists working in more traditional media.) The others—the 'me too' products, the cheap copies that take a brand and make it into a genre—constitute the environment in which new brands struggle to be born and in which they are absorbed once again. This effort can be mapped with our product lifecycle graph if you call the X-axis 'differentiation'.

I am not seeking simply to recuperate humanist values here within the context of consumer culture. It is not that the 'hero' still exists among the 'celebrities' but rather that the distinction between the two categories is no longer sustainable. However, the impulse for differentiation obviously pre-dates (and post-dates) humanism: the creation of difference and significance in an image can be expressed just as well in the medieval language of demonology and in the anti-humanist discourse of psychoanalysis. Pierre Klossowski has shown us this in drawing upon the theological concept of 'the collaboration of demons in the work of art' as a metaphor for what he calls the 'pathology' of artists and 'the obsessions, the joys, the anguish' provoking and provoked by their work.[20]

As always, Klossowski is instructive, here in his detaching of the image from the ideological sphere of meaning and reanchoring of it in the terrain of affect. While certain 'simpatico professors in blue jeans' and their flocks dither around the spurious dichotomy of 'effect versus affect', Klossowski, the cranky old man with the foulards, delves beneath the humanist moment in art to the basis of the power of the persona rendered as image. So, for instance, one could conclude, after Klossowski, that at the heart of merchandising and children's entertainment lies not the rejection of humanism in a festival of aimless effect but rather the recruitment of the power of affect liberated from its humanist bonds.

The massive resurgence of animation and flourishing of merchandising during the 1990s—while significant commercially and for the industry, the fans and the cultural theorists—do not mark a new era for the image. For me, these phenomena are useful examples with which to demonstrate a collaborative, corporate model of authorship, one conceived of as operating within strategic responses to competitive marketplaces around the globe. In such a context, a survey of the criticisms leveled at marketing and entertainment for children provides a decent forum for exposing the futility of attempts to sustain a humanist intellectual opposition to a society which has commodified intellectual and creative work as 'properties'.

Indeed, there is nothing in particular to draw intellectual dilettantes to the movies or to the concept stores these days, except for the spectacle of the accumulation of evidence for the disappearance of marginality.

NOTES

*As it was written in the mid-nineties, this essay makes no mention of such relevant latter-day phenomena as Cartoon Network, *South Park*, *Pokémon*, Pixar, *No Logo* and MBAs in Entertainment Business. However, its findings remain pertinent; and it still marks out some fruitful directions for future inquiry in animation theory and film theory.

1 The figures are from Deyan Sudjic, *Cult Heroes: How to Be Famous for More Than Fifteen Minutes* (London: Andre Deutsch Limited, 1989), p. 61.

2 See Gilles Lipovetsky, *L'empire de l'éphémère: La mode et son destin dans les sociétés modernes* (Paris: Editions Gallimard, 1987), p. 127.
3 Irving J. Rein, Philip Kotler and Martin R. Stoller, *High Visibility* (London: William Heinemann Ltd, 1987), pp. 109-111.
4 Ellen Seiter, *Sold Separately: Children and Parents in Consumer Culture* (New Brunswick: Rutgers University Press, 1993).
5 Stephen Kline, *Out of the Garden: Toys, TV, and Children's Culture in the Age of Marketing* (London: Verso, 1993).
6 Tom Engelhardt, 'The Shortcake Strategy', in *Watching Television: A Pantheon Guide to Popular Culture*, ed. Todd Gitlin (New York: Pantheon Books, 1987).
7 ibid., pp. 84-85.
8 Seiter, *Sold Separately*, p. 170.
9 Pierre Bourdieu, *Distinction: A Social Critique of the Judgement of Taste*, trans. Richard Nice (Cambridge: Harvard University Press, 1984), p. 6, as quoted in Seiter, *Sold Separately*, p. 46.
10 Seiter, *Sold Separately*, pp. 191-193.
11 ibid., p. 224.
12 Robert Hodge and David Tripp, *Children and Television: A Semiotic Approach* (Stanford: Stanford University Press, 1986).
13 Patricia Palmer, *The Lively Audience: A Study of Children around the TV Set* (Sydney: Allen & Unwin, 1986).
14 Ben Crawford, 'Saturday Morning Fever', in *THE ILLUSION OF LIFE: Essays on Animation*, ed. Alan Cholodenko (Sydney: Power Publications in association with the Australian Film Commission, 1991).
15 Kline, *Out of the Garden*, pp. 18-19.
16 Seiter, *Sold Separately*, pp. 37-38.
17 Daniel J. Boorstin, *The Image* (Melbourne: Pelican Books, 1963).
18 ibid., p. 70.
19 ibid., p. 84.
20 Pierre Klossowski, 'On the Collaboration of Demons in the Work of Art', *Art and Text* 18, July 1985.

5 More General Theoretical Pieces on Animation

Porky's Stutter: The Vocal Trope and Lifedeath in Animation

ANNEMARIE JONSON

The trace is...anterior to sound as much as to light...[1]
Jacques Derrida

The *Salute to Mel Blanc* tape in Warner Bros.' *24 Karat Golden Jubilee* video series makes much of Blanc's virtuosic voice characterization of Porky Pig.[2] Porky, often the naive offsider or comedic foil to the star turns of Daffy and Bugs, has one characteristic which marks him as the apotheosis, if not of Warners' characterology, at least of Blanc's work: Porky stutters, badly. He, of course, is not the only Warner Bros. star to be afflicted with a speech impediment. Blanc endows Daffy with a seriouth lithp, Bugs with a verbal tic ('*eeeeeer*—What's up, Doc?'), Elmer with a pathological inability to pronounce 'r' ('that *w*abbit!') and Tweety with an intractable case of consonant trouble. ('I *t*awt I *t*aw a pu*dd*y *t*at'.) Foghorn Leghorn's speech is interrupted by an involuntary tic ('boy—*I say*—boy!'); and Wile E. Coyote is rendered aphasic in the face of Road Runner's disingenuous '*Meep Meep!*', the motif that signifies the bird's effortless victory over Coyote's sisyphean struggle.

The very prevalence of the speech affliction in the realm of animation begs a number of questions. Why are vocal afflictions—impediments to articulation—endemic in the animated cartoon? What is it about the nature of animation that renders it a hotbed of speech pathology? And why in particular—since, in this instance the affliction is the character's *sine qua non*—does Porky stutter? This essay attempts to deploy Porky's vocal trope to think the question of animation, to use Porky's stutter as a clue to theorizing aspects of animation's conceptual universe.

My approach takes its cue from a certain analogous or homologous relationship in the conventional theorizations and definitions of, on the one hand, speech or voice, and on the other, animation. Speech, the voice, is ontologically understood, as Jacques Derrida has shown, as the condition of conscious life—the breath of soul or life itself.[3] Animation, too, is intimately connected to the notion of life. To 'animate' is, etymologically, both to 'breathe life into' and to 'give the appearance of movement' (*The Oxford English Dictionary*—hereafter *OED*). Yet, following a number of existing theorizations of animation and of the voice or speech—theorizations which challenge, or better, complexify and confound these definitions and their philosophical bases—I will adduce the vocal trope of the stutter to think animation itself not as life but as a figure that bridges the threshold between, reveals the compossibility or undecidability of, *both* vivification and deanimation, life and death, the animate and the inanimate.[4] The putative complicity of voice and animation will ultimately be revealed not in their co-plenitude, their shared life-likeness, but in the intervallic cut—the stutter or stammer[5]—which renders at once possible and impossible both animation and voice, as it imbricates animation as animism and animation as mechanism.

THE STUTTER AS WRITING

> *Stammer: v. i., speak...with halting articulation esp. with pauses or rapid repetitions of same syllable (OED).*
> *Stutter: v. i., involuntarily repeat parts, esp. initial consonants, of words in effort to articulate... ME f. Gmc* stut- *knock (OED).*
> *Stutter: Speak with checks at and repetitions of certain sounds...* stut - *'strike against' (Oxford Dictionary of English Etymology).*

Some brief reflections on animation and voice illustrate their intimate etymological and philosophical relation. First, the etymology of the term 'animation' returns us to early post-Socratic philosophy.

For Aristotle, *anima* (or in the Greek, *psyche*) (the soul) is the principle of animation, the principle of life: it is 'that in virtue of which something is alive'.[6] But what is of particular interest here is the correspondence of *anima* with voice. Soul is the condition of voice insofar as, in Aristotle's estimation, '...voice is a kind of sound of an ensouled [animated] thing'.[7] Voice, as the sound of the soul, is, however, not merely any sound made by an animate entity. Rather, it is sound made by an ensouled thing with a 'kind of imagination'. Since voice in Aristotle's schema is 'sound *with meaning*',[8] it is speech. Voice, finally, is inextricably linked to motion. Entities can only give voice when 'holding the air', since, Aristotle contends, 'as one holds it in one produces a movement with it'.[9] Thus commensurate with both *anima* (life/soul) and movement, voice becomes for Aristotle the sound of the motion of life.

Aristotle further distinguishes the signifying capacity of the voice from mere interruptions of speech, its nonsignifying perturbations. The cough or click of the tongue, mere sounds of the 'striking of air [breath] against the windpipe', are not voice—they lack the 'meaningfulness' of ensouled speech. In this, they are akin to mechanical sounds, sonorities that the animate entity shares with the world of inanimate things. As Aristotle notes, '...none of the things without soul [inanimate things] gives voice,...'[10] The sound of a musical instrument, for example, would be merely mechanical and unrelated to *anima*. Like the air striking the windpipe in the case of the cough or click, it would be sound but never meaningful voice.

It is instructive here to trace the etymological derivation of the term 'stutter'. Our epigraph shows that it derives from '*stut*', to strike against or knock. Like Aristotle's cough or click which 'strikes' air against the trachea, the irruptive striking of the stutter might be thought to enagage not *anima* but merely the impact of inhaled air—perhaps the mechanism subjacent to the *anima*.[11] Indeed, as Aristotle posits elsewhere, the stammer is merely a mechanical problem—a kind of machinic failure or breakdown—which disables one from moving the tongue quickly enough to articulate successfully.[12]

Aristotle's characterization of voice makes it possible to theorize the relationship of stutter or stammer to voice, and correlatively, to animation, on a related level. If voice is the sound made by an ensouled thing, an animate entity, then its brief absences—its mechanical interruptions and syllabic redundancies—perhaps advert to a correlative absence of life, an *in*animation coterminous with animation. Put simply, the periodic suspension or elision of voice would raise the corresponding possibility of an intermittent ellipsis of soul. The break in voice perhaps approximates an intervallic negation of the very 'animation' ostensibly evinced in phonality. Thought in these terms, the voice that stammers or stutters is voice inflected by the 'knock' or the 'striking against' which are other than the *anima*. The sound of the movement of soul—voice—is interrupted by silent interregna and repetitions of nonsignifying sound during which voice is ineluctably withheld, deferred and reduced to a merely mechanical, inanimated sonority.

This is perhaps to speculate tendentiously on Aristotle's postulate. Interestingly, however, Sigmund Freud also mobilizes the notion of 'soul', or rather its *suspension*, when discussing speech vis-à-vis the stutter. Equating the aetiology of parapraxes with affections such as stuttering, Freud refers to the stammer as a suspension, precisely, of the 'soul' of the speaker. He writes:

> ...speech-disturbances which cannot any longer be described as slips of the tongue...affect...not the individual word but the rhythm and execution of a whole speech: disturbances like, for instance, stammering and stuttering... [H]ere, too, as in the [case of parapraxes], it is a question of an internal conflict, which is betrayed to us by the disturbance in speech.[13]

Stammering, the disturbance of speech, takes place for Freud only in the *disengagement* of soul—the juncture at which soul is temporarily absent. This absence, while ultimately thanatic (redolent of death), of course is not immediately fatal. Rather, it is an analogue for the irreducible presence-absence that subsists in the life of the psyche. In Freud's estimation, parapraxes and idiopathic stammering arise from an 'internal conflict': repressed conative trends—*un*conscious desires and wishes—are conflicted with conscious thought, the place in and through which the soul presences for Freud, disturbing and impeding articulation.[14] Here, as in dreams and jokes (those other marginalia of conscious life), that which is *nonpresent* to consciousness—the radical alterity that renders the fiction of unified subjecthood and conscious life untenable—irrupts, vitiating the continuity or flow of speech's rhythm, differing and deferring its proper 'rhythm and execution'. Difference, here, inflects the 'soul' of articulation, as the unconscious inflects the presence of the conscious to itself.

This rupture or gap in articulation might also be thought as the diacriticity which shades for Derrida into the *différance* in the voice. For Derrida, 'full speech',[15] the putative 'presence' of the voice, is the founding trope of Western ontotheology. In theorizing selfhood, the metaphysical project has relied on the notion of ontological presence. The voice, the breath or life of soul, as adduced by Aristotle and others, becomes the paradigm of such consciousness and interiority.[16] Indeed, as Derrida notes, the voice has a pre-eminent relationship to animation thought as the 'life' of 'self-presence':

> Where does this complicity between...voice and ideality...come from?... When I speak,...[t]he signifier, animated by my breath..., is in absolute proximity to me... The living act, the life-giving act,...which animates the body of the signifier..., seems not to separate...from its own self-presence.[17]

Derrida's deconstruction of the ontologically animated voice and of the mandating subject will rely on an ellipsis—a gap or caesura immanent in voice. That gap or caesura is marked in his notion of *différance*, a figure of inscription whose terms—the 'gram', the 'trace' or the 'letter'—connote the primordiality of not speech but 'writing'. The voice, speech—what he asserts is the paradigm of self-presence in Western metaphysics—cannot so serve since ipseity and the putative presence of meaning themselves rely on an irreducible difference and deferral (of voice, of identity, of presence, etc.)—on writing as *différance*.

This *différance* takes, notably, the form of a silent interval—a break in the voice. What enables (and simultaneously disenables) voice, presence, etc., is precisely silence, absence, etc.—the '*brisure*' or 'hinge' of 'articulation' which suspends the terms' distinction.[18] Derrida names this intervallic ellipsis the '*spacing* (pause, blank, punctuation, interval in general, etc.) which constitutes the origin of signification'.[19] Elsewhere, it becomes for Derrida 'the silent token I must give'[20] in order to speak. Insofar as that which constitutes signifying voice, 'the difference which establishes phonemes and lets them be heard', always 'remains in and of itself inaudible',[21] the ideal of 'plenary' voice is irrevocably undermined. The difference which conditions voice renders voice and solipsistic certitude asymptotic. In the Derridean economy, voice is always simultaneously and differentially voice and not voice. The difference 'in and of' the animation of voice—or better, the diacriticity and adjournment of *différance* in voice—corrupt the living speech putatively animated in the temporal instantaneity of self-identical presence. The sound of the 'ensouled' thing is henceforth *primordially* vitiated by a kind of interval or arrest (which is, as we shall see below, itself deferred). This gap is (Derridean) writing.

We would ask: might not this writing, difference or spacing be something like the 'disengagement' of the soul/voice for Aristotle and Freud—perhaps something like the *stut* (knock/striking) and pause of the stutter? If the 'knock', a non-phonetic, meaningless moment like the click or cough, is redolent of inanimation (non-ensoulment) for Aristotle; and if for Freud the stutter is a symptom of the alterity which 'betrays' conscious articulation (the soul); then for Derrida, the stutter is perhaps writing—the 'death' which, he asserts, 'betrays' life. Developing the thematic of *écriture*, Derrida styles writing as precisely that which dissevers—'cuts'—voice (breath, life, *phonè*) from its intimate relation to animation. He states:

> What writing itself, in its nonphonetic [non-voiced] moment, betrays, is life. It menaces at once the breath [and] the spirit... It is their end, their finitude, their paralysis. Cutting breath short, sterilizing or immobilizing spiritual creation in the repetition of the letter,...it is the principle of death and of difference...[22]

Derrida's assertions appear to confirm our analogy between writing and the stutter. As the dictionary definition of the terms shows, the stutter or stammer is denotatively both a 'pause', 'halt' or *arret*—a 'cutting short'—and a 'repetition'—an iterative derangement of speech's normal 'rhythm', as Freud notes. These too are features of *écriture*. The stutter marks voice with ellipses akin to Aristotle's cough and click which perturb the 'breath' (the vehicle of 'living voice'), as does Derridean writing. The intervallic moment of the 'check' which conditions the stutter is precisely 'non-phonetic', as is the 'moment' of writing for Derrida. And as we shall see, to think Derridean writing as the stutter will bring writing in touch with the stutter not only of the voice, and indeed Porky's voice, but of the cinematograph, and with the death in its cut.

THE WRITING MACHINE/THE CINEMATOGRAPH/ THE ERASURE

Porky's voice, of course, is not a 'natural' voice. Rather, it is one mediated by the apparatus, by the cinematograph, or, as we shall see below, by what might be called the 'animatic' machine.[23] And even if cinema, or animation, its precursor,[24] have, like voice, an intimate correspondence with life and motion, then for Derrida both are conditioned (and both are animated and deanimated, as I hope to show) by the *gram*—by Derridean writing. Derrida writes:

> To affirm...that the concept of writing exceeds and comprehends that of language...presupposes...a certain definition of...writing... And thus we say 'writing' for all that gives rise to an inscription in general, whether it is literal or not and even if what it distributes in space is alien to the order of the voice: cinematography, choreography,...pictorial, musical, sculptural 'writing'.[25]

As Jean-François Lyotard affirms: 'Cinematography is the inscription of movement, a writing with movements…'[26] The cinematograph must accordingly be thought, first of all, as a machine which writes, and writes with movement and moves with writing. And the writing of movement, for Derrida, must itself be thought outside of an appeal to the order of the voice, the avatar of animation, presence and consciousness. Indeed, the scriptive apparatus for Derrida is theorized as precisely that which precedes, differs and defers voice, presence, animation, in the constitution of consciousness. The apparatus takes the form of a kind of primordial or prototypical writing device whose register as a grammatological metaphor for the psyche is developed in Freud's story of the 'Mystic Writing-Pad'. As Derrida remarks: 'It is no accident that [in his exegesis of the Pad] Freud...has recourse to metaphorical models which are borrowed not from spoken language...nor even from phonetic writing, but from a script which is...never exterior and posterior to...the spoken word'.[27] In Freud's exposition, which Derrida will subsequently acknowledge as anticipating his own formulation of writing as *différance*,[28] writing is *interior* and *antecedent* to consciousness and voice. Consciousness is written—never voiced—in the very process of perception.

In his 'A Note upon the "Mystic Writing-Pad"', Freud compares the perceptual apparatus of consciousness with the 'magic slate' writing toy. The doubled plastic shield and waxed cover of the slate are analogues for the system perception-consciousness. The wax slab beneath these covers, upon which indelible marks are impressed by the writing stylus, corresponds in Freud's account to the unconscious. Freud writes: '...I do not think it is too far-fetched to compare the celluloid and waxed paper cover with the system *Pcpt.-Cs.* [perception-consciousness] and its protective shield, [and] the wax slab with the unconscious behind them...'[29] To use the Pad, one writes with the stylus upon the celluloid cover, 'the depressions upon which constitute the "writing"' (431). To remove the writing, one simply 'raise[s] the double covering-sheet from the wax slab' (431). The inscription is now 'erased by an easy movement of the hand' (431). The surface of the machine becomes 'clear of writing and once more capable of receiving impressions' (432). On the wax slab, however, there subsist 'permanent...[legible]...trace[s]' (432) of the inscription.

Here, perception imprints its mnemonic 'traces'—the term is notable—in the unconscious, just as the writing on the celluloid and waxed paper shield imparts to the wax slab beneath a tracery of signs. Writing on the surface of the Pad is at once imprinted as erased and erased as imprinted. This chiasmatic interplay of impression and erasure corresponds for Freud with the periodic operations of the psyche. He writes:

> ...cathectic innervations are sent out and withdrawn in rapid periodic impulses from within into the...system *Pcpt.-Cs.*... [The]

> system...receives perceptions (...accompanied by consciousness) and passes the excitation on to the unconscious mnemic systems; but as soon as the cathexis is withdrawn, consciousness is extinguished... (433-434)

The withdrawal of cathexes interrupts and 'extinguishes' perception, as the withdrawal of the slate's cover erases the inscription on its superficies. Freud concludes his analogy by referring to his own earlier work on the psyche, dreams and the pleasure principle to show this analogous relationship. The 'discontinuities' in the 'current of innervation' correspond, Freud writes, to the 'interruptions, which in the case of the Mystic Pad have an external origin...' (434). The 'periodic non-excitability of the perceptual system'—the period when perception is disengaged—is analogous to 'the actual breaking of contact which occurs in the Mystic Pad...' (434).

Perception here is only ever periodic. What constitutes perception (consciousness) for Freud is not its plenary continuity but its interruptions and discontinuity—its intermittence. Freud concludes: '[T]his discontinuous method of functioning of the system *Pcpt.-Cs.* lies at the bottom of the origin of the concept of time' (434). The consequences here are profound. As Gayatri Chakravorty Spivak observes, the primary bastion of selfhood—the continuity of time perception—is definitively breached.[30] The appeal to consciousness is thrown back on the inscription of the trace. If the conscious retains no traces whose continuity would constitute a unified self ('The layer which receives the stimuli—the system *Pcpt.-Cs.*—forms no permanent traces; the foundations of memory come about in other, adjoining, systems' (433)), then henceforth, Spivak asserts, 'What we think of as "perception" [as consciousness] *is always already an inscription*'[31] [my italics]. Moreover, she contends, if the impressions of stimuli on the psyche 'lead to permanent "memory traces"... which are *not* a part of conscious memory, and which will constitute the play of the psyche far removed from the time of the reception... there is no conscious perception'.[32] The memory, the apparent *continuity* of selfhood, is always already the writing which antedates and is supplemental to the *discontinuity* of perception/consciousness (selfhood).

The writing machine, the psyche, becomes a device of the interval and the supplement. It operates a liminal interplay between the stimulus and the trace, the discontinuous and the undifferentiated, the break and its adjunct, the effacement and its writing, the erasure and the inscription. It mobilizes a systematic network of caesurae and their supplementary palimpsest of scriptive traces. Showing the startling comparability of the psyche, the child's plaything, the cinematograph and, I would suggest, the philosopher's toy,[33] Freud writes:

> [T]he appearance and disappearance of the writing [on the Mystic Writing-Pad compare] with the flickering-up and passing-away of consciousness in the process of perception.
>
> ...On the Mystic Pad the writing vanishes...and the wax slab... preserves the impression. (433)

To pursue the comparison for my purposes here, the Mystic Pad functions exactly as a proto-cinematograph, the machine which produces series of intermittent appearances and disappearances, 'becomings visible' and 'becomings invisible'—the philosopher's toy—which, like Freud's 'writing toy', sets in motion (and effaces) cinematographic interregna of the flicker. As Thierry Kuntzel points out, at the most basic functionally analogical level, the celluloid strip of the film could be said to correspond to the wax slab of the Writing-Pad. The Pad's covering sheets are a planar surface corresponding to the cinema screen. Kuntzel notes the relation between, on the one hand, what Freud describes as the slate's 'ever ready receptive surface' and the screen, and on the other, the 'permanent traces' on the wax slab and the indelible images on the film strip.[34]

The conventional description of the mechanism of production of the cinematic or animated image goes as follows: discrete, discontinuous, sequential images, printed and enframed on a celluloid strip, are propelled through the projector and momentarily fixed individually in the gate, briefly 'becoming visible' as light passes though the celluloid, the open shutter and the lens, projecting the photogram onto the screen. The projection is interrupted by the borderline of the celluloid frame, the closure of the shutter and the extinguishing of the beam of light—the image 'becomes invisible'. This disappearance is itself in turn 'erased' by the successive appearances of further images. In Freud's terms, the 'flickering-up' of consciousness is succeeded by its intervallic 'passing-away', an effacement which is in turn effaced (redoubled, repeated) by consciousness' (next) 'flickering-up'. Just as the unconscious sends out its intermittent cathectic innervations accompanied by perception, so the photograms which comprise the strip are periodically illuminated by the projector lamp. As the 'current of innervation' is withdrawn—as the shutter closes and the projector light is 'extinguished'—perception ceases. The on/off mechanism of the cinematic apparatus corresponds, that is to say, to this discontinuous 'flickering' operation of the psyche. It, moreover, corresponds to the repetitive inscriptions and deletions, or 'appearances and disappearances', of writing on the Mystic Pad.

Yet I would argue that the cinematic machine, like the writing apparatus, suspends this periodicity in favour of the supplemental operation of the 'trace'—the interval which blurs the systemic discontinuities. As Jean-Louis Baudry points out, apparent motion in cinema requires that 'separate frames have between them differences [discontinuities] that are indispensible for the creation of an illusion of continuity, of a continuous passage (movement, time)'.[35] But the illusion of movement depends on a further condition: these differences, Baudry observes, 'must be effaced as differences'.[36] Thierry Kuntzel further elaborates this relationship. As he points out, discrete photograms roll through the projector 'hidden from sight'; the viewer sees 'only the movement within which they insert themselves...'[37] Cinematic signification—what Kuntzel calls the inscription of *l'émouvoir*[38]—is located in a kind of tension between the photogrammatic 'cleavage' (the discontinuity or *arret* of the discrete images) and the continuous syntagmatic 'unravelling' (the movement of the film).[39] Kuntzel styles this relation as the 'interaction between stillness and motion'[40] *le défilement*,[41] or, using a term which recalls for us Derrida, '*mouvance*' or the trace.[42] Continuity and discontinuity are in Kuntzel's view inextricably and undecidably co-implicated in the cinematic text, a text effected by an interplay of effacements (discontinuities, erasures). The object of filmic analysis, Kuntzel observes, is to be found in the 'generation of the projected [continuous] film by the [discontinuous] film-strip, in the negation of this [discontinuous] film-strip by the projected [continuous] film, by the erasing work (itself erased) of the work of signification'.[43]

In Derrida's view, as it is articulated in 'Freud and the Scene of Writing' and elsewhere, the 'trace'—the mark, what remains, of the erasure of the erasure—enables this process which Kuntzel describes as 'the work of [cinematic] signification'.[44] It is instructive here to investigate further the analogy between the 'traces' of the Writing-Pad, the unconscious 'traces' which supplement the discontinuities of conscious (time) perception in Freud's model of the psyche and the cinematic mechanism. In the phenomenon known as the 'persistence of vision', the retinal impression—perhaps, the trace—of the projected image remains temporally coextensive with the period or interval of the image's negation, a negation effected by the intervallic cut of the shutter, the frameline,[45] and the repetitive mechanism of the projector's drive, which propels the film strip through the machine frame-by-frameline-by-frame. It is the relation of the persistence of vision to the frameline, border or cut which is conventionally adduced to account for the contrivance of motion in film.[46] The photogrammatic image is periodically erased, just as the iterative withdrawal of the top sheet of the Pad deletes the writing on its laminar surface, preserving the traces below. The trace or afterimage supplements (for) the 'absence' of the projected image (or the uppermost writing), insofar as it retains and holds the image-trace (or writing-trace) in reserve, as it were, deferring the image's (or the writing's) full erasure. At the same time, the trace or interval *defers* the projected image's (the uppermost writing's) plenary 'presence'. Thus, any image or inscription in this system is neither ever purely present and self-identical nor ever purely absent and non-self-identical but always already at best liminally present-absent; that is to say, it is co-implicated irreducibly with that now 'absent'/not yet 'present' image/inscription, which spatio-temporally precedes and succeeds it and from which it thus *differs*.[47]

But the trace, in Derrida's interpretation of Freud, is also itself effaced. Like the projected image as I have read it through Derrida, the vestigial afterimage is never an incorruptible or eternal 'presence' as Freud would have his 'indelible' traces be, and after Freud,

Kuntzel would have his film strip be. (One might think here that if the positive afterimage never 'disappeared', the filmic experience would comprise a nonsignifying simultaneity of increasingly superimposed images and not a continuous succession of differing images.) On this point, Derrida's analysis of the writing machine parts company with Freud's. Derrida writes, against the putative 'permanence' of the marks imprinted on the wax slab in Freud's model: 'An unerasable trace is not a trace, it is a full presence, an immobile and uncorruptible substance...a sign of parousia...'[48] The trace's fugacious commerce corresponds, rather, to the cinematographic 'writing' of the projected photograms—the ludic network of at once presences and *absences*, intervallic appearances and *disappearances*, inscriptions and *erasures*. The economy of the trace presupposes such an interweaving of writing and effacement. Derrida styles the grammatological (and correlatively the photogrammatological) text as comprising serial 'syntheses and referrals [of elements of the signifying chain or system] which forbid at any moment...that a simple element be *present* in and of itself...'[49] Like the projected image, or the surface inscription on the slate, the subjacent trace is inscribed—'presented'—only to be effaced—'absented'. Derrida writes apropos the Mystic Pad: 'Traces...produce the space of their inscription only by acceding to the period of their erasure... From the beginning,...they are constituted by the double force of repetition and erasure, legibility and illegibility'.[50]

For Derrida, death lies in this 'erasure', this cut. In his exposition of Freud's metaphor for the psyche, the repetitive erasures and cuts of consciousness (and correlatively of cinema as writing) represent the inexorable death which accompanies 'living' consciousness. Derrida asserts, evoking the infinite regress and redoubling of erasures effected by the trace:

> The trace is the erasure of...presence, and is constituted by the threat or anguish of its irremediable disappearance, of the disappearance of its disappearance...
> *This erasure is death* itself...[51] [my italics]

But death, for Derrida, is never simply death. Rather, the 'discontinuous periodicity' of the psyche and of the Freudian writing machine—the apparatus' repetitive erasures and supplementations of the trace—will metaphorize in Derrida's exegesis the compossibility and simultaneity of death *and* conscious life.[52] Like the 'death' which 'betrays' life in the 'nonphonetic moment' (the instant when 'living' speech is suspended or erased) or the *arrets* which confound the cinematic illusion of life, the momentary ellipses of consciousness described in Freud's metaphor and redoubled in the repetitive erasures of the erasure evince what might be called the deanimation at the nucleus of animation.

The chiasmatic on/off operation of the perceptual system/ Writing-Pad/cinematic machine recalls, moreover, the pauses and repetitions which define the stutter. We observed that, in Freud's theorization, the stutter represents the irruption into speech of unconscious conative trends when the 'soul' (conscious life) is not 'engaged'. His Mystic Pad metaphor affirms and extends our observation. The interstices of disengagement which characterize the stutter correspond to those moments, in the model of the Pad, when consciousness is 'extinguished'—erased—and the current of innervation 'withdrawn'. During these intervals, the *other* of conscious life—what we now know to be the repository of fugacious traces of writing and therefore, Derrida will argue, of death—is exposed. But these intervals are themselves in turn 'erased'. Life 'flickers up' again, cathexis occurs, just as the voice flicks *on* in the staccato on/off/on/off of the stutter. It is never, however, simply a question of *either* the on *or* the off. There is in Derrida's account a peculiar invagination of the opposed terms (the 'innervation' and its 'withdrawal', the 'appearance' and the 'disappearance', the 'on' and the 'off') which effaces the distinction between life and death. An engagement with the iterative, redoubled 'erasures' of the on/off as they occur in the psychic and cinematic apparatus will now take us to the weird 'lifedeath'[53] at the stutter's core. This trope will be revealed to be the very chiasmatic operation of life and death which Alan Cholodenko, deploying Derridean logic to radically rethink animation, names the product of the 'animatic apparatus':

> ...animation always has something of the inanimate about it,...a certain inanimateness that both allows and disallows animation.

> Animation therefore could never be only animation. It is both and neither animation and nonanimation at the same time... The animatic apparatus...suspends distinctive oppositions, including that of the animate versus the inanimate...[54]

DEATH/THE BLINK/WRITING/THE STUTTER

Freud's machine metaphor revolutionizes the metaphysical concept of presence and its intimacy with voice. Correlatively, for Derrida it serves to demonstrate the 'originality' of writing as *différance* with respect to that privileged term in the ontological lexicon which concerns us here: animation. How is this so? The notion of conscious life, and it follows, of animation (etymologically and philosophically understood), relies on the existence of a self-sufficient plenum of consciousness, a consciousness which requires no support or prosthesis external to its internal auto-integrity, a consciousness which is replete. Christopher Johnson has called this phenomenon 'a living continuum of presence, the conscious self or *voice* that exists without interruption…'[55] [my italics]. (Consciousness, for example, is conventionally understood to 'animate' the body of spoken signs in the plenitude of an indivisible present, hence the privilege of 'full speech' in the determination of ipseity.) What Freud's metaphor illustrates for Derrida is the essential *non*-integrity of this 'plenum' of animate life and its irreducible relation to the exotericity—the writing—which adumbrates and corrupts it.

The machine model will also exemplify the 'interruptions' that confound the 'living continuum' of voice. Freud's appeal to the model of the machine, which notably 'inscribes' the 'trace' in the psyche, demonstrates the utter dependence of the psyche on an auxiliary apparatus. This very reliance is the mark of the psyche's nonplenitude: consciousness/life/animation periodically 'fade' away.[56] The illusion of 'full' consciousness, of plenary subjectivity and of 'life' itself is effected by the work of a writing machine which represses and supplements the 'differences' of conscious perception, in the same way that the cinematograph represses and supplements the cuts or intervals of the film strip, and in so doing, creates the illusion of continuity.

But life's dependence on the machine-for-supplementing-life simultaneously confounds life: the autonomy of that which the machine supplements is thrown into doubt. As Johnson writes, 'how can that which is auto-mobile and self-sustaining [life] also require the vehicle or support of the auxiliary?'[57] Life does so because it is not—it cannot be—self-sustaining and autonomous. Life, to require supplementation, must lack (life). Johnson continues: 'The co-operation of "death" and "life" in the mutual...economy of supplement and supplemented inevitably exposes the essential lack—or death—at the heart of the supplemented party'.[58] Inner life is revealed as thanatic: conscious life and the 'external', 'inanimate' machine are coterminous. Derrida puts it unambiguously: 'The machine...is death and finitude *within* the psyche'.[59]

There is here an aporetic logic. If the psyche is not plenary life, if it is compossibly death, then the 'death...within the psyche' must be (cannot *not* be) compossibly life. If one accepts that life is not *fully* life because there is death within it, then its 'outside'—death, the inanimate machine—now irreducibly co-implicated with, now 'within', life, cannot be *fully* death. Life's (death's) aporetic logic is to be both itself and not itself. Derrida here further problematizes the distinction between the inanimate (the machine) and the animate (conscious life). The term which disables this dichotomy is the trace. The chiasmatic co-implication of life and death is the effect of the 'technology' of 'writing'. Derrida observes:

> Here the question of *technology*...may not be derived from an assumed opposition between the psychical and the nonpsychical, life and death. Writing, here, is *technē* as the relation between life and death...[60]

Within life (animation) there lies death (deanimation), and vice versa. For Derrida, the life-writing-machine is always also the (proto-cinematic) death-writing-machine. And if voice *is* animation—if voice is the 'signifier *animated* by my breath', by the '*living* act'—then voice is also inflected by the relation to the death which is life's compossibility: what Cholodenko calls the animatic, what would be the 'dissemination' of animation. Cholodenko, applying to animation the notion of dissemination—a trope for practical purposes synonymous with the logic of Derridean writing or *différance*—writes:

> Dissemination is the condition of the simultaneous possibility and impossibility of...'animation' as the fullness of presence, the living presence of *logos*, speech as a living, animate discourse. Dissemination introduces dispersal, deferral, delay, suspension and death, making of animation not only a productivity—something that vivifies and composes—but a seduction—...something that decomposes, deanimates, brings lifedeath—at the same time.[61]

Finitude, as Cholodenko evinces, is always already integral to voice, which (in the history of Occidentalism) 'is' conscious life—is animation. And voice's finitude is Derridean writing—dissemination, the interval, the trace, the spacing—which relates life and death.

We saw above that in *Of Grammatology*, Derrida claimed that the 'nonphonetic moment', the 'end' or the 'paralysis' of breath, the moment within speech which 'cut[s] breath short' and 'betrays life', is also the moment of writing. Derrida confirms in 'Freud and the Scene of Writing' that spacing—the trace—erodes the plenitude of speech, just as he shows that it subsists *in*, and bedevils, life. On the theme of spacing, Derrida writes: '[T]he pure phonic chain...is itself *not* a pure continuum or flow... [It is] always already distended by [a] minimum of essential spacing...'[62] [my italics]. Spacing—the gap in the voice, the difference and deferral of Derrida's radicalized concept of writing—corrupts voice's plenary continuity. As Johnson observes, the metaphor of the writing machine demonstrates that the putative continuum of presence *qua* voice is only ever a product of the interval. This spacing for Derrida is also death. The relation is made quite explicit in *Of Grammatology*. Derrida continues: 'Spacing as writing is the becoming-absent...of the subject... As the subject's relationship with its own death, this becoming is the constitution of subjectivity'.[63]

The point, in Derrida's estimation, is incontrovertible. He proposes a metonymic series: spacing is writing is death is the *break* in the voice—the *de*animation in animation. In the *Grammatology*, the originary gap which at once constitutes and *de*constitutes, founds and *con*founds, consciousness and life is rendered as a chain of substitutions and supplements. It becomes the 'caesura', 'hollow', 'discontinuity', 'cut' and 'cadence' of *différance*.[64] These terms are notable for our purposes. 'Discontinuity', as Baudry and Kuntzel show, is the difference, the 'cut', indispensable for the filmic or animated text and the creation of the illusion of life and movement. The 'cadence' is the fall of voice at the end of a sentence (*OED*). 'Spacing', Derrida writes apropos the cadence, 'cuts, drops, and causes to drop... [S]ignification is formed only within the hollow of differance [*sic*]...'[65] Voice's 'drop' or 'cut' is also meaning's *urquelle*, its source point.

Notably, the stuttering voice of Porky Pig also is cadenced. The great Warner Bros. animator Chuck Jones observes: 'Porky's voice always drops at the end [of a sentence], I don't know why, so when you say "you cat, you", that little "you" at the end drops down...'[66] Derrida's use of the cadence as the analogue of the intervallic 'drop' or 'cut' is salient here in elucidating Porky's enigmatic vocal inflection. The 'hollow' of *différance* in the cadence corresponds to what would be in Derrida's estimation the 'discontinuity' inherent in language, a periodicity which in phonologistic linguistics had, Derrida observes, 'run up against a...*continuist* prejudice'.[67] The linguist Roman Jakobson, however, had recognized that speech consists in discrete 'informational units'. Derrida writes, quoting Jakobson: 'These ultimate discrete units...are aligned into simultaneous bundles...which in turn are concatenated into sequences. Thus form in language has a manifestly *granular* structure and is subject to a quantal description'[68] [my italics].

The 'granular structure' or quantal discreteness of the units of language highlights the primacy of the 'hinge' or *brisure* of articulation as the formal structuring principle of meaning. Language, like cinema, operates on the basis of the compossibility or interplay of the on/off. Since the voice can now be shown to be conditioned by the same principle as writing—the anteriority of the interval—Derrida contends that 'phonology must...renounce all distinctions between writing and the spoken word...'[69] That is to say, voice relies on its cadences, as writing is conditioned by its discontinuities. The trace—the interval or spacing (for our purposes, in the flow of speech or cinematic writing)—Derrida writes, 'is...anterior to sound [voice] as much as to light [the image/writing]...'[70] Like 'full' speech, the 'plenum' of cinematic writing—its illusion of continuous movement and life—is primordially vitiated by erasures (themselves effaced) which simultaneously endow and withhold life and movement.

Derrida's invocation of the hollow, *brisure* or cadence which conditions language suggests the discontinuous periodicity of the perceptual apparatus described by Freud—the interplay of appearance and disappearance, the flickering-up and passing-away of perception, or rather, the passing-away of the flickering-up and the flickering-up of the passing-away at the same time. Another of Chuck Jones' remarks is salient on this chiasmatic play. Pointing to the fact that, like Porky's voice, the cartoon character's eyelid also drops intermittently, Jones observes: '[Cartoon characters] blink when someone's talking... That's big stuff. To establish that the character is alive'.[71] As in the thematic of the Writing-Pad, the intermittent negation of perception—in Jones' instance, of vision—establishes diacritically the *existence* of perception. The animated character which blinks, like the consciousness which periodically 'fades' or 'disappears', is 'alive' (and, Derrida would add, 'dead' at the same time).

As it does in the cartoon, the 'blink' or flicker has a key place in experimental cinema. And Paul Sharits' meditations on the flicker film further illuminate this relationship. For Sharits, the flicker film makes the 'fundamentals...[of motion pictures] explicitly concrete'.[72] By visually reproducing the punctuating action of the shutter and the frame-by-frame—by heightening the 'blink' or 'stutter' constitutive of cinema—the flicker film emphasizes the 'quantal' structure (to use Jakobson's term) of cinematic signification, stressing the discreteness of the individual units (frames) which comprise the strip and foregrounding the intermittence of the projections. The rapid-fire periodicity of the on/off/on/off in the flicker film is intended, for Sharits, to induce a state of heightened consciousness. He writes of his process: 'I wish to abandon imitation and illusion and enter directly into the high drama of:...individual rectangular frames/...the viewer's retina screen, optic nerve and...

psycho-physical subjectivities of consciousness'.[73] For Derrida, after Freud, the intermittence foregrounded by Sharits' art is the very *principium* of 'psycho-physical...consciousness'. Insofar as Freudian consciousness is the product of 'discontinuities' in the 'current of innervation' (in which ellipses, Derrida asserts, resides death), Sharits, I would suggest, demonstrates, by heightening the interval, the thanatic economies of both cinema and consciousness.[74]

But the blink which allows and erases perception, or indeed the flicker which emphasizes appearance and disappearance, perception and its erasure, perhaps most appositely recalls Paul Virilio's account of picnolepsy. Virilio's theorization of the cinematic event as a play of appearance/disappearance may be seen as an anticipation of his work on the brief absences of consciousness afflicting picnoleptics.[75] The frequent picnoleptic 'crises' experienced by sufferers are such that, Virilio writes, 'a little of...life simply escape[s]'[76]—or, one might say, a little of death interrupts life. During a picnoleptic interval, Virilio observes, 'the senses...are...closed to external impressions'.[77] One has here an analogue for the cinematographic moment of darkness, of *arret*, and for the withdrawal of the covering sheets of the Writing-Pad. After the attack, Virilio writes, 'Conscious time comes together again automatically, forming a continuous time without apparent breaks'.[78] As in the case of the bringing into apposition of the strata of the Pad or the erasure of the interval in the cinematic realm, apparent continuity is restored. And like Freud, and Derrida after him, Virilio argues that a kind of (picnoleptic) perceptual discontinuity is an intrinsic condition of post-cinematographic consciousness: 'who isn't, or hasn't been [picnoleptic]?',[79] he asks. The fundamental principle of the illusionist Méliès' invention is for Virilio the 'non-seen of...lost moments'—the *dis*appearance which forms, Virilio contends, the '*basis of the production of appearance*' insofar as 'what [film] shows of reality is what reacts continually to the absences of the reality which has passed'.[80] As what Virilio calls a 'mass phenomenon', picnolepsy corresponds in the waking order to 'paradoxical sleep' (REM or dream sleep). We live in a state of 'paradoxical waking'—a state of consciousness inflected by the fleeting picnoleptic (or cinematographic/oneiric) moment.[81]

If the picnoleptic moment serves as the model of perception from cinema on, then it has an aural analogue in the stutter. Picnolepsy's brief perceptual absences are accompanied by what Virilio styles, significantly, as 'arrests' which 'interrupt' speech[82]—precisely, I would argue, the stutter.

The psychophysiology of the stutter affirms the correspondence between the picnoleptic moment and the stutter's intermittent arrests and interruptions of the voice. The medical literature on stuttering compares

> …stuttering blocks to the minute seizures associated with pyknolepsy [*sic*]… [M]omentary and intermittent characteristics [are] common to both disorders… [T]he information suggests some common...developmental abnormality...that operates periodically to cause momentary neuro-motor malfunctioning whenever the system is exposed to sufficient stress to trigger the breakdown.[83]

Periodic neuro-motor malfunctioning. The stutter reads here as a momentary neurophysiological death. In David Appelbaum's exegesis of voice, the stutter is likewise a little death.[84] Appelbaum's extended meditation on the various tropes which inflect articulation returns us to our speculation on Aristotle vis-à-vis the stutter. Appelbaum frames the stutter or stammer as an 'interruption' of speech precisely analogous to the Aristotelian cough, only, in his view, more 'pernicious'.[85] Appelbaum evinces, as Derrida has shown, that the voice is conceived philosophically as pertaining to *anima*. It is conventionally theorized along the soul (life) or spirit side in the body/mind divide and is putatively complicit with intellection, as is the case for Aristotle. The conceptual adequation of voice and soul means that voice's relation to corporeality is reduced.[86] In this schema, the cough and stutter come to represent the irruption of 'incarnate' experience—and accordingly, mortality and finitude—into the realm of pure noesis corresponding with voice. Appelbaum asserts that the 'erasure' from philosophy of the history of the cough (and therefore of the stutter) 'as propounded by Aristotle…'—the negation of those corporeal tropes which perturb apparently seamless and bodiless articulation—'is a history denying death'.[87] Hence, according to Appelbaum, metaphysics' *refusal* of the cough, the stutter, etc., is such that '[t]he death of the meaning-intention [manifested in voice], its absence, its lack, is voided—and life, meaning, and mental focus made eternal…'[88]

Roland Barthes' work on the voice is also suggestive on these points. For Barthes, too, the voice is always already inflected by death. Barthes' notion of the 'fading' or 'laceration' of the voice parallels both the periodic 'fading' of perception on which basis the Freudian psychic machine operates and the dropping away of the voice invoked in the Derridean 'cadence' or 'cut'. These terms collectively disclose absence and death. Barthes writes: 'The other's fade-out resides in his voice... [I]t is characteristic of the voice to die. What constitutes the voice is what, within it, lacerates me by dint of having to die…'[89] That is to say, voice's lacerations—its tears or cuts—are also its condition of possibility. Its 'fading out', moreover, evokes the transformation from speech to the inaudible interval which for Derrida conditions speech—the break in the continuum of voice, reconceptualized in the 'science' of grammatology as the thanatic moment of writing, speech's intrinsic cut.

Like speech, animation, too, turns on the cut. The Canadian animator Norman McLaren, in a startlingly Derridean assertion, has remarked that '*difference*...is the...soul of animation'.[90] For McLaren, the interval—which he defines as the invisible interstice that lies between each frame[91]—is animation's primary ontological fact. He observes: '...the *difference* between each successive frame is more important than the image on each single frame'.[92] A reading of Derrida extends McLaren's insight here. The interstice of animation—the writing/death within life—would be in Derrida's estimation both 'an invisible connection...between two spectacles'[93] *and* a 'silent mark'.[94] *Différance*, he contends, 'eludes [both] vision *and* hearing...'[95] [my italics]. The trace is 'not more sonorous than luminous'.[96] At once the condition of possibility and impossibility of animation, the simultaneously vivifying and deanimating ellipsis of writing is invisible *and* inaudible. Porky's stutter is, then, perhaps the aural counterpart of those visual differences which for McLaren define the obscure art of animation. Derrida's radicalization of the ontology of animation renders, jointly, the animated *image* and the animated *voice* the aporetic products of the interstices which simultaneously bedevil and bestow life: the animatic. Paraphrastically, then, and read through Derrida, McLaren's assertion, which makes of 'difference' the 'soul' or life of animation, might be recast thus: 'death is the life of animation'.

* * *

Derrida laments in 'Freud and the Scene of Writing' the latter's effort to sustain an intrametaphysical distinction between the 'memory aid' (the 'external' 'lifeless' writing apparatus) and the 'living' psyche.[97] Derrida writes: 'All that Freud had thought about the unity of life and death...should have led him to ask other questions here'.[98] For Derrida, Freud's revolutionary insight into the psyche, his discovery of the unconscious, had prepared the ground for the radicalizing confrontation with the nonplenitude—the death—within life, a program which remained unfulfilled in Freud's work on the Mystic Pad.

To set in train the deconstruction of the (Freudian) 'logocentrism' which strains to preserve the dichotomy between life and death, Derrida prescribes, at the conclusion of his exegesis of Freud, a course of action: further attention is warranted to the phenomenon Freud identifies as the *lapsus calami* (the slip of the pen), the scriptive analogue of his *lapsus linguae*[99]—the slip of the tongue or stammer which discloses the erasure of consciousness, revealing the alterity which always already fractures conscious life. For Derrida, as we have seen, this alterity is refigured as the trace, writing, *différance*. The theorization of the *lapsus calami/linguae*—the interval or gap which cleaves intellection, corrupting conscious life—would for Derrida be consistent with grammatology: the thought of the trace, of writing, as the death within life and the life within death.[100]

Porky's stutter is perhaps a small key to the conundrum of the *lapsus*. Since Porky's voice is intractably beset by *lapsus linguae*—by the erasures and *arrets* of the stammer—now reconfigured, via our reading of Derrida, as *always already writing*, he is perhaps a proto-grammatological pig. That is to say, Porky's stutter—the *lapsus linguae* or gap which marks his voice with erasure—is also the interval or the *lapsus calami* which for Derrida is constitutive of writing, and which therefore speaks death. Animatic writing—death—has always already circumvented (Porky's) voice—(his) life. Like the cinematic image misregistered in the gate, revealing the intervallic frameline and momentarily arresting the animatic continuum; like the tropes that periodically irrupt in the patois of Porky's co-stars, likewise rendering their speech 'dissonant' and intervallic; like Freud's stammer and Aristotle's cough—the pause and *stut* is the moment of insubordination of *différance*, the *lapsus* or interval which exposes the death (the technology, the non-self-identity, the writing) with which life (animation, presence, voice) irreducibly coexists: lifedeath. If, in Derrida's estimation, ontology consists in the 'reduction of the trace' to the 'full presence...[of] a speech dreaming its plenitude,...life without differance',[101] life without death, then Porky's stutter (animation's stutter)—insofar as it hyperbolizes *non*plenitude, disclosing the thanatic interval—inverts, transforms and disseminates this repression, soli-soli-soliciting the m-m-m-m-metaphysics of animation.

NOTES

1 Jacques Derrida, *Of Grammatology*, trans. Gayatri Chakravorty Spivak (Baltimore: The Johns Hopkins University Press, 1974, 1976), p. 65.

2 See Leonard Maltin's cover notes to the tape. He writes in reference to Mel Blanc, and, in particular, to Blanc's voice characterizations of Porky and Bugs: 'The greatest star of Warner Bros. cartoons was never seen on camera...'

3 This theme is developed in Derrida, *Of Grammatology*, and Derrida, *Speech and Phenomena and Other Essays on Husserl's Theory of Signs*, trans. David B. Allison (Evanston: Northwestern University Press, 1973).

4 This is the question thought by Alan Cholodenko in his Introduction to *THE ILLUSION OF LIFE: Essays on Animation*, ed. Alan Cholodenko (Sydney: Power Publications in association with the Australian Film Commission, 1991), pp. 9-36, and in his '*Who Framed Roger Rabbit*, or the Framing of Animation', ibid., pp. 209-242, in which the relation of life and death is discussed in terms of Derridean dissemination, the *parergon* and supplementarity. The idea for this essay is drawn from these works, and especially from the following observation: 'Death... means the necessity at least:...to think the speech impediment of so

many major cartoon characters, which impediment marks their association with the stutter of the camera and projector, with the on/off/on/off of the "frame by frame" and with writing itself'. ibid., pp. 237-238, note 16.

5 Since the technical difference between the stutter and the stammer is negligible, and of minor interest in the current context, I use the terms interchangeably in what follows.

6 Hugh Lawson-Tancred, Introduction to Aristotle, *De Anima (On the Soul)*, trans. Hugh Lawson-Tancred (Harmondsworth: Penguin, 1986), p. 12. Elsewhere in this text, *anima* is 'the first principle of living things'. ibid., p. 126.

7 ibid., p. 178. Square brackets indicate my own insertions in the text.

8 ibid., p. 179.

9 ibid.

10 ibid., p. 178.

11 See St. Thomas Aquinas:

> It is clear, then, that [for Aristotle] voice is not the mere impact of breath such as occurs in coughing; and that the principal cause of the production of voice is the soul, using this air, i.e. air inhaled, to force against the windpipe the air within it. Not air, then, is the principal factor in the formation of voice, but the soul, which uses [the impact of the] air as its instrument. *Aristotle's De Anima, in the Version of William of Moerbeke and the Commentary of St. Thomas Aquinas*, trans. Kenelm Foster and Silvester Humphries (London: Routledge and Kegan Paul, 1951), p. 298.

12 See Aristotle, '*De Audibilis*', in *The Works of Aristotle*, trans. W.D. Ross (Oxford: Clarendon Press, 1967), vol. VI, 804b. As Fay Fransella notes, 'mechanical theories' of stuttering, like that of Aristotle, gave way in the fourteenth century to 'physiological theories of causation' and later, psychological theories. Fay Fransella, *Personal Change and Reconstruction: Research on a Treatment of Stuttering* (London: Academic Press, 1972), pp. 30 and 36. The relation of the *stut* of the stutter to the mechanism of animation, the cinematograph, is treated below.

13 Sigmund Freud, *The Psychopathology of Everyday Life* (1901), The Pelican Freud Library, vol. 5, ed. James Strachey and trans. Alan Tyson (Harmondsworth: Penguin, 1975), p. 147.

14 See ibid., pp. 94-152.

15 See Derrida, *Of Grammatology*, p. 69.

16 Derrida claims that for metaphysics, 'the voice is consciousness itself'. Derrida, *Positions*, trans. Alan Bass (Chicago: The University of Chicago Press, 1981), p. 22. He reiterates this claim in *Speech and Phenomena*, p. 80. In *Of Grammatology*, Derrida traces the complicity of voice and 'soul' (à la Aristotle) throughout post-Socratic thought, citing, for example, Hegel's account of the role of sound in idealization. See *Of Grammatology*, p. 12.

17 Derrida, *Speech and Phenomena*, p. 77.

18 On 'articulation' and the *brisure* as *différance*, see Derrida, *Of Grammatology*, pp. 65-73, especially pp. 65-66 and p. 69.

19 ibid., p. 68.

20 Derrida, *Speech and Phenomena*, p. 146.

21 Derrida, 'Différance', in *Margins of Philosophy*, trans. Alan Bass (Chicago: The University of Chicago Press, 1982), p. 5.

22 Derrida, *Of Grammatology*, p. 25. As Derrida poses elsewhere: 'How is writing—the common name for signs which function despite the total absence of the subject because of (beyond) his death—involved in the very act of signification...and, in particular, in what is called "living" speech?' Derrida, *Speech and Phenomena*, p. 93.

23 I use 'animatic' here in the sense that Philip Brophy and Alan Cholodenko use the term. Brophy writes in 'The Animation of Sound':

> [A]n *animatic apparatus* [is] a means for constructing film... which is based on an understanding of the processes of animation rather than the principles of animism...
>
> An animatic apparatus would be a similarly generative machine of effects to that of the cinematic apparatus, but one that is interested in frames, images, cuts and parts more as events and occurrences than elements or components... *THE ILLUSION OF LIFE*, p. 68.

Diagrammatically, Brophy asserts that while the cinematic apparatus has to do with the creation of the illusion of 'presence', the animatic machine effects 'absence'. ibid., p. 70. The 'event' that interests me here is the 'cut' of the animatic machine, the very 'frame'-line or interval that, as Cholodenko defines the animatic and its apparatus, deconstructs animation as animism as it deconstructs animism as life, presence and being, and which, as I argue below, is analogous to the interval in voice which is the stutter. See Cholodenko, Introduction,

THE ILLUSION OF LIFE, especially pp. 28-29; and Cholodenko, '*Who Framed Roger Rabbit*, or the Framing of Animation', *THE ILLUSION OF LIFE*, pp. 209-242.

24 Despite the unhappy theorization of animation, by writers such as Donald Crafton, as a 'subspecies of film in general' (Donald Crafton, *Before Mickey: The Animated Film, 1898-1928* (Cambridge: The MIT Press, 1982), p. 6), an historical investigation into the origins of cinema (that is, into the mechanical animation of still, photographic or drawn images by prototypical cinematic devices) would invert this assertion, such that, as Alan Cholodenko states, 'film [becomes] a form of animation'. Cholodenko, Introduction, *THE ILLUSION OF LIFE*, p. 22. (Also see Cholodenko, '*Who Framed Roger Rabbit*, or the Framing of Animation', *THE ILLUSION OF LIFE*, p. 213.) Richard J. Leskosky's extensive historical researches on prototypical cinematic devices similarly lead him to posit the 'historical and ontological primacy of animation with respect to the cinema'. Richard J. Leskosky, 'Two-state Animation: The Thaumatrope and Its Spin-offs', *Animation Journal*, Fall 1993, p. 31.

25 Derrida, *Of Grammatology*, pp. 8-9.

26 Jean-François Lyotard, 'Acinema', *Wide Angle*, vol. 2, no. 3, 1978, p. 53.

27 Derrida, 'Freud and the Scene of Writing', in *Writing and Difference*, trans. Alan Bass (Chicago: The University of Chicago Press, 1978), p. 199.

28 See on this point Derrida's reference to Freud's influence in the essay 'Differance' [*sic*], *Speech and Phenomena*, p. 130. The term *différance* appears unitalicized and without the accent in this translation. I have retained throughout the translator's usage when quoting directly.

29 Freud, 'A Note upon the "Mystic Writing-Pad"' (1925), The Pelican Freud Library, vol. 11, *On Metapsychology: The Theory of Psychoanalysis*, ed. Angela Richards and trans. James Strachey (Harmondsworth: Penguin, 1984), p. 433. Further page references to this work appear in parentheses in the text.

30 See Gayatri Chakravorty Spivak, Translator's Preface to Derrida, *Of Grammatology*, p. xl.

31 ibid.

32 ibid.

33 On the correspondence between psyche and cinematograph enabled by the Mystic Writing-Pad, see Thierry Kuntzel, 'A Note upon the Filmic Apparatus', *Quarterly Review of Film Studies*, vol. 1, no. 3, August 1976. Early animatic and proto-cinematic devices were known as 'philosophers' toys'. See Cholodenko, Introduction, *THE ILLUSION OF LIFE*, p. 23.

34 See Kuntzel, 'A Note upon the Filmic Apparatus', pp. 268-269. Since, as we will see, Derrida argues in 'Freud and the Scene of Writing' against Freud that the traces on the wax slab are not permanent, I attempt below to speculatively align the traces described by Freud not with the indelible marks comprising the film strip but with the retinal after-image.

35 Jean-Louis Baudry, 'Ideological Effects of the Basic Cinematographic Apparatus', *Film Quarterly*, vol. 38, no. 2, Winter 1974-75, p. 42.

36 ibid. Baudry further notes here the correspondence between breakdowns in the projection of film, slips of the tongue (which as I have shown are equated by Freud with the stammer) and 'continuity destroyed,...the unexpected surging forth of...difference'. ibid. This difference is treated below.

37 Thierry Kuntzel, '*Le Défilement*: A View in Close Up', in *Apparatus, Cinematographic Apparatus: Selected Writings*, ed. Theresa Hak Kyung Cha (New York: Tanam Press, 1980), p. 238.

38 ibid., p. 241.

39 See ibid., pp. 239-240.

40 ibid., p. 239.

41 ibid., p. 238.

42 ibid., pp. 235 and 239. *Mouvance* in the Derridean lexicon is a metonym for the undecidably active/passive economy of *différance* or the trace. See on this point Derrida, 'Différance', *Margins of Philosophy*, p. 9. Evoking this undecidability, Kuntzel denotes *mouvance* as 'motionness'. Kuntzel, '*Le Défilement*', p. 235.

43 ibid., p. 241. Since this interplay between discontinuity and continuity may be said, as a form of (neither active/nor passive) *mouvance*, to both/neither endow and/nor withhold movement, Kuntzel reaffirms here, as he had suggested earlier, that the object of filmic analysis is located 'neither on the side of motion nor on the side of stillness, but *between* them...' ibid.

44 See Derrida, *Positions*, p. 26: '[E]very process of signification [is] a formal play of differences. That is, of traces'.

45 The frameline should be here understood as the border that at once separates and joins the discrete frames of the celluloid strip, or as Alan Cholodenko has it, as 'the frame of the frame...the interval, the spacing between...' See Cholodenko, '*Who Framed Roger Rabbit*, or the Framing of Animation', in *THE ILLUSION OF LIFE*, p. 237, note 13.

46 Peter Brunette and David Wills, for example, in adducing the Derridean '*parergon*' to theorize the frame-by-frame of the cinematic and the motion effect, write:

> The term "frame" names...a section of celluloid whose successive repetitions...pass in front of the lens in order to project a motion picture. Two of the sides of that piece of celluloid are defined by preceding and successive images and the borders between them, and the other sides by the sound track and sprocket holes. In each case there is a type of otherness that works to constitute the entity called a frame [as is the case in the Derridean *parergon*]. The celluloid border...represents, in conjunction with the action of the shutter, the moment of... lack of sight that permits vision to take place, to the extent that it allows for the temporal overlap between the time the image remains in front of the lamp and the time it remains imprinted upon the retina. It becomes clear...that the...[phenomenon] of persistence of vision...require[s] a peculiar relation of presence to absence in order to function;...in order for the illusion of motion to be produced... Peter Brunette and David Wills, *Screen/Play: Derrida and Film Theory* (Princeton: Princeton University Press, 1989), p. 104.

The relation of presence to absence as an effect of the 'animatic' trace, as Alan Cholodenko names such operation, is discussed below.

47 Derrida's description of *différance* or the trace (as difference and deferral) in *Speech and Phenomena* is apposite, especially if for the term 'element' we substitute 'photogram'. Derrida writes:

> Differance is what makes the movement of signification possible only if each element that is said to be "present"...is related to something other than itself but retains the mark of a past element and already lets itself be hollowed out by the mark of its relation to a future element. Derrida, 'Differance', in *Speech and Phenomena*, p. 142.

Further, in order for this *différance* to take effect, an 'interval', according to Derrida, must separate each element. Derrida writes of the interval: '*Différance* is the systematic play...of traces..., of the *spacing* by means of which elements are related to each other. This spacing is the...production of the intervals without which the "full" terms would not signify...' Derrida, *Positions*, p. 27. The 'movement of signification' in film as a grammatologic form is, then, a product of film's intervallic economy, as Baudry and Kuntzel point out. The interval, in the Derridean lexicon, is also, of course, the trace which concerns us here.

48 Derrida, 'Freud and the Scene of Writing', p. 230.
49 Derrida, *Positions*, p. 26.
50 Derrida, 'Freud and the Scene of Writing', p. 226.
51 ibid., p. 230.
52 As Derrida writes elsewhere of the trace: '[T]he trace [is] simultaneously traced and effaced, simultaneously alive and dead...' Derrida, 'Differance', *Speech and Phenomena*, p. 156.
53 Alan Cholodenko uses this Derridean term in his thinking of the imbrication of life and death in animation in his Introduction to *THE ILLUSION OF LIFE*, p. 29, and in his paper in this collection, 'Speculations on the Animatic Automaton', in which the imbrication of machine and organism, the nonhuman and the human, is theorized.
54 Cholodenko, Introduction, *THE ILLUSION OF LIFE*, pp. 28-29.
55 Christopher Johnson, *System and Writing in the Philosophy of Jacques Derrida* (Cambridge: Cambridge University Press, 1993), p. 107.
56 As Derrida says in 'Freud and the Scene of Writing', p. 225.
57 Johnson, *System and Writing in the Philosophy of Jacques Derrida*, p. 104.
58 ibid.
59 Derrida, 'Freud and the Scene of Writing', p. 228.
60 ibid. Or, as Derrida writes elsewhere in the essay: 'life *is* death'. ibid., p. 203. As Christopher Johnson notes: 'The ultimate effect of Derrida's reading of Freud [in 'Freud and the Scene of Writing'] is...to displace the absolute distinction between internal and external, when such a distinction is applied to the "human" or the "living" as against the "artificial" and the "dead"'. Johnson, *System and Writing in the Philosophy of Jacques Derrida*, p. 107.
61 Cholodenko, '*Who Framed Roger Rabbit*, or the Framing of Animation', in *THE ILLUSION OF LIFE*, p. 216.
62 Derrida, 'Freud and the Scene of Writing', p. 219.
63 Derrida, *Of Grammatology*, p. 69.
64 See ibid.
65 ibid. In *Of Grammatology*, the term *différance* appears unitalicized and without the accent. I have retained throughout the translator's usage when quoting directly.
66 Greg Ford and Richard Thompson (Interview), 'Chuck Jones', *Film Comment*, vol. 11, no. 1, January-February 1975, p. 34.
67 Derrida, *Of Grammatology*, p. 69.
68 ibid.
69 ibid.
70 ibid., p. 65.
71 Jones quoted in Hugh Kenner, *Chuck Jones: A Flurry of Drawings* (Berkeley: University of California Press, 1994), p. 53.

72 Paul Sharits, 'Statement of Intention', Fourth International Experimental Film Competition, Knokke-Le Zoute, 1967, quoted in Regina Cornwell, 'Paul Sharits: Illusion and Object', in *Movies and Methods*, ed. Bill Nichols (Berkeley: University of California Press, 1976), p. 364.

73 ibid., p. 366.

74 The relation between, on the one hand, the *repression* of the cut in the film strip, which characterizes the everyday cinematic event, and, on the other hand, the *disavowal* of death is well known. As Brunette and Wills, drawing on the work of Baudry, write:

> [I]t is discontinuity that, as much as movement, is recognized as constitutive of cinema... In addition, what is...constitutive of the spectator is a certain immobility... [B]oth discontinuity and sub-mobility can, rhetorically at least, be related to death... [Insofar as the cinematic event conceals the cuts constitutive of cinema,] [t]he spectator...tak[es] pleasure in a privileged form of perception that represses its own discontinuities,... a form...in which death is...disavowed. Brunette and Wills, *Screen/Play: Derrida and Film Theory*, p. 116.

75 See Paul Virilio/Sylvère Lotringer, *Pure War*, trans. Mark Polizotti (New York: Semiotext(e), 1983), pp. 84-85; and Paul Virilio, *The Aesthetics of Disappearance*, trans. Philip Beitchman (New York: Semiotext(e), 1991).

76 Virilio, *The Aesthetics of Disappearance*, p. 10.

77 ibid., p. 9.

78 ibid.

79 ibid., p. 14.

80 ibid., p. 17. Virilio notes that the making visible of the 'non-seen' of 'in-between' states of movement, the anamorphic passage between forms, is exemplified in the animations of Emile Cohl. ibid.

81 See ibid., pp. 14-15.

82 ibid., p. 9.

83 Frank B. Robinson, *Introduction to Stuttering* (Englewood Cliffs: Prentice-Hall, 1964), p. 28.

84 See David Appelbaum, *Voice* (Albany: State University of New York Press, 1990).

85 ibid., p. 3.

86 ibid.

87 ibid., p. 26.

88 ibid.

89 Roland Barthes, *A Lover's Discourse: Fragments*, trans. Richard Howard (New York: Hill and Wang, 1978), p. 114.

90 McLaren quoted in Georges Sifianos, 'The Definition of Animation: A Letter from Norman McLaren', *Animation Journal*, vol. 3, no. 2, Spring 1995, p. 66.

91 See ibid., p. 62.

92 ibid., p. 66.

93 Derrida, 'Differance', *Speech and Phenomena*, p. 133.

94 ibid., p. 132.

95 ibid., p. 133.

96 Derrida, *Of Grammatology*, p. 65.

97 Freud had posited that the comparison between the Pad and the psyche breaks down insofar as the machine cannot, as the 'living' psyche ostensibly does, spontaneously reproduce its traces. See Freud, 'A Note upon the "Mystic Writing-Pad"', p. 433.

98 Derrida, 'Freud and the Scene of Writing', p. 227.

99 See ibid., p. 230.

100 See ibid.

101 Derrida, *Of Grammatology*, p. 71.

Animation 1: The Control-Image

WILLIAM SCHAFFER

IF ANIMATION BELONGS...

Attempting to specify the possibilities of their favoured medium, the great heroes of film theory have rarely turned towards the art of animation expecting to find anything more than a limit case or a negative example. A student of film theory with a passion for cartoons is therefore unlikely to be surprised at how little space it takes to quote Gilles Deleuze's entire treatment of the cartoon film in *Cinema 1: The Movement-Image*:

> Any other system which reproduces movement through an order of exposures [*poses*] projected in such a way that they pass into one another, or are 'transformed', is foreign to the cinema. This is clear when one attempts to define the cartoon film; if it belongs fully to the cinema, this is because the drawing no longer constitutes a pose or a completed figure, but the description of a figure which is always in the process of being formed or dissolving through the movement of lines and points taken at any-instant-whatevers of their course. The cartoon film is related not to a Euclidean, but to a Cartesian geometry. It does not give us a figure described in a unique moment, but the continuity of the movement which describes the figure.[1]

Beyond this, Deleuze has nothing to say on the matter—as if animation were merely a peripheral example, belonging passively to the motion picture machine without contributing anything of its own. But can animation simply 'belong' to cinema or do we need to differentiate radically at some level between animation and cinema as modes of film? In the very paragraph in which he leaps so quickly over the question of animation, Deleuze identifies the technical possibility of cinema with four preconditions:

(1) The instant photo or snapshot, as opposed to long-exposure photography.

(2) The automatic temporal equidistance of these snapshots (18 to 24 frames per second).

(3) The transfer of this temporal equidistance onto the spatial equidistance of the film strip.

(4) A mechanism for automatically moving and projecting the frames of the film strip at a speed corresponding to the second condition.

Animation may conform to conditions 3 and 4 taken in isolation, and we shall consider shortly the implications of this; but the necessity that conditions 1 and 2 be fulfilled in the case of animation seems immediately debatable. As Deleuze rightly points out, cinema would be impossible in principle using long-exposures, since it needs to capture at least 18 frames per second in real-time in order to become the medium of 'translation' for all possible movements. The same is not true, however, of the animation process. Despite the obvious and immense advantages of the snapshot for the working animator, effective animations could be created using long-exposures for the recording of frames, since the individual frames take the form of photographed drawings. This fact, never explicitly considered by Deleuze, has more than merely empirical consequences.

The drawing of a figure, of course, is never instantaneous. The time of drawing can never correspond to the automated time of projection. The animation process is in this sense necessarily determined by processes which divide the image against itself at the level of production. Each cel is produced not as an instantaneous perspectival unity, as is the case with the snapshot, but as a layering of graphical processes unevenly distributed in time and space. It may be true for animation, as with cinema, that finished frames must be moved and projected at a rate of at least 18 frames per second if a coherent and continuously moving image is to be generated; but there is no such requirement in principle concerning their production.[2] There seems to be no need at any level for temporal 'equidistance' in the production or recording of frames in the case of animation, even if these frames must be produced in *anticipation* of the equidistances imposed by the film strip.

It cannot, however, be a matter of merely subtracting the first half of Deleuze's formulation of the conditions of cinema—conditions 1 and 2—leaving us with conditions 3 and 4 to define animation as a 'truncated' form of cinema. Since the four conditions taken as a whole are logically sequential, the 'subtraction' of the first two conditions necessarily and radically changes the status of the third. Instead of a *transfer*, which refers to the movement of already existing bodies, as with the Deleuzian account of cinema, there is in animation a double movement of *imposition* and *generation*. From the point of view of individual cels, considered in isolation, recording onto a film strip involves the imposition of an indifferent measure; from the point of view of the moving image, this same process involves a pure act of generation, a veritable 'giving of life' to animated bodies.

These essential discrepancies between cinema and animation as modes of the movement-image render highly problematic any claim that animation 'belongs fully to the cinema', not only insofar as this belonging is empirically identified with the technical conditions already specified but more importantly, insofar as the very *essence* of the movement-image is defined in terms of the *extraction of the motion of bodies*:

> [T]he essence of the cinematographic movement-image lies in extracting from vehicles or moving bodies the movement which is their common substance... This was what Bergson wanted: beginning from the body or moving thing to which our natural perception attaches movement as if it were a vehicle, to extract a simple coloured 'spot', the movement-image, which 'is reduced in itself to a series of extremely rapid oscillations' and 'is in reality only a movement of movements'.[3]

What kind of movement could animation be said to translate? From what kind of body might the 'common substance' to which Deleuze refers be 'extracted' in the case of animation? How does the manual temporality of drawing relate to the automated interval of the any-instant-whatever, which, according to Deleuze, is essential both technically and conceptually to the possibility of a movement-image?

As soon as we would look to see it in itself, the isolated any-instant-whatever captured with each frame is automatically dissolved in a flow of perceptually effective, if nonetheless virtual, movement. Such movement has the *effective integrity of a whole*. (But it is, as we shall see, necessarily a strangely disjunctive whole, a *whole of holes*.) The any-instant-whatever of film, embodied in the regularly separated frames of the film strip, *deterritorializes* any single 'pose' so that it can no longer be simply identified with itself, no longer be contained or apprehended in terms of a fixed or closed space. In the context of the any-instant-whatever, each frame is instead automatically lifted out of its 'own' context and raised to a *plane of immanence* where figures emerge only in and through a process of 'universal variation' which no fixed form or pose can transcend or control.[4]

It is in this sense that Deleuze can assert that the cinematic image should not be seen as arising from a simple 'addition' of an abstract quantity of movement (afforded by the projecting mechanism) to 'immobile sections' (equated with individual frames). Cinematic perception is not a matter of incrementally summing up single frames in sequence. Instead, for Deleuze, what we see on-screen is as much 'between' frames as it is 'in' any single frame: an *intermediate image* that moves *intrinsically* as a function of the any-instant-whatever, that exists only in, and as, intervallic movement-image.

Considered from this perspective, the *animated figure*, always already caught up in the any-instant-whatever as in its own life, can never be definitively 'figured' on any single frame of the film strip. It is always 'opened' up to the next interval by the same force which would 'close' it in relation to the preceding interval: the force of movement itself as any-instant-whatever. Each figure may appear closed and finished at the level of the single frame taken in isolation; but at the level of the any-instant-whatever, it can never be simply so. In this sense, Deleuze can convincingly claim that in the cartoon film 'the drawing no longer constitutes a pose or a completed figure, but the description of a figure which is always in the process of being formed or dissolving'. Chuck Jones says more or less the same thing:

> One of the odd misunderstandings about animation even by those who work in the field is that an individual drawing has the same importance as an illustration. Animation is a chorus of drawings working in tandem, each contributing a part to the whole of a time/space idea. If a single drawing, as a drawing, dominates the action, it is probably bad animation, even though it may be a good drawing.[5]

The cartoon film may be based on drawing; but the animator's practice becomes unlike any other form of drawing, becomes, that is, animatic, as soon as he ceases to relate to the drawing taken in isolation and projects himself into the automatic in-between of the any-instant-whatever. Filmic motion, in the case of cinema and animation alike, is possible not because we have a machine capable of 'adding' motion to single frames but rather because these single frames are *produced and deterritorialized* as functions of the any-instant-whatever from the very beginning. Since Deleuze precipitously and exclusively equates this production process with the automated 'extraction' or 'translation' of movement by cine-cameras, it is the question of exactly *how* frames are so produced in the case of animation, rather than the reason *why* they must be, which Deleuze's empirically restricted formulation of the movement-image does not allow us to answer.

Animation may belong to film, but its relationship to cinema is not one of simple belonging. Both are, rather, distinct modes of film, though eminently capable of interfering with each other; and both are forms of the any-instant-whatever. In cinema, as Deleuze argues, the automatic interval allows cameras to *extract* movement from bodies, even if it then decentres movement by raising it to a plane of immanence open to effects of false continuity. In animation, to the contrary, the automated interval *engenders* movement. Animation does not refer primarily to the camera as 'generalized equivalent of movement' as does the Deleuzian movement-image (though this is certainly one of animation's possible and most common figures, one of the ways it refers to cinema within itself). The rostrum camera is in fact fixed as rigidly as possible at the moment of shooting, whereas Deleuze tellingly claims that the cinematic movement-image only shows its specificity when the camera becomes mobile and capable of taking on the specific movements of bodies and things.

Animation, then, is obviously not primarily an art of the camera moving in space and time, nor can it be defined in terms of any particular recording method. You can, after all, make animation by just scratching straight onto the film. What decisively differentiates animation in *general* from cinematography is the fact that the animator must physically encounter the fact of each frame and deliberately provide its graphic content, manually controlling the relationship between successive frames conceived as any-instants-whatever in the movement of a whole. Animation in the most general sense is this unique art of direct interaction with every interval of the any-instant-whatever generated by film (a definition broad enough to embrace all forms of animation, even if there will only be space here to deal with drawn character animation).

An inescapable paradox of control thus emerges at the heart of the commercial animator's practice. The same conditions which allow an unprecedented, even unlimited, degree of control in the creation of moving-images—the need to *decide and provide* the content of each individual frame and manipulate the relation between all of them—soon necessitates a fragmentation of the drawing process in the division of labour. (In today's commercial animation industry, different stages of the process are often carried out in different countries.) Animation is thus always caught up in an interplay between, on the one hand, the established weight of *models* which dictate the global possibilities of movement and coordinate diverse graphical processes (including, very importantly, models of movement derived from cinema) and, on the other hand, the indeterminacy encountered with each interval of movement and each stage of the animation process. In one way or another, there is always a certain degree of 'tracing'; but there is also a certain degree of uncertainty and potentiality (which is why so much of the animation process is devoted to checking and re-checking). The process of animation necessarily involves the opening of a kind of feedback circuit between existing models for the possibilities of movement, the automated interval and the collective network of bodies and brains formed by animators themselves.

Here two very different evocations of the creative process—one reminiscing from the point of view of a great animator and puppeteer (Bob Clampett), the other written as a paraphrase of Deleuze's philosophy of time (Peter Canning)—begin to resonate irresistibly:

> If I'm doing Porky Pig I don't stand off removed from Porky directing him; I get inside of Porky and I think like Porky. I talk like Porky. I have a s-s-s-s-speech ppp-problem. I walk like Porky, and I feel like Porky... I'm helpful, trusting, concerned, kindly and sometimes a trifle pu-pu-pu-put out. S-s-s-s-shucks, I am Porky...
>
> ...Bugs' personality is quite opposite of Porky's. And much more fun to do. When I do Bugs Bunny I get inside of him, and I not only think like, feel like, and walk and talk like Bugs [whispers] but confidentially, Doc, [yells] *I am the wabbit!*[6]

> ...the strings of the marionette or the body of the actor are not connected to the will of the puppeteer or actor or author, but to the second order automaton of the human body-brain rhizome... From virtual to actual and back, in the ever-renewing feedback loop of self-motivation...
>
> [The] difference 'of' immediacy 'with' itself 'in' time forms the smallest internal circuit between the self and itself...as in the mirror or the mime...[7]

The animator finds himself reanimated in turn by the characters he animates and feels himself becoming a cartoon. Resonances of influence are conducted back through the pencil into the vibrating network formed by the strings of the artist's nervous system. According to Canning, the multiple strings of the moving puppet are never simply controlled from a single point embodying the 'will' of the puppeteer. In both cases, powers of influence are ramified in every direction across all the scales of a network of control that cannot be monitored from any point external to itself. The puppeteer or animator may initiate this dance of strings and displaced bodies; but once set in motion, it reverberates unpredictably, takes on a life of its own, in which the artist's entire body becomes but one of many dancing limbs.

It is in this light that I would view the animator's own experiment with the 'mirror stage', as enacted in the classical cartoonist's technique in which a character's takes and double takes are modelled on the artist's own facials caught reflected in a mirror. For it seems impossible here to decide whether the human is moulding the image by forcing it to mimic his own face or rather, to the contrary, the virtual image of a moving body that does not yet exist is *modulating* the human face by forcing it to anticipate and mimic its own absurd dynamics. All three terms involved in this automimetic loop by which the animator becomes his own special effect—face, model, mirror image—exchange identities in a cycle of ever-exacerbating effects, an open circuit in which, finally, the only controlling term is the speed of light interval simultaneously separating and relinking all the others.

From what kind of body, then, can movement be said to be extracted in the case of animation? From a purely virtual body generated by the process of animation itself as a mode of time's 'self-affection'. Animation alone automatically produces movement freed from any reference to a pre-existing body whose movement it would translate and whose existence could be verified in terms of photographic reference. Chasing itself through this irreducible circuit of self-affection, the animation process extracts the movement of a body that does not yet exist, yet which is always already on the brink of destruction, its defining lines always caught up in *virtual lines of movement* that dissolve and reconstitute figures across the interval of the any-instant-whatever.

The effect of the any-instant-whatever thus remains decisive in animation, as in cinema. In the case of animation, we must say that each frame *will have been* an any-instant-whatever in the movement of a body generated by the process itself. Animation is first of all the genesis of 'living images' out of nothing but a circuit of self-affection played out in time between human and machine. *The cartoon film arises out of a trial of control that laughs at itself.* Even and especially when we are lost in laughter, animation implies a singular *experiment* in the possibilities of perception and a profound *allegory* of the relationship between humans and machines.

Cinematic translation of movement, as formulated by Deleuze, assumes an initial correspondence between, on the one hand, the *analysis* of movement by the camera apparatus at the time of filming and, on the other hand, the *synthesis* of movement by the projecting apparatus at the time of viewing. In this way, cinema depends upon an initial correspondence of temporal equidistances at the times of image production and consumption which is physically mediated by the spatial equidistances of the film strip.

In animation, however, there is no necessary initial correspondence between the analysis and synthesis of movement. From the point of view of the animator's practice, each individual frame presents itself as an *arena of control*, indefinitely extendable on the side of production yet automatically related to the intervallic measure of the any-instant-whatever on the side of projection. The animated image has thus two faces: on the one side, invisible for the viewer, there is an open interval of manual manipulation; on the other side, a visible image moving inexorably at 24 frames per second.

It is this double, intervallic relationship definitive of animation which I call *the interval of control*. Here the life of the living image or of the moving body is inseparable from the cut which divides it. The life of animated bodies cannot be abstracted from this open relationship between the act of drawing and the automatism of the any-instant-whatever. The interval of control in this way renders the integrity of animated bodies—their self-enclosure, their very 'bodily' status—both possible and impossible at the same time. Keith Broadfoot and Rex Butler seem to suggest as much in their own reading of Deleuze on animation:

> [W]ould not this be the ultimate ambition of all great cartoons: the presentation—impossible—of this simultaneity of the figure and the breaking of the figure, of time (space) and movement? This is perhaps why the characters in cartoons are always fighting against themselves: they are trying to destroy themselves, erase themselves; but they would exist only in this erasure. The same line which forms them, delimits them from their background, also deforms them, makes it impossible to separate them from their surroundings.[8]

I would only add: if so many cartoon characters seem 'naturally' inclined to fight against themselves, this is finally because they tend at the same time to be engaged in a kind of perpetual mortal combat, which is also a loving dance, with the machinic forces, both human and technological, which determine their nature with the passing of every frame. It is in this context that one may understand the strategies of 'self-figuration' elaborated by Donald Crafton.[9] In a manner not accidentally reminiscent of a magic act, these strategies allowed animators working 'before Mickey' to make a performance of their own uncanny control over the image and, through it, over the audience and its perceptions. At the most primitive level, these self-centred performances could be perfectly literal and visible, as in the filmed *Lightning Sketch* (1907) performed with unnatural facility by J.S. Blackton or Winsor McCay's appearance on screen, taking a ride on the back of a dinosaur of his own creation after elaborately demonstrating the labour pains of the pre-industrial animation process (*Gertie* (1914)).

These strategies of self-reference were quickly extended, however, into *figures*, through which the animator made his presence felt while remaining invisible. Indeed, when Dave Fleischer puts his brother's living body in front of a camera and has a rotoscoped Koko the Clown materialize from within an inkwell at the beginning of a cartoon, he revivifies and celebrates an early tradition of direct presentation; when Koko gets fully absorbed into the animatic universe and discovers a lever marked 'the controller' which, when engaged, throws the very stuff of his cosmos into chaos, the Fleischers have begun playing a far more sophisticated, figurative game with the same theme of control (*Koko's Earth Control* (1927)).

Character animation thus often tends toward a kind of *gnostic scenario* in which characters themselves begin to suspect that the controller performs his invisible work purely in order to make a joke of his own creations. Relations between creators and created veer erratically between easy harmony and murderous distrust. A certain kind of underlined reflexivity, expressed through more or less extravagant deformations of spatial models and 'unmotivated' interruptions of regular movement (but it is precisely the *motivation of movement* that is in question), has thus been the *norm* in animation from the very beginning, and not at all a subversive transgression.

Drawn animation may not always set out to exploit its own powers. For any number of reasons, it may pursue the goals of the illustrative or the cinematic rather than the animatic. Wartime instructionals and public health announcements, for example, may be designed to evoke an integrated world unperturbed by the actions of a perverse controller. Animation remains nonetheless intrinsically 'two-faced' in this specific way: the visible image is always more or less obviously accompanied by the performance of an *invisible hand*. Later, I will try to show how these general principles may inform the analysis of a specific genre. In the third section of this paper, I will turn to the idea of a cartoon *allegory of control*, as proposed by Norman M. Klein, to articulate further the complex and constant communication between the visible and invisible dimensions of the cartoon form.

In the following section, however, I will need to take a brief detour from the specific question of animation to review the relationship between 'the interval', 'the whole' and 'living images' in Deleuze's general theory of the movement-image.

THE HOLE OF THE WHOLE...

How does one begin to conceive the perception of movement as such? How might this conception determine the specific possibilities of film in general and animation in particular? For Deleuze, following a line drawn by Henri Bergson, what is needed is a way of thinking, indeed, a way of imagining thought itself, that no longer assumes an inert world of represented objects constructed around the human subject as a controlling centre of reference. In Bergson's conception, according to Deleuze's rendition, 'the model would be rather a state of things which would constantly change, a flowing-matter in which no point of anchorage nor centre of reference would be assignable'.[10] Natural perception could thus no longer be thought as having fallen away from an ideal apprehension of original, changeless truth into a world of change and deception, as in the Platonic tradition.

Like Plato, Bergson does still seem to invoke a certain kind of fall and the echo of a certain kind of abyss; nonetheless, in his vision everything is inverted. Natural perception now falls *away* from absolute change and the powers of falsity *into* a frozen world of reified truths. It is just this fall from change into fixity which Deleuze, this time arguing against and beyond Bergson, believes may be 'corrected' by the experience of cinema:

> Instead of going from the acentred state of things to centred perception [natural perception], it could go back up towards the acentred state of things, and get closer to it…
>
> …[to a state] of universal variation, of universal undulation, universal rippling: there are neither axes, nor centre, nor left, nor right, nor high, nor low…[11]

In this sense, the 'correcting' of natural perception seems not so much a matter of regaining a lost ground as of 'saying yes' to an abyss which is at *one and the same time* always already there *and* created by the very act of affirming it, the act of thought itself—an abyss in which it becomes impossible to tell up from down, left from right, since all controlling reference points have been relativized. This abyss is the hole of the whole, a whole of holes. For Deleuze, cinema is a machine that potentially 'corrects' for natural perception's 'fall onto a ground' by allowing us to fall out of ourselves into the experience of time as groundless 'self-affection'.

It will no longer be a matter of a self-identical consciousness relating an image to a 'something' that exists 'out there' in space but of images conceived as interacting freely with each other on a single, open 'plane of immanence'. At the once-commanding place accorded to 'the subject' by Western psychology, Deleuze posits instead a 'living image' which has been decentred by defining relationships it cannot possibly control. The question for Deleuze is that of how a certain kind of image, a living image, relates itself to every other kind of image. And the answer is: intervallically. Quoting Bergson against himself, Deleuze writes:

> Thus the living image will be 'an instrument of analysis in regard to the movement received, and an instrument of selection in regard to the movement executed'... Because they only owe this privilege to the phenomenon of the gap, or interval between a received and an executed movement, living images will be 'centres of indetermination', which are formed in the acentred universe of movement-images.[12]

This 'living image' should definitely not, as I read it, be read as merely a figure of cinema. Rather, it is to be taken as both a figure of cinema and as a description or conceptualization of the conditions of our own lives of illusion, that is, of the conditions of natural perception. The living image is one that opens a *gap*, a zone of indeterminacy, in the universal translation of movements-as-images-as-movements which Deleuze makes his primary hypothesis. On one side of this gap or interval, there will be *perception*; on the other side, *action*; and the interval of the gap itself will be the site of *affection*. These three terms form for Deleuze a circuit of *sensory-motor continuity* which may be understood simultaneously in terms of natural perception and in terms of the system of cinema. The cinematic movement-image is therefore a system which determines the any-instant-whatever in terms of compositional relations between moments of perception, affection (typified by the close-up) and action. Within the domain of the movement-image, movement thus tends to be reintegrated and rationalized around the interval of the living image.

Thus, the movement-image necessarily remains an indirect image of time. Closure is never total and always artificial. At one extreme, the extreme of expansion and immensity, the image remains open at some level to a changing whole which cannot be spatially closed or controlled. At the other extreme, the extreme of contraction and the variability of the present, it evokes the possibility of an ever-diminishing interval of indeterminacy that can neither be rationalized nor accounted for. As indirect image of time, the movement-image remains open at two opposite but mutually implicating extremes:

> Whenever time has been considered in relation to movement,... two aspects of time have been discovered... Time as whole, the set of movement in the universe, is the bird which hovers, continually increasing its circle. But the numerical unit of movement is the beating of a wing, the continually diminishing interval between two movements or two actions.[13]

Within the regime of the movement-image, time is given indirectly as the sublime prospect of a whole which exceeds any possible enclosure or act of framing, that is, as that impossibility of total enclosure which ensures that all enclosures are relative. As well, within the regime, time appears indirectly in terms of the *interval*, that is, as indeterminacy in the centring relationship between perception and reaction.

'HMMM, IT DISTHINTEGRATED!'

> The more exactly these two images, that of a person and that of a machine, fit into each other, the more striking is the comic effect, and the more consummate the art of the draughtsman. The originality of a comic artist is thus expressed in the special kind of life he imparts to a mere puppet.[14]

How might the relationship between the whole and the interval of the movement-image work out in the case of the cartoon form? It is here that Norman M. Klein's theory of animation, outlined in the book *Seven Minutes: The Life and Death of the American Animated Cartoon*, becomes indispensable.[15] For Klein, cartoon characters function as allegories for the paradoxes of control which haunt the interstices of manipulated environments. The unforgettable, uniquely funny qualities of great animated characters emerge in the idiosyncratic ways they suffer and amplify all the chaotic possibilities generated by the totally designed worlds which surround, define and repeatedly destroy them. What Klein has begun describing for us, even if he never meant it this way, is precisely the peculiar way in which the animated action-image correlates the 'extraordinary movements' of its living images with the any-instant-whatever of the movement-image.

In his analysis of the seven minute cartoon form, Klein begins by recognizing that cartoon characters rarely develop within narrative, that, in a certain important sense, they are just not going anywhere. As I see this, it is not at all that cartoons cannot, in fact, evoke a deep sense of 'character'. Instead, it is as though, in exchange for their death-defying powers of ballistic movement, cartoon characters have been instantaneously frozen at birth, as in a snapshot. Development makes little sense in a cartoon world. Cartoon characters are destined by their very deathlessness to suffer the eternal return of death, to live through a perpetual cycle of reversion; and in this sense, they are amenable to analysis not in terms of character development but rather in terms of function.

For Klein, three functions are essential to the cartoon form. The *nuisance* gets everything started by provoking its antagonist, the *over-reactor*. Victimized by the nuisance, the over-reactor immediately ups the ante, demanding two eyes for every eye. An ever-accelerating cycle of assault and revenge begins. *The controller* directs this dizzying spin, becoming a figure for the animator and his perverse desire. Directly manipulating the animated environment, the controller introduces asymmetry into the conflict.[16] The most transparent demonstration of this principle of asymmetry remains the treatment Daffy receives in Chuck Jones' *Duck Amuck* (1953) at the hands of an unseen, controlling Bugs Bunny, who, it turns out in the cartoon's closing gag, has been nonchalantly creating and destroying Daffy's world over and over again from behind an animator's drawing board.

Asked to explain the significance of this much speculated upon cartoon, in which Daffy finds himself and his world spontaneously shape-shifting in the weirdest of ways, subject to the most outrageous powers of the false, assaulted, crushed and doubled by the represented interval of the film strip, Chuck Jones has famously remarked that he merely wanted to show how through all these metamorphoses, even at the moment of his own erasure, Daffy would nonetheless remain himself.[17] Daffy is thus always in character because he is always already out of character, always already beside himself, quite visibly so at several points in this cartoon, since the very substance and contours of his being are functions of the unseen controller's unpredictable whimsy. He is an imperishable identity without identity, plunged continually into the absolute abyss of an empty screen severed from contextualizing connections, pure form of the any-space-whatever. Bugs, playing the part of a despicable controller, can even use the other end of his cosmogonic pencil to rub Daffy out altogether; but the duck, like any creature of the interval, is *still there even when he is not there*.

In *Duck Amuck*, one of the most beloved cartoon characters ever invented is forced to face the fact that he consists in nothing but the maintenance of effects of sensory-motor continuity across the gap of the interval. The lesson which the duck ultimately receives so painfully at the hands of Bugs, and which might just as well have been applied to that stinker of a rabbit himself (as it soon would be in *Rabbit Rampage* (1955)), is a lesson definitive of the cartoon condition: a cartoon character is at once virtually immortal and totally vulnerable—and for the same reason. Here, as elsewhere, Daffy's uniquely memorable character manifests itself precisely in the way he confronts and avoids the repeated discovery that he *does not belong to himself*.

Hence the evident allegorical attractions of the cartoon form for children still exploring the limits of socialization and the challenges of mastering a human body. It is a commonplace that the negative horizon of a child's expanding world is defined less by the fear of death—for which it may have no concept—than by the recurrent experience of a violent disparity between expectation and actuality encountered in relationships with the world and with itself. The shifting limits of a child's expanding world seem to be defined and tested through ongoing experiments in which the body is often experienced as an errant machine. Children are drawn to cartoon characters of the kind invented at Termite Terrace, I am suggesting, because they are taken by the compulsive ways these eternally neonatal, pre-human, animated animals deal with a world where the very laws of nature—the laws of their very own bodies—are open to the possibility of being suspended at any moment. The cartoon form flattens out the pain of humiliation and makes a shared joke of the countless daily traumas suffered and overcome by still growing bodies fated to repeatedly find, in the words of the original *Looney Tunes* theme song, that 'the merry-go-round broke down'.

According to Klein, all three functions can be swapped among the characters in the determined anarchy of a good cartoon, although well-established characters tend to gravitate towards one function. One may surmise, however, that the function of the controller tends to become privileged insofar as it becomes something like the fixed object of animated desire and to that extent precisely what prohibits any development of character. The position of controller, invulnerable and all powerful, is the one all characters strive to capture for themselves as their chaotic encounters unfold, at least insofar as they are seen to 'think' at all. (We shall see that this is an important qualification.)

The function of controller in this way 'doubles' as an allegory for that specific relationship between the visible image and the invisible moment of its genesis, that supplementary dimension of filmic reference which is peculiar to animation. It refers the visible space of the cartoon and the actions of characters to another inaccessible, invisible world. Reference to the controller in character animation makes animated figures themselves, animated movements themselves, animated spaces themselves, intrinsically double and allegorical.[18] In terms of the interval of control—which always implies a relationship between the visible and invisible dimensions of the image—the character visibly playing the function of controller at any particular moment becomes the embodiment or vessel of an unseen force which is nonetheless active everywhere, controlling everything within the image, defining everything, insofar as it is referred to as the very possibility of all the functions, all the characters, and of the very scene in which they meet. The best cartoons never stop drawing new possibilities of invention from this animatic ambivalence of the 'everywhere' and the 'nowhere'.

It is in this sense that, within the animated action-image, the *figure* of the controller fills the void left by the absence of a cine-camera (capable of acting as 'translator of all movements'). The cinematic camera makes its moves from an implied point exterior but adjacent to the image, the point from which the image is framed. As André Bazin emphasized, the camera's act of framing the world automatically generates a reference to the out of field. According to Deleuze, the relative closure of the out of field is marked within the cinematic action-image, insofar as the principal function of that image becomes one of 'adding space to space'. As we have seen, at the expansive limit of the action-image, as described by Deleuze, time is experienced indirectly as the impossibility of establishing a spatial enclosure that would exhaust any further possibility of 'adding space to space'. The cinematic frame is in this sense haunted by the thought of an unseen whole from which the image has been cut out and from which something unexpected might at any moment yet appear.

In the case of animation, however, it is the drawing process itself which generates and encloses all the figures and all the spaces in which they meet. Here the 'unexpected' arrives as a direct trace of the controller's caprice, the act of a controlling force making itself felt less from 'outside the frame' than from *between frames*. Felix picks up a hole and puts it in his bag of tricks. Popeye transforms himself into a battleship. Stimpy disappears up his own belly button. At the beginning of every episode, as they once again innocently try to take up their rightful place in front of the TV, the entire Simpsons family finds itself prey to random fluctuations in space/time. Character metamorphosis, one of the native delights of the cartoon, from Emile Cohl to *Transformers*, regularly exploits the fact that animation allows the unexpected, even the impossible, to emerge at *any-point-whatever* of the world in which characters move, even and especially from within their own bodies. (It is evident that special effects, which similarly allow the turning inside out and transformation of figures from any-point-whatever, offer a way for cinema itself to become animatic.)

The animated frame, able to regenerate or collapse all its dimensions without apparent rhyme or reason, to wrap around itself or implode upon itself at any instant whatever, is haunted in a singular way by a drawing process which makes itself invisible through the interval of control, even as it renders the viewed scene visible, rather than by the intimation of a greater whole from which it has been more or less violently severed. Where the cinematic action-image refers to the controlled shifting of points of view upon and within objectifiable, integral space, the chase cartoon generates a supplementary reference to an unseen power of control *making space*, according to its own whim. It is this 'haunting' of the cartoon world by an invisible hand making its moves from a space that remains forever inaccessible to the living images fated to suffer its influence which is so memorably allegorized by *Duck Amuck*.

Animation automatically possesses the possibility of referring to an out of field not simply reducible to the function of 'adding space to space' in a movement of continuous expansion and contraction, since it does not primarily refer to the camera as a profilmic agent capable of cutting out a section of the world that exists beyond the limits of the image.[19] If only for this reason, the cartoon form should not be defined in exclusively negative terms which ultimately serve merely to reinforce the positive definition and evaluation of cinema, as if animation amounted to nothing more than film minus the referential gravity of cinema. New terms of analysis need to be introduced and others qualified to account for the relatively specific ways in which animation assumes a relationship to its own limit. The function of the controller marks a rationalization and relative closure of the process of animation, insofar as it becomes the *centre* to which all aberrations of movement are referred. It marks this closure at two levels: *within* the cartoon form, insofar as it provides a centre of reference for all the potentially decentred movements; *as* the cartoon form, insofar as commercial cartoonery becomes a time-managed, rationalized, industrialized process of command and control. Klein writes:

> Not only are cartoon characters trapped inside the borders of the screen in a whimsical power-struggle against the controller, they are also caught in a beam of electronic light. All the antics aside, theirs is an utterly deterministic world... It is almost as if the medium steps in, not as the message but as the allegory for a conflict that continues to plague the animation business: corporate marketing dominating the hand-drawn image.[20]

The figure of the controller, which seems at one level to celebrate the divine creative freedom and control exercised by the unseen animator, also allegorizes his simultaneous impotence and lack of control, the fact that he regularly finds himself in the position of a puppet manipulated by unseen controlling forces. The field of reference in which the controller functions thus constantly shifts and inverts itself, in this particular context simultaneously positioning the animator as both sovereign origin of movement and slave to the impersonal movements of capital.

The controller, in whatever dimension of reference the figure is developed, ultimately serves as a kind of vanishing point, the mere hypothesis of a place at which all the lines of control terminate in a single hand. The human animator, caught up himself in a network of control, can only be a figure for this hypothetical point at which all the strings of influence come together. In this sense, *the controller is the index of its own impossibility*.

Here further parallels and differences may be drawn between the movement-image as conceived by Deleuze and the cartoon form as it has emerged in this analysis. The cinematic action-image described by Deleuze is structured around a series of duels between opposed terms—between protagonist and situation, between protagonist and antagonist, between protagonist and himself—which tend to converge towards a point of resolution. For Deleuze, the *binomial* is implicit in every form of the action-image:

> [W]e should like to call the other *binomial*, in order to designate every duel, that is to say, what is properly active in the action-image. There is a binomial as soon as the state of a force relates back to an antagonistic force, and particularly when—one (or both) of the forces being 'spontaneous'—it involves in its very exercise an effort to foresee the exercise of the other force: the agent acts as a function of what he thinks the other is going to do.[21]

The *binomial* tends eventually to demand resolution, which Deleuze describes in terms of a 'third law of the action-image': there must be a moment where the duelling parties meet in a single shot and resolve their difference once and for all. In the world of cartoons, dominated by the invisible hand of the controller, this form of resolution and closure is simply not available. The controller acts as an implicit third party rendering any one-on-one resolution of conflict impossible within the animated action-image, since it can never itself be met face to face by any character. The controller can never turn up for a final showdown then, for it is ultimately inseparable from the forces which divide the character from itself with the passage of every instant, robbing the character of its integrity in and through the same movement which grants that integrity.

It is thus no mere accident that the ostentatiously self-referential *Duck Amuck* begins with Daffy brandishing his musketeer's sword and ready for a duel. He is looking for the one thing he is never really going to find: the coherent, cinematic world of a binomial structure.

Cartoon characters, like their cinematic counterparts, may indeed be engaged in a relentless and often desperate bid to anticipate the moves of their adversaries; but as *Duck Amuck* so memorably demonstrates, their real adversary, the controller, can never be directly encountered. In this regard, the cartoon action-image may be opposed directly to the cinematic action-image. The cinematic form is *convergent* and progresses irresistibly towards a moment of relative resolution; the cartoon form is *asymptotic* and repeats endlessly the momentary realization that resolution is impossible. The particular comic effect of the cartoon action-image is bound up with the spectator's implicit awareness that the characters are struggling with impossibility. Whether they know it or not, 'we' all know that cartoon characters are trapped in a mouse's wheel.

The cartoon action-image thereby achieves its own relative closure, through non-resolution and non-convergence, as opposed to the strategies of organic development and resolution which determine the cinematic action forms analyzed by Deleuze. Chuck Jones' *The Road Runner* series, originally conceived as a deliberate parody of the entire chase cartoon form, is exemplary in this regard.[22] In this meta-generic series, repetition becomes less an obstacle to the viewer's enjoyment than its unashamed foundation.

The one grim joke of *The Road Runner*—ingeniously and endlessly varied—lies in the juxtaposition between Wile E. Coyote's passion and the mechanical predictability of the situation in which he is caught. Each episode is thus like a randomly sampled 'any-episode-whatever' in a circular ritual of Sisyphean humiliation. Perhaps more transparently than any other series, *The Road Runner* shows how the chase cartoon form normalizes animated movement by referring it to a closed circuit in which characters find themselves trapped.

There is nothing more instructive in this regard than the look on Wile E. Coyote's face at that moment of painful peripeteia when the huge rubber band once again finds its limit or the boulder reaches the apex of its climb—that sickened and sickening look which dawns across the Coyote's face as he fleetingly realizes that he can never do anything but build machines which will guarantee his own destruction. Every attempt on the part of ambitious cartoon characters like Daffy and Wile E. to 'get a life for themselves' sees them inevitably plunged back into an abyss.[23] This is the paradoxical essence of the cartoon double take: *the look fails to see what it has seen until it is already too late.* Like characters in Deleuze's cinema of the time-image, reflective cartoon characters are thus *characters who have become viewers*. What they view, over and over again in endless takes and double takes, are the effects of an invisible controlling force which manipulates their world and makes it impossible for them ever to resolve their relationship with their antagonists in a simple one-on-one conflict.

Insofar as everything cartoon figures do in the hope of separating themselves from or controlling their cartoon condition somehow turns back against them, it is hardly surprising that the most relentlessly triumphant of all cartoon characters, the Road Runner himself, generally appears to be completely lacking in a will or a mind of his own. He is like a zero degree of cartoon character: completely fixed, even as he speeds along his trajectory. As if this were the inevitable price paid for the extraordinary speeds he routinely maintains, the Road Runner not only fails to develop in time, he exhibits no spectrum of emotion at all. If he wins as regularly as clockwork, is this not because he thinks nothing of it? Whatever happens, he continues to zoom obediently along the road laid out for him in advance. In his own way, the Road Runner, reduced to the compulsive, idiotic repetition of his 'BEEP BEEP', seems every bit as trapped in a mouse's wheel as his canine pursuer. At the asymptotic limit of his one defining characteristic—acceleration—he would disappear irretrievably in the blurring of his form to become a pure and empty sign for the speed of emergent animatic movement itself.

A trickster character like Bugs Bunny presents quite different complications. Bugs, unlike the Road Runner, is definitely a thinking and desiring being; and for that very reason he can never secure total control. Even if he wins out over Daffy and Elmer in the end, Bugs never becomes a master of the universe. Indeed, in the later episodes, we usually meet the rascally rabbit just after he has taken a wrong turn at Albuquerque. Like Daffy, in this sense, he seems to suffer some inexplicable, recurrent difficulty in moving through space. Nor does he exercise any effective sovereignty when it comes to the serious business of finding somewhere to rest. Indeed, throughout his career, Bugs finds himself repeatedly and unceremoniously evicted from his latest meagre domicile. Nonetheless, once dislodged from the domestic privacy of his personal hole, Bugs displays a genius for dancing on the infinitely thin line between control and chaos that defines the world of drawn cartoons from moment to moment.

An initial attempt on the part of some nuisance to displace the rabbit from his rightful home inevitably reverses itself, releasing a cascading series of paradoxical displacements across which Bugs will dance and pirouette, his movements and gestures describing a kind of invisible net in which his adversaries entangle themselves. Bugs even displaces himself from himself, cross-dressing again and again as a damsel in distress in order to lead his pursuers astray, turning the hunter into a suitor (see *Rabbit Fire* (1951)), or playing dead in all sorts of hammy fashions in order to turn the hunter into a ridiculous mourner (*The Heckling Hare* (1941)). In each case, it is a matter of emitting the wrong signs at the right time so that the hunter finds himself instantly reduced to an automaton, doomed to mechanically running out programs which perform no useful work upon the world around him. In Tex Avery's *The Heckling Hare*, Bugs distracts a hungry hound from its deadly business by engaging him in the infantile intimacy of a game of ugly faces. Wound up like a senseless clockwork toy, the dog becomes so engrossed in manically turning over a series of grotesque facials programed by Bugs that he completely fails to notice when his former prey withdraws from the exchange altogether and turns with familiar irony towards the audience, a pre-painted sign held in his three-fingered paw, 'ain't he ridiculous?'

Bugs is a creature of portable holes and subliminal connections. It is his ability to find strange loops in space or anomalies in the laws of the animatic universe which usually allows the rabbit to triumph. (Not always, however. Certainly not against the eleatic tortoise of *Tortoise Beats Hare* (1941).) Someone is always furiously digging at the earth, shoving a gun down into its depths in an effort to force Bugs out of a hiding place from which he has already elegantly absented himself. 'What ya doing, Doc?'... 'I'm looking for a wabbit'.

Bugs Bunny's power lies in knowing how to use the impossibility of control to achieve effects of control. His mischievous secret lies in allowing other characters to get tangled up in *traps of their own making*, feedback loops in which they watch themselves reduced to mere cogs in machines dedicated to the destruction of their every purpose. Elmer hardly ever gets time to consider the implications of this paradoxical truth, even as it is presented to him, time and time again, in the literal shape of his own gun barrel somehow twisting back to make a target of the hapless hunter himself. It is just this ultimate paradoxical displacement, this animatic inversion of the natural order, which is taken to the limit at the conclusion of the brilliantly twisted *Rabbit Fire*: 'Be vewwy, vewwy qwiet', Daffy and Bugs admonish the audience. 'We're hunting Elmers'.

There is a standard cartoon gag which shows a character dissolving himself, blurring himself, in a willed explosion of energy, only to find that he is soon effortlessly overtaken by some other character whose lines of definition remain stable and precisely defined, betraying no sign of stress or exertion. At any instant whatever, speed may suddenly convert into stasis, a potentially infinite movement may collapse without apparent cause into the very fissure which makes it possible—the fissure of the interval—and become asymptotic, giving us an infinite movement that moves nowhere.

Zeno's Paradox is in this sense the very stuff of a cartoon character's life.[24] When Wile E. falls yet again into the chasm, he is never delivered, as might be expected, to a final resting place. Instantly repaired, a few momentary Acme brand band-aids the only visible trace of his recent trauma, the unhappy Coyote always finds himself immediately returned to the initial point of his endless pursuit. The Road Runner and Wile E. return eternally and instantaneously to the same point of inconclusion. In their very failure to meet, they are inseparable. In this way, the two poles of the animated action-image—unrestrained movement versus the impossibility of movement—are embodied in the two characters and put into a direct conflict that can never be resolved and that tends to repeat itself infinitely, asymptotically. The Road Runner himself is a champion of unrestrained movement, his body actualizing the infinite speed allowed by pure false continuity. Wile E. Coyote is a victim of the interval, which appears spontaneously, yet with clockwork regularity, as a yawning abyss swallowing him whole, instantly reducing all his efforts to nothing. At both ends of its existential spectrum, then, the Warner Bros. cartoon universe—*the Looney Tuniverse*—is governed by a single natural law inverting nature itself, the law of the comic as defined by Bergson: *the mechanical encrusts itself upon the living*.[25]

The art of character animation is always more or less *comic* in this sense, even when it fails to be funny or comedic, whether through accident or design. For the animation process gives life with the same breath that it takes it away. The bodies it gives us, no matter how engaging and graceful, can show themselves driven by a motivity that is not their own at any instant whatever. The effective 'degrees of freedom' enjoyed by its 'living images' are visibly limited by the same flatness from which they emerge, undermined by the very same lines which body them forth, disrupted by the effects of that same interval which animates them in the first place. Character animation for this reason tends almost irresistibly towards the comic: at a fundamental level, it is uniquely suited to presenting the spectacle of an apparently vital and spontaneous force struggling with the stuck gears of its own life. The funniest and saddest cartoons alike constantly make a virtue of this fate.

At one extreme, the pole of expansion, the cartoon form seems to open the possibility of an absolutely unrestrained movement of false continuity, a movement of infinite inflation. (See the 'global inflation' of Tex Avery's *King-Size Canary* (1947).) At the other extreme, the pole of contraction, it reserves the power to make all movement revert instantly to zero. The cartoon form generally exhibits a unique capacity to take itself immediately to the limits of the movement-image—to demonstrate in a 'graphic' way the *aporia* of movement insofar as it is conceived in terms of space—yet it nonetheless achieves relative closure precisely in terms of that very paradox. The paradox of impossible motion is itself the invisible engine of cartoon movement.

Evoking the limits of the cinematic movement-image, Deleuze, we have seen, writes of a circling bird whose spiral path describes the limits of expansion and whose beating wings correspond to the interval of movement. The simultaneous closure and opening of the cartoon action-image would be better expressed, by contrast, if this bird were to suddenly and inexplicably fall into the abyss below. For the abyss combines within itself the traits of immensity and of the interval, of expansion and contraction, continuity and division, but as the collapse of one into the other. It is in this abyss, basis of the one cartoon gag every TV baby should remember, that we find the most commonly evoked figure for the interval of control and the relative closure of the cartoon universe.

Some crazy talking animal comes speeding along a road which seems to stretch out to infinity like an endless spool of film. Sooner or later, this same road brings the character to an abyss that opens up in the gap between two points in his path, like the gap between any two frames of the film strip, an abyss that only takes effect the moment he looks down to make sure the road is still there. Oblivious to his perilous situation, the character goes racing off the cliff's edge and continues racing across the void, magically suspending the laws of gravity until that inevitable catastrophic moment when he looks down to see what he is doing.

Look down and drop. The ultimate double take. It could happen at any instant whatever, to any cartoon character whatever (with a very few exceptions, such as the Road Runner). Here, it is clearly the character's very apprehension, his will-to-control, that guarantees his body will once again be sent hurtling back towards a degree zero of all movement. The moment of impossible, hovering delay, which must be shown before the character looks down and falls, a standard element of this standard gag, proves that it is not any representation of the natural law of gravity which is at stake here. The controller is happy to show that he can turn that law on and off at will.

This *animatic abyss* is a figure of the interval of control itself—the necessarily unobservable element which renders the life of illusion, the life of animated living images, possible and impossible at the same time. It is an animated figure of animatic figuration. *The character sees himself not having seen the thing that must be avoided, by that very action causing the thing he wants to avoid.* In this missed encounter, he sees that he has not seen, that he is always already too late to coincide absolutely with himself. It is in his fall that the character will come closest to directly encountering the controller, precisely as a ground that withdraws towards infinity. Which is perhaps why the eventual impact is never truly terminal. A brief puff of smoke is often all that we are given to mark and mask the interval between the character's destruction and his inevitable reappearance.

NOTES

Thanks to Alan Cholodenko for his insistence upon the need to think through the relationship between 'animation' and 'translation' after reading a very early draft of this piece.

1 Gilles Deleuze, *Cinema 1: The Movement-Image*, trans. Hugh Tomlinson and Barbara Habberjam (Minneapolis: The Athlone Press, 1986), p. 5. I suspect that when Deleuze discusses 'transcendental poses' in relation to animation, he is alluding in part to the use of dual magic lanterns in the pre-history of cinema and animation. Such systems, which are effectively duplicated today with the use of synchronized slide projectors, created a limited effect of movement in images by moving or fading at least two projected images across or into one another. Here, the viewer watches images slowly fading or 'transforming' into one another. In animated cartoons, however, as with film in general, frames representing 'any-instant-whatever' are arrested at the projector gate in a linear sequence and 'shown' in isolation at regular intervals, at a rate of at least 18 frames per second. Thus, we need to distinguish between the gradual 'transformation' of *poses or exposures* through convergent projection and the very different process through which *described figures* are instantaneously and simultaneously 'formed' and 'dissolved' with each separately projected frame of the any-instant-whatever.

Deleuze's claims here could also be related to Norman McLaren's famous assertion that 'animation is not the art of drawings-that-move, but rather the art of movements-that-are-drawn. What happens *between* each frame is more important than what happens *on* each frame'. Quoted in Charles Solomon, 'Animation: Notes on a Definition', in *The Art of the Animated Image*, ed. Charles Solomon (Los Angeles: The American Film Institute, 1987), p. 11.

2 In an historical sense, the development of animation was doubtless intimately entwined with the developing use of 'temporal equidistances' in the analysis and recording of moving bodies. There is every reason

to believe that pioneer animators were decisively instructed by the implicit lessons contained in Marey's and Muybridge's photographic analyses of movement, as well as by a familiarity with the principles of movie cameras. At this level, animation does 'belong to cinema' but as a *part that becomes greater than the whole*, that is, as its uncanny double or shadow, one which divorces effects of movement from any reference to independently existing things or integral space. This already seems to be at stake in the self-conscious 'incoherence' of 'the first proper cartoon', Emile Cohl's *Fantasmagorie* (1908). Here, we watch the implausible adventures of a metamorphic clown who alternately plays the role of controller and controlled in a time/space which defies any rational integration. Is it accidental that at one point we see a hapless spectator desperately struggling to assume his proper position in an impossible cinema?

For a declaration of animation's privileged relation to the uncanny, see Alan Cholodenko's Introduction to *THE ILLUSION OF LIFE: Essays on Animation*, ed. Alan Cholodenko (Sydney: Power Publications in association with the Australian Film Commission, 1991), pp. 28-29. For an exploration of animation as the uncanny double of cinema, belonging to it as that which upsets the very propriety of belonging itself, see Cholodenko's essay '*Who Framed Roger Rabbit*, or the Framing of Animation' in that book. For analysis of the techniques of 'self-figuration' in Cohl, see Donald Crafton, *Emile Cohl, Caricature, and Film* (Princeton: Princeton University Press, 1990).

3 Deleuze, *Cinema 1: The Movement-Image*, p. 23.

4 For a very different account of the relationship between animation and the any-instant-whatever, see Keith Clancy, 'ΠΡΗΣΤΗΡ: The T(r)opology of Pyromania', in *THE ILLUSION OF LIFE*, p. 257.

5 From an interview in John Cawley and Jim Korkis, *How to Create Animation* (Las Vegas: Pioneer, 1990), p. 39.

6 Clampett quoted in Jeff Lenburg, *The Great Cartoon Directors* (Jefferson: McFarland, 1983), p. 57.

7 Peter Canning, 'The Crack of Time and the Ideal Game', in *Gilles Deleuze and the Theater of Philosophy*, eds. Constantin V. Boundas and Dorothea Olkowski (New York: Routledge, 1994), p. 79.

8 Keith Broadfoot and Rex Butler, 'The Illusion of Illusion', in *THE ILLUSION OF LIFE*, p. 270. My arguments here could in fact be considered an attempt to take up the question asked at the very close of their essay: 'Is it only because the Road Runner does not know whether he can fly or not that he can cross the abyss?' (p. 296).

9 See the 'Conclusion' of Donald Crafton, *Before Mickey: The Animated*

Film, 1898-1928 (Chicago: The University of Chicago Press, 1993), pp. 347-349.

10 Deleuze, *Cinema 1: The Movement-Image*, p. 57.

11 ibid., p. 58.

12 ibid., p. 62.

13 ibid., pp. 31-32.

14 Henri Bergson, *Laughter: An Essay on the Meaning of the Comic*, trans. Cloudesley Brereton and Fred Rothwell (London: Macmillan, 1911), p. 31.

15 Norman M. Klein, *Seven Minutes: The Life and Death of the American Animated Cartoon* (London: Verso, 1993).

16 To avoid possible confusion, I will clarify. It is evident that each character would be capable, at least in principle, of reacting with equal or greater force to every action. Every 'upped' ante would be equally 'upped' by the other. In the sense that I intend, the *process* of such a reciprocal conflict must itself be defined as symmetrical, even if its *state* at any particular moment could not be, since one character would always have just upped the other.

17 Jones quoted in Leonard Maltin, *Of Mice and Magic*, rev. ed. (New York: Plume, 1980, 1987), p. 263, cited in Patrick Crogan, 'Bugs, Daffy and Deleuze: The Out-of-Field in Chuck Jones' *Duck Amuck*', *Hermes Papers 1990*, p. 12.

18 There will only be space here to explore in any detail the animatic allegory of control as it is understood and exploited within a very limited range of examples, and even this in a most schematic way. Elsewhere, I hope to show that all the great commercial character animators, from Walt Disney to Tex Avery to John Kricfalusi, develop their own ways of figuring the paradoxes of control and of modulating figures inherited from other animators. My aim here is merely to demonstrate the way in which animation, as a specific mode of film, enjoys the possibility of playing upon this 'supplementary dimension of reference' at any-instant-whatever. In relation to experimental animation, also, the whole task of elaborating descriptive terms for the theorization of a pure *chaos-image* remains to be addressed.

19 Edward Branigan has argued that 'the camera' referred to within the cinematic system of point of view should not in general be considered as identical with any real profilmic object, even turning his attention explicitly towards animation as a limit case for the theory of film. Branigan, it will be recalled, insists that the camera be defined as a 'term of reading'. Nonetheless, he certainly does not attempt to describe any supplementary dimension of reference opened up by

the cartoon film, which is precisely my theoretical project here. See Edward Branigan, *Point of View in the Cinema: A Theory of Narration and Subjectivity in Classical Film* (Berlin: Mouton, 1984), p. 54.

20 Klein, *Seven Minutes*, p. 79.

21 Deleuze, *Cinema 1: The Movement-Image*, p. 142.

22 For an important reading of *The Road Runner* which converges with and diverges from my own analysis in asymptotic fashion, see Richard Thompson, 'Meep Meep', in *Movies and Methods*, ed. Bill Nichols (Berkeley: University of California Press, 1976).

23 This necessity of self-defeat is confirmed by the second item in Chuck Jones' set of 10 rules for *The Road Runner*: 'RULE 2. NO OUTSIDE FORCE CAN HARM THE COYOTE—ONLY HIS OWN INEPTITUDE OR THE FAILURE OF THE ACME PRODUCTS'. Chuck Jones, *Chuck Amuck* (New York: Avon, 1989), p. 225.

24 Zeno's Paradox plays a crucial role in Deleuze's and Bergson's consideration of the relationship between natural perception and cinema. For reasons of space, I have had to forgo here any explication of the extremely suggestive ways in which Deleuze turns back against itself Bergson's disqualifying association of cinema with the spatializing illusions of natural perception, illusions codified in the logic of Zeno's repudiation of movement. See Deleuze, *Cinema 1: The Movement-Image*, p. 2.

25 See Bergson, *Laughter*, p. 37.

Speculations on the Animatic Automaton

ALAN CHOLODENKO

> I think, Sebastian, therefore I am.
>
> Pris the Nexus 6 *replicant* in *Blade Runner*

Animation bedevils definition, even (and especially) 'its' 'own'—double—definition: *endowing with life* and *endowing with movement*. By this doubling, this multiplying and dividing, even of 'itself', animation poses the very question of life itself, movement itself, and their relation, a complicated coimplicated relation in which each of the terms can only be thought through the other, in which each of the terms solicits and replies (to) the other. This is always already double trouble doubled.

Further, the modes of animating as *endowing with life* are coimplicated with the modes of animating as *endowing with motion*—in terms of the former, the ideas and processes of authoring, creating, engendering, etc., given us by religion, classical mythology, magic, mysticism, etc., and by the institutions and discourses of the arts and humanities, including philosophy, and science, too, which propound them; in terms of the latter, the kinds of movements proferred by science, technology, and philosophy, too, over the centuries. Indeed, for some time now, biomedical science and genetic engineering, and computer science and engineering (including the engineering of intelligence), have been issuing a challenge, claiming that they themselves endow not only with motion but *with life*, a life whose artificiality or genuineness has been subject at times to fervent dispute and questioning.

To say this is to suggest that any consideration of animation inevitably takes up a place in the debate from classical times onward between the animists, who believed that the world was alive with organic or spiritual substance, that all that moved was alive (even things that did not move could be considered as alive), and the mechanists, who believed that the motion of matter was obedient to physical laws and necessitated no presumption of organic or spiritual vivifying agency.

This essay follows on from the portions of two paragraphs in my Introduction to *THE ILLUSION OF LIFE* that I have in part quoted and in part paraphrased immediately above, portions devoted to the crucial relevance to the thinking of animation of the debates of the animists and mechanists over the nature of life and motion, of the human and the machine. As well, this essay takes off from my initial formulation in that Introduction, and in my '*Who Framed Roger Rabbit*, or the Framing of Animation' essay in that book, of a theory of the filmic/cinematic apparatus as *animatic apparatus.*[1] It not only focuses on and explores these debates and that formulation, it seeks to extend them by situating that apparatus within the debates, and vice versa.

In so doing, it continues the project I 'began' in *THE ILLUSION OF LIFE*—and the work I have done subsequently on animation—to develop not only a theory of animation but an *animatic* theory of it, the purport of which will be elucidated as the essay progresses. En route, it will bring to these debates and that formulation the ideas of many thinkers, especially J. David Bolter, Mary Shelley, Donald Crafton, David F. Channell, Sergei Eisenstein, Jacques Derrida, Sigmund Freud, Philippe Lacoue-Labarthe, Gilles Deleuze, Jean Baudrillard and Plato, and will 'conclude' with consideration of singular ways in which *Blade Runner* exemplifies and performs these debates, that apparatus and their commingling.

To highlight certain aspects of the history of these debates and what is at stake in them: it has been suggested by J. David Bolter, in his book *Turing's Man*, that every age has what he calls 'defining technologies', technologies *of* the human, where *of* means made by the human but also at the same time *making* the human.[2] Bolter argues that Man can only know himself and his image of the universe in terms of such technologies, which define the human, human body, mind or brain. In classical times, it was the clay pot or spindle; for Descartes, it was the clock; and in modern times, it is the computer. Bolter writes: 'A defining technology develops links, metaphorical or otherwise, with a culture's science, philosophy, or literature; it is always available to serve as a metaphor, example, model, or symbol'.[3]

Thus, a defining technology (re)defines, (re)makes—we would say *(re)animates*—the human. Bolter says of Turing's Man, 'By making a machine think as a man, man recreates [we would say *(re)animates*] himself, defines himself as a machine'.[4] Bolter is saying that it is the analogy or comparison between man and machine which preceeds the possibility—I would say at once *both* possibility and impossibility—of naming either of them as such.

Bolter proceeds to figure the 'technology of making Man' in the two great traditions of artificial life—the animistic and the mechanistic. The former is for him first represented in the classical era by the myths of Hephaestus, Daedalus and Pygmalion—to which I would add that of Prometheus. Hephaestus, the Greek god of fire, fabricated at his forge golden automata of girls to serve him, a bronze living statue for King Minos of Crete to guard the island against invasion, as well as twenty three-legged tables that moved about on their own.[5] Daedalus, designer of the Labyrinth, made not only artificial wings endowed with the power of flight but also, according to Hellenic fables, moving animals, including a cow, as well for King Minos.[6] Pygmalion sculpted an ivory statue of a woman of such perfect form that he fell in love with it and implored Aphrodite to help him. Prometheus, the Titan, not only fired the inanimate clay to fabricate the first humans but brought fire to Man. These are myths in which a divine or human master craftsman or the intervention of Aphrodite was necesssary to provide the spark or breath of life to animate the inanimate metal of the automaton, metal or ivory of a statue, or clay matter of the human.[7]

The mechanistic tradition is for Bolter first represented in the classical era by the Alexandrian School of the second century B.C., famous for its engineer-entertainers—Ctesibius, Hero of Alexandria, and Philo of Byzantium—who made automata driven by fluids, compressed air or steam, to instruct in natural principles as well as to entertain.[8] Such automata, which imparted what Bolter tellingly describes as 'the illusion of animation',[9] included Hero's vessel from which wine, water, or a mixture of the two mysteriously poured; his mobile automata theatre in which 'the god Dionysus came forth, sprayed water and wine from his staff, and then was surrounded by Bacchants who danced in his honor'[10]; and his temple, whose doors mysteriously automatically opened when a fire on an altar across the way was lit and closed when the fire was extinguished. As well, such automata included clepsydra (automatic water clocks).

Declaring the victory of the animistic tradition over the mechanistic in classical times, Bolter tracks these two traditions in Western Europe—the animistic in the alchemists and magicians of the Middle Ages and Renaissance (such as Paracelsus and his artificial man, the homunculus, and the Jewish golem) and the mechanistic in the mechanical automata of the Middle Ages and Renaissance, and beyond. Mechanical automata were found on clock towers from the mid-fourteenth century on; in gardens and grottos of the sixteenth and seventeenth centuries, notably the hydraulically driven automata theatres set in grottos made by Salomon de Caus for Charles V and by the Francine family for Henri IV at St. Germain-en-Laye[11]; and in royal courts and salons of the eighteenth century, the century of their greatest popularity—such wondrous curiosities as the three life-size spring-driven clockwork automata invented by Jacques de Vaucanson, including the most famous automaton of all, his gilded copper duck of 1738.

This duck quacked, ate, drank, flapped its wings, splashed about and eliminated its food—and was the toast of Europe![12] Indeed, no less a personage than Voltaire, after seeing the duck, crowned de Vaucanson 'Prometheus' rival'.[13] By this nomination, de Vaucanson became the mechanist rival of one of the four great figures of Western animistic myth.

Exceedingly popular as well in the eighteenth century were the life-size automata of Pierre Jacquet-Droz, especially his automatic boy writer of 1774, which dipped its pen in an inkwell and wrote messages, 'distinguishing between light and heavy strokes and lifting the pen between words and over the line'[14]; and his astonishing female harpsichordist, 'who actually played the harpsichord with artificial fingers and at the same time breathed, raised her eyes, and turned her head'.[15]

Significantly, Frederik L. Schodt, in his book *Inside the Robot Kingdom: Japan, Mechatronics, and the Coming Robotopia*, states that there is a story that the automata of Jacquet-Droz and his sons 'were so uncannily lifelike they are said by some to have inspired Mary Shelley to write her novel *Frankenstein*'.[16] Here it should be recalled that the full title of Shelley's novel is *Frankenstein: or, the Modern Prometheus*. Let us remember that Frankenstein was the name of the 'student of unhallowed arts'[17] who made the artificial man, not the man that was made, though later, in popular culture, the name would uncannily turn into that of the artificial man, confounding in the process the title of the book.

Thus, we see not only de Vaucanson but Jacquet-Droz, to the degree he was the inspiration, the model, for Victor Frankenstein, being figured, like Victor himself, as Prometheus, in that figuring doubling and (un)doing—that is, at once making and unmaking, reinforcing and challenging, conjoining and confounding—the animistic tradition with the mechanistic.

Bolter also tracks this mechanistic tradition in the mechanistic philosophers like Descartes, Hobbes and Leibniz, and declares the victory of the mechanists—philosophers like Newton and La Mettrie—over the animists in the eighteenth and nineteenth centuries. La Mettrie proclaimed in his book *L'Homme-Machine* (*The Man-Machine*) of 1748: 'Let us conclude bravely that man is a machine; and that there is in the universe only one kind of substance subject to various modifications'.[18]

Not only were automata known to Descartes,[19] Hobbes,[20] Leibniz, Newton[21] and La Mettrie but they philosophized in 'the light' of them.[22] Aram Vartanian, for instance, records that equal in importance to the image of the clock as 'the technical criterion that inspired La Mettrie's mechanical model of man' were

> the many ingenious automata so popular at the time, such as Vaucanson's famous flutist and duck, which embodied the

> engineering equivalent of the man-machine theory and undoubtedly prepared the imagination of La Mettrie and his contemporaries for the idea of psychophysical automatism.[23]

For Bolter, the ancient myths captured perfectly the prevailing world view of that age, the animist view 'that man was a material, like clay or stone, animated by the breath or spark of life',[24] while

> Hero and his mechanical toys expressed the minority opinion, arguing paradoxically against animism. But in Western Europe [during the Middle Ages and Renaissance], the animists, the alchemists who sought to make men from a recipe, were in the minority. The mechanical view triumphed: the bodies of animals and men were best approximated by clocks and best imitated by clockwork toys.[25]

With each passing decade of the nineteenth and early twentieth centuries, as automata became progressively more precise and complex, the triumph of mechanism became, for Bolter, more apparent.[26]

For Bolter and myself, the human is only ever defined by technology. Thus, there is always something technological 'in' and 'of' the human, one might say *in-forming* the human, a technological other, double, to the human that defines the human and at the same time indefines it, as well as at the same time defines and indefines itself, even as the human defines and at the same time indefines the technological, as well as at the same time defines and indefines itself.

Put another way, for Bolter and myself, not only is there always already something technological 'in' and 'of' the human, there is always already something human 'in' and 'of' technology, such vertiginous coimplications indetermining, disseminating, seducing the human, suspending the human, turning the human into the 'human', even as it makes of technology 'technology'. Indeed, insofar as the human is always already in-formed in and by the technological, the 'human' would itself never not be a defining technology.

Thus, Bolter's defining technology is for us *indefining* technology, which is what for us technology 'as such' is and does—including Bolter's 'metaphor, example, model, or symbol' as 'defining' technology, and vice versa—indefining as it defines, and vice versa, including itself. And that applies across Bolter's key defining technologies. To recall and elaborate: in classical times, Plato's metaphor and model—indeed, metaphorical model and model metaphor—of the universe as clay pot (*Timaeus*) or spindle (*The Republic*); in the seventeenth century, Descartes' metaphorical model and model metaphor of the universe as clockwork, his notion in the *Discourse on Method* of the animal as clockwork automaton—*bête-machine*—and the human as dual—body like animal like automaton, mind or soul as independent and immortal; in the nineteenth century, the metaphorical model and model metaphor of the universe as entropic steam or heat engine; and today, the metaphorical model and model metaphor of the universe as computer (and, we would add, the human as cyborg[27]).

For us, one such defining technology is, obviously, the automaton, linking and reanimating animistic myths and mechanistic inventions, at once joining and separating them, defining and indefining them, forming and unforming them, indetermining, disseminating, seducing not only their relationship but each 'in themselves'.[28]

Whether it be technology as 'actual', 'real' invention (including mechanical automata) or as 'virtual', 'fictional' invention (figured in and as the animating and animate(d) forces and forms of animistic myth, also including automata and living statues)—each of which inventions would stimulate, infiltrate and contaminate the other—a defining technology makes of technology a metaphorical model and model metaphor and at the same time makes a metaphorical model and model metaphor a technology.

In fact, the linking, bridging form of a defining technology is a form of the link, the bridge—link, bridge as metaphorical model and model metaphor and metaphorical model and model metaphor as link, bridge—that which inextricably couples, at once joining and separating, indeed at once joining in the separating and separating in the joining, a hybrid form at the same time part of and apart from what it links/bridges—what the automaton is for us here.[29]

In the 'rivalry' between the animistic and mechanistic world views, the perverse apparition of the double and the double redoubled should be noted. For not only are there two traditions for the 'making' of the human—the animistic and the mechanistic—each doubling and (un)doing the other, and itself at the same time thereby—but such a 'made' human doubles and (un)does the human, and in doubling and (un)doing the human, doubles and (un)does all of philosophy's questions of the human.

Insofar as 'Philosophy begins and ends with the question of the other',[30] as Mark C. Taylor declares, one of the 'others' which interests, in fact *fascinates*, me, is precisely the subject of this essay—the artificial human, which, as the double of the human, makes this subject likewise the subject of the double, indeed that of the double of the double. Whether created by means of animism—metaphorical model and model metaphor of/as technology—or fabricated by means of mechanism—technology of/as metaphorical model and model metaphor—this made human doubles and (un)does the human, making and at the same time unmaking it, including in every re-making of it.[31]

Thus, philosophy's enterprise as the questioning of the 'other', of the double, might be treated as the thinking of the human against what alarms the human, where 'alarms' might be thought as what at once both attracts and repels, charms and terrifies, makes and unmakes, the human—what I here call the *automaton*, but what might be called the other, the double, the spectre, the heliotrope, as Jacques Derrida characterizes them, or the Other, as Jean Baudrillard characterizes it.[32] While philosophy would wish to reduce that Other to the Same or to contain it within a logic of the Same, that Other will not allow it, instead mocking all such efforts.[33] No solution, resolution nor reconciliation is possible. Rather, indeterminacy rules. Like metaphor, the other, the double, the spectre, the heliotrope, the Other—the artificial human, thought here as the automaton, introduces the crepuscular, the twilight, of *the illusion of life* and *the life of* (that) *illusion* to the metaphysical enterprise of philosophy.

Philosophy's solicitations of the human and replies of the made human mark the human as 'always already made', always already doubled, not only machine in man's image and man in machine's image but man and machine in man's image and man and machine in machine's image at the same time, such indifferentiating making it impossible to say where man begins and machine leaves off. The human artificer is always already artificed, artificial, artifact.

In this sense, man is always already hybrid, 'man-machine'—'animate inanimate'. Furthermore, insofar as for me what operates in both domains of artificing the human—the animistic and the mechanistic—is simulation, the human is always already a simulation, though animation as *anima*, as animistic, would like such artificing to be not simulation but representation (a point to which I shall turn later).

Here, we (re)turn to Mary Shelley's *Frankenstein: or, the Modern Prometheus,* which offers compelling demonstration of this confounding process, performing the inextricable coimplication of maker and made, human and non-human—where the human maker is as much the non-human made as at the same time the non-human made is human maker—arguably the very thematic of the text—as it performs the inextricable coimplication of animism and mechanism in/and the operation of the simulacrum.[34]

It is thus most telling for me that animation historian Donald Crafton, writing of the earliest film animators, declares: 'Are these curious filmmakers playing with bringing their puppets and household objects to life far from Shelley's *Frankenstein* and similar homunculus themes in romantic literature?',[35] which literature for Crafton represents a metaphorical, 'imaginative attempt to assimilate the staggering developments of late-nineteenth-century science and technology'[36]—literature as metaphor, as science and as technology, and vice versa. At the same time, he writes:

> Perhaps the gothic and scientific subjects of early animation... are comprehensible as images of the turn-of-the-century fascination with self-propulsion. The automobile and the airplane were wonderful inventions because they represented totally liberating freedom of movement. These objects moving with what seemed their own internal life were reflected when the normally inanimate objects of everyday life—furniture, tools, toys, even pictures—lurched into sputtering motion on the screen. Unexpectedly, through the marvelous 'electrical' invention of the cinematograph, the whole world appeared to be in flux, as

> though electricity and internal combustion were secrets of the universe. For the most part the animation sequences in these first films serve no narrative function; they exist only as movement for its own sake. Although some may view this as 'primitive', it demonstrates that even at the beginning the makers of animated films were, like earlier romantics, fascinated with the materials of artistic creation. These subjects, then, however 'haunted', were also representations of animators' enduring concern with autokinesis, movement in itself, the stuff of animation.[37]

For me, Crafton's invocation of Shelley's *Frankenstein* opens the door to situating these early filmmakers and their films in the line that extends from Mary Shelley, Victor Frankenstein and his creation back to Jacquet-Droz and his automata, and beyond, to de Vaucanson, and back to the Alexandrian school and Prometheus, Pygmalion, Daedalus and Hephaestus. The fascination of these filmmakers is the enduring fascination with animation 'as such', with the endowing with/bringing to life and motion, with the artificing of life as such, an artificing that takes us back to classical times, to the artificial man of the automaton and to the 'rival' traditions of animism and mechanism.

In fact, *autokinesis*—the very stuff of animation for Crafton—has a relative not only in the word *automobile* but in that of *automaton*, from the Gr. *automatos*, *likewise* meaning self-moving. For me, even as their names indicate, the automobile, autokinetic technologies of transportation that Crafton references in terms of mechanism are as well themselves automata. And crucially, they are ancestors and relatives not only of what is animistically imaged in these films but of the mechanical imaging apparatus in and with which these filmmakers are working—the automaton that is the cinema, the cinematic/animatic apparatus, itself apparatus of transportation.

Thus, the automaton is marked not only in the 'animators' enduring concern with autokinesis' as subject of the early animation films, it is marked in the very apparatus of film animation, of cinema, itself. It is what links the subjects—human and nonhuman—in the film and the makers of the film with the mechanical apparatus of film. It is what links the two key features of curiosity and fascination of Crafton's analysis.

Therefore, such automobility, such autokinesis, allies not only with the romantics' fascination for Crafton 'with the materials of artistic creation' but with the 'self-creating', self-animating, self-moving at stake in inanimate inorganic objects being 'brought to life' by media and technologies of simulation, themselves inorganic and ostensibly inanimate but having the capacity to 'animate' and problematize thereby their characterization as only inanimate. It is to suggest that our media and technologies of automobility, autokinesis, automation, the automaton and simulation have 'a life of their own'—the life of *the illusion of life*—the life of the automaton—a point remaining for us a bit too implicit in Crafton's articulation, where he appears to give more weight to *who* images and what *is* imaged in animation films than to *what* images. For us, the cinematograph is itself animatograph as automaton—a self-moving machine like the automobile and airplane.

A fascination binds the proto-history of cinema, the advent of cinema and the advent of cartoon animation. It is the fascination with the mysterious imbrication and reanimation of life and motion by means of an apparatus.[38] It is the fascination with *the illusion of life*, as *the life*(-likeness) *of* (the) *illusion*. It is the fascination with the way in which an apparatus animates—gives movement and life to—inanimate images of inanimate people and things—as illusions, making them appear to appear to live and move. It is the fascination with the way in which that apparatus may be thought to have reanimated the world in and as simulation.

It is the fascination with the automaton.

This fascination has animated their makers and their subjects as much as their makers and their subjects have animated it, even as it has animated the invention of the cinematic/animatic apparatus itself, and been reanimated by it in turn, as it has animated and been reanimated by that apparatus' technological ancestors and relatives of transportation.

Thus, the filmic apparatus is neither merely a machine, nor what it images merely mechanical, for it confounds, disseminates and seduces the very opposition of organic and mechanical, animism and mechanism. It is a *vital machine*—to use the term David F. Channell employs in his book *The Vital Machine* to define the new bionic world view that for him arrived by the beginning of the twentieth century to supersede the opposition, exhausted by the middle of the nineteenth, of the animistic (what he calls organic) and mechanistic world views—a dualistic view which he defines as 'in one sense *neither* mechanical nor organic, and in another sense *both* mechanical and organic',[39] a 'Derridean'[40] formulation, though unacknowledged as such—*a vital machine* that is the inheritor of and invention issuing from the debates between and creations of the animists and mechanists.[41]

It is what I call automaton, *animatic automaton*.

For me, the logics and processes of the animatic automaton—and of Channell's vital machine and bionic world view—are, after Derrida and contrary to Channell, never not in operation, making that inextricably coimplicated bionic view never not applicable in the history of those debates. Such logics and processes are never not working to perturb the impossible aspiration of each 'opposing' world view—animistic and mechanistic—to purity, totalization and subsumption of the other, never not rendering each view always already impure, hybrid—interacting with, incorporating elements of, contaminating and at the same time contaminated by, its opposite—even as my figure of *the animatic automaton* is the very figure of that inextricable coimplication.

The operation of such logics and processes means that the reconciliation, integration and closure which both Bolter and Channell envision with Turing's Man and the bionic world view, respectively, would be impossible of realization, as would that totalization sought by the animist and mechanist views jointly and severally. No reduction of Derridean *différance* to simple difference nor presence, no reduction of the Radical Other to a simple other always already incorporated in a logic of the Same, no reduction of the Radical Exotic, Seduction, Illusion, Evil, Cruelty (Jean Baudrillard) to the system and its oppositions, is possible, for the Other will always already have its revenge.

Crucially, for me, the very distinction between animation and cinema can be read as replaying the 'debate' between the animists and the mechanists, even in definitional terms, the terms of the very double definition of animation—endowing with life and endowing with motion. On the one hand, the definition would tie animation to animism (its most stunning articulation is that of *Eisenstein on Disney*[42]) and its tradition of endowing with life; and on the other hand, it would tie cinema, which derives from the Greek *kinema<kinein* and means motion, to mechanism and its tradition of endowing with motion.

Animation as the animatic tells us that such a simple distinction is unsustainable. As I have proposed, life and motion are always coimplicated; and they are coimplicated in the very double definition of animation.

And yet this distinction between animation and cinema is momentarily intriguing because it suggests that animation allows us, indeed compels us, as does cinema's own definition, to see cinema as affiliated with mechanism, despite (or even because of) cinema's efforts to try to establish itself as a living animistic presence—live action—*against* animation as mechanical—the merely mechanical degraded form of cinema (or as a graphic form unrelated to cinema).

In my '*Who Framed Roger Rabbit*' essay, I focus on the graphic aspect of this marginalization of animation by cinema and its institutions and hypothesize that, contrary to the doxa of Film Studies, animation might be thought to engender cinema (both historically and theoretically), and thus cinema might be thought to be animation's step-child.[43] I go on to suggest that insofar as animation implicates both life and motion and animates cinema, cinema may be thought of as a reduction of animation. Cinema would thus be a falling off from animation, the removal (or increasing removal) of the life (*anima*) of animation. Cinema would render (or increasingly render) that life of animation anemic.[44]

If one conjoins this thought to the characterization by some commentators of film's initial appeal—its mechanical illusion of life and motion—of animation—simulating the world—it might be possible to think in another register that that which fell off from animation in cinema has always already had its 'revenge' *against animation*—that is, animation as *anima*—through the life of the mechanism of film. Such 'life' would be a form of animation as *dissemination,* as writing, as Derrida articulates it.[45] It would suggest that even *within* animation film and film animation—that is, film 'as such', film as a form of animation—there is an evil demon lurking to disseminate animation as a pure animistic presence (such as animation and its institutions might assert in its turn against cinema as a mechanical falling off from animation!). This means that any effort on the part of *animation theorists* to ally *animation* only with animism, while seeking to expel the mechanical *as cinema*, is subject to the same challenge that the mechanical issues to the effort on the part of *film theorists* to ally *cinema* only with animism, while seeking to expel the mechanical *as animation*!

Both animation theorists and cinema theorists can thus be seen to be defending the same principle—the animistic—against what they take the other as representing—the(ir) opposite, the mechanistic. It also means that animation as the animistic confusion of boundaries—the Bororo's 'I am bird and human at the same time' that Sergei Eisenstein invokes[46]—is disseminated by an analogous process associated with the 'mechanical' as simulacrum, what Gilles Deleuze would call rather 'the machinic'.[47] If Eisenstein proposes animation as *anima*, here one might think of the T-1000 of *Terminator 2: Judgment Day*—this mimetic polyalloy—as the 'equivalent' 'mechanical' or machinic form—'the deadliest machine ever built'—its 'mechanical' or machinic form a formlessness that can simulate all form, the simulation of Eisenstein's protean plasmaticness, which plasmaticness is for Eisenstein the essence of film as animation as animism.[48]

Insofar as film is a simulative mechanical apparatus that always already doubles the animistic, even as the animatic apparatus doubles both the animistic and the mechanistic, not only do film's multiple registers, modes and forms of mechanical simulation double Eisenstein's multiple registers, modes and forms of animism in animation and cinema but the animatic apparatus disenables, suspends or collapses such oppositions even as it at the same time enables them.

I would propose a vertiginously complicated double game is being played here by an evil demon, what I would call the game, the play, of the animatic automaton, whose gambits I have barely detected. It is a game which the animatic automaton has played with animation and cinema from their 'inception' and which more recently is played out in the relation of films like *Blade Runner* and *Terminator 2* to *Akira*. It involves the indetermining of animism and mechanism and their traditions. For example, in *Blade Runner* the Nexus 6 replicant, as organic simulacrum, is therefore at once in both the animistic tradition and the mechanistic tradition and in neither of them. And in *Terminator 2* the T-1000, as inorganic simulacrum simulating animistic plasmaticness, is at once in both the mechanistic tradition and the animistic tradition and in neither of them. And both *Blade Runner* and *Terminator 2* are live action/cartoon animation hybrids, 'versus' *Akira*, a cartoon animation/live action hybrid.[49]

Here I would wish to propose an analogous process. Not only is the return of Film Studies to animation and of animation to Film Studies a return to and of animation as the 'unsurmounted' of Film Studies, from which for us not only film but Film Studies came—an 'uncanny' return, a return to what is old and long familiar but which is become strange, too (again)[50]—but the 'gift' of what I call *the illusion of life*—of animation as *the illusion of life*—to Film Studies is a 'gift' of lifedeath, of not only the 'uncanny' return of live action and Film Studies to animation and animation studies but also the 'uncanny' return of *both* live action and animation, *both* Film Studies and animation studies, to animation as 'animation', animation as 'inanimation', animation as lifedeath—animation as the *animatic*—which process is for us never not happening in film.

And once one has said this, lifedeath means that Film Studies returns to animation studies as its 'unsurmounted', as animation studies returns to Film Studies as its 'unsurmounted', so that each becomes the 'unsurmounted' of the other, each indistinguishes the other... So that if one looks at live action, one sees (it 'uncannily' turn into) animation, and vice versa, each thus indetermining 'its' 'other'—a turn (marked as) always already there insofar as *live action* inscribes the two key terms of animation[51]—to endow with life and to endow with motion. Live action is always already animation, and vice versa, with the qualification of lifedeath that the animatic has never not set into play. The 'uncanny' turn of animation is 'itself' always already doubled—reanimation.

This disseminative, seductive process is what I call the animatic.

The animatic problematizes any simple distinction between life and movement, animism and mechanism, human and nonhuman, animation and cinema, film and world. Indeed, it problematizes definition 'as such', telling us that a certain indetermining and suspending of distinctive opposition in a complicated dizzying coimplication of opposing terms and attributes always already defers the possibility of definitive fixed understandings of things, including animation, which both needs to be and is impossible to be thought,[52] this necessity and impossibility engendered by 'animation' 'itself'—the *animatic*.

The *animatic* allows me to propose that both animation and cinema are reduced forms of 'it', 'it' being like Roland Barthes' 'third meaning', that is, beyond 'animation, flux, mobility, "life", copy'[53]; that if animation and cinema would wish to be pure *anima*, purely animistic, as pure presence, then animation as the animatic would be dissemination as Derrida articulates it—dissemination the condition of possibility and impossibility of animation and cinema, not only necessarily included in them but necessarily excluded at the same time for them to 'be', that incomparable that allows them to be 'compared', that inexchangeable that allows them to be 'exchanged', that undecidable that allows them to be 'decided' upon.

Insofar as this disseminative process—the *animatic*—implicates and is implicated in and by the play of a mechanical apparatus, I choose to characterize this 'animatic apparatus' as *automaton*. The animatic automaton reanimates, disseminates and seduces the animistic modelling of animation and cinema—the cinematic apparatus—as it likewise reanimates, disseminates and seduces the mechanistic modelling of animation and cinema.

It is more than a bit intriguing to discover that even the definition of automaton is itself uncannily disseminative, dramatically so in light of what we have traced and argued so far. The *Encyclopedia of the Nineteenth Century* defines it—a definition which Christian Bailly offers in his exquisite book *Automata: The Golden Age, 1848-1914*—as 'a machine which has the form of an organised being and contains within itself a mechanism capable of creating movement and *simulating life*'[54] [my italics]. It is a definition that at the least conjoins and confounds the organic and the mechanical, creating and simulating. Webster's Dictionary puts it thus: '1. anything that can move or act of itself. 2. an apparatus with a concealed mechanism that enables it to move or work of itself. 3. a person or animal acting in an automatic or mechanical way'. In both definitions, not only are both the human and the nonhuman subsumed—for the human, as much as the nonhuman, is capable of not only moving and acting of itself but of simulating life, of acting in an automatic or mechanical way—but the filmic/cinematic apparatus is, too, making it—the animatic apparatus—automaton.

Like Bolter's 'the illusion of animation', the illusion, the simulation, of life is, of course, not life but rather its double and (un)doing, for its mechanical repetition of the living being incorporates death within it, as Derrida suggests of any mechanical process and/as repetition, including writing, making the automaton a form of lifedeath.[55] That is to say that, figured from antique times on as the 'living statue', etc., the automaton is a hybrid form, an 'animate inanimate'—a form of lifedeath that simulates both the animate and the inanimate at the same time, the 'mechanical' 'equivalent' of the toon in *Who Framed Roger Rabbit*, which toon is both and neither animal and human at the same time, as the automaton is both and neither machine and living being at the same time.[56]

Freud writes of the automaton and its 'uncanny' doubled aspect, as well as its relation to animism, in his uncanny essay, 'The "Uncanny"' ('*Das Unheimliche*'):

> Jentsch has taken as a very good instance [of what arouses the feeling of the 'uncanny'] 'doubts whether an apparently animate being is really alive; or conversely, whether a lifeless object might not be in fact animate'; and he refers in this connection to the impression made by waxwork figures, ingeniously constructed dolls and automata. To these he adds the uncanny effect of epileptic fits, and of manifestations of insanity, because these excite in the spectator the impression of automatic, mechanical processes at work behind the ordinary appearance of mental activity.[57]

For Freud, one factor which turns something frightening into something 'uncanny' is animism. He hypothesizes that this primitive belief is, in civilized people, 'in a state of having been (to a greater or lesser extent) *surmounted* [rather than repressed]'.[58]

He continues:

> Our conclusion could then be stated thus: an uncanny experience occurs either when infantile complexes which have been repressed are once more revived by some impression, or when primitive beliefs which have been surmounted seem once more to be confirmed... [T]hese two classes of uncanny experience are not always sharply distinguishable.[59]

I propose that these two classes of uncanny experience are never sharply distinguishable, such indistinguishing itself the work of the animatic.[60] One might call this also the work of the automaton. The automaton (con)fuses the either/orism of *either* a living being turning into an inanimate thing *or* an inanimate thing turning into a living being. Uncertainty, undecidability, as to whether a figure is living or dead, animate or inanimate, human or machine, animistic or mechanistic, is precisely what the automaton—the 'animate inanimate'—induces. Thus, it would have to be a question for Freud of the maintenance of both 'it appears to be animate but is inanimate' and 'it appears to be inanimate but is animate' at the same time. This is what makes the automaton 'uncanny', that is, *at once* strange and familiar, frightening and delightful, malign and benign—or, to be more precise, at once strangely familiar and familiarly strange, frighteningly delightful and delightfully frightening, malignly benign and benignly malign.[61]

Therefore, it would be wrong to say that the double is only and simply strange, frightening and malign. Indeed, the double of the human was first thought as guarantee of immortality and therefore comforted the human. It is the modern double and the 'uncanny' turn from one to the other—including as marked in the 'uncanny' turn of the still photographic image into the moving cinematographic image at the first screenings in 1895 and 1896 that so fascinated and horrified spectators—that discomfited the human with the spectre of its mortality in this fatal double.[62]

The automaton would be that 'uncanny' figure not quite dead, not quite alive, that at once both delights and terrifies, reminding us that we return from death, live with death and return to the death from which we came, for the animatic automaton as 'uncanny' is bound to Freud's notion of the Death Drive—that drive of animate beings to return to the inanimate state from which they came[63]—for which all 'uncanny' returns are doubles, that is, it is death which returns, doubles back on 'itself', suggesting that there is always something 'inanimate' in animation, and vice versa. What returns as the return, the automaton, neither (completely) dead nor (completely) alive, both alive and dead at the same time, is of the order of the simulacrum, seduction (Baudrillard), *différance* (Derrida), the sublime (Immanuel Kant and Jean-François Lyotard), the evil demon (Baudrillard[64]), the diabolical third (Baudrillard, Michel Serres)—*the illusion of life* and *the life of illusion*. Something demonic is at work here.

For example, writing in 'To Speculate—on "Freud"' of the *fort: da* game—the child's tossing of the wooden spool/reel (already evoking one element of the filmic apparatus) away and making it return—and of its process as that of the movement of the 'narrative' of Freud's *Beyond the Pleasure Principle*, Derrida treats the demon performing in and on Freud's text as revenant automaton, binding writing, the uncanny, the Death Drive, the spectre and the automaton with the demon in a way that provides the constituent elements of what I call the Cryptic Complex of cinema as animatic apparatus, which apparatus after Derrida supplies 'finality without end, the beauty of the devil'.[65]

In his essay 'Typography', Philippe Lacoue-Labarthe suggests that Socrates is fond of speaking of the Daedalian (and Pygmalian?) artifice of the 'living statue', the animated statue, and that, as for Plato,

> what unsettles him, in the plastic realm or in 'fiction' (whatever form it might take), is, as P.M. Schuhl has suggested, *simultaneously* that the inanimate being should give itself as something alive and that this (falsely or illusorily) living thing should never be sufficiently alive, that is, it should always let death show through too much (in other words, 'brute' death, the bad death that the sensible world holds—and not that death that marks the 'separation of the soul and the body' as the beginning of the true

> 'life of the spirit'). The *deinon*, the *Unheimliche* (as the ex-patriation or exile of the soul, as well) is this unassignable, this 'neither dead nor alive', that disturbs, or always risks disturbing, the fundamental ontological opposition (between the present and the non-present). This is mimesis, the 'disquieting strangeness' of fiction: undecidability 'itself'.[66]

Marking 'the ex-patriation or exile of the soul', of the spirit, the uncanny spectre of the living statue, of the automaton, disturbs ontological opposition, including that of animism and mechanism, including that of mind, spirit and soul (varyingly, Gr. *psyche*, L. *animus, anima*[67]) on the one hand and body and matter on the other.

In the Introduction to *THE ILLUSION OF LIFE*, I characterize *the illusion of life* of animation as bearing a privileged relation to Freud's uncanny, as the uncanny reanimation by animation film, film animation and the animatic apparatus of the world in and as simulation. Not only is the animatic automaton that is this animating apparatus a simulator, it is a simulation—an 'animate inanimate'—an 'apparatus of the "uncanny"' that, doubling, replicating, world, indetermines and suspends *all* distinctive oppositions, including that of film 'versus' world, etc. (Derrida's *crise du versus*)—thereby indetermining 'itself'. Which is to say that *the apparatus of the animatic automaton is itself a 'defining' technology*.

In terms of this 'defining technology', the technology of the Mystic Writing-Pad that Freud offers as a model metaphor and metaphorical model of mind is one which has been taken up and challenged by Film Studies. In this regard, Thierry Kuntzel', in his 'A Note upon the Filmic Apparatus',[68] proposes the cinematic apparatus as a better model than the Mystic Writing-Pad of what Freud had in mind in modelling mind with the Pad. For his part, Derrida, in his 'Freud and the Scene of Writing',[69] proffers writing as a better model than the Pad. Derrida's naming of *cinematography* as a form of writing, a form of the graph and the gram—form invested with death—in *Of Grammatology* provides the link, the bridge, between the cinematic apparatus and writing enabling an articulation of the cinema and of Freud's model of mind (of *psyche*) as always already animatic apparatus.[70] Although Derrida has never to my knowledge specifically elaborated on his naming of cinematography as form of writing, what his naming means is that wherever he writes of writing—that simulacrum that would be for him a 'defining technology'—the cinema as animatic apparatus and animatic automaton are subsumed therein.

In simulating life, the 'mechanism' of the animatic automaton multiplies and divides it, making life, like 'itself', the same as and other than 'itself'—life-like, the semblance, the simulation, of life. For me, the cinema reanimates life as semblance, as simulation, engendered by the animatic apparatus, itself a simulacral machine like the clepsydra, which Sigvard Strandh, in his book *The History of the Machine*, calls in its most refined version a simulacrum that imitated the movement of the cosmos and which automaton Plato himself made in simple form to alarm his students, to wake them up![71] 'Wake up. Time to die', says Leon to Deckard in *Blade Runner*, recalling Plato's call to his students. For Plato, philosophy is preparation of the philosopher not for life—for life for the philosopher could only ever be the imitation, the simulation, of life—but for death—for death, as Lacoue-Labarthe puts it, 'as the beginning of the true "life of the spirit"'.

Here I am reminded of Deleuze's characterization of the philosopher in *Cinema 2: The Time-Image*:

> For philosophers are beings who have passed through a death, who are born from it, and go towards another death, perhaps the same one. In a very happy story, Pauline Harvey says that she understands nothing about philosophy, but is very fond of philosophers because they give her a double impression: they themselves believe that they are dead, that they have passed through death; and they also believe that, although dead, they continue to live, but in a shivering way, with tiredness and prudence. According to Pauline Harvey, this would be a double mistake, which amuses her. According to us, it is a double truth, although this is cause for amusement as well: the philosopher is someone who believes he has returned from the dead, rightly or wrongly, and who returns to the dead in full consciousness. The philosopher has returned from the dead and goes back there. This has been the living formulation of philosophy since Plato.[72]

In characterizing the philosopher thus, does Deleuze not make him into that uncanny 'being'—one of the living dead, an animatic automaton?!

To sum up, the animatic automaton marks the disseminative (con)fusion of the mechanistic tradition of automata with that animistic tradition (including of automata) which endows with life, offering an uncanny simulation of both, a simulation of both animism and mechanism, life and motion, animation and cinema, etc., which is to suggest not only that the animatic apparatus converges with Walter Benjamin's notion of the decline of the aura of the work of art in the age of mechanical reproduction—age of photography and cinema—but also that our machines have (and possibly increasingly) a 'life' of their own, which is also (of the nature of double invagination) ours—lifedeath.

Significantly, the cinematic apparatus as so theorised—as animatic apparatus—deconstructs the ways in which it has been thought in late '60s and '70s Marxist film theory as akin to the robot (work, production, the banal), disseminated by the animatic apparatus as automaton (play, seduction, the fatal, the sublime, the singular) or as cyborg. In this regard, when Baudrillard poses the question—what is sovereign principle today?—his answer for cinema seems to be that seduction (warm, enchanted simulation) has been overtaken by simulation (cold, disenchanted seduction). He writes:

> A whole generation of films is appearing which will be to those we have known what the android is to man: marvellous, flawless artifacts, dazzling simulacra which lack only an imaginary and that particular hallucination which makes cinema what it is.[73]

Baudrillard's configuring of cinema in a way that links his third order of simulation with the android—thinkable from his description and analysis as cyborg—opens it as well to be thought in a way that links cinema's earliest, what he calls 'most fantastic or mythical',[74] order to seduction, enchantment and the automaton. As his reference to android suggests, Baudrillard's history, or rather destiny, of the world as articulated in 'The Orders of Simulacra', including in for us the key section notably entitled 'The Automaton and the Robot',[75] finds a parallel in his treatment of cinema: from a first order of seduction, metamorphosis, animism and the automaton; to a second order of production (swallowed up in reproduction), metaphor, mechanism and the robot; to a third order of simulation, metastasis, cybernetics and the cyborg. Therefore, in asking, including of cinema—does seduction still live and is it still sovereign, or is all now cold, disenchanted simulation?—Baudrillard is also asking—do metamorphosis, animism and the automaton still live and remain sovereign or is all now metastasis, cybernetics and the cyborg?[76]

Which is to say that for Baudrillard, the automaton is an enchanted, theatrical, illusionistic, counterfeit form—the analogy, perfect double and interlocutor of man—a 'sublime and singular'[77] device of resemblance posing metaphysical questions of and to the human, questions of appearance and being, thus anything but an automatic worker machine—a robot.

Insofar as I would argue after Derrida that the automaton disseminates both animism and mechanism as well as propose after Baudrillard that it is sovereign 'principle', including in cinema, I would submit that it problematizes C.W. Ceram's highly loaded effort in *Archaeology of the Cinema* to seek to exclude it, animation and mechanism in general from cinema, cinema being for Ceram of the order of technology, which is for him dynamic as against the static nature of mechanics.[78] Arguably, the 'mechanical' is already 'dynamic' in advance of Ceram's 'technology'(!), to say nothing of the automaton, animation and the animatic.

Philip Brophy, in his essay 'The Animation of Sound', argues that the cinematic apparatus presumes and subsumes animation as animism—the bringing to life of what it animates—and poses instead the animatic apparatus, with animation as dynamism, the apparatus 'itself coming to life'.[79] I would suggest, however, that the apparatus does both, brings what 'it' animates to life as well as 'itself' to life, with the qualifications that bringing, or coming, 'to life' is not equivalent to life and that the apparatus (un)does 'itself', seduces 'itself' at the same time as it produces 'itself'. I would propose that lifedeath, like the Law in Kafka's Parable of the Man before the Law in *The Trial*, makes impossible the aspiration of cinema and animation to 'come to life', makes that 'coming to life' of the order of the asymptote and the simulacrum, even as it makes impossible the aspiration of cinema and animation to 'come to death'. No more than life can death be 'come to'. Like Kafka's Messiah, both arrive a day too late (or too early).[80]

Like the lightning sketch, the earliest form of the hybrid live action/cartoon animation film—bridge between 'pure' live action and 'pure' animation—the animatic apparatus as automaton is the bridge, the hybrid bridge, between animism and mechanism, animation and cinema, human and nonhuman (machine), etc., that third coming between any and every two things, including two opposing poles, as well as 'forming' the medium in which all 'come to life' and 'come to death'—which would be the simultaneous bringing of death to life and life to death—lifedeath.[81]

The 'uncanny' fascination in seeing life and movement, the life and movement of the world, simulated by a mechanical apparatus is, as I have proposed, the fascination offered by and as the automaton.[82] Crucially, to say the automaton 'simulates' and is a simulation binds it to issues of representation and simulation which have marked Western art and philosophy 'from Plato on'. In Book 10 of *The Republic*, Plato compares the original Idea (of Bed or Table) to the good copy (the bed or table that a carpenter makes)—the likeness to the original Idea or model, a likeness or resemblance because it partakes in the interior and spiritual essence of the original Idea—and compares both to the bad copy—the phantasmatic simulacrum (the image made of a bed or table by an artist or poet)—the mere exterior semblance without resemblance to the Idea and good copy.

For Deleuze, 'the Sophist himself is the simulcral being,...the Proteus who intrudes and insinuates himself everywhere',[83] which, in the form of the poet—that 'monster who is likely to assume all forms, a magician of metamorphoses—a Proteus'[84]—Plato condemned, writes Jean-Pierre Vernant. Poetry and art, species of the mimetic for Plato, have affinities for him, Vernant tells us, 'with the polymorphic and gaudy world of becoming and with the inferior part of the soul that is always unstable and in flux and is the seat in us of the desires and passion',[85] with the deceptive, phantasmatic, simulacral world of 'sensible becoming that belongs to ever-changing appearances'.[86]

Here we should recall Eisenstein's 'protean plasmaticness', explicitly associated by him with the myth of this sea god, whose appeal, he writes, is 'the omnipotence of plasma, which contains in "liquid" form all possibilities of future species and forms'.[87] Such would be Eisenstein's animistic, protean plasmatic 'essence of film', for me (non)essence, neither animistic nor mechanistic, both animistic and mechanistic, at the same time. For me, film 'as such' would be this sophistic, protean plasmatic, plastic, simulacral, metamorphosing automaton, which can mime, metamorphose into, hyperconform to, all forms—including animism and mechanism—always already seducing them thereby, always already leading them astray.[88]

The simulacrum is a false, groundless claimant that Plato banishes, along with those who artifice it, from the ideal state. Deleuze writes that for Plato, 'Simulation is the phantasm itelf, that is, the effect of the operations of the simulacrum as machinery, Dionysiac machine'.[89] The worst, most uncanny aspect of the simulacrum as Dionysiac machine—as what I call *animatic automaton*—is characterized by Deleuze as follows:

> Plato, by dint of inquiring in the direction of the simulacrum, discovers, in the flash of an instant as he leans over its abyss, that the simulacrum is not simply a false copy, but that it calls into question the very notions of the copy...and of the model. The final definition of the Sophist leads us to the point where we can no longer distinguish him from Socrates himself: the ironist operating in private by elliptical arguments. Was it not inevitable that irony be pushed this far? And that Plato be the first to indicate this direction for the overthrow of Platonism?[90]

In his turn, Baudrillard writes: 'Whereas representation tries to absorb simulation by interpreting it as false representation, simulation envelops the whole edifice of representation as itself a simulacrum'[91]—a characterization shadowing, challenging, all simple representational models of the image, all models assuming the good faith and candour of the image, including those modelling film,[92] and I would add, animation.

The animatic automaton as simulacrum not only enables the

cinematic apparatus but at the same time disenables it, is at once its condition of possibility and impossibility, making the cinematic apparatus the reduced form of the animatic apparatus, reduced form of the animatic automaton. The animatic automaton as simulacrum indetermines and suspends the distinction between representation and simulation, making it impossible to say not only which is which but what each 'itself' 'is'. Plato philosophizes in the shadow of the simulacrum, the animatic automaton, as does *all* of philosophy 'from Plato on'. And life is artificed in the shadow of the simulacrum, in the shadow of the animatic automaton, turning animism's original or good copy into protean, seductive simulacrum.

For Baudrillard, cinema is of the order of the simulacrum—the double, the phantasm, the mirror, the dream, the myth, etc.—of the order of the evil demon, evil, Seduction, Illusion, irreconcilability. Descartes tries to exile the evil demon with withering doubt until he can find something he is sure of—doubt itself. In his turn, Baudrillard is sure only that there is no sureness, which makes him in this sense like Descartes.

I would follow the suggestion of Rex Butler that an evil demon as evil would always be in play, unsettling even that sureness, suggesting that even doubt must be doubted, an evil demon, I submit, which is that third that forever makes impossible the simple fusion of mind and body in the human via the pineal gland that Descartes unsatisfactorily proposes in *The Passions of the Soul*. No more than Plato can Descartes or Baudrillard exile the evil demon. Indeed, any effort to exile it will include it, and vice versa.

The evil demon of the simulacrum, of the automaton, will double Plato, as his Sophist doubled Socrates and himself. The evil demon will double Descartes, as the automaton Francine that legend has it Descartes built as his daughter doubles him, as Rachael doubles her maker Tyrell in *Blade Runner*. The evil demon doubles and (un)does everything and everyone.

Parenthetically, I wonder if Descartes' Francine derived her name from the Francines who constructed the automata grottos in the gardens at St. Germain-en-Laye, grottos known to Descartes! A student whose name is now lost to me suggested in class that Deckard—the 'hero' of *Blade Runner*—is a variant of Descartes. (I suggested Tyrell is a variant of Turing.) This would therefore offer us a second relation: Rachael is to Deckard as Francine is to Descartes. This would suggest that Deckard's problem[93]—of distinguishing replicants from humans—is analogous to Descartes' vis-à-vis doubt, tying thereby the replicant and the evil demon.

Given such a logic, one that sees Descartes seek to exile doubt—the evil demon—only to, in the same move, incorporate it cryptically within his 'self', it is hardly surprising that *Blade Runner* leaves a textual hole in Deckard's not answering Rachael's question as to whether he himself took the Voight-Kampff test to determine if *he* is a replicant. As such, it could be proposed that *Blade Runner* plays Turing's Game, making cinema a form of the Voight-Kampff test for the viewer, its challenge to distinguish the human from the artificial human, a challenge impossible of success.

This is also to say that *Blade Runner* plays out the debates between the animists and the mechanists as one of its main subjects. In terms of animism, the film's dystopian depiction in the opening shot of a vast, dark, filthy landscape illuminated by refineries' fires shooting up into the black night sky joins with Roy Batty's pyrotechnical words, 'Fiery the angels fell', and his final words as well:

> I've seen things, seen things you wouldn't believe. Attack ships on fire off the shoulder of Orion bright as magnesium. I rode on the back decks of a blinker and watched c-beams glitter in the dark near the Tanhauser Gate. All these moments... They'll be gone.

All this, but especially the flood of fire shooting up the iris of an unattributed giant eye in the opening sequence, recalls for me the animistic creationist myths of ancient Greece, appealing to the figure of the spark of life as mobilized by Hephaestus and Prometheus. For me, the unattributed eye cannot but be attributed to these gods associated with animating fire, as well as with a universe animated by fire—Heraclitus' πρηστηρ (spinning fire), the Stoics' *pneuma*—as its elemental substance.[94]

In terms of mechanism, the first sequence in which Deckard and Rachael kiss shows that they 'have something in common'. A mysterious white sheen suddenly appears on Deckard's face. Then, on the other side of the bridging shot of the vast hypermediatized landscape, with its image of a Japanese woman popping pills (thinkable in terms of the *pharmakon* and its logics as Derrida articulates it[95]), we discover Pris white-faced, then sight J.F. Sebastian with his white-faced Kaiser Wilhelm automaton, then see Roy make his appearance. The white sheen thus can be read as retrospectively posing the question of whether Deckard is himself a replicant. That is, not only would Descartes' body be like the automaton but his double, Deckard, would be replicant!

J.F. Sebastian lives with his friends—automata, including the Kaiser Wilhelm toy and a teddy bear dressed as Napoleon. As well, he has a clock whose elaborate architecture and cuckoo's sound recall the great Strasbourg clock of the fourteenth century. Bolter suggests this latter clock, with its automaton cock that flapped its wings and crowed at twelve o'clock, sparked the thinking of Descartes and Leibniz.[96] At Roy Batty's death, a bell tolls, also recalling that clock; and Deckard releases a dove, one which has always struck commentators as a false, trite, saccharine Hollywood excuse for an ending. Yet for me, it recalls Archytas of Tarentum's simulation flying wooden pigeon, thereby continuing the film's debate between animism and mechanism, human and replicant.

Blade Runner plays out this debate in one register in terms of the gap between J.F. Sebastian's automata, which, like his dolls (also marking the inscription of Freud's uncanny in the text), are distinguishable from the human, and Tyrell's replicants, which are now indistinguishable from the human, except, that is, insofar as their animatedness—their endowments both of movement and 'life' (emotion, spirit)—is seen to belong to no human in the film, especially not to Deckard, whose mechanical nature is particularly pronounced at the beginning of the film, serving to establish not only the difference between the replicant and the human but also the condition for his possible reanimation. 'More human than human'—the Tyrell Corporation's logo—announces that in their outbidding and surpassing of the human, these hyperuncanny replicants—both more human and less human than the human at the same time—as their name suggests, *re-ply* (re-fold) the human, (re)animating Deckard, and as well the human viewer. And insofar as Rachael is not Nexus 6 but Nexus 7, with an unknown termination date, the film suggests that she is the most indeterminate of all, even possibly an immortal. And all this recasts the opening sequence as a kind of reply to Disney's *A World Is Born* segment of *Fantasia*, for here in *Blade Runner* a world is dying while another is perhaps being born.

Insofar as nothing stands outside the insinuating evil demon of simulation, I would suggest that this is true of all this essay proposes, suspended by the Artaudian spiritual automaton as the powers of the false, the unthinkable, which cannot, and cannot not, be thought, as well as by the psychological automaton,[97] by the interstice, the between, the third, dissemination, the evil demon—the animatic automaton. The animatic automaton is fatal to all efforts at the production of meaning, including the effort to produce 'its' meaning. For 'it'—this nothing and everything at the same time—is that which not only produces meaning but seduces it. And the fatal must be fatal to 'itself', or 'it' is not fatal. The evil demon that doubles Descartes replies, replicates—shall I not say *replicants*?!—everything, posts everything posited, charted, mapped.[98] Insofar as the replicant is 'virtually identical to the human', as the opening intertitle of *Blade Runner* declares, it is 'only' the asymptote of the virtual, of the animatic—the animatic automaton—that keeps them apart, keeps them double.[99]

Given that Rachael is ostensibly the closest to the human in the film, it would seem that it should have been she rather than Pris who doubles and (un)does Descartes in saying, 'I think, Sebastian, therefore I am'.[100] Its name written in the opening intertitle of the film (in italics—(the) ghost writing, the writing of the revenant, the spectre), the *replicant*—the 'more human than human'—retires/replies/refolds everything, including 'itself', like/as the evil demon of the animatic automaton. The first time written, *replicant*, like the title *Blade Runner* itself, is in red—a singular isomorphism—red the colour not only of blood but of fire! And, though not in red but in white—like all the other titles but for *Blade Runner*—in the remainder of the intertitle, *replicant* never ceases to be written in italics.

Therefore, not only does the blade runner 'retire' the replicant (in line with its role as stated in the opening intertitle), the replicant 'retires' the blade runner, the human, at the same time, where 'retires'—from the French *retirer*—means, against the implication of the intertitle, not to render merely inanimate but to *redraw*, thereby relating the animatic automaton to the Derridean graphics of supplementarity.[101]

Given all of this, should it surprise anyone that at various points in its history, the automaton has been linked with the devil?! Legend has it that Descartes' Francine was thrown off a ship during a storm at sea by an anxious captain afraid of having such a demonic, devilish creation on board. Strandh suggests that the basis of this legend is perhaps 'that Descartes had a daughter called Francine on the wrong side of the blanket, so that the legendary android Francine could have been a substitute for the girl'.[102]

This legend imitates two earlier stories of automata being regarded as the work of the devil. One has it that Thomas Aquinas smashed to bits the automaton constructed by his teacher, Albertus Magnus, the Bishop of Regensburg, whose doorkeeper of metal, wood, wax and leather 'greeted visitors by uttering "Salve"! and by asking them their business'.[103] The other relates how the abbot of the monastery of San Yuste in Estremadura, witnessing the amusing automata that Juanelo Turriano built for his melancholic Emperor, Charles V—again including an android in the form of a valet[104]—was convinced that Turriano was in league with the devil himself.

And given all this, should it surprise anyone that (the) (d)evil (demon) bedevils animation with and as the animatic automaton as Dionysiac simulacrum machine, replicating apparatus? Should it surprise anyone that 'Nexus *replicants*' marks the double ch(i)asmatic bind(ing) of the simulacrum?[105]

Here I draw to a 'close' with a 'demonic' image from *Blade Runner* to speculate on: the suspension of the *human* and the *artificial human* on the ledge across the chasm, the abyss, in the duel between the duo Deckard and Batty atop J.F. Sebastian's building. But, given the suspension, dissemination and seduction of polar opposites, which is which?

NOTES

This essay was presented at the third Society for Animation Studies conference, at the Rochester Institute of Technology, Rochester, New York, October 4-6, 1991. Though since enlarged and extended, it remains basically the 1991 essay, with nothing significant removed from or altered within it. I believe it is as 'current', relevant and important to animation studies today as it was then, which is why I have included it in the book. Its relevance is most recently confirmed by the Animation Research Centre of the Surrey Institute of Art & Design, University College, having as one of its suggested areas of addressal for its July 10-11, 2003 *Animated 'Worlds'* conference 'The figure, automata, simulacra and the "Doppelgänger"'.

1 See *THE ILLUSION OF LIFE: Essays on Animation*, ed. Alan Cholodenko (Sydney: Power Publications in association with the Australian Film Commission, 1991). The reader is advised to consult that Introduction and essay for the several points here drawn from them, as well as in general. Insofar as this essay is animated by texts it at once draws from and to, even as, at the same time, it reanimates and redraws them, it itself illustrates and performs a deconstructive, animatic process for us never not happening.

2 J. David Bolter, *Turing's Man* (London: Duckworth, 1984).

3 ibid., p. 11.

4 ibid., p. 13.

5 Isaac Asimov and Karen A. Frenkel, *Robots: Machines in Man's Image* (New York: Harmony Books, 1985), p. 2. The bronze living statue that Hephaestus animated—Talos by name—is depicted in Ray Harryhausen's *Jason and the Argonauts*.

6 Sigvard Strandh, *The History of the Machine* (New York: Dorset Press, 1979, 1989), p. 171.

7 Given that one definition of animation is to inspire, the giving of breath (inspiration) and its taking away (expiration) are privileged modalities of animation.

8 Bolter, *Turing's Man*, p. 203. While Bolter tracks the two traditions back to ancient Greece, Alfred Chapuis and Edmond Droz go further, to ancient Egypt with its 'living statues', which moved and talked through the 'presence' of the gods. Chapuis and Droz, *Automata: A Historical and Technological Study*, trans. Alec Reid (Neuchatel: Editions du Griffon, 1958), Chapter 1.

9 ibid.

10 ibid.

11 Such grottos offer a take on Plato's Cave and the modelling of cinema in terms of that Cave in late '60s Marxist film theory, turning that Cave, that modelling and that theory toward the grotesque as subcategory of the sublime and pressing the implications of the grotesque and the sublime for the thinking of animation and film.

12 Bolter says that ancestors of Vaucanson's duck surely helped to confirm Descartes' vision of animal and human as intricate clockwork mechanisms. *Turing's Man*, p. 205. For me, Vaucanson's duck has other ancestors to be reckoned with as well: Donald Duck and Daffy Duck, for starters.

13 Quoted from Voltaire's *Discourse on the Nature of Man*, in Isaac Asimov and Karen A. Frenkel, *Robots: Machines in Man's Image* , p. 5.

14 Bolter, *Turing's Man*, p. 205.

15 ibid. To these marvels of de Vaucanson and Jacquet-Droz one could add the toy-size automata of Juanelo Turriano.

16 Frederik L. Schodt, *Inside the Robot Kingdom: Japan, Mechatronics, and the Coming Robotopia* (New York: Kodansha International, 1988, 1990), p. 56.

17 Mary Shelley, *Frankenstein: or, the Modern Prometheus* (London: Penguin Books, 1994), p. 9.

18 La Mettrie quoted in Bolter, *Turing's Man*, p. 205.

19 See René Descartes, *Discourse on Method, Discourse on Method and the Meditations*, trans. F.E. Sutcliffe (Harmondsworth: Penguin Books, 1968, 1985), p. 73. On Descartes' knowledge of and influence by the automata grottos of the gardens at St Germain-en-Laye, see Leonora Cohen Rosenfield, *From Beast-Machine to Man-Machine: Animal Soul in French Letters from Descartes to La Mettrie*, new ed. (New York: Octagon, 1968), p. 6, as referenced by David F. Channell, *The Vital Machine: A Study of Technology and Organic Life* (New York: Oxford University Press, 1991), p. 34.

20 See Mark Rose, *Alien Encounters* (Cambridge: Harvard University Press, 1981) on Hobbes.

21 See Norbert Wiener, *Cybernetics, or Control and Communication in the Animal and the Machine*, 2d ed. (Cambridge: The MIT Press, 1948, 1961) on Leibniz and Newton.

22 To philosophize in the light of automata is to philosophize at the least in terms of a double(d) metaphor of the automaton and of light. On philosophy's dependence upon metaphor, including sun metaphors, see Jacques Derrida, 'White Mythology: Metaphor in the Text

of Philosophy', *Margins of Philosophy*, trans. Alan Bass (Chicago: The University of Chicago Press, 1982), including pp. 266-267, on Descartes' utilization of such metaphors. For Derrida, the heliotropic character of Western metaphysics contains the seeds of its own dissemination, for in turning toward and upon such metaphors as 'the light of the sun' and 'the light of day', philosophy opens itself to the danger that the heliotrope—and/as metaphor—holds for philosophy, the danger that Aristotle recognized in the Sophist in his simulating doubling of philosophy. For Derrida, metaphor 'always carries its death within itself' (p. 271), a double death—one reconcilable with philosophy, fulfilling itself within it; the other irreconcilable with philosophy, spelling philosophy's own death.

In this regard, an intriguing connection is to be found in the fact that Strandh remarks (*The History of the Machine*, p. 178) upon the influence of Descartes upon Father Athanasius Kircher, who was not only the maker of automata but the creator of the magic lantern, on which the motion picture projector is based. For me, insofar as the magic lantern simulates the light of the sun, which light certain animistic film-makers like D.W. Griffith and Frank Capra assume or desire cinema to be animated by and to animate and project with—what would be a metaphysical, theological project(ion) by means of which cinema would unveil truth as presence—that magic lantern (and its avatar the motion picture projector) replaces that sunlight with the light of the illusion of life and of automata—the light of the crepuscular, that of twilight—a light never without shadow, without Descartes' evil demon (for example, in the 'First Meditation' in *The Meditations*)—which is also the twilight of metaphor and of defining technologies. See my Introduction to *THE ILLUSION OF LIFE*, as well as my essay therein, '*Who Framed Roger Rabbit*, or the Framing of Animation', pp. 230-235, where I foreground after Derrida the light of the doubled sun—the light of the moon, of the lunar—of cinema.

23 Aram Vartanian, *La Mettrie's* L'Homme Machine (Princeton: Princeton University Press, 1960), pp. 67-68.

24 Bolter, *Turing's Man*, pp. 205-206.

25 ibid., p. 206.

26 ibid.

27 Bolter fails to mention the cyborg in this context, presumably regarding it as an embodiment and extension of the computer.

28 Including linking not only both varieties of classical automata with each other but both of them with Descartes' clockwork automaton. In

terms of animistic myths, the metaphorical model and model metaphor of technology and the technology of metaphorical model and model metaphor are doubled, for not only are myths technologies/ metaphorical models and model metaphors but these are myths *of* technology/metaphorical models and model metaphors, performing what they describe and describing what they perform at the same time.

29 Beyond such indefining, Derrida's assertion, after Freud, of 'the irreducible metaphoricity', the figurativeness, of 'the structure of scientific language' applies for me as well to the language of technology, indeed to language as such, spelling thereby the death of defining as pure, simple, literal, denotative positivity 'as such'. See Sigmund Freud, *Beyond the Pleasure Principle* (1920), The Pelican Freud Library, vol. 11, *On Metapsychology: The Theory of Psychoanalysis,* ed. Angela Richards and trans. James Strachey (Harmondsworth: Penguin, 1984), p. 334; and Derrida, 'To Speculate—on "Freud"', *The Post Card: From Socrates to Freud and Beyond,* trans. Alan Bass (Chicago: The University of Chicago Press, 1987), pp. 381-382.

See also Rosalyn Diprose and Cathryn Vasseleu, 'Animation—AIDS in Science/Fiction', in *THE ILLUSION OF LIFE.* Diprose and Vasseleu foreground the way fiction inescapably and inextricably informs 'reality', and I would add vice-versa, in their case the inescapable 'fictioning' and metaphoricity animating science's models, processes and representations of itself, in particular in the case of scientific research into AIDS, including in terms of the use of the metaphor of the bridge, of metaphor as bridge and of the bridge as model metaphor. For me, not only is the 'link' (Bolter's term) itself metaphor—that is, metaphorical model and model metaphor—not only are the links that defining technologies develop all in a sense so, but those links are—contrary to those Bolter poses 'with a culture's science, philosophy, or literature'—across a culture's science, philosophy *and* literature, as evidenced by the defining technology of the automaton as figured in and across science, philosophy *and* literature, across the animistic and mechanistic traditions, linking and coimplicating all of them inextricably.

30 Mark C. Taylor, 'Introduction: System...Structure...Difference...Other', *Deconstruction in Context*, ed. Mark C. Taylor (Chicago: The University of Chicago Press, 1986), p. 4.

31 On the complex logics of the remake, see Lisa Trahair, 'For the Noise of a Fly', in *THE ILLUSION OF LIFE.*

32 Baudrillard also refers to this Other as the Radical Exotic, after Victor

Segalen. See Baudrillard, 'Irreconcilability' and 'Radical Exoticism', in *The Transparency of Evil*, trans. James Benedict (London: Verso, 1993).

33 It is intriguing to note within philosophy a tradition of mechanistic philosophy already operating as contagion, challenging the pureness of the human, and as well 'within' it, the history of thinking the limits to philosophy. In his helpful Introduction to *Deconstruction in Context*, Taylor takes up major aspects of such thinking, as well as collecting in that book significant texts conducting such a project, including Derrida's essay 'Différance'.

34 Inspired/animated by the mechanist Jacquet-Droz, Shelley animates her text as Victor animates his artificial man. For Peter Hutchings, such animating in *Frankenstein* and its avatars is, after Julia Kristeva, a process of abjection that characterizes what he calls 'the work-shop of filthy animation'. Its collocations of textuality and *tekhnē*—literary, scientific, cinematic—not only confuse and conflate Shelley and Victor, her novel and the monster, the literary text/body and the monstrous, scientific text/body but the makers with the made. In light of Hutchings' treatment, we would speak of the *tekhnē* of textuality and the textuality of *tekhnē*. See Peter Hutchings, 'The Work-shop of Filthy Animation', in *THE ILLUSION OF LIFE*.

35 Donald Crafton, *Before Mickey: The Animated Film, 1898-1928* (Cambridge: The MIT Press, 1982, 1987), p. 32.

36 ibid.

37 ibid., pp. 32-33.

38 I articulate this fascination in my Introduction to *THE ILLUSION OF LIFE*, pp. 18-20.

39 Channell, *The Vital Machine*, p. 90. Thus, unlike Bolter, Channell refuses to grant victory to the mechanist world view. As well, tellingly, he asserts that the automata of the Middle Ages and Renaissance still supported the organic world view, the technology of these automata being for him 'closely associated with magical, spiritual, or organic forces' (p. 72).

40 I put Derridean in quotes because of the inconsistency in Channell's articulations of his definition.

41 For me, Channell's vital machine and bionic world view open themselves up to a reading of film animation and cinema in accord with our Derridean modelling of them. Channell himself never addresses them.

42 Sergei Eisenstein, *Eisenstein on Disney*, ed. Jay Leyda and trans. Alan Upchurch (New York: Methuen, 1986, 1988).

43 Cholodenko, '*Who Framed Roger Rabbit*, or the Framing of Animation',

pp. 212-214. See also my Introduction to *THE ILLUSION OF LIFE*, pp. 9-10.

44 Unless, of course, life is already anemic in comparison with motion; or there is a life of motion which is increasing while the motion of life is decreasing, that one has absorbed or is absorbing the other's energy and life to its own enhancement—its redoubling, in a fatal game of defiance, outbidding, hypertelia, metamorphosis and reversion. Here, after Baudrillard, one is forced to ask: is animism today more mechanism than mechanism, everywhere except in itself, everywhere except in what is alive, what is human, thus in the machine, in technology?! And is mechanism today more animism than animism, everywhere except in itself, everywhere except in what is a machine, a technology, thus in what is alive, what is human?! These are questions already engaged with in analogous ways in my '"OBJECTS IN MIRROR ARE CLOSER THAN THEY APPEAR": The Virtual Reality of *Jurassic Park* and Jean Baudrillard', in *Jean Baudrillard, Art and Artefact*, ed. Nicholas Zurbrugg (London: Sage Publications, 1997); and my 'Apocalyptic Animation: In the Wake of Hiroshima, Nagasaki, *Godzilla* and Baudrillard', in *Baudrillard West of the Dateline*, eds. Victoria Grace, Heather Worth and Laurence Simmons (Palmerston North, New Zealand: Dunmore Press, 2003).

45 I argued the affinity between animation and Derridean dissemination, writing, in '*Who Framed Roger Rabbit*, or the Framing of Animation', pp. 214-216. Insofar as Alexandre Alexeïeff adds a new name to the animistic list of Prometheuses—Emile Reynaud, inventor of the Praxinoscope (1877), the Praxinoscope Theatre (1889) and the Théâtre Optique of 1892 at the Musée Grévin, 'father' of animation film and film animation—in his Preface to Giannalberto Bendazzi's *Cartoons: One Hundred Years of Cinema Animation* (London: John Libbey, 1994), p. xix—such a naming for me is always already disseminated by mechanism, by writing, by the *animatic*, which is why in my Introduction to *THE ILLUSION OF LIFE* I proposed that Reynaud synthesized the *animatic* apparatus of film with his Théâtre Optique.

46 Eisenstein, *Eisenstein on Disney*, p. 50. Insofar as animism is itself a confusion of boundaries, as in the Bororo's disseminative *hama*, it is itself a hybrid 'form'.

47 See Gilles Deleuze, *Cinéma 1: L'Image-Mouvement* (Paris: Les Editions de Minuit, 1983), p. 123, for his term '*agencement machinique*'. Those English translators who translate '*agencement machinique*' not as 'machinic assemblage' but as 'machine assemblage' for me lose thereby its very pertinence. In that regard, see, for example, Deleuze, *Cinema 1:*

The Movement-Image, trans. Hugh Tomlinson and Barbara Habberjam (London: The Athlone Press, 1986), p. 85. Deleuze's machinic is for me of the order of the animatic.

48 Eisenstein defines plasmaticness as 'the ability to dynamically asssume any form', declaring,

> ..for here we have a being represented in drawing, a being of a definite form, a being which has attained a definite appearance, and which behaves like the primal protoplasm, not yet possessing a 'stable' form, but capable of assuming any form and which, skipping along the rungs of the evolutionary ladder, attaches itself to any and all forms of animal existence. *Eisenstein on Disney*, p. 21.

On the implications of the animatic for Eisenstein, see Keith Broadfoot and Rex Butler, 'The Illusion of Illusion', in *THE ILLUSION OF LIFE*. They propose that Deleuze's notion of the cinematic time-image is the veritable figure of animation to which Eisenstein's cinematic movement-image as Deleuze characterizes it aspired.

49 This is to suggest, after Derrida and contrary to Channell, that the opposition of animism and mechanism has not simply been exhausted or superceded, that *both* technology and the living organism remain at once mechanical and vital, neither mechanical nor vital, at the same time. See Channell, *The Vital Machine*, pp. 112-113. The teasing out of the complexities of Channell's modelling, including in relation to the logics of Derrida, lies beyond the scope of this essay.

I would add: if one wanted to be Baudrillardian, one would speak of the hypertelic, post-cinema situation of both *Blade Runner* and *Terminator 2* as cinema more animation than animation 'versus' the hypertelic, post-animation situation of *Akira* as animation more cinema than cinema. See my texts cited in note 44. Indeed, in terms of *Akira* in particular and Japanese animation—*anime*—in general, in my 'Apocalyptic Animation' essay I argue, after Baudrillard, that both Disney cute and Warner Bros. speed, violence and war have been surpassed and outbid—nuked even!—by post-World War II *anime*—the hyperreal, pure and empty, form of animation. Here, I would say, in accord with such a Baudrillardian logic, animism and mechanism, including Disney animism and Warner Bros. mechanism, would be so surpassed and outbid by such *anime*—the hyperreal, pure and empty form of animism and mechanism. All the while, we would need to remember that, prior to such hyperrealizing, any simple distinction/opposition posed between animism and mechanism, including Disney animism and Warner Bros. mechanism, calls for deconstructing on the basis of the inextricable coimplication of animism and mechanism, even as any simple distinction/opposition posed between Disney and Warner Bros. would likewise call for deconstructing. See Philip Brophy's 'The Animation of Sound', in *THE ILLUSION OF LIFE*, for his own complex take on matters animistic and mechanical in Disney and Warner Bros. animations.

50 See my Introduction to *THE ILLUSION OF LIFE*, pp. 9-10, on the at once extraordinary and predictable neglect by Film Studies of animation. I would suggest that, in line with the 'logic' of the uncanny that that Introduction not only seeks to ally with animation as the animatic but as well itself to perform, these terms 'extraordinary' and 'predictable' find cognates in those more obviously associated with the uncanny: 'strange' and 'familiar'.

51 A fourth year Honours student, Dominic Williams, pointed out to me that the two words making up 'live action' cover the two pertinences of animation—life and motion.

52 As I state in the Introduction to *THE ILLUSION OF LIFE*, p. 16.

53 Roland Barthes, 'The Third Meaning', *Image-Music-Text*, trans. Stephen Heath (New York: Hill and Wang, 1977), pp. 66-67.

54 Christian Bailly, *Automata: The Golden Age, 1848-1914* (London: Sotheby's Publications, 1987), p. 13.

55 See, for example, Derrida, *Of Grammatology*, trans. Gayatri Chakravorty Spivak (Baltimore: The Johns Hopkins University Press, 1974), p. 69.

56 See my '*Who Framed Roger Rabbit*' essay for the articulation of the complex logics of the hybrid as they apply to the toon.

57 Freud, 'The "Uncanny"' (1919), The Pelican Freud Library, vol. 14, *Art and Literature*, ed. Albert Dickson and trans. James Strachey (Harmondsworth: Penguin Books, 1985), p. 347. That the uncanny and the automaton cannot for us be reduced simply to 'automatic, mechanical processes' is perhaps figured in Freud's use of the term 'impression'. Rather, the uncanny and the automaton seduce, disseminate and confound the automatic, the mechanical, as they do their opposites.

58 ibid., p. 372.

59 ibid.

60 A proposal I made in my Introduction to *THE ILLUSION OF LIFE*, p. 28 and p. 36, note 36.

61 See Tom Gunning, 'An Aesthetic of Astonishment: Early Film and the (In)credulous Spectator', *Art & Text* 34, Spring 1989; and my extended comment on Gunning's essay in '"OBJECTS IN MIRROR ARE CLOSER THAN THEY APPEAR": The Virtual Reality of *Jurassic Park* and Jean Baudrillard', pp. 82-83, note 19, where, among other things, I argue that all that Gunning says of the character of the advent of cinema is already in Freud's 'logics' of the uncanny, that the attraction, film and *a fortiori* animation are of the order of the uncanny. See also my 'The Crypt, the Haunted House, of Cinema', presented at the *Cinema and the Senses* Conference at the University of New South Wales, November 1998, published in *Cultural Studies Review*, vol. 10, no. 2, September 2004.

62 See texts cited in note 61.

63 Freud, *Beyond the Pleasure Principle* (1920), p. 311.

64 See Baudrillard's comments on Descartes' evil demon in the interview conducted with him by Edward Colless, David Kelly and myself, published in Baudrillard's cogently titled *The Evil Demon of Images* (Sydney: Power Institute Publications, 1987), reprinted in *Baudrillard Live!*, ed. Mike Gane (London: Routledge, 1993).

65 Derrida, 'To Speculate—on "Freud"', p. 341. *Beyond the Pleasure Principle* is a text itself intimately and inextricably coimplicated with 'The "Uncanny"'. Indeed, Derrida himself remarks that the 'demonic demonstrates one of the trajectories which link *Beyond...to Das Unheimliche*' (p. 342).

66 Philippe Lacoue-Labarthe, 'Typography', *Typography: Mimesis, Philosophy, Politics*, ed. Christopher Fynsk (Cambridge: Harvard University Press, 1989), p. 93, note 79. See, too, Hélène Cixous' 'Fiction and Its Phantoms: A Reading of Freud's *Das Unheimliche* (The "uncanny")', *New Literary History*, vol. 7, no. 3, Spring 1976. For me, the automaton as Lacoue-Labarthe articulates its uncanniness makes it a phantom, a spectre, of fiction and fiction a phantom, a spectre, of it.

67 On the meanings of *animus* and *anima*, consult William D. Routt's '*De Anime*' in this volume. On *anima*, see also Annemarie Jonson's essay 'Porky's Stutter: The Vocal Trope and Lifedeath in Animation' herein.

68 *Quarterly Review of Film Studies*, vol. 1, no. 3, August 1976.

69 In *Writing and Difference*, trans. Alan Bass (London: Routledge & Kegan Paul, 1978). See Annemarie Jonson's engagement with Kuntzel's 'A Note upon the Filmic Apparatus' and Derrida's 'Freud and the Scene of Writing' in her essay in this volume.

70 Which link, bridge, informs my '*Who Framed Roger Rabbit*' essay 'in toto'.

71 Strandh, *The History of the Machine*, p. 170.

72 Deleuze, *Cinema 2: The Time-Image*, trans. Hugh Tomlinson and Robert Galata (Minneapolis: University of Minnesota Press, 1989), pp. 208-209.

73 Baudrillard, *The Evil Demon of Images*, p. 31.

74 ibid., p. 33.

75 See Baudrillard, 'The Orders of Simulacra', *Simulations*, trans. Philip Beitchman (New York: Semiotext(e), 1983). Note: this translation severely mistitles this section 'The Automation of the Robot'.

76 In terms of his two irreconcilable hypotheses—undecidable between them—of the Perfect Crime of virtualization and the Radical Illusion of Seduction—Baudrillard speculates that the former could be an avatar of the latter, thereby offering the unprovable hypothesis: the first order—of metamorphosis, animism and the automaton—is still sovereign. See Baudrillard, *The Perfect Crime* (London: Verso, 1996), pp. 5, 74, as well as his *The Vital Illusion*, ed. Julia Witwer (New York: Columbia University Press, 2000), pp. 53, 55.

Also see note 49 above. In terms of animation film, a simple application of Baudrillard's orders of simulacra would make Disney animism first order, Warner Bros. mechanism second order, and post-World War II *anime* and digital animation third order.

77 Baudrillard, 'The Orders of Simulacra', p. 95.

78 C.W. Ceram, *Archaeology of the Cinema* (London: Thames and Hudson, 1965). Ceram specifically mentions automata as playing 'no part in the story of cinematography', naming and excluding from that story: 'animated "scenes"', Chinese, Indian and Javanese shadow-plays, the baroque automatons, the marionette theatre, 'the writer' of 'Jacques Dros' [*sic*] and the suggestions advanced by 'Heron [Hero] of Alexandria' from his *Peri automatopoietikes* (Construction of Automaton Theatres) (pp. 15, 17, 21).

79 Philip Brophy, 'The Animation of Sound', *THE ILLUSION OF LIFE*, pp. 67-73 and p. 105.

80 See Baudrillard, *Forget Foucault* (New York: Semiotext(e), 1987), p. 49, on Kafka's Messiah arriving one day too late.

81 Insofar as the apparatus not only projects illusions but appears itself to be 'coming to life', it articulates for me with the comments by such thinkers as Deleuze and Baudrillard on the nonorganic life of objects, that 'life' in the 'dead', that 'animate' in the 'inanimate', which for me is at the least what we call 'magic'. As that nonorganic life of objects pertains directly to cinema, see Deleuze, *Cinema 2: The Time-Image*, p. 214. In terms of this magic of the movies, an intriguing historical note

is to be found in the fact that Georges Méliès, the 'first' magician of the cinema, learned magic from Jean Eugène Robert-Houdin, one of whose magic acts was the presenting of automata programs. Bailly, *Automata: The Golden Age, 1848-1914*, p. 20.

82 Please consult my Introduction to *THE ILLUSION OF LIFE* on these matters. Like the philosopher's toy and the cinematic apparatus, the automaton is at once amusement and science—at once for child and adult, disseminating which is which. In this regard, one can see how one of the inventors of cinema—Thomas Alva Edison—stands in the lineage of engineer-entertainers as early as his 1877 invention of a doll that said aloud, 'Mary had a little lamb'. In its wedding of phonograph and automaton, this doll is a precursor to Edison's wedding of the two to the motion picture camera and projector.

At the same time, to name Edison here cannot but evoke that 'fictional' Edison who invents the automaton Hadaly in Villiers de l'Isle-Adam's *L'Eve future*. Notably, Villiers has Edison declare to Lord Ewald: 'This is the arm of an Android of my making, animated for the first time by this vital, surprising agent that we call Electricity, which gives it, as you see, all the soft and melting qualities, all the *illusion* of life!' Villiers de l'Isle-Adam, *Tomorrow's Eve*, trans. Robert Martin Adams (Urbana: University of Illinois Press, 1982), p. 61. Beyond marking the crucial term—*the illusion of life*—this comment could equally be a characterization of the animatic apparatus of the cinema that Edison's work would come to produce, minus the soft and melting qualities.

83 Deleuze, 'Plato and the Simulacrum', *October* 27, Winter, 1983, p. 47.

84 Jean-Pierre Vernant, *Mortals and Immortals*, ed. Froma I. Zeitlin (Princeton: Princeton University Press, 1991), p. 175.

85 ibid.

86 ibid., p. 177.

87 Eisenstein, *Eisenstein on Disney*, p. 64.

88 Exemplary figures of this 'form' in cinema include The Thing in John Carpenter's *The Thing* (1982), Leonard Zelig in Woody Allen's *Zelig* (1983), Tetsuo at the end of Katsuhiro Otomo's *Akira* (1988) and the T-1000 of James Cameron's *Terminator 2: Judgment Day* (1991).

89 Deleuze, 'Plato and the Simulacrum', p. 53.

90 ibid., p. 47.

91 Baudrillard, 'The Precession of Simulacra', *Simulations*, trans. Paul Foss and Paul Patton (New York: Semiotext(e), 1983), p. 11.

92 Baudrillard, *The Evil Demon of Images*, pp. 13-14 and p. 23.

93 And one might add: Plato's problem re writing, the machine, simulation.

See Samuel Weber, 'The Unraveling of Form', in *Mass Mediauras: Form, Technics, Media*, ed. Alan Cholodenko (Sydney/Stanford: Power Publications/Stanford University Press, 1996).

94 On πρηστηρ, see Keith Clancy, 'ΠΡΗΣΤΗΡ: The T(r)opology of Pyromania', in *THE ILLUSION OF LIFE*, especially pp. 246-247. On *pneuma*, including its assocation with *psyche*, see Channell, *The Vital Machine*, p. 48. On fire as the most plasmatic of elemental forms for Eisenstein, see Eisenstein, *Eisenstein on Disney*, pp. 24-25.

95 Derrida, 'Plato's Pharmacy', *Dissemination*, trans. Barbara Johnson (Chicago: The University of Chicago Press, 1981). See also my '*Who Framed Roger Rabbit*' essay.

96 Bolter, *Turing's Man*, p. 204.

97 See Deleuze, *Cinema 2: The Time-Image*, pp. 164-174 and pp. 263-270, on Antonin Artaud and the great spiritual automaton, as well as on the psychological automaton that is always for Deleuze the automaton's other, coexistent, complementary sense—the automaton a figure for Deleuze of the 'essence' of cinema, what for me after Derrida would be the demon spectre animatic automaton. Insofar as André Pieyre de Mandiargues writes 'The automaton is a thing of illusion, and its proper place should be a house of illusions' (Jean-Claude Beaune, 'The Classical Age of Automata: An Impressionistic Survey from the Sixteenth to the Nineteenth Century', *Fragments for a History of the Human Body*, Part One, *Zone 3*, ed. Michel Feher (New York: Zone, 1989), p. 474), that house of illusions of the automaton is what I have called the crypt, the haunted house, of cinema, itself for me likewise demon spectre animatic automaton. See my 'The Crypt, the Haunted House, of Cinema'. After Baudrillard, it is the house of the evil demon animatic automaton of cinematic/filmic images.

98 See Derrida, 'To Speculate—on "Freud"', pp. 341-342.

99 Quite despite all the '90s commotion over virtual reality, this virtual in/of the animatic leads me to suggest that virtual reality is the only 'one' I have ever 'known'.

100 But Pris does contain Isis. See my '*Who Framed Roger Rabbit*, or the Framing of Animation', p. 232.

101 See my articulation of the relation of animation to those graphics: in terms of writing—in '*Who Framed Roger Rabbit*, or the Framing of Animation'; and in terms of drawing—in 'The Illusion of the Beginning: A Theory of Drawing and Animation', *Afterimage*, vol. 28, no. 1, July/August 2000.

102 Strandh, *The History of the Machine*, p. 178.

103 ibid., p. 175.

104 ibid., p. 177.

105 The coimplication of the devil and the double is far from surprising. For the etymology, ultimately derived from Sanskrit, that inextricably coimplicates *devil*, *two*, *double*, *death* and *God*, see 'How the Devil Became: Etymological' [a passage from Ernest Jones, *On the Nightmare* (1931)], in *The Vintage Book of the Devil*, ed. Francis Spufford (London: Vintage, 1997), pp. 61-62. See too 'How the Devil Became: Psychoanalytical' [a passage from Freud, 'A Seventeenth Century Demonological Neurosis' (1923)], pp. 60-61, therein.

Nor is it surprising that the opening landscape of *Blade Runner* also reads as the place where 'Fiery the angels fell', where Lucifer/Satan/ the Devil rules: Hell.

APPENDICES

Fred Patten's Annotated Chronology of Pertinent Works and Publications Relevant to *The Lion King* and to the Controversy

Note: dates in parentheses are actual dates of publication and appearance, supplied from outside sources, where those dates differ from those printed on the texts.

A. Works Pertinent to Osamu Tezuka and to *Junguru Taitei*

(1) 1950. Osamu Tezuka, *Junguru Taitei* (*The Jungle Emperor*).

Serialized in the monthly *Manga Shonen* (*Boys' Comics*) from November 1950 through April 1954. The serial has been collected and published as a cartoon novel in a variety of editions since the 1950s. The standard edition today is the three volume paperback set from Kodansha, Ltd., first published in June 1977. It has been regularly carried by several Japanese community bookshops in Southern California. The current printings at the time of the original version of this essay for *The Life of Illusion* conference were: vol. 1, 10th printing, Nov. 1994; vol. 2, 9th printing, Dec. 1994; vol. 3, 8th printing, Sept. 1994.

(2) 1951. Osamu Tezuka, *Bambi* (Tokyo: Tsuru Shobo, November 10, 1951).

An authorized comic book adaptation, credited to Tezuka, of the Disney film. Tezuka also drew *The Story of Walt Disney* (Tokyo: *Manga Shonen*, November 1951) and the authorized Japanese comic book adaptation of Disney's *Pinocchio* (Tokyo: Tokodo Shoten, June 5, 1952).

(3) 1966. *Kimba the White Lion*. NBC Films. 52 half hour episodes.

Syndicated TV series, premiered on Sunday, September 11, 1966 on KHJ-TV, Los Angeles, 5:30-6:00 p.m. 1/4-page display adv't in *TV Guide* (Los Angeles edition), vol. 14, no. 37, whole no. 702, September 10-16, 1966, p. A-29. NBC's contract with Mushi Production Co. was for twelve years from the month of the American premiere broadcast, that is, through September 1978. Distributed through syndicated sales by NBC Films through 1971, when NBC was forced by a federal antimonopoly ruling to get out of the syndicated TV market. Sold by NBC to National Telefilm Associates in 1971 and distributed by NTA through syndicated sales through September 30, 1978. Due to litigation in Japan arising from the bankruptcy of Mushi Pro in 1973 and conflicting claims to the ownership of *Jungle Emperor*, the American rights could not be renewed. NTA was instructed to ship its *Kimba* masters to New York City for storage pending a resolution of the bankruptcy trial in Japan. However, one of the Japanese claimants obtained some existing *Kimba* film prints and, representing himself as their owner, sold them to another distributor, Air Time International. ATI distributed them through TV barter sales, despite challenges of its right to do so, from 1979 until ATI disappeared in the early 1980s. Last broadcast in Los Angeles on Channel 52, KBSC-TV, on Mondays through Fridays from August 30, 1976 to January 11, 1977 at 5:00 p.m. and January 13, 1977 to July 8, 1977 at 3:00 p.m.

(4) 1976. *The World Encyclopedia of Comics*, ed. Maurice Horn (New York: Chelsea House Publishers, 1976). 784 pp.
Illustrated entry on *Jungle Taitei (Japan)*, pp. 347-348. Illustrated entry on *Osamu Tezuka*, pp. 656-657. Both by Hisao Kato.

(5) 1976. Vincent Terrace, *The Complete Encyclopedia of Television Programs, 1947-1976* (South Brunswick, New Jersey/New York: A. S. Barnes & Company/New York Zoetrope, 1976), vol. 1, A-K, 450 pp.; vol. 2, L-Z. 464 pp.

Entry on *Kimba the White Lion*, vol. 1, p. 441. Erroneous: states 'Caesar, the ruler, old and dying, bestows upon his son Kimba, the rare white lion, the sacred throne'. Repeated in *1947-1979*, 2nd ed., rev. (South Brunswick, New Jersey: A. S. Barnes, 1979). 1211 pp. in 2 vols.; in vol. 1, pp. 528-529. Entry without plot synopsis, but including the theme song lyrics, on p. 246 in Terrace's *Encyclopedia of Television Series, Pilots and Specials, vol. 1, 1937-1973* (New York: New York Zoetrope, 1986). 480 pp.

(6) 1980. *Sunday Special. Disneylando Daizenshuu—Tezuka Osamu no Disneyworldo Tanken Ryokou (Sunday Special. The Disneyland Grand Collection: Osamu Tezuka's Journey of Exploration to Disney World.)*

TV Special movie, broadcast on TBS television on April 20, 1980. A humorous tour of Disney World, starring Osamu Tezuka as a comical tourist bumbling throughout the park.

(7) 1980. *San Diego 1980 Comic-Con Program Book* (San Diego, California: San Diego Comic Conventions, Inc., 1980). 48 pp.

A group tour of around 30 Japanese professional cartoonists, led by Osamu Tezuka and Monkey Punch, attended the 1980 San Diego Comic-Con, July 31-August 3. Tezuka presented the American premiere of his 1980 animated feature, *Phoenix 2772*, which was so popular that a repeat screening had to be scheduled for attendees who could not get into the standing-room-only first screening. Tezuka drew many sketches of Astro Boy and of Kimba for the fans. Tezuka was presented with the Comic-Con's annual Inkpot Award, 'for excellence and achievement in: comic arts; cinematic arts; animation arts; science fiction; adventure fiction; and fandom service'. The 1980 souvenir Program Book includes a four page profile, *The Japanese Are Here!*, by Orvy Jundis, introducing the Japanese cartoonists. Osamu Tezuka is first, with a full page profile (p. 19) featuring portrait drawings of Astro Boy and Kimba. (The other cartoonists have a half page or less apiece.)

(8) 1980. *The World Encyclopedia of Cartoons*, ed. Maurice Horn (New York: Chelsea House Publishers, 1980). 787 pp.

Illus. entry on *Jungle Taitei* (Japan), by Frederik L. Schodt, p. 328. 'The animated versions of *Jungle Taitei*, like the comic strip, were a spectacular success—full of brilliant color and action, and incorporating Tezuka's favorite themes of idealism, perseverance and the vitality of life'.

(9) 1981. *The Encyclopedia of Animated Cartoon Series*, ed. Jeff Lenburg (Westport, Connecticut: Arlington House Publishers, 1981). 190 pp.

Illus. entry on *Kimba the White Lion*, p. 135. Erroneous: refers to Kimba as 'she' and says story is set 4,000 years ago.

(10) 1983. Frederik L. Schodt, *Manga! Manga! The World of Japanese Comics*, Introd. Osamu Tezuka (Tokyo: Kodansha, Ltd., July 1983). 260 pp.

The first major serious study in English of Japanese comic art literature, with a brief survey of the related Japanese animated cartoons. Osamu Tezuka is credited as a major founder of both. A note on the Japanese custom of bestowing flowery honorifics upon noted cartoonists such as 'master of comics' or 'king of comics' concludes: 'Osamu Tezuka, regarded as the pioneer of the modern Japanese story-comic, is the only artist accorded the supreme accolade: *manga no kamisama*, or 'the God of Comics' (p. 139). *Jungle Emperor* is noted in an extensive illustrated entry.

(11) 1983. Robert Hughes, 'Culture: The Art of All They Do', *TIME* Magazine, vol. 122, no. 5, August 1, 1983. Special Issue: *Japan: A Nation in Search of Itself.*

In a survey of *manga*, as part of Japan's literacy and gigantic publishing industry, Hughes observes: 'The top artists, with, at the very top, Osamu Tezuka, known as *Manga no Kamisama* (God of *Manga*), are treated by their adoring public of all ages with an enthusiasm unknown to Stan Lee or Garry Trudeau; they are stars in the way that Mick Jagger or Norman Mailer are stars, and are credited with some of the properties of both' (p. 48).

(12) 1983. George W. Woolery, *Children's Television: The First Thirty-Five Years, 1946-1981. Pt. 1: Animated Cartoon Series* (Metuchen, New Jersey: The Scarecrow Press, Inc., 1983). xvii + 386 pp.

Entry on *Kimba the White Lion*, p. 161.

(13) 1989-1990. *Junguru Taitei.* Tezuka Productions. 50 half hour episodes.

A remake of the 1965-1966 TV series, closer in mood to Tezuka's original graphic art novel. Broadcast in Japan on Thursdays at 7:30 p.m. from 12 October 1989 through 27 September 1990.

(14) 1990. *The 18th Annual ANNIE Awards, 1990* (Burbank, California: ASIFA-Hollywood, December 9, 1990). Illustrated souvenir program book of the 1990 annual ASIFA-Hollywood ANNIE awards banquet, Studio City, California. 28 pp., incl. covers.

Text reads: 'June Foray presents Winsor McCay Award to Osamu

Tezuka', and 'The Winsor McCay is based on merit and is awarded to an individual whose primary career function has been that of animator' (p. 20). Full page illus. biography of Tezuka, p. 10; full page group portrait of his major cartoon characters (Tezuka Prod. poster), p. 11; full page obituary by myself, p. 13.

(15) 1991. *The Encyclopedia of Animated Cartoons*, 2nd ed., ed. Jeff Lenburg (New York: Facts on File, 1991). xiii + 466 pp.

Illustrated entry on *Kimba the White Lion*, p. 356. The errors in the first edition about Kimba being female and the setting being 4,000 years ago have not been corrected.

B. Publications Relevant to *The Lion King* and to the Controversy

(16) Friday, November 22, 1991. *Paula Parisi*, 'Disney Animators Go Back to Drawing Boards for 2 Films', *Hollywood Reporter*, p. 17.

A news rewrite of a Disney press release about two of its forthcoming features, *Aladdin* and *King of the Jungle*. '*King of the Jungle* is being readied for 1993, according to writer Linda Woolverton, who segued into the project immediately following *Beauty*. Woolverton describes the original story, about the coming of age of a young lion, as a pet project of Walt Disney Studios chairman Jeffrey Katzenberg'. The *King of the Jungle* title is listed in the *Hollywood Reporter's* weekly 'Film Production' column as 'start' on June 15, 1992. It appears as *King of the Jungle* through the January 19, 1993 issue; in the January 26 issue it becomes *The Lion King* (formerly *King of the Jungle*).

(17) (mid-April 1994 release) Christopher Finch, 'The Story of *The Lion King*'. *Animation Magazine*, no. 29, May/June 1994, pp. 26-30.

Extensive feature article (publicity) on the forthcoming film. It emphasizes that 'Astonishingly, *The Lion King*—initially called *King of the Jungle*—is the first Disney animated feature to be based on an original story idea' (pp. 26-27), written entirely by a Disney development team from a suggestion by studio chairman Jeffrey Katzenberg.

(18) (May 9, 1994 release) Felicity Robinson, '*Lion King*', *Wild Cartoon Kingdom*, no. 4, 1994, pp. 52-57.

Extensive illustrated article (publicity) on forthcoming film. Includes sidebar, 'Simba, Meet Kimba and Zimba', by Fred Patten, noting two earlier cartoon lions with names based on the Swahili word 'simba': *Kimba the White Lion* by Osamu Tezuka's Mushi Productions (Japan & America, 1960s) and Zimba in David Hand's *Animaland* series (Great Britain, 1948-1950).

(19) Sunday, May 15, 1994. Flyer, Los Angeles Comic Book and Science Fiction Convention. Also published as an adv't in *Comics Buyer's Guide*, no. 1070, May 20, 1994, p. 76.

'A Special Look at This Summer's Major Films. Appearing in person: Rob Minkoff, Director of *The Lion King*. Rob Minkoff will be appearing along with several *Disney* animators to introduce a twelve minute *Lion King* reel and speak on the film. Plus a special *free Lion King* item will be given away courtesy of Walt Disney Pictures (while supplies last). *The Lion King* presentation starts at 1:00 p.m.'.

This particular event took place long after *The Lion King* had completed its major production; but it is an example of Disney's promotions featuring key animators and directors at fan conventions where *Kimba* videos were screened and sold and Japanese *Jungle Emperor* merchandise was on display and sold during the period when *The Lion King* was in production. To cite the promotional flyers of the (monthly) Los Angeles Comic Book Convention alone, 'T.V. Cartoon Marathon' at the March 1, 1987 convention and 'T.V. Cartoon Marathon #2' at the March 6, 1988 convention both advertised the screening of *Kimba the White Lion* episodes. The convention on October 8, 1989 featured 'the animators who worked on the film' at a presentation on Disney's *The Little Mermaid*. Rob Minkoff presented 'A behind the Scenes Look at the Roger Rabbit Cartoons' at the Sunday, April 8, 1990 session. The October 20, 1991 convention advertised 'Meet the Animators' at 'An Updated Presentation' on *Beauty and the Beast*. The October 4, 1992 convention featured '*Aladdin* Animators. Meet the animators of *Aladdin*, who will give preview scenes and give a behind the scenes look at this new Disney film. Appearing in person: *Beauty and the Beast* Director Gary Trousdale'. A similar fan convention where Disney animators regularly appeared to make presentations, while *Kimba* videos and *Jungle Emperor* merchandise were displayed and sold, was the annual San Diego Comic-Convention (see note 7).

(20) Monday, May 16, 1994. Richard Turner, 'Disney, Using Cash and Claw, Stays King of Animated Movies./Now, It Is Hoping

a Feature on a Lovable Lion Cub Will Extend Its Domain /Mr. Katzenberg on the Prowl', *The Wall Street Journal*, Sect. A, pp. A1, A8.

Feature article on the making of the forthcoming feature from the business aspect, emphasizing Disney chairman Katzenberg's role. Article alludes to Disney's worldwide search for potential rights conflicts: 'When Disney consumer-products officials suggested the Lion King's name, "Simba", might run afoul of copyrights of a German toy maker of the same name, Mr. Katzenberg wouldn't hear about changing the name'.

(21) June 1994. *Walt Disney Pictures Presents* The Lion King (Burbank, California: Disney, 1994). 79 pp.

Disney's official publicity booklet contained in '*The Lion King* Press Information' kit distributed for the film's premiere on June 15, 1994. The biography of co-director Roger Allers states that, around 1983, Allers in Los Angeles 'provided character design, preliminary animation and story development for the Japanese-produced feature, *Little Nemo: Adventures in Slumberland*. He went on to live in Tokyo for the next two years in his role as one of the animation directors overseeing the Japanese artists' (pp. 46-47). Another note in the booklet states that Allers 'joined the [*Lion King*] project in October, 1991' (p. 27).

(22) Monday, July 11, 1994. Charles Burress, 'Uproar over *The Lion King*', *San Francisco Chronicle*, Sect. A., pp. A1, A13.

Burress writes that Disney's film 'has aroused a roar of protest from those who say the record-breaking animation feature is not as original as Disney claims'. Parallels between the two are cited. Opinions are quoted from Tezuka fans Trish Ledoux, Toren Smith, Robin Leyden; *anime* experts Frederik Schodt, Fred Ladd, Naoki Nomura. Disney denials from Rob Minkoff, co-director; Howard Green 'no comment'. Report that Matthew Broderick, voice of Simba, originally thought the character was Kimba. The Tezuka Pro press release of July 12 is cited.

(23) Tuesday, July 12, 1994. *The President of Tezuka Productions Comments on* The Lion King. Tezuka Productions first press release.

'Comments [...] made in the context of a reply [...] to inquiries by Charles Burress of the San Francisco Chronicle and others'.

(24) Wednesday, July 13, 1994. Robert W. Welkos, 'A *Kimba* Surprise for Disney', *Los Angeles Times*, Sect. F, pp. F1, F6.

Same overview. More detailed synopsis of *Kimba*. Quotes Minkoff for Disney; Tezuka Pro press release cited.

(25) Thursday, July 14, 1994. Charles Burress, 'Disney—*Lion* Is Original', *San Francisco Chronicle*, Sect. D, pp. D1, D3.

'Disney officials yesterday denied that their wildly successful movie *The Lion King* owes any debt to a pioneering Japanese artist whose 40-year-old lion story has some striking parallels to Disney's tale'. Disney spokesperson Howard Green and principal screenwriter Linda Woolverton denied that any of 'the principals involved in creating' the story concept had ever heard of Tezuka or of Kimba. Skepticism from Schodt, Toren Smith. Similarities cited; Woolverton explained as naturally coincidental. Tezuka Pro press release acknowledging Disney's originality cited.

(26) Thursday, July 14, 1994. Ann Oldenburg, '*The Lion King* Shares a Jungle Crown', *USA Today*, Sect. D, p. 1.

Entertainment section front page story on charges of similarities from 'Japanimation' fans; Disney denial; skepticism of Ladd, Schodt; Tezuka Pro press release acknowledging Disney's originality cited.

(27) Friday, July 15, 1995. 'Did Japanese Animator Inspire *Lion King*?' (unsigned article), *The Washington Times*, p. C-15.

Reports the basic facts. Quotes Fred Ladd and Toren Smith on the similarities: 'Mr. Ladd and others did not accuse Disney of stealing ideas from Tezuka but said they simply want the creators of *The Lion King* to admit the influence of Tezuka on their work. "The thing that is bothering a lot of people is that Disney is making such a big thing out of trumpeting, 'Our first entirely original movie and aren't we terrific', says *Torren Smith* [sic.]"'. "No one associated with the film, no producer, or animator or director, has ever heard of this [television series]", *Terry Press*, a Disney spokeswoman, says. "They were asked about it in Japan. They said none of them had ever seen it"'. Illustrated with a photo of Matthew Broderick, the voice actor for Simba quoted as saying, 'he was confused when he was first cast, because he thought it was Kimba, the "white lion in a cartoon when I was a little kid"'.

(28) Saturday-Sunday, July 16-17, 1994. *Entertainment Tonight*.

TV news report, weekend broadcast, of the controversy. Robin

Leyden and Fred Patten interviewed; comparative film clips shown.

(29) Monday, July 18, 1994. Charles Burress, 'Some *Lion* Artists Knew of *Kimba*', *San Francisco Chronicle*, Sect. E, pp. E1, E2.

'Although Disney officials were quoted this past weekend on *Entertainment Tonight* as saying, 'The team that did *The Lion King* was completely unaware of *Kimba*', Disney spokesman Howard Green admitted to The Chronicle on Friday, 'Some of us had heard of *Kimba*'. But Disney only admitted that some of their production crew had heard of *Kimba* but were unfamiliar with it, or may have seen it as children 25 years ago but didn't remember any details. Continued denials that any of the main creative team who wrote and directed the story had ever heard of *Kimba*.

(30) Friday-Sunday, July 29-31, 1994. Anime America '94 convention, San Jose, Calif.

Anime fan convention. Three unauthorized T-shirts on sale by fans: (1) Kimba looking into mirror and seeing Simba, captioned (at top): *The Lying King*; (at bottom): *Mirror, mirror, on the wall, who created me after all?'*; on back of shirt: '*What I try to say through my work is simple. My message is as follows: "Love all creatures!" "Love everything that has life!" I have been trying to express in different ways through my work the message such as "Preserve nature". "Bless life". "Be careful of a civilization that puts too-much stock in science". "Do not wage war". And so on... Tezuka Osamu 1928 - 1989*'; (2) *Lion King* colouring book(?) portrait line-drawing of young Simba, coloured as Kimba (white with black ear-tips), in full-colour picture frame to emphasize colouring; (3) 1965 Kimba promotional portrait captioned, 'The *Real* Lion King!'

(31) (Monday, August 8, arrived) *Advance Comics* #70, October 1994, p. 288.

Capital City Distribution Company's October solicitations to comics shop retailers of comic books and related merchandise due for release that month.

Adv't/announcement for release of 'The Original Lion King' videos (The *Leo the Lion* cartoons shown on the Christian Broadcasting Network in the mid-1980s). Text says: 'As any hep person knows, the hit Disney movie *The Lion King* was inspired by Japanese animation great Osamu Tezuka's *Kimba the White Lion*, which appeared on U.S. TV in the mid-60s. In this sequel series...' Mailed with *Internal Correspondence* (note 32).

(32) (Monday, August 8, arrived) Tom Flinn, '*Lion King* Boffo; Big Merchandising Hit of the Summer, Too', *Internal Correspondence*, August 1994, p. 11.

Half on merchandising of *Lion King*, then, 'There are other ways to profit from the *Lion King* boom. One of the most interesting involves the Japanese cartoon *Kimba, the White Lion*'. Describes similarities between *Lion King* and *Kimba*, illustrated with cover of the *Leo the Lion* video being solicited in *Advance Comics*.

(33) Tuesday, August 9, 1994. Shauna Snow, 'Morning Report: Roaring about Similarities', *Los Angeles Times*, Sect. F, p. F2.

Public letter of complaint from Japanese professional cartoonists; Tezuka Pro 'rethinking its original stand'.

(34) Tuesday, August 9, 1994. Kozo Mizoguchi, 'Japanese Rush to See *Lion*', *San Francisco Chronicle*, Sect. E, p. E1 (early ed.)

The Lion King is a hit in Japan, but its success has renewed the controversy. 'A prominent Japanese cartoonist said she will send a letter to Disney this week expressing regret that the man who conceived the Japanese cartoon was not credited in the Disney movie'. Signed by 'dozens of cartoonists'. Also, Tezuka Pro rethinking its stand. Opened in Japan two weeks earlier; earned $5.7 million so far. In the U.S., Disney's highest grossing movie ever.

(35) Tuesday, August 9, 1994. Charles Burress, 'Japanese Artists Seek *Lion* Credit', *San Francisco Chronicle*, Sect. D, p. D1 (late ed.)

'52 Japanese comic book artists are sending a protest letter to Disney'. 'Prominent Japanese comic book artist Machiko Satonaka organized the protest letter, which is signed by 52 *manga* artists and 200 supporters'. No comment from Disney.

(36) Saturday, August 13, 1994. Steven Linan, 'Morning Report: *Lion King* Plans Vacation', *Los Angeles Times*, Sect. F, p. F2.

Disney will pull *The Lion King* from theaters on Sept. 23, when children are back in school, to clean the prints and to prepare a new ad campaign for a Thanksgiving/Xmas re-release in about 1,500 theaters nationwide. '...a dearth of films for youngsters during the holidays...'

(37) August 22, 1994. Emily Mitchell, *People* Section, *TIME* Magazine (Canadian edition), p. 55. .

'*Leonine Look-Alikes*. Those eyes, that flowing mane. Now that you mention it, *Simba*, the hero of Disney's *The Lion King*, does look a lot like the star of Japan's popular '50s and '60s comic book and TV series *The Jungle Emperor*, which was also known as *Kimba, the White Lion*. Disney says Simba is no copycat of the leonine creation by the late Osamu Tezuka, but there's a marked resemblance; both are orphans who become wise leaders. Concerned about the similarities, 42 leading Japanese cartoonists penned a petition of protest to Disney. Would Tezuka, a master cartoonist who admired Disney's work so much that he saw *Bambi* 80 times, have objected? A spokesman for the company that controls his estate says Tezuka was inspired by Disney films, "so if his works influenced *The Lion King* in the same way, then we are happy"'. Illustrated.

(38) Monday, August 22, 1994. *Mr. Takayuki Matsutani, the President of Tezuka Productions, Comments on* The Lion King-Kimba *Controversy*. Tezuka Productions second press release.

Expansion and clarification of the stand being taken by the company and by the Tezuka family personally, following the public controversy of the past month. They feel that *The Lion King* was definitely influenced by *Jungle Emperor/Kimba*; but they choose to consider this a tribute to Tezuka, who they feel would have been flattered, rather than as grounds for a lawsuit. Mr. Matsutani declares: 'That stated, we are nonetheless always prepared to act resolutely, to protect both the works of Dr. Osamu Tezuka and his honor, whenever we feel that our copyrights have been maliciously violated'.

(39) Tuesday, August 30, 1994. Cameron W. Barr, 'Cartoon Controversy over *Lion King* Percolates in Tokyo', *The Christian Science Monitor*, p. 13.

Chatty report by a self-styled cartoon-hating foreign correspondent in Tokyo. 'When the sniping started over Disney's *The Lion King*, with some people here saying the movie was too similar to work done by a famous Japanese cartoonist, I thought this was a story I would abstain from covering. As is so often the case with trivial controversies, the teacup starts to swell. Soon CNN and major newspapers are sloshing around, and suddenly childless adults who wouldn't spend three seconds thinking about *The Lion King* are talking about the controversy at social gatherings. Recently the leading Japanese grouser, a cartoonist named Machiko Satonaka, sent a letter of complaint to the Disney subsidiary that distributes the movie in Japan'. Barr notes Satonaka's list of parallels, and that 'Disney, incidentally, says *The Lion King* was inspired by Shakespeare's *Hamlet* and Disney's own *Bambi*, not Osamu Tezuka's work'. Barr 'rented a tape of *Leo, the Jungle Emperor* episodes (as *Kimba* was titled in Japanese) and then went to see *The Lion King*'. 'Without reviewing the entire *Jungle Emperor* series, it's impossible to track down all of Ms. Satonaka's parallels. I saw some, and the rest may be there. But the bigger point is that the Disney movie transcends the Japanese series'. 'Satonaka may be right about the parallels. Disney would do well to consider her charges and respond. But *The Lion King* does a much better job of entertaining the cartoon-averse'.

(40) (shipped late August) Trish Ledoux, '*Animerica* Special Report: Whose Lion Is It, Anyway?', *Animerica,* vol. 2, no. 8, August 1994, p. 38.

Full page report recaps the public controversy during July 1994, citing newspaper articles and the *Entertainment Tonight* video news story, noting that 'A film crew from the local [San Francisco] ABC affiliate interviewed both Toren [Smith] and myself on camera'. Report concludes, 'Whose lion is it, anyway? We leave it to you to decide', presenting two columns of similarities between *The Lion King* and *Jungle Emperor*. However, there are several inaccuracies. *Lion King*: 'Physically challenged evil male relative Uncle Scar (scar over one eye)'; *Jungle Emperor*: 'Physically challenged evil male relative Uncle Claw (has only one eye)'. This is erroneous. There is no suggestion in *Kimba* that Claw and Kimba are related. *The Lion King*: 'Anthropomorphic sidekicks include talkative parrot named Zazu'; *Jungle Emperor*: 'Anthropomorphic sidekicks include talkative parrot named Coco'. Zazu in *The Lion King* is a hornbill, not a parrot. Referring to the *Jungle Emperor* characters as Claw and Coco is an inconsistent mixture of their Japanese and American names. Claw is Bubu in *Jungle Emperor* and Coco is Pauley Cracker in *Kimba*.

(41) (shipped late August) John Beam, 'Cartoon Reviews: *The Lion King*', *Protoculture Addicts*, no. 29, July/August 1994, pp. 29-30.

A full page essay describing *The Lion King* as a thinly disguised copy of the basic story of *Kimba*, replacing the original elements in *Kimba* with stock clichés of melodrama. 'Another Quick Review', by Claude J. Pelletier: 'For all who are familiar with *Kimba*, it is quite obvious that Disney has largely been influenced by Tezuka's work for the basic concept of this animated movie'. 'Taken by itself (without the disappointment that all *anime* fans resent), it is a very good animation'.

(42) September 9, 1994. Donald Liebenson, 'Product Watch: The Cartoon That Would Be King?',*Video Business*, p. 46.

'Is *The Lion King* a copycat? Thanks to home video, consumers can judge for themselves, and the controversy can mean a marketing opportunity that could make *Leo the Lion* a roaring success'. Overview of the controversy, from the viewpoint of how it could be used to help promote the new *Leo the Lion* video release.

(43) (Sept. 1994 publication) Chris Gore. Review of *The Lion King*, *Wild Cartoon Kingdom*, no. 5, p. 68.

'Animation critics have accused Disney of borrowing quite heavily from Japanimation favorite *Kimba*—there are too many parallels to ignore. But when I watched the film, I wasn't thinking of that white lion at all. If only Disney would simply acknowledge that *Kimba* was an influence, then I don't think anyone would care'.

(44) September 1994. 'John Cawley's Get Animated! Calendar of Animation' (column), *Inbetweener* (newsletter of the International Animated Film Society), pp. 7, 12.

In this monthly newsletter of the professional animation industry, Cawley gives the Japanese *manga* and TV origins of Tezuka's *Kimba the White Lion*, and notes, 'This tale of a young lion cub whose father is killed and later must find the courage to reclaim his throne bears more than a passing resemblance to this summer's blockbuster *The Lion King*. The large number of "simbalarities" have been mentioned in print, on radio and TV. The studio management has maintained no one on the crew was aware of the cult favorite...but a number of the artists on the film (including at least one art director, one supervising animator and one story person) would probably privately disagree'.

(45) (shipped mid-October) 'Flash News: *The Lion King*', *Protoculture Addicts*, no. 30, September/October 1994, p. 5.

The public controversy over the resemblances between *Kimba* and *The Lion King* are noted, with several specific news articles cited.

(46) (shipped December 1994) *Advance Comics*, no. 74, February 1995, p. 290.

Capital City Distribution Company's February solicitations to comics shop retailers of comic books and related merchandise due for release that month.

Adv't/announcement for video release of *The Lion King*: 'The most successful animated film in history comes to home video! The politically correct were in a snit over it (so what else is new?), and *anime* fans were distraught over its uncredited origin in Osamu Tezuka's *Jungle Emperor/Kimba the White Lion*, but anybody who saw it without a chip on their shoulder had a great time'.

(47) (January 1995 publication) Helen McCarthy, 'Who's the King of the Jungle?', *Anime U.K.*, no. 17, December 1994-January 1995, pp. 6-7.

Analyzes the evidence and covers the controversy in the U.S. from July to its fadeout around late August, when Disney apparently never acknowledged the open letter by Japanese artists and fans. 'The story has died down in the American press and only attracted a few small mentions in British media. However fans are still left with the feeling that a major American studio has ridden roughshod over the contributions of a fellow artist, trading on the lack of cultural sophistication of their target audience and their own great reputation'.

(48) (February 1995 publication) 'Toon News', *Animato!*, no. 30, Fall 1994, pp. 9-11.

'*The Lion King and Kimba*. *The Lion King* may become the Disney Studio's most profitable animated film, but it will certainly be its most controversial. The questions over racist images in *Fantasia, Song of the South*, and *Aladdin* have not received as much attention as the numerous similarities between *The Lion King* and the Japanese series known in the United States as *Kimba the White Lion*. The Disney stand on the issue has been short and sweet; none of the production staff involved with *The Lion King* had ever heard of *Kimba*. Since the Japanese side has not been covered as thoroughly as it should, *Animato!* is printing the following press releases from Mr. Takayuki Matsutani, the President of Tezuka Productions in their entirety'. The Tezuka Prod. press releases of July 12th and August 23rd are reprinted without further comment.

(49) 'Letters to the Editor', *Mangajin*, no. 42, February 1995, pp. 4 and 34.

Kimba vs. Simba. A letter from Stephanie Tomiyasu, of Yokohama, asks for the magazine's opinion of the *Lion King* controversy, especially in regard to the fact that 'the Japanese say such things as that Tezuka would be pleased to have influenced a Disney film', while if the issue had arisen between two American companies, 'the case would have been in court long ago. Doesn't this whole thing say something about the Japanese?' The magazine asked Tezuka expert Frederik Schodt for his opinion. Schodt replied that '..."borrowing" is very common in animation', but that 'Disney's public assertion—that its hundreds of production staff members had never even heard of the late Tezuka Osamu or his work—is preposterous'. Schodt feels that the issue has become particularly inflammatory in Japan 'where years of American accusations that Japanese are mere "copycats" still smolder in the collective memory, and where Tezuka is regarded as a demigod'.

(50) James Bates, 'Footnotes', *Los Angeles Times*, Monday, February 27, 1995, Sect. D, p. D1.

'Circle of Cash: At Walt Disney's annual meeting in Florida last week, Vice Chairman Roy E. Disney said *The Lion King* would be the most profitable movie of all time, with about $800 million in profit from its box office, video sales, merchandising and other sources...'

(51) (March 1995 publication) Anthony Hayden-Guest, 'Who Killed Bambi?', *World Art*, 1, 1995, pp. 45 et seq.

Brief comment in a long article about *anime*. [The young Osamu Tezuka] 'was promptly commissioned to work on two new sets of cartoons. One was set in a jungle and gave the world Kimba the White Lion, the doubtless not wholly accidental ancestor of Disney's Simba, the Lion King'.

(52) Andrew Leonard, 'Heads Up, Mickey', *Wired*, April 1995, pp. 140-143, 180, 182, 184, 186.

Brief comment, in a long article about *anime*. 'Japanese animators also claim that large sections of Disney's *The Lion King* were lifted straight from a film created by Tezuka' (p. 186).

(53) *The Simpsons* (TV program). Episode #125, 'Round Springfield', aired April 30, 1995.

This brief parody illustrates how public awareness of the *Lion King/Kimba* controversy has become general public knowledge. Lisa Simpson's saxophone teacher, an old jazz musician known as Bleeding Gums, dies. Lisa goes to a hilltop to play a last tribute to him. His head appears in the clouds; but before he can speak, he is interrupted by a lion's head that says, 'You must avenge my death, Kimba... I mean Simba!' Similar portentous parodies of Darth Vader and a CNN announcer also appear, until Bleeding Gums roars, 'Will you guys pipe down? I'm sayin' goodbye to Lisa!'

(54) *Space-Time Continuum*, no. 17, May-June 1995, pp. 8, 15.

This fan-produced s-f & fantasy media newsmagazine publishes news about the controversy which is almost totally erroneous, demonstrating how the controversy has passed into the realm of urban myth. Under 'Animation' news, it is stated that '*Kimba the White Lion* is available on tape in the US. There is an Osaka, Japan, museum dedicated to Kimba's creator. Artists & merchandisers of the popular Japanese *anime* are suing Disney' (p. 8). Only the second statement is true, and it is misleading since the purpose of the Osamu Tezuka Museum is not to honor Tezuka as solely the creator of *Kimba*. Under 'Disney' news, it is stated, 'Claiming too-close similarity to the long-running & popular Japanese *anime*, *Kimba, The White Lion*, 43 suits were filed by Japanese artists, Sony Corp. (Disney got a court order to stop *Kimba* merchandising when *Lion King* opened), plus Pioneer, who distributes *Kimba* episodes. *Lion King* was pulled from US theaters for a "new print" until the cases are resolved' (p. 15). It is not true that any suits had been filed; the unavailability of *Kimba* in the U.S. was due to litigation in Japan unrelated to Disney or *The Lion King*; no company was distributing *Kimba* in America at this time; and *The Lion King* was pulled from U.S. theaters on Sept. 23 and rereleased on Nov. 18, which had nothing to do with the controversy being resolved but was seen by most industry observers as Disney's attempt to compete with the premiere of Nest Entertainment's first theatrical animated feature,

The Swan Princess, on the same day.

(55) Michael Lindsay, 'Open Yer Eyes!', *Overstreet's Fan*, no. 4, September 1995, pp. 96-97.

In the regular *manga/anime* column of this comics fan magazine, a brief biography of Tezuka includes the statement that, 'Mimicry being the sincerest form of flattery, Disney paid an unannounced tribute to Tezuka with their mega-hit *The Lion King* which was scattered with so many similarities to Tezuka's *Kimba the White Lion* (as it is known in the US) that the direct influence of that TV series is almost indisputable' (p. 96).

(56) Trish Ledoux and Doug Ranney, *The Complete Anime Guide: Japanese Animation Video Directory & Resource Guide*, ed. Fred Patten (Issaquah, Washington: Tiger Mountain Press, December 1995). v + 215 pp.

A thorough survey of Japanese animation available in America theatrically, on TV and on video from the 1960s through 1995. The 'Animated Television Series' chapter includes a two page profile of *Kimba the White Lion* which concludes, 'In 1994, Disney studios released the theatrical animated feature *The Lion King*, which although promoted as an "original story" was perceived by many *anime* buffs to be more than a little beholden to Tezuka's *Kimba the White Lion*. [A list of parallels is presented.] Disney issued a statement that none of their animation staff had ever heard of Kimba (*or* Osamu Tezuka!), despite a statement from Simba voice actor Matthew Broderick that he thought he was being cast for a remake of Tezuka's classic TV series. Coincidence? You be the judge' (pp. 15-16).

(57) Frederik L. Schodt, *Dreamland Japan: Writings on Modern Manga* (Berkeley, California: Stone Bridge Press, June 1996). 360 pp.

Schodt has been Tezuka Productions' translator for many years. Chapter 5, 'Osamu Tezuka: A Tribute to the God of Comics' (pp. 233-274) covers various aspects of Tezuka and his career. The final section of this chapter, entitled 'Jungle Emperor: A Tale of Two Lions' (pp. 268-274), is a report of the controversy which is the subject of this essay. Schodt notes, 'Tezuka visited the United States regularly while he was alive. I personally accompanied him in the 1980s to Disney World in Florida, to the Disney animation studios in

Burbank, California, and to the house of Disney animation luminary Ward Kimball. In 1964, at the New York World's Fair, Tezuka had even met Walt Disney, whom he considered his idol. As the story Tezuka loved to recount goes, he spotted Mr. Disney, ran up to him excitedly like an ordinary fan and introduced himself. To Tezuka's never-ending delight, Mr. Disney reportedly said that he was well aware of Tezuka and *Astro Boy*, and someday "hoped to make something like it"' (p. 272).

(58) Sonni Efron, 'Disney Dives into Japanese Film Business', *Los Angeles Times*, Wednesday, July 24, 1996, Sect. D, p. D4.

'Walt Disney Studios plunged into the Japanese film business Tuesday by acquiring worldwide distribution rights for the works of Japan's best-loved animated-film director, Hayao Miyazaki'. The article further states, 'Disney executives say they control 65% of the Japanese market for children's videotapes. Tokuma [the Japanese rights holder of Miyazaki's films] sells only to video rental stores, and a consumer wishing to purchase a Miyazaki classic would have to pay the rental store price of up to $140 per tape. Disney executives said they could market Miyazaki videos for the same price as Disney films, $42 each—a bargain by Japanese standards, but a highly lucrative market for Disney'. Also, 'Disney expects to make most of its money in the Japanese market as well as in Taiwan, where Miyazaki has a following'. These comments testify to Disney's knowledge of the Japanese children's video market, where Tezuka's *Jungle Emperor* has been available since at least 1984.

(59) Antonia Levi, *Samurai from Outer Space: Understanding Japanese Animation* (Chicago: Open Court Publishing Co., November 1996). x + 169 pp.

This book by a Ph.D. in Japanese history from Stanford University discusses the sociology of Japanese culture which underlies the superficial action adventure plots of Japanese animation. She mentions the 'modest success with American youngsters' of *Kimba* in 1966, and adds, 'Indeed, despite Disney Studio's vigorous denials, many American and Japanese *otaku* [fans of Japanese animation] remain convinced that *Kimba* was an important influence (possibly subconscious) on the animation team that produced *The Lion King*' (pp. 6-7). Levi also comments on the August 1994 letter of protest signed by over 200 Japanese artists and other animation industry personnel sent to the Disney Studio. A full-page (unnumbered) illustration from *Kimba* is captioned: 'Osamu Tezuka is sometimes called the Walt Disney of Japan. Tezuka was influenced by Disney as a young man, but his later work took an entirely different direction. Given the similarities between Disney Studio's *The Lion King* and Tezuka's earlier work, *Kimba the White Lion*, perhaps Disney should be called the Osamu Tezuka of America'.

(60) David Koenig, *Mouse under Glass: Secrets of Disney Animation and Theme Parks* (Irvine, California: Bonaventure Press, December 1996). 270 pp.

Koenig presents popularized reviews of each of Disney's theatrical animated features, humorously emphasizing flaws and inconsistencies in plot logic, and summarizing the public's reception upon their initial releases. *The Lion King* is covered on pp. 227-232, with the Disney/Tezuka controversy reported on pp. 231-232. Most of p. 231 is devoted to a 'Simba-Kimba Conspiracy' chart comparing similarities.

(61) Trish Ledoux and Doug Ranney, *The Complete Anime Guide: Japanese Animation Film Directory & Resource Guide*, 2nd ed., ed. Fred Patten (Issaquah, Washington: Tiger Mountain Press, February 1997). viii + 214 pp.

See note 56. This 'revised, updated, expanded' edition contains a slightly revised profile of *Kimba the White Lion* (pp. 14-16). A new entry (pp. 115-116) documents the 1996 *Kimba the Lion Prince* video release.

(62) 'Japanimation' (unsigned article), *Bridge U.S.A.*, no. 202, October 15, 1997, pp. 13-15, 17-20.

This is a Japanese language magazine for the Japanese community in Southern California. The cover feature article in this issue reported on the growing popularity of Japanese animation in America. It is in the section entitled 'Disney Also Influenced by Japanimation?' that the magazine interviewed Miyamoto, identified as currently working 'as a senior staff artist in the planning department at Disney' (p. 20). The interview was translated by Frederik L. Schodt.

The Life of Illusion Program

The Second International Animation Conference in Australia

March 3 1995 Japan Cultural Centre, Sydney
March 4-5 1995 The Museum of Contemporary Art, Sydney

Conference Director
Dr Alan Cholodenko

Assisted by
The Mari Kuttna Bequest in Film
The Power Institute of Fine Arts
The Faculty of Arts
The University of Sydney

The Museum of Contemporary Art

The Japan Foundation

Film Graphics

Network Ten

PROGRAM

Friday March 3
The Japan Cultural Centre

Alan Cholodenko: Welcome and Introduction

Kosei Ono: 'Post-War History of Japanese Animated Films and the Sense of Levitation in Hayao Miyazaki's Feature Works'

Pauline Moore: 'Cuteness (*Kawaii*) in Japanese Animation: When Velvet Gloves Meet Iron Fists'

Keith Clancy: 'JUST WHEN YOU THOUGHT IT WAS SAFE TO GO BACK IN THE WATER: Becoming-Other-Than-Oneself by Halves in Rumiko Takahashi'

Philip Brophy: 'SONIC-ATOMIC-NEUMONIC: Apocalyptic Echoes in Japanese Animation'

Patrick Crogan: 'Logistical Space: Flight Simulation and Virtual Reality'

Alan Cholodenko: '"OBJECTS IN MIRROR ARE CLOSER THAN THEY APPEAR": The Virtual Reality of *Jurassic Park* and Jean Baudrillard'—Part 1

SCREENING OF JAPANESE ANIMATION FILMS:
Kosei Ono: Introduction
Osamu Tezuka: *Legend of the Forest* (1987)
Hayao Miyazaki: *My Neighbour Totoro* (1988)

Saturday March 4
The Museum of Contemporary Art

Leon Paroissien, Director, Museum of Contemporary Art: Welcome

Fred Patten: 'Simba versus Kimba: Parallels between *Kimba, the White Lion* and *The Lion King*'

William Routt: '*De Anime*'

Jane Goodall: 'Animation and Species Confusion'

Ben Crawford: 'Intertextual Personae: Character Licensing in Practice and Theory'

SCREENING OF JAPANESE ANIMATION FILMS:
David Watson, Project Coordinator: Cinématheque, Museum of Contemporary Art: Welcome

Fred Patten: Introduction

Robot Carnival (1990). Produced by Kazufumi Nomura and Carl Macek. Adapted by Carl Macek.

Sumiyoshi Furakawa: *8 Man After*, vol. 1: *City in Fear* (1994)
John Conomos: 'The Odd Couple, or, Happy Happy, Joy Joy'

Sunday March 5
The Museum of Contemporary Art
Rick Thompson: 'Robert Clampett in Context'

Freida Riggs: 'The Infinite Quest: Husserl, Bakshi, Rotoscope and the Ring'

Edward Colless: 'Between the Legs of the Mermaid'

Rex Butler: 'The King Is a Thing'

Richard Rushton: 'The Mask of Truth'

Kristi Cooper: 'Entre-Action'

David Ellison: '*STREETFIGHTER*: Leisure Technologies and the L.A. Uprisings'

William Schaffer: 'Stimpy's Invention and the Interval of Control'

SCREENING OF JAPANESE ANIMATION FILMS:
Fred Patten: Introduction
Mashahara Okuwaki: *Great Conquest: The Romance of Three Kingdoms* (1992)

List of Contributors

PHILIP BROPHY formerly taught at the Royal Melbourne Institute of Technology. In addition to writing on Japanese animation, he curated *KABOOM!: Explosive Animation from America and Japan*, Australia's first animation exhibition, in 1994, as well as the subsequent Osamu Tezuka and Studio Ghibli programs for the Melbourne International Film Festival. He was Director of *Cinesonic: International Conference on Film Scores & Sound Design* and Editor of the volumes of its proceedings. His writings on sound, horror (gore, exploitation, violence), film, media, theory and technology have been published widely within Australia as well as overseas.

REX BUTLER is a Senior Lecturer in the School of English, Media Studies and Art History at the University of Queensland. He has written and edited a number of books on Australian art and is author of *Jean Baudrillard: The Defence of the Real* (London: Sage, 1999) and *Slavoj Žižek: Live Theory* (London: Continuum International, 2005).

ALAN CHOLODENKO taught film theory and animation theory in the Department of Art History and Theory, the University of Sydney and is now Honorary Associate there. He organized *THE ILLUSION OF LIFE*—the world's first international conference on animation—in 1988; edited the book of that event—*THE ILLUSION OF LIFE: Essays on Animation*—the world's first book of scholarly essays theorizing animation, published in 1991; and organized *THE LIFE OF ILLUSION*—Australia's second international conference on animation—in 1995, on which this book is based. He has published and lectured widely on animation theory in Australia and overseas.

EDWARD COLLESS is the Head of Art History Studies at the Victorian College of the Arts in Melbourne. His art criticism and journalism have been published in magazines, newspapers, catalogues and anthologies within Australia and overseas. A selection of his critical and theoretical writing, titled *The Error of My Ways*, was published in 1995 by the Institute of Modern Art in Brisbane and was shortlisted for the New South Wales Premier's Literary Award. He has taught art history, film studies, performance and art theory in several tertiary institutions, is a filmmaker, has worked as a theatre director and has curated a number of art exhibitions.

BEN CRAWFORD is President of LTB, the world's leading publisher of art-related periodicals (including *Art + Auction*, *Modern Painters*, *Gallery Guide*, and others), headquartered in New York. He was formerly Managing Director of the London-based SportBusiness Group, and Executive Producer of the world's (then) highest-trafficked website, IBM's olympics.com. His essay in *THE ILLUSION OF LIFE*, 'Saturday Morning Fever', provided the title for a book on television cartoons by Timothy and Kevin Burke (New York: St Martin's Press, 1998), which credits Crawford as a forerunner to Douglas Coupland in theorizing Generation X.

PATRICK CROGAN teaches film and media at the University of Adelaide. He has published work on computer games, film, animation and critical theories of technology in numerous journals, including *Angelaki*, *Theory, Culture and Society*, *South Atlantic Quarterly*, *Film and Philosophy*, *Animation Journal* and *Culture Machine*. He has contributions in *Paul Virilio: From Modernism to Hypermodernism and Beyond*, ed. John Armitage (London: Sage, 2000) and *The Video Game Theory Reader*, eds. Mark J.P. Wolf and Bernard Perron (New York: Routledge, 2003). He was co-editor of *SCAN: Journal of Media Arts Culture*, vol. 1, no. 1, January 2004 (www.scan.net.au).

DAVID ELLISON teaches in the School of Arts, Media and Culture at Griffith University in Queensland. He received his doctorate from Princeton University in 2001. He is currently researching connections between competing accounts of domestic comfort and Victorian supernaturalism.

JANE GOODALL teaches in the School of Contemporary Arts at the University of Western Sydney, where she specializes in the development of cross-disciplinary research. She is the author of *Artaud and the Gnostic Drama* (Oxford: Oxford University Press, 1994) and *Performance and Evolution in the Age of Darwin* (New York: Routledge, 2002) and two novels, *The Walker* (2004) and *The Visitor* (2005), both with Hodder Headline Australia.

ANNEMARIE JONSON has published and edited widely in the area of technology and the media arts, and has written for publications such as *Art & Text* and *Australian Feminist Studies*. Along with Darren Tofts and Alessio Cavallaro, she edited *Prefiguring Cyberculture*, co-published by Power Publications and The MIT Press in 2002.

PAULINE MOORE is a freelance writer based in Sydney whose principal areas of interest are film, television, animation and music.

KOSEI ONO is a film critic, writer and lecturer. His publications (all in Japanese) include: *The World Image of Donald Duck* (1981), a critical study of Disney cartoons; *The History of Chinese Animated Films* (1987), the world's first full-length study of the subject; *Story of Osamu Tezuka* (1989), a biography of Tezuka; and *Manga of Asian Countries* (1993), the world's first book on the work of the cartoonists and animators of Asia. From 1981 to 1993 he was a lecturer on American popular culture (mainly comics and animated films) at the University of Tokyo. He is also an enthusiastic translator of comics into Japanese, including Winsor McCay's *Little Nemo in Slumberland* and Art Spiegelman's *MAUS*.

FRED PATTEN has been studying *anime* since 1972. He co-founded the first American *anime* fan club, the Cartoon/Fantasy Organization, in 1977. He has written many articles on *anime* since 1980 for both popular and academic books and magazines, including current monthly *anime* columns for *Animation World Magazine*, *Comics Buyer's Guide* and *Newtype USA*. He was Director of Marketing at Streamline Pictures, an American *anime* specialty company, from 1991 to 2002 and has been a consultant for many *anime* film festivals. His first book on *anime*, *Watching Anime, Reading Manga: 25 Years of Essays and Reviews*, was published by Stone Bridge Press in September 2004.

FREIDA RIGGS has taught design theory at the University of Western Sydney and film theory at the University of Sydney and the University of New South Wales. The focus of her present research is the relevance of Husserlian Phenomenology to a contemporary analysis of cinema and its anticipation and absorption of successive theories of film. Her recently completed PhD thesis is entitled *The Community of Film: Husserl, Phenomenology and Poststructuralism* (2003).

WILLIAM D. ROUTT has done pretty much what he wants since leaving the Department of Cinema Studies at La Trobe University in Melbourne. Some of his work on film has appeared in the online journals *Intensities, Postmodern Culture, Rouge, Screening the Past* and *Senses of Cinema*. He has also been published in *The Oxford History of World Cinema, The Oxford Companion to Australian Film, Twin Peeks: Australian and New Zealand Feature Films, Cinesonic: Experiencing the Soundtrack* and *Value Added Goods*, as well as in *Cultural Studies Review, Postcolonial Studies, MIA* and *Animation Journal*.

WILLIAM SCHAFFER teaches film studies and the history of animation at the University of Newcastle. He has lectured on animation both in Australia and overseas.

RICHARD THOMPSON is Senior Lecturer in Cinema Studies at La Trobe University in Melbourne. In the '70s, he pioneered in writing about animation in the United States with his famous articles on Warner Bros. cartoons in *Film Comment* ('Meep-Meep!', vol. 11, no. 1, 1975; and '*Duck Amuck*', vol. 12, no. 3, 1976), anthologized in *The American Animated Cartoon: A Critical Anthology*, eds. Danny and Gerald Peary (New York: Dutton, 1980). More recently, his work on Manny Farber appeared in Farber's *Negative Space: Manny Farber on the Movies, Expanded Edition* (New York: Da Capo Press, 1998) and, with Tim Hunter, on Clint Eastwood, in *Clint Eastwood Interviews*, eds. Robert E. Kapsis and Kathie Coblentz (Jackson: University of Mississippi Press, 1999). He guest edited the Robert Aldrich special issue of *Screening the Past*, no. 10, June 2000, and is now editor of that journal.

Name Index

Proper names have been indexed. For subjects and concepts please refer to the Introduction in general, including Part III, where they are sketched in terms of the projects of both the different parts of and the individual essays in the book and presented as 'a network, a matrix, of subjects, of concerns', at that Part's end on pages 66-67. 'Fred Patten's Annotated Chronology of Pertinent Works and Publications Relevant to *The Lion King* and to the Controversy' has not been indexed.